INTERVENTION
IN HUMAN SERVICES

a guide to skills and knowledge

INTERVENTION IN HUMAN SERVICES

a guide to skills and knowledge

Eveline D. Schulman, Ed.D.

Human Services Consultant; Director, Center for Development
of Interpersonal Skills, Consultant to President's Committee
on Employment of the Handicapped; formerly Assistant Director,
Mental Retardation Administration, Maryland Department of
Health and Mental Hygiene; Professor, Mental Health,
Morgan State University; Chairperson, Psychology Department,
Community College of Baltimore, Baltimore, Maryland

THIRD EDITION

with **104** *illustrations*

The C. V. Mosby Company

ST. LOUIS • TORONTO • LONDON   1982

MOSBY

A TRADITION OF PUBLISHING EXCELLENCE

Editor: Diane L. Bowen
Assistant editor: Susan Schapper
Manuscript editors: Katie McCluskey, Rebecca A. Reece
Book design: Susan Trail
Cover design: Diane Beasley
Production: Carol O'Leary, Susan Trail

THIRD EDITION

The C.V. Mosby Company
11830 Westline Industrial Drive, St. Louis, Missouri 63141

Library of Congress Cataloging in Publication Data

Schulman, Eveline D. (Date)
    Intervention in human services.

    Bibliography: p.
    Includes index.
    1. Social service. 2. Interviewing. 3. Counsel-
ing. I. Title. [DNLM: 1. Counseling. 2. Interview,
Psychological. 3. Social work. HV 40 S386i]
HV40.S393 1982   361.3   81-16989
ISBN 0-8016-4371-6   AACR2

GW/VH/VH 9 8 7 6 5 4 3 2   02/C/245

For

MY HUSBAND

the consummate helper through the long journey of the writing maze

and for other members of my family

offering inspiration and contributions of ideas and artistic efforts

Mark, Kary, Susannah, Saranella, Saul

Ken, Barbara, Leah

PREFACE

It is said that a new generation with new ideas occurs every 4 years, and it does not seem too far-fetched now that this third edition has weathered two generations of students and other groups of human service workers in an era of rapid changes. Although the public is still uncertain of the meaning of "human services," it has "arrived" with recognition in the title of the recently organized department, The Department of Health and Human Services. Yet sociopolitical incidents have pushed the planning, programming, and payment of human services in many directions that portend unsuitable support for the care of those individuals confronted with problems of daily living, with cultural disadvantages, and with the other barriers and discriminations emerging from various disabilities. From the broader perspective, there are several paths that human service workers can choose. They can lean on the apparent comfort and security of their status quo, or they can staunchly seek solutions that prepare themselves and their students or trainees as change agents for a rapidly reconstructed world with many cataclysmic happenings.

I have eagerly sought opinions from the individuals who have been using the first and then the second editions, as well as from the varied learners with whom I have used this text. Originally the idea for the first edition of *Intervention in Human Services* (1974) sprouted from my students at the Community College of Baltimore. After bombarding students with books and pamphlets since the

initiation of the Mental Health Technology (MHT) program at the College in 1967, I became frustrated by the inadequacy of material pertinent to human services. The MHT program was arranged so that the acquisition of facts was coupled with skill training in the classroom laboratory and in the associated field experiences. Many texts supplied the didactic aspect; some satisfied the experiential skill training. However, no books integrated the didactic with the experiential, and none were suitable for undergraduates from diverse backgrounds.

Handouts formed the building blocks for the foundation of this book. Students used these handouts as their informational and skill-training guides in conjunction with books about human behavior and also other references to the human services field. The content was revised on the basis of students' criticisms, and revisions have continued with suggestions from the expanding number of readers who have adopted and applied the facts and practices of this book. Beginning students in an introductory course at Morgan State University, as well as advanced students at Morgan and in a variety of departments in other universities have volunteered their views. Trainers of adult mentally retarded persons and house counselors of group homes for mentally retarded persons; parents, teachers, and administrators of Headstart programs; groups of older persons; paraprofessionals in a short-term training project at an inner city community mental health center; and others have been involved in leadership training, observational and listening skills, and like learning experiences based on the concepts and procedures of this text.

In addition, psychologists, social workers, nurses, criminologists, gerontologists, and a host of other established and beginning professionals (paraprofessionals) responded to a questionnaire, submitting their opinions for the third edition. Most of these suggestions have been incorporated into this new edition. Any omissions are due not to disregard of the value of the notions offered but to the general format of the book and space limitations. Another significant source of material has been visits to innovative programs in several states. These visits yielded particulars about the competencies required in an assortment of human service programs and examples of unique and diverse roles and functions for both professionals and paraprofessionals.

The outcome of these revisions for the third edition is a shifting of subject matter so that there is a more definitive and organized layered approach, which is represented by the acronym ORRIC: *ob*servation, *r*ecording, *r*eporting, *i*nterviewing, and *c*ounseling. The layered approach begins with fundamental skill and knowledge about observation (Part One), builds recording and reporting competencies upon this basic skill (Part Two), then moves on to the more skillful layers of interviewing (Part Three) and counseling (Part Four). Each layer is preparation for the succeeding skills and knowledge. However, each layer also can stand alone so that the complexity of the layer can be selected in accordance with the existing skills of the learners. Thus competencies can be initiated and developed by beginning learners and refined by the more knowledgeable and experienced individuals.

Attitudes, *s*kills, and *k*nowledge continue to be the undergirding structures. Explanations of concepts precede exercises for developing the skills associated with the concept. New exercises and examples have been added, some are deleted, and others from the second edition have been altered, based on my use of the exercises and the views of

other individuals. In addition, references are updated, Chapter 8 is completely changed to an exploration of the present and future roles of human service workers (Beyond Counseling), and new skills and knowledge are presented:

Chapter 1: values clarification, problem solving, and decision making

Chapter 2: ageism, sexism, and handicapism; establishing a guiding ideology

Chapter 3: the recording process, recording methods

Chapter 4: reporting and confidentiality, the issue of privacy

Chapter 5: the many meanings of helping; helping as the essence of caring; hope, trust, and patience as the core of caring

Chapter 6: understanding the expectations for the outcome of the interview; selecting goals and problem solving

Chapter 7: the serendipitous counselor, primary and secondary process thinking

Chapter 8: new occasions and new duties; changing human systems and the human systems consultant; stress, burnout, and stress management; psychoeducators; psychosocial rehabilitation; corporate support for recreation; the scope of human services; the future of human services

The final pages contain appendices with a glossary and selected psychological tests, as well as sources of materials of interest to human service workers and more detailed descriptions of some of the innovative programs mentioned in the previous chapters, plus about 400 references concerning research, with more extensive discussions of specific subjects in the text, including other viewpoints.

The reading level is focused on a heterogeneous population ranging from individuals offered short-term training within an agency to college students from diverse cultural and experiential backgrounds. Graduate students in counseling, social work, and other programs have also found this text useful.

This third edition is indeed a compilation spanning several years' accumulation of information and communications germinating from a multitude of resources. Always there is a nagging doubt that someone is bound to be omitted from acknowledgments. If this does occur, I apologize. The memory may be obscured, but the appreciation is nevertheless assured. First and foremost is my deep appreciation for the assistance, leg-work, patience, and everything else of my husband, who acted as a research associate. My two sons—Mark, a professor and chairperson of a communications department, and Ken, a social worker and codirector of a consultation and education division in a counseling center—shared their insights and provided certain factual data. My daughters-in-law contributed information about dramatic expressions for the disabled and the aging population, some of the illustrations of the figures (Kary), and data about community services for the aging population and some photographs (Barbara).

Beyond this family collaboration, there are numerous others, such as:

Altro, Bronx, N.Y., S. Abel, J. Sloma; National Public Radio, Washington, D.C., B. Bird, Ed.D.; Caminar, Calif., J.S. DePetro, S. Ettcheson, R. Fuller, C.J. Richmond; Center Club, Mass., J. Bartek, E. Hamburger; Center for Independent Living, Calif., Z. Roberts; Creative Growth, Calif., F. Ludins-Katz, E. Katz, Ph.D., P. Rand; Cutler Counseling Center, Mass., R. Korwin, Ph.D.; Feeling Good, Yes, No, Project MENCH, Calif., G.J. Blum; Fountain House, N.Y., J. Schmidt; ICD, N.Y., J.C.

Folsom, M.D., B. Gastall, J. Grimaldi, Ph.D., S. Heymann, D. Maniscalo, I.P. Robinault, Ph.D., B. Rosenberg; Mental Health Association of Montgomery County, Md., M. Jachowski; Norfolk Mental Health Association, Mass., D. Uhlig, Ed.D.: OUR PLAC, Calif., J.M. Dix, E. Johnson; Paraprofessional Manpower Development Branch, Division of Manpower Training Programs, National Institute of Mental Health, Md., V.R. James; PACT, Calif., C. Gold; Postgraduate Center for Mental Health, N.Y., P. Wiemer; and Rehabilitation Mental Health Services, Calif., L.H. Goveia, V. Thompson—Litteral House, L. Beckles, D. Beckman, M.A. Donegon, J. Dykstra; Transitional Residential Program, M. Chan; Sub-acute Residential Treatment, J. Evans, P. Pilien; Community Care Home, L. Hernandez, A. Sardo; Quarters, D. Lake, M.D., J. Santistevan, B. Zanze.

These persons shared their programs, explained the roles of professionals and paraprofessionals, loaded my arms with materials, provided opportunities to observe and to some extent participate in their program activities, and patiently answered my unending questions. In addition, Pam Williams furnished the line drawings, and Pat Honey, who has been an unswerving assistant in the typing of two of my manuscripts, deciphered my scrawls and was ever ready to follow my idiosyncracies—to Pat, my profound appreciation.

Eveline D. Schulman

CONTENTS

Part Three

THE WHAT AND HOW OF INTERVIEWING: how to get out of the client's way

Appendices

Part One

OBSERVATION: THE FOUNDATION FOR HUMAN SERVICES

look and listen for the way to go

Everyone observes with more or less accuracy from birth to death. Human service workers develop the specific attitudes, skills, and knowledge that enrich the scope and accuracy of their observations. Note particularly the nonverbal cues in this drawing.

Chapter 1

HUMAN SERVICES
a special kind of helping relationship

Pam Williams

Human services depends on many segments of the continuum of social, medical, and other services. Interdisciplinary staff planning for the client involves a variety of medical and nonmedical disciplines and the participation of beginning professionals (paraprofessionals) and other direct care staff members.

THE DIMENSIONS OF HUMAN SERVICES

[1]

Mary walks slowly, leaning on her walker. Her left foot is bandaged and covered with a slipper unlike the black, laced shoe of her right foot. She stops and raises her eyes to look toward the open office door of Dr. T., which is inscribed with her name and "Ph.D." Dr. T. comes out of her office and greets Mary with a smile, "Hi, Mrs. M. I'm pleased to see you—brought some interesting items to show you. Remember you told me you liked to see pictures of . . ." Dr. T. is a psychologist who specializes in gerontology. She has prepared special materials for a session in reality therapy with Mary. *Dr. T. is a human service worker in a nursing home.*

[2]

Mr. B. wheels Tom to the front of the room and places his wheelchair so that Tom faces the audience of audiologists, psychologists, psychiatrists, educators, and others at this conference on nonspeaking persons. Tom's wavy black hair spreads out on the white pillowcase as his head jerks back periodically. His thin arms and hands move in spastic gestures as he grunts and smiles at the comments of Mr. B, who is bent over and whispering into Tom's ear. Mr. B. straightens up and faces the audience, placing his hand on the arm of Tom's wheelchair as he speaks, "I am Tom's social worker, and he has asked me to read his speech for you, since he cannot speak." Tom grunts and smiles, nodding his head and falling back on his pillow. Mr. B. continues, "Tom asked me to tell you first about his greatest handicap.

He says that cerebral palsy is not his handicap. He has learned to live with it and in spite of it. His greatest handicap comes from those people among you who feel sorry for him and from those who give forth bad vibes about his wobbly head and hands. Tom says that instead of me helping him adjust to the community to which he has recently moved, I should help those in the community who really can't accept him." *Mr. B. is a human service worker in the specially constructed, barrier-free apartment house to which Tom recently moved from a state hospital.*

[3]

Sam H., M.D., watches Ellen as she places the palm of her right hand on the chair and pushes downward, raising her hips from the chair. He notes that Ellen's left hand and leg tremble as she struggles to rise. When Ellen stands up, her back remains slightly bent as she slowly shuffles to the examining table. Dr. H. places a stool in front of the table and says, "This is quite a climb; may I help you?" Ellen nods as she draws her eyebrows together, deep marks creasing her brow. Dr. H. comments, "That surely did take a great deal of effort. Tell me about when you noticed some of these difficulties." *Dr. H. is a human service worker who specializes in neurology.*

[4]

Ms. R. drives slowly up the dirt road to the small clapboard house with peeling white paint. She knocks at the door and listens to the shrill voice of someone calling out, "Hey, Joe, get the door. Must be her." A middle-aged man in faded denims opens the door and motions Ms. R. to enter. Frank, a young man, is seated on the only cane-backed chair in the room, with his zipper undone and a part of his shirt showing through the open fly. The man (Joe) points to the sagging, brown, covered couch, says, "Please sit," and then calls out, "Reba, she's here. C'mere." Joe swiftly walks over to Frank and zips his son's fly. Frank looks at Joe and spreads his lips in a wide, toothy grin. When Mrs. D enters, she and her husband seat themselves on the couch next to Ms. R. Mrs. D. inquires, "Are you the one . . . the one to help us?" Ms. R. looks toward Mrs. D., responding, "Yes, Mrs. D., I spoke to you on the phone last week. I do want to assist you in finding some help for Frank—would like to speak with him for awhile. Then we can all talk about what needs to be done next." Mr. D. turns to Ms. R., shaking his head from side to side, "Yeah, but remember, can't afford much of anything—can't even take him someplace . . . our car can't go far. We do stay close to our farm." "Whoah, Mr. D., give me a chance," exclaims Ms. R. "Of course we will talk about what you can and cannot do. I'm here just for that—to help Frank get what he needs and to make things easier for you and Mrs. D. Am I right, Frank is 23 and has been at home with you two all of his life?" Ms. R. notes that Mrs. D. nods affirmatively, then Ms. R. continues. *Ms. R. is a human service worker who has been trained as a "broker" to help consumers obtain the services they need.*

[5]

Terry sits staring at the small white canvas board on the aluminum easel in front of him. He raises one finger of his right hand, which is resting on the table, and moves his hand with upraised finger closer and closer to the canvas board. Brian, who has been leaning against the wall near Terry silently watching him, walks over to stand at Terry's left side and speaks in a low tone, "Hello, Terry. Sure is a lot of white on that canvas, isn't there? Wonder what it would look like with some color on it?" Terry's shoulders are flung back as he turns toward Brian. Brian apologizes, "Sorry, Terry, sorry. Did I startle you?" Terry does not reply but turns his head sharply toward the container of paints and stares at them. Brian asks, "Terry, there's a space near you. I'm getting my paints and some brushes so I can finish my painting. OK?" Terry continues to stare at his paints as Brian walks toward the table with paints and brushes. *Brian is a human service worker studying for his associate of arts degree in mental health technology.*

[6]

Anne repeats her request and adds, "Look here, I'm a clinical psychologist, Bud's an advocate, Ted's a psychiatric nurse, Helga's a speech therapist, Larry's a mental health associate, Tom's a health assistant—and all the others have different titles; but listen, what are we arguing about? Let's talk about how we can serve the people's needs more effectively, no matter what our degrees or level of training." *This community health center is staffed with human service workers.*

The diversity of human service careers

The preceding six examples of human service workers indicate not only the diversity of human service careers, but also the complexity of the services provided (Fig. 1-1). Differentiations are apparent in the populations served, in the settings for the services, and in the services performed. New and different service needs have become evident with deinstitutionalization and the development of systems for serving mentally restored and mentally retarded individuals in the community. Additional service strategies are adopted by self-help groups that provide mutual aid for their members. The particular problems of minorities, the chronically disabled, older persons, persons in rural areas, and émigrés from Cuba, Mexico, Vietnam, China, and other countries have demanded that human service workers develop new roles and cultural understanding.

The importance of human services has been affirmed with the reorganization of the Department of Health, Education, and Welfare (HEW) into two separate departments, the Department of Education and the Department of Health and Human Services (HHS). President Jimmy Carter signed the public law establishing these two departments in 1979 and appointed Patricia Roberts Harris as the first Secretary of HHS. Both the Secretary of Education and the Secretary of Health and Human Services achieved Cabinet status.

The subdivisions of the Department of Education include the Office of Education for Elementary, Secondary, and Postsecondary Education and Research Activities; Special Education and Rehabilitative Services; the Office for Civil Rights; and

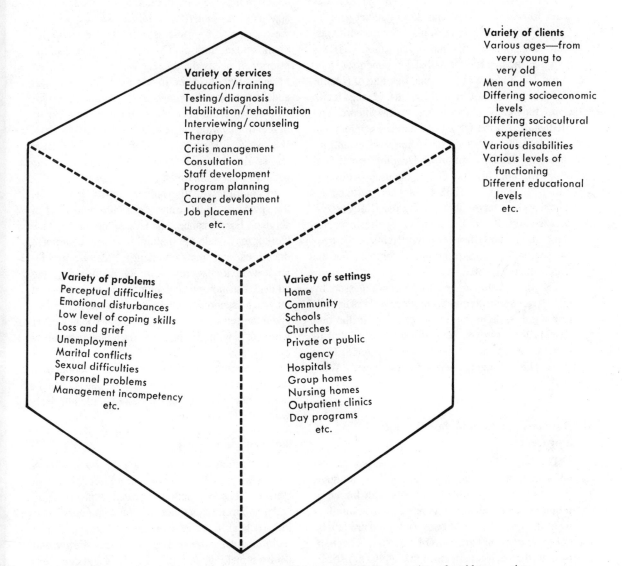

Variety of clients
Various ages—from
  very young to
  very old
Men and women
Differing socioeconomic
  levels
Differing sociocultural
  experiences
Various disabilities
Various levels of
  functioning
Different educational
  levels
    etc.

Variety of services
Education/training
Testing/diagnosis
Habilitation/rehabilitation
Interviewing/counseling
Therapy
Crisis management
Consultation
Staff development
Program planning
Career development
Job placement
    etc.

Variety of problems
Perceptual difficulties
Emotional disturbances
Low level of coping skills
Loss and grief
Unemployment
Marital conflicts
Sexual difficulties
Personnel problems
Management incompetency
    etc.

Variety of settings
Home
Community
Schools
Churches
Private or public
  agency
Hospitals
Group homes
Nursing homes
Outpatient clinics
Day programs
    etc.

Fig. 1-1. Four of the dimensions of human services: variety of clients, variety of problems, variety of services, and variety of settings. Human service workers perform many roles related to these dimensions.

the Architectural and Transportation Barriers Compliance Board.

The Department of Health and Human Services seeks to ensure "a just and decent society for all persons" through a range of partnerships with state and local governments and organizations. HHS's activities include four principal components: (1) the Public Health Service (National Institute of Health, National Institute of Mental Health), (2) the Health Care Financing Administration (Medicare and Medicaid), (3) the Office of Human Development Services (which focuses on social services and includes the Administration on Developmental Disabilities), and (4) the Social Security Administration. In addition, HHS administers refugee assistance programs authorized by the Refugee Assistance Act of 1980, the Office of the Inspector General, and an Office for Civil Rights of the people served by HHS programs (Programs for the Handicapped, 1980a,b).

The title "Human Services" encompassed by HHS gives status to human service workers as well as a national definition to the concept. In the discussion that follows, several questions related to human services are proposed and examined: How is the phrase "human services" explained? What is a "professional self?" Is the human service worker a professional?

Human services: a philosophy and a procedure

The holistic view. Human services is a philosophy that stresses care for the *whole* individual, including the person's interactions with the environment. This holistic view poses two straightforward notions: (1) One's body and mind are labels, not separated compartments of a person. What happens to the person happens completely, holistically. Individuals act and react as a unity. (2) Individuals are influenced by what happens around them; the same individuals influence what happens around them. These influences and counterinfluences shape an individual's thoughts and actions at any one moment.

The generalist-specialist spectrum. Human services is also a procedure based on the previously stated philosophy. Concern for the whole individual as well as the environment leads to a generalist approach. As *generalists,* human service workers view a person's problems as part of a socioeconomic and cultural matrix. For each individual the priority of needs differs; each person's quality of life must be considered in relation to both physical and psychosocial components. Human service workers who are generalists consider their clients in regard to various aspects of the helping process. If a specialist is needed, the human service worker knows about resources and makes certain that the person in need obtains help.

In contrast with the human service generalist, the specialist concentrates on a particular kind of service. For instance, a medical human service worker may be an ophthalmologist who examines, diagnoses, and treats a patient's eyes or a psychiatrist who treats only severely disturbed young adults. The nonmedical human service specialist may be a psychometrician who administers, scores, and interprets psychological tests or a social worker who works with groups of children in a community center.

The generalist is likely to help fewer people with the larger view of all their problems. The specialist, on the other hand, cares for more people but deals with specific problems.

The professional self

Are all human service workers professional? A "yes" or "no" response oversimplifies rather than clarifies. The distinction between a professional and a nonprofessional depends on a number of factors such as level of education, degrees, course requirements, extensiveness of responsibility and decision making, and the difficulties and complexity that might be encountered with things and data as these issues pertain to people's problems. Added to these differentiations is the criterion of the closeness of supervision required. Professional status also may depend on legal requirements (license requirements, for example), organizational criteria (membership), and experiential background (internships and other field work). Any combination of these numerous criteria may become the determinants of professional status. Thus a social worker with a master's degree in social work (M.S.W.) may be required to be accredited by the National Association of Social Worker's Academy of Certified Social Workers (A.C.S.W.) and/or in accordance with state laws become a Licensed Certified Social Worker (L.C.S.W.). To be certified or licensed in some states, a psychologist in private practice must have a Ph.D. or Ed.D. and pass an extensive oral and written test after having received internship training. Variations in standards for professional status are incorporated in the requirements for other human service workers.

Many terms and many levels. Human service workers, mental health technicians, and mental health associates and professionals are pigeonholed in many ways. Many terms are used to classify these workers into levels of professional status. The gap between ''professional'' and ''nonprofessional'' is filled with educational and degree credentials as well as other characteristics. The word ''nonprofessional'' has been used most often to indicate the non–traditionally trained worker without a degree. This term is frequently applied to volunteers, parents trained to help their disturbed or mentally retarded children (filial therapy), college students working as play therapists, and the like.

Other terms are associated with ''nonprofessional'' even though the criteria for the labels vary.

paraprofessional Alley, Blanton, and Feldman (1979) define a mental health paraprofessional ''as a regularly employed and fully salaried staff member whose formal degree in mental health does not exceed the baccalaureate (B.A. or B.S.) level . . . a person with a master's degree in psychology would not be classified as a paraprofessional, while an individual with a Ph.D. in philosophy would be categorized as a paraprofessional in mental health. Also, a volunteer with a B.A. would not be a paraprofessional, while a salaried staff member who has not completed high school would be classified as a paraprofessional.''

The Paraprofessional Manpower Development Branch of the National Institute of Mental Health

(1979) defines mental health workers as persons who are or will be employed to provide mental health services or to perform related functions such as mental health program planning but who are not considered to be within the core mental health disciplines of psychiatry, psychology, social work, or psychiatric nursing.

Furthermore, Alley, Blanton, and Feldman (1979) subdivide paraprofessionals into the following three major designations:

1. *Indigenous individuals* born and usually living in the community they are serving, or who have been and/or may be part of the subculture of the people seeking assistance. Indigenous paraprofessionals may be part of minority groups or the economically disadvantaged population. The New Careers Training Programs have prepared some of these paraprofessionals.

2. *Former clients* who have undergone rehabilitative experiences and thus have special insights into the difficulties involved in changing from alcoholism or other drugs or of renewing interpersonal skills after a ''breakdown.'' These paraprofessionals develop the competencies to help others and also become role models—persons who have ''kicked the habit'' or discovered more satisfying coping skills.

3. *Persons with some college education* who often are graduates of 2-year associate of arts or 4-year bachelor of arts programs in human services, mental health technology, mental health associates, or other forms of behavioral sciences. Their college training usually has consisted of studies related to human relationships, the delivery of mental health and other related social services, learning behavior, and the like.

The following phrases are also used to describe paraprofessionals:

functional professional This is a phrase coined by Carkhuff (1971) that describes individuals selected on the basis of their existing abilities in a given area who are trained to a high level of expertise in that area. ''Although they do not have the formal or educational credentials they can function effectively as professionals.'' These individuals are usually indigenous (native) to the area from which the clients come for help.

beginning professional McPheeters of the Southern Regional Education Board has often used this phrase to describe 2-year community college graduates who are trained in human service programs with a variety of program labels. This phrase is the preferred title for this new brand of professional, since it does not suggest inferiority or primarily assistant status. It also allows for differences in levels of professional responsibilities. "Beginning professional" opens up the prospect for continued growth as well as for the utilization of existing skills from life and job experiences. Professionals would become even more important in training and supervision. In fact, supervision may be arranged so that aspects of training and supervision may be divided among the various levels of workers.

The phrase "beginning professional" is not merely a game of words. It brings a stronger image to the role and functions of these individuals and raises their self-image several notches. Some beginning professionals supplement professionals, assisting them in their service delivery. Others, depending on their level of knowledge and skills, complement professionals. They might provide new services, such as case managers, brokers acting as linkages between the provider and consumer of services—the bridge between need and resource (Mermelstein and Sundet, 1980).

Definition of a professional self. No matter what phrase is employed to describe the human service worker, the major question is: What makes for the professional self?

There are at least two directions that a definition of "professional" may take. One definition sets up a closed system in which individuals with degrees establish a monopoly of knowledge, skills, ethical procedures, and other credentials to regulate and maintain a certain status and levels of performance determined by an agency or by an accrediting group. Another definition provides a more open system in which individuals are presented with expectations and levels of competency in knowledge, skills, and performance so that they may function in certain roles with specified levels of responsibility. Both definitions stress the obligations of a code of ethics responsive to individual rights, to service-related effectives, and to societal standards. The difference between the two definitions lies primarily in the acceptance of the non–traditionally trained, competent individual with no degree as a *beginning professional* under the second, more open definition.

"Self," the second word in the phrase, focuses on the actor or performer of the professional role assigned. Self includes the thoughts, opinions, feelings, and strivings of which the actor and others are aware and some of the observable (overt) and nonobservable (covert) behaviors that are hidden from the person, from others, or from both (see Johari's window, p. 16).

The *professional self* is therefore an individual who, as a result of certain general and/or specific training in skills and knowledge, meets established qualifications for certain levels of responsibility and competence. In the process of this training the individual develops certain attitudes toward the helping role that are related to the rights of the people being helped and the helper's responsibility in preserving these rights (Ennis and Siegel, 1973).

Professionalism versus "professionalitis." The essential tool for effective human services is the professional self, a defined identity with a prescribed social role. This identity or role imposes the required levels of competence and the opportunities for accomplishment in the worker's area of competence. Helpers advance in self-understanding during the helping process as a side effect of the interpersonal relationship between them and their clients. Reciprocal (mutual) growth of helper and client is an outcome of this relationship. The goal of the helping relationship is self-help—to help clients meet their needs through their own efforts.

"Professionalitis" is not the same as professionalism and is far removed from the meaning of professional self. The term describes those helpers who, because of feelings of inferiority, insecurity, or other negative self-evaluations, hide behind complicated explanations, high-sounding jargon, and professional clichés. The tone of voice as well as the manner of speaking reflect the ''professionalitis touch.'' Professionalitis encourages turf boundaries with clearly defined and carefully restricted functions and responsibilities.

There are many other differences between the helper who is professional and the helper who displays the grandiose, all-knowing airs of professionalitis. The professional role demands both skills and knowledge in interpersonal procedures and a helper who functions at a more life-satisfying level than the client. Professionals share understandings, while respecting the worth and dignity of clients. In contrast, helpers who exhibit professionalitis feel (or just act) impressive and seek to convince others of their authority, superiority, credentials, abilities, and so on; they barricade clients from the inner sanctum of the professional mystique. Examples 1-1 and 1-2 describe some clients' problems and the professional and professionalitis approaches of interviewers.

Example 1-1
MR. P.: PROFESSIONALISM OR PROFESSIONALITIS?

The group is seated in close contact around a table in a small room. One of the younger men, Sam, sits back on the hind legs of his chair, glancing through a notebook he holds in his hands. A young woman, Mikel, pushes her chair up to the table and leans her chin on her hands with her elbows perched at the end of the table edge. Mr. P. sits between Romano and Stan, with one arm encircling the back of Romano's chair and the other hand resting on the table near Stan's hand.

MIKEL: All my life it's been that way. Can't say ''no.'' Living with this guy for 4 years, except for the past year I was in that dump of a hospital. Better now, I guess, but still want to change . . . want to be able to shout at him—no, don't want to go to that dive—don't want to lend your friend my camera . . . don't, don't. It's not only him. I'm a patsy for anyone. Guess that's why I try to avoid people . . . to . . . to . . . hide myself from the world.

SAM: *(Glances over at Mikel and nods his head.)* Know what you mean. Been there, getting better though. Can assert myself, not easy though. Even have begun to lose some of that fat

that cushioned me from people. Think it's what's been happening in this group, the safety of expressing myself.

ROSE: Just like me with my mother, always felt I had to please her. One of 10 kids . . . just a little bit of love. So when I couldn't get her attention by being so-o-o good, tried the ba-a-a-ad routine. Pregnant, abortion twice, then went off the deep end. Five years in that crazy house. Thought the devil was planning some way to get me to hell. No, not really thought it . . . imagined it. But sometimes it was so real.

MR. P.: Feelings . . . to control . . . to express . . . sure does get in our way sometimes. Each of us can tell about these hang-ups. I've been wondering how we help one another. What, for instance, can we say to help Mikel?

STAN: Shit, man. How can we say anything to help Mikel? That's what you're here for, *miss-ter* P.—the ''great leader,'' Benny. Yeah, Benny, you're the guy with savvy, the one and only together person in this group. What are *you* going to say to Mikel?

ROMANO: Just one little minute, Stan. 'Sure, Ben has the know-how, but ain't we in this room, in this group, because we share our ways with each other?

MIKEL: *(Softly, almost in a whisper.)* Yeah, help each other.

MR. P.: Sure, Stan, think I'm the man with all the answers. Wish it was that simple. And even if I had an answer for each one of us in this group, including myself, how could you or Mikel or Gerta or Manny or anyone know it was the right answer, the right way? Maybe this time I would hit jackpot, but what about the next time, when we're not in a group?

TOM: Find our own answers. Talk freely here and try out a new way. Like maybe Mikel could do what I did yesterday when my mom put on the sad act, asking me to get the haircut *for her,* for how it looks to the neighbors. But she does not know me. In my small way this hair is my strength. Now I don't have to wonder if the world is looking at *me.* Sure they are, and so I fling my head about and my waist-length hair flows. So I laugh rather than cringe. And now I can say to my mom, ''When and if I'm ready, I'll cut it.'' Took a long time to feel that I have the right to tell my mom off.

MIKEL: Is that what you call ''assertion''?

MR. P.: Let's try something—we'll find out about assertion. Would you and Tom and Mikel try something? You remember role playing. Mikel, how about you being Chuck, and Tom, you be Mikel. Chuck is asking Mikel to lend her camera to a friend of his. Work it through.

After role playing, the group discusses what has occurred, and some of the participants present other ways of dealing with the situation. Then, at Mr. P.'s suggestion, Mikel performs as herself and Tom becomes Chuck. Throughout the role playing and the conversation that follows Mr. P. continues to be part of the discussion, encouraging interchanges and acting as a catalyst rather than imposing his own ideas.

Example 1-2
DR. Y.: PROFESSIONALISM OR PROFESSIONALITIS?

DR. Y: *(Seated in a large black leather executive desk chair behind a well-polished 6-foot wooden desk. Looks up as Ruth enters her office.)* Sit down, please. I'm almost finished with these notations. *(Dr. Y. points to the red leather chair in front of her desk.)*

RUTH: *(Looks around the office and then slowly slides into the chair, planting her feet firmly on the carpeted floor in front of her.)* But I. . . . *(Dr. Y., without looking up, holds up her left hand while she continues writing.)*

DR. Y.: Ah, that's done. And now I can give you my attention.

RUTH: Really don't know why I came here. Don't think anyone can do anything. Just got your name from the yellow pages and saw that you were certified as a psychologist. But, but my problem is so different. *(Ruth opens her purse, removes a facial tissue, and wipes the corners of her mouth and a tear rolling down her right cheek.)*

DR. Y.: Yes . . . go on.

RUTH: Bob, my husband . . . oh, I don't know. He would kill me if he knew I was talking about him. Don't know.

DR. Y.: How about free associating. Just talk about anything, without censoring your words. Tell me about your husband.

RUTH: Bob, he's a big shot in the business world, gets along with his workers, with his other executives. A lamb at work, a vicious alcoholic animal with me. He . . . *(Ruth begins to sob.)*

DR. Y.: Seems as if Bob's business self is the socialized part of him, and yet the pressures are such that he releases his frustrations, or whatever it might be, with you. What does occur when he is under the influence?

RUTH: Gotten beyond that . . . does it even when he is not drinking. Only rarely does he speak to me. He commands. And if I don't jump to bring him his dry martini when he comes home, if the kids bother him, if dinner is even a little late, if. . . . It was not this way for the first 5 years of our marriage. So much like my father, used to slam my mother until she was black and blue, sometimes even bleeding. But how can anyone stop him? No one stopped my father.

DR. Y.: Indeed, often we repeat the dynamics of our family interrelationships. Family systems recur. Yet there are strategies that may be employed to counteract these events. We need not reinforce abusive behavior just because our life experiences have established a pattern.

RUTH: Huh? I hope I'm not giving you the wrong ideas. Bob in many ways is a good husband. I never want for money. We have a wonderful home. It's just become more serious and violent since Jimmie was born. There's another thing. The doctors don't know how it happened. Anoxia, they said; maybe the baby suffered from lack of oxygen—brain damage because his birth took so long. Maybe the anesthetic they gave me during the difficult birth process hurt him. But Bob blames me. He says I must have done something wrong, even though our two other kids are just fine.

DR. Y.: A complex of reasons for Bob's acting-out behavior. So often the birth of a defective child precipitates a high level of stress, resulting in disinhibition, relaxing of one's usual socially appropriate behavior. Afterward your husband may feel guilt or remorse and wonder how he could have expressed such ego-alien behavior. Yet he suffers ambivalence, hitting out at you because he feels you have in some way failed him, yet feeling guilty about his behavior. He gives you and the children material advantages. And. . . .

RUTH: *(Interrupting.)* I'm not ready to cope with what you are saying, Dr. Y. It sounds worthwhile . . . but I'm so confused.

The conversation continues for about 20 more minutes; Ruth speaks of the bruises she has from Bob's most recent brutality, and Dr. Y. interprets Bob's and her behavior. A second appointment is arranged, but as Ruth leaves she wonders whether she wants to return.

■   ■   ■

Mr. P. and Dr. Y. both appear to be knowledgeable. One of them, however, abides by the principle, "If you have it, flaunt it." Who does this, Mr. P. or Dr. Y.?

SELF-UNDERSTANDING FOR ESTABLISHING A PROFESSIONAL SELF

What makes one person able to feel comfortable while also being comforting? What makes another person eager to press upon others a font of knowledge, an aura of expert authority? One basic tenet clarifies the differences in people's behavior—*self-understanding*. It would not be too farfetched to say that one may gather a great deal of information about oneself and yet have very little understanding. Understanding signifies awareness and clear perception of facts about one's characteristics. Understanding is a life-long ideal rather than an immediate achievement. To get more in touch with oneself, individuals should at least discover their learning style and identity-concept.

possible?

Learning style

People learn through their senses by interacting with an environment. This environment may be a book, a lecture or discussion, some physical contact with other people, or a combination of any or all of these channels for communication. Learning styles are conditioned in early childhood by means of the significant people (parents and others) around the child. For example, John thinks and learns best when he listens and then comments rapidly; Rose prefers reading and thinking before she responds to a question; Ingrid likes to learn by doing, touching, and interacting with others. John's learning style is auditory (depends primarily on his hearing), and he probably is a quick thinker who is impulsive (dashes off, blurts out) in his responses. Rose is a visual learner (depends primarily on seeing what she is learning) and is more cautious and slower (reflective) in her responses. Ingrid learns best through physical means (kinesthetic) and is more responsive to social learning situations (field dependent).

Knowing one's learning style and being able to recognize learning styles in others is important for the educator as well as for the human service worker. Teaching and helping methods should be adjusted to the individual differences in learning styles of students and clients. Smith and Martinson (1971) conclude from a study of counselor-client interview relationships "that counseling educators should consider the possibility that counselors' and counselees' learning styles have some influence on interview behavior. . . . Counselors should be sensitive to their own learning styles as well as to those of their counselees and should learn to make whatever adjustments are necessary during the in-terview in order to facilitate a genuine therapeutic relationship."

Alertness to various learning styles poses many questions for the human service worker. What is the impact of different cultures on learning styles? Are people from some cultures more likely to respond to visual rather than oral stimuli? Do oral cues predominate for people from other cultures? Does the lowered sensory acuity of older persons alter their learning styles? Should the counselor depend more on listening to the elderly person rather than speaking? Should the counselor speak more slowly, more loudly, with greater emphasis? What about the learning styles of the blind person, the deaf or hard-of-hearing person, and the mentally retarded person? These questions reflect only a small part of the issues raised regarding learning styles.*

Exercise 1-1 provides a means of seeking information about one's learning style.

---

*Information about the interaction between learning styles and other influences may be obtained as follows. *Aging:* Ganikos, 1979; Herr and Weakland, 1979; Sinick, 1977. *Culture:* Brownlee, 1978; Kleinman, and others, 1975; E.D. Schulman, 1981. *Disabilities (physical and psychiatric):* Anthony, 1980; Bitter, 1979; Rusk, 1977. *Mental retardation:* Bialer and Sternlicht, 1977; E.D. Schulman, 1980.

Exercise 1-1
WHAT IS YOUR "SENSE" FOR LEARNING? *(may be done alone or in a group)*

Part 1—*Time:* APPROXIMATELY 10 MINUTES

Answer the following questions by checking the answer that best describes your preference. Insert another response if none of those listed is applicable for you.

1. Where do you study?
   a. In your private room? Most of the time _____ Some of the time _____ Rarely _____
   b. In your dorm room? Most of the time _____ Some of the time _____ Rarely _____
   c. In the library? Most of the time _____ Some of the time _____ Rarely _____
   d. In _____ *(Insert other place.)* Most of the time _____ Some of the time _____ Rarely _____

2. With whom do you study?
   a. Alone? Most of the time _____ Some of the time _____ Rarely _____
   b. With a certain friend? Most of the time _____ Some of the time _____ Rarely _____
   c. With a group of people? Most of the time _____ Some of the time _____ Rarely _____
   d. With _____ *(Insert with whom.)* Most of the time _____ Some of the time _____ Rarely _____

Continued.

3. How do you study?
    a. In a quiet room? Most of the time _____ Some of the time _____ Rarely _____
    b. While listening to the radio? Most of the time _____ Some of the time _____ Rarely _____
    c. While watching television? Most of the time _____ Some of the time _____ Rarely _____
    d. While _____ *(Insert how you study.)* Most of the time _____ Some of the time _____ Rarely _____

4. How do you find it more effective to gain new facts?
    a. By listening to a lecture? Most of the time _____ Some of the time _____ Rarely _____
    b. By reading a book? Most of the time _____ Some of the time _____ Rarely _____
    c. By discussion with someone? Most of the time _____ Some of the time _____ Rarely _____
    d. By doing (performing) something (practicing, role playing, and the like) with the facts to be learned? Most of the time _____ Some of the time _____ Rarely _____
    e. By taking notes about what you see or hear? Most of the time _____ Some of the time _____ Rarely _____
    f. By _____ *(Insert your preference.)* Most of the time _____ Some of the time _____ Rarely _____

5. How do you respond when someone asks you a question?
    a. Take time to think things through? Most of the time _____ Some of the time _____ Rarely _____
    b. Give a quick response? Most of the time _____ Some of the time _____ Rarely _____
    c. By _____ *(Insert your method.)* Most of the time _____ Some of the time _____ Rarely _____

6. Which do you prefer?
    a. Talking to people? Most of the time _____ Some of the time _____ Rarely _____
    b. Listening to people? Most of the time _____ Some of the time _____ Rarely _____
    c. Watching people? Most of the time _____ Some of the time _____ Rarely _____
    d. _____ *(Insert your preference.)* Most of the time _____ Some of the time _____ Rarely _____

7. How do you greet your friends?
    a. With a handshake, a kiss, a touch on the shoulder? Most of the time _____ Some of the time _____ Rarely _____
    b. With some words of greeting? Most of the time _____ Some of the time _____ Rarely _____
    c. With _____ *(Insert your preference.)* Most of the time _____ Some of the time _____ Rarely _____

8. How do you tend to listen to a person talking?
    a. Until the person completes the thought? Most of the time _____ Some of the time _____ Rarely _____
    b. While thinking about something or someone else? Most of the time _____ Some of the time _____ Rarely _____
    c. While thinking of a question to ask? Most of the time _____ Some of the time _____ Rarely _____
    d. Blurting out a question about something? Most of the time _____ Some of the time _____ Rarely _____
    e. While admiring (or disliking) some item of the speaker's apparel (such as the texture of the speaker's velour shirt)? Most of the time _____ Some of the time _____ Rarely _____
    f. _____ *(Insert your procedure.)* Most of the time _____ Some of the time _____ Rarely _____

Part 2—*Time:* APPROXIMATELY 5 MINUTES PER PARTICIPANT

Have the group discuss the learning styles revealed by each person's responses.

Identity-concept

Although learning styles and identity-concept are discussed separately to clarify some issues, they are interrelated. Individuals may show certain characteristics in one setting and others in another setting. Yet each individual tends to maintain a consistent general pattern of learning style and identity-concept.

The term "identity-concept" refers to the unique ideas an individual has about his or her role and status in society. It includes thoughts about maleness/femaleness, brightness/dullness, affluence/poverty, Catholic/Protestant/Jewish/Moslem, and white/black. These thoughts are partially imposed by one's family, community, government, and even the world situation—from the moment of birth. They are *ascribed* roles and functions. The *achieved* roles and functions develop from what the individual learns and accomplishes throughout his or her lifetime and the expectations and opportunities available to the person. These acquisitions establish the person's self-image of being educated/noneducated, credentialed/noncredentialed, professional/paraprofessional/nonprofessional, capable/incapable, and so on.

From birth the identity-concept is tightly interwoven with the "who," "what," and "how" of a person's existence. Exercises 1-2 and 1-3 focus on these aspects of the identity-concept.

Only a few aspects of the identity-concept are examined in Exercises 1-2 and 1-3, yet the characteristics explored define some of the boundaries of one's feelings about oneself and one's place in the world. In Exercise 1-2 woman, wife, mother,

---

Exercise 1-2
WHO AND WHAT ARE YOU? *(may be done alone or in a group)*

Part 1—*Time:* APPROXIMATELY 20 MINUTES

You need a pencil or pen and paper for this exercise. Work rapidly. Spend no more than 2 minutes to reply to each set of three questions. Write your first thought even if you consider it silly. Interpret the meaning of "who" and "what" questions as you perceive them. There is no right or wrong answer, only *your* answer. Respond to each question in sequence. List a minimum of five items for each question.

SET 1

1. Who am I?
2. Who do others think I am?
3. Who would I like to be?

SET 2

1. What am I?
2. What do others think I am?
3. What would I like to be?

Part 2—*Time:* 5 MINUTES PER PARTICIPANT

After completing your answers, look them over carefully. Think about your responses. Do they tell you anything about who you think you are and what you think you have achieved? What identity seems most impressive to you—which is first in your lists? Does this exercise clarify any future directions for you? If this exercise is conducted within the group, a group discussion with sharing of insights would be helpful. Compare the answers to questions 1 and 2, questions 1 and 3, and among all three questions in Sets 1 and 2. Did you discover dissimilarities between the "who" and "what" of your responses? Did you note contrasts between the "who" and "what" of your current self-image and the "who" and "what" you consider your ideal self? Were there discrepancies between your self-image and what others think of you?

daughter may be some of the ''who'' responses. Psychologist, educator, advocate, helper may be some of the ''what'' answers. For some individuals *what* they have achieved rather than their gender or family role is foremost; their response to ''Who am I?'' is psychologist or physician rather than man/husband/son or woman/wife/daughter. If a vast difference is demonstrated between the ''who'' and ''what'' of a person's self-identity and the identity perceived by others, or between the person's *real* self and *ideal* self, trouble may be brewing. Such discrepancies may reveal dissatisfaction with oneself and unresolved self-seeking. On the other hand they may indicate that the individual assumes a phony image with other people.

A person's name is one of the trademarks of identity as well as the representation of family origins. Shakespeare pinpointed the conflicts of a name in the sad tale of Romeo and Juliet when Juliet spoke (Act II):

O Romeo, Romeo! Wherefore art thou Romeo?
Deny thy father, and refuse thy name. . . .

Individuals who develop negative feelings about their names are likely to sustain negative feelings about themselves and their identities. The children of film or stage stars, authors, and scientists sometimes perceive the parent's name too difficult to ''live down'' or ''live up to.'' In the past few years several such persons have expressed their distraught identity crises through their writings or dramatically and tragically through suicide. Ben Jonson realized this difficulty in his seventeenth century comment (Timber; or Discoveries Made upon Men and Matter, 1640):

Greatness of name in the father oft times overwhelms son; they stand too near one another. The shadow kills the growth . . . so much, that we see the grandchild come more and oftener to be heir of the first.

Still another characteristic of identity is an individual's preference for certain objects or people as illustrated in Exercise 1-3. The person or object selected reveals characteristics of an individual's interactions with the environment, and an explanation of the basis for the person's choice furthers understanding of the person. The following example of Gerta's choice of object indicates some interesting projections of how she felt about herself.

Exercise 1-3
WHAT DO YOU SEE—OBJECTS AND PEOPLE? *(should be done in a group)*

Part 1—*Time:* APPROXIMATELY 5 MINUTES FOR SELECTION OF OBJECT
AND 5 MINUTES FOR EACH PERSON TO DISCUSS THE CHOICE OF OBJECT

Arrange your group into a circle. Look around the room at the objects. Pick an object in the environment that catches your eye and impresses you as representing one or more of your interests or characteristics. Think about this object. What does this object mean to you? What do you like or dislike about the object? Have each member of the group tell about the object selected and what it represents.

Part 2—*Time:* APPROXIMATELY 5 MINUTES FOR SELECTION OF PERSON
AND 5 MINUTES FOR EACH PERSON TO DISCUSS THE CHOICE OF PERSON

After you finish your discussion about objects, look around the room again. Select a person in the room who catches your eye, someone who has certain characteristics that attract you and that you would like to develop. Think about your choice of person. Have the members of the group tell about the characteristics of the person selected that they find particularly appealing.

Consider to yourself or discuss with the group what this exercise has revealed to you about yourself.

Example 1-3
GERTA'S FULFILLMENT

"Not again," thought Gerta, "nobody remembers what people say. Why do they always use that group dynamics gimmick—around the room, tell us who you are and what you do. And to top the joke, now we play the game . . . choose something or someone in the room and tell about what made you select that particular object or person. Oh, to remove this weary carcass from the confines of this room. Why did I ever get myself into this discussion group?"

The person next to Gerta finished his description of the person he had chosen. He had rambled on "forever," Gerta thought, about the look of strength and thoughtfulness of the handsome bearded man opposite him. "So much crap, now it's my turn."

Gerta looked around the room and had almost given up when she saw a cranberry-colored leather briefcase in the corner of the room. "That's it," Gerta called out, "over there, that rich-looking, soft, shiny leather briefcase. Terrific showpiece on the outside, but empty on the inside. There is a zippered section and two other slots, one each side . . . and another section on the outside. When I open the zipper I am surprised to see several papers because all the other pockets are empty. I remove the papers and look at each one carefully . . . don't mean anything to me . . . they're in some secret code. Yet, although I can't decipher the code, there is something about it that makes me think about several possibilities for getting some understanding of this code. Either I was able to read this at some time in my life and have forgotten how to do it now or I need to know only one key word so that I can decode this mysterious message. Or there is someone who can, and in fact wants to, help me understand the contents and even the lack of contents in this briefcase." Gerta's voice gets lower while she stares at the briefcase and then she looks around the room.

■ ■ ■

Gerta did not realize how much she revealed about herself through her comments about the briefcase. During the past year she had been divorced soon after she had undergone a massive mastectomy on her second breast. She felt useless and often complained about a feeling of "emptiness" to her friend Selma. In fact, one of the reasons she joined the discussion group was to meet people, fill her time with some interesting explorations of human relationships, and be intellectually stimulated.

During the discussion that followed Gerta's selection of the briefcase, group members suggested that

□ Gerta might not be too comfortable with people at the present time. Perhaps she selected an object— a noticeable, attractive object—hoping that she might be attractive and yet hidden in a corner, hoping that the loss of her breasts might not be obvious.

□ the hidden coded message in the zippered compartment might represent the parts of Gerta that she was concealing from herself, from others, or from both.

□ there was a positive note in what Gerta was describing. She pointed to some way in which the code might be deciphered—by herself or by someone who would help her.

These interpretations were elaborated, and the group support encouraged Gerta and other members to delve into their own experiences and self-knowledge for greater self-disclosure.

Self-disclosure

Individuals' ideas and feelings about themselves are a private matter. People erect cocoons of privacy, showing different parts of themselves at different times and with different people. Some individuals reveal more of themselves than do others and are often referred to as "open" people. Others appear to be cold or withdrawn and unresponsive and are labeled distant or "closed" people. Closed people may hide distressing thoughts from themselves as well as from others. Penetrating their defensive walls is difficult and sometimes dangerous, since their defensive walls often provide a shield protecting them from more serious behavioral disturbances.

Johari's window. One way of looking at a person's degree of openness is by means of the Johari window, a graphic model of interpersonal behavior. Joseph Luft (1969) developed the concept of the Johari window with Harry Ingham. (The term "Johari" was derived from the combination of their first names.) The Johari window can further understanding of human interactions through its technique for exploring levels of self-awareness, intrapersonal reactions (internalized ideas, feelings, and reactions), and interpersonal occurrences and relationships.

The Actual Self

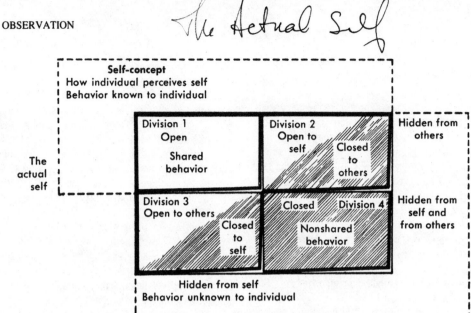

Fig. 1-2. The open and closed individual. (Modified from Group processes: an introduction to group dynamics by Joseph Luft. By permission of Mayfield Publishing Company [formerly National Press Books]. Copyright © 1963, 1970 by Joseph Luft.)

Fig. 1-2 is a diagram of Johari's window presenting a four-part division of the individual self. The entire figure represents the person's *actual self*, including all the person's attributes at any given moment. These attributes incorporate the psychological and physical characteristics emerging from the person's demographic and physical factors, developmental experiences, family structure, and the like. This actual self reflects a person's observable abilities and fulfillments as well as untapped, hidden, and unfulfilled potentials. Part of this complex of behavior, motivations, feelings, and potentials is known to the person (the self-concept) but may not be revealed entirely to others. As depicted in Fig. 1-2, self-concept includes divisions 1 and 2 but excludes 3 and 4. Division 3 represents behavior that is open to others but of which the person has little or no awareness; division 4 designates feelings, thoughts, acts that are controlled so that these are concealed both from the person and others. The following explanations detail these divisions more extensively.

Division 1: on top of the table. The behavior, motivation, feelings, and potentials that are open to oneself and shared with others. This portion shows the degree to which two or more persons can enjoy experiences together, can work together, and can freely give and take. The larger this area, the more available are the person's needs and abilities to self and to associates. In general, the larger the area of shared behavior, the stronger the person's contact with reality—with the world and other people.

Example 1-4 describes an "opening" of self after a person recognizes and deals with the problem of obesity.

Example 1-4
DON'S REALIZATION

Don smiled as he spoke of his rotund frame, "I have obesity. An eataholic, that's me. It's taken me a long time to say that out loud. But when my blood pressure began to jump as my weight increased, I got scared. You helped me at a crucial moment of my life, Doc. Do you know when I lost that first 30 pounds, I felt as if I had come out of a dark closet, even began to take some pride in what I was wearing. OK, I see that look again—yeah, I know your theory proposes that this is a lifelong job. Like a diabetic or an alcoholic or any of these forever ailments. I've got to be aware, careful, and continue contact with this program for a long time, maybe always. But for the first time in 10 years I don't mind meeting new people and speaking before groups.

Division 2: hidden agenda. The behavior, motivation, feelings, and potentials that are open to oneself and partially concealed from others. For instance, in a meeting a member may bring up a particular subject and keep "under the table" the subject he really wants to discuss (hidden agenda). Another person at the same meeting might suspect this concealment and resent some of the speaker's remarks but refrain from commenting despite the discomfort she feels. This form of concealment is sometimes referred to as ulterior motives. For example:

Bob may pretend that the only reason he wishes to tell Terry, his co-worker, about the boss's disparaging comments is to alert Terry to the hostility felt by Mr. M. Yet the ulterior motive may be that Bob hopes that such remarks will make Terry so uncomfortable in his job that he will resign. Then Bob will be able to move into Terry's job.

More and more lies become necessary to continue this kind of concealment of motives. This deceit propels the concealing person into ever-increasing demands for more elaborate pretenses. Eventually the snowballing lies can entrap the concealer.

Division 3: blind area. The behavior, motivation, feelings, and potentials that are open to others but not known to oneself. A person may be unaware of a mannerism in speech or gesture that may be obvious to others. For instance:

Bish purses his mouth when he listens to someone talking and sometimes when he is talking, Cora chews gum loudly and rapidly, and Tina tends to take over a meeting, directing the group's discussion into many tangential issues. Bish's pursed mouth, Cora's gum chewing, and Tina's domination are obvious to everyone but Bish, Cora, and Tina.

Robert Burns, the poet, wrote about behavior unknown to the individual but seen by others in his poem "To a Louse."

Oh wad some power the giftie gie us
To see oursels as others see us!

Mannerisms that may not be noticed by an individual are often caricatured by other people. The surprise and even shock of an instructor coming upon a student who is imitating the instructor's method of class presentation may range from mild distress to major disturbance. Characteristics of an individual become especially noticeable when the individual is involved in social events, particularly when large groups of people are present. Some traits of which the individual may be unaware may include physical peculiarities in walk, body movements, gestures, speech mannerisms, or distinctive approaches in social or business situations that reveal the need to command or to be commanded.

The reasons for the lack of awareness of certain characterisitics are complex. When these characteristics are just a part of the person's uniqueness, they present no impediment to the establishment of productive relationships. It is only when these actions interfere with satisfying one's goals that their discovery and alteration would be advisable.

Division 4: closet behavior. Behavior, motivation, feelings, and potentials closed to both oneself and others. Occasionally certain behavior or motives peep through the slightly opened closet door. At such times the individual and others discover the previously hidden behavior.

The most concealed area of behavior, motives, feelings, and potentials is closed to oneself and to others. A great deal of energy is expended by the individual who forcefully forgets and conceals from others present thoughts or past experiences so painful that to face them would be destructive to the person and sometimes to others. This hidden area may contain behavior of which the individual is ashamed, past actions that arouse feelings of guilt, or even unfulfilled acts the person has considered. There may be some less offensive events and beliefs that the individual has distorted to undue proportions. On the other hand, favorable characteristics may emerge. People in stress situations may surprise everyone by exhibiting unexpected assertiveness, organizational abilities, or great physical strength. Erica, Jerry, and Myra in Example 1-5 display uncloseted and closeted behavior.

Example 1-5
UNCLOSETED AND CLOSETED BEHAVIOR

Erica surprises herself and her friends by taking over the leadership of the group during a critical discussion that is "getting nowhere." Jerry discovers that he can mollify the warring factions in the group so that Erica can be effective in her efforts. Erica and her friends "didn't know she had it in her." Jerry never saw himself as a peacemaker, nor did anyone else realize his calming effect on the group. However, the potentials have always been present.

Myra presents another problem. She cannot understand why men do not interest her nor why she is uncomfortable during her sexual encounters with them. Her mother has often asked her when she would find "Mr. Right," and this irritates her more and more as her mother reminds her that she now is reaching the unmarried age of 33. Myra wonders what she should do. She is certain there is no man she wants to marry, yet she is not satisfied with her "singleness." "What can it be?" she ponders, "Where is the answer?" For Myra the dilemma remains closeted behavior, forbidden inclinations.

Openness. The question of openness must be approached cautiously. Openness is not good in and of itself. Some people may be open (speak and act without restraint) as a defensive measure. For example:

Ted may believe that self-revelation will cover up the discomfort that he really feels with Jane. Sandy may reveal certain information about herself because she wishes to shock or verbally hurt Mark. Her hostile act may satisfy her for the moment but does not promote constructive growth in her relationship with Mark.

Sincere, comfortably open individuals are committed to sharing ideas, feelings, and activities because of the mutual satisfactions involved in the interpersonal situation. Closed individuals are committed to nonsharing to protect themselves from real or imagined distress. However, these distinctions must be considered within the framework of the interpersonal and situational factors that are powerful determinants of each person's behavior (Chelune and others, 1979).

Expanding one's awareness about oneself and others often encourages understanding and improved interrelationships. Exercise 1-4 directs attention to one aspect of "consciousness raising," sharing of self.

The findings from Exercise 1-4 do not indicate whether an individual's self-disclosure is adequate or inadequate. This can be appraised only within the context of a given situation, a particular time, and with a given person. In other words when, what, to whom, by whom, and to what degree are all components related to the level of adaptive and maladaptive behavior self-disclosure tends to indicate. Johari's window represents areas of exposure or openness, not levels of coping skills. Furthermore, there is not a one-to-one linear relationship between increasing or decreasing self-disclosure and mental health (Jourard, 1971). For instance, increased self-concealment is frequent when an individual enters a new situation, particularly if one is likely to meet the same people again or if the people know one's friends, relatives, or others important in one's social, school, work, or other life space. In time, if an individual gets to know the person(s) better in a group and "feels more at ease," the extent of self-disclosure becomes wider and fuller. Fig. 1-3 diagrams these changes in self-concealment.

Self-disclosure can be a strategy for establishing a more intimate, acceptant atmosphere. When self-disclosure is appropriately used by the helping person, it can enrich the communication in a one-to-one situation as well as in a group. Two factors (Chelune and others, 1979) enter into this disclosure relationship: (1) the reciprocity of dyadic effect—the tendency of a target person to match the original speaker's level of disclosure, and (2) the "liking effect"—the tendency of the recipient to be more attracted to a speaker who discloses more

Exercise 1-4
HOW MUCH OF YOURSELF DO YOU SHARE WITH OTHERS? *(may be done alone or in a group)*

Part 1—*Time:* APPROXIMATELY 10 MINUTES   *Consciousness raising*

Think about the questions listed in this exercise. Answer them in terms of how you feel you act in most of your encounters with people. Remember there are no right or wrong answers. Check the reply that best suits your feelings about yourself.

1. Do you feel you are an open person? Yes _____ Sometimes _____ No _____
2. Do you prefer that people do not know too much about you? Yes _____ Sometimes _____ No _____
3. Do you feel free to tell people about yourself? Yes _____ Sometimes _____ No _____
4. Do you get upset if someone is told something about you that you prefer that person did not know? Yes _____ Sometimes _____ No _____
5. Do you like people to ask you questions about yourself? Yes _____ Sometimes _____ No _____
6. Do you feel exposed when people seem to know too much about you? Yes _____ Sometimes _____ No _____
7. Have other people told you that you are frank? Yes _____ Sometimes _____ No _____
8. Do you like people to know you better? Yes _____ Sometimes _____ No _____
9. Would you feel comfortable writing about your life experiences? Yes _____ Sometimes _____ No _____
10. Do you feel people are prying if they ask you questions about yourself? Yes _____ Sometimes _____ No _____

Part 2—*Time:* APPROXIMATELY 8 TO 10 MINUTES PER PARTICIPANT

After completing the questions, look over your answers. What do you see as the predominant trend in your answers? Discuss your ideas and feelings about yourself with the group members. If you are doing this exercise alone, write your analysis of the significance of your answers so that you coordinate your replies more meaningfully.

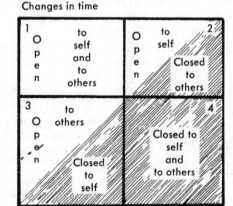

Fig. 1-3. Shifting self-concealment. (Modified from Group processes: an introduction to group dynamics by Joseph Luft. By permission of Mayfield Publishing Company [formerly National Press Books]. Copyright © 1963, 1970 by Joseph Luft.)

than to one who discloses less. In addition the skillful helper seeks self-understanding as well as motivation of others by means of self-disclosure.

Channels for self-disclosure. The discussion to this point has concentrated on the explanation of the significance of disclosure and the importance of appropriate self-disclosure in the helping event. The following methods are examples of procedures for identifying the degree of self-disclosure and the ways in which people reveal themselves.

☐ One method for assessing the degree of self-disclosure is the *self-report* or *self-rating questionnaire*. Self-report inventories and questionnaires, such as that in Exercise 1-4, are similar to *Jourard's Self-Disclosure Questionnaire (JSDQ)* (Jourard, 1971). They assess the person's degree of repression and comfort in sociability.

☐ Another technique, a *sociometric procedure,* requires peer observation with objective scoring. This form relies on the analysis of interpersonal relations in terms of personal reactions to each other or members of a group in a designated situation. Such observations also may be accomplished by the counselor.

☐ Still another source for determining self-disclosure is through the *esthetic pursuits* of individuals. Painting, poetry, fiction, and other channels for creative expression reveal thoughts about how individuals view themselves.

The following poem is taken from *The Me Nobody Knows,* a book edited by Stephen M. Joseph (1969). Joseph, a teacher, gathered the writings of students in New York City. One poem boldly states a great deal about the self-concept of Frank Cleveland, a 17-year-old high school student who used the pen name, "Clorox."

What am I?

I have no manhood—what am I?

You made my woman head of the house—what am I?

You have oriented me so that I hate and distrust my brothers and sisters—what am I?

You mispronounce my name and say I have no self-respect—what am I?

You give me a dilapidated education system and expect me to compete with you—what am I?

You say I have no dignity and then deprive me of my culture—what am I?

Exercise 1-5
WHAT ABOUT SELF-DISCLOSURE IN A POEM? *(may be done alone or in a group)*

Time: APPROXIMATELY 15 MINUTES

After you have read the poem "What am I?" (pp. 20-21), answer the following questions.

☐ What does the pen name "Clorox" tell you about the way Frank feels about himself and about other people?

☐ Do you think Frank perceives himself favorably? Unfavorably? Explain.

☐ How do you think Frank thinks others perceive him?

☐ How would you describe Frank's identity-concept?

☐ What prejudices for and against people, institutions, and ideas does Frank express?

☐ How much of Frank's feelings, thought, and behavior is he revealing, and how much is he concealing?

☐ How do you feel about Frank?

☐ Do you think Frank needs help from a counselor or someone else? If so, how would you help him? If not, what self-disclosures about Frank led to your decision?

These questions may be used for your consideration but would be more effective as springboards for small group discussion.

You call me boy, dirty lowdown slut—what am I?
Now I'm a victim of the welfare system—what am I?
You tell me to wait for change to come, but 400 years
    have passed and change ain't come—what am I?
I am all of your sins
I am the skeleton in your closets
I am the unwanted sons and daughters in laws, and
    rejected babies
I may be your destruction, but above all I am, as you
    so crudely put it, your nigger.

Frank discloses many annoyances with society for relegating him to a second-class citizenship status. The anger he expresses about his devalued identity emerges from background roots traumatized by a ghettoized existence. For some blacks the struggle against racism in the 1980s has become the class struggle. Others have accepted other paths and other channels for change. However, for all individuals identity begins at birth and proceeds from attachment to detachment and from detachment to involvement.

Development of identity

Each person begins life as part of someone else and must move away, become differentiated, before renewing involvement with these origins. In other words, detachment from one's parents and establishment of a separate identity must occur before one can view one's parents as people and become involved with them at another level of experience.

From attachment to detachment. The unborn child is an obvious example of physical attachment within the mother's womb—a symbiotic relationship. The mother and the developing fetus are intimately "living together," and the embryo and then the fetus are completely dependent on the mother. The lives of the developing organisms would be jeopardized if they were born before most of their vital processes were sufficiently mature. This mutual support results in satisfaction for the mother and the fetus; there is an interattachment.

The attachment continues after birth with an additional twist—newborn infants must learn to become dependent on others to obtain satisfaction of needs from them. Infants must, in fact, train the people around them to answer their cries and gurgles. A form of emotional attachment begins that is closely interwoven with physical attachment and comfort. Out of this arises trust or mistrust, which is the beginning step in the development of identity. For infants trust signifies that this is a fairly predictable and mostly pleasant world. It is essential that infants begin to feel, "I am important to someone." This feeling of importance, of belonging, of being cared for, of dependence, moves infants into self-exploration and into mastering themselves and the things and people around them. They begin to separate themselves and to become differentiated from the blurring confusion of people and things in the environment.

It is interesting to note the parallel of infants' progress with that of individuals who seek or are brought for help. Clients find the answer to their problems, whether large or small, with the assistance of a more knowing person. Seeking persons must feel that they can trust the helping person before any changes will occur. They attach themselves to a counseling transaction in which they feel that they are important to someone, belong, and are cared about. With this dependence on a helping person, clients are better prepared to explore and to master themselves and the things and the people around them. The confusion becomes explainable, and new relationships are initiated in which the clients detach themselves from the counseling situation toward independence. Every so often during this developing period they return for emotional refueling and start out again with renewed vigor. Just as crawling infants acquire steadiness to stand, to walk, and to assert themselves, so are clients able to begin to function on their own.

At first infants or toddlers require the physical and psychological nearness of the mother to develop self-esteem and autonomy (independence). Later, when they begin to move about on their own, they may become overenthusiastic and temporarily dismiss the frustration that comes from failure to get where they are heading. It is at this time, when toddlers venture farther away, that they most need their parents' warmth, understanding, and support.

The comparison of the infants' striking out on their identity adventure with clients' activities in establishing or reestablishing identity is apparent. Persons seeking help are more or less trying to define or redefine themselves. The college student puzzling with the counselor over the choice of college major and the alienated, hostile, or depressed individual are both trying to refine their identities. The college student wants to discover which major fits his or her identity best and hopes to discard some of the choices (detach self from them). The pressure of parents or of the counselor to fit the college student into certain molds encourages attachment or aggressive detachment and a blurred identity for the student. The student needs warmth, understanding, support, and also the opportunity for self-direction in defining self and goals more clearly. This process is rapid for some students, slow for others.

The alienated individual is enveloped in a more serious identity crisis. Such an identity crisis may occur during any change point in an individual's life. At each of these points the person is making another shift from attachment to certain characteristics and/or people to detachment. The first of these points occurs when infants physically leave their mother as they begin to walk. Toddlers detach themselves more and more as they develop confidence in their increasing ability to stand on their own, both physically and psychologically. Away they run, only to return periodically to make certain of their mother's presence if they should need her comfort. If the mother should leave the room so that the toddlers cannot find her, their activity slows down, and they show signs of alienation from their surroundings as their searching, moving about, and interest in surroundings decrease. It is almost as if the infants were saying, "It's all right for me to leave you [to become detached], but I need you around so that I can be me."

Several other change points result in identity definition for the individual. Adolescence, for instance, brings with it the even greater change point.

Adolescents must adjust to a physically changing body as well as to the push/pull of detachment from their parents and attachment to their peers. This is a period when identity conflicts with autonomy. Adolescents push away from the viewpoints of their parents in an effort to establish their separate self-identity; yet they still need some important others to whom they may relate. So they turn toward selected peers and identify with their codes of behavior. They adopt the life-style, the hairstyle, and the uniform of the day, becoming more anonymous in the peer crowd. They eventually resolve this clash between identity and anonymity if the social situations allow it.

This clash is more unsurmountable for individuals from minority groups. The black youth finds that in spite of the new enlightenment, to many he is still "boy," openly stated or secretly thought. To ensure his identity, the black man must choose from several options. He may detach himself from a black identity and become more like whites, or he may become more militantly attached to his black identity with subsequent detachment from "whitey." A third way is a little more subtle—he becomes hostilely seductive, particularly with white women.

Hispanics must phase out their Spanish-speaking identity and in the process assume a slow-learner identity in the English-speaking school. They, too, have several choices for the resolution of the clash between identity and anonymity. They may detach themselves from their parents' customs and speech, their Hispanic friends, and their life-style and show an Anglo identity. Conversely, they, like blacks or Indians, may adopt a militantly Hispanic identity in which they detach themselves from the Anglo world, speak Spanish, leave school, and attach themselves to the hairstyle and dress of Hispanic peers.

Change is inevitable for everyone. During the person's lifetime new strivings evolve from new orientations. The progressive growth occurring approximately in the mid-twenties becomes stability of growth through the mid-forties, after which there is gradual decline or regressive growth (Gubrium,

1976). As individuals reach mid-life, they are confronted with a number of transitions that require mastery of certain developmental tasks (Cytrynbaum and others, 1980). These tasks entail a review of primary relationships and a restructuring of sexual identity. Changes in work, career, creativity, and achievements may be necessitated by recognition of biological limitations and health risks and the realization and acceptance of one's mortality. Joined with these transitional tasks is the alteration of one's identity-concept. Although the age of the frailer individual, the "at risk" period, varies from person to person, it is inevitable that at some point vigor will be decreased, mobility will be curtailed, and assistance will often be needed in one's daily tasks. With further aging, therefore, the process from attachment to detachment is often reversed. The cycle of development is completed, and dependence, attachment, becomes more prevalent.

At each stage of development the potential for unresolved conflicts is apparent. Out of these conflicts rises identity confusion or a constant battle for identity survival. What does this mean to counselors? First, it means that counselors must experience accurate empathy. This special kind of understanding must begin with counselors themselves. There are other considerations. Do the counselors fit the client's needs? Do counselors know themselves well enough that they are able to be genuine with their clients, no matter what their race, color, creed, ethnic background, or age? Do the counselors trust their own identity so that they may encourage the clients to trust them? Have the counselors progressed from the attachment-detachment conflict to the next stage, detachment-involvement?

From detachment to involvement. Independence must emerge before the individual is able to reinstate more mature involvement. The desirability of independence has been written about in poetry and prose. Others have written vigorously in favor of involvement and interdependence. For instance, Thoreau referred to independence in Walden (1854):

If a man does not keep pace with his companions, perhaps it is because he hears a different drummer. Let him step to the music which he hears, however measured or far away (Thoreau).

Walt Whitman ("Song of Myself," Sec. 20, 1855) added another perspective in a humorous vein:

I wear my hat as I please indoors or out.

Caution and the need as well as the fact of involvement were urged by Benjamin Tucker (*Instead of a Book,* 1893):

Independence is good, but isolation is too high a price to pay for it.

and John Donne (*Quotation upon Emergent Occasions,* No. 6, 1624):

No man is an island, entire of itself.

Both Thoreau and Whitman stress self-expression as characteristics of independence. Tucker and Donne insert a precautionary note, that independence to the point of over-self-reliance (for example, not attending to other humans, not asking for assistance even in instances of great need) is overdoing the act of independence.

Adults supposedly are expected and permitted to be independent. What about children? Christopher Robin (Milne, 1924) brings to attention the growing independence of the young child:

I never did, I never did, I never *did* like "Now take care, dear!"
I never did, I never did, I never *did* want "Hold-my-hand";
I never did, I never did, I never *did* think much of "Not up there, dear!"
It's no good saying it. They don't understand.

Even these few examples of views about independence indicate the diversity of meanings it may have for individuals. Self-care and opportunities for self-expression are the nub of independence, but the channels for expression and recognition vary with such things as culture, age, sex, and intellectual and physical characteristics.

Attached (dependent) infants grow into interdependent adults because of the interest and caring of others. They move ahead to self-respect because of the intimacy others feel and experience with them. They learn responsibility because other responsible people are involved with them. Caring means both love/liking and restraints/discipline. Stunted psychological growth often results if the developing child, client, or counselor is exposed to only one aspect of caring: exclusive love or exacting discipline. These characteristics of interdependence, caring, discipline, involvement, and responsibility are essential for the effective counselor.

Independence is not easily achieved by the growing child, the struggling client, or the beginning counselor. Each forms a strong attachment to an important other person. Each becomes dependent (attached) to this person, from whom they learn to seek help. Yet each must also become independent (detached). For some 4-year-old children, gaining independence means walking alone, near a parent, perhaps, but not holding hands. The client and the counselor also need to be gradually released from the symbolic hands that guide them.

As the child, the client, and the counselor-trainee begin to form their own ideas of self-identity, they may be pleased with the care, the direction, and the outstretched hand. However, if the development stops at this point, complications arise from the continuing attachment. Instead of self-identity,

smudged carbon copies result. The individuals are not as confident or as competent as the original.

To move from detachment-independence to involvement-interdependence, individuals must feel comfortable with themselves and with others. In the process of detachment they become more aware of themselves, more alert to their ability to achieve, and more defined as individuals. They are on the way to finding their meaning for life; they become involved. Finding oneself signifies realizing one's strengths and weaknesses, appreciating the worthiness of one's abilities, altering when possible one's inabilities, and accepting what cannot be changed. There is nothing profound about this statement. It has been repeated in one form or another by many self-help groups such as Alcoholics Anonymous. Yet becoming aware and acceptant of one's strengths, imperfections, and weaknesses is not a simple matter. Exercise 1-6 is a beginning effort toward exploring one's strengths and weaknesses.

Alienated and/or depressed persons react differently from individuals developing a satisfying self-image. They cannot move from either severe detachment (alienation) or deep attachment with self-concern (depression). Unable to find joy or meaning, they may strike out for power, excessive pleasure, or even death. None of these goals leads to self-satisfaction, but rather to frustration or self-

---

Exercise 1-6
WHAT DO YOU INTERPRET AS STRENGTHS AND WEAKNESSES?
(may be done alone and discussed in a group)

Time: APPROXIMATELY 35 MINUTES

Complete Fig. 1-4 and then gather into a small group. You, of course, present only that information about yourself which you feel comfortable to share, so feel free to write comments about yourself and others on the list for your own clarification.

Write next to each person listed what you like most (the strengths) and what you like least (the weaknesses). A word or a short phrase is sufficient to pinpoint your responses. Next to numbers 9 and 10 fill in the names of other family members, friends, or acquaintances and list information about strengths and weaknesses as you did previously.

After completing the list, look it over to note whether any pattern emerges. Are your strengths and weaknesses similar to those of anyone else?

	The strengths I like most	The weaknesses I like least
1. My mother		
2. My father		
3. My sister		
4. My brother		
5. My friend		
6. My instructor		
7. My employer		
8. Myself		
9.		
10.		

Fig. 1-4. Strengths and weaknesses score sheet.

extinction. Alienated or depressed individuals suffer from what Frankl (1963) termed "hyperintention"—excessive attention to one's own and/or to others' needs. This overabundant attempt to satisfy needs is not the same as involvement. Persons who accept the challenge of first discovering and fulfilling themselves are more receptive and capable of becoming involved with others. The alienated or depressed individual is often tormented with attachment or involvement and threatened by the loss of security in the event of withdrawal from these pseudosatisfactions.

In essence, alienation is an example of another kind of involvement, self-involvement. Alienated individuals become more and more detached from others as they hide in themselves. This self-attachment is a protective device to conceal the anxiety they feel in person-to-person encounters. Alienated people stop growing outward, toward others, and grow inward, toward self. Their self-concentrated behavior is revealed in the way they handle relationships. Other people are considered as "better," "not better," "more important," or "less important." Often alienated individuals seek ways to exploit situations and people to satisfy their own needs. Rather than pursuing a working partnership with another respected individual, they persistently are directed toward self-seeking and self-gratification; their "I-ity" remains unsatisfied. They dehumanize the other person and think of and feel toward the other person as an "it," an object (Buber, 1958).

Dehumanization and anonymity are close allies. Anonymity results in treating another person as a formless "watchamacallit." "What's-his-name" takes up physical space but very little psychological space. "Who's-that" has no identity as a human being; he or she is anonymous. Why pay attention to a nonessential except to move him or her out of your space? That "wheelchairer" takes up too much time and money if provisions are to be made so that she can travel on the bus. That "retardate" should remain in the country so that "my children won't be exposed to him." That "former crazy" annoys me when she talks and yells at the air as she walks down the street. It is so simple to relegate

the disabled persons to anonymity and not much more difficult to use the same thought processes in relation to members of racial and cultural groups.

Dehumanizing another person or group of persons not only encourages disregarding their needs, but also makes violence and murder possible and almost inevitable. Violence does not need to be physical to be disturbing. It may be branding as "horse manure" the achievement record of the presidential incumbent seeking reelection. It may be tagging someone from a minority group a slow learner or mentally retarded. Both of these do violence to the identity of an individual. Murder takes many forms. It may be the sniping of the anony-

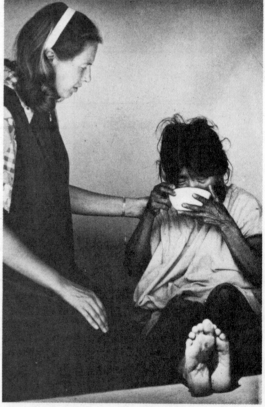

Fig. 1-5. The many segments of services to humans. Involvement of the helper's humanness in the helping situation requires that the helper care about the client and feel comfortable in sharing her human qualities.

Michael Hayman, Image, Inc.

mous enemy during a war, the killing of black children on the streets of Atlanta, or the slow torture (sometimes self-torture) of hunger and malnourishment.

How does knowledge of dehumanization enrich the helper's professional self? The importance of information about depersonalized relationships crystallizes the role of the helper and clarifies the impact of identity-destructive experiences for the person seeking help. "The only essential requirement for counseling is humanness, which is the capacity of an individual to be open to another human being without judging and without losing his own individuality" (Webster, 1973). Humanness includes an individual's weaknesses as well as his strengths. Involvement of the helper's hu-

manness in the helping situation requires that the helper feel comfortable sharing his human qualities. The primary objective of this sharing is to help clients accept themselves as they are so that they may start becoming what they want to be. There is a catch in this sharing. Helpers must be sufficiently detached from their own desires during the counseling or other helping transaction so that they do not become self-involved and self-therapeutic. The help is for the client, not for the helper.

Self-acceptance does not imply a static continuance for either the helper or the client. The quest for self-understanding involves exploration of one's needs, wants, and changes. Exercise 1-7 provides a method for such exploration.

Exercise 1-7
HOW DO YOU SEE YOUR NEEDS, WANTS, AND CHANGES?
(may be done alone and discussed in a group)

Time: APPROXIMATELY 25 MINUTES

Complete the following statements and then gather in groups of five to discuss your responses. Present to your group only that information you feel comfortable revealing. The statements you make should be current "here and now," not the past or the future. Interpret the differences between need and want according to your own meanings.

What I need most:

What I want most:

I will change by doing the following:

I don't think I can change because:

Self-understanding for establishing a professional self requires:

☐ More than information about learning style

☐ More than information about the development of identity and the identity concept

☐ More than information about self-disclosure

Helpers need to become aware of the origins of behavior to appreciate their roots and the effect of these background factors on their relationships with clients.

THE ORIGINS OF BEHAVIOR

Behavior is derived from a complex and continuous person-environment transaction (Ivey and Simek-Downing, 1980). When clients first meet the helper, whether in the interviewer's office or somewhere else, they step into a new world. This is the world of the interviewer, which is distinguished by all the interviewer's values, feelings, and surroundings, as well as the attitudes and influences on the interviewer of other people.

Clients bring with them the predominant culture of their parents, the way they feel about themselves, and the argument with their mother or spouse over their uneaten breakfast, overtime at the office, lack of money to buy a down coat, or job refusal received that morning. Along with the client arrive fears about the exam in psychology, whether a new roommate will "work out," and how much longer it will be possible to cover up an increasing loss of memory. The smile on the client's face reflects the recollection of the exhilaration felt while skiing down the winding slope of the mountain last weekend. The frown was etched there from years of feeling that he or she is a failure and not knowing who or what to become.

The helper also has memories of poverty or affluence, parental or marital squabbles, and recognition or nonrecognition and introduces his or her style of humanity into the interview. Out of these determinants shared by the helper and the client comes the behavioral transaction—a dynamic interaction of persons and environments.

Since both helper and client bring a life-style to the interview, the social system of the interview is not a clean sheet of paper. Every interview is different because of factors such as the participants' differing demographic, familial, physical, intellectual, and developmental experiences.

Demographic factors

Demographic factors, those vital statistics gathered by the U.S. Bureau of the Census every 10 years and most recently in 1980, refer to the distribution of people in neighborhoods and certain characteristics of the inhabitants of each household. Such items as birthplace, race, ethnic origin, sex, age, socioeconomic status, education, religion, and geographical origin produce primary cultural effects on the person.

Fig. 1-6. Background roots: family history. (Copyright © 1973 by Norman Hurst. Courtesy Stock, Boston, Inc.)

Familial factors

The family into which the person is born (family of origin or orientation) molds the future family style before the child becomes adult. The patterns of interpersonal relations practiced by the individual's family of orientation will be continued in a more or less modified fashion in the individual's family of procreation, which the person initiates after establishing his or her own home. Factors such as parental relationships, parents or other significant adults with hereditary illnesses or emotional disorders, and the relationships between siblings (brothers and sisters) are significant.

Examination of demographic and familial factors was given much attention during the 1970s. Background roots opened up a vast field of inquiry in literature, films, and television. Games and charts were constructed to examine "roots." Alex Haley spent 12 years searching for his ancestry and wrote the book *Roots* (1976), from which a successful television program emerged. *The Autobiography of My Mother* by R. Brown (1976) presents the confrontation and antagonism between mother and daughter within the context of contrasting and conflicting backgrounds and life-styles. Family dynamics also are depicted in Philip Roth's story *The Ghost Writer* (1979) about the young writer in search of a "spiritual father" who would comprehend and validate his art and support him in his flight from a conventionally constrictive yet loving middle-class home. Other portraits of families are presented in novels, plays, and television shows such as *Centennial* and *Eight is Enough*. The realization that demographic and familial factors affect personal life-styles does not mean that an effective helper *must* delve into the client's past. However, exploring these roots clarifies for some helpers the contribution of these factors to life-style. Exercise 1-8 presents a means for examining demographic origins and familial history.

Exercise 1-8
HOW DO YOU DESCRIBE YOUR BACKGROUND ROOTS?
(to be done alone and, if desired, discussed in the group)

Time: VARIABLE, DEPENDING ON EXTENSIVENESS OF INDIVIDUAL'S EXAMINATION OF BACKGROUND ROOTS

Part 1

☐ Write as much as you know about your demographic origins and family history. Refer to the description of these two areas of information earlier in this chapter to determine the items to be included.

☐ Interview two people close to you, such as one of your parents and preferably a grandparent, to discover their views of their demographic factors and of the intergenerational family history. Write a separate description of the information each person relates to you. If you are interested in obtaining a fuller picture, you might interview other relatives, including siblings.

Part 2

Consider and write your answers to the following questions.

☐ What have you learned about yourself that you did not realize before you wrote about your background roots? If your answer is "nothing," think about whether you really have been open and thorough in your comments and explorations.

☐ Do you notice any differences between your recollections and those of the people you interviewed? If your reply is "yes", how do you explain the differences? Do the similarities have any relation to how you feel about yourself, your family, and others?

Continued.

HOW DO YOU DESCRIBE YOUR BACKGROUND ROOTS?
(to be done alone and, if desired, discussed in the group)

Part 3

Draw a family systems chart as diagrammed in Fig. 1-7 to show the people living in your home at present. If you are living with your parents, draw one chart; if you and your family have different living arrangements, draw two charts.

☐ Your family systems chart should show the distance between you and the people living with you. Interpersonal distances are indicated by the length of the arrows—the further apart you consider the distance between persons, the greater the length of your arrow; closer relationships would be indicated by shorter arrows.

☐ Draw a square or rectangle (your chart space). Place yourself (''me'') on the chart in relation to the other people to indicate whether you believe yourself to be at the center of the family relationships, nearer certain persons, or on the fringe of the family relationships. Consider how comfortable you feel in this family.

☐ Your arrows or circle should portray the type of interrelationships you consider yourself to have with your family members. A full, reciprocal relationship of mutual respect and acceptance is shown by drawing a circle of arrows as follows:

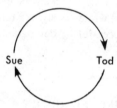

This indicates that there is a satisfying *transaction* most of the time between yourself and the family member.

If you feel that your relationship with another family member is satisfying some of the time, but you feel uncertain of the other person's acceptance of you because some of the time there are arguments, lack of listening, impositions on your striving for independence, lack of understanding, or other reactions you consider undesirable, draw your arrows as follows:

$$Sue \longleftrightarrow Tod$$

This indicates *interaction*, a close relationship but with some flaws more often than you prefer.

If you feel a lack of respect, acceptance, or both most of the time, if communication is often one-sided and not too satisfying, then draw your arrows as follows:

This indicates an *action/reaction relationship*, the inadequacy of response and responsiveness.

☐ Place significant people not living within the home outside of the enclosure (square or rectangle) of your household. Draw arrows to indicate the distances from these persons and the type of relationship—transaction (circle), interaction (double arrows), action-reaction (one arrow).

Does your family system chart give you any hints about how you feel about yourself? In your description of your background roots, which events in your background seem to have had the most influence on you? Do your background roots reveal anything about how some of your ideas, beliefs, values, feelings have evolved?

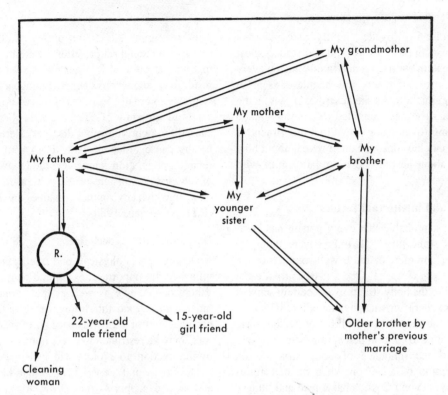

Fig. 1-7. Family system chart of 19-year-old woman representing her description of family relationships within her home and with some significant people not living in her household.

Exercise 1-9
HOW DO YOU DESCRIBE ROZELLE'S FAMILY SYSTEM CHART?
(may be done alone and discussed in group)

Part 1—*Time:* APPROXIMATELY 25 MINUTES

Look at Fig. 1-7. Note the position of Rozelle ("R") and the position of and distance between people as well as the type of arrows. Then answer the following questions:

- □ Which individuals have an action-reaction (⇄) relationship with "R" and with each other? What do those action-reaction relationships tell you about the interpersonal communications of "R" with these people?
- □ Which individuals have an interaction (⟷) relationship with "R" and with each other? What do these interaction relationships tell you about the interpersonal communications of "R" with these people?
- □ What does the family system chart tell you about the 19-year-old woman?

Part 2—*Time:* 10 MINUTES

Divide the larger group into subgroups of four members. Discuss your answers to the questions in Part 1 with your subgroup members.

In Exercise 1-9 Rozelle's family system chart is diagrammed. She is 19 years old and stutters most of the time with her friends and family and on every occasion when she meets new people or is in an unfamiliar situation. As she describes it, within the past 5 years she has attempted to commit suicide by "OD-ing (overdosing)" with an assortment of drugs What clues does the chart reveal about how she feels about herself and her relationships with other persons?

Physical and intellectual factors

It is most probable that every person has commented at some time, "If only I were taller, or shorter, or slimmer, or more well-rounded in the 'right' places, or . . ." One's genes provide the beginning to the body structure and certain sensory or physical characteristics, but an individual's feeling about the satisfaction with his or her body are closely related to cultural perceptions. Shakespeare recognized the influence of body structure on the perception of a person when he had Julius Caesar say, "Yond Cassius has a lean and hungry look; He thinks too much: such men are dangerous."

Attitudes toward well-rounded women differ among cultures. Hairstyles among different races as well as for men and women of the same race have fluctuated in length and spread. Physical factors affect the behavior of the people around an individual as well as the individual himself. These physical factors include body structure (large or small boned, obese or slim, tall or short), facial features, general state of health, medical history, and physical defects.

Intellectual factors often become sharply embroiled in the heredity-environment issue. Many myths have evolved about the origin and impact of genetic and experiential influences. Just as with physical factors, intellectual functioning is dependent on the attitudes of others—how society feels and acts toward "people who are different." The causes of retardation in persons considered mentally retarded, for example, may be exogenous (initiated by external events). Retardation may be caused by injury, infection during or after birth, or environmental deprivation. Cerebral malformation and cultural-familial retardation primarily result from exogenous causes. Endogenous causes originate internally from genetic makeup. Down's syndrome (trisomy 21) is an example of retardation caused by a chromosomal disorder. Heredity may be the cause of about 10% to 15% of the total retarded population. However, the largest number of retarded persons are of the cultural-familial variety, in which environment assumes the major role (E.D. Schulman, 1980).

Developmental experiences

Demographic, physical, and intellectual factors influence the opportunities offered to individuals. Where people live as well as the extent of their movement beyond this immediate dwelling place becomes part of their life space. Life space, therefore, may be restricted to one's home or expanded by the freedom to explore wider vistas.

Developmental experiences (what happens to and around people as they grow up) provide environmental opportunities; individuals' use of these opportunities is modified by the degree of sharpness of their vision, hearing, and other senses. The developmental experiences that may expand or decrease individuals' potentials depend on their interpersonal relations with family, neighborhood people, peers, and teachers. What happens at home, at church, at school, and in the military will affect an individual's feelings about people, sex, and interpersonal relations in general.

The ecological approach takes into account the individual's interaction with many aspects of the environment. These subenvironments include objects, people, geography, climate, and all other variables in an individual's life space at any given moment as well as during the individual's lifetime. A two-way process exists: the subenvironments impinge on the individual's development, for better or worse, and the individual affects the environment, favorably or unfavorably. (E.D. Schulman, 1980).

In essence, it certainly helps to be "born well"

in accordance with the prevailing standards of the "good life." It also "makes life easier" if the person is able to "live well," encountering developmental experiences that are enriching and fulfilling. Yet the person that evolves from these so-called excellent experiences is the consequence of a complex of factors. Human service workers who are knowledgeable about the interactive quality of their own background roots realize their potential effect on the helping situation and are alert to the added impact of the background roots of the person seeking help. It is no surprise that because of the interplay of these factors, characteristics such as race, religion, and birthplace may evoke certain prejudices that interfere with the flow of an interview. (See Chapter 2 for further discussion of prejudices.) It is no surprise that sexual role perceptions, socioeconomic class, ethnic differences, and value orientations (Turner, 1978) are the staples of

Fig. 1-8. Developmental experiences: the father's role is important.

the helping process. It is no surprise that life-coping skills emerge from these roots and that attitudes toward people and their differences affect the quantity and quality of attention and helpfulness in interpersonal situations.

VALUES CLARIFICATION

Basic to life-coping skills are values—the helper's values as well as the client's values. Therefore one of the preparatory aspects for the human service worker is *values clarification*—the sorting out of actual values, ideal values, and conflicting values (Cormier and Cormier, 1979; Simon, Howe, and Kirschenbaum, 1972).

Raths, Harmin, and Simon (1966) evolved the values clarification theory and differentiated two distinct entities that relate to values: value indicators and actual values. *Value indicators* indicate what a value is in the process of becoming; *actual values* are reflected in the person's behavior. "Beliefs, goals, attitudes, ethics, morals, feelings, thoughts, interests, and aspirations" (Simon, 1980) are value indicators. What individuals *do* about racism, sexism, political issues, family relationships, and academic and occupational pursuits represents their actual values. Exercises 1-10 and 1-11 provide beginning steps in values clarification. Exercise 1-11 seeks values clarification by means of a values grid in which "each of the seven columns corresponds to one of the seven criteria for a value that make up the values-clarification theory. A person can put anything from his or her life on the values grid to see if it is a value" (Simon, 1980).

Exercises 1-10 and 1-11 just skim the surface of value identification. There are other instruments, such as the *Allport-Vernon-Lindzey Study of Values* (1960), *A Measure of Moral Values* (Hogan and Dickstein, 1972), *Kluchohn Value Orientation Instrument* (Kluchohn and Strodtbeck, 1961), and *Rokeach Value Survey* (1973). Although only a beginning, the two exercises initiate considerations regarding values clarification. This is important, since values are the roots for caring, sharing, and helping (Mussen and Eisenberg-Berg, 1977). The

Exercise 1-10
HOW DO YOU COMPARE VALUES? *(may be done alone and discussed in the group)*

Part 1—*Time:* APPROXIMATELY 20 MINUTES

Draw two squares to represent (1) your values and the values of someone with whom you usually disagree, (2) your values and the values of a close friend with whom you agree most of the time, and (3) your values and the values of your parents. Show by the amount of overlap within the squares the value similarity between your values and the values of the persons listed in items 1, 2, and 3 above. Fig. 1-9 is a guide to the procedure to use to depict similarity and differences in value systems.

Part 2—*Time:* 10 MINUTES

Think about and then compare your value squares and the values of (1) someone with whom you usually disagree, (2) a close friend, and (3) your parents. Discuss with the group your findings about the similarities and differences in your values with the values of the three people for whom you drew diagrams. Discuss also how and to what degree these similarities and differences in values affect your relationships with people.

Exercise 1-11
HOW DO YOU ACHIEVE VALUES CLARIFICATION WITH A VALUES GRID?*

Time: APPROXIMATELY 25-30 MINUTES

Refer to Fig. 1-10. The seven columns in the values grid refer to the following questions:
Column 1—Is this something you truly prize and cherish?
Column 2—Are you willing to publicly affirm your choice, preference, or belief?
Column 3—Have you examined the consequences of your decision?
Column 4—Has this choice been made from among several alternatives?
Column 5—Has this been a free choice?
Column 6—Have you acted on your value, and done so repeatedly?
Column 7—Is this item consistent (compatible) with your other choices?
Answer these questions for each topic by placing a check mark or a zero in the box on the line near the topic and under the appropriate column. You must be able to give a strong "yes" answer to check the box. If you have any doubt or cannot respond clearly, write a zero in the box. Five topics have been inserted on the grid. You complete the list of topics with five more items. It is important that you respond to the questions from your own viewpoint, not as you believe someone else would prefer you to answer. After you respond to all of the items, note how many topics you have checked seven times. Compare your responses for each topic. Topics that have received seven checks can be labeled as your values.

---

*Modified from Simon, S.B.: J. Specialists Group Work **5**(3):140-147, 1980.

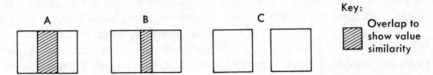

Fig. 1-9. Graphic comparison of similarity of values.

Topics	1	2	3	4	5	6	7
1. Present-giving ritual							
2. Equal rights for women							
3. Prestige							
4. Family loyalty							
5. Loyalty to friends							
6.							
7.							
8.							
9.							
10.							

Fig. 1-10. Values grid.

development of a system of personal values is one of the areas involved in learning life-coping skills, "those skills needed by the individual to ensure a degree of mastery over the environment with which he or she must cope" (Schumacher, 1980).

Values and life-coping skills

From birth onward, individuals "must learn to cope [with] . . . friends, family, money, politics, sex, love, death, health, sexism, racism, work, religion, leisure, media, recreation, time, future, influence, autonomy, and intimacy" (Simon, 1980). Table 1-1 categorizes developmental modalities into four broad classifications and presents a selected sample of life-coping skills associated with these modalities.

The modalities in Table 1-1 offer a framework for assessing level of functioning and effectiveness of coping strategies. To cope signifies preparation—the savvy to contend with and confront the reality of the environment, what Vontress (1979) has entitled the *umwelt*. Each person tends to cope with life events influenced by three factors: (1) the *umwelt*, (2) the positive or negative contributions of the interpersonal world, the *mitwelt*, and (3) the special, individualized methods the person develops, the *eigenwelt* (Robinson, 1980; Vontress, 1979). When the statement is made that the helper

Table 1-1. *Developmental modalities and selected sample of life-coping skills*

Developmental modalities	Selected sample of life-coping skills
Psychosocial development	Communication skills: personal, interpersonal, and group relationships Self-identity and self-image Emotional refinement, awareness, expression, and control Affectional relationships: receiving and giving affectional responses Family relationship skills Friendship skills Value identification: establishment and maintenance of ethics and morals Self-appraisal and correction Generative skills: creative and procreative Consumer skills Citizenship skills Skills in utilization of community resources
Psycho-physical-sexual development	Body image Health awareness and maintenance Physical fitness Sexual awareness, acceptance, expression, and control Transition from family of orientation to independent household
Cognitive development	Learning skills Fact acquisition skills Problem-solving and decision-making skills Skills in the suitable application and modification of information
Vocational skills	Career development skills Job readiness skills Pertinent occupational skills Job-seeking and job-obtaining skills Job-maintaining skills

Modified from Gazda and Brooks, 1980; Havighurst, 1972; and Schumacher, 1980.

must be at a higher functioning level than the one seeking help, the reference is to these life-coping skills. "Concepts of 'mental illness' will need to be changed to 'life-skills deficits' for which teaching/training is the preferred treatment" (Gazda and Brooks, 1980). An ideology stressing development of coping skills supports the following contention expressed by Gazda and Brooks (1980): "One of the primary weaknesses of traditional counseling and therapy is that the client is not given enough time to practice new skills and to integrate them before he or she is expected to use them independently to solve life problems." This educational viewpoint emphasizing training rather than therapy opens up a booming box of job opportunities and skills for human service workers to provide the "balanced services" of both prevention and rehabilitation. (See Chapter 8.)

SKILLFUL INTERPERSONAL FUNCTIONING

The description and definition of the professional self is heavily laden with landmarks for self-understanding and self-improvement. Interwoven with these concepts is skillful interpersonal functioning. Some of these characteristics of interpersonal functioning are listed in Table 1-1. In the following paragraphs, after consideration of involvement, perception, and expectation, three of the basic helping attributes of psychosocial and cognitive functioning are discussed: controlled nondirection, friendliness versus friendship, and problem solving and decision making.

People are not born with the information and skills that are essential for relating effectively to other humans. They learn their particular approaches and avoidances. They learn their way to be happy and to fulfill their needs with other humans. They also learn to be sad and to be unfulfilled. Cooperation and competition are learned. Dependence, independence, and interdependence are learned. Skillful interpersonal functioning is also learned. Thus how a person acts and reacts and what he or she says are learned skills (Gerrard, Bonniface, and Love, 1980). Awareness of the

origins of behavior and of the behavior of the helper and the client in the helping event is accentuated in this chapter. Brammer (1977) stresses the significance of awareness of the following elements for an effective helping relationship:

☐ The cultural roots of the helper and the client
☐ How these cultural roots influence communication*
☐ The empathy that can enrich or hinder interpersonal relationships
☐ Influences that people have on one another

Involvement, perception, and expectation

As human service workers acquire self-understanding, self-awareness leads to positive involvement with their clients. Caring (nurturing) is essential for effective helpers but is not enough. Helpers must ask themselves, "Do I really care for this person? Do I really regard this person as worthy of respect? Do I think of myself as the expert who must help this misguided client for the social good?" If helpers see themselves as dominant and powerful, they set a trap for clients as in the wishful fantasies of the *Wizard of Oz*. These helpers primarily are interested in satisfying their own needs through leading the client down the "yellow brick road" toward the "good life" (Baum, 1900, in Hearn, 1973).

Satisfying the clients needs to achieve, to be confident, and to grow in interpersonal skills does not restrict helpers from feeling worthwhile and in this way satisfying their own needs for recognition, accomplishment, and personal growth.

Furthermore, since expectations provide the framework for interpersonal functioning, the human service workers' perceptions of their clients impact strongly on what happens during and after the helping event. How helpers see, hear, and feel (emotional reactions) the client and the helping event—their level of perceptual accuracy—as well as their skills in communicating and relating de-

---

*Vontress (1979) cautions, however, that the commonality of all persons should be recognized and an overconcentration on the cultural differences avoided.

termine the effectiveness of the outcome. Thus relationships emerge, are maintained, and progress or regress on the basis of these ever-changing perceptions; perceptions and expectations are interlaced in the responses to people. Exercises 1-12 and 1-13 examine these characteristics.

Perception and expectations regulate communication procedures such as who starts the conversation and who manipulates the direction of the discussion and the frequency of "talk," "non-talk," "listen," "silence," and "interference-talk" communication. Prestige, power, attending skills, and other particulars of the interpersonal circumstance are the determinants.

Helpers who have developed professional selves do not deem themselves to be all-powerful experts or masters of knowledge and answers. They value themselves and others. They respect and encourage others to find their way out of helplessness. They are competent in controlled nondirection.

Exercise 1-12
HOW DO YOU RESPOND TO PEOPLE? *(should be done in a group)*

Part 1

Think about how you would end these situations. Write your responses for later discussion with members of your group.

During the group discussion each person selects one of the situations and presents the situation ending. The basis for selecting a particular ending is discussed with the group.

[1] You have attended your practicum four times. A new person enters the room in which you are working. You do not know whether this person is a new client or a new worker. The person stands at the door, looking around the roomful of clients. What do you do?

[2] You are training a mentally retarded child who is 10 years old but who is functioning at the level of a 2-year-old. One of the volunteers comes over to you and says in a loud voice, "That's a helluva messy job. . . I tried to do something for that kid but these dummies can't learn anything." You say, "Let's talk about this later." The volunteer laughs and says, "Come on, now, that idiot doesn't even know I'm here . . . doesn't understand a word I say." What would you do or say after these remarks?

[3] You are working in a mental health center. One of the other workers comes over to you, yells, and shakes his pointed finger at you, "Hey, what are you doing over there? You're not supposed to use that desk!" What do you do or say?

[4] You are home with your parents. Your mother says, "It's wonderful having you here. Wish you would visit more often. You don't look as if you are taking too good care of yourself." What do you do or say?

Part 2

Use the information presented in the box on p. 39 to get a rough measure of interpersonal functioning as determined by your responses to the situations described in this exercise.

Each group member measures the individual's level of interpersonal functioning using this information and then records these assessments in the rating scale in Fig. 1-11. During the group discussion the group members compare and explain the bases for their ratings.

Check the appropriate column in Fig. 1-11 to indicate your estimation of the responses presented by the group member.

Levels of interpersonal functioning: explanation of ratings

1. Poor response, tends to put barriers in the way of interpersonal exchanges of ideas and feelings. Suggests disorganized interpersonal functioning. Negative comments directed toward the other person rather than the issue(s) involved.
2. Inadequate response that is not concrete or to the point of the issue. Does not recognize the other person's feelings. Offers advice without appearing to understand.
3. Minimally adequate and effective interpersonal functioning. Basic level of adequacy that deals at least minimally with the situation.
4. Appropriate responses in terms of the situation and the issue(s). Higher level of interpersonal skills.
5. Accurate, full response that is appropriate and adequate. Recognition of other person's feelings and possible reasons for feelings.

Modified from Carkhuff (1969) and Egan (1975).

	Poor	Inade-quate	Ade-quate	Good	Very good
	1	**2**	**3**	**4**	**5**
The responses presented:					
1. Appear to focus on the issue(s) in the situations					
2. Are positive					
3. Are concrete					
4. Offer alternative approaches to the situation					
5. Attempt to help the other person explore his behavior					
The person giving the responses:					
6. Does not give advice					
7. Does not threaten the other person					
8. Seems to be aware of (in contact with) what is happening					
9. Looks at (not stares at) the other person					
10. Turns toward (not away from) the other person					
11. Asks just the adequate amount of questions					
12. Gives the other person a chance to respond					

Fig. 1-11. Rating scale for interpersonal functioning.

Exercise 1-13

HOW DO YOU EXPECT ANOTHER PERSON TO RESPOND TO YOU?

Time: APPROXIMATELY 30-35 MINUTES

Part 1

You have invited several people to your home to "celebrate" your divorce. One of your invited quests is your close friend who just phoned to tell you he or she cannot come to your party because she or he is not feeling well. This friend knew you and your spouse even before you were married. After the friend's phone call, you begin to conjecture about the reasons he or she is not coming to your party. Write at least five alternative reasons for your friend's absence. Circle the responses with which you would be most comfortable.

Part 2

When the group has completed Part 1, the larger group is divided into groups of five members to present the alternatives. After a discussion of the similarities and differences in the alternatives presented, the members of the small groups discuss the following two questions:

☐ What did each person learn from this activity?

☐ How did each person feel during the activity?

Controlled nondirection

A Chinese proverb typifies what Kahn and Cannell (1957) call controlled nondirection: "You give a man a fish, he has one meal; you teach him to fish, he can feed himself for the rest of his life." In the context of the relationship between the interviewer and the client, this proverb affirms the idea that the interviewer's role is *not to do* for the client but to reinforce the client in learning *how to do for himself*. This idea incorporates both client direction and the nurturing of the client direction by the interviewer. The client absorbs some of this learning from attending to his problems during the interview situation, some from the prompts or reinforcements of the interviewer, but most from the accepting atmosphere of the interview situation.

The process of enlarging on and clarifying the client's problems is lubricated by the interviewer's questions or statements. The controlled nondirection arises from the nature of the interviewer's questions (control) and from the shifting of the responsibility for information and searching to the client (nondirection). Minimal encouragement as well as the eductive technique follow the same line

of thought—client direction within an interviewer framework.

The purpose of any interview is the stimulation of communication. The important consideration is to provide this stimulation without narrowing or modifying the meaning of the client's responses. Both the kind of questions and statements used and the manner in which the interviewer words these quests for information influence whether the client is given the fish (the answer and completion) or is taught how to fish (to find his own answers).

Friendliness versus friendship

Another characteristic of the professional self is friendliness. The distinction between friendliness and friendship on the surface may appear to be a fine line. Yet there is more to it than just a play on words.

Friendship and friendliness have different implications. *Friendship* suggests joining with another in a kinship of mutual intimacy and a free exchange of values and understandings, of thoughts and feelings. *Friendliness* indicates certain characteristics suitable for friendship, such as intimacy, free exchange, support, help, and dependability. The primary difference between friendship and friendliness resides in the degree of intimacy and free exchange. Friendship veers off into a "no-holds-barred" situation in which each individual opens up without any interviewer "stops" of intimacy and revelation. Such a relationship is usually pleasing rather than releasing. In contrast, the friendly interviewer has an awareness of the client's needs and adjusts his intimacy and friendly exchange to the client's needs.

Numerous problems may arise from a relationship of friendship. Helpers may hold back because of their reluctance to reveal too much and hurt the friendship or relationship. Clients may try to latch onto the friendship and in this effort withhold their true feelings to avoid hurting their new-found friend, the helper. An even more jarring problem may emerge when clients distort their own reactions to conform more nearly to what they think will please the helper. Both helper and client lose in this type of encounter, and both become involved emotionally but not professionally.

Problem solving and decision making

Controlled nondirection and friendliness set the stage for the kind of problem solving necessary for the effective helping relationship. Problem solving, especially when the issues are complex, is a process comprising both planning and doing—activities in which everyone is involved daily—with different levels of complications. Only in the *Wizard of Oz* are perplexing problems resolved by the magic touch of a wizard. Only in Oz do the characters attain the sharpness of a brain from a head filled with bran mixed with pins and needles or from a diploma for questionable achievement (the Scarecrow), obtain courage out of a bottle (an alcoholic beverage) or from a medal for bravery (the Lion), or gain ability to love from a sawdust-filled silk heart shape or from a ticking clock (the Tin Woodman). Even though it takes a little more effort for Dorothy to return to Kansas, she does accomplish this trip with ease through the intervention of the Good Witch.

No easy solutions. Gardner (1980) is concerned with children's easy acceptance of these procedures for resolving problems, so he wrote a turnabout tale as a sequel to the Baum story. In *Dorothy and the Lizard of Oz* Gardner depicts the continuing trials of the four characters. No one wants to hire the Scarecrow in spite of his "bran-new brains" or his diploma. The Tim Woodman still cannot love or be loved, no matter how much he tells about and shows the square patch where his heart was inserted, or even when others hear his clock-ticking heart. The Cowardly Lion still finds that his fears have not been overcome, even with his medal boldly pinned on his chest or with the spirits he has imbibed. And Dorothy, although back in Kansas, still finds that the problem that caused her to flee Kansas in the first place—the conflict with Miss Gulch, who had seized Dorothy's dog Toto—is still no closer to being solved than it was prior to her departure. With the help of the Lizard of Oz—a wizard who was transformed into a lizard because people were dissatisfied with his complex solutions—the foursome discover more realistic and gratifying solutions to their troubles.

A great deal can be garnered from the tales of the Wizard and the Lizard of Oz. One glaring revelation is what Puryear (1979) entitles "magical set" solutions: "I'll tell you my problem, and you'll solve it"—simply, rapidly, and completely. Yet, realistically, one becomes shockingly aware that problem solving is *work*. In addition, for lasting effectiveness the problem solver must develop self-reliance rather than dependency on someone else to make decisions. There may be individuals who resolve their problems with ease without resorting to the five steps presented in Fig. 1-12. However, there is always the danger that a simple solution actually becomes ineffective because not all of the facts are known. This frustrating discovery of the failure of the "magical set" is related in Gardner's sequel to the *Wizard of Oz*. Gardner depicts the characters confronting their problems with more thoughtfulness.

The ability to discriminate which problems require more extensive planning and doing is essential to problem solving. This recognition actually is the first step in the problem-solving procedure.

Five steps in problem solving and decision making. Fig. 1-12 diagrams the five steps of the behavioral processes of the problem-solving and decision-making procedure.*

Step 1: detect a problem. An individual is confronted by a problem when a question, situation, or another person becomes perplexing or difficult, so that the individual feels more and more uneasiness ("something is wrong"), uncertainty (unsure of one's efforts and the effectiveness of the outcome), and lack of closure ("something is unfinished"). In other words, a problem is an unsettled situation requiring the application of knowledge, thought, and skill for solution (Gerrard, Boniface, and Love, 1980). Step 1 is a general orientation to recognizing that a problem exists. At this beginning stage it is essential that impulsive decisions be avoided and that problems be considered part of the experience of living that can be coped with—a challenge rather than a threat.

Step 2: define the problem and the goal. After the event has been identified as a problem and information about the characteristics of the problem have been gathered, the problem must be formulated so that it is in relatively concrete, workable terms. In this process the details are further clarified, and the conflicts, issues, and goals are identified. The problem is analyzed by responding to three questions: (1) Where is the problem? (2) What is the problem? (3) What makes the problem exist and persist? The problem might be within the person (not listening to directions), between persons (conflict in expectation between a supervisor and worker), within a group (dissension among the group members as to group goals), or within a system (lack of integration of mental health services so that gaps occur). It also is essential that the real problem be discriminated from the surface manifestations and descriptions of the problem. A more detailed explanation is sought with questions

such as the following: What do you mean by that? Can you explain further your "upset feeling"?

The businessman's drinking is his manifest problem, but his *real* problem is a half-dead marriage. Husband and wife are dependent on each other and so afraid of any disturbance in their relationship that they do not admit to outsiders and even to themselves the magnitude of their marital disagreements, pretending a congeniality to their friends but feeling an uneasiness. For the husband the problem is resentment of his wife's narrow interests and boredom with their relationship. For the wife the problem is feelings of unworthiness beside her competent husband who travels in broad circles with numerous acquaintances. Dealing with the husband's drinking without acknowledgment of the more far-reaching actual problems would be the simple solution that might provide short-term help and long-term failure.

Step 3: identify alternative solutions and courses of action. Once there is a handle on the real problem and the characteristics of the problem and the problem experiencer, strategies for solving the problem are sought. Throughout this problem-solving process the helper and the problem experiencer must continue to focus on the problem, not on tangential issues such as the annoyance of the parents at the marriage which "started all the trouble 15 years ago." It is up to the helper to aid in tying these offshoots of the central problem to the present concern. It is also essential that the helper and the problem experiencer channel their energies on the issue, the problem situation, rather than on the person. "Who is to blame?" "Who started the messy situation?" Neither of these questions is essential to the solution. The tactics for resolution must be directed to the unembellished problem.

For the troubled 17-year-old boy, Conrad, in Judith Guest's book (later made into a film) *Ordinary People* (1976), the manifest problem is his suicide attempt, his lack of confidence, his lack of definition of normality. His mother's annoyance with Conrad's apparent inability to mobilize himself and her inability to deal with his explosiveness place the onus of guilt on him. Underlying his concerns is Conrad's feeling of helplessness and guilt

---

*Modified from Carkhuff, 1973; D'Zurilla and Goldfried, 1971; Gerrard, Boniface, and Love, 1980; Kanfer and Goldstein, 1980; Kaufman, 1976; and Puryear, 1979.

at the drowning of his older brother, who was the favorite son of his mother. Both mother and son perceive the problem in terms of the person, not the issue of Conrad's need for belonging, hope, and confidence. The family becomes three isolated and troubled members until a psychiatrist becomes a friendly helper who directs Conrad toward the real problem of unmet needs. Then Conrad, with the help of the psychiatrist, seeks alternatives for resolving his problems.

One procedure for generating alternatives is by means of "brainstorming," a form of free association based on the assumption that quantity eventually breeds quality (Kanfer and Goldstein, 1980; Osborn, 1963; Parnes, 1967). It is important that judgment of the practicability of proposals be suspended, temporarily, so that there is an unhindered flow of alternative strategies (tactics or courses of

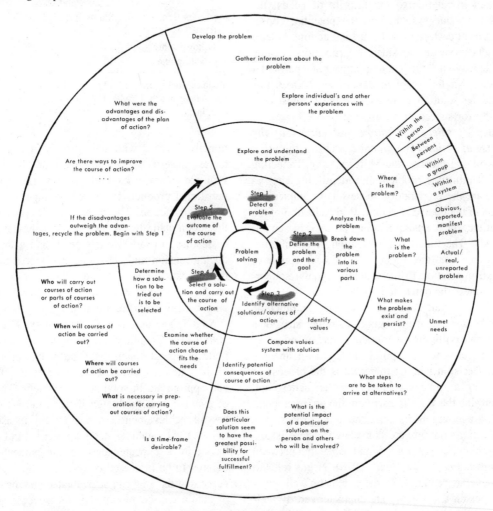

Fig. 1-12. Problem-solving and decision-making processes. (Data from Gerrard, B.A., Boniface, W.J., and Love, B.H.: Interpersonal skills for health professionals, Reston, Va., 1980, Reston Publishing Co., Inc.; and Carkhuff, R.R.: The art of problem-solving: a guide for developing skills for parents, teachers, counselors and administrators, Amherst, Mass., 1973, Human Resource Development Press.)

action). The uninhibited stream of alternatives has a greater prospect of producing a "good" solution, since the earliest alternatives are frequently the superficial, simple solutions and further delving encourages keener analysis. No effort is condemned. At this stage no suggestion is evaluated as good, bad, foolish, or impossible.

When the list is exhausted, each solution is examined in relation to the priority of needs, the person's value system, and the potential consequences of each proposed course of action. At least two questions are considered during this weeding process: What is the potential impact of a particular solution on the problem experiencer? Does this particular solution seem to have the greatest possibility for successful fulfillment?

Step 4: select a solution and carry out the course of action. The *planning* steps of the problem-solving process now shift to *doing.* Detecting and defining the problem and identifying alternatives are the preparatory phase for the implementation of the course of action. With selection of the solution, the decision-making process is accomplished. The functional evaluation of the alternatives considers the "goodness" of each course of action in relation to the outcome (goals) sought. In business the outcome may be increased productivity or a financial payoff; in obesity the outcome may be a sense of belonging, a smaller size, or a more chic outfit; in government it may be increased cost-effectiveness or a political ploy to win an election. Decision making therefore is the process of choosing a strategy, elaborating the tactics, and specifying the ways to carry out the arrangements.

Throughout this planning and doing process certain differentiations are considered. There is differentiation between *needs* and *wants* and between *means* and *ends* (Kaufman, 1976). Needs refer to whatever is required for the health or well-being of a person and usually are characterized by feelings of tension or dissatisfaction, impelling the person toward behavior that may lead to tension reduction and satisfaction. Wants are the personally and socioculturally determined cravings and desires for goods, services, and other items that satisfy and stimulate. The hunger need is most nutri-

Table 1-2. *Needs versus wants and means versus ends*

Means	Ends	
Feet, bicycle, motorcycle, camper truck	Transportation for work, shopping, visiting doctors, pleasure, and so on	*Needs*
Mercedes Benz, BMW, Jaguar, sailing yacht, private plane	Status, prestige	*Wants*

Modified from Kaufman, R.: Identifying and solving problems: a system approach, LaJolla, Calif., 1976, University Associates, Inc.

tionally satisfied with staple foods such as vegetables, cheeses, and breads, but many individuals want ice cream, cake, and other calorie-high, less nutritional products to reduce feelings of tension or dissatisfaction. The means are the procedures, the action plan, the tactics, and the behavioral processes used to satisfy one's needs and wants. Reducing tension and achieving one's goal through these means attains the ends, the outcome or the product needed or wanted. Table 1-2 provides examples of these differentiations.

Step 5: evaluate the outcome of the course of action. The planning and doing would be meaningless without a step that focuses on verification of the extent to which the alternative is effective and appropriate in solving the problem. The task of evaluation is facilitated if the criteria for successful achievement are worded in measurable terms. If the outcome states a specific kind of behavior to be expected or a certain percentage or number to be increased or reduced, the degree of success of the goal can be evaluated and the course of action can be modified if the success is only partial. If the problem is not resolved, the problem-solving and decision-making processes are recycled.

Exercises 1-14 and 1-15 seek to put into practice these steps of problem solving. Exercise 1-14 focuses on identifying unmet needs that may be pre-

Exercise 1-14
HOW DO YOU DIFFERENTIATE NEEDS FROM WANTS AND MEANS FROM ENDS?
(may be done alone and then discussed in a group)

Time: APPROXIMATELY 25 MINUTES

Complete the following statements and then gather in groups of five to discuss: Do these needs or wants reflect any persisting problems confronting you? What alternative means might achieve the same ends you are seeking? Are the ends you seek realistic? Are these ends measureable so that you know when and whether you have attained them?

If after reconsidering your ends you consider them impractical or unrealistic, restate them so that they become achievable. Respond to the questions that follow in terms of ''here and now,'' the present, not the past. The future is considered only in relation to the ends sought. (This exercise is similar to Exercise 1-7 with the addition of considerations of means and ends and the problem-solving approach.)

What I need most:
(Place in order of priority, the first item representing the most important need as you see it.)

What I want most:
(Place in order of priority, the first item representing the most important want as you see it.)

What means might I use to satisfy my
Most important need:

Most important want:

What ends (results) would I achieve by satisfying
(If you use the means you state, what would probably be the most likely result[s]?)
My most important need:

My most important want:

DO YOU DEFINE A WORKABLE PROBLEM?

Time: APPROXIMATELY 25-30 MINUTES

Step 2 in the problem-solving and decision-making processes states that a workable problem is one that is concrete and fulfills certain characteristics that clarify the issues and goals involved in the problem and the solution sought. "He retired last year" is too general a statement to help a person learn to deal with the more significant problem the retiree's wife presents: "I can't stand him around doing nothing all day. Sleeps, walks the dog, sometimes reads the paper, but gets in my way all the time." The retiree's wife may be annoyed by her husband's presence, his demands for attention, his constant requests for food, or any number of other interferences with the previous flow of her activities. The essential issue should be planning with the husband and wife for time together, as well as for the husband's leisure activities. Thus the wife's need for privacy and other undertakings can be arranged to the satisfaction of both spouses.

Part 1

In Fig. 1-13 reword the "unworkable problems" so that they become "workable." Consider the questions in Step 2, and make your answers specific and brief.

Part 2

After rewording the unworkable problems, have groups of five members discuss their workable problems. Determine restatements that best respond to the criteria for workable problems.

cipitating problems. Exercise 1-15 concentrates on defining a workable problem. Further clarification is sought of those aspects of an individual's behavior sparked by socioculturally determined wants that may not be critical for the survival or safety of the society or the individual. Finally, the exercise seeks to demonstrate that the means of obtaining need or want satisfaction are not the same as the ends desired.

Barriers to problem solving. Not all problems require the five steps of the problem-solving process. The choice of a green sweater or a blue sweater is a simple event unless the person is unable to distinguish these two colors (color-blind) or the interpersonal situation presents difficulties that make the choice more complex. Certain skills are essential to the problem-solving process: accurate observation, active listening, and competency in clarification and the expression of opinions. Clarification skills make the helper understandable and also help the problem experiencer identify the problem; observation and active listening provide the

necessary information and ease the expression of opinions and suggestions for handling the problem.

The helper who is deficient in these interpersonal skills fails to fulfill the role of a problem-solving facilitator. Premature closures and omission of exploration of information from past experiences with similar problems are added interferences. Very often an individual who experienced failures in the past with similar problems will steadfastly refuse to deal with the situation and will instead give up too soon with too little effort and assume a suffering martyrdom. Misguided expectations, therefore, lead to a narrowness of exploration. The astute human service worker observes these difficulties and helps the client bring about solutions.

THE "ASK" CONCEPT

"ASK" is an acronym for *a*ttitudes, *s*kills, and *k*nowledge. A human service worker can be versed in the study of behavior and the methods of observation, recording, interviewing, and counseling, yet still lack what it takes to be an effective

Unworkable problems	Workable problems
He had a serious motorcycle accident.	He has not learned to cope with his paralyzed legs and feels isolated from his active friends because of reduced mobility.
Her mother died.	
She lost her job.	
Mr. and Mrs. H. were hostages in a bank robbery last year.	
The 13-year-old girl is pregnant.	
Sara was born deformed.	
The M.'s mother was moved to a nursing home.	
Mr. Y. is depressed.	
Ned says he's afraid that he is a homosexual.	

Fig. 1-13. Unworkable problems made workable.

helper. This same worker may develop the skills to put the knowledge gained into practice. Yet the knowledge and skills may be empty accomplishments if the human service worker is directed more by self-interest or by a hidden or even obvious dislike and distrust for certain people.

The development of a professional code of ethics is one more basic component essential to round out this chapter's introductory discussion of human service workers. The "ASK" concept recognizes that mere understanding of learning styles, identity, or other characteristics leaves wide gaps in the suitableness of the helper's functioning. Knowledge of origins of behavior and values clarification are important but insufficient, and skillful interpersonal functioning is essential but not enough. A code of ethics is another detail that must be included.

This helper may mouth the "right" answers, may even put the words into action. The words may be correct according to the book, but if the ethical attitude is missing, the helper is nonhelpful. At a cocktail party this helper is likely to say, "Had the wackiest dame come into the office . . . wildest name . . . Minnie Giva . . . hmmm . . . Givonas, no, it was Givonese. This Minnie character should have been named Minnie Mouse . . . the squeaky way she talked and looked. . . ." It does not matter whether this helper has several degrees after his name—he's a loser. He is an unethical helper who pulled at least two boners. He named and talked about his client at a social event, and he attached some unpleasant descriptions to his comments.

A PROFESSIONAL CODE OF ETHICS

"Ethics as a science is an integral part of hominology, the science of the whole man, because ethics is man's concern for what he ought to do to attain the most of what is best in his life, and ethics as a science is man's effort to understand what is best and thus what is oughtness . . . obligation, duty, rights, rightness, wrongness, justice, conscience, choice, intention, responsibility."* Ethics interdepend with values (axiology), and therefore

the development of ethical behavior is directly related to values clarification as the foundation for the ethical person.

The ethical person

The competent human service worker develops a professional self that includes a professional code of ethics. Basic to ethical behavior is the belief in the worth, dignity, and uniqueness of each human being. The ethical person recognizes that each person, no matter what his or her physical, intellectual, emotional, social, ethnic, or racial status, has the right to life, liberty, security, and the pursuit of happiness. These beliefs and values of the ethical person may be the ideals to which a person strives. The important fact is that ethical persons—and even more so professional persons—are obligated to strive toward these ideals.

Guidelines for human service workers' professional code of ethics

Professional organizations develop codes of ethics, and these ethical codes become the basis for regulating the conduct of their membership. These ethics also become the essential characteristics for the self-regulation of each member of the organization. Because human service workers represent a wide variety of professionals, the ethical statements presented in this discussion are based on a mosaic of ideas from current statements by several professional organizations:

American Academy of Cerebral Palsy
American Anthropological Association
American Association on Mental Deficiency
American Medical Association
American Nurses' Association
American Personnel and Guidance Association
American Physical Therapy Association
American Psychiatric Association
American Psychological Association
American Speech-Language-Hearing Association
Association for Advancement of Behavior Therapy
The Association for Specialists in Group Work
National Association of Social Workers

*From Baum, A.J.: Ethics as a behavioral science, Springfield, Ill., 1974, p. v. Courtesy of Charles C Thomas, Publisher.

National Education Association

National Rehabilitation Association

The following principles are based on remarks gathered from the ethical codes of these professional organizations. These statements are guidelines to stimulate thinking about the characteristics of ethical behavior.

In fulfillment of human service workers' professional code of ethics:

1. They shall accept as their *first goal the performance of competent services*, not the selling of themselves as experts. They shall not compete with other workers for clients.

    1.1 They shall not use professional relations with clients for private advantage.

    1.2 They shall refrain from promising greater results than can be reasonably expected.

    1.3 They shall be responsible for recognizing the limits of their competence and shall perform only those functions for which they have been prepared.

    1.4 They shall correct any misunderstanding about their qualifications.

    1.5 They shall not seek self-enhancement through expressing evaluations or comparisons that are damaging to others.

    1.6 They shall be cautious about misleading persons by direction or implication and about guaranteeing any results from any intervention procedures that cannot be predicted from sound evidence.

    1.7 They shall be responsible for clarifying the goals of group work and group services.

2. They shall accept as their primary obligation the *protection and promotion of the client's dignity and welfare*. They shall diligently seek to assist the client toward goals that assure and respect the client's needs and development toward a satisfying and satisfactory life-style.

    2.1 They shall examine their own values, life-styles, plans, decisions, and beliefs so that they may be better prepared to refrain from molding the client to accept their judgments and values as the "best" basis for the client's choices and behavior.

    2.2 They shall construct *an individual program plan and goals for the client* on the basis of appropriate measures of the client's functioning with other suitable professionals as well as,

whenever possible, with the client or, when appropriate, with the client's parent or guardian.

2.3 They shall be aware of the significance of socioeconomic, ethnic, and cultural factors in the selection and meaning of the testing instruments and test results.

2.4 They shall accept responsibility and accountability for their decisions and actions.

2.5 They shall present alternative approaches to the solution of a problem so that the client may select the "best" fit for his or her life-style and ability.

2.6 They shall conduct periodic examination of their methods and of the client's progress toward his or her goal to determine the effectiveness of the procedures used.

2.7 They shall interpret for the client the information that is essential to the client's training or treatment progress.

2.8 They shall preserve the client's right to freedom of choice within the individual's capacity to make decisions and within the limitations imposed on all persons.

2.9 They shall establish reasonable, deserved, and fiscally sound individual and group fees commensurate with the services rendered.

2.10 They shall take all reasonable precautions to avoid injuring persons during the provision of professional services.

2.11 They shall respect the law but shall seek changes in those requirements which are contrary to the best interest of the client.

3. They shall preserve the *confidentiality and privacy* of the information acquired concerning the client.

    3.1 They shall secure permission from the client, the guardian, or parent to release information if, for the advancement of the client's good, it is deemed necessary to share information with others.

    3.2 They shall make certain that unauthorized persons do not have access to the client's records.

    3.3 They shall protect members of the group of which they are the leader/facilitator by explaining what confidentiality means and the difficulties and procedures for its enforcement.

    3.4 They shall maintain in the client's file all information about professional services rendered that is essential to the assessment of the client's progress and the client's goals.

4. They shall *not discriminate* because of race, religion, age, sex, or national ancestry.

    4.1 They shall examine their biases carefully and refer clients to other professionals if they consider their prejudices barriers to their effectiveness with clients.

5. They shall try to persuade the client either to *report to the appropriate authorities* or, after advising the client that it must be done, they shall report to the appropriate authorities when the client's behavior tends to be destructive to himself or herself or to others.

6. They shall use every resource available, including referral, as needed, to *provide the best possible service* for the client.

    6.1 They shall accept and maintain those clients whom they are prepared to help because of their knowledge, skills, and experience.

    6.2 They shall not make false statements about their professional qualifications.

    6.3 They shall know the legal or regulatory limits of their services, and they shall operate within these limits.

    6.4 They shall fully inform persons of the nature of possible effects of their professional services in one-to-one or in group relationships. They shall report these effects in accordance with the client's (and significant others') capacity to understand and within the limitations imposed on all persons.

7. They shall *safeguard the client* from violations of human dignity and from physical and psychological harm.

    7.1 They shall avoid using persons for teaching or research in a manner that constitutes invasion of privacy.

    7.2 They shall inform persons participating in research or teaching activities of the nature and possible effects of these activities (in accordance with the participant's and significant others' capacity to understand and within the limitations imposed on all persons).

    7.3 They shall afford participants informed free choice to participate.

    7.4 They shall remain alert to any attempts to distort reports of their research findings or of the impeding of the appropriate use of their findings.

8. They shall accept *responsibility to the institution in which they are employed.* Their acceptance of employment in the institution implies that they are in substantial agreement with the general policies and principles of the institution.

    8.1 They shall alert their employers to conditions that may be potentially disruptive or may limit their employers' or their own effectiveness.

    8.2 They shall leave their employment in the institution if they are in ethical disagreement with the philosophy and procedures of the institution.

9. They shall participate in activities that contribute to the ongoing *development of their professional knowledge and skills* throughout their careers.

    9.1 They shall seek to influence the development of the profession of human service workers by continuous efforts to improve professional standards and practices, services, research, and teaching.

    9.2 They shall report alleged incompetence, illegal activities, and unethical conduct to the appropriate authority.

10. They shall be committed to *increase the public's understanding* of the needs and potentials of their clients.

Individuals who are being trained to enter the human service workers' profession would profit from a careful examination of the 10 principles described as guidelines of a professional code of ethics. These principles are stepping-stones for the discussion and interpretation of the meaning of the beliefs (values) from which the code is built.

SUMMARY

This chapter has painted the dimensions of human services with a broad brush. The large canvas contains considerations regarding human services as a philosophy and a procedure, the examination of the professional self, and the elements of self-understanding. The origins of behavior are surveyed in relation to such factors as demography, family, physical and intellectual aspects, and developmental experiences.

A general summary description of the characteristics of the individual likely to be an effective human service worker would be as follows: Effective human service workers perceive themselves, and their role as helpers, high on their list of "who-ness"; they also perceive others as seeing them as helping persons. They are at ease with themselves and with their identity, although not completely satisfied or problem-free. People rather than things catch their interest and concentration. They have developed knowledge about human behavior and the interpersonal skills of controlled nondirection, friendliness, and problem solving and decision making. They demonstrate appropriate characteristics of intimacy and comfortably share themselves and their experiences with their clients. This sharing is offered not for boasting but instead to further a closer relationship primarily for the benefit of the client and secondarily for the satisfaction of the human service worker. Fundamental to the practices of the human service worker is the professional code of ethics. These ethical considerations set the framework for the provision of services.

With the establishment of a concept of a professional self, the human service worker is prepared to take the first step into the skills essential to the competent helper. Observation, recording, and reporting form the building blocks for all human service workers. Chapters 2 to 4 examine these three basic skills.

Chapter 2

OBSERVATION
attitudes, skills, knowledge

The person's "second skin"—clothing. What does the accurate, unbiased helper perceive?

She sat across from me behind her desk with her braille typewriter in front of her and next to it her cassette recording machine. With her right hand she picked up the ringing phone, raising her other hand toward me as she rapidly said, "Excuse me a minute, the secretary is out to lunch. Need to answer the phones." After a brief conversation she said, "Hold on," and typed on a 4″ by 5″ card the information requested and the person's name, address, and telephone number. Two more calls interrupted our discussion, and she followed the same procedure—speaking and then typing on a large sheet of paper or on an index card information that would be the mnemonic devices for fulfilling the requests or appointments she planned. After each call she turned to me and spoke eyeball to eyeball, "observing" just as I was observing and marveling at her efficiency and responsiveness to what was occurring around her. We spoke about the cues she used to sharpen her observations. "Simple," she said. "There are many ways to compensate for a lack or diminishment of visual cues. What is most important is that the physically challenged person look at the person who is speaking. This shortens the distance between them." This was exactly what she had been doing. She even moved her head slightly in the direction that I had shifted my body as I spoke.

She continued, "Become attuned to the meaning of sounds, interpret muffled sounds." (She cupped her chin in her hand, demonstrating the effect of a pushed up chin and lips.) "The direction of a person's voice is a clue as to the position in which that person is sitting." Then I discovered how she knew that I had shifted my body: "The rustling of clothes and the movement of feet indicate movement, and then, of course, tapping fingers and swinging or tapping feet are additional 'visual' cues.

In other words, I see with my ears—I listen for changes."

Blindness does not deter observation. Encounters with visually impaired persons assures one of their keen ability to pick up cues. Nevertheless, the bias of language continues to focus on vision as the only door to observational alertness. For instance, narrowmindedness and pettiness are associated with the words "shortsightedness," "nearsightedness," "blinders," and "blind spot." Of course, vision helps, but just as essential to observation is the other attending skill—listening. There is one ability that the human service worker must have in large quantity—the ability to observe. Everyone observes from the moment of birth. This is the route for learning. Infants attend to their mother; they watch and listen. On the basis of observations infants, children, young adults, and older adults get the information they require to respond to the world around them. During their development infants pick up some quirks that affect the accuracy of their observations. Perhaps the infant thinks, "Momma is good; she has blonde hair; she does not wear glasses; she has a high-pitched voice." The association made with Momma—her hair, her eyes, her voice—reinforce certain ways of seeing, hearing, and relating with other women. Observations are tainted by the experiences an individual has with other people. Thus all people observe others, yet few people observe without being influenced (contaminated) by their past experiences. Those who work with people must decontaminate themselves of these influences before they can improve their ability to observe.

This chapter is about observation and about the numerous factors manipulating the accuracy of observations, including attitudinal influences, observational skills, and basic knowledge about observational procedures.

FACTORS INFLUENCING THE ACCURACY OF OBSERVATION

At least three broad categories of influence may enrich or hinder the accuracy of observations: (1) factors related to the observer, (2) factors related to the location of observation, and (3) factors related to the person or group observed.

Factors related to the observer

Accurate observation is an active and reactive process. When "something happens out there," something also happens to all persons in the vicinity of the happening. One person may be *aware* of what is happening, another may not be alert to the changes occurring in the environment, and a third person may watch so closely that he or she is able to provide close-knit details of the happening. The observation would vary with each person and be directly related to the level of awareness, of active observation, demonstrated. Physical, psychosocial, and cognitive-affective factors and observational skills are involved.

Physical factors. Most people believe that they are alert to the physical influences on their observations. A more careful examination of this physical aspect, however, reveals some potential sensory blunders and health factors that often are hidden or disregarded.

Degree of sensory acuity. When individuals begin to view a world made fuzzy by nearsighted eyes, they are very likely to get corrective lenses to sharpen their vision. As people age, they need more bright light to read comfortably, but the headlights from an approaching car can deter their vision longer than at a younger age. Such changes

in eyesight are usually fairly readily noticeable to the individual. Loss of hearing, such as the fuzziness of sounds, is not as readily detected. It is easy to fill in with one's own words what one does not hear. Special inflections (changes in voice tones) also may be lost when the individual with a slight hearing loss strains to hear the main parts of the message.

As individuals get older, they experience some degree of hearing loss. Sometimes this takes the form of not hearing parts of a sentence or becoming unaware of background noises that may be important. Very often individuals cover up these losses by pretending to themselves and/or to others that these losses do not occur. Yet, in developing and maintaining observational competency, the helper must learn to deal with these hearing losses, not to pretend or compensate by fill-ins. Not only the sharpness of one's senses (sensory acuity) but also the position from which one is observing may influence what one observes. One more factor that applies to the use of eyes and ears is the way in which the individual attends to what is happening in the environment. There are the more observant and the less observant and the many individuals in between these two poles. To reiterate, attending behavior, that is, looking and listening, affects the level of alertness to sensory cues.

The following example demonstrates the different observational results caused by different degrees of sharpness in hearing.

Example 2-1
WHAT DID IT REALLY MEAN?

Estelle says, "Marty was busted for selling dope." This is a statement of fact with no specific changes in tone and no emphasis on particular words. Estelle appears to have accepted the possibility that Marty might get busted and also that he might be selling dope. However, Estelle might have emphasized the words "Marty," "busted," and "selling," and the more alert observer would hear, *"Marty* was *busted* for *selling* dope." In this statement Estelle shows her surprise and shock that Marty, of all people, has been arrested for selling. Thus one sentence may have different meanings depending on the loudness or softness of the words and the rising or lowering of the voice tone. Keen observers note these characteristics if their hearing and attending are adequate.

Words themselves have different meanings depending on the individual's background. Estelle's statement in Example 2-1 provides an example. "Busted" for some individuals may carry another message rather than being arrested. For some people "busted" refers to the well-proportioned, ample bosom of a woman. Another example of the need not only to hear clearly but also to understand the meaning of the words and how they are being used is in the statement "That's really bad." The tone of voice, the loudness or softness, and the person making the statement are taken into consideration. Thus this one sentence might be telling someone, "I do like your faded jeans," "That must have been interesting or exciting," or "Sorry to hear that; must be unpleasant." The point is that accurate hearing is one part of accurate observing.

State of health. An aspect that is related to sensory acuity is the individual's state of health. Physical well-being has a great deal to do with both one's ability and desire to look and listen.

Fatigue, a clogged nose, an itch on the arm—all may have an effect on the efficiency of an individual's observations. How interested might an individual be in observation if he or she is experiencing hunger pangs? Is it possible to be exact and complete in one's observations while feeling physically uncomfortable?

These points are not stated to stop individuals from observing under less than ideal physical circumstances. Instead, they are mentioned to alert the observer to the dangers involved in depending on only one brief observation. These physical factors are often more obvious than those which stem from interpersonal relationships and environmental influences, the psychosocial factors.

Psychosocial factors. Psychosocial factors are concerned with the individual's development of interpersonal behavior. This behavior involves social interactions based on cultural tasks that are established in a sequential order from simple to more complex responsibilities. During the process of "growing up" biases appear and life experiences are enriched or diminished—always in the aura of cultural impositions and personal capacities.

The origins of the selective perception of bias. Observers' degree of awareness, their flexibility, and their life experiences regulate the thoroughness of their observations. The basic question is "How open are observers to their own life spaces and to the life spaces of the people they observe?" "Life space" refers to all the factors that influence the behavior of a person at any moment. These factors include objects, persons, goals, thoughts, and other environmental events. More aware observers know the many complex transactions going on at the time of their observations. These observers heed basic differences in language usage and understand that words mean different things to different people (semantics). In addition, they painstakingly sift through their prejudices to work at lessening the effect on their observations. Alert observers know that biases against anyone because of race, religion, or appearance shut them into a tight box of inaccurate and incomplete observations. Biased individuals tend to see only what they expect to see, hear what they think should be said, and are more likely to observe something happening because they expect it to happen. Observations by such observers are fixed according to their prejudices. Even biases in favor of the person being observed can pigeonhole the observers' thinking.

Biased observation is referred to as *selective perception*. Selective perception is interwoven with selective behavior, selective viewing, and a self-fulfilling prophecy. When individuals *prophesy* a particular result to an event, they expect the particular result or response. Then, usually without realizing it, they fulfill the prophecy by their behavior. They view the world through glasses shaded by preconceived notions and encourage what they believe is "gonna be" to be. In the following example three people experience the same event differently. Which person is more prejudiced? Which person demonstrates the self-fulfilling prophecy?

Example 2-2
THE EVENT

The time had arrived for the presentation of the award. Everything was ready. The plaque had been printed, and the speech had been written. Invitations had been mailed to the 100 people who belonged to the organization. Chairs had been arranged on the stage so that seating would be ready for four guests who were to comment on the person to receive the award.

[1]

Mr. W. was the person to present the award. This was the first time he had done anything like this. He walked on the stage and with a smile greeted the four guests. As he walked past the person who was to receive the award, he said in a low voice, "Congratulations." His thoughts returned to the speech he was to make and he felt his throat muscles tighten. "I don't know. These people really aren't interested in what I have to say. They don't care about me. If they did care, they might have considered what I have done for this organization. Look at them . . . sitting on their hands out there. A little applause . . . just some recognition. This schnook they chose. She . . . she . . . that's it. They just picked her because she's a woman . . . and a black woman. That's it. Nothing to do with quality of work. Nothing to do with importance of what she has done. Nothing to do with anything. Look at her . . . a squat woman of 40 . . . dolled up to kill. And, now, as soon as I say anything . . . they're so prejudiced, they'll shut me off. Why should I even try? This speech . . . this speech will not be appreciated by them. Besides, I would probably flub it anyway. I'm not gonna give them the chance to make fun of me." When it was Mr. W.'s turn to introduce the person receiving the award, he said, "I w-w-w-wish to re . . . I mean introduce . . ." Two people in the front row of the audience looked toward one another. One of them, Ms. S., said, "As usual, the jerk made an ass of himself."

[2]

Ms. S. was sitting in the front row with her friend, Dr. P. She moved her hand toward his and touched his fingers gently. Dr. P. turned toward Ms. S., nodded his head, and then bent toward her, whispering in her ear, "I love you." Ms. S. squeezed Dr. P.'s fingers and then looked up at the stage. She commented, "There they are, the four 'liberals' choosing her as the best poet of the organization. What a farce! Just because black is in—whitey, not. She can't write. Look at her sitting up there with a smirk on her face. Almost feel as if she's looking at me with those thick bifocals that she always wears. Look at those red—bright red—frames and that flowered dress. Has she no sense?!"

[3]

Dr. P. listened to Ms. S. and then looked up at the woman sitting on the stage. "Little too fat," he mused, "but I like the way she sits there. She seems so poised. I wonder why Paula is so hard on that woman. I heard her tell about her life in Harlem . . . living in a flat with her sister, brother, and three other families. Those lines on her face . . . hard lines . . . but those are the lines that resulted from a hard life. Her poetry came out of her misery." Dr. P. looked at Ms. S. and said, "Paula, I wonder if you know from what sorrow and reality her poetry was written. Did you know that the flowered dress is the first one that is not a hand-me-down?" Just then the speaker began to introduce the person receiving the award. Dr. P. looked at him wondering, "That guy . . . he's so uptight, I expect him to burst. What's his problem, I wonder?"

How open are Mr. W., Ms. S., and Dr. P. to the poet receiving the award? Are they seeing and hearing "like it is" or "like they think it is"? Are they all viewing this event from the same perspective? How do the background and the life spaces of these individuals affect their ways of seeing, hearing, and observing?

Life experiences. Life experiences are another characteristic that enters into the observational process. How extensive and varied is the observer's experience? Prior experience with a variety of people in many situations is more likely to lead to openness of observing, openness in seeing relationships, and greater flexibility in searching for cues. In addition, educational experiences that prepare the observer with developmental information, knowledge of needs, and awareness of behavior patterns also sharpen observational ability. Life experiences are closely intertwined with the cultural background of the individual.

Cultural aspects. There is a simple truism, so simple that it is sometimes forgotten by an observer—"each individual acts differently depending on the other people around him." This statement points to the fact that when an individual is at home with his parents, wife, or children, he behaves accordingly. The same individual in the office, in the classroom, or in church acts differently. In other words, individuals behave in accordance with the expectations of the social situation in which they find themselves. These social selves are dependent on learned cultural differences in behavior.

Observers have to realize this cultural effect. They must take into account not only the factors mentioned up to this point, but also their and the observed person's social, economic, and ethnic background. In this sense observers must realize that their presence, the color of their skin, the clothes they wear, and even the way they sit influence the behavior of the person they are observing. The observer and the observed person act differently when they are together than when they are apart because of their cultural differences. This is just another point of which the observer must be aware.

Cognitive-affective factors. The selective perception of bias, life experiences, and cultural influences is an essential consideration in understanding cognitive and affective development. Cognitive factors include thought processes involved in comprehension, judgment, memory, and reasoning for problem solving; and these competencies are prominent in directing one's conduct. The capacity to learn is important, but the opportunities for learning and for utilizing this learning are also consequential.

The ability to learn and to think. There is much uncertainty as to just what intelligence is, and therefore definitions of intelligence are varied. Intelligence may be measured *quantitatively* by means of standardized intelligence tests; often this type of measurement implies a definition of intelligence as that which the intelligence test measures. Intelligence may also be measured *qualitatively* as proposed by Piaget (1952), who defined intelligence developmentally according to four main stages of increasing competence toward the achievement of logical thinking. A third way to estimate intellectual status is by means of the client's *school and job record and the vocabulary he or she uses.* The assumption underlying this method of assessing intelligence is that intellectual capacity or cognitive ability is a tool used for adaptive behavior and for solving problems.

The measurement of intelligence provides only a small section of the picture of an individual's cognitive processes. In fact, the ability to break up or analyze a problem as a step toward solution is intertwined with background experiences, knowledge, general competence, and affective factors. A cognitive style (field-dependent or field-independent) emerges from these characteristics, and this style regulates the human service workers' responsiveness to their clients. The *field-dependent individual* exhibits a ''with-people'' orientation and a sensitivity to social situations. Such a person is more likely to be more limited in analysis and structuring approaches to perception and cognition and more inclined to seek experiences with other persons. The *field-independent individual* emphasizes analysis and structuring. This person is more likely to demonstrate social distancing and more limited social sensitivity (Witkin and others, 1962). These two characteristic cognitive styles may be viewed as two ends of a continuum; most people's style is somewhere between the two extremes. One's primary cognitive style also varies in different situations and with different people. In essence, the effectiveness of the helping event depends on more than cognitive style or the intelligence quotient.

It is interesting to note, for instance, that people with high intelligence quotients are not necessarily more interested in or more capable of dealing with people or their problems than are others. Such individuals are likely to be cognitively able, and they tend to be self-critical and probably critical of others. They may be coping and thoughtful adults interested in intellectual pursuits, but not necessarily adept in observational techniques, especially when these techniques are focused on people.

What does this information about cognitive functioning signify for the human service worker? Basically, that inclination toward people and interest in helping them discover methods to satisfy their needs is a more fundamental characteristic in the helping event. This explanation does not deny the importance of adequate intellectual capacity; it merely seeks to point out the fallacy of considering that high IQ is enough.

Affective factors. Affective factors are another dimension of the helping function that are interwoven with self-concept and cognitive factors. Affective functioning is essential to the effectiveness of the helper and provides data about the client. The emotional controls and defenses adopted by the helper impact on the helping relationship and add or subtract from the open expression of the helper's intellectual capacity. The effect of the adaptive techniques governing the discharge and restraints of the helper's impulses and anxieties interacts with the controls of the client. The emotional status of the client may be inferred by the observed degree of emotional control and of mood changes during the interview as well as the descriptions offered by the client of emotional behavior outside the interview situation. Competent helpers are keenly aware of the client's behavioral responses to them. Emotional characteristics that may be revealed by the client's behavior include suspicion, reserved reactions, embarrassment, evasiveness, and ingratiation.

Some clients reveal their need to avoid emotional upheavals by blaming others for everything that they think is going wrong in their lives. Other clients take the opposite route. They blame themselves for everything. The alert helper picks up these cues and observes that the client's way of escaping issues is to blame but not to explain and deal with the issues. The alert helper also notes whether these same reactions are emerging during the helping event.

Determining the level of functioning of both the client's and helper's cognitive and affective abilities is essential to helping the client. Frequently the intellectual capability of an individual may not be demonstrated because of overanxiety, lack of motivation, depression, sweeping mood disturbances, or fear. At other times an individual may evidence intellectualization, a defensive maneuver

using intellectual activity to conceal turbulent emotions or undesired thoughts. When either rigid or blocked intelligence or intellectualization is evidenced, the individual's flexibility in confronting new situations and in coping with problems is reduced. The freeing of the client's intelligence becomes an integral part of the interview transaction.

One further caution concerning the assessment of intellectual status must be noted. Performance on most tests of intelligence depends on cultural experiences and especially on culturally biased verbal and academic information. Because of racial, ethnic, economic, or geographical dissimilarities, this cultural bias makes these tests unfair to people from different cultural backgrounds. People who do not have the same opportunities as those individuals for whom the intelligence test was constructed originally will be less likely to achieve high scores on these tests.

Observational skills. A theme may be drawn from the preceding discussion: observational skills are the root from which emerge data for effective helping. Observational skills originate with self-observations and self-reports, are enriched with observations of other persons, and are confirmed or discounted by observational reports (feedback) from others. The sharpening of these observational skills is essential for every helper, particularly since it is the helper who assists clients in increasing their self-awareness by means of observations. Generalizations about the many other skills necessary for human service workers are difficult because of the diverse roles they perform (D'Augelli and others, 1980) and the variety of settings in which these roles are performed. However, there is no question about the crucial value of observational skills.

Factors related to the location of observation

Factors related to the observer initiate the influences on the accuracy of observation; the location of observation enriches or distorts the efficacy of the observation. How much, when, and to whom individuals reveal themselves depend on their life experiences (background roots) and certain features of the situation they experience at the interview moment. Thus situational features also are determinants of the atmosphere and outcome of the interview transaction.

Many factors are established even before the interview begins. Interviewers who are in their own private office, the physical location of the office, and what the client has heard about the interviewer are significant preinterview features. On the other hand, if the interviewer's office is located in an agency, the agency's functions and its physical location set the stage for the interview.

Psychoecological factors. The psychoecological label places in one bag a number of variables (factors). "Psychoecology" is formed from two words, "psychology" and "ecology." Psychology is the scientific study of the behavior of living organisms. This leads to a study of individuals' feelings about themselves and about their relationships and transactions with people. Ecology, particularly human ecology, is the examination of how the environment affects individuals and how individuals handle transactions with their environment. The psychoecological viewpoint encourages the observer to develop an increased awareness of the numerous factors that enter into human transactions. Psychoecology brings into focus the effect of people, animals, things, and physical surroundings on an individual's behavior.

Situation of the observation. The starting point for the observation of an individual is what is happening in the environment at that particular moment. Other people present just prior to or during the observation, the weather, the temperature, and the atmosphere inside and outside the room are part of the observational picture. Not all of these factors may have equal significance. Yet some of them may be manipulating the observed person to respond in a certain way. A room that is too hot or too cold will affect behavior. These facts should be noted so that later observations may be compared if temperature changes do occur. The following observations of Bob's behavior on different occasions discloses some interesting differences.

Example 2-3
THE DIFFERENCE THAT DIFFERENCE MAKES

[1]

The sun is shining brightly, and the crocuses in front of 5-year-old Bob's doorway have begun to bloom. Bob walks out of the doorway his mother is holding open for him and trips over the doorway ledge. His mother rapidly extends her hand and grasps his arm. "Are you okay, Bob?" she asks. Bob looks up at his mother and smiles. Just then the school bus draws up to the curb. Bob runs to the bus and slowly pulls himself up the steps by the railings that have been built low for the small children the bus carries to kindergarten. The bus driver says, "Hi, Bob. How you doin'?"

[2]

The sun is shining brightly, and the crocuses in front of 5-year-old Bob's doorway have begun to bloom. Bob walks to the door and calls, "Mommie, I can't open." Bob's mother responds, "Wait a minute; can't you see I'm trying to wipe up this cereal you spit up? First, your father . . . yelling . . . then you . . . can't stand it . . . can't, can't." Bob's mother walks to the door slowly and while opening it she pushes Bob toward the opening doorway: "Come on. Do you think I have all day!" Bob moves out of the doorway slowly, dragging his brown bear on the ground. He trips over the doorway ledge. "Clumsy," his mother yells. "Can't you watch what you are doing?" Just then the school bus draws up to the curb, and Bob runs toward the bus. He looks back toward his mother, and tears are streaming down his cheeks. "Don't wanna go. Wanna stay home. Mommie, Mommie, stay home." The driver gets up and walks to the top step of the bus, wondering to himself, "What happened to this poor kid *this* morning?" Bob's mother walks to the bus with short, rapid, jerky steps. She says, "Cut it out; don't be a stupid crybaby. Boys don't cry. Do you want to be a sissy?" Bob sits down on the ground at the foot of the steps to the bus. His mother drags him to his feet, picks him up, climbs the bus steps, and dumps Bob on the first empty seat. She walks out of the bus mumbling. Bob continues to cry during the entire bus trip.

[3]

The clouds are black; and the wind is blowing. Some of the crocuses that had bloomed outside of 5-year-old Bob's doorway have begun to wither. Bob is dressed in a heavy jacket with a woolen hat pulled down over his ears. He squirms and shifts his shoulders as he walks toward the doorway. Bob walks out of the doorway his mother is holding open for him and trips over the doorway ledge. His mother rapidly extends her hand and grasps his arm, but he falls forward. His mother picks him up gently and brushes the mud from his jacket. "Sorry, Bob. I know it's difficult to walk with all those clothes on. Are you okay, Bob?" Bob looks up at his mother and shakes his head slowly. Just then the school bus draws up to the curb. Bob walks to the bus slowly, stopping for a moment to look up at the clouds and the raindrops that have begun to fall. Slowly Bob walks to the bus, and slowly he pulls himself up the steps by the railings that have been built low for the small children the bus carries to kindergarten. The bus driver says, "Hi, Bob, are you set? All OK? Let's go."

Same child, same people—different weather, different behavior of people. The meaning of the difference in behavior is not interpreted by these two incidents. However, Bob in the first observation did act differently than in the second and third observations. Additional facts and observations are needed to better understand which pattern of Bob's behavior is more likely to recur.

Interviewer's office. The amount of space, the degree of enclosure, and other conditions in the interviewer's office contribute to the physical and psychological comfort or discomfort of the client.

Interruptions. The number of interruptions may have an effect on the interview. The degree of disruption will depend on the frequency and length of these disturbances, how the client views the interruptions, and how the interviewer handles the interruptions.

Telephone calls and individuals who intrude into the office will disrupt the continuity of the interview even with the most experienced and competent interviewer. Perhaps the only value of such interruptions might be in providing the opportunity to observe how the client responds. A general rule that may prove effective is not to permit interruptions so that a free, uninterrupted flow of conversation may ensue. However, the interviewer must decide what emergency or other situation would permit an interruption.

Furniture arrangement. Privacy may be increased by the physical arrangement of the office. Even in unsatisfactory circumstances the arrangement of the furniture as well as the type of furnishings can provide a semblance of privacy.

Whether there is a desk between the interviewer and the client or they sit on two chairs facing each other is something the interviewer must determine on the basis of preference. A desk may prove to be a barrier for a feeling of intimacy; yet some interviewers are more comfortable behind a desk. The ease of relationship depends not only on the location of the desk but also on the ease of the interviewer.

Some clients may also get "uptight" with two chairs facing each other, particularly in the beginning stages of the interview. The positioning of the chairs and the kinds of chairs (straight-backed or upholstered) should be determined by concepts of comfort, genuineness, and respect as well as the feelings and needs of the client and the interviewer.

Other mechanics. There are other mechanics involved in the physical arrangements and furnishing of the office, such as the lighting and pictures. Is there too much or too little lighting? Is the sunlight or electric light shining in the client's or interviewer's eyes? Are the pictures on the walls provoking, calming, or stimulating? Are they appropriate for the particular clients most likely to visit the interviewer's office?

Agency's functions. The purposes of the child guidance clinic, the family service agency, the community mental health clinic, the comprehensive health clinic, and the state or private hospitals vary in scope and intent. These differences will affect the kinds of services provided as well as the particular focus taken for the problems.

Beginning professionals trained as human service workers, mental health technicians, mental health associates, or any of various titles used in such programs often find their status threatened in a subtle fashion. Acceptance by the agency and by the nurse, the social worker, the psychologist, the psychiatrist, and others becomes a complex process that depends in part on the positive self-attitude and degree of confidence and competence of the beginning professional.

Agency's priorities. The priorities set forth by the agency will also translate into such widely diverse aspects of the interviewing situation as whether privacy and protection from interruption during interviews will be provided.

The interview that must be conducted in a doorless semienclosure has an atmosphere much different from one held in an enclosed room with a shut door. Lack of privacy may affect the client's responses and it may also reflect the agency's unfavorable attitude toward the interviewer.

Physical location of agency. The physical location and appearance of the agency or interviewer's private office may have a significant impact on getting the client to come to the agency in the first place, and the various individuals in the agency or private office may encourage or discourage the client to continue the interviewing situation.

The storefront and the building in the inner city may be more acceptable locations for the client from the inner city. The middle-class individual who is impressed by distinguished addresses is likely to select and to be more open with the interviewer whose office is in an expensively designed and elaborately decorated building. For the status-seeking client a more sizable fee may be related to expectations for successful interviews.

Two ends of the continuum. In one situation the simplicity and proximity of building and interviewer make for a favorable interview atmosphere. In another situation the affluent status of luxurious surroundings is assumed to enhance the helping capability of the interviewer. Physical location has more or less of an effect on the outcome of the interview depending on the client's perceptions.

Other people to whom the client must relate in the agency. In addition to the interviewer, the client often must relate to one or more other people. The first individual the client meets, whether this person is the interviewer or other agency staff member, will become interlaced with the feelings the client has about the interview. For this reason some interviewers prefer to be the first person to whom clients speak over the telephone or whom they meet in person. This is a matter of interviewer preference and is also related to whether the other people come on too strong or in some other way would disturb clients.

Brusque or annoyed secretaries, receptionists, or other agency personnel may distress the client and consequently decrease the degree of openness the client feels in the interview situation. The client's attitudes toward individuals surrounding the interviewer in an agency or private office should be taken into consideration. Just as significant is how the people around the interviewer affect him or her.

Availability of other specialized services. In the fulfillment of the client's needs the availability of specialized services becomes an important issue. Ease of access to medication, specialized examinations, and other services make for a more effective and efficient helping situation. An adequate referral service is a must for the agency or interviewer in private practice where diverse services cannot be offered.

Behavioral effects. The contributing factors just described suggest two main concepts. One concept is that all behavior is caused; that is, there are stimuli (prompters) and reinforcements that perpetuate (strengthen) certain ways of responding and others that weaken, or extinguish other forms of behavior. Second, behavior is caused by many interrelated factors.

In other words, the client and the interviewer learn their verbal and nonverbal behaviors. Furthermore, behaviors that occur in the interviewing transaction add another influence to the outcome of the session.

Example 2-4 describes the interrelationships among an interviewer's and client's background roots, life experiences, behavior, and the location of the observation.

Example 2-4
TED AND DR. L. JUST DON'T FIT TOGETHER

Ted, 14 years old, is in the psychologist's office. One of the conditions of his release from the juvenile evaluation and referral facility was that he return home and receive psychological help. Ted had been picked up drug-wandering through the streets.

Ted is slouched in the chair opposite the interviewer, Dr. L. He just doesn't dig this guy who looks so much like his "damned father" with his straight suit and his straight haircut. The office fixtures turn him off. All furnishings are in an elaborate, expensive green-and-blue plan. They remind him of his own carefully arranged, affluent home. "Even the way this dude speaks is bookstuff. In fact, this guy's secretary sounds like Mother when she is trying to impress people."

Ted is weary of listening so he decides he will think about 2 weeks ago when he and Terry left the lunchroom at school and found Tricia for a fix. Ted looks at his hands and is determined that he will say as little as possible.

"Ridiculous," Dr. L. is thinking. "This character has everything going for him. I had to do it the hard way, working and studying at the same time. My parents couldn't afford to give me all the luxuries this kid has. They thought I should be earning money, not attending college. This pip-squeak just doesn't know what's good for him. My 5-year-old had better appreciate what I'm doing for him. Well, at least the fee is good. Let's see if I can penetrate this kid." Dr. L. briefly stares at Ted and then pulls his lips into a smile. He sits back in his chair, folds his arms across his chest, and begins speaking.

Ted looks up when he hears Dr. L.'s voice and mechanically mumbles his answers. Meanwhile, his right leg begins moving up and down rhythmically with a motion that seems to begin at the thigh. He slowly leans back in his seat and once more looks around the room, noting the diplomas and certificates on one side and the landscape paintings on the other wall. Ted thinks, "Even his walls are covered with lousy straight stuff." Then Ted's eyes move to Dr. L.'s face, and he notices the thin bottom lip held by Dr. L.'s teeth. Ted slumps further into his chair.

Dr. L. untangles his arms and picks up a pencil from his desk. He moves the pencil back and forth between his fingers.

The example just described is exaggerated in order to condense several of the aspects of the factors related to the client and interviewer (the observers) and to the location of the observation. The ethical interviewer would refer Ted to someone else, since the hostile responses of both the client and the interviewer appear to be insurmountable.

Factors related to the person or group observed

Recent surveys and research indicate that considerable prejudice about disabilities, aging, races, and religions continues to persist among school-age children, teenagers, and young adults (Allport, 1979; Glock and others, 1975; Mortenson, 1980). The strength of these prejudices and associated stereotypes is of serious concern. People are programed to be prejudiced positively or negatively. Favorable or unfavorable biases are initiated at the preverbal level of infancy and early childhood; they are emotionally loaded and not subject to critical evaluation of validity. These prejudices usually are reinforced by those significant persons who instigated their origin and later by the behavior and misguided or exaggerated perceptions of the growing and maturing child, young adult, adult, and elderly person. Prejudiced individuals conduct themselves in such a fashion that their actions encourage the manifestation (or at least perception) of the behavior they expect of a person or group (self-fulfilling prophecy). Their prejudice warps their observation of what actually does occur; their expectations distort the event to fit into a preconceived mold. Such expectations are especially dangerous for the human service worker, whose biases result in misinterpretation of information.

In the following discussion the words "bias" and "prejudice" refer to an inaccurate belief, a preconceived idea based on insufficient and/or faulty observation of events and experiences. This twisting of facts spreads to inflexible generalizations about the similarities in characteristics and behavior of other individuals. Prejudices vary in terms of intensity; in terms of the specific object, belief, individual, or group; and in terms of direction—positive (favorable, likes) or negative (unfavorable, dislikes). The problem with prejudice is that it narrows the rational assessment of someone or something (Wicks, 1979). Such interference may enlarge to such an extent that decisions about someone or something become erroneous and even destructive. Thus the helping relationship is skewed toward or away from the client by these often subtle, unyielding prejudices. Important information about the client is missed if the helper lapses into favorable attraction to or unfavorable annoyance with the client. A prejudicial reaction also is possible on the part of clients, whose attachment to or displeasure with the helper tends to blemish their relationship and openness to communication.

Prejudices may emerge from many different sources. The beginning counselor may feel uncomfortable with older clients or with less intelligent or gifted clients. The counselor may be prejudiced against homosexuals, as was, for example, Jung (Moore and Strickler, 1980; Worell, 1980). Women human service workers may find intolerable dependence and passivity in their male clients; male workers may be put off by dominance and assertiveness in their woman clients (Storr, 1980). The list of possibilities is extensive—prejudices may be linked to racial, ethnic, ability, disability, age, sexual, socioeconomic perceived differences, and so on. Exercise 2-1 uses occupations as the starting point to examine certain biases.

Bird (1980) has written a trenchant article tying together handicapism, sexism, and racism. She states that "unequal and unjust treatment of women evolves from attitudes and practices that have similar stereotypes." She mentions the following five attitudes commonly held by the general public about the physically challenged (handicapism), women (sexism), and minorities (racism):

□ They are all three treated like children.

□ They are innocent—unable to defend themselves from the cruel world.

□ They are not very bright—do not learn very fast and do not seem to be able to handle high level jobs.

□ They are incompetent—bungle almost everything you ask them to do.

□ They are unable to recognize or to resist evil—cannot resist temptation.

Bird admits that "many of these five comments have been tongue-in-cheek, but . . . they drive home the serious problem of stereotype . . . that all members of a group are alike." It is this catch-all trap of the undifferentiated response to people that thwarts the effectiveness of the prejudiced human service worker.

Prejudices are complex in their motivations and behavioral expressions. The following discussion deals specifically with prejudices based on racial and ethnic differences.

Racial and ethnic differences. Studies by Banks (1971) and others about the effectiveness of white interviewers with black clients indicate that a slower establishment of rapport takes place than when the client and the interviewer are of the same race. Black clients reveal less information pertinent to the immediate problem when interviewed by white interviewers. This reluctance to be as free with a white interviewer as with a black may stem from a social conformity syndrome rather than from a racist attitude. This syndrome (pattern of behavior characteristics) is evidenced in the inhibition of hostility and the decrease in openness on the part of the black client. Black clients may tend to act out what they consider to be the behavior expected by the white interviewer. This type of stereotyped interpersonal behavior leads to greater anxiety in the client and often a lowered performance on psychological tests (Baratz, 1967; Heine, 1950). However, studies (Yamamoto and others, 1967) have found that when the interviewer's level of prejudice is lower, the number of interview contacts with the black client is increased and a more productive relationship is established.

Butts (1972) describes the effect of black-white relationships from the viewpoint of the black psychoanalyst treating white patients. On the basis of his own analytical experiences with patients as well as those of other psychiatrists, Butts states that the black psychoanalyst with the white patient is afforded a unique opportunity for the following reasons. The analyst is able to examine the characteristics and changing expressions of racism of which the white patient may be unaware. Interracial analysis enables the white patient to work

---

Exercise 2-1
WHICH PEOPLE SHOULD FILL THESE JOBS?

Time: APPROXIMATELY 45-60 MINUTES

Indicate what kind of person usually fills each occupation in the following list. For example, if you consider that the job usually is filled only by a man, insert a check in the box under "M"; if both men and women fill the job, check the boxes under "M" and "W". Insert checks in the other boxes you consider appropriate for each occupation. The key to the symbols above each column is as follows:

M—Man
W—Woman
Min—Minority (ethnic or racial) group member
B—Blind person
D—Deaf person
P—Physically disabled person (paralyzed person or amputee)
MR—Mentally retarded person
MD—Mentally disabled (mentally ill) person

Occupations	M	W	Min	B	D	P	MR	MD
Airline attendant	☐	☐	☐	☐	☐	☐	☐	☐
Architect	☐	☐	☐	☐	☐	☐	☐	☐
Artist	☐	☐	☐	☐	☐	☐	☐	☐
Author	☐	☐	☐	☐	☐	☐	☐	☐
Ballet dancer	☐	☐	☐	☐	☐	☐	☐	☐
Ballplayer	☐	☐	☐	☐	☐	☐	☐	☐
Counselor	☐	☐	☐	☐	☐	☐	☐	☐
Crane operator	☐	☐	☐	☐	☐	☐	☐	☐
Diplomat	☐	☐	☐	☐	☐	☐	☐	☐
Dishwasher	☐	☐	☐	☐	☐	☐	☐	☐
Doctor	☐	☐	☐	☐	☐	☐	☐	☐
Electrician	☐	☐	☐	☐	☐	☐	☐	☐
Engineer	☐	☐	☐	☐	☐	☐	☐	☐
Executive	☐	☐	☐	☐	☐	☐	☐	☐

Exercise 2-1—cont'd
WHICH PEOPLE SHOULD FILL THESE JOBS?

Time: APPROXIMATELY 45-60 MINUTES

Occupations	M	W	Min	B	D	P	MR	MD
Garbage collector	☐	☐	☐	☐	☐	☐	☐	☐
General	☐	☐	☐	☐	☐	☐	☐	☐
Hospital attendant	☐	☐	☐	☐	☐	☐	☐	☐
Human service worker	☐	☐	☐	☐	☐	☐	☐	☐
Janitor	☐	☐	☐	☐	☐	☐	☐	☐
Judge	☐	☐	☐	☐	☐	☐	☐	☐
Lawyer	☐	☐	☐	☐	☐	☐	☐	☐
Mathematician	☐	☐	☐	☐	☐	☐	☐	☐
Movie producer	☐	☐	☐	☐	☐	☐	☐	☐
Newscaster	☐	☐	☐	☐	☐	☐	☐	☐
Nurse	☐	☐	☐	☐	☐	☐	☐	☐
Pharmacist	☐	☐	☐	☐	☐	☐	☐	☐
Pilot	☐	☐	☐	☐	☐	☐	☐	☐
Professor	☐	☐	☐	☐	☐	☐	☐	☐
Receptionist	☐	☐	☐	☐	☐	☐	☐	☐
Sales clerk	☐	☐	☐	☐	☐	☐	☐	☐
Scientist	☐	☐	☐	☐	☐	☐	☐	☐
Secretary	☐	☐	☐	☐	☐	☐	☐	☐
Senator	☐	☐	☐	☐	☐	☐	☐	☐
Street cleaner	☐	☐	☐	☐	☐	☐	☐	☐
Telephone operator	☐	☐	☐	☐	☐	☐	☐	☐

Divide into groups of five and tally the responses of the group members for each of the columns. Discuss the meaning of your group's responses in relation to biases about the status of the jobs and the significance of status as applied to sex differences, racial and ethnic considerations, disability prejudices, and the like. How do you think these findings about prejudices will affect your relationship as a helper with your client? What have you learned about your own biases?

through certain feelings of inferiority/superiority that might not surface as easily when both individuals are of the same race. Racial differences may induce patients to explore feelings against their own families that may resemble their racial stereotypes and hostility.

Butts's interpretation of the meaning of racism to his patients is based on psychoanalytical concepts of transference (the patient projects ideas, feelings, desires, and conflicts stemming from the past onto the analyst) and countertransference (the analyst does the same to the patient and uses the patient to gratify his or her needs). Nonpsychoanalytically oriented interviewers may not agree with some of the historical aspects of Butts's explanation of racism. Whether the interviewer is psychoanalytically oriented or not does not detract from the potential impact of at least four important points that unfold from this interpretation:

1. Racial and other prejudices stem from one's past experiences in the family and in other social groups (background roots).
2. Interviewers may be effective in interracial interviews if they are capable of expanding their awareness of their racial attitudes and of controlling their reactions in the interview situation (psychosocial bases and situational features).
3. The interracial interview may provide the springboard for exploring feelings of prejudice and hostility toward people (situational features and psychosocial bases).
4. Racial differences (and other differences such as age, socioeconomic status, and religious beliefs) need not curtail expressiveness and sharing but may be used as sources for further understanding (background roots and behavioral effects).

Even more subtle in their effect on the helping relationship are the assumptions, research, and generalities originated by white counselors with black clients. The myths that are perpetrated are exemplified in stereotypical statements about black clients, such as that they have poor self-concepts;

are nonverbal; are very verbal (but speak poorly); or profit only from a highly structured, action-oriented counseling approach (Smith, 1977). Surely, some black clients are some or all of these things; some are no different from white, Anglo-Saxon, middle-class clients; still others are unique in other ways. Avoidance of prejudice does not deny racial, ethnic, and other differences. It urges alertness to individuality.

Age differences. Racial and ethnic stereotypes are not the only barriers to clear thinking. Age-related expectations clouded by outmoded and inappropriate misconceptions about what a person can do at different ages also restrict perceptual accuracy (Okun, 1976). Butler and Lewis make the following comment about health and other services for older persons (see Fig. 2-1):

An examination of the services offered in community mental health centers . . . documents the fact that older people share health and social services to a far lesser degree than the total services provided to the clients. Elderly people make up only 4% to 5% of the clients of the community mental health center and rarely is there any adequately formulated program of outreach to assist the elderly to obtain services. In addition, suitable services are discouraged because the staff of community mental health centers have at best only a superficial understanding of the culture, life experiences, and needs of their clients and are unable to bridge the cultural chasm between themselves and the poverty stricken. The aged person who also happens to be black, poor, widowed, and a woman suffers "multiple jeopardy."*

The signs of ageism take many forms (Brody, 1980; Butler and Lewis, 1977; Holmes and Holmes, 1979; Sudnow, 1971; Usdin and Hofling, 1978). Some common stereotypes and negative attitudes are presented in the following list:

☐ Physicians and medical students call older female patients "crocks."
☐ Ambulance drivers sound their sirens more slowly when the patient is an older person.

---

*From Butler, R.N., and Lewis, M.I.: Aging and mental health: positive psychosocial approaches, ed. 2, St. Louis, 1977, The C.V. Mosby Co.

Fig. 2-1. Multiple jeopardy: age, blackness, poverty, widowhood, womanhood. (From Butler, R.N., and Lewis, M.I.: Aging and mental health, ed. 2, St. Louis, 1977, The C.V. Mosby Co.

- □ The prognosis for elderly patients is more often pessimistic. Senility, irreversible organic brain syndrome, and paranoia are prevalent diagnoses, although depression or a toxic reaction to medication may be the more significant factors. Ageism, in fact, has become professionalized in the mental health field.
- □ Professionals prefer to work with younger persons. They rationalize their preference on the basis of priorities and the potential for rehabilitation and productivity in the younger person.
- □ Professional schools narrow their course content to adulthood that ends at an early age, usually no later than the forties. Only token representation may be afforded the aging phase of life.

- □ Older people are discriminated against in the job market, and vocational counselors discourage their efforts to continue to work or to seek jobs.
- □ The terms "old man" and "old lady" have assumed a pejorative and condescending quality.
- □ Advertising glorifies youth, and youthful characteristics are considered the criteria of beauty.

Brody (1980) discusses the problems of elderly persons in institutions:

The ageism that pervades the attitudes toward all the elderly is intensified with respect to those in institutions. Because so many are mentally impaired they also bear the stigmata attached to patients in the institutions called *insane asylums* that antedated modern psychiatric hospitals. Because many are frail, dependent, and confused, they are objects of a particular subtle form of ageism that has been perpetuated by incorrect psychodynamic formulations such as "generational role reversal" and "second childhood. . . ." The behavior of a brain-damaged old person may appear childlike, but he is not a child; half a century or more of adulthood cannot be wiped out.*

Just as serious is the plight of the older woman, who is confronted with social, sexual, and financial problems to an increasing extent. The sexism imposed on her potentially is aggravated by her greater longevity with more prolonged needs for services. In the beginning of the twentieth century the ratio of women to men 65 years of age and older favored the male population—98 women per 100 men. However, statistical projections predict that by the beginning of the twenty-first century, by the year 2000, the ratio of women to men will be 150 to 100 (Table 2-1).

The problem goes beyond prejudices to more serious considerations of the factors of stress and other threats that are detrimental to the longevity of men. Human service workers cannot afford an-

*Published by permission of Transaction, Inc. From Growing old in America by Beth B. Hess, Copyright © 1980 by Transaction Books.

Table 2-1. *Comparison of population of women and men 65 years of age and older from 1900 to 2000*

Year	Total population (millions)		Ratio (women/men)
	Women	Men	
1900	1,525	1,555	98/100
1930	3,309	3,325	100/100
1970	11,605	8,367	139/100
1977	13,925	9,569	146/100
2000	19,105	12,717	150/100

Modified from Office of Human Development Services, Administration on Aging: Facts about older Americans, DHEW Pub. No. (OHDS) 79-2006-1978, Washington, D.C., 1978, U.S. Department of Health, Education, and Welfare.

noyance with the demands of older women nor disregard the difficulties of men. Too much is at stake.

Factors encouraging the continuance of ageism. At least three factors encourage the continuance of ageism: (1) the outdated definition of "old age," (2) economic difficulties and the lack of jobs, and (3) the memories and the identification processes of the young.

• *The outdated definition of "old age."* Usdin and Hofling (1978) address the question of old age as follows:

Generally speaking, we have accepted chronological age in a rigid fashion as a measure of the adequacy or inadequacy of people and we have failed to appreciate the significant physiologic and psychologic difference between any two individuals, whether they are in their 20's or in their 70's. Personalities differentiate further and become more unique in proportion to the time they have lived and developed.

Neugarten (1968) suggests that older persons, those over the age of 65, should be differentiated according to whether they are "young-old" or "old-old." The involved, comparatively healthy and more youthful-appearing individuals would be included in the young-old group. Hess (1980) enlarges on these differentiations as follows:

In terms of capacities, needs, and resources, we may be moving toward a two-tiered old age, especially if retirement from work and from child-rearing continue to occur at earlier ages than in the past for large numbers of men and women. A first period of post-parental joint survival in relatively good health and financial condition will be followed by what we typically think of today as "old age," that is declining social, psychological, physical, and financial resources.

Economic difficulties and the lack of jobs. During periods of economic recession experienced in the United States, and to greater or lesser degrees in other societies, older people as well as young adults, disabled persons, women, and minority group members are construed as unjustly competitive in the narrowing job market. They are the scapegoats for the battered economy (Butler and Lewis, 1981; Holmes and Holmes, 1979; Rosow, 1980; E.D. Schulman, 1980; Schulman, 1981). Why support them with welfare? They do not want to work. Why not urge retirement so that younger blood can step in and be given a chance? Affirmative action be damned. Priorities must be shifted to the "family man," the able-bodied family man, who is most productive. Isn't it about time to stop this favoritism? The comments are extensive. The debate finds strong supporters. In an affluent society there is a demand to discover quick solutions or at any rate quick explanations for disturbances of affluence. Paradoxically, "the greater the poverty and the struggle to survive, the relatively better off old people are by the standards of this group. . . . the contribution of each additional pair of hands to the small gross product is valued [and] the greater interdependence among members promotes mutual aid in meeting survival problems" (Rosow, 1980). In an affluent society "the old are with us, but not of us" (Rosow, 1980). Who considers the ethics of these views or the quality of life? Should human service workers be change agents?

Recent data from a Harris survey indicate that 31% of Americans (approximately 4 million people) would like to continue working after the age of 65. Yet the Bureau of Labor Statistics defines an "older" worker as one over the age of 45, suggesting that this is the age when labor market problems are first encountered (Holmes and Holmes, 1979). Unfortunately, the legislative mandate of the Age Discrimination in Employment Act of 1967 and its more recent 1978 amendments remain primarily a paper lion without courage or bite. Even though the amendments have removed the upper age limit restriction from federal employment, the retirement of eligible employees has been encouraged by certain financial inducements. The boomerang effect of this will become more apparent with the full impact of the American post–World War II baby boom population, when the 76.4 million people born from 1946 to 1964 become part of the elderly population (Jones, 1980). If the current mortality and fertility rates continue, the increase of individuals over 65 will be greatest in the twenty-first century—just about two decades from the present. Thus the young people described as the "greening" of America will be part of the "graying" of America. Approximately one in five persons (17% of the total population) will be over 65 by the year 2030, in contrast to the 4% of the total in 1900 (Table 2-2).

Priorities and arrangements for retirement, job selection, maintenance, credit, insurance, and housing will be affected by this shifting toward an older population. Ageism becomes even more dangerous, leading to inadequate social and medical plans and caring and economic insufficiencies. Such neglect harms not only the older population, but the entire society. Table 2-3 details further the pattern of older age groups from 1970 to 2040.

The projected statistics present the magnitude of the potential problems for human service workers who are unaware of their own ageism and also who should be prepared to educate others about the danger of their ageism. The wise human service worker seeks the expansion of services for the elderly and

Table 2-2. *Percentage of persons 65 years of age and over compared with total population of the United States from 1900 to 2030*

Year	Percent total
1900	4.1
1930	5.4
1970	9.8
1977	10.9
2000	12.2 to 12.9
2030	17

From Office of Human Development Services, Administration on Aging: Facts about older Americans, DHEW Pub. No. (OHDS) 79-2006-1978, Washington, D.C., 1978, U.S. Department of Health, Education, and Welfare.

becomes knowledgeable and skillful in assisting older people with their problems and in the attainment of their rights. The role of the gerontological human service worker is promising in the present as well as the future.

The memories and the identification processes of the young. Before beginning professionals are prepared for a helping relationship with the aging population, they must unravel some of their own hang-ups. They must examine their memories about their own parents and other experiences with older persons. Belittling, overindulging, or infantilizing the older generation, actually, may be a shield protecting the helper from the fact of his or her eventual aging and death and the possible confrontation with the social and economic problems of increasing numbers of older people. The human service worker who is over 30, and even more so the one who is over 40, may avoid the older person who is feeble and depressed in order to dodge the reminder that he or she is just 10 or 15 years away from the age of the older person (Butler and Lewis, 1977; Usdin and Hofling, 1978). These shams and concealments serve only to confuse and delay improved relationships with the aging population.

Sex differences. Sexism, like ageism, pigeonholes people and denies them the opportunity to be

Table 2-3. *Percentage of United States population 55 years and over from 1970 to 2040*

Year	55 years and over (%)	Increase or decrease (%)	65 years and over (%)	Increase or decrease (%)	75 years and over (%)	Increase or decrease (%)
1970	38.7		20.1		7.6	
		+6.9		+4.4		+1.5
1980	45.6		24.5		9.1	
		+7.9		+6.1		+4.4
2000	53.5		30.6		13.5	
		+29.0		+21.0		+7.2
2030	82.5		51.6		20.7	
		+2.3		−1.3		+3.5
2040	84.8		50.3		24.2	

Modified from Bureau of Census, U.S. Department of Commerce: Statistical abstract of the United States, Washington, D.C., 1979, U.S. Government Printing Office; and Jarvik, L.F.: Aging into the 21st century, New York, 1978, Gardner Press, Inc.

individuals with unique ways of living their lives (Butler and Lewis, 1981).

There is a reason why women are coy about their age. For most purposes, society pictures them as "old" ten or fifteen years sooner than men. Nobody in this culture, man or woman, wants to grow old; age is not honored among us. Yet women must endure the specter of aging much sooner than men, and this cultural definition of aging gives men a decided psychological, sexual and economic advantage over women (Bell, 1980).*

The plight of women is exacerbated because they live longer than men (see Table 2-1), and if their primary occupation has been homemaking, they are often poorer and lonelier during their widowhood. In addition, women have a more difficult time than men to remarry so that more of them spend their older years without husbands. Many myths are maintained about women; often these myths are applied to minority groups also. For instance (Mortenson, 1980):

Discrimination against women and minorities is largely their own fault. They just don't aim for the top, and they don't prepare themselves.

*Published by permission of Transaction Inc. From Growing Old in America by Beth B. Hess, Copyright © 1980 by Transaction Books.

It is hard to find women and minority group members qualified to hold any of the more skilled positions.

Women should stick to "women's jobs" and should not compete for "men's jobs."

Employing and promoting ethnic minority women would be a good way to satisfy the demands of both women and minority groups.

Washing dishes and cleaning are "women's work" and aren't suitable for a man.

Delinquent girls are more vulnerable and self-destructive than boys. A recent study by Barnorst brought to focus the prejudicial attitudes toward delinquent girls. The researcher found that police refer girls with less extensive records than boys to court, and that judges send girls more often to training schools for less serious crimes than those committed by boys (Behavior Today, 1980b). This sex-role stereotyping demonstrates the sexism that begins at any early age and becomes even more serious and evident against the teenager.

The changing roles of men and women have received a great deal of attention in recent years. It has become apparent that both men and women have experienced attitudinal and behavioral changes. Benton and Bowles, Inc. (1980) reports the results of its survey of husbands of its consumer panel members. The tripartite goals of the study were as follows:

☐ To assess the husband's attitudes toward his family role

☐ To examine the husband's involvement in performing household chores

☐ To explore the husband's role (vis-à-vis his wife's) in influencing family decisions and brand choice

The highlights of the findings indicated the following:

☐ Men are taking a wide variety of nontraditional family roles.

☐ Despite their growing involvement in these nontraditional areas, however, the men surveyed are experiencing a great deal of conflict and ambivalence about their changing family roles. There is evidence that these new roles and the values they represent are being met with some upheaval at the emotional level.

☐ Men with employed wives are more willing to accept the new values than are men whose wives are not working.

☐ Younger husbands (under 35) are much more comfortable with these "new values" than are older men.

As a consequence of these findings it has been suggested that the advertising for household products should begin to portray men more often in domestic activities and that advertising can make use of men's current ambivalence toward changing family roles by recognizing and articulating men's concerns about their new roles. Doyle Dane Bernbach, Inc. (DDB) (1980) added support to the Benton and Bowles findings. DDB's national study of married men discovered that two thirds of them agree that the role of women in American society is changing, but most of them do not like it because it interferes with their personal comfort and well-being. The husbands balk at the expectation that they should assume responsibility for the "drudgery of household chores." These findings suggest strategies for the advertiser. What do they suggest for the human service worker?

In spite of changing roles, a woman's difficulties persist in the "man's world" that determines her education, recreation, occupation, medical treatment, and so on. Societal stereotypes are insinuated in the mass media and other environmental influences. In addition, women reinforce sexism by their own attitudes and responses. Nevertheless, feminism is not the answer for all women. Solutions depend on the unique needs, value systems, and even defenses of each person in addition to cultural features (Ivey and Simek-Downing, 1980).

This issue of sexism goes beyond concerns with women's societal roles and opportunities. In societies that are strongly achievement oriented, such as the United States, behavioral expectations for men continue to be harsh. The "breadwinner" label perseveres. Personal growth and success usually are estimated in terms of financial success, physical stamina, and certain other aspects of a "macho" image. Both women and men still are victims of these cultural impositions.

Ability and disability differences. The concerns about differences of race, ethnic origin, age, and sex are interlocked with considerations of ability and disability. For some, ability signifies the pursuit of perfection. For others, it means building on whatever strengths one has so that a disability does not become a handicap. Abilities vary just as much as disabilities. Each person has disabilities in certain areas of competency. The essential consideration is the label "handicapped"—this is a social restriction. It stresses limitations and does not recognize the individual's capability as well as disability.

For example, epileptics often are viewed with superstition and prejudice. In some states they are not permitted to marry or to drive a car. Laws restricting the person with epilepsy from participating in certain rights disregard estimates of the Epilepsy Foundation of America (EFA) that through good medical care and drug therapy about 50% of individuals with seizure disorders can live completely free of convulsions and another 30% can have their seizures reduced to a minimum. In spite of these estimates, the unemployment rate of medically controlled epileptics is nearly 25%, according to the EFA (Howell, 1978). Negative responses and lowered expectations, shame, avoidance, handicapist humor, distaste, and sadness are some of the marks of prejudice. Both pity and excessive praise have traces of prejudicial viewpoints. Humor that plays on the fancies and feelings of superiority addresses the real or perceived disability rather than the abilities of the individual. Dunham and Dunham (1978) describe the effects of these responses as follows:

> People with disabilities have a wide variety of experiences regarding prejudice. Some individuals may encounter few evidences of prejudice in their lifetimes; others feel that their entire existence is marred by their being trapped in a stereotypical box. The most common experience of persons with a disability is to encounter a range of subtle and not so subtle prejudices almost every day of their lives. . . . Many disabled persons have been known to join the general population in accepting prejudicial attitudes toward other disability groups. A person confined to a wheelchair marvels to learn that a blind colleague is traveling alone to a distant city although she has traveled the world in her wheelchair.

Even more serious for the disabled is the *fatalism syndrome* (FS) of human service workers (E.D. Schulman, 1980), which proposes that "nothing can be done" to develop self-sufficiency in retarded, blind, deaf, physically disabled, or chronically mentally ill persons. FS-oriented professionals predict that failure is inevitable in any attempts to alter and/or compensate for disabilities and that attempts to develop abilities would be unsuccessful. If professionals propose such doom, can the public be far behind in its thinking?

Rooting out prejudices would be simpler if every person were aware of these negative attitudes. In fact, awareness is the first step toward a more understanding approach to the disabled. Exercise 2-2 explores opinions about the handicapped to open up thoughts concerning some of the barriers to accepting disabled persons as worthy and capable persons.

Socioeconomic and sociopolitical differences. Handicapism, racism, ageism, and sexism have much in common. These isms pervade people's lives. They are destructive in many areas of human endeavor. Yet they can serve a useful function as a vital tool by means of which human service workers can scrupulously examine professional, personal, and societal behaviors toward other people. Socioeconomic and sociopolitical differences and the isms that are associated with economic factors and political ideologies may actually be the origin of many prejudices.

Economics and politics are closely interwoven in the societal scheme; each fosters or undermines the other. The isms of prejudice do not explain group hostilities of the magnitude that often prevails. When security and abundance in community life exist without sharp contrasts of life-style, conflicts are less likely. When insecurity and scarcity spread in an atmosphere of affluence, conflict conditions are exaggerated. It is the contrasts of differences that annoy and frighten. In addition, poverty leads to more poverty and increased illness.

The foregoing statements about the effect of differences and insufficient financial and other resources may be interpreted in several ways. An example may be drawn from the prevailing perspectives regarding public welfare in the United States, which may be viewed from two perspectives, the residual and the institutional.

> According to the residual outlook, welfare should be used only when usual sources—the labor market and the family—are unable to meet the individual's needs; welfare programs are viewed as providing temporary, emergency assistance. From the residual perspective, being on welfare carries a stigma. It is the poor person's own fault that he or she is poor. The institutional view, on the other hand, attaches no stigma to the receipt of welfare. The provision of public welfare is looked on as a proper and legitimate institution within society, and the need for comprehensive, continual support is recognized. Structural inefficiencies in society are seen as the cause of poverty; the individual is not blamed for being poor. . . . the residual view seems to be more prevalent in the United States, even among welfare recipients (Osgood, 1980).

Hubert Humphrey mentioned the significance of the political climate in supporting an institutional

Exercise 2-2
WHAT ARE YOUR OPINIONS ABOUT DISABILITIES? *(completed individually and discussed in the group)*

Time: APPROXIMATELY 45 MINUTES

Circle the number that best represents your agreement or disagreement with the items listed.

KEY: 1—Strongly disagree
2—Disagree
3—No opinion
4—Agree
5—Strongly agree

agree

1. Disabled people are good workers.   1 2 3 4 5
2. Disabled people prefer to associate with other disabled people rather than   1 2 3 4 5
   with nondisabled people.
3. It is unwise and uneconomical to build special devices to help disabled persons   1 2 3 4 5
   travel because so few disabled people use public transportation.
4. Disabled people can fit into the general life pattern.   1 2 3 4 5
5. I would feel uncomfortable working with a disabled person.   1 2 3 4 5
6. Disabled persons should earn as much money as nondisabled if they are   1 2 3 4 5
   willing to work and study as hard.
7. Disabled persons want sympathy.   1 2 3 4 5
8. I would like to know more about the problems of disabled people.   1 2 3 4 5
9. Disabled people have an advantage when applying for a job.   1 2 3 4 5
10. I feel sorry for the disabled.   1 2 3 4 5
11. I feel inadequate to help the disabled person.   1 2 3 4 5
12. I would date a disabled person.   1 2 3 4 5
13. Disabled persons should be placed in regular classrooms.   1 2 3 4 5
14. I would like to know more about how I can help the disabled.   1 2 3 4 5
15. I have no objection to living next to a disabled person.   1 2 3 4 5
16. Most disabled people should not be allowed to have children because they   1 2 3 4 5
    are unable to assume full parental responsibility.
17. Disabled people cannot live alone.   1 2 3 4 5
18. Disabled people are treated unfairly.   1 2 3 4 5
19. Disabled people can be as intelligent as nondisabled.   1 2 3 4 5
20. If three people were applying for a job and the one who was disabled got   1 2 3 4 5
    the job, I would believe that the person received the job because of his or
    her disability.
21. Since there are no disabled people in my family, I do not need to be concerned 1 2 3 4 5
    about problems of the disabled.
22. Disabled people often feel sorry for themselves.   1 2 3 4 5
23. Disabled people are often ill.   1 2 3 4 5
24. Buildings should be made more accessible to disabled people.   1 2 3 4 5
25. More than enough is being done to help the disabled.   1 2 3 4 5

After inserting your opinions on the list of items, look over your responses. Count the number of times you marked "agree" or "strongly agree" for items 2, 3, 5, 7, 9, 10, 16, 17, 20, 21, 22, 23, and 25. Count the number of times you marked "agree" or "strongly agree" for items 1, 4, 6, 8, 11, 12, 13, 14, 15, 18, 19, and 24. Count the number of "no opinion" responses for both sets of questions.

Do you note any pattern of favorable, unfavorable opinions, or of nonopinion?

In a group discussion, do you note any similarity in the pattern of responses?

Modified from Holmquist, D.: Opinionaire regarding the handicapped. In Mortenson, R.A., editor: Prejudice toward hiring the handicapped, New York, 1980, Anti-Defamation League of B'nai B'rith.

perspective in his address to the Democratic National Convention on July 13, 1976, as follows:

The moral test of government is how it treats those in the down of life—our children, those in the shadows of life—our needy, our sick, our handicapped, and those in the twilight of life—our elderly.

The election of Ronald Reagan as President and the increased representation of conservative Republican senators in the United States Congress have been cited as a consequence of the majority of the voting public's disenchantment with the programs and politics of the "bleeding-heart liberals." Smoldering within these political changes are the ashes of budgetary support for many social service programs. One may question whether the biases related to the views of conservatism are to be replaced by the prejudices associated with liberalism, welfarism, communism, socialism, and other isms.

How will these changing views and priorities affect the system of services for people, such as public assistance, vocational training, guaranteed annual income, and public day care? Will this altered outlook reinforce programs with built-in biases against rural areas? How will this impact on the special treatment and rehabilitation needs of the mentally ill who are poor?

The last question is of particular interest because of the incorrect notions about mental illness and poverty. Early studies concluded (1) that since the lower socioeconomic class has a higher rate of mental illness, this statistic signifies that poor people are more prone to mental illness and (2) that one may conjecture that inheritance is the originating cause. Miller and Mishler (1964) questioned the conclusion relating social class to mental illness, pointing out that other interpretations of the data do not support a clear-cut relationship between social class and mental disorder:

One cannot conclude from prevalence data that the rate of morbidity varies by social class, or by any other characteristic. Prevalence rates (all the active cases discovered during a given interval of time) are affected by a number of factors that are particularly misleading in the understanding of the relationship between social class

and mental disorders. For example, a higher rate of mental disorder among one segment of the population being studied might mean that this group had less access to the treatment resources available. In this case, a large number of untreated mental disorders would be accumulated over a period of time. It might also be that the particular kind of treatment offered is congenial and effective for only part of the population, again causing an uncommonly high morbidity rate in the remainder of the population.

For the human service worker the implication of prejudices is clear. These biases constrict the efficiency and effectiveness of relationship. Differential treatment occurs—of races, of ethnic groups, of women and men, of the elderly, of the poor, of the people of certain political persuasions, of inhabitants of rural areas, of the disabled, and so on. In fact, anyone who varies from the culturally current perception of normality tends to be subjected to many greater difficulties in obtaining effective and appropriate help. Frequently the YAVIS (*y*oung, *a*ttractive, *v*erbal, *i*ntelligent, *s*uccessful) person receives more positive responses, expectations, treatment, and social responses than the HOUND (*h*omely, *o*ld, *u*nattractive, *n*onverbal, *d*umb) person (Goldstein and Simonson, 1971; Schofield, 1964). The human services professional is challenged to become aware and to educate others about the unjustness and serious consequences of these intolerances as they relate to attitudes and the helping relationship.

ATTITUDINAL INFLUENCES ON ACCURACY OF OBSERVATION

Three categories of factors operating on attitudes have just been discussed: (1) factors related to the observer, (2) factors related to the location of observation, and (3) factors related to the person or group observed. Throughout an individual's life these factors vacillate in their effect on the development of attitudes for or against people, things, and so on. These attitudes are important, since positive or negative attitudes underlie the predispositions that dictate the responses associated with behavior. Thus attitudes, acquired and organized through life experiences, become neural states of readiness that influence people's ideas, opinions, beliefs, prejudices, values, purposes, and interests (Wright, 1980).

Inferring attitudes from behavior

These attitudinal sets—readiness to act—can be inferred only from behavior. As with actual values, mere words expressing an attitude are not to be confused with the actual performance that confirms the actuality of the attitude. (See Chapter 1.) "My best friends are . . ." means very little unless goodwill, acceptance, interpersonal relationships, and other such acts affirm such friendship. Attitudes are implied by behavior—direction or movement toward or away from an object, event, person, or situation. Statements such as "I'm for (or against) ERA" and "I'm for (or against) nuclear power" are confirmed as attitudes if the speaker becomes actively involved in working for or against the expressed beliefs. This view that action is essential to the reality of attitudes is succinctly expressed in a passage from Jordan's (1971) book. Linda, one of the characters in this book, is annoyed about the uncertainty of her friend Eric's commitment to an act of political protest. Linda speaks as follows:

I can't play the verbal political game. Taking a position is easy. I have to act on it. My parents—they're good, decent bourgeois liberals—played that parlor game all my life. I used to boast about them to my friends. Not any more. They love all the comforts of the system they're always shouting against. But they never lifted a finger against it, only their mouths.

For human service workers therefore it is not enough to state, for example, "I believe in helping clients to learn to help themselves." These workers also must demonstrate their nonpossessive, controlled nondirective behavior in the helping relationship.

Blake and others (1979) constructed a grid to represent differing helping attitudes. The grid is based on a nine-point system for two dimensions: (1) concern for the client as a person and (2) concern for problem solving. As seen in Fig. 2-2, 81 combinations of helping style may be drawn from the grid. Although the grid was designed for social

Table 2-4. *Helper's attitudes and client's self-reliance*

Scale	Location on grid	Attitudes	Degree of concern for client's problem solving	Degree of concern for client
1,9	Upper left corner	Support-oriented	Low—helper's direction more apparent	High—client-centered
1,1	Lower left corner	Take-it-or-leave-it–oriented	Low—helper as more or less passive observer	Low—more emphasis on agency's expectations
5,5	Center	Tried-and-true–oriented	Intermediate—helper tries to strike some balance between concern for problem solving and concern for client	Intermediate
9,1	Lower right corner	Push-the-solution–oriented	Low—helper takes initiative, advises client, and controls process	Little or no concern
9,9	Upper right corner	Mutual-problem-solving–oriented	High—helper presents options; client selects	High—helper is supportive and encourages self-reliance

Modified from Blake, R.R., and others: The social worker grid, Springfield, Ill., 1979, courtesy Charles C Thomas, Publisher.

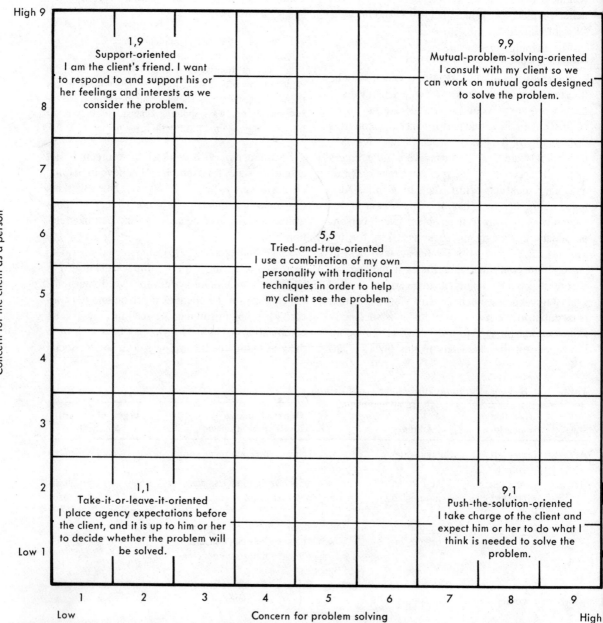

High 9

1,9
Support-oriented
I am the client's friend. I want
to respond to and support his or
her feelings and interests as we
consider the problem.

9,9
Mutual-problem-solving-oriented
I consult with my client so we
can work on mutual goals designed
to solve the problem.

8

7

6

5,5
Tried-and-true-oriented
I use a combination of my own
personality with traditional
techniques in order to help
my client see the problem.

5

4

3

2

1,1
Take-it-or-leave-it-oriented
I place agency expectations before
the client, and it is up to him or her
to decide whether the problem will
be solved.

9,1
Push-the-solution-oriented
I take charge of the client and
expect him or her to do what I
think is needed to solve the
problem.

Low 1

Concern for the client as a person

1   2   3   4   5   6   7   8   9
Low   Concern for problem solving   High

Fig. 2-2. The helping relationship grid. (From Blake, R.R., and others: The social worker grid, Springfield, Ill., 1979, courtesy Charles C. Thomas, Publisher.)

workers, it has implications for all helpers in their relationships with clients. Table 2-4 briefly states some of the differentiating characteristics of the scales arranged for the grid.

The helping relationship grid in Fig. 2-2 and Table 2-4 serve as the rating tools for Exercise 2-3, which explores attitudes toward the helping relationship.

Contagion of attitudes. A subtle effect, the contagion of attitudes, is instigated by the counselor's concern for the client as a person. In other words, what the helper does because of his or her attitudes affects the client's behavior and attitudes. In a review of studies reporting on what makes psychotherapy work, Berman (1980) concludes that the most significant client changes occur not so much

---

Exercise 2-3
WHAT ARE YOUR ATTITUDES TOWARD THE HELPING RELATIONSHIP? *(should be done in a group)*

Time: APPROXIMATELY 60 MINUTES

Read the following discussion between a counselor and his client. Then follow the directions after the discussion.

ORIN: So-o-o-o, here I am in the grand salon of *the Doctor* Pickwick. Terrific! Whatta layout!

DR. P.: Hmmm. *(Smiles.)*

ORIN: Well, so, I'm here. And my lousy father and that bitch-of-a-mother have their say.

DR. P.: Tell me, why *are* you here?

ORIN: C'mon, Doc, you got the message, the fact sheet right there. You know what I'm all about.

DR. P.: Sure, fact sheet—all laid out. But it means more to me to hear it from you.

ORIN: Like my name, Orin, a heavy dose for 15 years, and now just because I got picked up while "under the influence." What a jazzed up phony that is. So, I had a few extra. So. What happens? The judge says if I get counseling and do something about my alcoholism—alcoholism shit—I drink or don't drink, as I want. So-o-o on probation for one year. Damn him.

DR. P.: You say being picked up and having to get help is like your name. How come?

ORIN: My parents gave me my name. And now the judge has given my parents custody of me and my name. They don't have that much *(snaps his fingers)* savvy of what I'm all about. They don't have *(sobs)* that much *(snaps his fingers again)* interest in what I do. Listen, the real dirt is I've been drinking since I was 8—more, more, more. Now, hell, if only I could have a drink right now! *(Orin covers his eyes with his hands and lowers his head.)*

DR. P.: Tough, tough, sure tough. How . . .

ORIN: *(Suddenly raises his head and looks to the right of Dr. P., then turns his head sharply, stares at Dr. P., and raises his hand palm forward as if to signal stop.)* Whoa, Doc, you don't know the quarter of it. What my hollow-as-a-macaroni drinking parents don't know is that my older sister is a souse—just hasn't been caught.

Divide your larger group into five smaller groups. Have each group select one of the sets of scale numbers from the grid in Fig. 2-2 (see Table 2-4 also) and write counselor's and client's responses until Orin leaves the counselor's office. Follow the characteristics described in your group's assignment.

When this has been completed, have the entire group reconvene. The different endings are presented by each of the smaller groups and then considered as to whether the counselor actually has represented the degree of concern for the client as a person and concern for problem solving exemplified in the five portions of the grid. Alternatives should be suggested if necessary.

because of specialized techniques but rather because of the considerate attention of a therapist, the opportunity for the expression of emotions, and the belief that the treatment will help. Thus attitudes that lead to the belief in and expectation of client improvement have the most significant impact on the helping relationship. In essence the human service worker's attitude is contagious; it spurs on the helpfulness of the worker as well as the client's motivation to "get better" or "change." Another attitudinal component identified by Berman is that a more favorable therapeutic outcome is assured when the client feels liked and respected by the therapist. Once again it is the helper's positive attitude that is contagious. The client develops self-respect in this atmosphere of acceptance.

Rational emotive therapy (RET). This concept of the contagion of attitudes has reference in another context, RET. Ellis (1966), the founder of RET, postulates that the way we think (our beliefs, or attitudes) in large measure influences how we feel and eventually act. Ellis's mode of attitude therapy proposes a basic ABC model in which A is any stimulus (object, event, interpersonal encounter) in a person's life; B is the way in which the person interprets A (the attitude developed, the meaning attached to the stimulus); and C is the feeling, pleasant or unpleasant, that becomes associated with the stimulus. RET intervenes at the second step in this process by reeducating the client's attitudes and helping the client alter inappropriate, unhealthy, illogical, and faulty thinking (Schmidt, 1976; Schneider and Robin, 1975; Trexler and Karst, 1972).

Insidious myths. RET is a technique for attitude change that seeks to alter the insidious myths that individuals develop. The problem with myths is that they distort and perpetuate unsatisfactory relationships. At least two of the characteristics of myths make them insidious: (1) they are not based on fact and (2) attitudes supporting myths tend to generalize, to gain strength and momentum. Prejudices emerge and build stereotypes that lead to acts of exclusions and to forms of discrimination.

Scapegoating follows discrimination with verbal aggression or hostile acts against the "unchosen" persons (Selee, 1980).

The manipulative impact of attitudes is readily perceived in words that become heavily laden with special meanings. For instance, negative connotations accompany such words as "crippled," "paralyzed," "maimed," "deformed," "retardate," "old age," and "poor." Another kind of myth emerges from an attitude that fate, one's destiny, and one's personal growth are completely beyond one's control. Such an attitude negates any attempts to develop oneself or to help others change.

Establishing a guiding ideology

Contagion of attitudes and insidious myths are interwoven with value systems and a guiding ideology. Values with which human service workers view themselves, others, and the world in general were at one time relegated to the discussions of philosophers and theologians. Currently human service workers recognize the fallacy of this omission. Not only the helper's attitudes, beliefs, and values, but also those of the client, must be considered. The crucial question is "How do both the client and the human service worker perceive the helping process?"

Attribution theory. Clients who attribute changes in their behavior to their own efforts experience behavioral and attitudinal changes that are more long lasting. Human service workers who uphold such an attribution theory (Thibaut and Kelley, 1959) provide tools, skills, schedules and opportunity for practice, and reinforcements so that the clients may select, develop, and change in accordance with their own psychological learnings (Krasner and Uhlmann, 1973). Such an approach supporting client problem solving and decision making is based on an "educational attitude" stressing relationship enhancement (RE) (Guerney, 1977). The outgrowth of such enhancement is an ideology that proposes the role of the human service workers as the facilitators, the teachers of new skills, so that the clients are prepared to change their own behaviors. Furthermore, in changing their own behavior, clients influence changes in the response of others to them. The circle of changes continues with positive reinforcements for the more appropriate behavior.

Self-reliance. An ideology committed to the client's skill training rather than directive help also pledges the helper's assistance to the people with whom clients spend most of their time. Thus the interpersonal environment may be restructured to become more supportive of the client's efforts and more conducive to the client's self-respect, self-mastery, and self-reliance. On the other hand, the helper may suggest that the client consider leaving an environment that is uncooperative and cannot be restructured. The fundamental ideology therefore secures the client's development of independent functioning in the least restrictive environment, one in which the individual can function satisfactorily and satisfyingly in his or her cultural milieu.

The stage is set for further learning when the human service worker begins to accept the validity of the attitude emphasizing an ideology of client self-help with the helper's support and assistance. The next step in the "ASK" process moves from attitudes to the development of the fundamental helper skill—observation.

BASIC OBSERVATIONAL SKILLS FOR EFFECTIVE HELPING RELATIONSHIP

Which is more important, the content of what one says or the way it is said? Which is more important, the message or the massage (McLuhan and Fiore, 1967)? There probably is no answer that would apply to all people, about all kinds of situations, in all settings. The most effective balance between verbal and nonverbal elements in an interpersonal encounter varies from person to person.

Listening and looking

If we wish to have others listen to us, if we wish to have influence with them, we must first listen to them (Koile, 1977) (Fig. 2-3).

Verbal cues. Verbal messages tell the observer a great deal about the observed person. The choice of words and speech patterns used can reveal the speaker's socioeconomic status, ethnic group, religious orientation, subgroup, feelings about self, and feelings about other people. The language used by less-read or less-educated individuals reflects the social and economic setting to which they have been exposed. The geographical area they are from will be reflected in their words. Although the poor individuals (both economically and educationally) may appear to have verbal inadequacies and difficulty in verbal expression, this is an inaccurate conclusion. Children from slum areas use words differently. They use a more informal, "public" language with simple grammatical construction and frequent use of such conjunctions as "so," "then," and "because." The precision of their words seems inadequate to middle-class listeners, since these children do not use "school words." Instead they are open to more imaginative expression because they are less word-bound than the middle-class individual (Deutsch, 1964).

The observer who writes "poor vocabulary" to describe an individual from a slum area is not listening very carefully to the vast potential beyond the individual's words. Such an observer also does

Barbara Haimowitz

Fig. 2-3. Active listening involves the whole person in the communication event.

Is this paragr. stereo-typing individuals by groups?

not see the rich gestural language this "deprived" individual is demonstrating. Ethnic group language often is intertwined with the speech mannerisms characteristic of a particular socioeconomic status. Such words as "macho" (manly), "chutzpah" (shameless, impudent bravery), and "soul food" (chitterlings, corn bread, turnip greens) are now in the dictionary. Hispanic persons, Jewish persons, and black persons originated these words.

Religious orientation also insinuates itself into the words used. The language of the person close to a church or to certain religious convictions is sprinkled with words referring to the deity or to some other words such as "guru" (a spiritual teacher of the Hindu). Sometimes the words lose their religious significance or original religious attachments and become part of a culture or subculture, such as the golden rule ("Do unto others as you would have them do unto you"). Many young people who have turned to oriental philosophy as

their guide to living speak of the Hindu concept of Karuna (the cultivation of wisdom and compassion for other human beings), which is, incidentally, an excellent guideline for the human service worker.

The language of subgroups varies from the strung-out, hung-up language of the counterculture to the middle-class "bookish" speech of the teacher to the self-centered speech of the aging. Each of these groups has its own vocabulary, which is not only similar for the group but also is individualized. For the youth group, the black group, and the drug group the words used and their meanings change so rapidly that a dictionary published today would change within the hour of its publication. Some words remain, such as "pad" (room), "dig" (to understand), "jazz" (worthless talk), "cool it" (take it easy), "bread" (money), "knocked up" (made pregnant), "skinpopping" (injecting a needle under the skin), "nickel bag" (single packet or dose of a drug costing 5 dollars). Some so-called

---

Exercise 2-4
ARE YOU LISTENING TO THE WORDS? *(should be done in a group)*

Time: APPROXIMATELY 20 MINUTES
Part 1

Two members of the group volunteer for this exercise. They move their chairs into the center of the circle of group members. The group members turn their chairs around so that they are facing away from the two volunteers. This is done so that they may concentrate on words and sounds and not be distracted or influenced by the nonverbal behavior of the volunteers. Fig. 2-4 is the tally sheet for keeping track of the number of times certain words are used by the volunteers.

For a total of 3 minutes the volunteers discuss one of the following topics. Person A agrees with the topic as stated; person B disagrees.

☐ I can be whatever I want to be.
☐ Human service workers are welcomed as beginning professionals.
☐ My approach to studying is effective.
☐ Mentally retarded people can learn.
☐ Mentally ill people can be cured.
☐ Abortion is the most effective contraception.

Part 2

The volunteers return to the group. Everyone turns around to face one another in the circle, and a general discussion of the tallies follows.

Words used to refer to oneself	Tallies		Words used to refer to other people	Tallies	
	Person			Person	
	A	B		A	B
1. Words of self-direction Expect to			6. Words directing others Expect		
Can			Can		
May			May		
Ought to			Ought to		
Should have			Should have		
Would have			Would have		
2. Thought words: self-referral Think			7. Thought words: referring to others Think		
Consider			Consider		
Plan			Plan		
Reason			Reason		
Study			Study		
3. Evaluative words: self-referral Judge			8. Evaluative words: referring to others Judge		
Good			Good		
Bad			Bad		
Inferior			Inferior		
Superior			Superior		
4. Qualifying/conditional words: self-referral If only			9. Qualifying/conditional words: referring to others If only		
But			But		
Unless			Unless		
Yet			Yet		
Providing			Providing		
5. Personal/interpersonal words I			10. Other verbal cues		
You					
They					
Ours					
We					
He/she					

Fig. 2-4. Verbal cues.

ordinary words have been given new meanings. "Trip," for instance, signifies one thing to the "square"—travel by car or other vehicle. For the drug freak, however, this word means a self-trip induced by a psychoactive drug, which may be a "bummer" (unpleasant or frightening) or a "slide" (a beautiful, glorious, or even spiritual experience). The list of subgroup words is not by any means exhausted.

For the older person as well as for the young child, feelings about self are revealed by words. The aging person and the child use self-centered (egocentric) speech. They talk to themselves and carry on monologues. Sometimes two monologues are conducted between two aging people; they are talking simply to hear themselves talk, just as the young infant babbles and mouths words. For the young child this egocentric speech serves as a device for learning; for the aging person it is often a sign of loneliness and depression. Words can reveal

---

Exercise 2-5
DO YOU REALLY LISTEN TO THE OTHER PERSON ON THE TELEPHONE?
(should be done in a group.)

Time: APPROXIMATELY 30 MINUTES
Part 1

Two individuals volunteer as role players; one plays the client, the other the interviewer. The remainder of the group (the observers) arrange themselves so that they are seated in a circle with their chairs turned around so that they cannot see the role players. The role players also arrange their chairs so that they are back to back and cannot see one another.

The role players select one of the following situations and assume appropriate roles. For 3 minutes they carry on a telephone conversation, assuming the roles of the people described in the situations. The observers, using the list of cues in Fig. 2-4 as a reference, record as many verbal cues as they can during the role-players' conversation. Half of the observers focus on the client's verbal cues; the others concentrate on the counselor's verbal cues.

[1]   Marcus and Sally have been married for 26 years. Marcus is at home preparing the roast for the oven. He puts the roast in the oven and sets the clock for 2 hours. The phone rings, and Marcus slowly walks to it, licking the thumb he has just burnt on the oven door. He picks up the phone and says, "Yes?" Sally answers, "Hi, there, homemaker. Just wanted to warn you I'll be an hour late tonight."

[2]   Manny is talking to the counselor on the telephone, "I . . . I . . . dunno what's wrong with me. Just now I got rippin' mad at my screwed-up sister. I slapped her, and when she screamed I slapped her harder and harder. If my older brother hadn't come in just then, I dunno . . . dunno . . . woulda k-k-killed her maybe. And as I think about it . . . I don't feel sorry . . . don't feel anything." The counselor says, ". . .

[3]   Sandra is calling her home to tell her parents that she has been busted for "possession." She wants to ask her mother to arrange bail, but her father gets on the phone.

[4]   Hello, you don't know me, but I need to talk to someone. *(Short laugh.)* I'm about to have a party . . . a pill popping party . . . an OD trip . . . to hell. What do you say to that, huh? Hot-line answerer responds.

Part 2

After 3 minutes of the telephone conversation, the entire group gets together to examine the accuracy and completeness of observations and to arrive at some interpretations of the observed behavior. This discussion lasts 10 minutes.

much about how individuals feel about themselves and about other people. The observer should keep tab of the word choice. Does the observed person use words of certainty such as "I can" or words of doubt such as "If I could"? How close does the observed person seem to be to people? Is the observed person using words such as "I" and "we" or "they" and "you"? The following two statements indicate different degrees of warmth or closeness—"It seems inevitable that your needs will be met" and "We'll work on getting what you need." Which conveys the warmer message?

The intervention of words may help or hinder the smooth flow of the counseling transaction. Effective counselors rarely get into the "word act." When they do, it is to encourage clients to do some more self-exploration about how they contribute to their problems. Counselors tend to push for "here-and-now" words that refer to the present situation rather than the past. Thus counselors use words to keep clients from straying too far from their immediate behavior or the present problems.

Refining one's skills in listening to words— one's own and those of others—is essential to effective helping. For the vision impaired person, verbal cues and other sounds are crucial. For the hearing impaired person, clues such as lip movements and body language are more important. For many others with difficulties in listening because of learning disabilities, other forms of compensation must be developed. Exercise 2-4 is designed to sharpen skills in listening to words so that attention is focused on both the speaker and the responder in discussions of agreement and of disagreement.

Although verbal cues are only part of the observational setting, sometimes the helper must rely solely on these cues. Observation over the telephone concentrates on these verbal cues as well as other sound patterns. Attending to these cues becomes crucial in "hot-line" situations, in which the helper must think and speak rapidly to help a person considering suicide or another catastrophe. Exercise 2-5 involves practice in observation of verbal cues.

Exercises 2-4 and 2-5 might be tape-recorded. Then the observers could check their observations to determine their completeness. The use of the tape recorder is vital to this check on observational accuracy. Whenever possible, the tape recorder should be included in the exercises.

Sound cues. "One can observe without interviewing but one cannot interview without observing" (Kadushin, 1972). This statement refers to the looking, listening, smelling, touching, and tasting channels for observational cues. Observation therefore must be extended beyond merely word-listening cues. The effective observer is tuned in to the multichannels of communication—eyes (visual), ears (auditory), nose (olfactory), hands (tactile, touching), body, arms, and legs (motion and gestures). The sound messages include the non-word punctuation marks called paralinguistics, the pitch of the voice, the change in voice control, and breathing patterns.

Tonal qualities have a wide range of possibilities that may indicate positive or negative feelings. The tone of voice may sound close or distant, loud or quiet, tense (strained or tight) or smooth. A tone that is close, quiet, and smooth is more likely to suggest a higher level of empathy, genuineness, and warmth than is a tone that sounds distant, loud, and tense. Emotional responses are also conveyed by such sounds as sighing, crying, coughing, and laughing.

Exercise 2-6 is similar to Exercise 2-5, except that the observers are asked to note sound cues as well as verbal cues.

It is very likely that many participants in Exercise 2-6 discovered that they missed several of the verbal and/or sound cues. This is not unusual. Often questions are asked, but the replies do not reach the awareness of the questioner, as Lewis Carroll (1923) describes in *Through the Looking Glass:*

"Who are you, aged man?" I said,
"And how is it you live?"
And his answer trickled through my head
Like water through a sieve.

Exercise 2-6
DO YOU LISTEN TO THE VARIETY IN WORDS AND SOUNDS? *(should be done in a group)*

Time: APPROXIMATELY 30 MINUTES

The group divides into small groups of six to eight participants. Two group members serve as role players. The remaining participants arrange themselves into a circle with their backs to the role players, who are in the center.

Part 1

For 3 minutes the two volunteers role-play a debate in which one person supports and the other person is opposed to a topic of their choosing or any one of the following: legalization of abortion or marijuana, discontinuance of grades for college courses, revolutionary changes in the educational system, acceptance of a group home or halfway house in your neighborhood for mentally retarded or mentally ill persons who have been institutionalized for 10 or more years. Using Figs. 2-4 and 2-5 as tally sheets, half of the observers tally the number of times the role player in favor of the topic uses certain words and sounds; the others tally the words and sounds of the role player opposed to the topic discussed.

Part 2

The entire group compares tallies, noting any differences in verbal and sound cues for the role player supporting the topic as compared with the role player opposed to the topic. Each group member totals the number of verbal and sound cues he or she observed. These totals are listed on some large surface so that the entire group may see the results. How complete were your observations of word and sound cues? Have you missed cues?

	Tallies			Tallies	
	Person			Person	
	A	B		A	B
1. Pitch			5. Sound of voice		
Rises			Nasal		
Falls			Hoarse		
Louder			Others (specify)		
Softer			6. Speech sounds		
2. Pronunciation			Ummm		
Clear			Ah		
Slurred			Hmmm		
"Put on"			Mmmhmmm		
"Bookish"			Uh huh		
3. Speed			Huh		
Slow			7. Breathing		
Rapid			Deep		
Jerky			Rapid		
Smooth			Even		
4. Voice control			Sighs		
Voice breaks			Laughs		
Trembles			8. Groans		
Chokes			Moans		
Clears throat					
Smooth control					

Fig. 2-5. Sound cues.

For many people who have trained themselves to receive messages "like water through a sieve," practice in listening provides the initiation of suitable communication. Exercise 2-7 furnishes an additional opportunity to listen to sounds.

Attending. Active listening depends on active attending—looking as well as listening. Attending is a two-way process. Helpers must pay attention to themselves—to what they are saying, to what they are doing with their hands and body, to what they are feeling. This is the *in*-side of attending. Helpers also must pay attention to the client, the *out*-side of attending. Certain activities support the notion that interviewers are *with* the *client*. Ivey and Authier (1978) and Ivey and Simek-Downing (1980) call these activities attending behavior.

When attention is paid to the client, the helpers express their attending behavior both verbally and nonverbally. The helpers' choice of words tells the client that they are listening to what the client says.

What helpers say falls into line with the client's needs for clarification, not interviewers' oversolicitude or curiosity. Alert helpers avoid the frequent use of "I" and are cautious about the inclusion of the client into "we" until the client indicates readiness and willingness to become part of the social dyad (a group consisting of two people with some degree of organized interpersonal relationship).

Some individuals are primarily *in*-side attenders. They are involved in how they feel and often are overcautious of what they think. Some individuals are *out*-side attenders. They are so sensitive to what other people are saying or doing that they are unable or unwilling to consider their own thoughts or feelings. Helpers must be trained to recognize their focus of attending so that they may develop a balance between self-awareness and other-awareness. Effective helpers balance observation of verbal cues with sound and body language cues. Posture, eye contact, physical space, and other verbal

---

Exercise 2-7
DO YOU HEAR THE CUES AROUND YOU? *(may be done alone or in a group)*

Time: APPROXIMATELY 25 MINUTES
Part 1

Group members shut their eyes and open their ears to listen to the sounds around them for 60 seconds. Then all persons open their eyes and for 1 minute rapidly write down the sounds they have heard.

Part 2

The participants read their lists to the group and compare their lists with other participants' observations.
□ How many sounds did you hear?
□ What kinds of sounds did you hear? Do you note any pattern?
□ Have you heard more or fewer sounds than other groups members?
□ What sounds did you not hear?

Part 3

After 10 minutes of discussion and comparison, all individuals shut their eyes again and listen for sounds for 60 seconds. Then all persons open their eyes and write down the sounds they have heard. During the group discussion that follows the second period of listening, consider (for 10 minutes):
□ Did you hear more or fewer sounds than during your first listening period (Part 1)?
□ Did you hear more or fewer sounds than other group members?
□ What sounds did you not hear?

and nonverbal responses are part of attending to this constellation of cues that are listed in Figs. 2-4, 2-5, and 2-8.

Nonverbal cues. The words used and sounds made give only a partial picture of a message. Words in particular, because they are so dependent on individual interpretations, may distort rather than assist understanding. Body language and other nonverbal behavior are learned during infancy long before words become part of the child's behavior. As the child develops, cultural demands step in and shape the gestures and body movements according to the prevailing customs. More personal influences of the people caring for the developing child also enter into the expression of nonverbal behavior (Fig. 2-6).

Since nonverbal behavior is more revealing than words, perhaps some individuals condition themselves not to show their feelings through facial expressions. The "poker face" is a good example of concealing emotions.

In spite of the attempts to control the overt display of nonverbal behavior, feelings are not so easily squelched. There are numerous channels

Ruth Silverman, Editorial Photocolor Archives

Fig. 2-6. The eyes of men converse as much as their tongues with the advantage that the ocular dialect needs no dictionary but is understood the world over. (Ralph Waldo Emerson, The Conduct of Life: Behavior, 1860.)

through which feelings manage to be revealed to the observant counselor. Similarly, the client may "feel" the attitude of the counselor by observing the counselor's body language.

A rigid body keeps sending messages to which the individual must attend. Relaxed persons do not have to squirm and shift position because of muscle tension. They can attend to another individual and not so much to themselves. Comfortable helpers feel relaxed. Some helpers who are attending closely cross their legs; others keep their feet flat on the ground as if ready to spring forward. Crossed or uncrossed legs are part of the language of attention that the helper learns. Attentive helpers tend to turn their shoulders and legs toward the client and to lean forward slightly in a relaxed position. Leaning slightly forward and moving the body slowly backward and then toward the client accent certain points that the client makes and reassure the client of the interviewer's attentiveness. Contrasted with the rocking motion and the sideways position, the counselor's face-to-face position demonstrates a greater closeness with the client and also a less tense, more concentrating attitude. What message is being conveyed by the body language of the helper in Fig. 2-7?

Inexperienced helpers may attempt to appear attentive but will reveal their discomfort and even fear by a rigid, upright position, which is often aggravated by the closed-in look of tightly crossed

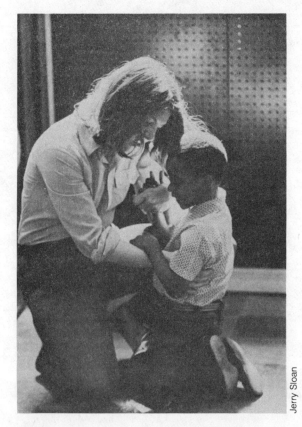

Jerry Sloan

Fig. 2-7. Nonverbal behavior can be more revealing than words. The child is especially responsive to the show of care expressed by a smile and gentle caress.

legs, folded arms, and stiff jaw. To unlock themselves, fearful helpers may need to learn how to relax. When individuals relax, they let their body unwind. The cat is a wonderful model to follow. When the cat awakens, he stretches his back into an arch, extends his legs, and opens his jaws wide. Slowly he blows himself up. Then the air slowly comes out. The cat now hangs loose. Exercise 2-8 considers a body-unwinding procedure.

Body language. Neither constant rigidity nor constant movement is desirable in the helping relationship. Body language includes (1) the study of the distance between people and the orientation or direction of the body (proxemics) and (2) the study of the motion of the body (kinesics).

Hall (1966) wrote about the person's use of environmental and personal space in *The Hidden Dimension,* describing the impact of such characteristics as the size of the room, the seating arrangement, a person's positioning himself near or far away from an object such as a desk or table, and the distance between persons. Proxemics also include territoriality, possessiveness about the space around a person. Comments such as "Don't crowd my space" and even perhaps "Don't rain on my picnic" go beyond the obvious physical reference to the social meanings of the environment.

Birdwhistell (1970) includes physical characteristics such as body physique, height, weight, and general appearance in the concept of kinesics. Other aspects of kinetic behavior are observed in general body movement (postural change and the like),

specific gestures, facial expressions, and eye behavior (Cormier and Cormier, 1979; Knapp, 1972).

Fig. 2-8 lists body language and other nonverbal and nonsound cues. Increased awareness of body language opens up a wealth of data to enrich the interpersonal moments of the helping relationship. Exercise 2-9 concentrates on "what a body reveals" and offers an opportunity to test one's alertness to nonverbal cues.

The body does "speak" in many ways, through the degree of tension demonstrated and through numerous other nonverbal cues. Another observational dimension is expressed in the manner in which an individual uses physical space.

Physical space and body motion (proxemics and kinesics). The preferred distance between individuals has cultural implications. There seems to be a graduated preference for distance that varies with the culture, with the social situation, and with men and women. People in the United States are generally inclined toward larger distances than in some European cultures, and American women are much more cautious about distances in physical space than are men. For the helper the importance of physical distance depends on the client's functioning level. Being too close too soon may result in the client's confusion and embarrassment (Scheflen and Aschcraft, 1976; Sielski, 1979). In general, a closer distance between client and helper indicates a more positive helper attitude (Fig. 2-9). However, the empathic helper is aware of the appropriate distance for client comfort. Ex-

Text continued on p. 95.

Exercise 2-8
HOW DO YOU GO ABOUT BODY UNWINDING? *(may be done alone or in a group)*

Time: APPROXIMATELY 15 MINUTES (IF DISCUSSION FOLLOWS THE UNWINDING PROCESS)

Sit upright in your chair. (A straight-backed chair is preferable.) Push your shoulders back and shut your eyes. Try to feel the points of contact of your body with the chair. Slowly, try to make yourself more comfortable. Concentrate on what you are doing as you move your body to make yourself more comfortable. Twist, stretch, sigh, and yawn as you please. Note how you stretch the muscles of various parts of your body as you plan and do the steps in your unwinding.

	Tallies			Tallies	
Total body			**Arms and hands**		
Posture			Arms and hands gesturing		
Stiff and rigid			*Arms*		
Bent			Crossed at waist		
Loose, relaxed			Akimbo (elbows bent out-		
Movement			ward in a semicircle or		
Rocks back and forth			arc) on chest		
Squirms			Unfolded		
Stiffly erect			*Hands*		
Sits on edge of chair			Rubs eyes		
Leans forward			Chin on hand		
Bends forward			Hands and arms drop over		
Shrugs shoulders			back of chair		
Stooped, rounded			Sits on hands		
Slouches			Hand(s) on hip(s)		
Orientation			Hides hands behind desk		
Sits squarely facing			*Palms*		
Sits sideways			Up		
Distance			Down		
Sits closer			Out		
Sits farther away			Circular movement		
Accessibility			Slow, continuous		
Open (arms and hands placed on			Semicircular, back and		
lap, legs uncrossed)			forth		
Closed (arms held crossed across			Swing an arc		
chest, legs crossed near thigh			*Chopping gestures*		
Odor			Rhythmic (up and down		
Perfume			Nonrhythmic (emphasizes		
Aftershave			certain words)		
Other (specify)			*Expansion/contraction*		
Legs and feet			*waves*		
Legs and feet still and unmoving			"Goodbye" motion		
Legs			Wavy lines		
Sway in circular motion			Others (specify)		
Kick back and forth			*Handshake*		
Move up and down at bent knee			Firm		
Slaps thigh			Flabby		
Hands clasp knees			*Fingers*		
Crosses one knee over other			Point		
Crosses ankle of one leg over knee			Drum on table		
of other			Extend		
Feet			Pick things (lint) from		
Tap			clothing		
Kick			Scratch		
Shuffle			Pull earlobe		
Slide back and forth			Rub nose		
			Squeeze facial tissue,		
			pimple on face		

Fig. 2-8. For legend see opposite page.

	Tallies			Tallies	
Snap pencil			One or both wink		
Head region Nods, moves from side to side			*Facial expression* Nostrils open wide (flared)		
Bobs (shakes up and down)			**Lips** Smile		
Bent down toward chest					
Hair Runs fingers through (combing motion)			Curl		
Plays with			Tremble (quiver)		
Curls hair around fingers			Turn up		
Neck Tense muscles			Turn down		
Stiff, rigid			Open (pursed together)		
Rapid hand-to-neck movement			Closed		
Forehead Wrinkles			Moistened by tongue		
Furrows			Bites lips		
Eyebrows Lifted (arch)			*Jaws* Opens mouth without speaking		
Contract (pull together)			Yawns		
Frown Twitching brow			Clamp		
			Teeth grind		
Eyes Wide open			*Chin* Thrust forward		
Narrow slits (squints) Moisture or tears			Drawn in		
Eye contact Looks toward directly			Quivers (trembles)		
Looks away, shifts gaze			Hides face behind hands		
Lowers eyes (looks down or away)			Covers mouth or eyes with hands		
Wears sunglasses			Beads of sweat on face		
Removes sunglasses			**Breath** Unpleasant		
Removes corrective lenses			Smell of liquor		
Pupils dilated			**Adjust** (straighten, pull) Clothes		
Pupils constricted					
Eyelids Close slowly			Things in hand or on desk		
Flutter rapidly			**Rub** (desk, arms, chair)		
Blink rapidly			**Pound** (table)		

Fig. 2-8. Nonverbal/nonsound cues. (Modified from Wiener, M., and others: Psychol. Rev. **79:**185-214, 1972; and Cormier, W.H., and Cormier, L.S.: Interviewing strategies for helpers: a guide to assessment, treatment, and education, Monterey, Calif., 1979, Brooks/Cole Publishing Co.)

Exercise 2-9
DO YOU SEE WHAT THE BODY REVEALS? *(should be done in a group)*

Time: APPROXIMATELY 30 MINUTES

The group divides into small groups of six to eight participants. Two group members serve as role players and sit in the center of a semicircle formed by the other trainees. The observers face the role players. Each of the observers needs a copy of Fig. 2-8.

The observers tally the number of times they see certain nonverbal actions listed in Fig. 2-8. The first column is used for the first 3 minutes of role playing, and the second column for the second 3 minutes.

Half of the observers rate one volunteer; the others rate the other volunteer. The observers also write comments about their overall impressions of the nonverbal behavior of the role players they have watched.

Part 1

For 3 minutes the two volunteers role play a situation of their choosing or use one of the following:

[1] The two volunteers role-play a parent and child. The parent has found a bag of "white stuff" and a hypodermic syringe. The parent suspects what the white stuff may be but is uncertain. The parent confronts the child with these items and tries to discover where they were obtained.

[2] An employee is in the office of the personnel officer of a federal agency. The employee is white, and the personnel officer is black. The employee has sent a grievance report to the Equal Employment Opportunity Commission about discrimination by his black supervisor. The employee is certain that he or she has not been given equal opportunity to obtain a promotion.

[3] The mother of a 24-year-old mentally retarded woman is speaking to the counselor in a sheltered workshop. The counselor has recommended that the daughter, Teda, move into a supervised apartment and begin employment in an office as a clerk. The mother does not want her daughter exposed to the sexual and other dangers of the people on the "outside."

Part 2

The role players join the observers, and for 10 minutes the group discusses the ratings and comments about the role players' nonverbal behavior.

Part 3

The role players resume their roles and continue their probing attack and counterattack of their confrontation. Another 10-minute discussion is held with the addition of a comparison of the accuracy and completeness from the first to the second sessions in the observers' comments and other observations.

Fig. 2-9. Body language: proxemics and kinesics, and other nonverbal cues. **A,** The beginning of the discussion. **B,** Getting closer and more involved. **C,** Nonverbal clues, including proximity and facial expression, revealing the concerted attention to the discussion.

Barbara Haimowitz

Exercise 2-10
HOW DO YOU TUNE IN TO BODY CUES IN PHYSICAL DISTANCE? *(should be done in a group)*

Time: APPROXIMATELY 35 MINUTES
Part 1

The goal of this exercise is increased awareness of body cues and the feelings associated with these cues. Two circles are formed. Five participants seat themselves in an inner circle so that they face the participants in the outer circle. Thus, depending on the size of the outer circle, there should be two or more participants observing each participant in the inner circle.

All inner-circle participants should be seated comfortably so that they face those in the outer circle. All should close their eyes and sit quietly for a minute. Then, individually, they should describe to the outer-circle participants what they feel.

Part 2

Now each inner-circle participant is a counselor. Individually the counselors select someone in the outer circle to be their client, walk over to the client, extend their hands to touch this person, and describe to the client what they feel. The procedure continues until all five inner-circle participants have completed their descriptions.

Part 3

The five inner-circle participants join the larger group, and a general discussion is held of the recorded observations. Comparisons are made of the differences between verbal and nonverbal behavior for the inner-circle participants when their eyes were closed and when they role-played counselors with a client.

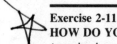

Exercise 2-11
HOW DO YOU PERCEIVE PHYSICAL SPACE AND DISTANCE BETWEEN PEOPLE?
(may be done alone and discussed in a group)

Time: APPROXIMATELY 30 MINUTES

Draw stick figures of yourself and the following persons:
- ☐ Your father
- ☐ Your mother
- ☐ Your sister or brother
- ☐ Your teacher or employer
- ☐ Your friend

Draw the stick figures of yourself and the other persons listed as you usually feel when talking to each person according to size (smaller than, the same size, or larger than the other person), physical distance (near or far from the other person), and position (body facing toward or away from the other person).

After you complete the five stick drawings *as you usually are,* make five more drawings representing yourself and the same people, but this time make their sizes and the positions and distance as you would like them to be.

What have you found out about your relationships with the five people of whom you drew pictures as you usually feel about them? How do you feel the space around you and the distance between you reveals your interrelationships? What have you discovered about how you would like your relationship to change?

ercises 2-10 and 2-11 offer experiences in sharpening awareness to body cues and to the use of physical space.

In effect, physical distance and positioning have several implications. The distance established by clients often is indicative of how free and comfortable they feel in the counseling situation. However, cultural differences in acceptance of closeness may affect the space clients permit (Miller, 1973).

In general, among Anglo clients a distance of between 3 and 5 feet (1 to 1½ meters) seems to be conducive to greater client comfort and verbal productivity (Knight and Blair, 1976; Sommer, 1974; Stone and Morden, 1976). Therefore the distance between helper and client regulates their interpersonal transactions, listening accuracy, and nonverbal behavior. Exercises 2-12 and 2-13 examine these aspects of distance and position.

Exercise 2-12
HOW DOES PHYSICAL DISTANCE AFFECT HOW YOU LISTEN? *(should be done in a group)*

Time: 30 MINUTES

Two members of the group volunteer to be partners. They seat themselves at opposite corners of the room, diagonally across from each other. The rest of the group members form a circle and move their chairs so that they are able to see and hear the partners. The group members write notes about their observations of the eye contact, posture, tone of voice, and positions of the partners' hands and feet as they move toward each other from the corners of the room. (Refer to Figs. 2-5 and 2-8.)

The partners talk to each other about any topic for 2 minutes. If they are stuck for a topic, they might talk about "What should we talk about?" Then they discuss for 3 minutes how they both feel. Did they look at each other? Did they feel comfortable? How did their voices sound? The group members listen to the partners' discussion and then add their own comments for 5 minutes.

The same procedure, as described in the first position, is repeated two more times. Each time the partners move a little closer, talk for 2 minutes, and then discuss the same questions as before. They note the differences in responses that the closer distance makes. The group members comment on these differences.

Finally, the partners are close enough that they are face to face, with their knees almost or actually touching, whichever is more comfortable. They discuss the same questions. Does physical distance make a difference in the ability to communicate effectively?

Exercise 2-13
HOW DOES YOUR LISTENING POSITION AFFECT HOW YOU LISTEN? *(should be done in a group)*

Time: 15 TO 20 MINUTES

Each person should have the chance to be the "low" one in this exercise. One person sits in a chair, and another person sits on the floor in front of the chair. The person in the chair looks down at the person on the floor, and the "low" person returns the look. They talk for about 1 minute. Any longer than that will probably make the neck of the person on the floor uncomfortable.

After talking together in these positions, the two get into a more comfortable position and for 5 mintues discuss how they both felt about their "high" and "low" positions. How did their bodies feel? Were they able to attend to what they were saying? Do they feel different now that they are seated more comfortably?

After this discussion the two should switch positions and the entire procedure should be repeated.

More specific observations of nonverbal cues focus on one part of the body or of motions of the body. The cues in the following description are those listed in Fig. 2-8. Observational skill development is the thread of this exploration. One must be cautious in the interpretation of nonverbal (or any) cues, since so many factors enter into their meaning.

If a dictionary of nonverbal cues could be compiled, it would be very helpful. However, except for a comparatively small number of nonverbal cues, the meaning of the cue depends on the time, the place, and the person using it. This need for specificity does not detract from the importance of the cue but does urge the observer to be concrete in observation and recording. Nonverbal behavior embraces many different languages and many different parts, positions, and motions of the body (kinesics). The caveat mentioned previously merits repetition: the emphasis must be on what each client "tells" by his or her nonverbal cues and what each helper suggests by his or her own behavior rather than on a generalized explanation of meanings.

Head movement. The constantly moving head or the stiffly held, erect head has negative values for the client. Greater warmth, genuineness, and empathy are exhibited when the head is periodically nodded up and down or tilted to one side in a "listening" position. Clients receive more acceptance when the counselor's head is held slightly forward rather than backward or bent down.

Facial expression. The wrinkled brow, the smile, the blink of the eyes, and the gaze or stare of the eyes all regulate, communicate, and express ideas and feelings. Hands may be hidden in one's pockets, placed on one's lap, or sat on. Legs and feet may be concealed behind a desk. The face, however, is constantly exposed and, unless hidden behind a hand or mask, cannot conceal the feelings communicated. The interpretation of the meanings of facial language requires an alert, knowledgeable, emphatic (keenly with-it) individual.

Facial expressions are probably the most frequently observed cues. The smile of the warm, empathic counselor is much more effective than the tight-lipped, frown of the harassed, uncaring counselor. Eyebrows have varied possibilities for expressing disbelief (one eyebrow raised), surprise (both eyebrows raised), and concern or distress (both eyebrows raised with creases in the forehead). The meaning of the movement of the eyebrows must, of course, be interpreted in the context of the client-counselor relationship.

Communicating with these nonverbal cues of head movements and facial expressions is constant. Yet the unskilled observer is too often unaware of the complexity and pervasiveness of these cues. Exercise 2-14 explores these two cues of nonverbal communication.

Eye contact. Eyes are even more "eloquent" than head position and facial expression.

Eye contact may be so intense that it annoys one, or eye movement may start or stop a conver-

---

Exercise 2-14
HOW DO YOU "SPEAK" WITH NONVERBAL CUES? *(should be done in a group)*

Time: APPROXIMATELY 15 MINUTES

The group pairs off with partners facing each other. For 1 minute both partners try to tell one another something without speaking. They use head movements and facial expression to accomplish this communication. They then discuss for 5 minutes what each was trying to communicate. The procedure of nonverbal "speaking" is repeated for another minute. Once again the partners discuss what they were trying to communicate. It should be noted whether and how either or both partners improved their ability to communicate.

sation. Wearing sunglasses makes the individual less available to others; this makes the removal of the sunglasses a significant sign of becoming available. On the other hand, individuals who wear corrective lenses may be removing themselves from the world when they remove their lenses.

The significance of eye contact in interpersonal relationships is demonstrated by the reactions of disturbed individuals. The more uncomfortable an individual feels with another person, the more likely he or she will avoid eye contact. Paintings of people done by severely emotionally disordered individuals often show the eyes in a bizarre (odd or absurd) manner.

Eye contact also depends on the status of the individuals involved. Individuals who are perceived as being of a higher status are afforded more eye contact than individuals considered to have a lower status. The student is likely to look at the college professor more frequently than at a graduate student assisting the professor. Dependent individuals, seeking self-status, are inclined to reveal a relatively high level of eye contact as part of their approval-seeking behavior.

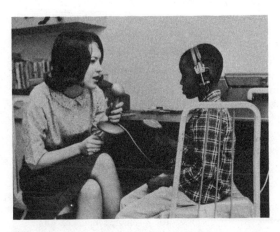

Fig. 2-10. Speech therapist trains child in developing listening skills. The first step is establishing eye contact. (From Barber, J.M., Stokes, L.G., and Billings, D.M.: Adult and child care: a client approach to nursing, ed. 2, St. Louis, 1977, The C.V. Mosby Co.)

Effective counselors maintain their gaze toward the client. Their eyes are turned in the direction of the client's and occasionally shifted—not shifty. Thus they avoid a constantly or rapidly changing eye movement just as much as they refrain from staring, glaring, and squinting (Fig. 2-10).

Eye contact is often used to reinforce the client to go on with a particular topic (by looking at the client) or to shape the talk behavior away from a blind-alley discussion (by looking away from the client). This discriminative use of eye contact assists the client in exploring problems and finding solutions. Helpers must learn to interact visually so that their eye contact not only shows the client their interest, but also reinforces the client's personal growth.

Restful, comforting eye contact comes easy to some people but must be learned and practiced by others. The deliberate learning of the skill of eye contact may feel artificial at first, but with practice the approach becomes automatic and satisfying. Contact between people is built on being on eye level with them. People must be close enough, must face one another, and must be at similar heights to be able to communicate successfully (note Exercise 2-13).

Exercise 2-15 provides an opportunity to experiment with degrees of eye contact.

It takes time and practice to observe accurately and to realize how much nonverbal cues disclose. However, the additional effort is productive since nonverbal messages are more spontaneous than verbal behavior. The "leakages" coming through nonverbal behavior are not as easily controlled as words (Passons, 1975). Verbal behavior can be regulated and managed so that "what we say isn't necessarily what we mean." Exercise 2-16 calls attention to nonverbal behavior as observed by cues from the total body—all aspects of body language.

Gestural movements. Individuals gesture with their arms, hands, legs, and feet. They may move their arms and legs up and down or from side to side. Finger-tapping, knuckle-cracking, leg-shaking individuals shout forth their tension, impatience, and displeasure. Open, accepting individ-

Exercise 2-15
DO YOUR EYES MAKE CONTACT? *(should be done in a group)*

Time: APPROXIMATELY 15 MINUTES

For 3 minutes two people sit directly opposite each other close enough so that they can touch. They talk about what they think the characteristics of an effective helper should be. During this conversation both people should be looking at something or someone, but not at each other.

During the next 3 minutes they talk about how they felt during the first 3 minutes. During this period only one person looks at the other. The other person continues to do what he or she did before—look at something or someone other than the partner.

For the last 5 minutes the two persons talk about the differences between the first and second 3-minute periods. The participants look at one another during this conversation and report on how this feels. Does eye contact make a difference?

Exercise 2-16
DO YOU LISTEN ONLY TO THE WORDS? *(should be done in a group)*

Two volunteers are needed for this exercise. The remaining group members divide into seven small observation groups. Each group selects one of the following sections from Fig. 2-8: (1) posture and movement, (2) orientation and distance, (3) accessibility, (4) legs and feet, (5) arms and hands, (6) head region, or (7) facial expression. All seven sections must be covered. The group members form a semicircle facing the two volunteers. The volunteers select one of the following situations and follow the directions as stated.

Nonverbal behavior with responsive and nonresponsive listener
Time: APPROXIMATELY 18 MINUTES

One volunteer speaks to the other volunteer about any topic of interest for 3 minutes. The listener sits quietly and shows no response. The nonverbal behavior of the speaker is tallied by the observers. Then the speaker discusses the same topic for another 3 minutes. On this second occasion the listener shows interest, listens intently, and uses gestures (if he or she wishes) to indicate interest. Again the nonverbal behavior of the speaker is tallied by the observers. After these two 3-minute encounters the group members discuss the differences in nonverbal cues between the first and the second discussions (10 minutes). Does the speaker show more or less nonverbal behavior when the listener is responsive?

Nonverbal behavior with a child
Time: APPROXIMATELY 18 MINUTES

One volunteer speaks for 3 minutes to the other volunteer, who is supposed to be a child. The nonverbal behavior of the speaker is tallied by the group. Then the speaker discusses for 3 minutes the same topic with the listener who is now in the speaker's age range. The speaker's nonverbal behavior is again tallied by the group. After these two encounters the group members discuss the difference in nonverbal cues between the first and the second discussions (10 minutes). Does the speaker show more nonverbal behavior with the child or with someone who is nearer his or her age?

uals are more likely to have their arms open, their legs uncrossed, their fingers still, and their hands loosely clasped on their lap.

The language of gestures includes pantomimic and nonpantomimic motions of the hands and fingers. *Pantomimic* gestures are actions that substitute for words. The game of charades is an example. *Nonpantomimic* gestures are actions that accompany words and modify or regulate the meaning of the words. Some pantomime is formal and has specific meanings that are known by most people in a particular culture—waving good-bye, "V" for victory, making two wavy lines in the air to demonstrate the well-proportioned female, putting one's thumb to the nose with the remainder of the fingers extended to signify extreme distaste and annoyance, forming a circle with the index finger and thumb with the remainder of the fingers extended to signify "OK" or "going well," and making a sign of a circle next to the temple to represent "he's nuts." Subgroups also have their formal pantomimic language—the hand language of deaf mutes, the military salute, the gesture of the hands in prayer, the clenched fist salute and the handshake of soul brothers, and the thumb up to save the bull and thumb down to kill him at the bullfight. There are also informal gestures whose meanings depend on the situation and the context. These gestures may involve parts of the face that are touched by the hands or fingers such as pulling the earlobe, rubbing one's nose, adjusting clothes, squeezing a pimple on the face, and other characteristics mentioned in Fig. 2-8.

Nonpantomimic gestures include pointing, chopping the air, and turning the palm. Pointing movements draw attention more specifically to a particular person or object—saying "that girl" with the index finger pointing toward her makes certain that the particular girl is noticed. Palms may be turned up in uncertainty or down or facing toward the message receiver to indicate emphasis. "Cut the static" and "Don't interrupt" are both more commanding when a palm faces the message receiver in a "stop" sign. Circular movements may demonstrate the generality of a statement ("Sometimes this works and the . . .") and semicircular movements of the hand back and forth suggest "either/ or." Chopping gestures are used for emphasis and may be used to highlight one word over another in a sentence. "You have to think about verbal and nonverbal cues" may be accompanied by two hand chops that emphasize that both cues are equally important or one chop after "verbal" or "nonverbal" to stress that one or the other is more important. There is the fish-story kind of gesture of expansion and contraction. Like an accordion, the size of the fish or other object is made smaller or larger during the telling of the "fish story."

Paralinguistics. The "what" (content) and the "how" (paralinguistics) of communication have been presented in the preceding exploration of verbal, sound, and nonverbal cues. Paralinguistic cues include silence as well as voice level, pitch, and speech fluency. Repeated words or letters, lisping, whining, and rapid, slow, or jerky speech provide hints about the emotional reactions of a person. A clammy hand, shallow or rapid breathing, paleness, blushing, and the like are most likely broadcasting the individual's embarrassment, fear, or anger. In other words, paralanguage gets at the core of the person who is sending a message—verbally and nonverbally. Exercise 2-17 expands observations to the items related to paralinguistics in Figs. 2-5 and 2-8.

Language of objects. The language of objects is one more aspect of nonverbal cues that everyone sees, yet few notice. Personal adornments such as clothes, hairstyle, makeup, jewelry, and tattoos are expressive extensions of the self. This describes the significance of home furnishings also. There are some uniforms of group identification—for example, long hair, beard, headband, patched jeans, tie-dyed tee shirt, and beads portray a different lifestyle than do studded leather jacket (usually black), boots, and red, white, and blue helmet. Both of these attires contrast with an Afro haircut and dashiki or Bermuda shorts with an Indian madras shirt. The picture of the home of each of these people would differ also. Books, hi-fi records, plants, art on the wall, and the furniture style also express the life-style of the individual. These non-verbal cues from objects are part of the script that helps interviewers gain better understanding of their clients.

Communication skills: active listening

Effective helping is built on the abilities of observation and communication. Observation of verbal and nonverbal cues is the bottom line, the foundation for the helping process. Communication builds on observational skills and is interwoven with receiving, understanding, and responding to messages.

Hearing and listening

Wise men talk, because they have something to say; Fools talk, because they have to say something (Plato).

There is no more inclusive property of the effective helper than listening. Listening and observing form the center around which all other

---

Exercise 2-17
ARE YOU LISTENING TO SOUNDS AND WATCHING MOVEMENTS AND GESTURES?
(should be done in a group)

Two volunteers are needed for each of the three parts of this exercise. The remainder of the group selects different sections of the lists of characteristics in Figs. 2-5 and 2-8 on which they concentrate. The number of different assignments depends on the size of the group.

After selections have been made and all the characteristics in both figures have been covered, the two volunteers move into the center of the group. The group members form a semicircle facing the two volunteers. (If the group is too large for all members to see the volunteers, smaller groups may be formed with several pairs of volunteers.)

Part 1—*Time:* APPROXIMATELY 4 MINUTES

One volunteer takes the role of a woman who has just arrived from Mars. She does not know how to speak but instead conveys her message through electrical vibrations from her brain. Her eyes are hurting because she is not used to strong sunlight. She wants to tell the second volunteer two things: (1) she needs someone to help her decrease the pain in her eyes, and (2) she is very hungry and wants to known where she can get some food. For 2 minutes the Martian woman and the other volunteer attempt to communicate. They are both unsuccessful. During the next 2 minutes the Martian woman gets annoyed and shows by her nonverbal language that she must have help or else her people will revenge her discomfort when they arrive. The other volunteer responds to the Martian woman as he or she wishes. Remember, no words are to be spoken throughout these 4 minutes.

As the volunteers attempt to communicate; the other group members tally the nonverbal characteristics they observe using Figs. 2-5 and 2-8 and concentrating on those particular characteristics for which they are responsible.

Part 2—*Time:* 10 MINUTES

The volunteers return to the group, and the group members discuss what they have observed. Particular attention should be paid to whether there was any difference in the nonverbal cues used during the first 2 minutes and the second 2 minutes.

Part 3—*Time:* APPROXIMATELY 20 MINUTES

The entire procedure should be repeated. Before beginning, the group should decide on a nonverbal scene for the volunteers. The discussion that occurs after the nonverbal scene has been completed should include whether there has been improvement in the number of nonverbal cues observed.

characteristics of the facilitative interview revolve. In spite of the vital impact of listening on the success of the interview, helpers too frequently fall short of skills essential to listening.

Several points pertain to the skill of listening. It has been said that an individual may hear but not listen, look but not see. Listening and seeing require concentration in the here and now. Effective listening is built on the cooperation of both the speaker and the listener in advancing toward better understanding. Intelligence as well as sharp vision and hearing supports the abilities of looking and listening but are just the channels for these attributes. They are like the camera lens with a blurred film or the microphone that is turned off. They are sterile skills without the attention—the active attention—of the listener and looker. An efficient listener is actively engaged in receiving, recording, and decoding (getting the meaning of) the client's message. Empathic listeners develop large eyes, big ears, a small mouth, and positive actions that reveal their interest and acceptance of the client. The active listener "enters in a relation" with the communicator—becomes aware of the speaker's reality (Banville, 1978).

Exercise 2-18 initiates try-outs for listening skills focusing on the differences between *hearing* words and *listening* to the meaning and message of the words.

Listening has become even less of a skill since the coming of television in the mid-1940s. The "tube" reinforced passive behavior, and the young have grown up on a diet of pictured words garnished with commercial snacks. Television's instant exposure to events does not demand much of the viewer. Pushing buttons and turning dials are often the extent of the experiencing involved.

"Tube plopping" has at least two unfortunate effects. It undermines the process of learning to respond on the basis of listening, and it detracts from individuals' feedback to their own words. Learning to listen to others begins with listening to oneself. The process leading to the achievement of the listening skill includes input (speaking), response (as a listener), and self-feedback (listening to oneself). Communication may break down at any of these stages. The growing child may not have had ample opportunity to speak, to listen, or to respond because other people were absent, uninterested, or doing all the talking for him or her.

Exercise 2-18
DO YOU REALLY *HEAR*—DO YOU REALLY LISTEN? *(should be done in a group)*

Part 1—*Time:* APPROXIMATELY 15 MINUTES

The group divides into subgroups with five participants. Four people are observers; the fifth person talks into the microphone of a tape recorder as rapidly as possible. The speaker discusses any topic, including himself or herself; for 5 minutes. The four observers take notes about verbal, sound, and nonverbal cues and about what the speaker is saying. One observer concentrates on each kind of information using Figs. 2-4, 2-5, and 2-8 for reference.

All observations are recorded. A 5-minute group discussion follows in which the observers and the speaker compare notes about their observations and the speaker's apparent feelings about the entire process. Then the tape recorder is turned on, and notes are taken by all five members of the group of the cues from the recording. An additional 5-minute group discussion is conducted concentrating on the added cues derived from the tape.

Part 2—*Time:* APPROXIMATELY 15 MINUTES

The entire procedure of Part 1 is repeated, the only difference being that this time the speaker discusses a topic as slowly as possible.

Exercise 2-19
DO VERBAL AND NONVERBAL CUES "MATCH"? (ARE THEY CONGRUENT?)
(should be done alone and then may be discussed in a group)

For 1 week keep a notebook with you in which you write your observations of people in at least 10 different situations for periods of at least 5 minutes for each observation. Jot down your 10 observations and your impressions, answering the following questions immediately after each observation:

□ What about the behavior of these individuals assures you that they mean what they say?
□ What about the behavior of these individuals assures you that they don't mean what they say?

Be specific in your observations and in your support of your impressions. Refer to Figs. 2-4, 2-5, and 2-8 for verbal and nonverbal cues.

Bring your findings to your next group meeting to discuss with the other group members. If you find that the others are more complete than you are in observations and supporting facts or that your findings need additional observations, you should repeat this exercise.

Exercise 2-20
HOW DO YOU KNOW ME? LET ME COUNT THE WAYS *(should be done in a group)*

Poetry fans will recognize the origin of the idea behind the title of this exercise (with apologies to Elizabeth Barrett Browning's "Sonnets from the Portuguese"). Several situations are suggested as starters for the "games." However, the group members may decide on other situations they prefer to use.

[1] *Time:* APPROXIMATELY 16 MINUTES

DIRECTIONS FOR THE ROLE PLAYER: You are not "you" today. You are speaking, moving, and in general acting as if you were someone in your family, one of your friends, or someone in your group. For 2 minutes act this role and then without saying or doing anything startling, change to "you" for 2 minutes.

DIRECTIONS FOR THE OBSERVERS: You respond to the role player as you deem appropriate and also observe all cues—verbal, sound, and nonverbal. Jot down these cues. Refer to Figs. 2-4, 2-5, and 2-8 if you need any suggestions for cues to observe. Tally the total number of the cues you observed. After the tallying is complete, the entire group discusses the observations for 10 minutes.

[2] *Time:* APPROXIMATELY 20 MINUTES

DIRECTIONS FOR THE ROLE PLAYERS: Four people role play this situation. There are two islands to which these four people must move—Etirabys or Dellortnoc. In Etirabys people live in a group home (commune), share all possessions, and do anything they want to do. Dellortnoc is an island where people live in their own homes, can have all the money they want, and must follow Seyegib's commands. Two of the role players want to move to Etirabys, and the other two to Dellortnoc. All four people decide that they will pretend to want to go to Dellortnoc. They do this because they do not trust the Council members who will decide which of the members may have their choice of island. (The four role players meet briefly, away from the observers, and decide who will be the truthful two role players and who will be the untruthful role players.) The four people discuss and support their real or feigned preference of island.

DIRECTIONS FOR THE OBSERVERS: You are the Council members who are watching closely to identify the two honest applicants. These applicants will be relocated in their choice of island. Jot down the verbal, sound, and nonverbal cues. Refer to Figs. 2-4, 2-5, and 2-8 if you need any suggestions for cues to observe.

After the notations are complete, the entire group discusses the observations. The Council members point out whom they consider worthy of moving to the island of their choice, supporting their decision with their observations of the "truthfulness" of the role players. Congruence is used as one of the clues to support their "honesty." Evidences of noncongruence are also discussed for applicants considered to be "lying."

Congruence. Since listening is the bridge between hearing and understanding, it is imperative that the interviewer attend equally to verbal and nonverbal cues. Competent listening presupposes a receptive state in which clients' glances, muscular twitchings, gestures, and other body reactions as well as their tone of voice, pauses, and words are noted.

The nonverbal cues must be tied together with what is said out loud. Helpers must ask themselves, "Do the client's words agree with what is being exhibited in nonverbal behavior?" Essentially the question becomes "Does the client's behavior fit his or her words?" This "fit" of messages of facial expression, of gestures, and of posture with the tone and choice of words is called congruence.

Exercise 2-19 explores this concept of congruence from the standpoint of whether verbal and nonverbal cues "match."

Comparing verbal and nonverbal behavior for cues about the observed person's honesty in expressions brings the observational process back to the whole person. Exercise 2-20 attempts to be three things—an experimental observation, a game, and a look at the whole person.

When the primary characteristics of capable listeners are put together, they include accurate observation of both verbal and nonverbal cues, active concentration on the spoken words, and caution in interpreting the client's meaning. Effective listeners *stop* to listen. They are occupied with the client, not preoccupied with their own thoughts.

The three r's of listening. Effective listeners are listening to the total message rather than selectively hearing what they choose to hear. Psychological deafness is a device used by the individual unable to, or unwilling to, listen to the speaker. Both helpers and clients must be trained to realize that "earshades" may be keeping out certain ideas or feelings that are unpleasant to them. Both helpers and clients must be trained to listen to themselves as well as to one another. They must learn to listen so that they are able to *recall* what they are thinking at the moment of the discussion

---

Exercise 2-21
CAN YOU ACCURATELY RECALL, RECOGNIZE, AND REPEAT? *(should be done in a group)*

Part 1—*Time:* APPROXIMATELY 15 MINUTES

Divide the group into subgroups of three people. Arrange chairs so that each member of the subgroup is comfortable and is able to see the other members of the subgroup. Read all of Part 1 before beginning.

For 1 minute each subgroup talks about what the members would prefer discussing when Part 2 of this exercise is begun. Then for 2 minutes each person recalls the ideas presented by the members of the subgroup:

   □ What he or she remembers about the discussions
   □ How he or she felt about the discussions (recognition of feelings)

After each member (the speaker) relates what he or she recalls (ideas) and recognizes (feelings), the other members of the subgroup (the listeners) discuss whether the speaker was accurate in the presentation. Each person reacts for no more than 2 minutes.

Part 2—*Time:* APPROXIMATELY 12 MINUTES

After the members of the subgroup have completed their presentations, they talk about their selected topic for 3 minutes. Then for 2 minutes each person discusses the following:

   □ How he or she feels about what the group was saying and doing (verbal and nonverbal observations)
   □ What he or she thinks the other group members were feeling
   □ How could the group members have improved what they were doing and how they were listening

and to *recognize* their feelings. If they can recall and recognize them, they will be able to *repeat* what transpired with accuracy. When these initial listening skills have been developed within the helping session, then clients must be trained to listen in the environment of their daily encounters with people.

It is unlikely that these three r's of listening are sufficiently developed in many people so that accurate responding occurs. Exercise 2-21 (p. 103) examines these three ingredients of responsiveness.

Looking and listening—observational skills—are the crucial elements of effective helping that are discussed in this chapter. Factors influencing the accuracy of observation have been examined; and attitudes and skills as parts of the observation understructure for human service workers, have been presented. Certain basic knowledge about observation is reported in the following section.

BASIC KNOWLEDGE ABOUT OBSERVATION FOR EFFECTIVE HELPING RELATIONSHIPS

The purpose and techniques of observation, the degree of involvement in the observation and the method of observation are three general considerations in the observational procedure.

All people with intact sensory apparatus believe they see, hear, touch, taste, smell, and gain knowledge about the world through these "doors to perception." The important consideration is what kind of knowledge is acquired. All observation is the process of obtaining facts or data through one's senses. The difference comes from the degree of orderliness and planning, and even more from the degree of awareness of contaminating influences. When the act of observation and the qualifications for accuracy are combined, observation can be defined as the cautiously planned, orderly act or process of fact gathering through one's senses.

The "what for," "how," and "what" of observation

The three monkeys huddled together are examples of the opposite of observation. Like the proverbial ostrich who hides his head in the sand, the three monkeys "see no evil, hear no evil, and speak no evil." The monkeys' kind of nonobservation is what the effective human service worker must avoid. Watching, listening, and appropriately using the information are the routes to take to understand behavior. Human service workers must be able to answer three questions about their observations: "what for," "how," and "what."

What for? To know "what for" is to know the purpose of the observation. If an individual is to be evaluated to determine, for example, qualifications for a job, the observations focus on the specific education, experience, and skills needed for the job. This may be accomplished by means of an interview, tests, a questionnaire, or other methods that provide facts about the level of the individual's competency. Observational procedures for the job seeker usually are much less time-consuming than for the individual who is troubled and requires more extensive interviewing, counseling, or psychotherapy. Diagnosing and planning objectives to be accomplished demand more observational time and a larger variety of techniques. Yet observation is the basis for the decisions about the job seeker as well as for the individual with problems. Information about "what for" merely gives direction to the specific procedures to be used; it does not alter the basic procedure of observation.

How? The "how" of observation is to some extent dependent on the "what for." "How" also requires an understanding of the differences between observations (facts) and inferences (guesses, interpretations). The "what for" sets the purposes, the goals; the "how" decides the procedure of fact gathering. "How" may vary from complete isolation from the scene in which the client is involved (for instance, by observing the client through a one-way mirror) to involvement with the client in a counseling situation.

What? "What" refers to the specific points to look for when observing. Most important to thorough observation is what is observed. People see, hear, and feel *selectively;* that is, their reality is colored by the way they look at things. This leads to *selective inaccuracy.* Anyone who has played the game "Gossip" knows how a sentence can be altered when it is whispered from one person to another around a circle. This is how rumors are born and grow with added twists as the message is passed from one gossiper to another. Anyone who has been a witness in court soon becomes aware of the variety of descriptions that can be given for the same event. Observers of human behavior must therefore develop skill in objective reporting. "What" calls to attention possible slanting of observations according to the observer's pet likes and dislikes. "What" also asks for a detective-like search for cues (clues): "talking cues"

and "doing cues." These two types of cues were considered earlier in this chapter in the discussion of developing observational skills.

Gestalt

Observing the gestalt means picking up cues about the observed person through all channels of communication and putting these all together for the pattern of behavior that emerges. Exercise 2-22 directs attention to the whole person, who in this situation is role-playing an interviewer. The measurement scale in Fig. 2-11 examines the interviewer's listening and responding skills.

Exercise 2-22
DO YOU LOOK AND LISTEN TO THE GESTALT—THE WHOLE PERSON? *(should be done in a group)*

Time: APPROXIMATELY 20 MINUTES

Remember the discussion in Chapter 1 about learning style? Do you learn best through your ears? through your eyes? through touching? through any combination of these and your other senses? Whatever your channel for learning—your learning style—expand your learning and your observational awareness by means of this exercise. See and hear the whole person.

Part 1

The group divides into subgroups of no more than seven participants. Five members of each subgroup form a semicircle. Two members of the subgroup sit in the center of the semicircle so that they are visible to the other five. For 3 minutes the two people in the center of the circle act out one of the following situations.

[1]   Tom pushes open the door to his supervisor's office. "Bitch!" he yells. "You lousy honky. On what did you base the two unsatisfactory ratings you gave me on my work ratings?" The supervisor rises, walks toward Tom, and then says . . .

[2]   Five-year-old Mattie is pulled into Dr. L.'s office. Mrs. T. is holding Mattie's wrist with one hand and a wad of facial tissue with which she dabs her eyes in the other. "Come on, come on, can't wait all day for you," moans Mrs. T. Dr. L. looks up at Mrs. T., rises from the chair, and . . .

[3]   Cynthia and Hank are seated with their knees touching. Hank passes what appears to be the very short end of a cigarette to Cynthia. The counselor enters the room just then and smells a sweet odor. The counselor goes over to the desk and sits at the edge of it, looks at Hank and then at Cynthia, and says, "Ms. McHenry asked me to speak to you. Do . . ."

At the end of the 3 minutes each observer completes his or her assessment of the "interviewer's" listening and responding skills, using Fig. 2-11. For 5 minutes the group discusses its findings and makes suggestions as to how the "interviewer" may improve listening and responding.

Part 2

The two volunteers continue their interview for 3 more minutes. The observers note the listening and responding skills on the measurement scale. The group discusses its new findings, points out how the "interviewer" has improved, and makes additional suggestions for improvement.

Directions: Place a check (✓) next to the rating that most closely approximates your observation of the interviewer's behavior. Check under each behavioral characteristic.

Eye contact: Maintains appropriate gaze, which is not a stare, but does not look away.
1. Gaze is persistent and comfortable._____
2. Gaze is appropriate most of the time._____
3. Shifts gaze a little too often._____
4. Frequently shifts gaze._____
5. Persistently shifts gaze or stares._____

Attending: Maintains appropriate posture; bends slightly forward from waist; maintains comfortable distance from client.
1. Persistently shifts position and moves about._____
2. Frequently shifts position and moves about._____
3. Shifts position a little too often._____
4. Most of the time maintains appropriate posture._____
5. Persistently maintains appropriate posture._____

Hand gestures: Moves hands slowly and appropriately; gestures appear to be comfortable.
1. Gestures are persistently comfortable and appropriate._____
2. Gestures are usually comfortable and appropriate._____
3. Some signs of "jerky" hand movements, which are disturbing._____
4. Tense, sudden movements frequently occur._____
5. Persistently uses inappropriate and annoying hand gestures._____

Facial expression: Smiles or shows other expressions that are appropriate and pleasant.
1. Persistently maintains unpleasant and inappropriate facial expression._____
2. Usually maintains unpleasant and inappropriate facial expression._____
3. Occasionally has unpleasant and inappropriate facial expression._____
4. Usually maintains pleasant and appropriate facial expression._____
5. Persistently maintains pleasant and appropriate facial expression._____

Voice tone: Voice is pleasant, sounds relaxed, and has appropriate volume for hearing.
1. Persistently has unpleasant tone that varies in loudness, either too loud or too low._____
2. Usually has unpleasant tone that varies in loudness._____
3. Occasionally has pleasant tone with appropriate volume._____
4. Usually has pleasant tone with appropriate volume._____
5. Persistently has pleasant tone with appropriate volume._____

Comment: Write a brief comment about the interviewer that you think the supervisor should know.

Fig. 2-11. Measurement scale: listening and responding skills.

■ ■ ■

After helpers have identified the "what for," "how," and "what" of observation, the degree of involvement during the observation and the method of observation are considered. These aspects are determined in accordance with the purpose, goals, time allotted, and focus of the observation.

The degree of involvement during the observation

The closer the observer moves into the scene, the more the observer becomes part of what the observed person is saying or doing, the more involved the observer must be. The methods the individual uses also vary depending on the level of structure, of planning, and of manipulation of the person or events in the observed situation. The competent observer often employs a variety of methods and is able to alter the degree of involvement in accordance with the requirements of the situation being observed.

The observer is most involved with a client in the interviewing and counseling situation and the most uninvolved when examining a report in the client's case record—a form of secondary source.

Secondary sources. Instead of speaking directly to the person observed or watching the person's nonverbal behavior, the observer goes to files in which reports and other aspects of the case history are kept. Additional secondary sources that may be explored are other people who have had some contact with the person being observed. Thus the individual is observed indirectly by means of records, reports, or comments made by other people as well as by results of physical and psychological tests. Except for the tests, which are based on information acquired by means of some standardized measuring procedures, these impressions of others are likely to be based on prejudices for or against the observed person. These impressions should not be discounted even if they are biased, since these ideas and feelings have had an effect, more or less, on the observed person's behavior. The next level of observation gets a little more into the act.

Spectator observation. In spectator observation observers attempt to keep their presence from influencing the observed person. They attempt to place themselves outside the focus of attention of the observed person. One way of doing this is to sit out of the immediate range of vision of the observed person. Another method is to talk with someone other than the observed person far enough away so that the conversation cannot be heard by the observed person. If the observers become part of the immediate activity of the observed person and still continue their observation, they involve themselves much more in what the observed person is thinking and feeling. The observers also are adding another element, themselves, which influences what the observed person does or says.

Participant observation. In this kind of observation the observers are actively involved with the observed person. They may be playing a game, reading a story, assisting in arts and crafts, or discussing something. At the same time the observers are noting what the observed person says or does. They are also mentally recording what is happening between the observed person and themselves as well as with the other people and things in the surroundings. The remarks of both the observer and the observed person become an essential part of this observation.

Interview. The interview begins to wrap the observer and the observed person into an even closer net of care and concern. The interview may be brief and seek only quick, surface information for job placement or credit extension. The interview could be in depth to determine more about the thinking and particularly the feelings of the observed person. Another distinction in degrees of involvement also may be made between interviewing, counseling, and psychotherapy. Each of these transactions becomes more absorbing and more consuming of time and attention.

The methods of observation

The six methods of observation listed in Table 2-5 differ in approach and in exactness. Yet the categories do overlap, and one category may lead

Table 2-5. *Methods of observation*

Type	Examples	Degree of control
Casual (random)	Observation of natural events— sky, trees, birds, other people	Observations are more or less undirected and are often inaccurate, contaminated by prejudices and past life experiences
Naturalistic	Running record (log or diary) in clinic, classroom, or other individual or group situations; observations in the field; case studies	Observed events are uncontrolled; observer exerts orderly approach and cautious observing
Clinical	More organized naturalistic observation; may be a case history, physical or mental status examination	Language used in writing the observation is in accordance with the terms of the particular profession of the observer; observer focuses on careful fact gathering and interpretation of the data as required by professional knowledge and skills
Specific goal	Observation of specific behavior and for specific purpose	Observed events are carefully controlled in terms of events to be observed or ends observation is to serve
Standardized	Time-interval observations and psychological tests	Conditions of observation are specified and must be followed; however, observed person is not controlled by changing any events around him or her
Experimental	Laboratory study of specific kind of behavior	Control of variables is more or less extensive, depending on what is being studied

to another. For example, a random (casual) observation may become a carefully planned observation according to certain time intervals and later be set up as an experimental situation.

Casual observation. Everybody indulges in casual observations that are based on a commonsense approach. Out of this kind of observation often emerge such statements as "He's a brat," "She is happy," "She is hostile," and "He is a general nuisance." None of these labels actually describes behavior. Casual observation is hindered by past experiences, expectations, conventional labels, and the observer's ability to look and listen. Observers' beliefs about themselves and about the people more familiar to them interfere with the accuracy of the observation. An observation of someone known very well in familiar surroundings tends to be highly contaminated with feelings. It is much easier to observe the behavior of strangers than the behavior of close relatives, lovers, or friends. Accurate observation is not a skill born with the individual. It must be learned and practiced.

Naturalistic observation. The aim of scientific observation is to gather precise and useful information about an individual. Information must be stated in such a way that it can be verified by another observer who is qualified to observe accurately. This may be partially accomplished by naturalistic observations, which are running records of observation that begin and end at any point of time. This on-the-spot record is the one used most frequently. Observers jot down notes during the observation or wait until they leave the presence of the observed person. Observers who take this latter route must remember that the longer they wait to write notes, the more inaccurate their memory of the observations will be.

This running record contains observations written in an anecdotal or story form. Since the observers do not make any planned attempt to change the situation of the observed person, this kind of observation is considered to be naturalistic. Field observations that explore the behavior of animals or of humans are an exampe of naturalistic observations. These observations may be written, photographed, filmed, or taped. Sometimes a combination of these methods is used. The disadvantage of naturalistic observations comes from substitution of imaginative inserts to fill out genuine observation. An observer who writes, "David looks at Cecily with hate in his eyes and hands," is recording his own interpretation and bias about David and Cecily ("with hate in his eyes and hands"). The observer must ask, "How do I know there was hate? What did I see? What did I hear?" A statement to the effect that David walks over to Cecily with his fist raised hints at a similar idea but does not provide unsupported conclusions about David's actions.

Clinical observations. Clinical observations are a more structured (organized) example of naturalistic observation. These clinical studies often are referred to as case histories or mental status examinations. A case history is a scientific biography of an individual, an institution, or a group of people. The observer helps the client reconstruct his or her past history as well as present complaints. All these facts are pieced together to gain a fuller understanding of the forces affecting the individual's present problems. One disadvantage of the case-history method of observation is that contemporary observation depends on the observed person's memory, which may not be accurate. However, this does not detract from the value of observing how the individual responds to his or her memory. Clinical observation also includes the on-the-spot observation of the client during the time of a physical or psychological examination.

Specific goal observation. The observer may set specific goals in terms of observing specific behavior or in terms of a specific purpose for the observation. Both of these goals require precise planning. Observation of specific behavior may concentrate on verbal or on nonverbal cues. It may also focus on such specific acts as the cooperation of one child with another, the shifts of leadership within a group, or the frequency of the use of of certain words. Specific purposes for observations may pose such questions as "How accurate are the interviewer's skills of observation?" and "How does the individual control his emotions?" Specific behavior and specific purpose very often fuse.

Standardized observation. There are many forms that standardized observation may take. Two are time-interval observations and psychological tests. Both varieties of standardizing procedure are based on obtaining a sample of behavior. Time-interval sampling requires observations at predetermined times of the day and usually for a set length of time. The length of time may be set from a few seconds or minutes to several hours. Sometimes the time samples may be half-hour or hour observations conducted at different times during the day. At other times the observation may be in terms of the number of times a certain behavior occurred within a specified unit of time. For example, the question may be "How many times during an hour does the child get out of his seat?" An observer who uses the word "constantly" to describe the frequency of such movement is providing inaccurate information, since "constantly" means a different amount for different people.

Psychological tests are standardized (experimentally constructed and scaled) as to their administration and method of scoring. These tests provide a method to measure the observed person's abilities, interests, attitudes, and achievements. Although the rules for administration of the tests and the norms for comparison may be scientifically established, there are still two obvious factors that are not so easily controlled. The observer and the observed person have their own "bags" of behavior, and the contents of these bags, the personal characteristics of each individual, may influence the outcome of a particular sample of behavior at a particular time. Therefore tests alone or any form of one-shot observation does not ensure exactness of the observed person's life-style.

Experimental observation. The experimental observation is carefully planned and controlled. Consideration is given to variables and the method of measurement of the observations. Another word for variable is "factor." Variables are factors such as drugs, events, and people that exert some influence on the observed event or person. When observers set up an experimental observation or design, they are searching to determine the relationship between certain variables. For example, they may study the effect of different amounts of marijuana on the memory of an individual. The procedure for observation would require that the observers think about the numerous variables that might affect memory. Such factors as age, sex, situation, and past experiences are considered. The observers control as many of the variables as they can and/or think necessary for the exactness of the experiment. They control the age variable by selecting only a certain age group. They arrange the setting so that unwanted noises and other distractions are not present. They select individuals who have or have not used marijuana, depending on the effects they want to study. In other words, the observers control certain variables and manipulate the independent variable (antecedent events)—in this case, the amount of marijuana. They change the amount in some predetermined manner so that they may observe the memory effect of different quantities of marijuana. The memory effect is the dependent variable (the consequent event), which is the change in the observed person's memory behavior. This is called a single-variable experimental observation.

Summary of Part One

■ Part One introduces the roles and functions of the human service worker and the fundamental attitudes, skills, and knowledge on which the helping relationship is built—observational competency. Chapter 1 explores the dimensions of human services as a philosophy and a procedure, the holistic view of human services, and the diversity of services provided. A distinction is made between human interrelationships involving anyone who gives attention and assistance to another person and professional human service workers who are equipped with appropriate attitudes, skills, and knowledge (the "ASK" concept). A code of ethics is essential to the professional self of the human service worker. Distinction also is made between the generalist, who concentrates on the needs of the whole person in the person's environment, and the specialist, whose provision of care is directed only to certain needs.

The professional self—not to be confused with the person exhibiting professionalitis—is an outgrowth of self-understanding, the development of an identity, appropriate expressions of intimacy, and values clarification. The origins of behavior, that of both the helper and the client, can be traced to demographic, physical, and intellectual factors and developmental experiences. Skillful interpersonal functioning is added to the list of characteristics of the professional helper. Competent helpers function comfortably and appropriately in their interactions with their clients. Such helpers maintain a controlled nondirection approach, which stresses that the best advice is "self-advice." Such helpers practice friendliness rather than friendship with their clients. Such helpers are skillful in their own problem solving and decision making regarding clients' needs and are able to assist clients in developing similar skills. (Yet, because these helpers also have human fallibility and difficulties, they sometimes make mistakes, get angry, are uncomfortable, and experience other shortcomings.)

Chapter 2 presents the beginning layer of the helping process—observation. Human service workers must clear away any cobwebs in their thinking and acting before the skills and knowledge related to observation can have any impact. Therefore this chapter begins with a discussion of the factors influencing the accuracy of observation related to the observer, the location of observation, and the person or group observed. Prejudices are presented as they affect the relationships between people, and the way these positive and negative biases interact with attitudinal influences to contaminate the accuracy of observations is discussed.

Awareness of all the factors that influence the accuracy of an observation does not magically do something about them. However, it is the beginning of learning to deal with possible distortion that might result from physical or psychoecological interferences.

The psychoecological approach of observation is particularly pertinent to the philosophy about people that is developed in this book. This model of thinking about people draws attention to the need to go beyond a one-shot, one-cause relationship between stimulating factors and resulting behavior. The helper who accepts this philosophy takes on added responsibilities to involve the home, neighborhood, school, and agencies in a coordinated plan to help the questioning and/or troubled individual. New patterns of interpersonal relationships are sought in a helping system that reaches out beyond the interview or counseling room. Many individuals become part of the helping team.

A large portion of Chapter 2 deals with the development of observational skills for effective helping. Verbal, sound, and nonverbal cues are identified separately and then drawn together in consideration of the singular importance of listening skills and of the gestalt—the whole person in the context of environment. The final portion of the chapter provides basic knowledge about the "what for," "how," and "what" of observation, the degrees of involvement in observation, and the methods of observation.

Part Two builds on the skills in Part One with an examination of recording and reporting. Reporting flows from the recorded observations that have been analyzed and organized in the form of a report.

All things by immortal power
  Near or far
  Hiddenly
To each other linked are,
That thou canst not stir a flower
Without troubling a star.

(Francis Thompson, "The Mistress of Vision," nineteenth century)

Part Two

RECORDING AND REPORTING
observation feedback

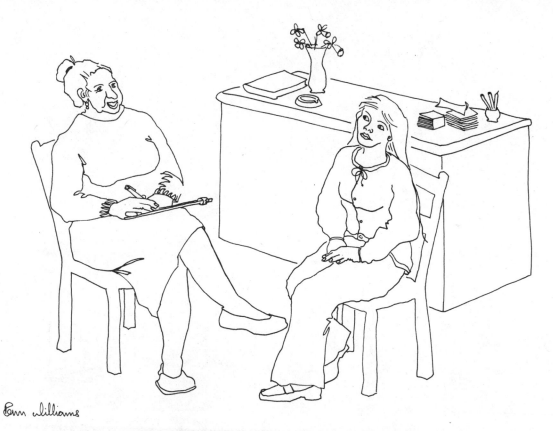

Accurate recording is the foundation for accurate reporting.

Chapter 3

RECORDING
organized note taking

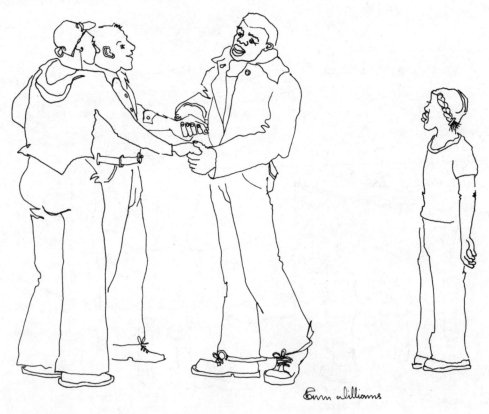

Recording begins with observations from the moment of initial contact—for the child and the adult.

The term "recording" has many meanings. It can refer to an act, the process of writing or imprinting words or music on paper or by means of some mechanical or electronic device. It can refer to the actual words or notations, what is recorded. It can refer to a piece of paper, a case study, a cassette, or any other form of recording. And there is as much variation in the opinions of the preferable quantity and purpose of recording as there are meanings for the term. The definition of recording is not the major concern of this chapter, since all the mentioned meanings are applicable. Instead the focus is on certain other issues.

THE RECORDING PROCESS
(Kadushin, 1972; MacKinnon and Michels, 1971; Wilson, 1980)
The quantity of note taking

The neophyte human service professional frequently becomes concerned about the appropriate quantity of note taking. Very often this distress is greater for the individual whose student note taking has been extensive and whose learning style is primarily kinesthetic and visual. Many times agitation is increased because of inconsistent messages from more experienced professional human service workers. Some seasoned professionals urge lengthy note taking with much detail; others advise against taking any notes so that the helper may concentrate on what the client is saying and doing. The helper is instructed to rely on memory to reproduce the interviewing event. There can be only clarifying statements but no definitive response to the question of quantity, since the appropriate amount depends on for whom and for what purpose the recording is accomplished.

One may envision the quantity of note taking on a continuum from verbatim recordings to the absence of note taking during the interview. In between these two extremes are many modifications. For example, the beginning of the interview may require extensive notes with comments on initial impressions and historical data. Later notations may contain new historical information, important events in the client's life, general comments about progress, and reminders for the interviewer of actions that he or she has promised to accomplish in response to the client's needs before the next interviewing session.

Verbatim recordings. Even the verbatim recording is not actually verbatim, or complete. Neither the dedicated, exacting note taker nor the sophisticated audio or visual recorder records the entire script of what transpired during the interview. In the midst of an important discussion notes are set aside, and it is only when communications slow down that note taking may be resumed. Emotional reactions and nonverbal cues are disregarded in the shuffle of body movements and continuing conversation. Many innuendos—both verbal and nonverbal—are lost if the helper's looking and listening have been narrowed to the act of note taking.

"Mental notes" can fill in the gaps if the helper arranges to record immediately after the interviewing session. Improved note-taking skill requires the development of keen observational competencies and the creation of a shorthand of key phrases or words identifying the essentials of the client's behavior, affective reactions, and the interactions between the interviewer and the client. These catchwords depend on sharpened awareness of the "threads" running through the client's interpersonal actions, reactions, and body movement during the discussion of specific topics. It takes time to develop this kind of expertise.

The purpose of note taking

The quantity of note taking depends not only on the whim and inclination of an instructor, agency supervisor, or helper, but also on the purpose of the note taking.

- ☐ To provide information for diagnosis for a plan of treatment and rehabilitation
- ☐ To jog the helper's memory concerning each client
- ☐ To obtain specific, necessary information such as name, address, birthdate, and members of family (Such information may be required for statistical purposes, to document services offered, and for federal grant information. In addition, some clients expect this kind of information to be set down immediately; if it is not, they might consider the interviewer disinterested and indifferent.)
- ☐ To assess the interviewer's competency and help the interviewer to become more effective
- ☐ To provide content for preservice and inservice teaching and/or training
- ☐ To meet supervisory and administrative requirements
- ☐ To supply data for research

The most important purpose for recording often is assumed but not specified—to organize interviewers' thoughts regarding the client as well as their perceptions of the interpersonal relationships in the helping event. Any one of these previously mentioned purposes or a combination of them would affect not only the quantity but also the selectivity of note taking. Therefore the recording purpose must be identified, since it dictates the content, form, and frequency of note taking.

The time for note taking

If there is to be any note taking during the interview, clients should become part of the decision to take such notes. They should be informed of the reason for the note taking and their permission obtained. This permission may be granted automatically even by clients who are opposed to or suspicious of the recordings. Although this permission is only the polite submission to authority, at least the client has been respected and given a choice. It is up to the interviewer to be alert to any clues of the client's dissatisfaction during the recording. The client actually may resent the note taking because it appears that the interviewer considers the notes more important than the client. To avert such feelings of lessened inportance, the interviewer should assess the effects of the note taking periodically; signs of displeasure, discomfort, or hesitancy should be discussed with the client. If these signs continue, and particularly if they become exaggerated, the wise interviewer discontinues the recording.

If the client is suspicious and voices, or in some other manner reveals, concern about a breach of confidence, other tactics may be used. The interviewer explains the circumstances under which the notes may be seen and who will be permitted to read them. When appropriate, the client is told that he or she may look at the notes of the interview. Another precautionary measure is full-view note taking so that the client does not build up antipathy toward the possibility of mysterious jottings or hidden unfavorable notations.

Of course, there is some advantage to note taking during the helping event—the more notes taken during the interview, the less note taking is required afterward. In addition, if the interviewer waits until the end of the day to write the notes, there is likely to be some loss of detail and some distortion. These inaccuracies are even more prominent if the interviewer puts aside recording for several interviews.

One interview may be confused with another. The preferred time for taking notes therefore is during the interview (at a minimum, key words and phrases should be recorded at this time); an alternate procedure is to write notes as near to the termination of the interview as is feasible.

The advantages of note taking

It is obvious that notes written during the interview have the greatest potential for accuracy. These notes ensure continuity between the helper and the client and assure the client of the importance of the communication interchange. In addition, the note taker can prompt a feeling of strengthened intimacy when pencil or pen and paper are put aside. This hiatus in note taking is especially important during the disclosure of certain material that may be of heightened emotional import for the client. In general, also, the recordings are a form of accountability for the interviewer, the agency, and the community and often are the core elements in the reports required by funding agencies. For the beginning professional a by-product of the act of recording is the establishment of a professional identity in the processes involved in organized note taking. On the other hand, this presumption of professionalism can also interfere with the interpersonal attentions and transactions between helper and client.

The disadvantages of note taking

The distraction presented by note taking is the most serious adverse consequence. The process of taking notes tends to reduce the interviewer's eye contact and other attending behavior. With experience the helper might find it simpler to minimize the preoccupation with note taking and to record with reduced loss of contact. Some interviewers develop the ability to write short reminders with only a brief glance at what they are writing. However, even if some method of note taking is devised that decreases absorption in the act of writing, the disadvantage of the selectivity of what is to be noted remains. What *has* been said must be the notation rather than what *is* being said. This selective perception is also affected by the factors affecting the accuracy of observation mentioned in Chapter 2. Focusing on certain content may be intentional or unintentional, but unless there is a cogent basis of selectivity for the client's welfare, the interviewer may be compounding errors.

Another difficulty emerges from this directing of the note taking, and subsequently the discussion, to certain items. The interviewer may reinforce certain trends of thought and direct the client's discussion away from more essential issues. In effect, because of this potential for manipulation, note taking may be self-defeating. It can disrupt the continuity of the client's conversation. The client notes the down-swept eyes of the interviewer and stops speaking to permit the interviewer to finish writing. The client hesitates not only out of politeness, but also because the interviewer does not appear to be listening.

When note taking depends on audio or video tapes, the effect on both client and interviewer must be considered. The recording devices may stifle the spontaneity of the communication interchange and may lead to either a "safer" and more stereotyped and intellectualized interview or to dramatic expressions "playing up to" the equipment. Some of the consequences can be averted if the interviewer and client are alert to these possibilities, know what is expected, and understand the meaningfulness of honest and open interactions.

The discussion of advantages and disadvantages is not exhaustive; nor is it intended to deter note taking. Instead, the intention is to affirm the usefulness of recordings if they are suitably and efficiently accomplished. The most important contribution to the comfort of the client in the interview session remains the attitude, skills, and knowledge of the interviewer. The disquieted, irritated, or uncommitted interviewer maximizes the use of note taking as a refuge from emotional contact with the client. Recording allows this interviewer to steer clear of eye contact and to divert thoughts to other matters. Copious notes and scanty notes are not the problem; the issue is the degree of authenticity and openness in the interrelationship between interviewer and client as well as the accuracy of decoding the observed messages.

DECODING OBSERVED MESSAGES

During an interview the helper may suddenly realize that although the helper and the client have been talking the same language, they actually are talking about different interpretations of events, or even about different events. Something has gone astray in their frames of reference.

Everyone thinks he has a direct pipeline to a piece of reality—and perhaps everyone does. In addition, everyone believes he has a clear grasp of some symbol that represents the idea in his head—and perhaps everyone has this, too. But what lacks is assurance that his symbol is the same as another's for the identical event in the real world. It is possible for one symbol to refer to different pieces of reality or for several symbols to refer to the same bit of reality.*

For instance:

What does 5-year-old Tina mean when she says, "I'm running away from this home"? How about 65-year-old Libby's complaint, "I can't take this depression any-

---

*From Bloom, M.: The paradox of helping: introduction to the philosophy of scientific practice, New York, 1975, John Wiley & Sons, Inc., p. 14.

more"? What is the significance of 8-year-old Annie's nightmare and 20-year-old Roger's distrust of the government? Do age, experiences, and other factors enter into the linkages between the words, ideas, and the individual realities of Tina, Libby, Annie, and Roger?

The Humpty Dumpty syndrome

The meaning of words varies with individuals, with a particular period of history, and with the place in which the communication takes place. This variability has been called the Humpty Dumpty syndrome. Lewis Carroll called attention to the need to hear the intended message rather than the words spoken by delightfully and insightfully pointing up the importance of searching beyond the words.

"But glory doesn't mean 'a nice knock-down argument'," Alice objected.

"When *I* use a word," Humpty Dumpty said, in rather a scornful tone, "it means just what I choose it to mean—neither more nor less."

"The question is," said Alice, "whether you *can* make words mean so many different things."

"The question is," said Humpty Dumpty, "which is to be the master—that's all."

Exercise 3-1
ARE YOU AWARE OF THE EFFECTS OF THE DISSIMILARITIES BETWEEN DENOTATION AND CONNOTATION? *(should be done individually and discussed in the group)*

Time: APPROXIMATELY 30 MINUTES

The group selects a word considered controversial, such as "liberal," "punk," "waste," "coke," "gay," or "abortion." Each member of the group lists all the synonyms he or she can think of for the word selected. Then these synonyms are reported to the entire group and listed on large sheets of newsprint, on a board, or in some other manner that allows all group members to view the list. The similarities and differences of the associated words are discussed in the group.

After the listing of synonyms and discussion, respond to the following questions. This may be accomplished in the group or individually.

□ Which words do you object to most? Least? What is there about the words that makes them more or less objectionable?

□ What did you learn from this exercise about language?

□ How does a particular social situation determine the word you would use?

Modified from Johnson, J.M., editor: Instruction strategies and curricula for secondary behavioral science, Plattsburgh, N.Y., 1973, State University of New York, College of Arts and Sciences.

Since words signify many different things for different individuals, effective interviewers must master communication so that both verbal and nonverbal messages are as clear as possible to themselves and their clients.

Denotation and connotation. The achievement of clarity is not simple because of the denotation and connotation of words. Denotation refers to the actual, direct, explicit meaning of an observable act or object; a word or term's denotation is uncontaminated by cultural evaluations and individual emotional significances. Connotation dresses up each word with ideas, notions, and biases derived from cultural abstractions and loaded individual associations. The word "food," for instance, denotes some form of nourishment to satisfy tissue deficit needs. But is that all there is to the meaning of food? Food connotes one thing to the starving person who may beg, steal, or borrow to obtain even water to drink. It means another thing to the prisoner in isolation who may be so secluded that the hand offering food may provide the only solace of awareness of an outside to the surrounding walls. It means another thing to the obese person for whom food is associated with affection and even a way to build a fortress of girth against the intrusions of other people. It means another thing to the author, the speaker, the psychologist, the nutritionist, and so on.

The Humpty Dumpty syndrome pertains to this dissimilarity between connotation and denotation. What a word connotes in the culture and for an individual leads to a pattern of characteristic acts that occur together. Consequently, the Humpty Dumpty syndrome relates to a specific type of behavior that is not conducive to suitable communication between interviewer and client. If the interviewer is stuck with his or her own connotation, the client's connotations are lost; misunderstandings and misinterpretations are inevitable. Exercise 3-1 is designed to establish discriminations between denotation and connotation.

Coding, encoding, and decoding. The processes involved in denotation and connotation have relevance for coding, encoding, and decoding. To decode, the listener must be alert to the connotative quality of the words spoken. Obviously, foreigners unfamiliar with the English language and not versed in the code would not be able to satisfy even their simplest needs. Yet not only foreigners have difficulty; individuals speaking the same language often experience mixed messages in communications. In Exercise 3-1 the code "gay" might have elicited synonyms such as "joy" and "happy" or synonyms describing homosexuals. "Gay" in and of itself is merely a group of three letters—a word—that has become a substitute form, or symbol, representing environmental and personal events. Spoken and written words and numerals are codes that convey a message just as are the dots and dashes, short and long sounds, or flashes of the Morse code.

Fig. 3-1 diagrams the path of a message from sender to receiver. It shows several points at which personalized interpretations (connotations) can color the cultural language or other symbols (the code) so that message distortion is likely. The message sender encodes (puts into code) the original communication using words derived from the culture, but these are personalized with the message

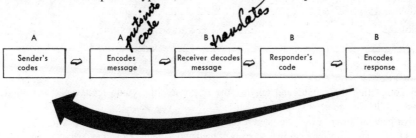

Fig. 3-1. Coding, encoding, and decoding the message.

Exercise 3-2

HOW WOULD YOU DEAL WITH SEMANTIC DIFFERENTIALS? *(should be done in a group)*

Time: APPROXIMATELY 30 MINUTES

Part 1

The group separates into evenly divided subgroups of from 6 to 10 participants. There should be the same number of men and women in each small group. If this is not feasible, the groups should be arranged with 6 to 10 participants of the same sex.

The small group participants individually rate each of the words or phrases on the seven-point rating scale by checking the space that most appropriately describes what they think and feel about the word. (A separate copy of the scale is needed for each word or phrase.) For instance, those who believe that the Democratic Party is strong would check the space near "strong":

Democratic Party

strong: __✓__ : ____ : ____ : ____ : ____ : ____ : ____ :weak

On the other hand, those who consider the Democratic Party weak would check the space near the word "weak." If neither extreme of the scale represents one's belief or feeling, a check may be placed farther away from the extremes. The center space represents uncertainty or neutrality about the word.

After completing the rating for each of the following 10 items, the small groups tally their responses, keeping the responses from the men and women separated.

WORDS AND PHRASES TO BE RATED

1. Republican Party
2. Father
3. Capitalism
4. Moslemism
5. Busing
6. Communism
7. Mother
8. President of United States
9. Friend
10. Democratic Party

RATING SCALE

strong: ____ : ____ : ____ : ____ : ____ : ____ : ____ :weak

helpful: ____ : ____ : ____ : ____ : ____ : ____ : ____ :harmful

dumb: ____ : ____ : ____ : ____ : ____ : ____ : ____ :smart

excitable: ____ : ____ : ____ : ____ : ____ : ____ : ____ :calm

bad: ____ : ____ : ____ : ____ : ____ : ____ : ____ :good

peaceful: ____ : ____ : ____ : ____ : ____ : ____ : ____ :violent

generous: ____ : ____ : ____ : ____ : ____ : ____ : ____ :greedy

disagreeable: ____ : ____ : ____ : ____ : ____ : ____ : ____ :agreeable

responsible: ____ : ____ : ____ : ____ : ____ : ____ : ____ :irresponsible

decent: ____ : ____ : ____ : ____ : ____ : ____ : ____ :indecent

Part 2

After completing the ratings and tallying the responses, the group reconvenes and all participants consider the following questions:

☐ What general differences have been revealed in the responses?
☐ Are there specific differences in responses of men and women? How do you explain these differences?
☐ What have you learned about semantic differentials from this exercise?

sender's associations with the words. Then the message receiver decodes (translates the coded message), and once more the interpretation of the code is personalized. If this is a helping event, the cautious interviewer is alert to the personalized effects at these message change-points. The interviewer realizes the potential intrusion of connotation, the semantic impact.

The semantic impact

The study of sematics renews the earlier discussion of Humpty Dumpty. Dumpty unequivocally states that the meaning of words is determined by each person. Semantics focuses on meaning. It is the study of symbols and their current meaning as well as the changing meanings of these symbols. Semantics also includes consideration of the feelings associated with the meanings that are attached to symbols. Thus *what* a person says and *how* he or she says it are linked with meaning. This last statement recalls the content of Chapter 2 regarding congruence of verbal and nonverbal behavior. Does the smiling person say, "I hate you"? Does the man say, "Doesn't hurt a bit," while his eyebrows move closer and closer into a frown and his jaws and fists become tighter and tighter? The meaning of words does not exist in a vacuum. Words are touched by feelings and influenced by experiences; they vary in effects and thus differ in meaning (semantic differential). The semantic differential also reflects an individual's underlying attitudes. Osgood (1952) developed a technique to measure differences in the meaning of words by means of a seven-point scale. Interpretations of objects, words, and events can be examined by the series of scales that reflect the rater's attitude toward the item rated—the meaning (semantics) or significance of the item to the rater (Osgood, Suci, and Tannenbaum, 1957). Exercise 3-2 is an example of the semantic differential approach.

Descriptive and interpretive words

The Humpty Dumpty syndrome and its implications in terms of the semantic impact tie in with

the observational clues to be noted in the recording process. Added to these considerations are the qualifying and conditional words listed in Fig. 2-4. Qualifying words manage to take something away from the meaning of the sentence either by adding a statement or by suggesting that the action implied is unlikely to occur. "But" is one of these qualifying words. "You had a good grade on the test, *but* you might have done even better." "If only" is another teasing insertion. "*If only* I had the time, I would help you." How often does the observed person, and the observer, too, use these words? The underlying idea for this discussion of words is the difference between interpretive words and descriptive words. Interpretive words evaluate and pass judgments; they label. Descriptive words explain what is seen or heard in behavioral terms, unblemished as much as possible by personal bias.

He's really paranoid. He always talks about CYT ("cover your tail"). "Get it in writing," he says. He looks at you and then looks around him. Truthfully, I can't stand the guy.

She's a retard. She slurs her words and speaks slowly and takes a while before she answers. Her eyes don't focus, and she walks with her left foot dragging after the right foot.

In the first set of sentences "paranoid" may fit the behavior. However, more would have to be known about the interpersonal transactions before a label is attached to the behavior. In the second group of sentences the slow person may be functioning at a retarded level, may be drugged, may have been hurt, or may have suffered a stroke with resultant brain damage. In both sets of sentences the first sentence infers, interprets, and hypothesizes; the other sentences describe behavior. This distinction is particularly important when the observer records the event being examined. A much-labeled account says very little about the observed person and much more about the observer.

Exercise 3-3 explores differences between descriptive and interpretive words.

Exercise 3-3
CAN YOU TELL THE DIFFERENCES BETWEEN DESCRIPTIVE AND INTERPRETIVE WORDS?
(should be done individually and discussed in a group)

Time: APPROXIMATELY 25 MINUTES

The following passage contains several interpretive words. Identify these words or phrases and alter them to be descriptive (action words describing behavior). (Use the box shown below as a reference.) After you and the other participants have completed this task, compare your selections and corrections with the other members of the group.

Alyson laughed out loud and shook her head from side to side. Once again she was being uncooperative and snobbish. She refused to answer any questions and shut her mouth tightly as I probed for an explanation. She may have been considered normal by others, but to me she was just a troublemaker who saw everyone as someone to manipulate and conquer. Each new man became a challenge to her ego, and she would "slither" to him, making her ever-present perfume more apparent. She became elated when a man became a slave to her extravagant whims. In common parlance she is "bad," and by this I don't mean what some people consider bad to signify. I mean she is evil, promiscuous, a crock, a sinner who betrays everyone—a no-goodnik.

Descriptive and interpretive words: some examples

DESCRIPTIVE WORDS		INTERPRETIVE WORDS	
Tell	Cry	Know	Troublemaker
Identify	Talk about	Understand	Lonely
Describe	Ask for	Think	Extravagant
List	Work with	Believe	Bad
Look	Say	Alert	Snob
Smile	Tickle	Elated	Anxious
Laugh	Stir up	Sad	Indifferent
Spend money	Provoke	Cooperative	Sensitive
Walk	Stimulate	Normal	Introvert
Frown			

THE RECORDING SEQUENCE

The first part of this chapter brought attention to the recording process and the language used in recording. The following comments explore the sequence of recording events to make certain that the essential characteristics of the observation are included. Two areas are discussed: linear and branching approaches and the ABC sequence of recording.

Linear and branching approaches

Recording would be simplified if events happened in a straight line—in a linear form. However, it is only in the imagination of the playwright or the author of fiction that life events are linear, that is, that people speak and act, receive responses and respond in turn. In the branching approach conversational offshoots, interruptions, and tangential issues are brought forth. Examples 3-1 and 3-2 describe the same event, the first by means of the linear approach and the second by means of the branching approach.

Example 3-1
BILL'S LINEAR HAPPENING

Bill sat down next to Elsie in the one remaining empty chair. "What's it all about?" he whispered.

Elsie replied, "We just began the meeting. Ted started his report on housing needs for the deinstitutionalized mentally ill."

Bill sat quietly, listening to Ted's report. When it was completed, he asked, "What do you suggest that our advisory committee do about this, Ted? Sounds like housing is not sufficient."

"You're right and it doesn't look as if the county will have a large enough budget to do anything about it during the next year."

"Are you saying that we shouldn't do anything?"

"No, I'm . . . "

The dialogue continues with everyone silent when Bill and Ted speak with one another and others joining in when Bill or Ted is not involved (see Fig. 3-2). Does this seem "real"? Does the group process move from one person to another with no comments from other members of the group?

Example 3-2
BILL'S BRANCHING HAPPENING

Bill sat down next to Elsie in the one remaining empty chair. "What's it all about?" he whispered to Elsie.

Elsie replied, "Where were you? Do you always have to be late?" and turned to look at Ted. Bill shrugged his shoulders and repeated his question, this time a little louder.

Chuck, who was sitting on the other side of Bill, turned to Bill, scowled, and poked Bill with his elbow, saying, "Shhh!"

Bill said, "Cut it."

Ted looked toward Bill and Chuck and then returned to the presentation of his report.

Bill bent closer to Elsie's ear and once more questioned, "What's the report about?"

Elsie turned to Bill with clenched fists. "You are . . . oh, well . . . We just began the meeting. Ted started his report on housing for the deinstitutionalization of the mentally ill."

Bill nodded his head, bent forward with his hands clasped between his spread-out legs, and sat quietly listening to Ted's report.

Marcie interrupted Ted, "Hey, Ted, that statistic you just quoted about the increasing incidence of mental illness—what's your source?"

Before Ted could respond, John exclaimed, "That's ridiculous! Those numbers can't be right. It means that we'll never catch up with the community needs for the mentally restored, not at the rate we're going."

"Marcie, those are from the U.S. government estimates. I can give you the exact reference later—have to look it up in my notes," replied Ted, after which he continued his report until it was completed.

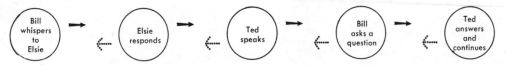

Fig. 3-2. Bill's linear happening.

Bill asked, "What do you suggest that our advisory committee do about this, Ted? Sounds like housing is not sufficient."

"That is so true," added Bert. "My son can be released from the hospital, but living at home is not what he wants, and we know it's best for all of us if he lives independently. He's . . ."

Ted said, "It is a problem. You're right, and it doesn't look as if the county will have a large enough budget to do anything about it during the next year."

"Are you saying that we shouldn't do anything?" asked Bill.

Ted replied, "No, I'm . . ."

The dialogues continue with asides and interruptions, and with several participants involved. Fig. 3-3 diagrams the branching approach.

Actually, events in life are sometimes linear and sometimes branching. Some occasions form a direct line sequence; on other occasions variations in comments and acts become branches of the interaction episode. There is danger of cue loss or distortion from errors in recording. Several possibilities can crop up that push the interviewer into a twisted round of errors. Perhaps the most frequent midjudgement appears when interviewers hear only what they expect the client to say. These warped statements are often rounded out, amplified, or otherwise modified by interviewers to fit their preconceived notions.

Furthermore, interviewers may embellish these imperfect recordings with a change in the sequence

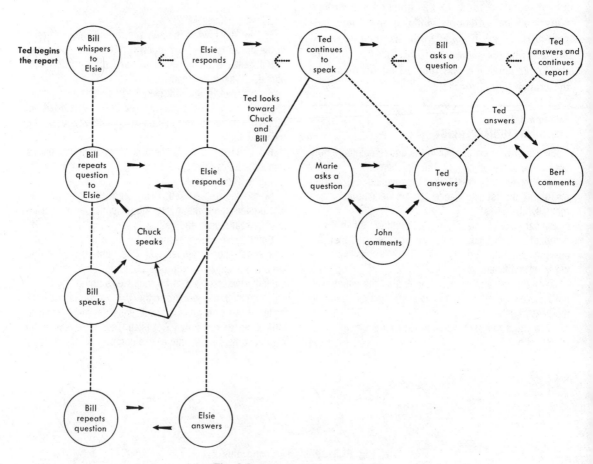

Fig. 3-3. Bill's branching happening.

of what the client says to make the continuity more logical—to the interviewer. This may be a very serious infraction, since hopping from one subject to another may be a distinct characteristic of the client's behavior. Another form of incorrect recording is the omission of selected statements of the client that threaten or run counter to the interviewer's own attitudes or to the interviewer's belief in the progress the client should be making.

Recordings that are finished pieces of composition are unlike actual conversation. In a one-to-one interview, just as in Bill's branching happening, conversation does not usually flow in a straight line from thought to thought (linear communication) but actually hops from idea to idea centered about a theme that may be obvious or concealed (see Fig. 3-3). Thus the communication process is actually a hodgepodge of thoughts from which the interviewer must glean the themes revealing the client's concerns. Polished recordings tend to distort cues. These refined recordings are just the products of the interviewer's pen.

In a group situation the facilitator or leader is aware of the branching away from the central topic. If the group objective is task oriented, the members are eased back to the predetermined issue. Linear and branching processes are made meaningful if recordings of the group event are arranged according to the ABC sequence.

The ABC sequence of recording

The antecedent event (A), behavior (B), and consequent event (C) represent the ABC sequence of recording behavior. These three events are intertwined and often occur in rapid succession, almost simultaneously (within seconds of each other).

Antecedent event. Recording in terms of ABC provides observers with points of reference from which they may determine the events that encouraged certain behavior to begin and the events that reinforced the behavior to continue. For example:

Kay moves up and down, in and out of her seat, when the subject she hates must be worked at "quietly in her seat." Kay's behavior (leaving her seat) reveals the reinforcements (rewards) she obtains from her behavior.

First, she avoids the necessity to "play around" with sums, subtractions, and divisions (self-reinforcement). Second, the teacher pays attention to Kay (teacher's reinforcement). At no other time during the day does Kay become the center of attention.

Stating the ABC of behavior helps explain the antecedent (beginning event), the resulting behavior, and the consequent reinforcement (ending of the event). Using this approach, the observer can point out to the teacher the cues from his behavior that prompt Kay's constant motion to linger on.

Part of the antecedent, the behavior, and the consequence is *overt;* that is, it can be seen or heard. Part of these three aspects is *covert;* that is, it is not observable and cannot be directly seen or heard. Since overt factors are observable, they are objective and reportable. Covert factors are more or less hidden and must be guessed at or inferred from the observable behavior.

Often it is simpler to notice the consequent event rather than the event that precedes an individual's behavior. One reason for the difficulty in isolating the antecedent event is the tendency to attempt to establish cause-and-effect relationships. However, behavior does not result from one isolated stimulus (antecedent event) but instead from a number of stimuli (events), which are interrelated into a stimulus-situation (pattern of antecedent events). Another name for an antecedent event is an independent variable. In an experimental situation occurring in the laboratory the independent variable can be manipulated (changed) so that the changes in behavior, the dependent variable, may be observed. In real life it is much more difficult, if not impossible, to control factors so that only one item (variable) changes. Exercise 3-4 begins this more objective recording process with consideration of the antecedent event and the resulting behavior.

Another detail involved in antecedent events is the setting in which the behavior occurs. The setting shares in the effect of the antecedent and touches on such questions as:

☐ What is going on (the event or events) around the observed individual (external factors, physical setup)?

Exercise 3-4
HOW DO YOU FIND THE EVENT THAT IS THE ANTECEDENT TO BEHAVIOR?
(may be done alone or in a group)

Time: APPROXIMATELY 20 MINUTES

Read the three examples of behavior that follow and fill in Fig. 3-4 to show the antecedent event and the behavior. After completing the chart, discuss what you wrote with other members of the group.

[1]   Hally is standing up in the courtroom explaining to the judge: "Judge, I know mebbe it sounds wild . . . but I didn't know about the candy. It tasted so good. Sure it had a kick, but how did I know it had lotsa kick? As I drove home I felt swell . . . but woozie . . . that's why . . . that's what made me go through the stop sign. Didn't even see it. Damn that John. He gave me that candy. It was only later when I looked at the wrapping I noticed that it said it had a kick. All the others ate some . . . but . . . OK . . . so I was the driver."

[2]   "I've got to do it . . . got to," yelled Dick. "I can't stay in this house . . . too much. They nag. They fight. They constantly push one another around. So he has no job. So what is he to do? Sometimes it gets me so down that I feel like junkin' this life. She calls herself 'mother' but she's really a witch."

[3]   Albert and Alfred are 12-year-old identical twins. Mrs. T. meets Albert in the hallway of his school. She is speaking to Albert, "Hi, there . . . Alfred? Is that you, Alfred?" Albert replied, "Dunno. Sometimes Alfred, sometimes Albert. Dunno right now." Mrs. T. thinks to herself, "That mother of theirs—dressing them alike all of their lives. Can't she see that they walk, they talk, they are as one? Can't she see that they should be separate?"

	ANTECEDENT EVENT	**BEHAVIOR**
Hally		
Dick		
Albert		

Fig. 3-4. Antecedent events.

□ Who are the people around the observed individual?

□ What are the demands and expectations of people and things around the observed person?

To demonstrate how the setting makes a difference, Exercise 3-5 uses the behavior and antecedent events in Exercise 3-4 and the settings are supplied by the participants.

Behavior. The antecedent event answers such questions as "What happened before the activity (behavior)?" "What was the beginning of the event?" "What stimulated the activity?" "What spurred the individual to action?" "Who or what began the activity (behavior)?"

Some other points to remember about the antecedent event (the stimulus, the excitant, the independent variable) are that it may be obvious

---

Exercise 3-5
WHAT IS THE SETTING OF BEHAVIOR? *(should be done in a group)*

Time: APPROXIMATELY 20 MINUTES

Read the situations in the three examples in Exercise 3-4 and make up settings that change either where the observed person is or who is around him at the time of the antecedent event. Fill in Fig. 3-5 with short phrases showing how the behavior is the same or is altered by the setting. In the fourth column explain what makes the change in behavior.

After you have completed your chart, discuss your ideas with other group members.

	SETTING	ANTECEDENT EVENT	BEHAVIOR	EXPLAIN
Hally				
Dick				
Albert				

Fig. 3-5. The setting of the antecedent event.

(overt)—something or someone outside that can be seen or heard. On the other hand, the spur to activity may not be seen or heard (covert), such as an inner excitant or impulse (a feeling).

Behavior is what an individual does or says after the antecedent event. This observed behavior should be stated in such a way that it describes the action seen or heard. For example, it is *description* if a person records, "Dee pushed her red wagon from the back and Frank pulled it by the handle. They sang about a 'Little Red Wagon' as they pushed and pulled." On the other hand, it is *interpretation* if Dee and Frank's activity is recorded as, "Dee worked hard pushing her wagon and Frank pulled without trying and they joyously sang as they pushed and pulled." In the first example, the description of behavior, the actions performed by Dee and Frank can be seen and heard. In the second example, the interpretation, there are more opinion words and fewer action words.

☐ Opinion words: worked hard, without trying, joyously

Exercise 3-6
HOW DO YOU DESCRIBE BEHAVIOR? *(may be done alone or in a group)*

Time: APPROXIMATELY 20 MINUTES

Some of the brief statements about behavior in Fig. 3-6 are observable and measureable. They describe behavior. Other statements are vague and interpret behavior. Place an X in the descriptive column for those statements you consider contain observable and measurable action words. Place an X in the interpretive column for those statements you consider contain vague and nonmeasurable opinion words. In the third column change the interpretive statements to descriptive statements. Note the two examples.

After completing the chart, discuss your opinions with the other members of the group.

STATEMENT	DESCRIP-TIVE	INTER-PRETIVE	CHANGE TO DESCRIPTIVE
Example: He walked to the door.	x		
Example: He's a good walker.		x	He walks with a straight back.
1. She raised her left eyebrow.			
2. She seems tired.			
3. He changes his mind.			
4. She took off her sweater.			
5. He said, "Yes, I do."			
6. He feels good.			
7. He says, "I feel good."			
8. They marched around the yard.			
9. She acted dumb.			
10. You will understand.			

Fig. 3-6. Describing behavior.

☐ Action words: pushing, pulled, sang, pushed and pulled

Opinion words can be misleading and dangerous. They can be misleading because they might not be accurate and even may reflect prejudice or dislike of the observed person by the observer. Opinion words also can be dangerous. They hang a label on a person that can affect not only the person's behavior but also the behavior of the people who are in contact with the observed person. For instance, the comment "without trying" in the report about Dee and Frank gives an impression about Frank's efforts without knowledge about Frank or about whether the remark is an accurate assessment of Frank's efforts.

Exercise 3-6 focuses on the difference between an observable and measurable statement about behavior and an interpretation.

Consequent event. Consequences are the events that immediately follow behavior. Often individuals who set out to change behavior actually reinforce the behavior they want to change. For instance, the mother may say to her child, "Again you didn't come in when I called you. Wait until your father comes home. He'll get you!" The threat is there and Mother may tell Father, but the consequence has little or none of the planned effect that the mother hopes to accomplish. The consequence is too far removed from the behavior. The influential consequence is the mother's admission that she is not doing anything about the undesired behavior. In this way she is strengthening (positively reinforcing) the undesired behavior. Behavior continues mainly because of the consequences (effects) that it produces. Thus observation of the relation between behavior and its consequences (contingency) becomes very important for the human service worker. Exercise 3-7 examines contingencies.

Exercise 3-7
WHAT COMES AFTER BEHAVIOR? (CONTINGENCIES—BEHAVIOR PLUS CONSEQUENCE)
(may be done alone or in a group)

Time: APPROXIMATELY 10 MINUTES

In the example of behavior in Fig. 3-7 insert the antecedent and the consequent events. Write one consequent event that is likely to continue the behavior and one that would tend to decrease or stop the behavior.

ANTECEDENT EVENT AND SETTING	BEHAVIOR	CONSEQUENT EVENT
	Skippy sat at the table and looked down at the plate in front of him. With his left hand, he picked up a piece of meat from his plate and then stuck his hand into the peas, squeezed them, and brought his hand to his mouth with the squashed peas. Ms. P. came over to Skippy and	Likely to continue behavior: Likely to decrease or to stop behavior:

Fig. 3-7. The consequence of behavior.

THE OBJECTIVE-SUBJECTIVE OBSERVATIONAL CONTINUUM

Neither objectivity nor subjectivity makes the perfect human service worker. Both ends of the continuum leave aspects of observation out of the picture. It is important to note that subjectivity reflects one's private and unique experience of an object, person, or event, a covert (private, inner, not outwardly observable) observation. Therefore it tends to be biased and unscientific and is only inferred from the outward behavior or self-reports of the experiencing person. When subjectivity leads to labeling, it can be harmful. Studies of elementary school children from minority groups reveal the negative effects of labels such as "aggressive," "untrustworthy," "incorrigible," and "academically dysfunctional." These tags can stick with a child throughout the elementary school years, can limit that child's participation in class, and can cause the child to live up to the reputation the words have built (American Personnel and Guidance Association, 1980). These labels are the consequence of subjective observations that do not describe but rather interpret; they reflect teachers' biases and misperceptions. Even when the label has some validity, it tends to be inaccurate, incomplete, or unfair.

The inferences that evolve from these subjective comments reinforce distorted assumptions about behavior. This does not suggest that subjectivity should be eradicated from observations. It does suggest that competent human service workers should recognize their prejudices so that conclusions are not based on unscientific guesswork. The influences of the covert facets of behavior should be tested by observations of overt behavior (that which can be seen or heard).

Objectivity in observational notations relies on the screening of biases and distortions in perception. It emphasizes description that centers the observer's attention on what can be seen, heard, touched, and the like—through the observer's sensory apparatus. When a number of individuals agree and report about their subjective experiences,

the coordinated subjective responses become accepted reality that can be shared.

Understanding the decoding of observed messages and the recording sequence are introductory steps toward accuracy in recording. The next step is to develop discriminations among the types of notetaking: objective observations, subjective inferences, and suitable blending of the two.

"Purely" objective observations

Pure objectivity in observations is questionable even in the most rigidly scientifically organized experiment. Many personal characteristics are bound to become involved. Therefore the phrase "pure objectivity" more precisely refers to the accumulation of observational data from looking and listening. Such data state, "John lost his job," "Marcia raised her hand," and "The woman coughed." These are the kinds of data that can be verified and about which observers from similar cultures would agree. However, these cold, unembellished, unfeeling facts about human behavior leave out the subjective feelings, the inferences, that color the observations and make them more personalized.

"Purely" subjective inferences

Observations that are totally based on impressions, hunches, and hypotheses tend to lose something because of their subjectivity. Inferences arise from the observer's reactions—the observer's feelings that accompany the objective events. Too many inferences may color the facts with the observer's bias and often distort what the observed person is actually saying or doing.

Inferences and observations combined

The most effective notes about observations have inferences supported with objective evidence from observations.

Example 3-3 presents observational notes illustrating purely objective observations, purely subjective inferences, and the melding of these two forms of notation.

Example 3-3
COMPARING OBJECTIVITY AND SUBJECTIVITY IN RECORDING

Purely objective observations	Purely subjective inferences	Inferences and observations combined
Mary hits John three times. Her lips are in a thin line and her eyes stare.	Mary angrily hit John.	Mary hits John three times. Her lips are tightly held in a thin line and her staring eyes glare her anger.
Mr. Jones says to Sue, "I saw Mary angrily hit John." (This comment by Mr. Jones merely restates what he said and does not infer anything about the statement.)	"Mr. Jones obviously told Sue about Mary's anger at John." (This latter statement does not repeat a comment by Mr. Jones but, instead, infers an act.)	Mr. Jones says, "I saw Mary angrily hit John." Mr. Jones' opinion is supported by other observations. Mary's tight lips, glaring eyes, and hitting John show her anger.
The teacher told Tommy to open his book and to start reading. Tommy lowered his head and did not open his book. The teacher repeated her request in a louder voice. Tommy, head still lowered, after 1 minute opened his book and began to read slowly.	Tommy is obviously hostile toward the teacher. He refuses to do what she asks him to do. The teacher doesn't realize that she is encouraging Tommy to be more hostile by her own hostility. Although Tommy finally does what the teacher commands, he remains hostile.	The teacher told Tommy to open his book and start reading. Tommy lowers his head and does not open his book. (Tommy's apparent refusal to do what the teacher asks him to do suggests hostility.) The teacher repeats her request in a louder voice. (Teacher's hostility and attention to Tommy's inappropriate [undesired] behavior are probably reinforcing Tommy's behavior.) Tommy, head still lowered, after 1 minute opens his book and begins to read slowly. (Tommy gave in, but his feelings of hostility appear to continue. Tommy's relationship with the teacher needs further exploration.)

DISCERNING AND DIFFERENTIATING FEELINGS

The previous discussion of objectivity and subjectivity in recording stressed the importance of incorporating feelings, since they are essential to the more complete understanding of the observed person. Facts are not to be neglected; objectivity is important. Nevertheless, content without recognition of feelings assembles an incomplete record. Several difficulties can interfere with the accurate discernment of feelings.

One of the most frequent occurrences is the substitution of one emotion for another. Many men in the United States repress sadness and crying and restrain joyful expressions such as greeting other men with a hug and a kiss because these expressions are not "manly." There have been alterations in these expressions, among younger men particularly. Yet many men continue to cover up their sadness with anger or a "macho" image and their joy of meeting other men with a casual handshake and a smile. In other words, these men substitute a secondary emotion for a primary one (Bolton, 1979). Such substitutions make the counselor's job more difficult because the helper must help clients not only determine their primary emotions but also assess the intensity of their feelings. Women are permitted, in fact expected, to express emotions in the American culture—but only in reaction to certain events. It is only with the growth of feminist ideas that women have been encouraged to accept their sexuality and to affirm their associated emotional pleasures and displeasures.

Another deterrent to differentiating feelings is an

outcome of the dilemma posed when individuals are asked to label and describe emotions. Part of this hindrance is due to the lack of recognition of one's emotional expressions, and part is due to the barriers individuals erect to conceal, falsify, and thus repress their emotions. Furthermore, in their attempts to "tell it like it is" both clients and helpers may become judgmental rather than expressive. To say "I feel abused by you" is at a great emotional distance from "I feel mad as hell at your lousy treatment of me."

Recognizing, recording, and handling feelings

This "constipation of emotions" (Salter, 1949) frustrates helpers and clients just as much as does logorrhea (excessive flow of words) that conceals feelings.

The beginning interviewer who has successfully accomplished ways of greeting a client and has begun to be able to set limits is still confronted with the task of handling feelings. Both the release and the control of feelings are involved in the interview transaction. In this transaction the interviewers must become aware of both the client's and their own feelings.

Note the differences in feelings exhibited in Figs. 3-8 and 3-9. Effective group leaders are alert to the variations in facial expressions and adapt their procedures appropriately.

Differentiating feelings. The first step in coping with the feelings brought forth during the interview session requires the ability to differentiate feelings. Unfavorable barriers and misdirection result from mistaking the meaning, intensity, or direction of the client's feelings.

One of the consequences of the client's manipulation through emotion may be *triangulation*. Triangulation refers to pulling in the interviewer or some other person as an ally against someone

Barbara Haimowitz

Fig. 3-8. "The way to be happy is to make others so." (Robert G. Ingersol, "Creed," 1896.) (Volunteer/Supportive Services Program meeting, Somerville-Cambridge Elder Services, Somerville, Massachusetts.)

Fig. 3-9. Discussion of grief and mourning as a normal part of life. Group meeting of volunteer and respite visitors in Somerville-Cambridge Elder services supportive program. Volunteers are residents of the community and Harvard University students who are members of the Elderly Affairs Committee affiliated with Philips Brooks House at Harvard University.

else. Sometimes the exploitation or manipulation is accompanied by weeping, by destructive or seductive remarks, or by helpless and hopeless behavior. In each of these behavior patterns the end result is to drag the interviewer into the client's battle on the client's side. Example 3-4 shows the difference between triangulation and the role of a helping ally.

Example 3-4
TO BE OR NOT TO BE TRIANGULATED

MS. S.: *(Beginning to sob quietly.)* Do you have a Kleenex, Doctor? I'm getting overwrought. But . . . but . . . *(Ms. S. takes the tissue, wipes the tears from her face, and noisily blows her nose.)* He says such cruel things. Just yesterday he called me a bitch. Me! Can you imagine that?

[1]

DR. M.: Yes, that does sound mean. What happened then?

MS. S.: He banged on the table and asked for his supper. He must have been crazy, thinking I would get it for him after he acted that way.

DR. M.: Hmmm, yes, I see.

MS. S.: Oh, I do feel better, Doctor. You do understand. See how much I am put upon.

Ms. S. goes home to tell her husband that the doctor agrees that he is cruel and mean and does not deserve anything from her.

[2]

DR. M.: *(Silent.)*

MS. S.: Imagine that. *(Wipes her tears with the back of her hand.)* He's a brute, a beast. He even banged on the table and asked for his supper. He . . . he . . . *(Wipes her eyes again.)* Doctor, do you have another Kleenex?

DR. M.: From what you say you do seem to be having a difficult time. *(Places the box of tissues on the edge of his desk near Ms. S.)* It would help if you would tell me more about yourself in this situation—how you feel about yourself. . . .

Note the difference between Dr. M.'s first answer and his alternative answer. In Dr. M.'s first response triangulation is apparent. Ms. S. manipulates Dr. M. to her side in the clash with her husband. Dr. M.'s second response places him in the role of a helping ally, not an ally against Ms. S.'s husband.

In the second answer Dr. M. redirects the client's thinking and feeling to an examination of her role in the conflict with her husband. Dr. M. also notes the persistence of the client's request for tissues. When Ms. S.

first requests a tissue, Dr. M. automatically hands her one. In the alternative answer, at her second request Dr. M. places the box of tissues near Ms. S. so that she might remove the tissue herself.

Manipulative and expressive feelings. Some clients use feelings as a strategic maneuver to steer the interviewer into compliance with a hidden plan they have devised (manipulative). Other clients attain relief by releasing their feelings (expressive). Releasing feelings is a necessary part of the interview transaction. However, the purposes for the release are also important and these purposes must be noted. Clients who use their feelings as a weapon to urge or embarrass others are repeating destructive behavior that probably has worked outside of the interview. Such clients have probably been using emotional "wheeling and dealing" to manipulate people to do their bidding. The interviewer who gratifies (reinforces) these clients' requests during and after the clients' emotional maneuvering is simply perpetuating the clients' self-defeating behavior.

Sometimes requests for tissues, cigarettes, or other items are efforts at manipulation of the interviewer through helplessness. When such requests continue, the interviewer may be catering to dependency needs rather than the client's personal growth.

Requested items should not be refused without consideration of the immediate needs and functioning level of the client. Offering the client a tissue may serve to assure the client of the interviewer's interest and empathic understanding of the client's feelings. The interviewer should be aware, however, of the possible manipulative quality of the client's emotional expressions. The more experienced interviewer is able to distinguish with greater assurance between manipulative and expressive feelings.

When clients ventilate their feelings expressively, they achieve relief of their tension. Unlike the manipulative emotional outbursts directed against some person or against the interviewer, the expressive emotional release permits clients to achieve new understanding about their problem. Emotional expression frees clients so that they are better able to do something about what they want. The effective interviewer must first help clients recognize their feelings and then assist them in finding a middle ground between release of and control of emotion.

The interviewer *encourages* the client who is fearful of yelling at people, showing anger, and crying to yell, be angry, and cry. When this client finds it is all right to feel and to express these feelings without losing the interviewer's respect, a great burden of suppression is removed. Clients are encouraged to accept and admit their feelings but not to harm themselves or someone else by acting out their feelings.

The interviewer *discourages* the games some clients play when they assume helpless or "dumb" behavior and speak or cry constantly about being abused or confused. The interviewer also discourages the client who attempts to manipulate with such remarks as "I feel like crying. He does it. Now why don't you see how wrong he is? I'm right, yes?"

The interviewer is alert to signals that the client is holding back expression of feelings. Although the client is assured of the right to feel, the interviewer is also alert to the false tranquility of repetitive emotional outbursts. The interviewer should help the client extinguish this inappropriate behavior that brings only temporary relief. The objective of emotional release is obvious. It is to give the client added freedom in using energy to confront and to resolve problems. By means of exploring the way a client feels about problems, these problems take on a new clarity.

Exercise 3-8 focuses on manipulative and expressive emotional styles.

Categories of feelings. In Exercise 3-8 an additional differentiation is added to manipulative and expressive feelings. In the first interview, feelings were broadly differentiated into three categories: positive, negative, and ambivalent. Fine (1968) identifies positive feelings as those which are ego-constructive (self-constructive). Negative feelings are those which are ego-destructive (self-destructive). Ambivalent feelings are conflicting or contrasting feelings or attitudes about the same thing, event, or person.

In the interview situation the client is afforded an unusual opportunity—the freedom to feel without guilt and without loss of face. The interviewer does not deny the importance of any feeling to the client. In fact, the interviewer supports the client's experience by the psychological closeness of acceptance and empathic understanding. Acceptance does not mean approval or agreement. It means respect, client self-direction, kindness, interest, empathy, equality, and communication.

The interviewer stimulates free-flowing expression so that clients may open new pathways to working through their problems. The interviewer guides clients through their emotional maze, helping them see feelings that are not fulfilling because they are weapons against self. These self-destructive (ego-destructive) feelings must be explored so that their threatening power will be diminished. The clients eventually ask themselves, "What makes me say or feel those horrible things about me? What makes me feel others are OK and I'm not OK? What do I want of me?"

Some clients become agitated when they express their emotions. They feel they reveal too much about themselves. They may even fear they may lose control of their emotions. Loss of emotional control may be of particular concern to clients who pride themselves on being cool. Other clients are flustered when they unveil both love and hate about a parent, a spouse, a child, or, in fact, anyone. Such ambivalence (contradictory attitudes) has often been carefully hidden for a long time.

When clients believe that the interviewer is interested in them as people, they are less likely to leave the interview with an unfinished feeling of "Why did I say it, why did I go so far?" The burden of handling feelings is on the interviewer. A shocked or surprised interviewer causes clients to respond more intensely or to "clam up."

Exercise 3-9 offers the opportunity to practice responses to the three categories of feeling.

Exercise 3-8

HOW DO YOU RECOGNIZE, RECORD, AND DEAL WITH MANIPULATIVE AND EXPRESSIVE EMOTIONAL STYLES? *(should be done in a group)*

This exercise requires a group of four participants and a tape recorder. An interviewer volunteers or is selected and then chooses someone to be the client. Both the interviewer and the client then select "doubles." These doubles will act as extensions of the interviewer's and client's thoughts and feelings. The doubles will not interpret or explain what the interviewer or client says but will reflect what they believe the interviewer or client leaves unspoken. The interviews should be recorded. Select from the following interview situations:

[1] Katra is a 24-year-old woman dressed in faded blue jeans and a jacket to match. She is wearing a knitted hat, the brim of which floats in scallops over her forehead. In her hand she carries a crushed shopping bag from which she pulls out an application blank.

KATRA: Here it is, my application.

MS. P.: Hello, Miss L. Please be seated. *(Ms. P. takes the application and looks at it.)* I see you have a bachelor's degree in psychology, and . . .

KATRA: Yes. Hasn't helped a bit. Waste of time. Can't get a job.

[2] Grant, 12 years old, walks into Dr. L.'s office slowly. Dr. L. rises to walk toward Grant, but Grant walks past Dr. L.'s extended hand and begins to take large steps around the outer edges of the office. As he walks he holds out his hand and rubs it along on the wall, making a soft swishing sound.

Suddenly he sits down on one of the straight chairs facing Dr. L. Grant slumps down so that his legs extend out far enough that the soles of his shoes almost touch Dr. L.'s shoes. He places both fists between his legs and stares at Dr. L. Then be begins to scrape the heels of his shoes on the rug and watches the ridges his heel marks make in the rug.

Slowly he raises his hand to his nose and places his index finger into his nostril, moving it back and forth, digging at the interior of the nostril. While he is doing this nose probing, he stares at Dr. L. and pulls his lips into a thin line.

[3] MS. E.: *(Bursts into the interviewer's office and plops down on the long, black leather couch. Looks at the interviewer, Dr. T.)* Why did you do it?

DR. T.: Do it? Do what?

MS. E.: Tell me to talk to him that way.

DR. T.: Tell you? Him?

MS. E.: Yep, last time. I told you about Carl's constant nagging and you said . . . *(Opens her purse and yanks out a tissue with which she begins dabbing at her eyes.)*

Part 1—*Time:* APPROXIMATELY 25 MINUTES

The interviewer and client and their doubles seat themselves so that the interviewer and the client face each other directly, while the interviewer's and client's doubles are at their sides but slightly to the back of them.

The client and interviewer continue the interview for 5 minutes after the particular situation is described. The doubles comment as they see fit, depending on whether they feel that some unspoken thought or unexpressed feeling is omitted. The client and interviewer may use the comments of the doubles to change their procedure, may disagree with them, or may ignore them.

The tape recording is then played back, and for 10 minutes the interviewer and the client as well as their doubles discuss how they felt about themselves during the interview and how the interview might be improved. Some topics to discuss are the following:

☐ How were feelings expressed?

☐ Describe the feelings expressed. Were the feelings predominantly manipulative or expressive? Were the feelings positive (favorable, pleasant, satisfying), negative (unfavorable, unpleasant, destructive), or ambivalent (partially favorable, sometimes unfavorable)?

☐ How do the interviewer and client feel about the comments of their doubles?

☐ How should the interviewer change the procedure to handle the emotions expressed more effectively?

Exercise 3-8—cont'd
**HOW DO YOU RECOGNIZE, RECORD, AND DEAL WITH MANIPULATIVE AND
EXPRESSIVE EMOTIONAL STYLES?** *(should be done in a group)*

Part 2—*Time:* APPROXIMATELY 20 MINUTES

The interviewer and the client as well as their doubles seat themselves as they were for the first interview. A second interview of 3 minutes is taped, with the doubles commenting as they did before.

After the playback of the second interview, the four participants hold a 10-minute discussion that concentrates on the following questions:

- □ What improvements were there in the way the interviewer handled the interview situation?
- □ What evidences were there of positive growth for the client?
- □ What might the interviewer do to have a more effective interview?
- □ What differences were there in the expression and handling of feelings?

Exercise 3-9
HOW DO YOU RESPOND TO POSITIVE, NEGATIVE, AND AMBIVALENT FEELINGS?
(may be done alone or in a group)

Time: APPROXIMATELY 15 MINUTES

Fig. 3-10 presents three expressions of feelings. In the first blank column write a reply that would help the client grow in understanding and self-acceptance. In the second blank column write the client's response that indicates understanding of the interviewer's remarks.

After completing the replies, discuss them in your group.

CLIENT SAYS	INTERVIEWER REPLIES	CLIENT SAYS
I know I should love my baby. But . . . but . . . sometimes I hate her so much it . . . it is frightening.		
I never knew I could feel so beautiful. A glory trip. Spiritual orgasm. Heard—saw the finely etched lines of a leaf swaying back and forth sounding soft sitar sounds. But now, 5 months later, flashbacks . . . now it hurts. What's happening to me?		
Cut the crap, Doc. Who the hell do you think you are, telling me you understand? Whitey understanding a black man. Shit talk. Nothing. Whatever I do is nothing. Try, try so hard. But nothing.		

Fig. 3-10. Expression and response to feelings.

Feelings versus content. The wise interviewer responds to the client in accordance with what seems most important to the client. At times the *feeling* of the client's remarks might be more important than the content. For instance:

MAIME: I shouldda stayed in bed. Woke up this morning with a tension headache. As soon as I got to the office, Mr. Schnottin, the big one, called me in to find out what was delaying my report. Headache worse and worse. Then, that dame who thinks she's the female machismo yelled at me because she didn't like my suggestions for changing the petty cash procedure.
INTERVIEWER: Terrible day, wasn't it? Irritating!

The interviewer's empathic reply noted that Maime's feeling of distress and frustration was more important than the actual events, the content of the day.

Sometimes the interviewer responds to the *content* because it seems that comments about feeling might disturb the client or because the client actually was pointing to the events of the day. Maime speaks of her roommate:

MAIME: Frustrating, we've been living together for a year. Today he tells me I should spend some time with other men. Says he thinks I'm getting bored and that's why I'm having problems at my office. Seems a little stupid. Have been wondering whether he's trying to tell me something. . . .
INTERVIEWER: Hmmm . . . wondering? What do you think he might be telling you?

In this dialogue the interviewer's reply notes that at this early stage of the interviewing session the client may not be ready to look more closely at her feelings and that the content of what Maime is saying appears to be more significant (Egan, 1975).

Cover-ups for feelings. Culture imposes numerous restrictions as to how, when, and where it is proper to show feelings. These restrictions extend to different requirements for the kind and intensity of feelings for men and for women. Unfortunately, these approved and disapproved expressions are not based on biological considerations. As a result, most individuals learn to reg-

ulate the expression of their emotions, and the resulting cover-ups are the basis for tension and distress. Sometimes this distress and the anxiety involved are channeled into bodily complaints (psychosomatic symptoms) and even serious illness. Cover-ups may take the form of headaches, ulcers, allergies, or other coping strategies such as defense mechanisms. This does not mean that the physical symptoms are "all in the mind," for the stress of anxiety and the chemical disruption in the body may eventually result in organ destruction. Defense mechanisms also require energy and tend to increase distress. For these reasons cover-ups may serve as temporary relief, but, if continued, they block the way to self-fulfillment. (Chapter 8 elaborates on the discussion of stress and stress management.)

In the interview the client may conceal feelings by blocked communication. The client either utters partial thoughts or responses or does not respond at all. At other times the restricted disclosure of feelings is shown in irrelevant or distorted remarks.

Many factors may restrain clients from open expression. They may feel threatened by the interview situation or may be reluctant at that particular interview moment to share their feelings. Conflicting feelings and confused impressions may make it impossible for clients to find a response they consider appropriate. Even more important is the clients' belief that the interviewer cannot or will not understand their feelings.

Culture, the client's personal reactions to the interview situation, and the interviewer's behavior are three factors that may restrict the feeling-message. Of these three factors the interviewer's behavior is the most relevant, since it is the interviewer who must clearly understand the "stop" and "go" signals revealed in the client's behavior. It is also the interviewer who must alter the interview environment so that clients may more successfully free themselves from the restrictions on their expressions.

Interviewers must look first at themselves to determine whether they make some question, remark, or nonverbal cue that discourages the client. If the general pattern of the interview transaction has been favorable and open and then the client changes the tenor of verbal and nonverbal responses, the most immediate cue would be particularly important. On the other hand, if the client has avoided certain topics and kept to a private world during most of the interview, other difficulties are apparent.

Thus empathic interviewers who put themselves into the client's shoes will not necessarily open all channels for client expression but will be constantly alert to the client's level of communication and resistance. In the dynamic flow of the interview the distressed client shows difficulties through blocked communication and the observant interviewer demonstrates skills of communication by helping the client break down the barriers.

Exercise 3-10 uncovers some of the problems that may be encountered with cover-ups of feelings.

Support or identification. The interviewer who is "with it" in the client's scene is able to differentiate feelings and also to help the client "hang loose." To hang loose implies an openness for both the interviewer and the client to explore prevailing hang-ups. When clients or interviewers face a problem that is too heavy to manage, they may disregard or even deny the problem, thus draining it, for the moment at least, of its power to trouble them.

Clients who reject a problem regard it as *ego-alien*. In other words, the problem does not belong to them because it does not fit into what they think of themselves. However, if, through exploring, the clients are made aware of the problem's relationship to them, an emotional overcharge may result, leaving them even less able to ponder solutions. Thus the problem becomes *ego-syntonic* and so much a part of the clients that they will not or cannot put the problem aside. The clients identify with the problem; they become concerned that if they or someone else does anything about the problem, then they are being attacked and might even be emotionally destroyed.

Interviewers may reveal similar responses in their relationships with clients. When interviewers are too far removed from a client's drama, they will not understand the client's script. The client's problem will be ego-alien. The interviewers may go so far as to reject the client's problem as ridiculous, illogical, or unwarranted. Such interviewers will not be able to establish rapport or harmonious communication channels.

In contrast to this ego-alien stance, the interviewers may become involved in the client's feelings because they remind them of some of their own emotional struggles. Thus the client's problems become ego-syntonic for the interviewers. Interviewers who wrap themselves in a client's problems to the extent that they act out the client's script are overidentifying with the client.

Dory Previn's haunting lyric (1971) penetrates the depth of feeling resulting from the frustration of overidentification.

i was you

i smiled	i lived
your smile	your life
till my mouth	till there was
was set	no me
and my face	i was flesh
was tight	i was hair
and it wasn't right	but i wasn't there
it was wrong	it was wrong
i was you baby	i was you baby
i was you too long	i was you too long
i said	and baby baby
your words	the worst thing
till my throat	to it
closed up	is that you let me
and i had no voice	do it
and i had	so who was weak
no choice	and who was strong
but to do your song	for too long baby
i was you baby	i was you
i was you too long	

It is not always easy to note the differences between supporting and identifying with a client. Empathy does not require identification. The "as

Exercise 3-10
HOW ARE FEELINGS UNCOVERED? *(should be done in a group)*

Time: APPROXIMATELY 35 MINUTES
Part 1

The group is divided into subgroups of at least four participants. The groups have 15 minutes to decide which emotional factors influence the clients in the five following examples.

[1] Ms. L. is having problems with her 15-year-old daughter Emmy. She has come to the high school counselor to find out about Emmy's behavior at school. Ms. L. says, "We would like to know how Emmy is doing at school. At home she is a young tyrant. We don't know what to do with her any more."

[2] The interviewer, Dr. L., is annoyed with the way in which Martin has been avoiding her questions. Dr. L. is certain the questions she is asking are important to get the information she thinks is necessary. Dr. L. says, "Now, Martin, I do want to help you. How come you refuse to answer my questions?" Martin lifts his head slowly and stands up holding a paper, which he puts on Dr. L.'s desk. On the paper is the following:

Pain is personal

Pain is	When i cut	But you
the most personal	my wrists—a scratch	do not feel the
event in the world.	small blood oozes	pain before and
You can share	my blood/	after because
my house;	my hurt—you	pain is the most personal
You can share	look and ask "Why?"	experience i possess—
my thoughts—but you	You look and	mine not felt or known by
can't share my pain—	try to understand,	any one but me.

[3] The interviewer, Mr. T., is a court-appointed social worker whom Celia has been ordered to visit. Mr. T. says, Come now, Celia, are you crying because you were picked up for prostitution or because you can't see your baby?"

[4] Tom is 16 years old and has been discussing his problems with Ms. M.
TOM: Yep.
MS. M.: Yep? Are you speaking to me, Tom?
TOM: Just thinking. Came out. *(Silence.)*
MS. M.: We were talking about your hands . . . about where they are, or what they are. . . . I think you were saying . . . .
TOM: *(Frowns and slumps down in the chair with his hands hanging loosely at his sides.)* Gotta go soon.

[5] Juan looks down suddenly and begins tapping his fingers on the desk in front of him. He moves his head slowly from side to side with his eyes downcast. In the 5 minutes of silence he occasionally moves his lips and glances upward.

Part 2

One of the examples is selected. One participant role-plays the client, another participant role-plays the interviewer, and the two remaining participants observe and record the interview session for 5 minutes.

The group discusses the favorable, positive procedures used in the interview to help the client understand his emotional responses. Then for 10 minutes the group discusses ways in which the interview approach might improve.

Part 3

For 5 minutes the participants role-play the same situation. After the role playing the group discusses for 10 minutes any improvement shown and then makes suggestions for further improvement.

if'' quality of empathy suggests that interviewers remain themselves but feel "as if" they were perceiving the world through the client's eyes. Support is empathic and implies two people—one helping person, one person being helped. Overidentification erases one's own self-identity and substitutes the self-identity of another. The two selves, client and interviewer, merge into one.

Identification may work both ways. Interviewers may find the client's feelings and conflicts so similar that they become ego-syntonic to the interviewer. Clients may find the interviewer's clothing, confidence, and behavior so appealing that they imitate the interviewer in an attempt to be like the helper. Interviewers lose their value to help when they identify with the client, but clients profit from the model provided by the higher functioning interviewer.

In the process of imitating and identifying the clients learn new behaviors. These new behaviors are essential to their personal growth. However, the interviewer must be keenly aware of the transition the clients must eventually make to their own behavior style. As Dory Previn so aptly disclosed in her lyric "i was you," "i" must not always be "you" or "i" becomes overshadowed and even merged with "you."

The importance of the interviewer's being *with* the client but *not being* the client cannot be denied. The former is support; the latter is overidentification. This overidentification clouds the issues of the helping event, blurs client-helper roles, and interjects intense feelings that hinder clarity of direction and interfere with accurate recording. Errors of recording are more likely when interviewers' perceptions are distorted by overidentification.

ERRORS IN RECORDING

The viewpoint maintained in this chapter is that observation, recording, and reporting are concurrent, not sequential, acts that continue throughout the client communication transaction with the interviewer. Lack of skill in any of these three processes curbs the development of effective inter-

viewing and counseling relationships. Inadequacies in observation thwart accurate recording and sabotage satisfactory reporting; a vicious cycle of defeated attempts to achieve a helping relationship ensues.

Therefore the potential origins of errors in recording demand careful scrutiny to check the snowballing failures that are bound to occur. Perception is the core concept in these errors. This concept has been alluded to previously, but it is worthy of additional exploration in the context of the discussion of recording processes.

Perception

Perception is one key to understanding what goes on in an interview. The teenager may see the policeman as a pig harrassing him for doing his thing, whereas the citizen espousing law and order may see the policeman as a person who wields a strong arm in keeping those "dirty longhairs" in line. The medically oriented human service worker may think "mental illness" is the best phrase to describe the problem of a troubled person, whereas the learning and behaviorally oriented worker may believe "mental illness" is an undesirable phrase for an individual's inappropriate habit patterns.

The way in which individuals see (perceive) the world, and what has happened and what will happen to them has a long history. Although perception of the world originally comes through the senses, these sensory impressions are modified and given meaning by the learning that takes place during life experiences. In other words, perception (seeing, hearing, smelling, tasting, and touching) is not the same for everyone. It is individuals' associations with these impressions that make them different.

Perception = Sensory impressions + Experience

To start at what may be the beginning, one may observe what happens to the infant. For the infant the mother's breast or the bottle provides warmth and comfort. These pleasant feelings arise from the satisfaction given by milk flowing into the baby's mouth and to the stomach. Later the breast or the bottle, and even later the mother herself, takes on meaning over and beyond the nourishment provided. The meanings of trust/mistrust, good/bad, and worthy/unworthy become associated with the mother. The word "mother" itself takes on these meanings as well as the emotional experiences originally associated with the person. Some of these meanings and emotional overtones affect the way the infant feels about himself or herself and later about others. Perception molds the events of living. Often the outcome is the self-fulfilling prophecy.

Self-fulfilling prophecy. From the beginning the growing infant constructs a self-fulfilling prophecy. Mothers in general, a particular woman, or perhaps all women are presumed to be good/bad, interested/disinterested, and dependable/undependable according to perceptions that have sprung from these early experiences. It is from these early learnings and their later modifications that self-fulfilling prophecies are built.

Self-fulfilling prophecies unfold from the world each individual creates from experiences in dealing with the environment. Individuals' reality and resulting behavior tend to be shaped by the way they view the world and, more pertinently, the interview situation. In turn, individuals act (behave) as if the world is as they perceive it to be. Even more important, individuals selectively, and perhaps mistakenly, appraise what happens around and to them in terms of this individualized idea of reality.

Self-fulfilling prophecies are both the cause and effect of prejudices. For example:

Because Hal believes that all white people are seeking ways to put down the black person, he views his white supervisor as someone who perceives him as unable to accomplish very much. Hal decides, "Why try?" and he slows his work pace. He perceives his supervisor as insensitive and "out to get him." If his supervisor comments favorably about Hal's work, Hal is annoyed. "Wise honky," Hal thinks. "He's trying to make me work more. Equal opportunity does not exist in this office." Hal perceives his supervisor as impossible. By his actions Hal makes his perception come true. Hal does not work to the best of his ability. The supervisor perceives Hal as incompetent. Hal's prophecy comes true. The relationship between Hal and his supervisor becomes more unpleasant.

Prejudices. The appraisals of people and things are brought into the interview room and affect the behavior of both client and interviewer in positive and negative ways. Prejudices, both for and against people, become the "eyes" through which each person perceives the other. These prejudiced eyes spur the self-fulfilling prophecy to come true.

The loner who believes himself incapable of establishing a relationship with someone will act as if these prejudices were facts and will seek responses in others that support this point. The prophecy becomes true—not because it *is* true but because the individual has pushed the prophecy into becoming real.

The parent who assures and reassures the son of his brilliance by repeating over and over again, "You are so capable. Why don't you try harder?" may be encouraging the son to failure. The son has two people to prove that he is not capable—himself and his parent. In this kind of failure he knows he can succeed. Hasn't it been proved over and over again?

The person who believes that "all people on welfare want to do is to live off government money" will find those characteristics in the "lazy" behavior of the sloppily clothed slum-dweller. This person will prove he is right. "Why, I even offered the parasite a job, and the lazy bum just said he had no shoes to wear to the job. What a feeble excuse."

Prejudices that are supported by self-fulfilling prophecies become even more dangerous to the interviewer who sees the client with the jaundiced eye of prejudgment. Awareness of these prejudices sometimes helps. Exercise 3-11 is directed to increase such awareness.

Words and associated feelings often reveal the distorted perceptions that evolve from selectivity in looking, listening, touching, and the like. It is this selective perception that frequently encourages negative prejudices and self-fulfilling prophecies.

Exercise 3-11
DO WORDS HAVE FEELINGS? *(may be done alone or in a group)*

Time: APPROXIMATELY 30 MINUTES

Part 1

At the top of a piece of paper write the word "race." As rapidly as you can, write the words that come to mind when you think of "race." Take no more than 2 minutes to do this. Follow the same procedure with the lead words "equality," "ghetto," and "power." Remember, write the lead word and then, for 2 minutes, without too much "think-time," write a list of words you associate with the lead word.

Part 2

Compare your lists for the four lead words. In the columns of Fig. 3-11 write those words you consider favorable (positive, pleasant) and those you consider unfavorable (negative, unpleasant).

Part 3

Answer the following questions:
□ What similarities and differences did you find in your four lists of associations? Refer to the comparison you completed in Part 2.
□ How many favorable terms did you list for each lead word? How many unfavorable words? Do you find any patterns in your responses?
□ How do you explain the associations you wrote for each word?
□ What has this exercise revealed to you about your perceptions? Your self-fulfilling prophecies? Your prejudices?

Discuss and compare your list with the lists of others who have done the same exercise; this is often an eye-opener, since you see different viewpoints. You may also try this exercise with other groups of words such as "grades," "professors," "college," "success,"and "failure," or "marriage," "mother," "father," "sister," and "brother."

FAVORABLE	UNFAVORABLE
Race	Race
Equality	Equality
Ghetto	Ghetto
Power	Power

Fig. 3-11. Favorable and unfavorable word associations.

Selective perception

People are selective in their attention. No person sees, hears, or feels all of the sensory impressions in the environment. People are conditioned to sift out certain stimulations and attend to others. Otherwise the bombardment would be overwhelming. The effective counselor is aware of this selectivity and works harder at observing and listening. The error of improperly selecting the predominant feelings in the client's problem results primarily from at least three deficiencies of the counselor—a low level of observational and listening skills and, particularly, a lack of empathic understanding. Some psychologists explain selectivity in terms of people's basic attitudes toward themselves and the people around them. An individual sees events and people not as they are but as the individual thinks and /or feels they are. This individual narrowing of the perceptual field is one of the factors in selectivity (selective perception).

When counselors selectively attend to clients' feelings, they help the clients explore their emotional responses to increase the clients' self-understanding. This procedure is less useful if the counselors are out of line with the clients' concerns. When the counselors' directional signals are off, they might urge clients to examine feelings that are too threatening for them at the present or, perhaps, not significant to the immediate problem. Ms. T. not only shows her bias but also her inappropriate and insensitive response to Gus in Example 3-5.

Example 3-5
GUS AND MS. T.

GUS: Ms. T., I've chosen to come to see you because you are a woman, and I thought you might be better able to clear up some of my confusions and conflicts. I'm married, have been for 20 years. For 18 of those 20 years my wife has taken care of the house, our two children, and has been active in community groups. OK, along comes women's lib. Two years ago my wife joined an awareness group and since then talks all the time about how she has been locked or "thinged" as a household sex object. Ms. T., it's not that I want to keep her back, never did. She decided to stay home. But she's making me feel so defensive. So guilty that I can't relax. Even my

sexual responses are beginning to suffer; think she might consider me too aggressive. It bothers me so much; sometimes I'm even impotent. Whew! Said a lot.

[1]

MS. T.: Yes, indeed, I do understand you. You feel that the awareness group is unfairly competing with you for your wife's attention. You sound as if you're depressed. (UNSUITABLE RESPONSE.)

[2]

MS. T.: Mmmmmmm. I hear you telling me several things—pressures, feelings of guilt, sexual unfulfillment, and perhaps also you are expressing a great deal of anger. (MORE SUITABLE RESPONSE.)

Close inspection of Ms. T.'s unsuitable response shows introductory remarks that seem mechanical ("you feel," "you sound"). Ms. T. also comments about the awareness group before she has sufficient observational clues to assess its full impact. Gus's more significant concern appears to be his apparent loss of virility (impotence); he seems to feel pushed and is pushing himself into a passive role. Ms. T.'s shallow remark inaccurately selects certain parts of Gus's statement that are less essential at this counseling moment. Another error may be related to Ms. T.'s own feelings about women's liberation. Possible bias is revealed when she uses the words "unfairly competing" to explain Gus's reaction.

Another dimension of Gus's concerns is Ms. T.'s mention of Gus's depression. Gus may be depressed, although his comment does not state this. Depression does not seem to be the problem most important to him at the moment. Gus is asking Ms. T. for some reassurance in the crisis that is almost immobilizing him. Ms. T. must provide this reassurance by what she says and how she looks when she makes her remarks.

The second response from Ms. T. more suitably directs attention to what Gus is saying rather than to the selective perception and consequent tendency to emphasize certain issues that are of more interest to her. Ms. T.'s selective perception dramatizes the inferences that detract from recognition of the client's concerns. Such perception acts as a sieve through which observed behavior sifts and becomes partially correct and probably distorted. Errors in perception may be minimized by greater accuracy in observed behavior but later may appear because of the memory losses in recalling unrecorded observations. Observations are given substance and meaning through recordings, but recording only serves a useful function when the recorder recognizes the value of the records.

RECORDING METHODS
(Cormier and Cormier, 1979; Turner, 1978; Wilson, 1980; Wright, 1980)

It is obvious that recording methods depend on the purposes and time limits for recording. Decisions must be made about for whom the records are to be maintained, what is to be recorded (the details), when the information is to be recorded, how it is to be recorded, and how confidentiality will be preserved—internally (within the office or agency) and externally (for referral and legal requests). These decisions are necessary in both the private office and the large agency. To ensure confidentiality, some human service workers maintain separate files. One file contains background facts about the client, the client's visits, and general and certain specific behavioral observations such as behavioral changes that are favorable (progress) or unfavorable (regressions). A second file contains the more intimate data about the client's personal events. The information in this file may be brief and is sometimes coded. For human service workers the question is not "Should there be records?" but rather "What format is necessary to help the client and worker discover and crystallize their own strengths, limitations, and external barriers to improvement as well as aid in recall?" Several procedures follow.

The narrative technique

The narrative recording technique has been the focus of discussion up to this point. This method records behavioral events, preferably in the ABC sequence presented earlier in this chapter. Narrative or anecdotal recording of behavior requires a minimal structuring by the observer (Wright, 1980). Yet, because narration depends on the ability to write succinctly, accurately, and with careful attention to the infiltration of prejudices, it may lead to distortion unless it is confirmed with caring, concern, and ethical monitoring. In spite of the possibility of distortion, translating thoughts, feelings, fantasies, and daydreams into words is the first step in establishing clarity for what often amounts to the client's internal monologue (Storr,

1980). For the helper these narrative recordings provide an observable opportunity to coordinate and critically appraise the "here and now" of the client's concerns and of the helping relationship. For the client a narrative recording offers outlets for self-observation and reflection of experiences as well as documentation of progress and needs for improvement. In addition, the client's examination of emotions and thoughts in the presence of the empathic helper promotes power over these anxieties and facilitates exploration of misinterpretations of events.

The client prepares a narrative record in the form of a log or diary. The content may be free flowing or may concentrate on specific moods, behavior changes, or other events. These logs are composed between sessions with the counselor and are shared with the counselor, in whole or in part, in accordance with the wishes of the client. Not all clients profit from such recordings, and the perceptive helper decides with the client the advisability of any form of log. Sometimes the "narrative" is painted or drawn rather than described in words. The value of the painting is enriched if the counselor is proficient in responding to the subtleties of such artistic representations without imposing artistic criteria or superfluous interpretations.

Scaling techniques

Two other recording formats serve as more structured methods for behavioral observation: scales and checklists (Wright, 1980). The hierarchical scaling method derives from the client's self-recording of incremental degrees of discomfort related to certain life experiences. This method differs from the rating scale, which begins with zero or one with a range of five points. Ranking arranges scores, events, feelings, and so on in order of size of importance from highest to lowest and assigns numerals indicating the location (rank) of the items among a list of items. Examples 3-6 to 3-8 present samples of hierarchical scaling, rating scales, and ranking.

Hierarchical scaling method. The SUDS scaling method refers to the *Subjective Units of Dis-*

comfort Scale (Wolpe and Lazarus, 1966). SUDS illustrates the hierarchical scaling method. The items of SUDS are arranged in a point system representing increasing "suds" of emotional discomfort; with zero indicating relaxation, and usually 100 as the high score characterizing the most stressful reaction (Cormier and Cormier, 1979; Wright, 1980). If clients have difficulty in assigning numbers to the degree of distress, they are directed to use the letters "L," "M," and "H" to symbolize low, moderate, and high degrees of discomfort. However, the 0-to-100 scaling permits greater flexibility and finer assessments of degree of distress. Clients record various events in a specified period of time and then assign numerals or letters to indicate the degree of distressful reaction a particular situation produces. Nora's portrayal of her job-interviewing incidents (Example 3-6) traces her levels of discomfort during one day.

Example 3-6
NORA'S JOB-INTERVIEW ANXIETY

Nora's counselor, Ms. H., suggested that Nora record the events of one day of job seeking. Nora and Ms. H. had been discussing Nora's feelings about employment and her antagonisms to her family, especially her father whom she considered domineering and insensitive to her needs. Throughout these discussions Nora balked whenever the topic "got too hot" for her. She changed the subject to "more pleasant news" about her forthcoming marriage. Since the counselor considered the relationships that Nora inadvertently revealed essential to Nora's ability to deal with her anxieties, she asked Nora, during their third session, to itemize events and scale the degree of anxiety she had experienced. The following is Nora's list of her anxiety hierarchy:

Hierarchy with numerals	Scaling with letters	Events
80	H	At breakfast thought about my meeting with the personnel officer where I was applying for a job.
60	M	Decided on the clothes to wear to appear more mature.
85	H	Rode downtown with my father while he gave me his usual lengthy advice.

Hierarchy with numerals	Scaling with letters	Events
95	H	Looked for the office on the board when I suddenly blanked out the name of the company.
50	M	Finally remembered the name of the company and took the elevator to the fourteenth floor.
65	M	Walked into the office.
65	M	Went over to the receptionist to tell her my name.
75	H	Called to see the personnel officer.
95	H	Personnel officer asked me to speak to three other people.
100	H	Spoke to the group of executives.
90	H	Began to feel a splitting headache.
95	H	Thought I might not be able to think straight but managed.
75	H	Afterward, went to my father's office.
90	H	My father third-degreed me about what happened.
85	H	Headache bigger.
40	M	Met my mother for lunch.
20	L	Went shopping for my wedding gown with my mother.
10	L	Finally, home and flopped into bed.

Although the previous example lacks many details such as Nora's age and other characteristics, it does present a number of probable problem areas confronting Nora. Exercise 3-12 seeks helping procedures that emerge from the data of the hierarchy scaling of Nora's anxieties.

Rating scales. Rating scales differ from hierarchical scaling in two ways: smaller range of a point system and prior listing of specific behaviors and situations. The items listed are not recorded and personalized by the client, and the meaning of each point on the rating scale is defined to reduce the rater's confusion or misinterpretation. Example 3-7 demonstrates this rating method.

Exercise 3-12
CAN YOU HELP NORA WITH HER ANXIETY HIERARCHY?
(should be done individually and discussed in a group)

Time: APPROXIMATELY 40 MINUTES
Part 1 *(to be completed by each participant individually)*

Nora has brought her list of discomfort items (see Example 3-6) to you, her counselor.

[1] Each item at the lower end and middle part of the scale (66 and below) should not be separated from the preceding item by more than 10 points; and at the upper end (67 and above) by no more than 5 points. Assume that you are discussing the list of items with Nora to help her to think about events that occurred in between each item. For instance, you assist Nora to recall the events between breakfast and dressing that decreased her estimation of her anxiety level from 80 to 60. You fill in the gaps that supposedly resulted from your cooperative effort with Nora. Use [1] as a guide for determining the gaps and then complete [2].

[2] After additional items have been inserted, organize the items into three groups representing low scores (L—0 to 33), middle or moderate scores (M—34 to 66), and high scores (H—67 and above). Rank each item in the three groups in order from most to least anxiety.

Part 2

After each group member has completed Part 1, the entire group discusses the primary discomforts and satisfactions Nora appears to have experienced on the recorded day. Then the group considers the following questions:

□ What strengths do you note from Nora's record?
□ What limitations do you note from Nora's record?
□ Would you suggest that Nora continue her recordings? If "yes," explain the basis for your decision and the recording format you would suggest. If "no," explain the basis for your decision and what other techniques you would substitute.
□ How would you use Nora's recording to aid her in improving her job-seeking behavior?

Example 3-7
RATING SCALE METHOD OF BEHAVIORAL RECORDING

The counselor translates Nora's expressed anxieties into a rating format that Nora assesses in degree of anxiety from 1 to 5. The following key explains each point on the rating scale:

1—Little or no anxiety or discomfort; most relaxed feeling

2—Some degree of anxiety or discomfort; beginning to feel some tension

3—Moderate degree of anxiety or discomfort; beginning to feel noticeably uncomfortable and tense

4—Strong feelings of anxiety or discomfort; tension

5—Intense and overwhelming anxiety or discomfort; tension annoying

The following is Nora's rating for 10 items:

Event	Rating
Choosing a wedding gown	1
Choosing clothes for my job interview	3
In the morning, telling my father about the job interview	4
After the interview, telling my father about the job interview	4
Speaking to the personnel officer	4
Speaking to the group of executives	5
Speaking with my mother	3
Speaking with the salesperson when buying the gown	2
Speaking to the receptionist	3
Getting a headache	4

The counselor refers to Nora's ratings and the following comments result:

COUNSELOR: Nora, do you note any pattern in your recordings?

NORA: Hmmm . . . yep . . . something I know about . . . and—and—another kind of thing I'm surprised about.

COUNSELOR: *(Nods her head and remains silent.)*

NORA: *(Continues after a brief pause.)* Knew that the most pleasant part of living is my forthcoming marriage to Tod . . . so warm about anything related to it. Maybe it's silly, since we have been living together for 3 years and marriage is really just the conventional frosting. Hey . . . maybe that's it! Besides my usual reluctance to "sell myself" in a job-seeking situation, I resent doing this at this time. *(Nora looks down at her hands, clasping and unclasping them. Then she raises her head, looks directly at the counselor, and begins to speak in a louder voice.)* That's it! I'm so very tired of my father's domination—his pushing me into things—his arranging this job interview—

his . . . There I go again. Whenever I think about it, I trigger a pain in my head. Isn't that ridiculous?

COUNSELOR: Really got to a great deal starting with your rating sheet. Might stir up some more if we look at each item together. How would you like to begin?

The counselor's reference to Nora's recording of her ratings became the starting topic for further considerations. Another dimension of recording is achieved and utilized to expand Nora's contemplation of her anxiety. Thereafter these discussions can be the foundation for Nora's self-monitoring of her behavioral change.

Example 3-8
RANKING NORA'S ANXIETIES

Nora's listing has been rearranged to concentrate on the events that might be grouped in the middle or moderate range of discomfort. Nora ranks these five events from those producing the least anxiety or discomfort (1) to those producing the most anxiety or discomfort (5). Each ranking can be assigned to only one event. If Nora wants to rank two items as similar in their rank order, then she would assign both events the average of the lower and the next higher rank. Note the ranks of events 1 and 3. Each of these events receives the rank of 3.5, derived from averaging the ranks 3 and 4.

Event	Rank
Deciding on the clothes for the job interview to appear mature	3.5
Finally remembering the name of the company and taking the elevator to the fourteenth floor	2
Walking into the office	3.5
Going over to the receptionist to tell her my name	5
Meeting my mother for lunch	1

The counselor discusses Nora's rankings with her to help her clarify her feelings about several aspects of her discomfort. The selection of clothes has a special connotation for Nora, and her remark "to appear more mature" may actually reflect lack of self-esteem. The degree of anxiety amplifies as Nora approaches the proximity of the interview site, decreases with her mother and events related to the forthcoming wedding, but increases during Nora's encounters with her father. Nora's data and the analysis of this information derived from her recording become springboards for seeking ways in which Nora learns to deal with her life experiences more effectively.

Checklists

Although hierarchical scaling, rating scales, and ranking are discussed for the client's use, these devices also serve as recording procedures by human service workers. Workers use them for scaling their own anxieties, to scale procedures, or to note the client's needs and progress. Checklists are similar to rating scales except that the observer can check only whether a behavior is present, not the degree of its presence.

For example, the counselor might train Nora in job interview behavior. The counselor prepares a list of verbal and nonverbal job interview skills. Then Nora demonstrates her existing skills through role-playing a job interview, and the counselor checks on the checklist the skills that Nora exhibits. The content of the training program emerges from the skill deficiencies discovered from the checklist recordings. Skill training is achieved by means of the counselor's modeling and Nora's role playing. From the base line of Nora's existing skill accomplishment through the continuing training process the checklist serves as the recording device for monitoring progress. If videotape records are added to the training strategies, these recordings afford an edifying adjunct to the process of skill development and behavior change. Biofeedback has become both a therapeutic intervention with certain ailments such as hypertension and migraine headaches and a recording medium to note muscle tension for verifying, for instance, the client's self-recordings of degrees of anxiety and of anxiety reduction.

Charting

The charting method has smatterings of the narrative technique and follows to some extent the more structured organization of information suggested by scaling and checklists. SOAP and POR are two methods used for charting.

SOAP. Data gathering is accomplished by means of a SOAP chart, consisting of the following items (Alley and others, 1979):
- □ *S*ubjective account of what the client says about the difficulty

- □ *O*bjective statement about behavior
- □ *A*ssessment of why the therapist thinks the problem exists
- □ *P*lan of action to work out the problem

The treatment team convenes for a staff meeting to discuss the SOAP chart, and a treatment plan based on the SOAP findings is developed. Effectiveness of the treatment plan is logged in each client's SOAP chart, and ongoing evaluation alters the procedures of the plan as needed. Diagnoses, client problems, and treatment strategies are reexamined constantly at regularly scheduled meetings. Records are maintained in the SOAP chart of progress, changes in strategies, and by whom and when procedures are accomplished.

POR (Ryback, Fowler, and Longabaugh, 1981). The format of POR differs from that of SOAP, but the general procedures and usage are similar. POR refers to the *problem-oriented record* indicating the nature of the problems presented by the client, the plans of treatment, and the expected time for the plan. POR is used for organizing treatment sessions and in some instances as a peer evaluative mechanism. Alley and others (1979) comment about POR as follows:

> It is felt that the POR may help the clients to understand why they have to come for help. It also provides a written record so that continuity of treatment is maintained when, for example, a client moves from individual therapy to group treatment.

Mental status recording

The four recording formats just discussed—narratives, scaling, checklists, and charting—vary in their usage. Prior training, agency requirements, and individual preferences are some of the determinants of where and how these methods are applied. Psychiatrists, for instance, often administer the mental status examination, which represents a coordination of several of these recording formats.

Mental status assessment is usually administered during a psychiatric interview with the more severely disturbed individual (the psychotic) whose degree of contact with reality needs to be determined or when organic brain damage is suspected because of symptoms of brain injury or of cerebral deterioration suspected as part of the aging process.

Mental status concentrates on the individual's current functioning. Although the information sought is recorded according to subdivisions, the framework for gathering the information should not be regimented by the order of the categories of information. Instead the sequence of topics and the flow of conversation should be based on cues from the client.

Examining for mental status requires a great deal of skill that is acquired through observation of a more experienced interviewer and by means of practice under supervision. Skill is needed not only for the gathering of the information but also for the eventual organization and evaluation of the data to determine the degree of disturbance and the possible directions for treatment.

The information covered in the mental status examination includes preliminary data identifying the client and the source of referral; general description of the client; determination of the client's orientation, memory accuracy, and intellectual functioning; exploration of the client's affective level, reality orientation, and coping mechanisms; and determination of the client's socialization level as evidenced in the client's interpersonal relationships.

RECORDING HUNCHES

Two steps must precede interpretations of behavior—observation and recording. Accurate reporting depends on these steps. Interpretation requires an orderly presentation and analysis of behavior and formulation of the meaning of the behavior to the behaving person and to the persons around the behaving person. This process of interpretation is initiated by means of hunches.

Multiple hunches or hypotheses to explain behavior

Hunches make the following assumptions about human behavior:

☐ The causes of behavior are multiple and interrelated.

☐ The same behavior may have different causes.

☐ The same cause may result in different behavior.

The causes of behavior are part of a system of causes. For example, an explanation of Tommy's behavior described in Example 3-3 is oversimplified when the teacher is made the "fall guy." Tommy, the "hostile" boy, may be tired, hungry, upset about his mother or father, or thinking about Bud who called him a "nigger." As more explanations or hunches about Tommy's behavior are considered, the observer becomes aware of the multiple and interrelated causes of behavior.

Mary may be hitting John because she is angry at someone else. John just happened to be the switch that turned her anger into action. On the other hand, John may have reinforced Mary's angry display because he enjoys it just as much as she does. This is a game called "anger," which they often play as part of their boy-girl relationship. Furthermore, this kind of interpersonal transaction—anger—is the only way that Mary has learned to show her interest in boys.

Fig. 3-12 is based on the approach developed by Prescott (1957). The method is useful for practicing the analysis of the observations obtained from field experiences (practicum) or for notes taken about incidents in a group or other places. The important point is that there must be ample opportunity to observe in order to support or deny the hunches.

Observational support for hunches

Accordingly, to analyze behavior, one must consider multiple (many) hypotheses. The next step is an examination of observations to discover which of the hunches are supported. These hunches, or inferences, that arise from the observer's interpretations of the feelings and reasons for the observed person's behavior must be handled cautiously. An example of a twisted tale arising from unsupported hunches emerges from the possible interpretations even with a simple, direct statement such as "Marcia raised her hand." One observer says that Marcia raised her hand to strike Hank. A second

Specific behavioral event: _____

MULTIPLE HYPOTHESES (interpretation/inference about observed person's behavior)	SUPPORT (observation/facts supporting interpretation)	REFUTE (observation/facts not supporting interpretation)
1. _____	a. _____	a. _____
_____	b. _____	b. _____
	c. _____	c. _____
	(Add more items if available.)	
2. _____	a. _____	a. _____
_____	b. _____	b. _____
	c. _____	c. _____
	(Add more items if available.)	
3. _____	a. _____	a. _____
_____	b. _____	b. _____
	c. _____	c. _____

Fig. 3-12. Form for multiple hypotheses for specific behavioral event.

observer is certain that Marcia raised her hand because her deodorant stung and she wanted to air her underarm. A third observer believes that Marcia sees Alan in the distance and is getting ready to wave to him. An illustration of how some of these hunches are supportable or even incorrect comes from Marcia's version of what happened.

[1]

MARCIA: Oh, my hand. *(She smiles.)* That really was far out. I was using this new deodor jazz . . . supposed to not sting, ye know . . . hah . . . stings . . . wow!

Was I glad that Hank came along . . . asked him whether the deodor really worked . . . at least *that* . . . raised my hand . . . felt sorta funny about it . . . saw Alan and waved to him. . . .

[2]

MARCIA: Oh, my hand. *(She smiles.)* That's a new kind of salute we've gotten together . . . means we're on the scene. . . .

Fig. 3-13 provides an example of the processes of multiple hunches related to a specific behavioral event involving Joe and his foreman.

Specific behavioral event: Joe was told by the foreman, "Since the brickwork is finished, your job is finished."

MULTIPLE HYPOTHESES	SUPPORT	REFUTE
1. He is depressed.	a. He says, "I feel lousy." b. He begins to cry. c. He bangs his hand on the desk in front of him. d. His shoulders slump, and his back becomes rounder. e. He refuses to go to the bar across the street with the other men.	a. He smiles broadly as he says "good-bye" to the people in his office. b. He tells jokes to the men in his office.
2. He is happy.	a. He smiles broadly as he says "good-bye" to the people in his office. b. He tells jokes to the men in his office.	a. He says, "I feel lousy." b. He begins to cry. c. He says, "This hurts, didn't expect such a lousy break."
3. He is angry.	a. He bangs his hand on the desk in front of him. b. He stares straight ahead. c. He says, "I feel lousy." d. He refuses to go to the bar across the street. e. He says, "That fink. What in hell does he think he's doing?"	a. He smiles broadly as he says "good-bye" to the people in the office. b. He tells jokes to the men in the office. c. His shoulders slump, and his back becomes rounder.

Fig. 3-13. Supporting multiple hypotheses: specific behavioral event.

Multiple hunches for recurring behavior

Multiple hunches aid in the analysis and interpretation of behavior and also accomplish two other purposes:

□ They urge caution in arriving at conclusions about a behavioral event.

□ The act of seeking more than one explanation for behavior tends to break down some biases and to dig deeper into understanding.

To arrive at even tentative conclusions about feelings and reasons, the observer must try not only to support hunches from written notes but also to determine whether any observations can punch holes in the hypotheses.

Multiple hypotheses may be constructed for one particular behavioral event such as Joe losing his job, Marcia raising her hand, or Susannah shutting her mouth when the spoon reaches her lips. Hunches may also be formulated for behavior that is repeated, *recurring behavior*. There is one additional procedure for the analysis of recurring behavior. Observational notes must be sifted to discover the behavior that is repeated several times. Fig. 3-14 examines Tommy's behavior in the classroom to discover his feelings and possible explanations for his behavior.

What other hypotheses might there be for Tommy's behavior? How may these hypotheses be further verified or discarded? Which of the hypotheses seems to have the most support? Which of the hypotheses seems to have the least support?

Recurring behavioral event: Tommy reads slowly, asks for help with several words, and in a paragraph of 35 words makes 12 errors.

MULTIPLE HYPOTHESES	SUPPORT	REFUTE
1. Tommy feels hostile toward his teacher.	a. Tommy does not open his book when the teacher asks him to do so. b. Tommy does not look at teacher when she talks. c. Tommy reads slowly with his head bent.	a. Tommy complains of headaches on three observations. b. Tommy rubs his left eye on four observations. c. Tommy walks up to the blackboard to "see better."
2. Tommy feels uncomfortable when he reads.	a. Tommy moves about in his chair during reading time. b. Tommy says "I can't" when asked to read.	
3. Tommy does not know how to read.		a. Tommy reads most words, particularly when he gets close to the book.
4. Tommy does not see well. He needs corrective lenses.	a. Tommy complains of headaches. b. Tommy comes up to the blackboard to see better. c. Tommy rubs his left eye. d. Tommy reads most words, particularly when he gets close to the book.	
5. Tommy has perceptual difficulties.	a. Tommy reads a "d" for a "b." b. Tommy reads "was" for "saw." c. Tommy rubs his eye and complains of headaches.	

Fig. 3-14. Supporting multiple hypotheses: recurring behavior.

Tentative implications of findings from hunches

The process of constructing multiple hypotheses and then supporting or discarding these hypotheses from the facts gathered during observations leads to tentative conclusions. The observer pulls together the hypotheses that appear to have the most observational support then decides what other information is needed and what other observations must be made before the interpretations of behavior can be considered correct or at least tentatively correct. The observer diligently applies the scientific method for analyzing behavior.

This does not suggest that observation is the beginning and the ending role of the human service worker. Instead the ability to observe accurately, to analyze, and to arrive at interpretations cautiously is the foundation for helping. With practice trainees achieve the ability to observe and hypothesize. They learn how to accept or reject hypotheses. Meanwhile, they are functioning as helpers to the client while with the client and analyzing their observations later so that they are better prepared to help the client and not just "walking on air."

SUMMARY

Two layers of helping skills have been discussed in the preceding chapters—observation and recording. These integral foundations of the helping event engender the inception of the subsequent layers of reporting, interviewing, and counseling. In this chapter recording is considered from the viewpoint of organized note taking. Note taking in this instance is conceived broadly to comprise handwritten, mechanical, and electronic recordings in the form of narrations, scaling techniques, checklists, charts, and mental status reports.

Several questions must be answered prior to note taking: For whom are the records maintained? How will the notations be used? What method of recording will be used? When will notations be accomplished? How will confidentiality be assured? The quantity and format of records depend on the responses to the foregoing questions plus the exigencies of administrative, legal, and political obligations. It is, of course, possible that these latter three requirements may unduly lengthen the recording process. Added to these confusions are the mixed messages about quantity of note taking proposed by some experienced professional human service workers. The discussions in this chapter provide guidelines for appropriate recording.

All recording begins with observational messages. These messages must be decoded accurately. Speaking the same language does not automatically ensure similar meaning, since each person's perception of reality is unique. For this reason it is urgent that helpers clear their ears, eyes, and the remainder of the sensory apparatus of the barriers to accuracy—prejudices. Individual realities vary because of the personalized beliefs that are demonstrated, for instance, in the semantic impact of the Humpty Dumpty syndrome. This syndrome is characterized by connotations for words that are so narrow that they have significance just for the message sender, rarely for the message receiver. Denotative communication, on the other hand, is untainted with emotional tones and evokes similar meanings from individuals in the same culture. The framework for coding, encoding, and decoding

messages must take account of the processes involved in denotation and connotation so that distortions are minimized. In other words, to record valid information, the listener must be aware of the cultural and other effects on the message sender (the connotation) so that the code (language, symbols) may be clearly and accurately decoded (interpreted).

Interpretive words are similar to the extreme personalizations represented by the Humpty Dumpty syndrome. These interpretive words are based on assumptions that often lack factual support. They label and infer rather than concretely particularize observed behavior. "Brat," "brute," and "braggart" are interpretive words, as are "mannerly," "manly," and "modest." Both unfavorable and favorable biases are exemplified in these words. None of the words depicts what is happening, rather they communicate what the decoder perceives or experiences. Descriptive words are action words based on observable behavior. The objective-subjective continuum considers dissimilarities between descriptive and interpretive words in the context of recordings based on observed behavior (objective) and inferences (subjective).

The ABC sequence is another aspect of recording to be mastered. This sequence focuses recording on the *a*ntecedent event, the *b*ehavior, and the *c*onsequent event. Branching approaches to recording follow actual events more accurately than do linear descriptions. These differentiations become significant in recording incidents leading up to behavior and its consequences. Feelings also must be incorporated into recordings, and this requires that the helper develop the skill to discern, differentiate, and deal with cover-ups for feelings. In addition, this skill must be coupled with competency in expressing appropriate response to the client's feelings or to the content of the client's remarks in accordance with the client's inclinations.

Errors in recording evolve from many sources. Some of these are a consequence of observational deficiencies, and others are due to lack of information of the procedures for observation, but most spring from perceptual rigidity and selectivity—self-fulfilling prophecies and prejudices. These errors of perception are more likely to occur in the narrative or anecdotal format of recording but also can affect scaling, checklist, and charting techniques. Hierarchical scaling is more likely to be subjective than are rating scales, since the hierarchy is created solely from the recordings of the client. Unlike hierarchical scaling, the rating scale has well-defined points that must be used for rating, and ranking produces a somewhat different portrayal by concentrating on the assessment of the influence of events from greatest to least impact. Checklists, which are similar to rating scales, are useful for noting the presence or absence of specific behaviors but not the intensity of these behaviors. Charting techniques such as SOAP and POR combine some of the methods of narration with the more structured format of scaling and checklists.

Mental status recordings are cited as an example of the coordination of several recording procedures.

Finally, recording hunches is presented in preparation for the next layer of the helper's skills—reporting (Chapter 4). Multiple hunches, or hypotheses, are the tools for interpreting the meaning of behavior. They must be examined in relation to observational recordings to identify which "guesses" are supportable by observed behavior, which require additional observation, and which are unsupported by observed behavior. The nature of problems and the sources of these problems can be derived from this process of identifying and verifying multiple hunches. These processes lead to the next step, reporting, as an aid for determining strategies needed for the client's development and the monitoring procedures to be made available in the helping relationship.

Chapter 4

REPORTING
organized feedback procedure

Eivm Williams

**Reporting accurately and fairly depends on
thoughtful and unbiased analysis of recordings,
which evolves from attentive and thorough
observations.**

RECORDING AND REPORTING: CONCURRENT PROCESSES

The previous chapter featured recording set apart from reporting. However, this differentiation is merely an expedient to accentuate certain particulars. In fact, there is a kinship between recording and reporting, and both are related to the origination of data for these processes—observation. Recording and reporting are concurrent procedures. When recording observations, one is self-reporting. Frequently these self-reports of interview sessions are referred to by others in an agency in addition to the counselor involved in the helping relationship with the client. Furthermore, recording and reporting are vehicles for communication—information-gathering and feedback procedures that provide problem-solving data for the individuals involved in the helping event.

Reporting as feedback

There are two directions for information exchange, *feedforward* and *feedback* (E.D. Schulman, 1980); reporting represents both directions. Reporting functions as a form of feedforward communication, since the report conveys data specifically about the client as well as other related information. Reporting also provides feedback, since the data are composed, recorded, organized, and analyzed with implications by the person who gathered the facts. Thus this person is expressing a reaction in the notation (recording). Reporting as

feedforward and feedback is a two-edged sword in which the biases that prompt misinterpretation and selectivity of observations and recordings add to the fallacies and misunderstanding erupting from unsuitable communication skills.

Feedback assumes critical importance when one realizes that the feedback of the reporting person becomes the stimulator of responses (the feedforward) for other persons reading the report. Rumors begin this way. Labels persist this way. Human services can be made suitable or unsuitable in this way.

Feedback in the communication system. Several characteristics of feedback govern the effectiveness of the helping relationship, such as the degree to which feedback is constructive or destructive, whether feedback is general or specific, and the anxiety-producing potential of negative feedback.

Constructive feedback. An act such as dropping one's clothes as one undresses can become the irritant for a confrontation.

[1]

Cut out the pig-acts; pick up your dirty clothes!

[2]

You sure make things easier when you pick up your dirty clothes.

The first feedback shouts forth the onlooker's annoyance. The act is painted in electric colors of red; hostility reigns supreme. "Cut out the pig-acts" as feedback tends to discourage favorable action; instead it stimulates adrenaline as a challenge to protest. The second feedback may not resolve the situation, yet it is less likely to escalate antagonisms and stir up a power fight as to whose will is dominant. The destructive statement demeans, threatens, coerces; the constructive remark urges cooperation and promotes approval for achievements.

Feedback may lose its constructive character if it is excessive or if it emanates from an external source when it is not desired or required. These comments can be applied to reporting. Reporting as feedback facilitates the helping relationship if it is specific, if it fits the dose of information needed, if it is suitably timed, and if its inferences and recommendations are positively based on observed behavior and unbiased analyses.

Specific feedback. The more general the feedback, the less the message receiver has to latch on to for changing or reinforcing behavior.

[1]

You have a skillful approach to listening. You sit forward and your eye contact with the speaker is natural and direct.

[2]

You're a good listener—looking at the speaker as you do does help.

In the first feedback the communicator concisely states the specific attending behaviors that reinforce the listening performance. The second feedback primarily evaluates and encourages but leaves much to the imagination about suitable listening responses. Similar criteria of suitability are applied to reporting. Reporting is meaningful as feedback if it specifically identifies the strengths and limitations of the client, states the goals and action plans, and assesses progress and regression during the implementation of the plans.

Positive feedback. Neither of the following internal monologues is free of negative feedback.

[1]

There I go again, talking too much . . . starting up when I really want to be quiet. Jerk that I am!

[2]

Whoops! Flubbed it! Oh, well, really would like to be quiet . . . but, then I would feel uncomfortable later.

The first monologue is adversely critical, reflecting and escalating anxiety. The second feedback allows some leeway for bungling, condemns less sharply, and realizes the necessity for expression. Similar comments apply to the following examples of external feedback.

[1]

Don't you ever learn when to shut up? Can't you see this kind of talk is nowhereland!

[2]

You got it. Sure needed to be said—but, now?

Exercise 4-1 refers to the characteristics of feedback just discussed and directs attention to feedback as reporting.

Levels of communication skills. The characteristics that control the effectiveness of feedback are dominated by the attitudes, skills, and knowledge of the reporting person, and especially by that person's level of competency in communicating. A low level of communication in spoken language, a written statement, an audio tape or videotape, or a film is a barrier to accurate feedback. Therefore, at the onset, the level of communication skills must be considered alongside the previously mentioned characteristics of effective reporting.

Human relationships have many levels of communication that range from speaking alone to speaking together. There are five different forms of speaking—the soliloquy, the monologue, the duologue, the duelogue, and the dialogue.

The *soliloquy* is a form of solitary speaking in which one talks out loud but to oneself. Infants soliloquize when they babble sounds. They hear their own sounds and learn to use certain sounds and certain combinations of sounds later by means

---

Exercise 4-1
DO YOU USE FEEDBACK TO REPORT EFFECTIVELY? *(should be done in a group)*

Time: APPROXIMATELY 30 MINUTES

Read the directions completely before beginning the exercise.

The group divides into triads. A participant in the triad reports a negative (annoying) feedback experience, preferably recent, and describes it for not more than 2 minutes. The speaker and the two listeners then use the rating scale in Fig. 4-1 to check certain characteristics of the report. Discussion follows, concentrating on how the feedback can be altered to be more positive, favorable, and helpful. The report then is changed in accordance with the suggestions offered. Once again the report is rated; improvements are noted, and further suggestions made.

Then the two other persons follow the same procedures as the first speaker.

After all three participants have completed their feedback, they discuss the following questions:

☐ What have you learned about feedback from this exercise?
☐ How might this information help you in writing a report?

Feedback is	Yes	?	Yes	
1. Constructive				Destructive
2. Specific				General
3. Positive				Negative
4. Descriptive				Evaluative
5. Timely				Unsuitably timed
6. Presenting options				Presents final solutions
7. Appropriate in length				Excessively lengthy
8. Informative				Dogmatic
9. Concise				Vague
10. Practical				Impractical

Fig. 4-1. Rating feedback characteristics.

of the reinforcements of the significant people around them as well as by the self-reinforcements of their own sounds.

Shakespeare used the soliloquy often in his plays. Hamlet's six soliloquies are similar to free association in which he expresses his feeling of helplessness and disgust with the smell of rottenness and corruption around him. At first Hamlet speaks out loud to himself and does not act. Afterward Hamlet's soliloquy spurs him on to action.

Soliloquizing may occur during an interview. The client's rambling on about concerns may help him or her put thoughts in order. Instead of silent contemplation, the client sticks thoughts together out loud. On the other hand, if the interviewer gushes forth a soliloquy, this has little value for the client. The client needs to be involved in the communication process.

The *monologue* is a little different from the soliloquy. The monologue *demands* an audience; the soliloquy *may* have others who happen to be listening. The monologue monopolizes a conversation. One person makes a long speech with little interest in receiving conversational feedback. The interviewer who carries on a monologue clicks away the precious minutes of the client's time unmindful of the client's needs very much like the television set in a recent cartoon—the television set permits viewers to "think without thinking . . . to feel without feeling, [and] live without living" and leaves "no visible scars" (Johnson, 1980).

A form of monologue occurs in the *duologue*. In this communication style both the interviewer and the client carry on separate monologues. It is as if two television sets in the same room were facing each other. Obviously both persons in this so-called conversation are speaking as if they were alone, although they happen to occupy the same room.

Sometimes this duologue is argumentative, and then it becomes a *duelogue*. The combatants arm themselves with word weapons and carry on a verbal duel. Unfortunately for the client the contest is frequently frustrating and destructive, since the issues are not considered. Instead the weaknesses of the participants are attacked. An empathic interviewer avoids such word-fighting encounters.

The *dialogue* contrasts with these one-sided speeches. The dialogue takes into account both the sender and the receiver. The client and the interviewer form a circle of communication, a transaction, in which they openly talk together, seeking the harmony of mutual understanding. In a dialogue the interviewer is alert to the client's leads and encourages the client with a minimal amount of words and direction.

Exercise 4-2 directs attention to the differences among the soliloquy, the monologue, the duologue, the duelogue, and the dialogue.

Feedback in the helping relationship

The authority of communication as feedback is most obvious in the helping relationship. From the moment of contact both client and helper size up their degree of affinity. For some clients privacy is the ingredient that is crucial to their comfort. These clients almost cry out, "I won't violate your space—don't push yourself into my space." They demand social distance—some friendliness without the intimacy, trust, and confidentiality of actual friendship (Victor, 1980). (See Chapter 1.) These conditions make the helping relationship more difficult, but if the human service worker accepts and works within the established boundaries, eventually these clients may express their need for feedback of some kind.

"How am I doing?" This question asks for *feedback*. Feedback helps people to improve their performance, to correct their errors, to behave more appropriately. The process of giving and responding to feedback is often extremely difficult because it involves risk and trust. Individuals must be able to take the risk of making themselves vulnerable when they "tell it like it is" or when they ask for an honest appraisal of their efforts. Feedback also involves trust, since individuals must feel comfortable with another person's opinions and reactions.

HOW DO THEY SPEAK—"ALONE" OR "WITH ANOTHER PERSON"?
(may be done alone or in a group)

Time: APPROXIMATELY 35 MINUTES

Read the five communications and decide which is the soliloquy, monologue, duologue, duelogue, and dialogue. Then rewrite them so that they are all dialogues. After you have completed the exercise, discuss your answers and revisions with the group.

[1] PETER: Hah! Caught ya signifying again. How the hell can you live with yourself, spying like that?

ALFRED: Signifying! Where are you at, man? Trying to find out, just find out. Have a right to know what you were doing there. You're off your beam, man.

PETER: Signifying—worse than stealing. Trying to find out about where I got the stuff. Son of a . . . .

ALFRED: Drop dead!

[2] MR. L.: Come in, come in. Sit down.

ROGER: *(Walks over and sits down on the chair next to Mr. L.'s desk.)*

MR. L.: Now, let me see. You were told to come here by your teacher, Ms. Perry. No, that's not her name, it's Ms. Percy. Or is that it? Well, doesn't matter. Now, let me see. Oh, yes, you haven't been doing very well, have you? Clowning, hmmmm. Not studying . . . aha! And you have fallen asleep in class. Well, well. And you also have been annoying what's her name, Margie, drawing odd-looking pictures of her. So that's what it is.

[3] MELANIE: *(Enters the nurse's office and sits down on the chair next to the nurse's desk.)*

MS. R.: Hello, Melanie. How may I help you?

MELANIE: *(Slowly moves her head from side to side.)*

MS. R.: *(Remains silent for a few seconds, meanwhile noticing that Melanie's eyebrows are drawn together across the bridge of her nose so that sharp lines cut into her forehead.)* Hard to begin?

MELANIE: *(Nods her head up and down.)*

MS. R.: *(Smiles and places her hand on Melanie's hand, which is resting on the desk.)*

MELANIE: *(Begins to weep. Ms. R. gives her a tissue.)* I'm . . . I . . . I think . . . oh no . . . can't . . .

MS. R.: *(Remains silent but leans forward slightly.)*

MELANIE: I think I have syphilis.

[4] SAM: *(Squirms in his seat, looks around, and then settles back with a vacant stare in Mary's direction.)* This just can't be. I feel so good, yet so bad—warm, cold. How long can it last? This magic of discovery . . . then distress of finding . . . I speak and no one hears. I feel and no one cares. When will there be peace? Peace of knowing what I want, where I'm going? Should we be together, alone, apart? Isolated in a crowd, crowded with thoughts when alone. I . . .

[5] ANGELO: I'm talking to you, and you're not hearing.

FATHER: What do you mean? I hear better than you. You're just a know-it-all.

ANGELO: Just don't want to stay in college . . . a year or more. I want time to find out what I want. Don't have to worry about making good; don't have to be pushed into education. Want to work, travel, be me. No *have-to*, just *want-to* every day.

FATHER: Know-it-all . . . this generation. All the advantages, takes . . . and takes. Don't appreciate the opportunities to get an education. In my day, my parents couldn't afford to send me to college. If only . . .

ANGELO: You've got to listen. I'm telling you that life is more than college. Education is life. Life is education. College is not real.

FATHER: All the advantages. All they want to do is ruin their lives. This generation don't care about responsibilities.

ANGELO: Yes, I want responsibility—for myself. I want to find out what the world has to offer; I want to . . .

Empty feedback. Praise, verbal encouragement, a nod of the head, applause, a smile, a pat on the shoulder—all are examples of feedback. None of these positive forms of feedback should be offered unless it is deserved. Empty feedback, which is automatic and without basis, is unwise and even dangerous because the person receiving the feedback does not learn about the appropriateness and effectiveness of behavior. Effort should be recognized and failure or errors mentioned but not dwelt on.

Competent helpers are alert to the feedback role. They make certain that the information they give is to help the other person to improve his or her

---

Exercise 4-3
HOW DO I ANSWER YOU? *(may be done alone or in a group)*

Time: APPROXIMATELY 15 MINUTES

For this exercise refer to Fig. 4-2. Read each statement in column A carefully. Then write an inappropriate feedback in column B and an appropriate feedback in column C. Note the two samples, then write two more statements (column A) and complete columns B and C for these.

A Statement	B Inappropriate feedback	C Appropriate feedback
What a job! Did so much today. So much more to do. I really feel burned out.	Good. Haven't I told you, many times, to cut down. When are you going to learn?	I admire you. You are a persistent, thorough person. I wonder, though, is your fatigue telling you something about your pace?
I yelled back at him, "You pompous ass, what gives you the right to talk to me that way!"	Hey, wait a minute. You really put your foot into your mouth that time. Can't you see what a mistake you made?	You sound as if you were ticked-off. Can we talk about what happened?
He always talks so fast I don't know what he wants me to do. I try but am not successful very often.		
I try—really I do—but I just don't come across. I'm so self-conscious that I end up getting out of the scene.		
I helped her with her homework. When I asked for a date, she said "No."		

Fig. 4-2. Appropriate and inappropriate feedback.

performance toward specific goals, not to punish the other person, not to get something off their chest so that they feel better, or to show how much smarter they are than the client. Skillful helpers also are aware of how the other person is receiving the feedback. Helpers ask themselves, "Is the client ready for feedback? Does the client feel the need for feedback at this time? How much is the client prepared to hear about himself or herself?"

Feedback and trust. Feedback tells people what they are doing in an effective way—their strengths—and what they need to improve. Both of these aspects of feedback can be a problem if the atmosphere of trust that encourages giving and receiving information has not been established. The receiver of feedback may suspect the motives of the helper. Tom may wonder what Mr. Perry is driving at: "Why is this fink telling me I handled Beezie good? What is he pushing me into?" Butch may say, "Cut the bull. You don't tell me nothin'. I know where it's at—I know my own thing."

The feedback circle always returns to communication plus observation, and the caveats regarding the semantic impact are to be considered particularly in the context of verbal feedback. Verbal feedback is often misunderstood and misused if the helper's communication skills are unsuitable for the client's needs. Appropriate versus inappropriate feedback is considered in Exercise 4-3.

Feedback loop of cue distortion. How simple communication would be if every person listened attentively, understood the message accurately, and responded appropriately. Communication is much more complex than this, and feedback often is based on loopholes in facts, strong feelings, and other factors that distort it. Added to these hindrances is the very definition of feedback. A humorous recent cartoon portrayed a wife responding to her husband's protests: "That's not nagging, that's feedback." One may conjecture what this cartoon conversation reveals about the cartoonist's beliefs and about the prevailing view of women. One may wonder whether the wife's comment represents misleading perceptions, nagging, feedback, or something else.

There is no doubt of the importance of developing accurate cue perception. This importance extends beyond the interview transaction into the daily lives of people and farther into the international scene. The distortion of cues too often results in a feedback loop that increases to monstrous proportions. Each new misperception is added to the previous one until all perspective is befuddled.

A vicious cycle ensues that cannot be broken until the individual involved becomes more skilled in picking up cues and less prone to permit distortion. Fig. 4-3 diagrams this feedback loop of cue distortion.

The erroneous perceptions that emerge from some degree of cue distortion can evolve into strong hostilities or strong attractions. The murder of more than 20 black children in Atlanta during a 20-month period in 1980 and 1981 added fuel to latent (and open) racial antagonisms. Comments abounded about the police's lack of activity and insufficiently militant searching for the murderer.

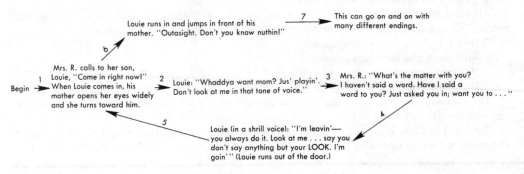

Fig. 4-3. Feedback loop of cue distortion.

Exercise 4-4
HOW DOES LISTENING BECOME GARBLED? *(should be done in a group)*

Time: APPROXIMATELY 25 MINUTES

The people in the group arrange themselves in two circles. The inner circle should contain half the number of people that the outer circle does. Someone in the inner circle starts a one-sentence statement (rumor) about the outer-circle members, and someone in the outer circle starts a similar one-sentence statement about the inner-circle group. Any individual may begin the rumor with either a positive or negative remark stated in one sentence.

The starter writes down the rumor on a piece of paper and then whispers it to the person on his or her left. The next person writes down what he or she heard and then whispers it to the next person. This procedure of writing (concealed) what is heard and then communicating it to the person on the left continues around the circle until the starter has been told the rumor and has written it down below the original statement.

When the two groups have finished, there should be a discussion of the various changes in the original statement as the rumor moved from one person to another. The discussion should also include the degree of difference in distortion (changes from original statement) by the smaller inner circle as compared to the larger outer circle.

After the discussion, which should take no longer than 10 minutes, the same procedure should be repeated with a new starter and new rumor.

Compare the recorded whispers in terms of their accuracy to the original statement from the first to the second whispering campaign.

Exercise 4-5
HOW DOES VIEWING BECOME BUNGLED? *(should be done in a group)*

Time: APPROXIMATELY 20 MINUTES

The group is divided into pairs. The chairs of the partners should be arranged so that the two people are seated back to back. Each person has 3 minutes to write down what the other person is wearing and what the other person looks like in general. The observation should include a general description of the other person, with specific details about clothing. The description should focus on what the describer actually recalls seeing, not how the describer feels about the person.

After both participants have completed their descriptions, they discuss (5 minutes) their notations. The partners face one another now and note the degree of accuracy and completeness of their observations.

□ How many cues have been recorded?

□ How many cues have been omitted?

□ How many cues are inaccurate?

□ How many notations are interpretations or expressions of feelings rather than observable facts?

The accuracies, the omissions, the inaccuracies, and the emotionally toned observations should be tabulated as suggested in Fig. 4-4.

The entire exercise is repeated with another person. Then a comparison is made of the extent of improvement from the first to the second observation, as indicated in the two columns of Fig. 4-4.

(Cue distortion or reality?) Several people pointed out that there would have been a more concerted effort if white children had been murdered. (Feedforward—cue distortion or accurate perception?) A newspaper columnist wrote that on two other recent occasions large numbers of white children had been molested and killed and the discovery of their murderer occurred after many lives were lost. (Feedback—cue distortion or accurate perception?) Danto, a psychiatrist, remarked that "the murderer has a psychopathological reason to ease some of his own score of childish hurts by taking it out on kids" (Behavior Today, 1981d). (More feedback—distorted cue interpretation or appropriate explanation?) Some parents of murdered children banded together in a supportive relationship to deal with their grief and to sensitize professionals and the public to the unique problems of the murdered victim's families (Behavior Today, 1981e).

In the first instance hostility and negative feedback cues expanded. In the second instance parents were attracted to other parents with similar problems of bereavement. The Atlanta story exhibits in an extreme form the innuendos that can be associated with feedforward and feedback. The potential for misconceptions is more apparent in this situation because of the heightened emotionality and the serious affront to the humanity of the children in Atlanta as well as to their families. Yet because each individual is enveloped in his or her own perceptual cocoon, the possibility of misperceptions is ever-present.

The problem with perception and feedback emerges from the fact that these two processes tend to be enveloped in the personally colored reality of the moment. Therefore there is an ever-present possibility of garbled listening as well as bungled viewing. Exercises 4-4 and 4-5 explore these two misperceptions and underscore a simple yet compelling point of view: if cues are incomplete, inaccurate, and biased, the observation, recording, and reporting are bound to be incomplete, inaccurate, and biased.

Cues are the subtle sources to which both the interviewer and the client react. These may be such observable characteristics as skin color or facial scars or the more subtle individual gestures or vocal features to emphasize or deemphasize what is said.

From these cues evolve expectations regarding the client's apparent economic status, probable attitudes on certain topics, and levels of information in certain fields. Unfortunately these cues may be distorted out of proportion while other cues are ignored. How these cues are interpreted depends solely on the viewer. As a result of an individual's selective perception and interpretation of cues, insurmountable restrictions may clog the flow of communication and understanding. The following discussion examines additional factors that influence the effectiveness of reporting.

FACTORS INFLUENCING THE EFFECTIVENESS OF REPORTING

Recording and reporting, concurrent feedback, are subject to similar factors that facilitate or impede productive communication. Some of these components are background and experience barriers; blocked communication; patterns of com-

	First observation	Second observation
Number of accurate cues		
Number of omitted cues		
Number of inaccurate cues		
Number of interpretations		

Fig. 4-4. Accuracy of observational cues.

munication and interpersonal relationships; and tolerance-acceptance.

Background and experience barriers

Barriers to communication that arise from differences in background and experience are not always recognized by the helper. Even when helpers and clients are from the same racial, religious, and socioeconomic groups, subtle differences in looking at the world may interfere with establishing a free exchange of ideas and feelings. Even when helpers have been able to recognize and largely free themselves from satisfying certain needs of their own, defending themselves in relationships, and expressing problems of their own life dramas—even then, unique differences are present in every interview.

The meaningfulness of diversified experiences. The helper who has had experiences with many different people, has read, and has had encounters with various problems is one step ahead in developing an effective relationship. If interviewers are able to honestly come to grips with the consequences of their own background and experience, several changes are likely to happen.

☐ Interviewers will learn to listen less selectively. The tendency to hear what one wants to hear because of the way one thinks will be avoided. Instead the interviewer will listen to and observe the meaning to the client of the interviewer's as well as the client's words and behavior.

☐ Interviewers will expand their experience and increase their response repertoire so that they will have a larger store of communication content. Interviewers will be able to demonstrate more flexibility and better understanding in their communication.

☐ Interviewers will realize that both the interviewer's and the client's backgrounds and experiences are sources of discriminations. These discriminations will not only determine

---

Exercise 4-6
HOW DO YOU TUNE IN TO IDEAS AND FEELINGS? *(should be done in a group)*

The group is divided into smaller groups of five; three people will act as observers and two as participants. One observer records nonverbal cues, one observer records verbal cues, and one observer records the entire process related to the people involved in speaking together. (Refer to Figs. 2-4, 2-5, and 2-8 for observational cues.)

Part 1—*Time:* APPROXIMATELY 15 MINUTES

The two participants tape-record a 3-minute discussion of a topic on which they have differing views. Before the listener may voice his or her views, both the ideas and feelings of the speaker must be reported by the listener (feedback) and accepted by the speaker as accurately expressing his or her ideas and feelings.

If the listener's feedback describes the speaker's meaning correctly, it is assumed that the listener heard and understood the speaker. If the listener's description is unacceptable to the speaker, either the listener placed obstacles in the way of understanding or the speaker was not clear. By this process of listening, reporting, and speaking, both the listener and the speaker are given opportunities to clarify their thinking, to examine their prejudices (obstacles to understanding), and to concentrate on what is being said rather than on the reply to be made.

After the tape of the discussion is played back, all five group members discuss the level and adequacy of communication.

Part 2—*Time:* APPROXIMATELY 15 MINUTES

The procedure may be repeated to determine the degree of improvement achieved in tuning in.

the level of communication effectiveness but also the manner in which new experiences will be accepted by the client.

☐ Interviewers will avoid the dim-sightedness of prejudices that tune them out of the client's wavelength. It is not easy to eliminate prejudices, but with practice interviewers can screen them out for the duration of the interview.

☐ Interviewers will recognize that warped communication often results from words and behavior that are beyond the client's background and experiences. On the other hand, when the client's world is unfamiliar, the interviewer will not make a phony attempt to speak the lingo of the client. Instead the interviewer will converse with (not to, about, at, or above) the client. The client is the only one who can convey whether the interviewer has tuned in to the client's wavelength.

The implication of these changes is that tuning in is the helper's obligation. Exercise 4-6 focuses on increasing awareness of the meaning of communication between two persons.

The notion that diversified experiences favorably affect the helper's openness to differences suggests to some individuals that human service workers are less competent, even incompetent, unless they have been junkies, alcoholics, mentally ill, or physically disabled. Extending this argument further leads to the notion that unless the helpers are mentally retarded, they cannot capably work with retarded persons. These convictions deny the value of empathy. Empathy supplies the vicarious experience that bolsters the helper's observations, experiences, and communication. The helper observes "as if" he or she were the client and experiences "as if" he or she were the client. These "as if" conditions enrich and expand the helper's experiences so that the report that is fed back to client or at a staffing about the client more consistently reflects the client's view of the world. The helper vicariously "walks in the client's shoes and tries on the client's point of view," thus to some extent experiencing the client's feelings.

Empathic helpers record and store information that serves the client's needs for improvement, not primarily statistical data. Example 4-1 relates the difficulties experienced by two people because of the negative attitudes, misperceptions, and prejudices reflected in their records.

Example 4-1
THE TILLYERS ARE MARRIED

About 40 years ago Warren Tillyer, at the age of 9, became a resident of Forest Haven, a District of Columbia institution for the mentally retarded. Tillyer, who had a speech impediment, became a victim of the court's tendency to institutionalize children of parents on the verge of separation because of continuing marital problems. These children were earmarked for institutionalization if they did not communicate capably and if they demonstrated any evidence of slow learning ability, no matter what the causative factors might be. Ten years later, in 1949, Viola Smith also became a Forest Haven resident when she was 28 years of age. The reasons for her institutionalization are unclear. Her records note that she was a vagrant when admitted and tested in the moderately mentally retarded range.

Warren's records labeled him as mildly retarded with notations that he was an apprehensive child and a repeated runaway. What the records did not indicate was Warren's determination to work and live independently in the community unencumbered by an institutional setting. Although he returned to Forest Haven periodically, his recurrent departures were his demands for freedom. In 1961 Warren settled down to learn vocational skills that would prepare him for a steadier income and eventual self-support. All went well until 1965, when an accident resulted in crushed and then amputated toes. He met Viola Smith, who gently and kindly assisted him in his wavering maneuvers on his crutches and comforted him during his recuperation. Their attraction to one another and mutual dependence grew and sharpened their resolution to break down the restrictions blocking their marriage.

In 1978 Warren Tillyer was discharged from the supervision of Forest Haven. This fact, plus his prior 10 years of living independently in the community as well as his government custodial job, reassured the institution that Warren Tillyer and Viola Smith would care for one another. The Tillyers are married and live in the community. Viola Smith, who is now 59 years old, is being trained for eventual job placement either in mailing or housekeeping. They travel to work by bus and maintain themselves, their home, and their budget. Help is available from Forest Haven if they should require it.

The path to this liberation has not been easy. The curbs that inhibited their rights are numerous, partially because their records supplied data and programs based on the prevailing ideology about mental retardation of several decades earlier—unsupportable assumptions about the capacity (or rather lack of capacity) of mentally retarded persons to take responsibility for themselves. Three empathic people, in particular, a residential director, a unit chief, and a social worker, took the initiative to pave the way for this couple's eventual marriage.

Modified from Mann, J.: Society catches up with the Tillyers, Washington Post, pp. B1 and B3, Dec. 24, 1980.

This tale of the Tillyers is repeated many times with other mentally retarded people. The 1980 film *Best Boy* relates the plight of Philly, whose independent life away from his parents begins at the age of 52 when the efforts of his cousin spur him to move into a group home and to become part of a training program. There are other incidents of human service workers who foster behavioral change and an improved quality of life. This positive helping is marked by *caring about* rather than *caring for* and is interlaced with the interpersonal skills of communication.

These remarks about vicarious experiences do not discount the probability of enriched practical knowledge by helpers who have experienced difficulties and therapeutic and/or rehabilitative measures similar to those of their clients. The salient point is that experience alone does not develop the requisite skills for the human service worker. In fact, background and experience barriers can be decreased if blocked communication is avoided.

Blocked communication

Earlier in this book the "great philosopher" (?) Humpty Dumpty was quoted as saying that words meant just what he chose them to mean. Mr. Dumpty sacrifices communication to his own glorified choice of meaning. He may be the master of the word, but he is not equal to the task of con-

veying his meanings. Yet Mr. Dumpty is a symbol representing the kind of communication that is prevalent in the discussions of most people. He reflects the self-centered (narcissistic) communication that frequently occurs in interpersonal discussions. All too often speech conceals rather than communicates.

Fast and Fast (1980) propose another dimension of the Humpty-Dumpty syndrome. These authors describe the superlanguage characteristics exemplified in Humpty Dumpty's communication. Distinctions emerge from the meaning behind words—the metacommunication. The Fasts posit the semantic impact of nonverbal cues that are subtly associated with words, namely resonance, pitch, stress, melody, dialect, accent, and emotional overlay. "So, it's not always *what* you say that counts, but the *way* you say it" (Krucoff, 1981c). Listening, reading, or looking that concentrates only on the literal or surface presentations omits a wealth of cues. Speaking, writing, or acting that disregards the underlying feelings or thoughts may appear ambiguous and confusing to the receiver of the report who is alert to the tones and clues of concealment. Even a report couched in specialists' jargon may be a vehicle expressing power, sending signals that encourage feelings of inadequacy in the recipient. Effective reception and transmission of unblocked communication are central conditions for proficient reporting. The reporting process therefore should begin with considerations of the "what," "how," "where," and "why" of communication.

The "what" of communication. Since it is through communication that people relate to one another, the ability to communicate adequately is particularly important for human service workers. By both verbal expressions and nonverbal gestures plus grunts, ahs, ughs, hmmmms, and pauses, the helpers deliver messages (reports) to the listeners, readers, and lookers and receive return messages from these sources. How clearly helpers send and receive messages depends on their appreciation of their own and the clients' background and experiences. The differences that do exist need to be recognized rather than swept under the cover of "I didn't even notice that. . . ." Connected to this recognition must be acceptance of the message receiver's *right* to be different, *to be themselves,* and to appraise the message in terms of their own value system.

When helpers accurately perceive and honestly accept other persons, communication becomes easier. This feeling that each person is worthy motivates each one to speak *with,* not *to* or *at,* the other person, and to report for the clarification of issues, not solely for self-gratification. For the helper this means developing the skills of the "what" of communication.

The "what" of communication obliges the helper to recognize where the audience for a report is intellectually, verbally, and philosophically. Simple feedback strengthens communication. The vigor of this simplicity comes from its directness and its freedom from double meanings.

Simplicity is not that simple, however. What's simple for one person may be overly simple for another. Example 4-2 shows two contrasting views of communication that point up different approaches to getting a message across.

Example 4-2
TRANSLATING THE COMPLICATED MESSAGE

Complicated message	Translation
Her esophageal contractions emitted decelerating auditory responses as a 5-minute schedule of negative reinforcement was presented.	She began to slowly stop talking when Tom called out "shut up" every 5 minutes.
Smart Sam pools the bread and runs out to score some barbs. He brings back and shot up five Mexican Reds. Sam got offed.	Smart Sam collects the money and runs out to purchase some barbiturates. He brings back and injects a mixture of 20 mg secobarbital and 10 mg strychnine. Sam dies.

Effective communication demands an atmosphere of trust and respect in which the meaning of both verbal and nonverbal symbols is familiar to the participants. Interviewers are responsible for the kind of communication established. They must choose words that express their meaning to the client and that are radared into the economic class, education, ethnic background, age, geographical region, and other factors of importance to a particular client.

Example 4-3 presents two types of communication. One passage is a humorous report in obsolete language; the other passage is the same message translated into words of contemporary usage.

Example 4-3
TRANSLATING THE OBSOLETE MESSAGE

Obsolete message*	Contemporary message
Cynthia fadoodly misglazed Hal's lovedrury. Hal was really a magsman and a hufty-tufty. If only she had not fallen for the color of his wink-a-peeps and his lip-clap, she might not have become so trunchy and venenated him when he left her.	Cynthia foolishly misinterpreted Hal's token of love. Hal was really a swindler and a braggart. If only she had not fallen for the color of his eyes and his kissing, she might not have become so very angry and poisoned him when he left her.

*Words and meanings from Sperling, S.K.: Poplollies and bellibones: a celebration of lost words, New York, 1977, Clarkson N. Potter, Inc.

The words in the obsolete message are centuries old and have been lost to the twentieth-century language. This ancient message makes an interesting point—sometimes communication becomes jargon because of culture-bound language that is too complex, confusing, or dated, and therefore misleading. The words that seem humorous in today's usage dramatize the impact of language in communication. Benjamin Lee Whorf once said, "The limits of my language are the limits of my thoughts" (Allen, 1980). This statement can be expanded: the limits of one's thought become a hindrance to the fulfillment of the helping relationship.

There is one important caution. When helpers adjust *what* they say in accordance with the characteristics of their clients, they must avoid the phoniness of trying to talk in the client's vernacular if this way of speaking is not comfortable for them. Helpers must find the middle ground in which certain words familiar to the client may be interjected to show that the client's language is accepted and understood. In addition to speaking in the client's words the helpers must understand the meaning of their client's facial expressions, tone of voice, posture, and gestures. What are even more important are the helpers' skill and genuineness in managing positive feedback of nonverbal cues for the client's comfort and trust. The same caveat about language use in speaking is applied to the writing of a report. A report can be a mass of double-talk, saying very little yet primed to impress, or it can punctuate the client's needs and procedures for psychosocial changes. The development of effective communication in reporting is not happenstance; it takes a great deal of practice. Simultaneously with the "what" of speaking or writing, the "how" must be considered.

The "how" of communication. "How" refers to the tool, the agent, the means used to communicate, as well as to the general atmosphere surrounding the helping event and the report. Consequently, "how" acknowledges the skills related to listening and responding, the attributes of recording and reporting, and the content and common problems of reports.

Listening and responding competently charge interviewers to accomplish the following:

☐ Maintain the richness of closeness while respecting the client's boundaries of privacy and helping the client eradicate or at least diminish the stigma, shame, and guilt that have erected barriers of secrecy and shut off communication and satisfactory interactions

☐ Maintain a minimal level of interruptions of the client's flow of conversation

☐ Hear what the client says and not speak the client's answers

☐ Avoid loaded questions that maneuver the client into the interviewer's thought patterns

☐ Refrain from negative statements such as "I don't suppose you thought about . . . ?" "You didn't . . ." and "Sorry about that"

☐ Pace the speed and rhythm of their communication so that it is not too slow, too fast, too much, or too little

In addition to these six points about verbal content, interviewers must be alert to their own nonverbal cues. Preoccupied with their own problems, interviewers may discourage the client's spontaneous discussion. Body-shifting, clock-watching, sighing interviewers are playing a game in which the client is an intruder. Such interviewers must solve their own problems first.

Recording and reporting have a wide variety of channels of communication from the pen or the pencil to the most complex computer. The keen observer and meticulous recorder rigorously seeks data as part of the entry steps in the preparation of reports. Effective reports are based on sufficient and accurate data and have the following characteristics (Wright, 1980):

☐ Answer questions previously posed by the prospective reader

☐ Contain verifiable information

☐ Have well-organized facts that lend themselves to generalizations, deductions, or implications for the present as well as the future

☐ Are in a brief, concise writing style that avoids wordiness

☐ Convey the message with simple, action-oriented (descriptive) words rather than polysyllabic jawbreakers and passive, indirect words, for instance:

Direct, active, brief statement	Ornate, complex, ostentatious statement
On her daily walks to the small waterfall, she cupped her hands to catch the dripping water.	On her quotidian peregrinations to the miniature cascade of surging water, her hands were formed into scyphi shapes so that they might become inundated by the interminably drizzling moisture.

☐ Use concrete language, descriptive details, prepositional phrases, and connective devices to contribute to transitions between thoughts and paragraphs

☐ Intersperse some long sentences with the more frequent short sentences to add variety and thus make the report more readable, more interesting, and less boring

The content of the report often is determined by certain prescribed requirements. However, the following general statements describe the most prevalent contents:

☐ Beginning: *identifying information* such as the date the report was written, the period covered, the report writer's full name, and the client's full name, case (or number or other code as required), address, telephone number, and birthdate

☐ Body: *summary material,* including a composite picture of the client, identification of goals and objectives, and time-frame and alternatives for consideration; *recommendations* that are precise, constructive, and realistic in terms of economy, personnel, and productivity

Report writing is a skill that often is neglected in human service education and training courses. It is not surprising therefore that several typical problems occur.

Common problems of reports are described by Wright (1980), who expresses concern for the depreciation in the report's usefulness because of these shortcomings. The following list was adapted from Wright's discussion:

☐ Inadequacies in data presented (Report neglects to answer questions or to provide information needed by prospective readers; omits essential information gathered, leading to insufficient content; or disregards constructive and realistic negative opinions and information.)

☐ Excessive inclusion of data (Report provides more material than is useful or repeats information previously presented.)

☐ Confusion in data presented (Conflicting material is included unwittingly or without explanation of reason for inclusion.)

☐ Incomplete interpretation and summary (Interpretation of observations and other findings or other aspects of summary content are omitted.)

☐ Unsupported, insufficient, or omitted recommendations (Report makes suggestions that are not documented by data or clarified

as to rationale, offers unrealistic plans, or omits consideration of alternatives.)

The "where" of communication. The deficiencies just discussed are intensified if the "where" of the report is not clarified. "Where" directs attention to the internal (within office or agency) and external (outside of office or agency) distribution of the report. The report's intended destination and readers affect its content as well as its length and format. Example 4-4 describes a reporting procedure in Montgomery County, Md.

Example 4-4
REPORTING PROCEDURES FOR GUARDIANSHIP RECOMMENDATIONS

In Montgomery County, Md., a social worker is assigned to prospective clients for public guardianship, and this worker is responsible for compiling information for a report to be distributed to the members of the Disabled Person's Review Board (a legislatively authorized board that reviews the guardianship needs of disabled and elderly adults). The report contains specific psychosocial and physical data that characterize the client's capacity for self-care, level of judgmental ability, and potential for independent functioning. These reported observations serve as evidence to support or refute the need for guardianship of the person and/or of the person's finances and other property. The board members read, discuss, and question the contents of the social worker's report at a hearing and then write brief recommendations that will be presented to the judge before whom the semiannual review of guardianship status is conducted. The judge's decision is based on the social worker's report and the board's recommendations.

At each stage of this process there are different kinds of reports, depending on where the report is sent. In the agency that originates the social worker's report, a constellation of subreports are gathered from persons involved with the client such as the physician in charge, the neurologist, the psychiatrist, the psychologist, and the social worker. Comments from the person being studied as well as significant others are incorporated in the report.

Each respondent in this fact-gathering process articulates the content, length, and objectives for the report according to his or her discipline and in consideration of where the report is to be distributed. Blocked communication might emerge at any of the sources of reports.

The communication system bogs down when any professional or paraprofessional delays his or her subreport and whenever one of the reports demonstrates any of the common problems listed previously. Often the most serious error in reporting is "shooting from the lip," using too many and too complex explanations. Possible determinants for this problem may be lack of esteem for oneself or for the client, paucity of information, or limited understanding of the "why" of the report. Antagonism toward the bother and time involved also can interfere with the report writing.

The "why" of communication. The "why" of communication attends to the reason for the communication—the purpose of the report. This "why" is the rationale that precedes the report writing and becomes the mainspring that spurs on the entire recording system.

Reports integrate information in accordance with distinguishable functions. Private practice professional human service workers and public and private agencies vary in their utilization and forms for reports. The following list, derived in part from Corbitt (1978), Turner (1978), and Wright (1980), exemplifies some of the many types of reports.

Intake report
Medical examination report
Psychiatric report
Psychological test report
SOAP chart report (see Chapter 3)
POR chart report (see Chapter 3)
Written behavioral observations report
Sequential videotape views of evolving development of helper-client transactions
Vocational skills report
Work evaluation report
Training report
Placement report
Progress report
Status report
Counseling/psychotherapy report
Incident report
Termination report
After-care report (Follow-along report: immediately on discharge from hospital, or other institution; frequency depends on client's status. Follow-up report: spaced at wider intervals than follow-along reports; usually briefer and characterized by less supervision.)

Do helpers who have been alerted to the "what," "how," "where," and "why" of communication automatically become perfect report writers? This transformation is desirable but not readily attainable. Other factors related to communication interfere with suitable interpersonal relationships and penetrate the texture of the report.

Patterns of communication and interpersonal relationships

Even the most objective report writer is not a recorder of untarnished facts, but to a lesser or greater degree an interpreter of facts. A kaleidoscope of events and stimulations potentially can destroy recording and eventually reporting. Some of these concerns have been discussed in the previous chapters. In this section the concentration is again focused on communication, particularly with respect to the impact of patterns of interpersonal relationship on the effectiveness of communication and eventually on the thoroughness of reporting.

The two end points of the communication chain are zero communication and messages—delivered, accepted, and understood. Zero communication occurs when one or both individuals do not listen and do not understand. The meaning is lost. The message is cluttered and confused. Such zero communication is more likely to result in an *action-reaction* communication style rather than *interaction* or *transaction*. These three styles present varying degrees of relationship between the message sender and the message receiver.

Action-reaction. The least degree of communication relationship is represented by the action-reaction interview. In an action-reaction interview one individual acts on another—asks a question, for example. A reaction in the form of an answer is not necessarily desired, expected, or even awaited. A nonrelationship exists.

Many times during the day the question "How're you doin'?" is flung through the emptiness between people. Sometimes an answer is flung back; "fine," "OK," or perhaps just a mumble, smile, or silence is the answer. An empty question is met by an empty response. No one really cares; they are just creatures of habit performing a social duty.

Communication is not always an easy task. It requires active listening, acceptance of but not necessarily agreement with another person's viewpoint, and empathic responding. Action-reaction contains a scant measure of these characteristics. It is most similar to the soliloquy, monologue, or the duologue. Exercise 4-7 explores this type of communication.

Interaction. As communication leads to more interpersonal involvement, toward more sharing of ideas and feelings, the form becomes an *interaction*. Interaction allows for more regard of people as people rather than as things. This kind of interview appreciates the possible effect of each person in the interpersonal situation. Interaction prompts back-and-forth, two-directional meshing of messages sent and responses returned.

The interaction interview is more than patch yap, since there is a greater degree of involvement of the people conversing. More listening effort and more responsiveness are required. A duelogue is an example of an interaction, since the auger of the communication requires that each person work at discovering words that efficiently prod the other person into losing the word battle. A "power" fight with words usually results in a draw. Even if one person seems to win, nothing constructive comes out of the duelogue—no growth in understanding. Interactive communication need not be a duelogue; it can border on a dialogue during which the people are seeking to move toward a solution or toward a more accurate view of the meaning of the communication. Rather than polite conversation and the mechanical responses of the action-reaction interview, the interaction interview follows a different

---

Exercise 4-7
PATCH YAP? *(should be done in a group)*

Patch yap is a Citizens' Band (CB) radio term that refers to polite conversation. Seldom does polite conversation reach any depth of interpersonal involvement, since its primary goal is the maintenance of a tight hold on what is said in order not to offend or to expose oneself to social difficulties. Patch yap, therefore, is an example of action-reaction communication.

Part 1—*Time:* APPROXIMATELY 5 MINUTES

Two "good buddies" (volunteers) seat themselves so that they face one another, separated so that they are not too close yet can hear one another speak (about one chair apart). The rest of the group members seat themselves in a semicircle so that they can see and hear the good buddies.

The setting is a large truck. One of the good buddies "breaks" (begins the conversation). A microphone from a cassette tape recorder should be used for the conversations. The microphone should move from one conversationalist to the other so that the entire patch yap is recorded. After a 2-minute patch yap, the two good buddies "go break" (make contact with another person) in the larger group. They continue their patch yap for 2 more minutes, taking turns on the mike. (More participants may be added to the patch yap.) The other group members write down the verbal and nonverbal cues they observe.

Part 2—*Time:* APPROXIMATELY 20 MINUTES

The group members listen to the recordings and add to their observational notes (5 minutes). A general discussion (10 minutes) follows, focusing on what verbal and nonverbal cues support the conclusion that the communication form was action-reaction.

pattern. Example 4-5 diagrams the difference between action-reaction communication and interaction.

Example 4-5
ACTION-REACTION VERSUS INTERACTION

Action-reaction communication would be drawn as follows:

Marta ——————→ Jill
"Like your hair."

Marta ←—————— Jill
"Thanks—had it blow-dried."

Marta ——————→ Jill
"See you later."

The interaction would be drawn as follows:

Marta ←——————→ Jill

1. "Like your hair."	1. "Thanks—had it blow-dried."
2. "It does look as if you take good care of it."	2. "Yes, I wash it every day."
3. "Really, how do you find the time?"	3. "Get up a little earlier."
4. "Hmmm, see you later."	4. Jill does not reply, just walks away. (Did she hear? Did she listen?)

Psychodynamic forces. Although the interaction type of interview is a step ahead of the action-reaction interview, one ingredient for an effective interview is still lacking. This ingredient stems from the ever-changing psychodynamic (interpersonal) forces in the interview that may make the interview a hotbed of emotions.

Psychodynamic forces involve ideas, impulses, and emotions. These forces develop, influence, and change each participant in the interview. Psychodynamic forces push or pull the client and the interviewer because they are both humans with particular ways of viewing the world and of viewing one another (frames of reference).

Measuring interactions. If these psychodynamic forces are disregarded, one way to determine the proficiency of the interviewer is to measure the frequency of verbal and gestural interactions in a specified time. By counting the number of times the interviewer speaks and/or the number of words spoken as well as the number of interruptions, the degree of client-initiated and interviewer-initiated verbal behavior may be determined. The same numerical determination may be conducted for gestural or other nonverbal responses of the interviewer.

Fewer verbal and nonverbal expressions by the client indicate less client participation and probably greater interviewer interference. However, the essential elements that are glossed over by this counting method may be those which would decide the outcome of the interview. Example 4-6 provides some forceful concerns that may influence the dynamics of the interview.

Example 4-6
THE INTERACTION INTERVIEW: SOME CONCERNS

The interviewer, Mr. N., has been requested to speak to Marty, a 12-year-old boy with a mental age of 6. Marty's housemother reported that Marty is frightened by something. Marty's record reveals that he is able to speak, though not too clearly, and that until now he has been able to take care of his toileting and feeding needs.

MR. N.: *(As Marty enters the room.)* Hello, Marty, remember me? I'm Mr. N.

MARTY: *(Mumbles something while keeping his head down.)*

MR. N.: Say, Marty, here's a chair for you. I'll put the chair right here so we can see each other. *(Mr. N. moves his chair to face Marty.)*

MARTY: *(Goes over to the chair and leans against it.)*

MR. N.: Marty, I have a candy someplace in my drawer. *(Searches in desk drawer and, finding the candy, holds it out toward Marty.)*

Marty does not move toward the candy. Without a word Mr. N. takes Marty's hand and walks with him to the housemother, who is waiting outside the office. Mr. N. shrugs his shoulders and puts his hand out, palm upward, in a gesture the housemother interprets as frustration.

Many questions arise when this interview is examined:

- ☐ How does Mr. N. feel about the mentally retarded individual?
- ☐ How does he feel about Marty in particular?
- ☐ Was everything done to make the atmosphere of the interview comforting and secure for Marty?

□ If the verbal and nonverbal expressions of the interviewer were counted, would an adequate evaluation of the effectiveness of the interview be obtained?

□ Are there other facets of the interview that should be scrutinized?

Blocked communication and insensitivity to Marty interfered with a favorable interview atmosphere. Offering (bribing?) Marty candy was not enough. Politely introducing himself to Marty was not enough. Neither of these attempts takes into account the covert (hidden) contents of the interview situation.

Even though Mr. N. went through the motions of trying to relate to Marty, he failed. He may have failed because he was not really sufficiently interested in Marty as a person, or his failure may have been due to his preconceived notions of what might happen during the interview. His failure may have partially resulted from the quick acceptance of failure—giving up too soon before Marty had a chance to respond.

Separation of interactors. It is even more important to realize that interviewing as an interaction implies that there are two separate and independently existing persons who may be sharing the same moment in space but not the same world. In other words, if the interactors of the interview are not viewed separately, empathy is missing.

Transaction. The greater degree of involvement occurs in the *transaction* form of communication. The message transmittal becomes coaction with a mutuality of communication—a "working together" to be understood. A dialogue results during which both individuals are actively listening and appropriately responding. Dialogue does not signify agreement. When two or more persons are conducting a dialogue, they are examining the issues and not directing their barbs against each other.

Constancy of change in social system. The interview as a transaction may be drawn as a circle to symbolize the constancy of change that continues throughout the interview. A circle also represents unity and the wholeness of the living processes in the interview. These living processes, feeling and behaving, become an interpersonal unity—a social system in which the interviewer and the client establish rules, games, barriers, or openness in the drama that unfolds between and around them. The interview as a transaction becomes a laboratory in human relations; the client and the interviewer experience self-discovery and reciprocal personal growth.

Exercise 4-8 introduces the concept of transaction with a simplified communication procedure in which each partner attempts to describe an object

---

Exercise 4-8
CAN YOU ACCURATELY REPORT ON A NONVERBAL COMMUNICATION?

The large group divides into dyads. One person in each pair is the communicator, and the other person is the receiver. The communicator draws an object on a sheet of paper and conceals it. Without words the communicator describes the object and responds to nonverbal questions communicated by the receiver. The receiver draws (reports on) what he or she thinks the communicator described nonverbally. The communicator then verbally discusses the receiver's report (drawing), identifying inaccuracies and omissions. The partners switch roles and again follow the directions above. The entire procedure is then repeated. After both partners have role-played each part twice, the following questions are considered:

□ Was it easier the first or second time the drawings were described and drawn? How do you explain your reactions?

□ Would verbal explanations aid in the "report"? How do you account for the enrichment or nonenrichment of communication effectiveness when verbal communication is added?

□ What pattern of interpersonal relationship was established by the first partner? By the second partner? Explain your responses.

without words. This description is followed by feedback, a "report," about the object in the form of a drawing as the observer of the nonverbal communication perceives the message.

Whether or not the partners in Exercise 4-8 effectively communicate and the pattern of their interpersonal relationships can be clarified by the *social penetration theory* (Altman, 1973; Altman and Taylor, 1973). This theory proposes that advancement in proficiency of nonverbal communication is a gauge that can measure the level of intimacy in a dyad. The underlying assumption is that the transaction form of interpersonal association provides more intimate relationships—a transpersonal alliance. Therefore partners in such an affiliation develop greater sensitivity to one another's nonverbal expressions. Both the communicator's sending accuracy and the recipient's observational and reporting skills are affected by the increased level of interpersonal intimacy in this transaction form of communication.

Research has not been initiated to determine the significance of nonverbal cues in the intimacy of interpersonal transactions when compared with that in action-reaction and interaction modes of communication. A recent study that approaches this type of investigation was accomplished by Sabatelli, Buck, and Dreyer (1980). These researchers studied 17 couples dating on the average of 14 months. The findings did not support the idea that increased intimacy and length of relationship are significantly associated with increased efficiency in nonverbal communication. However, this research focused only on spontaneous emotional responses in a nonsocial situation without any impellents to make specific efforts toward intimacy or toward more intensive transactions. Clinical evidence supports the hypothesis that intimacy evolves in long-standing dyadic relationships and even in relationships in which larger numbers of people are involved. The parent's stare, glare, or smile is rapidly interpreted by the growing child; parents also are able to note their children's reactions from nonverbal cues. Marital or other partners who have known one another for many months, and particularly those who have known one another for years, convey messages of humor, sadness, and anger with a glance or gesture. Instructors manage their teaching approach on the basis of nonverbal cues from their students, and students manipulate their instructors with their spontaneous or contrived actions. The competent human service worker is alert to the revelations embedded in these nonverbal cues and appropriately encourages the collaborative efforts of transactions, forming a consociation with the client—a partnership of client and helper working toward a common goal.

Partners in interview pattern. This concept of transaction, of the interview as a social system, includes interaction but goes beyond it. The client is welcomed as an active partner in the interview. The client is accepted as a person with knowledge, attitudes, values, and potentials. The client is considered to be someone for whom the awakening and fulfillment of creative potentials are more important than passive adjustment.

The *here and now* becomes the center of the pattern evolving from the interview transaction. The client's present conflicts, orientation toward goals, and fulfillment or nonfulfillment of goals are not fitted into any theory in order to explain what is happening. Such a straitjacket makes a poor fit because of the uniqueness of each client. Uniqueness signifies that no two individuals are alike. There may be some general similarities among people from similar cultures, yet dissimilar life experiences and physical factors induce each person to see, hear, and feel a little, or even a great deal, differently from everyone else, even in the same culture. Thus uniqueness is linked to the transaction forces influencing the interview.

The transaction contract. When all these facets of give and take occur in the unique helping event with an outcome of mutual growth, the transaction assumes the status of a contract—orally expressed or more formally written. The transaction contract is mutually designed by client and interviewer, who make promises such as the following:

I, the interviewer, promise to listen to you, the client, with empathic understanding. I do accept you and will help you accept yourself with all of your strengths and weaknesses. I will share your public world and hope that by means of my genuineness and warmth I may encourage you to explore your private world. By means of this self-exploration, I hope that together we may find some choices for change from which you may choose.

I, the client, promise to work at self-understanding. I accept the responsibility for making choices from the findings of my self-exploration. I will try to accept you into my private world so that you may help me find the alternatives open to me to resolve my conflicts, clarify my goals, and find the pathways to achieve my goals.

Of course, both of these contracts are imaginary and need not be verbalized in the exact words stated. However, some understanding of roles, responsibilities, and individual rights needs to be made clear.

Transaction interview and transactional analysis. Transaction, a contract for caring, and transactional analysis, a theory of personality and social dynamics, are similar. They both refer to social behavior as an important consideration in developing self-understanding and active inclusion of the interviewer and client in the interview process as both agents (doers or initiators) and receivers of interview transactions.

The dissimilarity between transaction and transactional analysis stems primarily from the fact that transactional analysis is a theory of personality development and method for change that is applied in group and individual psychotherapy. Berne (1961) formulated the concept of three ego states (organized systems of feelings and behavior)—parent ego state, adult ego state, and child ego state.

These three states grow out of the individual's social experiences beginning at birth and continuing throughout life. Each ego state (behavioral style) represents certain influences and certain behavior.

The *parent ego state* arises from experiences with a parental figure and exhibits a judgmental and moralistic attitude of approval or disapproval (the critical parent). Concern about what others think and say is likely to result in compulsive behavior to avoid criticism. Thinking is likely to be other-directed or bound by "what will the neighbors think?" Voice and posture are likely to exhibit rigidity, control, and tension. Nurturing (providing definitions of acceptable behavior) and caution (wariness about danger) often are predominant characteristics.

The *adult ego state* arises from self-fulfillment in facing reality responsively and responsibly and exhibits a rational and data-processing approach to problem solving. The person in this ego state is inner-directed and not bound by conformity out of guilt but rather out of a careful choice of rights and responsibilities. The person is likely to exhibit relaxed body posture.

Early experiences in a dependent role give rise to the *child ego state*. This individual exhibits autistic thinking (self-centered) and expects to be on the receiving end of social relationships; this is revealed through behavior, voice, and speech. As an adult such a person may be irresponsible and impulsive. This person may perceive authority as parentlike and respond as to parents, either rebelliously (the rebellious child) or submissively (the adapted child). An unrealistic attitude toward problem solving usually occurs in the child ego state. This ego state also has the seeds for creativity and spontaneity that enrich life (the natural child). Freedom to express these characteristics of the natural child belongs to the innovators.

The CHILD is above all the feeling part of the personality. In it reside feelings of happiness, joy, sadness, depression, anxiety, anger, rebellion. When you feel these emotions, you are experiencing your CHILD ego state (Gerrard, Boniface, and Love, 1980).

Fig. 4-5 is a diagram of the transactional model of the three ego states.

These three ego states are present to some extent in all individuals. It is only when one of the unfulfilled states of the parent or the child contaminates or overcomes the adult potential that the individual may find transactional analysis essential. Transactional analysis then progressively analyzes how the ego states are organized and how they interact. Thus a *structural analysis* is made of the client's use of the parent, adult, and child ego states. The client becomes more aware of the methods of manipulation in social situations. These methods are demonstrated in the way the client and others communicate (verbally and nonverbally). Transactional analysis of the games clients play (Berne, 1964) to defend themselves or to attain their ends (self-gratification) reveals more about their transactions and points out the lengthy and complex operations or maneuvers the clients en-

gage in with others. The client outlines the life-plan script (psychological drama) on which he or she bases maneuvers. Script analysis helps the client understand the elaborate fantasies that may be interfering with a freer and more open existence. The script also reveals the private logic from which the client's behavior flows.

Transactional analysis clarifies the interplay among people in daily living as well as in the interview situation. The changing spectrum of relationships, the kaleidoscope of changing patterns in the interview transaction, may be partially explained by the degree of dominance (parent), dependence (child), or empathic understanding and

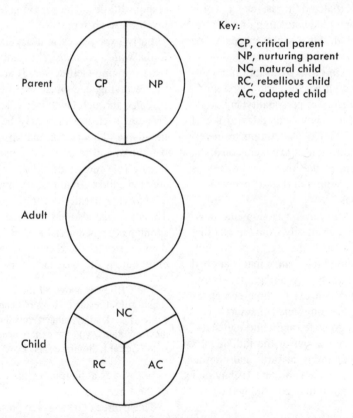

Fig. 4-5. Transactional model of ego states. (Modified from Gerrard, B.A., Boniface, W.J., and Love, B.H.: Interpersonal skills for health professionals, 1980, p. 46. Reprinted with permission of Reston Publishing Co., a Prentice-Hall Co., 11480 Sunset Hills Road, Reston, Va., 22090.)

genuineness (adult) expressed by the client and the interviewer.

Games may be played in the interview to cover up certain anxieties as well as to open or to conceal needs, requests, or demands of the client or the interviewer. Games also reflect the effect of self-fulfilling prophecies discussed earlier in this chapter.

Since the interview is a "mini" social event, it cannot be likened to a color snapshot of a frozen moment. The only constancy in a social event is change. Change is always occurring; therefore change can be depended on to be constant. This is a significant idea, for it is this idea of change that provides a positive, forward-looking approach to interviewing and, in fact, to all interpersonal relationships.

A conviction that what *is* will continue in the same fashion makes for the static view of behavior expressed in Examples 4-7 and 4-8. In both examples there is evidence of bias, self-fulfilling prophecies, and interpersonal games of defense and gratification. Closer examination may also reveal

the attitudes conveyed by the parent, adult, and child ego states. Exercise 4-9 applies the concepts of ego states in a role-playing event.

Example 4-7
THE SWITCHBLADE: WEAPON OR STATUS SYMBOL?

Al and Johnny were talking as they climbed the steps to their classroom. Al removed his switchblade from his coat pocket and demonstrated the speed with which the button released the blade. Mary, walking nearby, heard the snap of the knife and, turning swiftly, saw the blade as it sprang out. Al and Johnny continued to talk and walk. Mary stopped, looked around, and pressed close to the railing.

The incident of the switchblade may be somewhat more obvious in intent and effect than that in Example 4-8. The bias of the critical parent ego state becomes less distinct when concealed by self-righteousness. Exercise 4-10 focuses on the difference between self-righteousness and empathy.

Exercise 4-9
THE SWITCHBLADE: WEAPON OR STATUS SYMBOL? *(should be done in a group)*

Part 1—*Time:* APPROXIMATELY 15 MINUTES

The group members read Example 4-7. Four individuals volunteer to role-play Al, Johnny, Mary, and the school counselor. They role-play an interview between the counselor and the three students to demonstrate three different ways of handling the situation from Mary's perception of the switchblade as a weapon of attack, from Johnny's perception of the switchblade as a symbol of a cool cat, and from Al's perception of the switchblade as a status symbol in his group.

Show in the interview the ways in which self-fulfilling prophecies might encourage different endings to each story as seen through the eyes of the three individuals.

Part 2—*Time:* 10 MINUTES

The group discusses the following questions:
□ What was the significance of the ego states in the approaches of Al (adultlike), Johnny (childlike), and Mary (parentlike)?
□ How did the differing perceptions, self-fulfilling prophecies, and prejudices influence the behavior of Al, Johnny, and Mary?
□ How might the interview help each of the individuals grow in understanding of one another?

Example 4-8
INTERVIEWER-CLIENT MISMATCHING

Mrs. T. is visiting one of her clients at home. Her client's son has been skipping school, and Mrs. T. has to discover the reasons for his truancy. Mrs. T. is not too pleased about visiting this client because of the dirty, run-down neighborhood. In fact, she wishes that someone else might have taken over this case. Of course, she is not prejudiced, but why has her supervisor assigned a white woman to deal with black clients? When she arrives at the drab and chipped door, she notices someone peeping from behind the torn curtain. Mrs. T. knocks on the door, carefully avoiding the rotting and splintered wood. "Not only dumb, deaf too," she thinks. As she raises her fist to bang at the door a third time, she hears someone shuffling. The door is suddenly pulled open, and a man in a dirty white shirt and baggy pants leans against the door. "Yeah, waddya wan'?" he slurs. Mrs. T. stares at the man and coldly asks, "Where is Mrs. M? I want to speak to her." She thinks to herself, "This drunken bum. What's he doing here?" After a few more attempts to fulfill her assignment, Mrs. T. says, "We'll just have to get the truant officer here." Then she swiftly walks to her car and drives away.

Later she describes the incident in her report to the supervisor, ending with the statement, "Uncooperative, unable to make contact. Man in the house. Welfare payments should be investigated."

The discussion of patterns of interpersonal relationships is clearly applicable to the interview situation and, in fact, to any social event. Its corresponding significance for reporting is not as apparent unless the ingredients of interpersonal relationships are considered in relation to the report. Two factors enter into the report as an interpersonal phenomenon: (1) the procedures that originate the data for the report and (2) the interpersonal stance of the reporter. The first item has been discussed in the preceding chapters on observation and recording; the second item is concerned with questions such as:

□ Are the helper's communication skills suitable for collecting, organizing, and writing the report?

□ Does the helper rebel against writing the report or against the persons for whom the report is requested (the rebellious child)? Is the helper apathetic or rigidly compliant, with the result that he or she writes an uninteresting, even insensitive report (the dependent child)?

□ Does the helper dogmatize the lecture (the critical parent) and lace the report with value judgments molded into the helper's value structure (the domineering parent)?

Exercise 4-10
HOW IS SELF-RIGHTEOUSNESS DISCLOSED? *(may be done alone or in a group)*

Time: APPROXIMATELY 25 MINUTES
Part 1

   Write an interview between yourself and a client with whose appearance, opinions, race, or religion you feel annoyed or uncomfortable. Show by three statements that you feel that your feelings are justified, that you are "right" feeling this way. Then revise the content of the interview to show that you are striving for empathic understanding rather than to judge and disapprove self-righteously.

Part 2

   Get into subgroups of four and discuss your interviews. Compare your interview statements with those of the other members of your group. Do you and the other members of your group agree that you have succeeded in changing the tone of your interviews? (Discuss for 12 minutes; 3 minutes for each member of your subgroup.)

□ Does the helper affirm and support the client, the content of the report, and the recipients of the report (the adult ego state), perhaps including some creative alternatives for problem solution (the natural child)?

□ Does the helper merely tolerate (the rejecting parent) or actually accept (the nurturing parent) the client and the readers of the report?

Pattern of tolerance and acceptance

Background roots and experiences affect the way individuals treat differences. Sometimes the pretense of nonbias works in the guise of tolerance. However, in the close emotional relationship of an interview the deception is frequently revealed.

People may think that to be tolerant is great. It makes them feel so good and liberal to tolerate that "other-race" family who just moved in on their block, that radical who is disenchanted with the political scene, or that person whose religious ways are peculiar.

Tolerating differences is not the same as accepting them. Accepting differences implies nonconditional respect. This differentiation between tolerance and acceptance is not just word maneuvering. The intent of these sentences is to bring awareness to the contrast between *tolerance,* which is judgmental, and *acceptance,* which is nonjudgmental; and furthermore to pinpoint the perceptual blur that injects indistinctness and/or concealed stigma into racial, ethnic, religious, political, and sexual differences (see Chapter 2).

Perceptual blur. Tolerance suggests that one individual indulges or permits another individual to maintain certain beliefs or behavior. Tolerant people ("we") see others ("they") as fleeting perceptual blurs. They perceive neither themselves nor others clearly or honestly. A tolerant person *endures* the peculiarities and differences of others.

In contrast to tolerance, acceptance embraces ideas and feelings that support the worthiness of each individual with no judgmental gradations of better or worse. This does not suggest that acceptance is passive or neutral. Acceptance does not necessarily express agreement or approval. Acceptance is a complex of attitudes that consist of a number of characteristics.

Tolerance as well as intolerance decreases the trusting component of a relationship and increases stress for both helper and client. Helpers must exert intensified control and deceit to conceal hidden feelings of client rejection. Their intolerance of real or imagined imperfection urges helpers to "see" these characteristics in the client more sharply. Slips of the tongue and other verbal and nonverbal cues such as brusqueness and brevity of discussions demonstrate their annoyance and anger and by osmosis become part of the client's reactions. Both tolerance and intolerance consume a great deal of unnecessary energy. Acceptance establishes an atmosphere of respect, affirmation, and endorsement of the client's worth. These characteristics are more likely to be demonstrated in the transaction relationship.

Acceptance. The term "acceptance" is considered from several perspectives in the succeeding discussion: as perceptive awareness, as attitude, and as technique. From every nuance discriminating acceptance from tolerance, intolerance, and nonacceptance, the essential distinctions emphasize positive regard, impartiality, and the uniqueness of the client. Rogers (1961) defines acceptance as follows:

By acceptance I mean a warm regard for him as a person of unconditional self-worth—of value no matter what his condition, his behavior or his feelings. It means a respect and liking for him as a separate person, a willingness for him to possess his own feelings in his own way. It means an acceptance and a regard for his attitudes of the moment, no matter how much they may contradict other attitudes he has held in the past.

Acceptance: what it is and is not. Acceptance is client-directed and includes positive regard, caring, noncritical kindness, genuine interest, empathy, and rapport. It upholds the credo of human equality—all people create egos that are equally worthy; and it depends on effective communication through understanding. Table 4-1 describes acceptance in greater detail.

Table 4-1. *Acceptance: what it is and is not*

What it is	What it is not
Respect (positive regard and caring)	
Clients' self-experience is *real* to them. No experience should be considered more or less worthy of positive regard.	Agreement
	Approval
Interviewer maintains attitude of warm goodwill (calmness and understanding) regardless of what clients talk about, even if it is not socially acceptable or to the interviewer's personal liking. (Respect or liking is expressed in spite of client's unlikable characteristics.)	Neutrality
	Cold detachment
	Idle and/or avid curiosity
	Thinking or feeling the way clients do or having same values
Clients are valued because of their aliveness ("They are") and their being ("They think and feel"). Clients are persons with dignity, not objects to be pulled apart for study.	Assessment of clients' values
Interviewer believes that there is validity in the distinctive values of dissimilar ethnic, religious, and socioeconomic backgrounds. (Each person has the right to feel, think, and value differently.)	
Client-directed	
Clients are encouraged to make their own choices and to determine their own life, providing they do not infringe on the lives and rights of others.	Changing clients in interviewer's image
Interviewer encourages clients to be their own source of self-evaluation while affirming clients' worth and potential to become fully functioning individuals who are open to experience.	Disregard of limitations of external reality
	Clients' submission to controlling interviewer
Noncritical kindness	
Because of assurance of complete confidentiality, clients feel safe in discussing any topic they choose. They feel free to relate experiences that they may be ashamed of or that frighten them as well as those of which they are proud and satisfied.	Avoidance of discussion of alternative behaviors for clients' consideration
	Judgmental
Clients feel accepted by interviewer while still feeling unacceptable to themselves.	Blaming person
	Releasing clients from responsibility for their acts
Interviewer expresses continuing willingness to help no matter what the behavior of the clients and no matter whether the interviewer approves or disapproves of clients' behavior.	Allotting all responsibility to clients for their acts
	Condemnation or punishment
	Hostility
	Rejection
Genuine interest	
Interviewer is concerned about meaning of each item of discussion to clients' welfare and comfort.	Evasiveness
	Distorted interpretations
Interviewer constantly tries to clarify his or her own understanding of clients and to communicate that understanding during the interview.	Disregard of appropriateness of clients' way of functioning
	Unrealistic appraisal of clients' capacity
Interviewer recognizes and takes pleasure in clients' achievements, expresses confidence in clients' ability to handle certain tasks or situations, and honestly appreciates clients' efforts.	Insensitivity to clients' conception of their abilities
Empathy and rapport	
Interviewer is able to participate in clients' expression of feelings and assures clients of naturalness of anger as well as of joy. Interviewer is able to see events through clients' eyes.	Sympathy (too much emotional involvement by interviewer)
	Feeling uncomfortable with clients' outburst
Clients feel trust in interviewer and therefore are able to ventilate (express) their feelings.	Fear of not being able to control clients' emotional expressions
	Oversolicitude
	Distrusting clients
	Attacking clients' opinions

Table 4-1. *Acceptance: what it is and is not—cont'd*

What it is	What it is not
Human equality (all people create egos that are equally worthy)	
Clients are co-workers on a common problem. Clients' opinions and feelings are worthy of consideration.	Interviewer's advice as primary direction for change
Interviewer conveys feeling of quiet friendliness as well as of strong desire to help clients.	Extreme cordiality and effusiveness
Effective communication through understanding	
Interviewer's comments are on the same wavelength as those of clients. Interviewer follows clients' line of thought.	Interviewer attends to his or her own line of thought because he or she knows the score
Interviewer attempts to anticipate events the way in which clients anticipate them. Interviewer communicates this understanding according to clients' way of thinking while still maintaining a professional overview of clients' problem.	Interviewer anticipates events according to his or her theoretical outlook
	Attempt to fit clients' behavior into a statistical pattern

Table 4-2. *Acceptance: how it is shown*

Nonverbal behavior	Verbal behavior
Facial expression	**Verbal following behavior***
Relaxed, not frowning, appropriately smiling	Appropriate choice of words and statements that follow client's comments as well as nonverbal cues
Eye contact	Avoids excessive interviewer talk time
Visual interaction not forced	Feedback to client of an undistorted communication of what client said
Looks at client but does not stare intensely and makes varied use of eye contact	**Free client verbal expression encouraged**
Body posture	No interruptions; reinforces client's verbal expressions by nonverbal signs such as smiles, nods, and body posture
Comfortable posture, relaxed movements, and "towardness" posture conveyed by slightly leaning forward or sitting forward on chair	**Language used according to client's level of understanding**
Gestures	Words used to aid understanding, not to impress; use of special words (colloquialisms) of client only if they are understood by interviewer
Loose and natural arm, hand, leg, and foot movements	**Congruence between verbal and nonverbal behavior**
Distance	What is said fits nonverbal expressions; interviewers look like they mean what they say
Comfortable distance face to face	

*Ivey and Simek-Downing (1980) describe verbal following behavior as one of the behavioral characteristics of attending, which is a crucial reinforcer encouraging the client to continue talking.

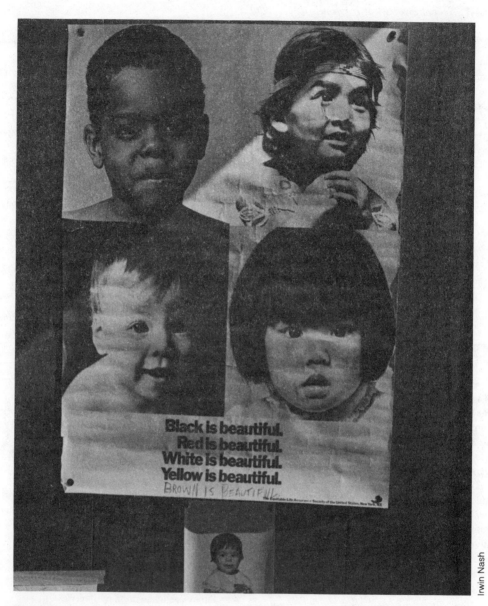

Fig. 4-6. Acceptance: all people are worthy of respect. (From Hernandez, C.A., Haug, M.J., and Wagner, N.N., editors: Chicanos: social and psychological perspectives, ed. 2, St. Louis, 1976, The C.V. Mosby Co.)

Acceptance: how it is shown. Nonverbal and verbal cues communicate acceptance. Facial expression, eye contact, body posture, gestures, and physical distance are nonverbal behaviors that can facilitate or deter the helping relationship. Suitable nonverbal and verbal cues stimulate and elaborate discussions. Table 4-2 lists and explains verbal and nonverbal behaviors as they relate to acceptance.

The words come easier than the acceptance itself. Many people can explain their concept of acceptance but falter when confronted with someone whose dress, ideas, or other attributes differ from their own (see Chapter 2). Walt Whitman chose fitting words to specify his ambivalence about himself and his reaction to other persons:

> I am of old and young, of the foolish as much as the wise,
> Regardless of others, ever regardful of others,
> Maternal as well as paternal, a child as well as a man . . . .
>
> Walt Whitman, *Song of Himself, Leaves of Grass*

These reactions of uncertainty of acceptance are not unusual, and they may interfere with the helping relationship if they are not recognized. Exercise 4-11 (p. 186) contrasts the supportive and negating potentials of acceptance and nonacceptance.

■   ■   ■

The discussion of reporting has taken many turns in the word-journey through this chapter. The issues are numerous and complex, revolving around communication styles, perceptual clarity, and appropriate interpersonal transactions. Yet, because ongoing reporting can have tremendous impact on problem solving and decision making in the client's treatment and rehabilitation, the subject matter is essential to the helping event. Reporting takes practice as well as the foundation of suitable attitudes, skills, and knowledge. Recognition of the import of feedback as reporting turns attention to those elements which enrich or deter effective feedback, such as background and experience barriers, patterns of interpersonal relationships, and all the fac-

ets of the helping relationship that become partners in the level of communication expertise. Mastery of questioning skills is one more prerequisite to proficient reporting.

CLARIFYING AND EXPANDING RECORDING AND REPORTING WITH QUESTIONS

Questions can open up or close down communication. Questions can add to the final clarity and accuracy of reporting or muddy the report with unnecessary tangential trivia. Questions can energize or deplete the comfort of the helping relationship. The "fool will ask more questions than the wisest can answer" (Jonathan Swift, *"Polite Conversation II"*), and "it isn't very intelligent to find an answer to questions which are unanswerable" (Bernard Le Bovier de Fontanelle, *La Pluralité des Mondes,* "Cinquieme Soir"). Questioning has been considered by philosophers, poets, theologicians, and many others for centuries. Aristotle (340 BC) wrote about begging the question, and others have agreed with and expounded on his statement. Still others have argued that questions are a noose, silly, momentous, and two-sided. The poet e. e. cummings (*Collected Poems,* Introduction, 1938) wrote, "Always the beautiful answer who asks a more beautiful question."

Questioning is indeed a crucial technique. However, it can disturb the flow of communication if the questions are excessive and not purposefully related to the overall goal of the helping event. In general, questions must be clear, brief, undogmatic, and without censure of the client.

Questioning and responding

The prime objective of the helping interview should be a movement toward trust and openness and away from anxiety and closed behavior. Getting into the center of the interview presupposes some degree of client-interviewer interdependence and mutual searching. To spur the client toward greater self-realization, the interviewer must watch for nonverbal cues and listen for verbal cues in addition to being aware of the sounds of silence.

The process of growth for both the client and the interviewer is further enriched by the interviewer's ability to formulate questions. Several considerations enter into the skillful use of questions.

General characteristics of effective questioning. Often it seems that the interviewer thinks that interview work consists of bombarding the client with questions. The interviewer who relies too much on questioning is in error; questioning is only one of many tools. The questioning tool becomes a weapon when the client is overwhelmed by the type, the frequency, or the procedure of questioning. The client is then likely to hide in a shelter of silence.

When questions are asked, they must be worded to correspond to the client's level of information. The client should understand what is being asked. The wide-awake interviewer knows that the question itself may be a subtle form of suggestion, permission, or challenge because of the way it is worded, by the tone of voice used, or by the particular words emphasized by the interviewer. For instance, the interviewer may encourage the client to do something: "Did you *ever* tell your teacher what you *really* think of him?" On the other hand, the interviewer may challenge the client: "Do you think another person would react as you did?" "Suppose you can't make it, what then?" "What if she doesn't care for you; what would you do?"

On the positive side, questions may be instruments to open the channels of communication be-cause they energize thought and expression of feeling, redirect the client into some new considerations, or link the client's comments together.

Productive and unproductive questions

Productive questions are the positive form for questioning. These questions create a scene for fertile communication and produce transactions that lead to abundant payoffs for the client, the helper, and the recipient of a report. In contrast, unproductive questions may tease forth some information yet yield limited and disputable responses, and they can be an intellectualized way to cover up emotions, an attempt to pick at the client, a syrupy approach, or woolgathering to avoid threat or self-exposure. Table 4-3 contrasts the characteristics of these two broadly categorized types of questions.

It is obvious that questions can go in many different directions; they can bring a client and interviewer to understanding or result in a confusion of sound. The productivity of questions can be bolstered by inquiries that encompass the "when" and "how" of questioning.

The "when" and "how" of questioning

The suitable timing and place in the helping discussion for questioning depend on the degree of details necessary to clarify the issues so that goals and solutions may be accomplished. The helper who is sufficiently empathic to the client's ability to cope with particular questions can judge the best occasion for questioning.

Exercise 4-11
DO YOU EFFECTIVELY EXPRESS ACCEPTANCE? *(may be done alone or in a group)*

Time: APPROXIMATELY 30 MINUTES

The large group divides into small groups of five participants. Each participant writes two replies in Fig. 4-7. In the first column write replies that indicate disregard for and lack of acceptance of the client. In the second column write replies that show recognition and acceptance of the client. After these responses are noted, they are discussed by the five group members, and a composite reply that is deemed "best" is integrated. Then the large group discusses the composite replies of the small groups.

Statement about client	Interviewer's nonacceptance	Interviewer's acceptance
Tim pushes the door open with his shoulder. In between the loud noises he makes while gum chewing, he says, "Yes, showed 'em, de noive of dem. Jus 'cause don' say dose woids. It's me hands . . . I kin do wid me hands . . . so los' me temper . . . gave 'em a finga . . . smacked 'im in da . . .		
Minna crosses her black-stock-inged legs and arranges her short skirt. Her tight-fitting tee-shirt reveals a well-rounded bosom and small waist. She moves her hand through her long blond hair and begins tapping her left finger on the long bell earring, "Address," she says softly, "changes with the night."		
May, a 14-year-old, comes into the office carrying the book *No One Here Gets Out Alive*. May had been picked up for selling drugs. Her parents say they cannot handle her at home anymore. She has been in the deten-tion home for girls for the past 2 weeks. She begins to speak as she enters the room. "Mixed-up place. All I know is don't want to stay here anymore. Not sure about anything."		
Stan sits down in the comfort-able chair upholstered in orange imitation leather. He looks around the office and notes how sparsely it is furnished. His hands are trembling and his body twitches as he moves around. "Listen, Doc, cut out talk-crap. I'm a fag. Nuthin' more to it. And that's what I want to be."		
Edna, a 19-year-old woman, was admitted 3 months ago for attempted suicide. A quick smile spreads over her face as she says, "Mr. T., last week was hellish. Looked around for a razor blade again. My mother brought my baby. Mom cried. Has no money for her-self. No money for the baby's milk. Too much."		

Fig. 4-7. Interviewer acceptance and nonacceptance.

Table 4-3. *Productive and unproductive questioning*

Productive questioning	Unproductive questioning
Energize thought What makes you think so? What is happening in your head right now? How do you explain his behavior? **Express feelings** What makes you feel this way? What is happening between us right now? **Redirect ideas** I wonder what makes you so concerned about how Kristen feels? Is it possible that you are thinking about something else, too? Is it possible that you talk about Paul to avoid talking about yourself? **Link comments** Client says, ''My mother constantly calls me dumb. I guess maybe I don't work hard enough. But the work is too hard for me.'' Interviewer answers, ''I hear something in what you are saying. I wonder, are you agreeing with your mother that you are dumb?''	**Head-trip** I have been observing Susannah very carefully. Have you noticed her sybaritic (self-indulgent) behavior? How would you explain her constant requests for affection and food? Do you have any comments to make? **Pick at client** Now, really, do you think you should have done that? Who gave you the authority to go ahead with that plan? Come now, that wasn't right, was it? What *is* the matter with you? Why do you always say that? Why don't you ever do what I say? **Syrupy** I am just here to help you find happiness. What I feel or think just doesn't count. What would you like me to do to help you? Yes, indeed, that's right. What would you like me to tell you [or do for you] next? **Woolgatherer** So . . . you have to share a room with your younger brother. Do you have color television in your home? Do you think that this chat can be supportive?

The "when" of questioning. *When* should questions be asked? Questions should be asked sparingly when they serve the following purposes:

- Interviewer or client clarification: "I'm sorry, I didn't understand. Would you repeat that?" "I'm spouting forth. What do you think about what I've just said?" "I wonder what you felt when Delores refused to go to your senior prom?" "Would you give me an example of what you meant by . . . ?"
- For exploration: "You mentioned that your father always made you feel unimportant. What do you mean?" "What further thoughts do you have about this . . . ?" "What are you feeling as we talk about this?"
- For additional information: "I think I got your message about Bud's reaction to his paralysis.

When did Bud have his last operation?" "What are the required subjects in the major to which you have transferred?"

- To hear better: "Sorry, I didn't hear that. What did you say?" "Did you say that . . . ?"
- Encourage client to talk: "You said something about Barbara a little while ago. Are you interested in talking about her some more now?" "Your comments about Sid are very interesting. Let's get down to some gut-level feelings. How do you feel about Sid?"

The "how" of questioning. *How* should questions be asked? Questions are asked as an invitation for the client to talk. They should be clearly stated in words that the client can understand. They should be as neutral as possible so that the words themselves have little influence on the nature of the answer. They should be open-ended more often than closed.

The varieties of questioning

Knowledge about the skillful application of a variety of questioning forms are as essential as knowledge about the previously described characteristics of questions and productive and unproductive questioning. Sometimes it is more reliable to assess the helper's level of proficiency by means of the "when" and "how" as well as the form of questions he or she uses rather than by the flow of conversation in the helping event. Focus on questions rather than answers can disclose the use of questions as a shield to conceal a lack of self-confidence, a negative attitude toward the client, or deficient skills in and knowledge of human services. Some helpers overuse questions or ask "top-of-the-head" questions that often are unrelated to the client's feelings and problems. Unsuitable questions introduce an aura of an inquisition, which precipitates the client's inquietude and elicits piddling details with few consequential particulars. Competency in questioning can be enriched with skill and knowledge of the various forms of questioning, some of which are explained in the following discussion.

Closed versus open questioning. "Do you want to learn about your problems?" Obviously this question can be answered with one of two answers, "yes" or "no," or perhaps a third answer, "not sure." This is a closed question. The client must select from a series of possible answers what best fits his or her wishes or feelings. Although the client has three options—"yes," "no," or "not sure"—these lead to a dead end. The question restricts the answer and is so narrowly focused that the client is not afforded leeway for self-discovery.

Rewording the question makes a difference: "Let's look at this mix-up together. How do you feel I might help you find out more about your problem?" The revised question allows the client fuller scope. Open questions invite the client to voice views and feelings. In this way the contact between client and interviewer is widened and deepened, since the client is included in the undertaking. Note the differences among the following:

When did you first notice you were getting depressed?	Tell me about your feelings . . . about your depression.
Do you think your grades will be higher or lower this semester?	How do you feel you are going to do this semester?
Do you feel your family is helping or hindering you with your decision?	Tell me about your family. How do they enter into your decision?

Closed questions readily display their factual, more focused purpose, whereas open questions leave more space for clients to structure their own answers as they see fit. The effective interviewer uses both kinds of questions, leaning a little more heavily on the open questions. Both kinds of questions have their advantages and disadvantages, depending on the objectives of the interviewer. Anxious clients may feel more comfortable beginning with a more defined (closed) question-and-answer format, which requires less effort and less involvement. As they begin to feel more accepted and worthy, they will be able to handle the looser, open question. On the other hand, reluctant clients may be less threatened with the open question, which provides freedom to move as they please.

The skilled interviewer knows how and when to use both open and closed questions. This helper is likely to start the interview with an open question such as "How have things been going with your roommate this past week?" The interviewer is careful to interject some structure in the form of closed questions with the rambling client who appears to be avoiding the issues. Yet, since listening to the client is the essential of the interview, the interviewer abstains from the comfort of frequent closed questions. Closed questions force the interviewer to concentrate on what to ask next rather than taking heed of what is happening with the client.

Closed and open questions are related to two

other types of questions—leading and responding questions.

Leading versus responding questioning. Closed questions are constructed to lead. Open questions follow the client's lead and thus respond to the client. In the first instance the interviewer functions as a guide for the client. The interviewer controls what happens during the interview, and because the helper remains in the center of things, he or she often suggests the client's answer. Frequently, leading questions become a cross-examination in which it is implied that the interviewer already knows the answer: "You loved your father, didn't you?" or "You're 34 years old now, aren't you?"

An interviewer may justify the use of leading questions with the assurance that he or she is well informed about the client's level of understanding. This may actually be a cover-up for the fact that the interviewer enjoys directing the client. Another reason the interviewer may offer is that the client is wandering from the topic too much or is getting bored. Once again, this may conceal the interviewer's discomfort or inability to get interested in the client's concerns.

At other times the leading question helps the client who is confused and vague to pin down a particular idea or feeling. In such a case it is similar in value to the closed question; that is, it should be used discreetly in times of need.

Contrary to leading, responding to the client impels the interviewer to speak in the client's terms and to follow the ideas and feelings the client communicates. Rather than the interviewer leading the questioning, responding demands that the questions place the client in the center. The interviewer whose philosophy is that the client has solutions sets about helping the client work out his or her problem.

Instead of saying to the client, "Tell me whether you are for or against amnesty for deserters from the Vietnam War," the interviewer says, "I'd like to know more about your thinking about amnesty." The helper encourages the client by one-word comments or well-timed pauses to talk a little more about what the client has just briefly mentioned.

The interviewer nods and by other body movements shows interest in what the client is saying. The following comments also indicate interest: "I see. Would you explain a little more what you are thinking about?" "Ummmmm-hmmmmm." "Tell me more about it." "Not sure I understand. Did you say . . . ?" "You said that you didn't like the way John answered. Suppose Suzie said the same thing?"

In essence, responding questions follow the client's leads; leading questions prompt the client to follow the interviewer's cues. Leading questions have much in common with answer-agree questions.

Answer-agree questioning. The answer-agree question is a form of leading question. The interviewer asks, "You didn't mean to do that, did you?" or "You were upset and lost control, didn't you?" The question includes the answer, and the interviewer expects the client to agree. The client may comply to maintain the goodwill and warmth of the interviewer and thus avoid the interviewer's displeasure and rejection.

A question that demands that the client go along with the interviewer is also a closed question. The client is boxed in when the interviewer says, "No one would rip-off unless he knew why, would he?" "It must be perfectly clear to you why your father lashed out at you as he did . . . after you did that. Isn't it?" "Surely you can understand that you should keep away from your old crowd. They'll drag you down again, won't they?" "Just because you're angry with me right now doesn't mean you have to leave right away. Do you?" "Come now, you know your mother loves you, don't you?" Often these questions require no more than a "yes" or "no" answer from the client, and they are likely to be stated in an impersonal way.

If these questions are opened up, they permit clients to give their answers, not the built-in answer of the interviewer. "What are your thoughts about what makes you rip-off?" "Let's talk about your father. After you . . . , what do you think he might have done?" "Have you considered what would happen if you returned to your old crowd?" "I feel that you are angry with me. It would help us both

if you stayed and we worked this out together."
"I see how you feel about your mother. Do you think perhaps that's the way she shows her love?"

Answer-agree questions have features similar to closed questions, to leading questions, and also to direct questions, which are discussed next.

Direct versus indirect questioning. There is a place for a direct question in the interview when the interviewer requires some information immediately or when the client is floundering or anxious and needs some additional interviewer support. On the other hand, the indirect question is preferable, since it puts the client in charge of the answer. Direct inquiries usually have a question mark at the end of the statement. Indirect inquiries explore without a question mark at the end. The following remarks contrast direct with indirect queries:

What do you think about . . . ?	You must have many thoughts about. . . .
How do you feel about . . . ?	I'd really like to hear your feelings about. . . .
It must be burdensome to attend college during the day and to work at night. How do you do it?	That takes some doing, working at night, college during the day. Tell me about how you manage it.
Does your stuttering bother you very much today?	I'm really interested in what's happening in your head today.

The concept underlying the unmarked question is a cooperative searching by interviewer and client. The direct question ("What procedures have you considered for changing her opinion of you?") may open more response doors for the client than the closed question ("Do you have any procedure for changing her opinion of you?") However, when the interviewer learns how to converse effortlessly without the hook, the question mark, he gets closer to a meaningful sharing with the client. Then the helper is also less likely to become involved in questions sprinkled with multiple ideas.

Exercise 4-12 differentiates between direct questioning and indirect questioning; the former is more likely to be leading and controlling.

Multiple-idea versus single-idea questioning. Questions may take in a large territory of ideas but should have only one reference point. Thus the interviewer should inquire, "How do you feel about your field work (practicum) experience?" rather than, "Do you like your field work placement and your supervisor?"

The difficulty with the multiple-idea question emerges from the client's inability to decide which question to answer first. Sometimes the client wants to answer only one part of the question and would be uncomfortable in replying to another aspect. Consequently, the client may not respond or may go off on a tangent that has nothing to do with the original question.

Exercise 4-12
HOW DO YOU ASK NONCONTROLLING QUESTIONS? *(may be done alone and discussed in a group)*

Time: APPROXIMATELY 30 MINUTES

To distinguish between leading (controlling) and nonleading (noncontrolling) questions, select a subject about which you wish to get some information. Decide on the information you want to get (objectives). Write five leading (controlling) questions that would get the information you want. Then ask someone to answer these questions. Write down the person's answers to these questions.

Use the same subject and objectives as before. Write five questions that are not leading (noncontrolling). Ask the same person the revised questions. Write the answers to the questions in the answerer's words.

What were the characteristics of your questions that made them leading (controlling)? What were the characteristics of your questions that made them nonleading (noncontrolling)? Discuss with your client how he or she felt about the two sets of questions.

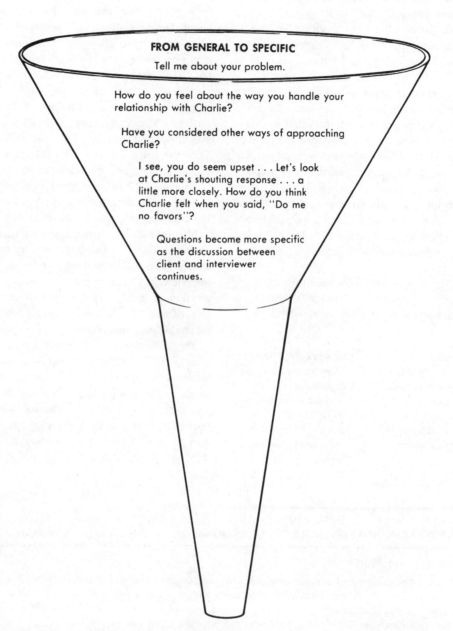

FROM GENERAL TO SPECIFIC

Tell me about your problem.

How do you feel about the way you handle your relationship with Charlie?

Have you considered other ways of approaching Charlie?

I see, you do seem upset . . . Let's look at Charlie's shouting response . . . a little more closely. How do you think Charlie felt when you said, "Do me no favors"?

Questions become more specific as the discussion between client and interviewer continues.

Fig. 4-8. Funnel questioning. (Modified from Kahn, R.L., and Cannell, C.F.: The dynamics of interviewing, New York, 1957, John Wiley & Sons, Inc.)

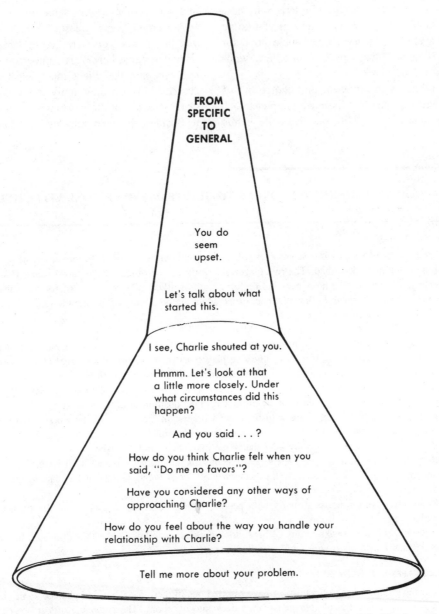

Fig. 4-9. Inverted funnel questioning. (Modified from Kahn, R.L., and Cannell, C.F.: The dynamics of interviewing, New York, 1957, John Wiley & Sons, Inc.)

Multiple-idea questions such as the following get too complicated for a reply: "Do you see interview behavior as an action-reaction, interaction, or a transaction?" "Do you believe that, if you do no harm to a client, you have done some good for him, or is there some aspect of interview withholding involved here?"

Even questions that present one choice out of two present some hitch. It is much simpler to answer two questions—"Do you like college this semester?" and "Do you like your professors this semester?"—than to reply to "Do you like college and your professors this semester?"

A seemingly easy question such as "When did you first notice you were getting tense, before or after you came here?" is cumbersome because it suggests that the client must select one of two choices and also must reply in terms of the time of tenseness, not the meaning or extensiveness of it. Besides, the client may answer "I don't know"

Exercise 4-13
WHAT DO YOU NEED TO KNOW IN ORDER TO QUESTION AND RESPOND EFFECTIVELY?
(should be done in a group)

Part 1—*Time:* 5 MINUTES

One member of the group is selected or volunteers to go out of the room. Before he or she leaves, the following situation is described. The role player has worked in an office for the past 4 years. His work is efficient, and he thinks that he is next in line for the job of office manager since the former manager has resigned. He plans to speak to the personnel office about the possibility of getting the job.

Part 2—*Time:* 5 MINUTES

After this explanation the role player goes out of the room to plan how he will handle the request for the job from the personnel officer. With the role player out of the room, a personnel officer is selected, and the group with the personnel officer plan how they will approach the situation when the role player asks for the office manager's job. Their plan should include one of the following problems that would prove unfavorable for the role player to be promoted to the position of office manager:
[1] Role player does not get along with the other workers. In fact, some of the workers have come to the personnel officer to complain about role player's brusqueness.
[2] Role player has a peculiar body odor that some individuals find offensive.
[3] Role player has been absent a great deal recently. Although he functions well when he is working and makes up for his absences, the personnel officer is wondering what has caused the frequent absences.
[4] Role player comes across strongly with people. He has been called a pompous ass by one of the employees.
[5] Role player rarely speaks to any of his fellow workers. A fellow worker has discussed him as "the quiet man" with his friends and has called him a "snob."

Part 3—*Time:* APPROXIMATELY 30 MINUTES

After the group and personnel officer have selected one of these problems and planned some questions and areas to examine, the role player is called back into the room. The personnel officer conducts a 5-minute interview, and the other participants keep a record on Fig. 4-10 of the frequency and type of questions. The group then discusses for 10 minutes the questions and responses of the role players and makes suggestions for improvement.

The interview, tallying of questions, and 10-minute discussion are repeated, with the additional consideration of improvements of the second interview over the first one.

rather than explore further because of inability to pinpoint the originating moment in terms of "before" or "after."

The intent of this discussion of questioning is to make the question the servant rather than the master of the client. The interviewer is charged with the responsibility to develop a more comfortable feeling about the interrelationship with the client using open, responding, answerable, indirect questions as often as possible.

Funnel versus inverted funnel questioning. Kahn and Cannell (1957) write of the difference between the "funnel" sequence and the "inverted funnel" sequence of questioning. The funnel sequence indicates that the interviewer asks questions from general areas to more specific points. In other words, beginning questions are less restricted, and as the interview goes on, questions become narrower and more informationally related to interview goals (Fig. 4-8, p. 192).

Several characteristics emerge from the questions listed in Fig. 4-8. The first question listed is an open, indirect remark that aims to bring to light the client's point of view ("Tell me about your problem"). The client has the chance to present the ideas and feelings that he considers most important. As the conversation progresses, the interviewer grasps the client's feelings and ideas and narrows the questions to the more specific issues that seem to be involved ("How do you think Charlie felt when you said, 'Do me no favors'?"). Gradually more specific issues and perhaps some closed questions may be used to help the client perceive his or her own behavior in relation to what is happening in the environment.

The opposite procedure is the inverted funnel sequence. In this approach questioning urges the client to think through subareas of the primary concern. The questions move from the specific to the general (Fig. 4-9, p. 193). The sequence from specific to general helps the client gather points that may be influential in the problem. Then the client is helped to tie them all together to reach some solution. The particular sequence that is best depends on the client's and the interviewer's learning styles (see Chapter 1) as well as the objectives of the interview. The more experiential the interview, the more likely that the preferred procedure will be the funnel approach. The more data-gathering the interview, the more likely it will proceed from specifics to generalities, the inverted funnel approach. In Exercise 4-13 the dependence of the

Items	Tally number of each
Number of open questions	
Number of closed questions	
Number of leading questions	
Number of responding questions	
Number of answer/agree questions	
Number of direct questions	
Number of indirect questions	
Number of multiple-idea questions	
Number of single-idea questions	
Approach primarily funnel sequence (check this or item below)	
Approach primarily inverted funnel sequence	

Fig. 4-10. Frequency and type of questions.

client's response on the interviewer's questioning and responding skills becomes apparent.

The question of "why"

Questioning serves many purposes. The interviewer's questions may lead to the discovery of solutions and to the linkage of events so that their meaning is clarified for both the client and the interviewer. Fuzzy or nonanswerable questions asked by the client are indicative of the client's level of development and degree of distress.

Consideration of questioning now moves to a new phase of inquiry, that is, the question of "why." The word "why" suggests surprise, probing, perhaps even prying, and also carries with it some negative effects.

"Why(?)" is a crooked letter. It is not only crooked, it is a hook that often pulls the listener into the fury of an emotional storm.

For the very young child "why" is a searching word, an effort to understand. Soon the child finds out that when mother says "Why did you do it?" she means that the child was wrong and bad. Thus the "why" becomes corrupted. It loses its reasonable search for information and takes on a critical meaning.

"Why" frequently implies scolding, faultfinding, impatience, depreciation, and dissatisfaction as well as other harmful responses. When the student asks the instructor, "Why don't you lecture us on the principles of interviewing so we'll be able to apply them?" is the student interested in reasons or is he or she really saying, "You have failed as an instructor"?

Thus "why," which originally asked for information, now is more likely to pose a threat to clients. "Why" prods and pushes and too often suggests to clients that they are to blame for something. When clients feel the disapproval of the interviewer's "why," they withdraw to escape the situation. The clients defend themselves instead of extending themselves so that they may grow in further understanding. Exercise 4-14 has a list of "why" questions that indicate how these questions suggest disapproval.

Sometimes the question of "why" suggests the

Exercise 4-14
IS "WHY" A CROOKED QUESTION? *(may be done alone and discussed in a group)*

Time: APPROXIMATELY 30 MINUTES

Change the following list of "why" questions into questions beginning with "what" or "how" or, better still, change them into statements rather than questions. Use the following example as a model for this exercise.

EXAMPLE: "Why did you say that?" Change to: "Would you explain what you meant?" "I hear you saying that you think I have been undermining your efforts. Tell me what I did to make you feel this way."

☐ Why do you think your parents are not helping you?
☐ Why do you come in here looking that way?
☐ Why do you keep touching your hair while you are speaking?
☐ Why do you act this way today?
☐ Why don't you like this course?
☐ Why don't you keep away from people like that?
☐ Why are you always in such a hurry?
☐ Why are you so disorganized?
☐ Why are you silent now?
☐ Why do you argue with me so much?

"tyranny of the should" (Horney, 1954). The "should" interviewer becomes irritated with the rebellious client who does not accept the interviewer's directive remarks. This same interviewer is elated with the client who blindly follows the scheme of behavior presented by the interviewer. There are many subtle ways that "should" interviewers jab at the client. The interviewer asks, "Shouldn't you consider what others think of your behavior?" "Don't you think you should consult your wife about that decision?" "Why do you think you should do that?" Often the client or interviewer who is full of "shoulds" may lose sight of the helping goals—to develop the coping ability of the client.

Questioning and coping ability

Hamlet proposed a profound question: "To be, or not to be: that is the question" (William Shakespeare, *Hamlet,* act III, scene 1). Since the seventeenth century there have been numerous analyses of Hamlet's intentions and emotional status, including the following remarks by Rowse (1978) and Wright and LaMar (1961):

□ Contemplated suicide ("by sleep we say we end")

□ Was mad ("tis nobler in the mind to suffer")

□ Thought about murdering the king ("sweep to revenge"; "I have sworn it") (act 1, scene V)

□ Anguish evoked by inability to cope with the "sea of troubles" stemming from the "mortal coil" (stress of life); as a result bemoaned the interference of "conscience" that "does make cowards of us all" (act III, scene 1)

Questioning the question in effect leads to deepened understanding of the questioner's coping ability. The coping significance of questions is exemplified in the following discussions of developmental questioning, nonanswerable questioning, ventriloquizing questioning, and historical questioning.

Developmental questioning. Questioning and answering are processes in which individuals have participated all of their lives. Questioning begins

in early childhood. Children use questions as a means of attracting and holding adult attention and also to gain information. At first most of the children's questions begin with "why." "Why" questions reach their peak in the second or third grade. Gradually children add "what" and "how" questions; and as they grow older, their questions become more specific. *Developmentally,* therefore, the individual employs questions to learn how to cope with the world.

Nonanswerable questioning. Clients' questions disclose a great deal about the way they view themselves, events, and the people around them. Disordered individuals often reveal their *confusion* in the fuzziness of the questions they direct to themselves or to the interviewer. Answers may be relaxing for some clients, but for the disturbed client the answers just lead to more complicated questions. These clients frame their questions in such a way that they are unanswerable. They ask, "Why was I born?" "Why does everybody hate me?" "What is the meaning of life?" No matter how these questions are answered, they do not bring satisfaction, because these clients are not ready to accept solutions. They always find some aspect still unanswered. If interviewers try to grapple with questions such as "Why was I born?" they prompt these clients to ask many other questions, as exemplified by Mr. G., the interviewer, in the following situation:

MR. G.: That's a difficult question to answer. Each person finds his own reason for life.

STELLA: Yes, but how does one find a reason?

MR. G.: I can only tell you how I would find my reason. I would plan some goals and work toward them.

STELLA: Goals . . . but that's where I'm stumped. Who can tell about goals?

On and on this interview could go with no progress unless the interviewer confronts the client with the clear and frank statement that there is no answer to the client's question. In fact, the path to problem solving might lead to a rewording of the question.

MR. G.: Born? There is no satisfying answer to that. But I do hear you saying, "How do I find my way? What are my goals?"

STELLA: Mmmmmmm. I think so. How do I know there is a reason for me to *be?*

MR. G.: Another hard question. It might help if you tell me some of the feelings you have when you ask that question.

Notice the different direction the revised interview is following.

Ventriloquizing questioning. Sometimes the client's question demonstrates distress *by ventriloquizing* (Johnson, 1946); in other words, the client speaks with the voice of another. The client says, "My husband wants to know when Jimmy is going to get over this identity thing you were talking about," or "Lots of people have been asking when you are going to make up your mind about Shirley."

Historical questioning. Another coping device to avoid the reality of the moment occurs when the client asks historical questions. The client wonders, "Hey, Doc, do you think it was because of what happened when I was 16?" "When I was little, everyone thought I was such a sweet, obedient child." "If only my father had not hit me on the head when I was younger, I wouldn't have these headaches now. That's important, isn't it?"

REPORTING AND CONFIDENTIALITY

The discussion of reporting would be remiss if the issue of confidentiality were omitted. In the present context the problem is not a matter of governmental secrecy such as occurred in Daniel Ellsburg's disclosure of the Pentagon Papers to the *New York Times* and other newspapers in June 1971. Nor is the issue concerned with subsequent governmental attempts to suppress the information followed by the national debate concerning secrecy (Lowry, 1980). Instead it is a matter of the ethics of actions such as the Watergate cover-up on September 3, 1971, during which the "plumbers" burglarized the office files of Ellsburg's psychiatrist to attempt to discredit Ellsburg by uncovering potentially derogatory facts about Ellsburg's emotional status and mental health. It is a question of access to private files.

Privacy of records

The issue of privacy of clients' records was proposed most recently in the Ninety-sixth Congress when the Privacy Protection Act of 1979 was passed (P.L. 96-440). This act "protects all innocent third parties from possible abuse of the search warrant procedure [and] . . . mandates Justice Department guidelines for searches of innocent third parties, such as psychologist's files" (Voorde, 1981).

Societal protection and clients' privacy

Another bill, in 1980, (S. 503/H.R. 5935) did not pass. This legislative effort sought to further ensure the confidentiality of the patient-therapist relationship, "to protect the privacy of patient's records by establishing rules for the use of and disclosure of medical information maintained in medical facilities" (Voorde, 1981). In spite of the "growing public and professional concern about confidentiality . . . [the bill] strangled in a snarl of complex issues that promise to resurface every time such legislation is contemplated" (McNett, 1981). Many researchers objected strenuously because of the many barriers to research with human subjects that were in existence; this new bill would make research even more difficult. On the other hand, Marth Kraft Goin, a psychiatrist, asserted (McNett, 1981):

Unless patients can be assured that their privacy will be protected, they will be reluctant to disclose sensitive information essential to the success of treatment. . . . Unrestricted access to psychiatric, psychological or mental health treatment notes by third parties, even for legitimate reasons, can cause serious problems for patients. . . . When medical information "gets around" it can lead to social embarrassment, strained or broken ties with family, friends, and co-workers, career damage and jeopardized insurance benefits, or refusal of admission to graduate school.

The unsolved issue of confidentiality

The answer to these concerns is perplexing and intricate. The issues do not appear to be resolvable at the present time. Awareness of the difficulties and the requirements for ethical conduct are the primary caveats for the human services professional. The issues continue to be discussed, as stated in the following (McNett, 1981):

When crimes have been committed, how far should the police be allowed to go in penetrating medical records to solve these crimes? Clearly, supporters believe legislation is needed in this area. State laws range from non-existent to fairly stringent. . . . An overall federal statute that balances individual and societal rights could correct many of the flagrant abuses that now exist.

The debate is not settled. Human service workers should press for solutions that are satisfactory for the protection of society and satisfying for the confidentiality of clients' disclosures.

ROLE PLAYING

There is only one step* for the helper from the fundamental skills of observation, recording, and reporting to the interview setting of the helping event. To accomplish this step to competent interviewing it is essential that helpers *feel into* the meaning of events for clients as well as for themselves. For the helper, role playing experiences such as those in this book provide a bridge between skills and knowledge and interviewing. For clients, this may be the giant leap that aids in clarifying and discovering new approaches to persistent problems and in identifying enriched channels for the quality of life.

Role playing as experiential learning

Role playing is a method used for developing observational, recording, reporting, and interviewing and counseling skills. Role playing involves the individual in a variety of roles and offers opportunity for self-observation as well as observation by other trainees.

The Latin origin of the word "role" is "rotulus," which refers to a rolled-up script. (The directions given in the exercises of this book may be likened to a script.) Later the French added the definition "social function" to the meaning. With the Latin and French meanings together, role playing is defined as a method of performing certain acts and/or speaking certain lines according to a planned script, combined with spontaneous acts and lines. These acts or lines refer to specified social or other events. Role playing may serve as a projective and/or therapeutic technique or as an educational or training device.

Role playing is best accomplished if the particular skills to be learned are broken down into the specific behavior involved. For example, individuals who have been hospitalized in a mental institution for several years profit from role-playing sessions with individuals who ask them about where they have been. They practice how they will respond to people's questions about their prior whereabouts when they leave the hospital. Job seekers devise effective approaches for communicating with someone in a personnel office. Children become more comfortable when they role-play the steps in the hospital procedure and how they should act when they go to the hospital to have their tonsils removed. Human service workers experiment with eye contact, body position, and gestures to develop better listening skills.

Several purposes of role playing

Role playing provides an approach that involves the whole person in an active process of self-exploration. The person thinks, feels, and does. The performance of a variety of behaviors also serves other purposes:

- ☐ Feedback is immediate and is also a response to many different aspects of the individual's behavior. The role player is not only seen and heard but has a more direct effect on others in the drama.
- ☐ Role playing offers a way in which an individual may learn about other people's values, feelings, and problems by experiencing events *as if* the role player were the other person. The role player practices empathy.

---

*Paraphrased from comment by Neil Armstrong, July 21, 1969: "One small step for a man. One giant leap for mankind."

□ The role player may act as a model for others by demonstrating skills, responses, problems, and so on.

□ The lessons learned in the process of role-playing one particular situation are likely to apply (generalize) to other similar situations, particularly if the similarities are noted.

For some beginning human service professional the movement into the performances associated with interviewing presents insurmountable obstacles. Uncloseting these apprehensions frees them and bolsters their confidence through recognition of the problem and of the areas of skill and knowledge that must be advanced. Exercise 4-15 strives to assist in this progress.

Exercise 4-15
WHAT ARE YOUR CONCERNS ABOUT INTERVIEWING* *(should be done in a group)*

Time: APPROXIMATELY 40 MINUTES

Draw two wheel diagrams with diameters of 4 inches each and with circles in the center of these circles that are 1 inch in diameter (see Fig. 4-11). Write the word "concerns" in the inner circle of the first wheel. Close your eyes and consider your "hang-ups" about your role as an interviewer with a client in an imagined helping situation. Write four concerns in the spokes of the first wheel and then focus on these concerns until you identify which is the most important.

Write this concern in the center of the second wheel. Try to "get in touch" with your feelings (fear, distress, anger, and so on) about the selected concern. Insert these feelings in the four spokes of the wheel (see Figs. 4-12 and 4-13).

After these two wheels have been completed, subgroups of four participants discuss their concerns. One person should speak at a time. The subgroup members compare the mutuality of their concerns and propose solutions. If the subgroups do not resolve their concerns to their satisfaction, the entire large group may reconvene to discuss these matters.

---

*Modified from Nisenholz, B., and McCarty, F.H.: Teaching concerns focus game: exploring solutions. In Thayer, L., editor: 50 Strategies for experimental learning: book one, San Diego, Calif., 1976, University Associates, Inc.

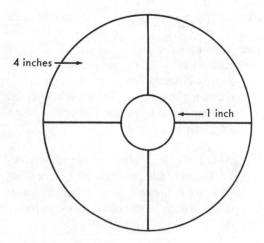

4 inches
1 inch

Fig. 4-11. The concern circle. (Modified from Nisenholz, B., and McCarty, F.H.: Teaching concerns focus game: exploring solutions. In Thayer, L., editor: 50 Strategies for experiential learning: book one, San Diego, Calif., University Associates, 1976. Used with permission.)

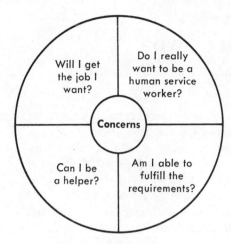

Fig. 4-12. Filling the concern circle. (Modified from Nisenholz, B., and McCarty, F.H.: Teaching concerns focus game: exploring solutions. In Thayer, L., editor: 50 Strategies for experiential learning: book one, San Diego, Calif., University Associates, 1976. Used with permission.)

Fig. 4-13. The concern circle with feeling. (Modified from Nisenholz, B., and McCarty, F.H.: Teaching concerns focus game: exploring solutions. In Thayer, L., editor: 50 Strategies for experiential learning: book one, San Diego, Calif., University Associates, 1976. Used with permission.)

Summary of Part Two

■ The main point proposed in Part Two is that recording and reporting are aspects of the communication process. Thus language communication behaviors, including reading, writing, speaking, and listening (Jones and Mohr, 1976) depend on observational skills as well as competency in organizing and crystallizing the data from observations into words. Although recording skills and reporting skills have been discussed in separate chapters, the division is one of convenience, not of fact. Recording and reporting go hand in hand in the compilation of a report. For explanatory purposes recording has been discussed in relation to its purpose, quantity, and quality and the advantages of on-site versus later note taking. The discussion of the semantic impact of the Humpty-Dumpty syndrome concentrates on the concepts of denotation and connotation; coding, encoding, and decoding; and descriptive and interpretive words. All these analyses are integrated in the presentation of the significance of the objective-subjective continuum and the ABC sequence of recording.

Discerning and differentiating feelings clarifies their impact on the accuracy of immediate and long-term recall of events for the helper and for the client. The recognition of underlying feelings is particularly important in the helping event, since these may blur perceptions and enter into the self-fulfilling prophecies and prejudices that distort recording. The influence of feeling-tone is usually greatest in the narrative technique of recording, may be noted to some extent in the hierarchical and rating scaling techniques, and is less apparent in checklists. Mental status recordings exemplify a constellation of these techniques.

Interpretations and inferences are part of the eventual report. Recording multiple hunches supplies a procedure for the conclusions that may be incorporated into the report. This method requires keen observational skills plus seeking many guesses for behavior rather than jumping to conclusions. Then pertinent and supported hunches are kept, and those which are unsupported by observable data are investigated further to ascertain their accuracy.

Chapter 4 continues to explore recording and adds a new dimension to the feedback process—reporting. Reporting as feedback is examined in regard to its constructive characteristics, its specificity, its positive rather than negative tone, and whether it encourages or discourages trust, distortion, and an empty inquiry and recording product. Further consideration of communication deliberates level of communication as exemplified by the closed systems of the soliloquy, monologue, and duologue as contrasted with the more open systems of the duelogue and, particularly, dialogue.

Several factors that are influential in the effectiveness of reporting are inspected. The meaningfulness of diversified background and experiences in the helping relationship is presented with descriptions of substitute channels for certain experiences through empathic relationships. Throughout the search for effectiveness in reporting, its alignment with the communication process is emphasized. In this context the ''what,'' ''how,'' ''where,'' and ''why'' of communication become germane to the recording process. Patterns of interpersonal relationships and of tolerance and acceptance are reviewed, and the positive value of acceptance in transactions that enrich interpersonal relationships is contrasted with the negative tone of tolerance and interpersonal patterns of action-reaction and interaction.

Questioning the question as a technique for gathering and reporting facts turns the probing of recording and reporting toward consideration of productive and unproductive questioning, the "when" and "how" of questioning, and questions as a clue to coping ability. These characteristics of questioning are expanded with descriptions of the varieties of questioning and the question of "why." The discussion of closed versus open questioning, leading versus responding questioning, answer-agree questioning, direct versus indirect questioning, multiple-idea versus single-idea questioning, and funnel versus inverted funnel questioning enlarges the scope of approaches to the collection and arrangement of information.

The confidentiality of reports draws together the societal needs for protection, governmental demands for secrecy, and the ethical considerations for clients' privacy. The answers to the issues presented are complex, and legislation cannot satisfy all contingencies that may arise. The human service worker must be alert to the difficulties and ethical considerations surrounding the maintenance of records and the presentation of reports.

Finally, role playing is set forth as one of the cornerstone skills of the human service worker. This form of experiential learning is an integral part of the exercises that are part of this book and serves as the introduction to the discussion of interviewing in Part Three.

Part Three

THE WHAT AND HOW OF INTERVIEWING

how to get out of the client's way

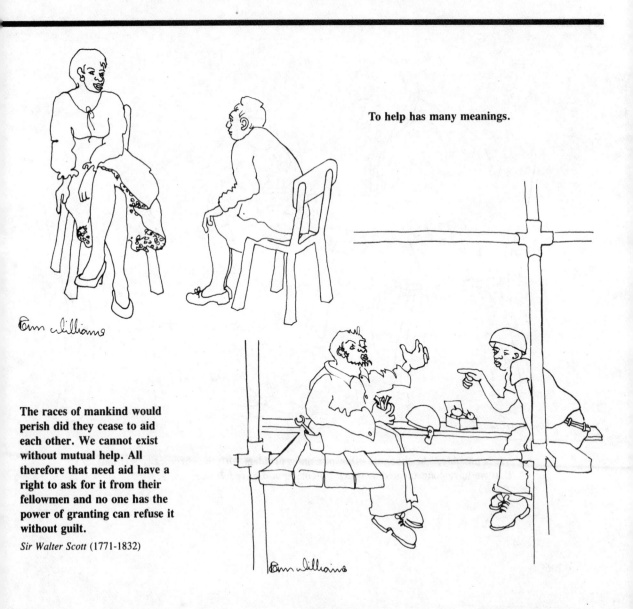

To help has many meanings.

The races of mankind would perish did they cease to aid each other. We cannot exist without mutual help. All therefore that need aid have a right to ask for it from their fellowmen and no one has the power of granting can refuse it without guilt.

Sir Walter Scott (1771-1832)

Chapter 5

DIMENSIONS OF THE INTERVIEW RELATIONSHIP

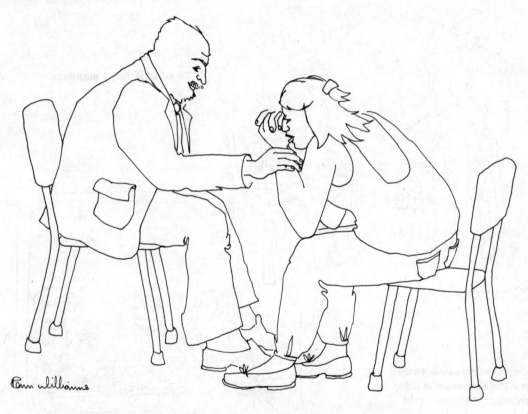

"It is possible," he thought, "that our main problem with the chronically mentally ill is that we have concentrated so much on curing and have left out caring."

CARING VERSUS CURING

The interview relationship is a special kind of caring, a special kind of helping, with many ramifications. Whether caring encourages curing depends on the meanings associated with the acts attendant with caring. Shakespeare denied the significance of care when the character in *Henry VI* states "Care is not cure. . . ." In fact, Shakespeare labeled care as "corrosive." This distinction regarding caring is one of the many perspectives from which the term "caring" may be viewed. From this standpoint care is really a troublesome, worrisome, burden disturbing the equanimity of persons. Other meanings consider care as follows:

☐ To pay close attention to a particular act, one's health, and the like ("Drive carefully." "Take care of that sore throat." "Study carefully.")

☐ To look after, take charge of or custody of, or provide for another person ("Watch her as she crosses the street." "They are unable to decide about that; you'll have to help them." "He'll need support to enter college—reassurance as well as money.")

☐ To obtain the satisfactions of a caring relationship—to care for and to be cared about

Caring: the fountainhead of helping

Mayeroff (1971) describes caring as follows:

Caring is helping another grow and actualize himself, is a process, a way of relating to someone that involves development, in the same way that friendship can only emerge in time through mutual trust and a deepening and qualitative transformation of the relationship.

The focus of this chapter is oriented toward the explanation mentioned by Mayeroff and the "I-and-Thou" philosophy of Buber (1958), which espouses the personal reactions of an individual "I" to another person as a truly human being, "thou." Out of all these thoughts emerges the following interpretation of caring as this term relates to the human service worker:

Caring is an interpersonal skill demonstrated by helping another to grow, change, and actualize as a separate person in accordance with his or her needs and potentials.

Seneca stated in *Hippolytus,* "It is part of the cure to wish to be cured." Caring aids in curing. Therefore it is more likely that the troubled, ill person who cares for and about himself or herself would be spurred on to perform acts that cure. The caring of another person—a helper, a relative, a friend—also can help the person in need to better endure and persevere even if cure (restoration to health or a sound condition) is a long-term or can only partially be achieved. However, without caring there is scant hope and stunted help.

TO HELP HAS MANY MEANINGS

The salesperson says it to the customers examining the double-knit suits hanging on the "Sale Today" rack:

May I help you?

The receptionist in an employment agency office says it to the puzzled job seeker:

May I help you?

The Frenchman says it to the weary sightseer wandering through an unknown street, confused by a foreign language:

May I help you?

The interviewer says it to the anxious client troubled by her inability to remain alone in her home because her friend has been raped recently:

How may I help you?

The essence of caring is helping

To help has many meanings:
- ☐ For the salesperson it may signify an added commission and making points with the supervisor.
- ☐ For the receptionist it serves to direct to the personnel interviewer a body that may be cluttering up the office.
- ☐ For the Frenchman it may be the selling point for other tourists to visit the "friendly" city.
- ☐ For the effective interviewer it means *caring*.

Caring is the characteristic to be sought in the interviewer. Care means giving serious attention to someone. The cared-for person feels that the caring person respects and accepts him or her as worthy. Interviewers who care encourage others to explore their beliefs and the influences that are helping or hindering them in making a decision or in solving problems. Interviewers who care are genuine, warm, and understanding and avoid intruding their ways of living (life-style) on the psychological field of the persons being interviewed.

Two essential ideas spring forth from these views about caring. First, it is obvious that helping *may* include caring, but caring *always* includes

helping. Second, to accomplish being with and not acting for another person is not easy.

Hope, trust, and patience: the core of caring

A triad of characteristics form the foundation for caring. *Hope* sets the stage, not with unrealistic thinking or unfounded expectations, but by directing attention to possibilities for solutions, by activating new energies, by encouraging risks that do not hazard safety and security, and by reassurances that errors do not mean failure or the final chance. Caring introduces hope and bolsters confidence.

Hope looks forward to change, and the degree of hopefulness measures the level of expectation of potential goal achievement (Stotland, 1969). Caring by another person provides the nutrient that invigorates hope.

Trust is basic to the maintenance of hopefulness. The caring helper expresses positive feelings of trust in the client's ability to change and to cope, in his or her own time and fashion. Thus the helper does not dominate the client's decisions but assures the client that the helper is there to follow the client's leads and to make suggestions at suitable times—above all that the helper *trusts* the client's decision-making ability. The client, in turn, does not have to wallow in overprotection but instead learns to trust the responsiveness of the helper and also his or her own capacity for problem solving.

Hope and trust demand *patience*. It is essential that the helper be patient and be alert to the time for waiting and the time for encouraging movement. "Patience is not waiting passively for something to happen, but is a kind of participation with the other in which we give fully of ourselves" (Mayeroff, 1971).

Caring is learned in the nurturing relationship of parent-child closeness and strengthened by parental protection, tenderness, and encouragement of the child to develop as a self apart. For the interviewer caring signifies attending to the client—looking, listening, and responding with empathy. Caring is helping with hope, trust, and patience so that reciprocal experiences lead to reciprocal growth.

To help has many meanings.

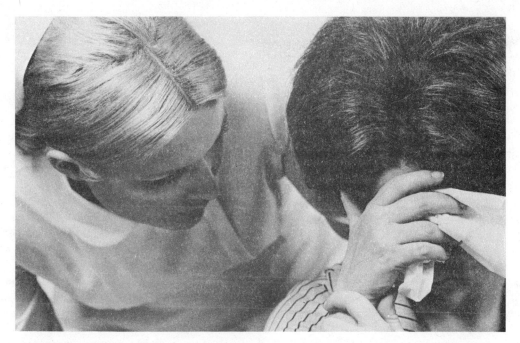

Fig. 5-1. From Mereness, D.A., and Taylor, C.M.: Essentials of psychiatric nursing, ed. 10, St. Louis, 1978, The C.V. Mosby Co.

Barbara Haimowitz

Fig. 5-2. Somerville-Cambridge Elder Services Office, Somerville, Mass.

DIMENSIONS OF MUTUALITY

The give-and-take of the interview transaction depends on mutuality of goals and expectations in a caring relationship. This relationship becomes more effective when it is punctuated with a communion of interests and planning. Out of this synergy emerge reciprocal effects—reciprocal affects gravitating toward reciprocal growth.

Reciprocal effects

Since both the client and the interviewer are discovering each other, mutual progressions and regressions (reciprocal effects) are inevitable. Improvement or deterioration of the interview situation depends on the level of functioning of the client and particularly of the interviewer as well as on the ways in which they perceive (see and hear) each other.

In any interpersonal situation there is bound to be some influence of one person on another. The degree to which feelings become part of the interviewer's responses relates to reciprocal affects.

Reciprocal affects

The principle of reciprocal affect (Truax and Carkhuff, 1967) states that when one person expresses a certain emotion (affect), this emotion is likely to call forth a similar emotion in the other person (reciprocal). Accordingly, anger encourages anger, joy encourages joy, sorrow encourages sorrow, defensiveness encourages defensiveness, and so on. Unless one of the individuals alters this snowballing effect of reciprocal affects, the emotional intensity builds up. In the counseling situation it is the counselor who must cut the anger short by means of a change in his or her own behavior. For instance:

EVA: It's that 18-year-old clod who is causing the trouble. We'd be okay. Lazy, good-for-nothing goof-off. Won't work, won't go to school, talks only of people power—demonstrating, noisemaking. What does he want? He's got a beautiful home, so he doesn't like the suburbs, stifles him, middle-class morality. Lives with a tramp; she's 26-years old and has a child. Both of them I spit on.

MS. G.: Wow! You've really got it in for him. Have you ever considered his side of the picture? His values?

EVA: Whaddya know about a son? You're too young to know what it's like; you . . . Well, you don't know what you're saying.

MS. G.: Hell! You have a lot of nerve saying that to me. I have studied to work with people. You don't know any . . . Heavens, what am I doing? I really am angry, really lost my cool. Let's look at this again.

The interviewer who is nondefensive is able to admit errors to the client: "I really jumped to conclusions just then" or "There I go, giving my opinion instead of listening to yours."

When the helper reacts to the intense feelings of the client, as Ms. G. does, the helper's perceptions (ways of seeing, hearing, and feeling) of the client become blocked. The interviewer is not only less able to listen to the client but also less able to recall what the client has just done or said. Too much threat increases the anxiety level of both the client and the interviewer to the point where they may both lose sight of the purpose of the interviewing session. Too much emotional reaction by the helper leads to helper burn out rather than reciprocal growth.

Reciprocal growth

Effective interviewers reduce the psychological and physical distance between themselves and their clients. They move together toward a statement of the clients' problems and toward the development of action plans to solve the stated problems. In this process both the interviewer and the client grow in knowledge about themselves and in understanding of one another. They experience reciprocal growth in coping skills so that interviewer and client are more capable of dealing with the events in their daily situations. The upswing in "cope-ability" (Up Front, 1980) accompanying positive reciprocal growth occurs in many forms, depending on the interview goals.

VARIETIES IN INTERVIEW GOALS

Caring, helping, and mutuality are part of any classification of the interview. In some interviews the depth and breadth of communication style and analyses are intense and wide in scope. In others the acquisition of specific information does not demand as much time or involvement. Accordingly the extent and intricacy of communications and disclosures stretch from the more rudimentary information-oriented interview through behavior management interviews to the more complex experiential interview. These interviews all depend on the same fundamental skills of observation, recording, and reporting and vary in the degree of interpersonal searching and conflict resolution.

Information-oriented interview

The information-oriented interview has the least depth in regard to interpersonal searching. The information-seeking interview is directed to gathering data about people, places, or products. The information-sharing interview goes a step further than information-seeking; since the data gathered are used for more than achieving the interviewer's own goals. Information-sharing interviews serve to help the client make a decision, for instance, about educational or vocational plans.

Information-seeking interview. Information may be collected by means of:
- A survey or public opinion poll
- A journalistic interview by a reporter
- A personnel officer interviewing a job seeker
- A testing situation to obtain the current status of an individual's knowledge and skills or level of intellectual, social, or emotional functioning

Survey interview. The telephone rings, and one more opinion about television is sought. "What program are you watching now?" "When did you begin watching?" "How many television sets are there in your home?" The survey takes many forms—preferences in television programing, in food packaging, in magazines bought and read, and so on. Usually the queries serve to inform the television sponsor or the marketing agent how to increase the product's appeal to the consumer.

The survey may consist of a questionnaire with written or spoken answers. For instance, a survey was conducted (Behavior Today, 1977a) to determine the number of mothers working outside the home. The survey found that nearly 40% of mothers were working in 1977, compared with 10% in 1940. The increased number of working mothers with children under 6 years of age (6 million children) makes a convincing appeal for licensed daycare centers of all types. However, other surveys of the childcare practices of working parents assemble data disproving the acceptance of daycare for the children of working mothers. During the late 1960s and early 1970s many companies sponsored daycare centers on their premises and soon afterward closed their doors because of lack of enrollment. Mothers were placing their children in the care of a relative, another mother, a babysitter, and, less frequently, in a licensed daycare center near their home. Several surveyers compiled the information. Other surveys will be conducted to determine care for the children of working mothers (Behavior Today, 1977b).

Public opinion poll. A survey may center on public opinion. For instance, the Gallup Poll asks carefully planned samples of the population selected questions about such things as their presidential candidates and their political opinions. Obtaining opinions from the public may also take the form of talking with public officials and private citizens about their attitudes toward, for example, the mentally retarded. Lippman (1972) conducted such attitude surveys in Europe and in the United States. In general, the major difference Lippman discovered was the more positive attitude toward retarded persons in European countries, with people in the Scandinavian countries expressing the most favorable and constructive attitudes, as contrasted with the United States. Public officials, citizen leaders, journalists, and professional people working with retarded persons expressed opinions that revealed their respect for mentally retarded people as human beings with the right to individual dignity. Lippman collected the data for his public opinion poll by means of a journalistic interview that was drawn from a basic outline. He took "highlight" notes and taped many of the interviews.

Journalistic interview. Reporters who make inquiries for a newspaper story must have at their fingertips a large selection of questions to use to probe for information to organize into a story. The reporters seek facts to cover the five W's: *Who? What? When? Where? Why?* In writing copy the reporters answer all these questions in the lead paragraph. In addition, the interviewer may add a *how* question to the inquiry. News and feature reporters must be skilled in interviewing people to collect interesting and accurate information for their articles. The successful interviewer picks a knowledgeable interviewee, asks the right questions, and knows where to begin as well as when and how to end the interview.

Personnel interview. Another sort of information is sought when an employer is reviewing the qualifications of applicants for a job. The suitability of candidates is determined by a discussion of educational background and experience. Often applicants are asked about their interests and what makes them believe they would like to and can successfully perform a particular type of work. Certain hypothetical incidents may be posed and the applicants asked to discuss how they would handle them. On the basis of such observation and questioning one applicant is selected.

Personnel interviewers in larger organizations frequently go beyond the job placement functions of preliminary recruitment, screening of applicants, and recommendations of the more qualified candidates to some form of counseling. Thus these interviewers expand their functions to a broader based helping relationship.

Testing. The tests that often plague students are forms of an information-seeking interview. The information (answers to questions) sought by the interviewer (the instructor) from the client (the student) depends on whether regurgitation (spilling back what the instructor has said) or self-understanding and interpretation (student oriented) are desired.

■   ■   ■

Surveys, journalistic interviews, personnel interviews, and tests differ in their format but have

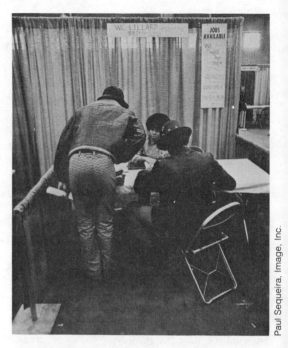

Fig. 5-3. Personnel interview—information seeking.

two important similarities: (1) they all primarily seek information, and (2) they all have a basic plan for the kinds of information they are seeking. To obtain information, the interviewer must establish objectives and questions leading to the achievement of these objectives before the information seeking is begun.

Information-sharing interview. The ultimate purpose of information sharing is similar to that of the diagnostic interview, in which the function of the sharing is to provide both the interviewer and the client with information about the causative factors and the procedures needed for therapy. For the physician the clinical examination of the patient, the x-ray films, the electroencephalogram, and the stethoscope help in determining possible factors involved in the patient's illness as well as the seriousness of the illness. *How much* and *how* this information is shared with the patient becomes a matter of the physician's particular approach and the physician's evaluation of the patient's needs. Fig. 5-4 is one example of information sharing of

Barbara Haimowitz

Fig. 5-4. Information sharing of human service workers in Somerville-Cambridge Elder Services Office, Somerville, Mass.

two colleagues in a human service agency, and the mental status examination discussed in Chapter 3 is an additional illustration of information seeking that may lead to sharing. Example 5-1 represents a psychiatrist's approach to a mental status examination of a recently hospitalized 62-year-old woman. Exercise 5-1 raises several questions about this interview.

Example 5-1
INFORMATION SHARING IN THE MENTAL STATUS EXAMINATION

Ms. P. enters the psychiatrist's office slowly. She walks with her head down but moves her head up and to one side as she quickly stares over her shoulder. She slips down into the seat that faces the psychiatrist, keeping her head bent with her chin held tightly downward. Her hair hangs loosely over her forehead, and the hem of her flowered dress droops down on one side.

The psychiatrist, Dr. L., starts to say "hello" but gets no further than "He . . ."

MS. P.: *(Rapidly raising her head and looking backward over her shoulder.)* Hear it? It's again. Again, again! *(She looks with upturned eyes at Dr. L. and then quickly pulls her head down.)* (NOTE: Auditory hallucinations and poor reality orientation.)

DR. L.: No, I did not hear that this time. Tell me about it.

MS. P.: Hear it? Tells what to do. Since I came here 10 years ago. (NOTE: Present memory inaccuracy.)

DR. L.: Ten years ago. How old were you then, Ms. P.?

MS. P.: Forty-two—no, maybe 44. Don't remember. Ten years ago came here to this hotel.

DR. L.: Hotel? Ms. P., this is a hospital. Do you remember that your daughter and your husband brought you here?

MS. P.: *(After a few minutes.)* So tired today. That new medicine gave me on Tuesday.

DR. L.: Medicine on Tuesday?

MS. P.: *(Pulling her eyebrows together and wrinkling her forehead.)* Must have been in the morning yesterday, Wednesday, or Thursday. Hard to remember. *(Raises her head suddenly and looks over her shoulder.)* Again! (NOTE: Difficulty with present and past memory accuracy.)

DR. L.: Tell me about it. Where does the sound come from? (NOTE: Testing for reality orientation.)

MS. P.: Have arranged for an investigation by the FBI and a supersonic witness. Must reconstruct the ions to induce closure. Have to go now. More to do. Remember too much. (NOTE: Vocabulary level high and intellectual functioning poor.)

Ms. P. appears to have some difficulty raising herself from the chair. After she manages the initial spurt of movement, she pulls herself up and slowly walks from the room. Dr. L. notices a slight shuffling limp in her left leg. Dr. L. follows Ms. P. to the doorway. He looks out and beckons to the woman seated on the wooden bench outside his office.

DR. L.: Please come in, Ms. R. Now that I have spoken to your mother, we can talk about the questions you asked the other day. As you said when we talked, your mother is an intelligent woman but is not functioning in accordance with her intellectual capacity.

MS. R.: Doctor, do you think she's ever going to be as she was—an alert, active woman?

DR. L.: We need some more tests to determine her prognosis. There are some evidences of brain pathology, but I'm not certain enough to state the nature of the pathology. A thorough physical examination, including an encephalogram, is indicated.

Dr. L. discusses the patient's poor reality contact and hallucinations as well as his other findings. In this information-sharing interview the data gathered about a person is shared with someone other than the patient.

Behavior management interview

A change of approach is necessary when moving from the primacy of information seeking or sharing to behavior management. The latter form of interview requires knowledge of learning principles and skill to use these principles appropriately. The acquisition of information about learning principles can be accomplished more readily than can competency in applying the techniques.

The behavioral counseling or behavior therapy interview is both symptom removal and action oriented. The primary goals of behavior approaches are to change behavior according to the client's needs and to maintain these changes (Rimm and Masters, 1974). The techniques to be followed depend on which theories and principles of behavior management an interviewer favors.

Behavior therapy operates in a highly visible and concrete fashion. For example, a client may present a problem of sexual dysfunctioning; where the psychodynamic therapist would tend to look for unconscious reasons for the problem, perhaps rooted in childhood experiences, the behavioral therapist seeks to understand the sexual problem through directly examining the immediate situation. Through changing the overt behavior of the client or key situational variables, it has been demonstrated that rapid and lasting changes in the sex life of an individual are possible (Ivey and Simek-Downing, 1980).

The formulas of behavior modification are founded on the experimentally discovered principles of learning. Basic to the practice of behavior therapy is the hypothesis that both appropriate ("normal") and inappropriate ("abnormal") behavior are learned and therefore may be unlearned. Inappropriate behavior is weakened and eliminated and appropriate behavior is initiated and strength-

Exercise 5-1
HOW IS THE MESSAGE DISCOVERED IN THE INFORMATION-SHARING INTERVIEW?
(may be done alone and discussed in the group)

Time: APPROXIMATELY 20 MINUTES TO ANSWER QUESTIONS,
             10 MINUTES FOR GROUP DISCUSSION

Dr. L.'s interview with Ms. P. in Example 5-1 not only opens up many areas for further exploration but also offers many cues. Examine the interview carefully and answer the following questions:

□ What additional information does the doctor require to obtain a more complete picture of Ms. P.'s problem?

□ How might Dr. L. have obtained more information and a better understanding of Ms. P. during the interview?

□ On the basis of the information presented during the interview, what inferences would you make about the causative factors of Ms. P.'s behavior and the diagnosis?

□ If you were the interviewer, what would you have changed in the interview with Ms. P. or with her daughter, Ms. R.?

ened by means of schedules of reinforcement. This process is called operant conditioning or contingency management. (See the ABC of recording in Chapter 3.)

Operant conditioning. Operant conditioning is defined as emitted (voluntary) behavior that is repeated, decreased, or extinguished (conditioned) when followed by a class of events called reinforcements. Thus the behavior is controlled by the consequences (reinforcements) occurring immediately after the behavior. Behavior is operant because it *operates* on the environment. An individual who comes to a locked door puts a certain key in the lock, turns the key in a certain direction, turns the doorknob, pushes the door open, and walks into the house. The individual's behavior has been shaped to perform several operants (actions) that have now become habits or persistent behavior: to discriminate stimuli—the appropriate key for the lock, the appropriate way to turn the key; to discriminate responses—move arms, fingers, and legs in the appropriate way; and to maintain neuromuscular control—use certain muscles in opening and shutting the door. All these acts of behavior have been chained together by the reward (reinforcement) of entering the house. Entering the house is the contingency, the arrangement between the behavior and the subsequent changes in the environment that happens at the right time and the right place to reinforce the behavior of using the key to unlock the door.

The behavioral interview is based on the concept of consequences or reinforcements of behavior. Reinforcement may be positive (a reward in the form of praise), negative (the removal of something unpleasant such as completing an assignment to avoid failure), or punishment (poor grade, electric shock, rejection, penalty, criticism). The interviewer is part of the reinforcement environment. Truax and Carkhuff (1966) speak of the differential reinforcement of the interviewer's high levels of accurate empathy, nonpossessive warmth, and genuineness. These interpersonal characteristics set up a reinforcing climate that supports and strengthens the client's self-exploration efforts, which lead to consequent changes in behavior (see Chapter 7). Helpers must be alerted to their role and impact on the behavior management process and also must develop a bag (repertoire) of approaches to accomplish behavioral change in order to teach problem-solving skills and methods of behavior change so that clients can control their own behavior.

Behavioral analysis. The first step in deciding the procedures to be followed for behavior management is to define with the client the target behavior or behaviors to be eliminated. As the interview progresses, the terminal behavior to be strengthened evolves. The behavior that is the target to be changed is reviewed with the client to determine the cues (stimulating or antecedent events) and consequences (reinforcements) that perpetuate the behavior.

The behavioral analysis of the obese individual who gorges on rich food leads to data about the frequency, quantity, and types of foods eaten. The interviewer and the client plan a behavioral contract (Krumboltz and Thoresen, 1969) that spells out a program of reduction of food intake and the specific rewards doled out. The rewards may be the weight loss indicated by a scale, the interviewer's social approval as well as the approval of the client's family and friends, a smaller size in clothing, or any other form of reinforcement applicable to this particular client. Further reinforcement for change may come from snapshots of the individual before, during, and after the weight loss. Signs of progress may be shown in snapshots revealing the flattening of the bulge. Reinforcement may be sustained by the client between interview visits by looking at the "before" snapshots (self-monitoring contingency) when sitting down to a luxurious spread (self-regulation or self-management). Furthermore, the stimulation to eat fattening foods may be controlled by limiting the cues around the client—removing any such food from the client's home and substituting less fattening food and drinks for candy, cake, and bread.

These parts take into account the methods the interviewer may use to help the client change his behavior.

Reinforcement menu. After the target behavior has been determined (for example, less food intake) and the terminal behavior decided on (for example, maintaining a certain lower weight), then the other parts of the reinforcement menu are considered.

Thought stopping. Wolpe (1969) writes about obsessive thoughts that may be diminished by a "thought-stopping program." Clients are told to close their eyes and to talk out loud about continuing, annoying thoughts, which may include food, sex, writing a book—anything. At certain intervals (intermittent reinforcement) the interviewer sharply calls out, "Stop!" (negative reinforcement). The clients' eyes snap open, and the interviewer calls their attention to the change in thought (annoying thoughts suddenly stop) that has occurred. This procedure is repeated several times.

The interviewer suggests that the clients close their eyes again and this time talk about something that is pleasant (substitute behavior) to them. If the clients return to obsessive thinking, the interviewer once again utters the loud command, "Stop!" In addition to what happens during the interview, the clients are given the directive to practice stopping disturbing thoughts by quietly reminding themselves to stop. Extinction, or the gradual weakening of a response, is thus accomplished by a schedule of both negative ("stop") and positive (interviewer's approval) reinforcement.

Verbal and nonverbal conditioning. Besides the three interpersonal characteristics of empathy, nonpossessive warmth, and genuineness (see Chapter 7), at least two other forms of reinforcement are always part of the interview setting. These are verbal and nonverbal conditioning (Woody, 1971). Verbal conditioning refers to the words the interviewer uses that influence the client's responses. The interviewer smiles, nods, or performs some other nonverbal act when the client performs some specified act or statement. Conversely, the interviewer ignores the client (avoids responding) when the emitted act or statement has not been specified. By means of verbal and nonverbal reinforcement, appropriate behavior is strengthened and inappropriate behavior is weakened. It is therefore essential that the interviewer be alert to his or her own responses as well as to the client's for the establishment of an efficient and effective reinforcement menu.

The controlling power of verbal and nonverbal reinforcements is apparent. Not only the client's behavior but also the interviewer's behavior is modified by verbal and nonverbal conditioning. In fact, this is an everyday occurence. The mother calls out to her child, "Stop that and come here right away!" Whether the child does come right away depends on the consistency of consequences for coming or for not coming. Sometimes it becomes more reinforcing (more fun and rewarding) not to come because then the mother will come into the room and thus give the attention that the child desires. Attention is the reinforcement.

Desensitization. Another circumstance in which attention modifies behavior is when the interviewer helps the client get down to gut anxieties. By attending to the anxieties, by talking them out, the client becomes increasingly desensitized to the anxieties. When the strength of the anxiety-provoking stimuli is not sufficiently reduced by means of exploring the anxiety, then Wolpe (1969) describes the behavior therapy procedure that is based on the construction of a heirarchy of anxiety stimuli. This hierarchy is planned so that the least anxiety-producing stimuli are tackled first, and by gradual steps the more anxiety-producing stimuli are attempted. Throughout this process of extinguishing anxiety and fear responses the reinforcing relationship with the interviewer is crucial. Example 5-2 shows how desensitization may be used with a client whose anxiety is produced by speaking before a group.

Example 5-2
DESENSITIZING SPEAKING ANXIETY

This was Sally's third visit to Mr. R. She thought about the last two sessions as she walked along the corridor to his office. "Guess I really dig the guy. Didn't when he pushed himself into my life at first. At any rate, thought he did. When, where, how—dig a little, dig some more. Now, can do two of the things we planned. Talk to two people at the same time. Was that a drag! In classroom think about what will say but don't feel have to answer. That was easier, yet at one time would have been so tied up, felt had to answer, wouldn't have worked. Sit and think—know my answer is mine to give if I wanted to. Well, here goes number three."

Mr. R. was in the anteroom as Sally entered the office. He looked toward her, smiled, then gestured toward his office door, and followed Sally as she went in. They both sat down in the facing chairs.

MR. R.: Hi, Sally. Hey, what's this? Looks to me like you're uptight today. Let's slump a little, Sally.

SALLY: Cut it, Mr. R. Just thinking about number three.

MR. R.: Number three?

SALLY: Yeah. Don't think I'm ready for it. Speechicating to you about anything.

MR. R.: Speechicating—excellent word.

SALLY: Planned it. Have been thinking about what we've done— the tight knot in my stomach was not there with the first and the second, but now.

MR. R.: *(Smiling.)* Planned it?

SALLY: Yes, I've been thinking about the meaning of some of the games people play, you know, Berne's book. I see how it applies to me—the child afraid to speak. The games I play, the "If-it-weren't-for-you" game; my parents did it—my boyfriend does it—they are the ones that stop me from doing things. "If it weren't" . . . a nice game to hide in. Whaddya know . . . here I've been rambling, speechicating, and am unknotted.

Mr. R. smiled and nodded his head, and Sally continued her discussion of Berne's ideas. Exercise 5-2 continues the discussion of Sally's problem with an opportunity to apply information about desensitization procedures.

Items on reinforcement menu. The following lists give some examples of appropriate and inappropriate behaviors that are modifiable by reinforcement contingencies.

Appropriate behaviors to be strengthened include the following:

☐ *Communication:* enunciation of comprehensible sounds or words
☐ *Use of materials:* appropriate use of blocks for building, not for striking another child
☐ *Following directions:* learning to comply with requests and to follow certain procedures in becoming desensitized to certain fears
☐ *Social development:* gradually moving toward social encounter with another individual or toward dealing with a social situation with someone who arouses anxiety

Inappropriate behaviors in the same areas that should be weakened include the following:

Exercise 5-2
HOW DO YOU ESTABLISH AN ANXIETY HIERARCHY? *(should be done in a group)*

Time: APPROXIMATELY 25 MINUTES

Use the example of Sally's difficulty (Example 5-2) as the starting point for the following activities.

Set up a group of four people. Allow 10 minutes to plan the steps in the anxiety hierarchy that will lead to the fulfillment of Sally's terminal behavior of speaking before a group.

Two members of the group role-play a 3-minute taped interview showing how Sally's attempts to achieve step four may be reinforced. The other two members of the group take notes on all of the verbal and nonverbal reinforcements used by both interviewer and client.

The tape is played back, and all four members of the group take notes on the verbal cues and reinforcements. For 5 minutes the effectiveness of the reinforcements is discussed, and suggestions for improvement are made.

The same two group members resume their roles and conduct a 2-minute taped interview. After playing back the tape and noting the cues and reinforcements, the four members dicuss for 5 minutes the improvement in the effectiveness of the reinforcements.

☐ *Communication:* planned steps toward extinguishing stuttering

☐ *Use of materials:* prohibiting use of the record player (object removed) for 1 day because it was roughly handled

☐ *Following directions:* removal of some privileges as a result of smoking in bed

☐ *Social development:* tantrums ignored or followed by isolation from group, for instance, in a time-out box

Reinforcement is most effective if it is tuned in to the interests of the client. Negative and positive reinforcements are therefore relative terms that depend on the client for their impact.

Table 5-1 compares positive and negative reinforcement.

■ ■ ■

Modifying behavior is a many-sided phenomenon that takes into account the principles of learning, the client, the interviewer, and the environment in which the client lives. The client must learn to cope with more than the environment in the interview office. To accomplish this mastery of the environmental effects on behavior, the client must learn self-assertion. The interviewer advances this behavior change by reinforcing positive features of the client's self-image (self-concept) and by establishing a more flexible and more satisfying self-reinforcement system.

The task of behavior change can be simplified if the persons and events in the client's natural environment are programed to respond so that these factors reinforce the client's appropriate behavior and positive self-concept. The husband who approves of his wife's drinking by subtle reinforcements such as "I know you're trying, but if you don't stop right away, I'll understand" is really part of her problem of alcoholism.

Assertive training. Another way out of this dilemma or social and behavioral differences is to condition clients so that they are better able to cope with the direct and indirect reinforcements in the environment that are perpetuating their unsatisfying (to them) and inappropriate (to others) behavior. Even before coping skills, the clients must spot when and how their behavior tends to be assertive, nonassertive, or aggressive.

Differences among assertive, nonassertive, and aggressive behavior. Each person has the right to self-expression but also has the responsibility to facilitate the personal growth of others. Differen-

Table 5-1. *Positive and negative reinforcement*

Positive reinforcement *(reward for behavior tends toward repetition and maintenance of behavior)*	Negative reinforcement *(consequence of removal of unpleasant or painful situation tends toward repetition and maintenance of behavior)*
1. Receiving approval from your parents for doing well in your college courses.	1. Remaining at home to study a disliked course to avoid your parents' disapproval if you should fail.
2. Reading a book that you find interesting.	2. Pretending to read a book to avoid answering your wife's questions.
3. Having an enjoyable conversation with a friend.	3. Remaining to listen to a conversation you consider boring because your boss is involved and he will demand an explanation if you leave.
4. Receiving a certificate honoring you for your volunteer work with the juveniles in a detention home.	4. Volunteering to help tutor young elementary school children so that you will not have to write term papers.
5. Receiving social approval in nonverbal form from interviewer who smiles and with a pat on the shoulder says, "You did it well."	5. Handling situations as the interviewer has suggested to avoid the interviewer's frown and remarks such as "I'm disappointed; you could do better."

tiation between expression (assertion) and aggression (unbridled release) is essential to produce a favorable atmosphere for fulfillment of self and of others. Dealing with these differences and knowing when and how to stand up for their rights is often difficult for clients.

Western culture encourages the individual to move toward nonassertive or toward aggressive behavior. The quiet, obedient child is often the most praised and accepted at home and in school. When children are impelled to exercise their feelings and their rights, they often learn to be aggressive rather than to assert themselves. Unfortunately the consequence of aggression increases anxiety. Asssertive behavior, however, acts as an anxiety decreaser.

When the interviewer helps the client to become assertive, the client becomes the master rather than the victim of disturbing symptoms. Table 5-2 indicates the dissimilarities among nonassertive, assertive, and aggressive behavior.

Establishing the baseline. Baseline data refer to the frequency of the behavior to be changed. Such data provide information of where to begin in the conditioning process and how serious the behavior is for the client and for others. To obtain baseline data, one must follow several leads: (1) the extensiveness of the behavior under study, (2) the specific situations under which the behavior occurs, and (3) the recognition of the inappropriateness of the behavior.

Extensiveness of behavior. The extensiveness of the client's nonassertive and aggressive responses is one of the leads to pursue. The accumulation of evidence of inappropriate behavior frequently supports the picture of an oversocialized client who has been conditioned to the underdog position of nonassertive behavior or to the upperhand status of aggressive behavior. If the life history of the client were examined, the selected reinforcements discovered would reveal that as the child grew into adulthood the reinforcements overemphasized social obligations. Thus the rights of others were embellished with greater vitality than were the client's rights.

Dan illustrates nonassertive behavior issuing from this distortion of obligations. He tells the interviewer about what happened just last night when he was waiting in the line to buy a ticket to *Star Wars*. Some fellow ran alongside the line, stopped suddenly next to Dan, and elbowed himself into line in front of Dan. Dan's impulse was to "push the guy out"—but he didn't. Instead Dan comments about his feelings of "uneasiness" and "embarrassment" because, as usual, he proved himself "incompetent in standing up" for his rights.

"Besides, Mary was annoyed with me," says Dan as he raises his shoulders and slowly drops them. "Mary is not a silent woman. She bristles when she doesn't like something—no one easily puts something over on Mary." Dan continues to explain how Mary's yelling at the guy just made him feel smaller and more defeated, particularly when the guy looked back at them and smirked.

From Dan's description one may assume that Dan is generally nonassertive whereas Mary is usually aggressive in response to distasteful social encounters. Some individuals do not assert themselves or become aggressive in most situations. Others are nonassertive or aggressive with certain people and/or with certain groups of people. Alberti and Emmons (1978) discuss the differentiations among general nonassertiveness and aggression and situational nonassertiveness and aggression.

The extent to which an individual bends to the domination, exploitation, and offensiveness of one certain person, several people, or most people hinges on the degree of the individual's positive or negative self-esteem. The lower the level of self-esteem, the more restricted is the indivdual's expression of feelings and assertion of rights. The choice of behavior, nonassertiveness or aggression rather than assertiveness, depends on what works, that is, what kind of behavior has been reinforced in the past and is still being reinforced in the present.

The interviewer helps the client sort through the maze of circumstances to discover the instances when the client is apt to inhibit actions, words, or

Table 5-2. *Nonassertive, assertive, and aggressive behaviors*

	Nonassertive	Assertive	Aggressive
Self-expression	Self-denial; others feel sympathy or sometimes contempt toward this person	Enhances feelings of self-worth as well as self-worth of others	Enhances self but denies worth of others; others feel put down and even humiliated
Exhibiting feelings and/or acts	Does not feel free to say or do what is reasonable or right; conceals feelings because easily hurt and wants to avoid criticism	Expresses what he or she feels and thinks and encourages others to do so; usually has friendly, affectionate, nonanxious feelings and is sufficiently self-assured to accept or reject criticism	Expresses what he or she feels and thinks but denies opportunity for such expression by others; usually feels resentment and anger and considers criticism unjustified
Selecting path of action and/or decision making	Easily maneuvered into undesired situation because of compliant surface behavior; fears rejection or ridicule of own decisions	Chooses in accordance with own needs without infringing on rights of others to choose	Usually chooses only in accordance with own needs, disregarding effect on others
Reaching goals	Often stops short of goal or doesn't try too hard to achieve it; feels inadequate to task and lacks self-confidence; others may push ahead, achieving his or her lost goal	Usually achieves goal and encourages others to achieve their goals	Achieves goal by downgrading others; thus others usually do not achieve goals
Feelings	Feels hurt, crushed, anxious, self-conscious because does not assert self; others may feel guilty or angry at incompetent behavior	Assertive responses make him or her feel less anxious and more competent; others feel comfortable and at ease in expressing themselves to him or her	Depreciates (nonverbal and verbal "put downs") others so that they feel hurt, defensive, and incompetent
Responses to unreasonable request	Probably concedes to request; others may feel guilty and annoyed with his or her inability to stand ground	Politely refuses and explains reasons; others may not be happy about refusal but usually feel there is some justification for the refusal	Refuses sarcastically with innuendos, which makes others either defensive or angry (anger, as such, is not aggression; it becomes aggressive when it is buried and not expressed assertively)
Attitude toward origin of difficulties	More often is intrapunitive (blames self for whatever goes wrong) and punishes self (form of self-reinforcement)	More often is impunitive (free from punishing responses); more likely to evaluate events rationally	More often is extrapunitive (blames others for whatever goes wrong) and tries to punish others (form of reinforcement for others)

Modified from Alberti, R.E., and Emmons, M.L.: Your perfect right, San Luis Obispo, Calif., 1978, Impact Publishers, Inc.

exhibition of feelings. To determine the extent of restraint, the client is encouraged to talk about the scope and strength of these social chains with which he or she has become locked. The interviewer observes the client's verbal and nonverbal signs of anxiety as he or she erects a pattern of "people walk all over me," "everyone gets ahead of me," "can't get anything I want," "constant battle to get anywhere," "claw and scratch my way through life," or "there's a sucker born every minute; why not take what you can get?" Discovering the specific or generalized particulars of the interpersonal anxiety that results in either decreased or belligerent action assists the client and interviewer in planning a behavior modification program based on reinforcement of assertive behavior.

Specificity. Several factors in addition to individual life experiences induce a person to respond with more assured assertion in one situation than in another. The different reinforcements prevailing in Western culture have regulated masculine and feminine behavior. This is evidenced not only in distinctive mannerisms but also in the exercise of assertion.

In measuring the meaning of the client's behavior, cultural impositions must be taken into account. This holds true not only for the reinforcements for behavior according to sex but also in regard to subcultural distinctions originating from ethnic and economic expectations. Thus what may be characterized as assertive behavior in one social situation or social group would come across as aggressive or even nonassertive behavior in another situation.

The translation of the script that contains the client's behavior depends on the social situation from which the client comes and the degree of rewarding consequences open to the client because of this behavior. Armed with data about when, where, and how, the client takes on the tasks of social living and self-fulfillment.

Recognition. Before any behavior change can be effected, the client must realize the inappropriateness of the behavior. The client may feel uncomfortable and want events to turn out differently but may not be fully aware that it is past and present behavior that is important. This returns to the concept of self-fulfilling prophecy. It is almost inevitable that the client is going to be a loser. He or she not only looks and acts the part of the loser, but manages to get into situations in which a loser is the only part that is left in the drama. The client must begin to notice the bad smell of the place and must learn that sometimes leaving the scene is the most feasible assertive behavior.

Others may help or hinder the client in continuing a certain character part. Another factor in the role continuation is the client's reaction and ability and/or desire to institute a new action. Sarah in Example 5-3 and Exercise 5-3 exemplifies this difficulty to note one's own self-reinforcement of a part in a self-written script.

Example 5-3
SARAH WRITES HER SCRIPT

Sarah trudges through the waist-deep snow and feels her hand getting stiffer. Soon she doesn't even feel her left hand, and the initial pain is gone. She walks into the classroom, drops her books on the floor, and sits down. Then she begins to feel an uncomfortable tingling sensation in the tips of her fingers. She thinks to herself, "Defrosting, that's what's happening. Hell, it hurts." She gets up from her seat and with a brief look at the professor up front she runs out of the room.

"Stupid," she says to herself, "Stupid, why didn't you say something? He's going to think you're some kind of a nut. What a jerked-up thing to do." She walks as rapidly as she can to the nurse's office, looking straight ahead as she walks. Some of the people walking by look at her and smile or say hello, but since Sarah does not respond, they walk away.

Sarah enters the nurse's office and explains to the nurse, Ms. D., "Guess my hand is frostbitten, Is there anything that can be done about it?" Ms. D. puts some warm packs on Sarah's hand, and, although the severe pain of returning circulation as the hand thaws is tremendous, Sarah speaks to the nurse about the depth of the snow and how unusual the storm is. When Sarah recovers the use of her hand, she is careful to thank the nurse and to commend her on her assistance.

As Sarah leaves the nurse's office, she realizes that she feels unusually tired; as she walks along the corridor

---

Exercise 5-3

HOW DO YOU REWRITE SARAH'S SCRIPT? *(parts 4 and 5 or this exercise might be carried over into a second meeting of the group)*

Time: PARTS 1 TO 3, APPROXIMATELY 36 MINUTES;
      PARTS 4 AND 5, APPROXIMATELY 36 MINUTES

Part 1

Group members arrange themselves into subgroups of four participants. Each subgroup participant selects one of the following roles: Sarah, the nurse, the professor, the counselor. During the total time of 2 minutes each role player tapes (audio cassette or reel-tape) what he or she thinks and feels about Sarah. Listen to the tape. This is part of your information about Sarah.

Part 2

Everyone should have read Example 5-3 and also the following:
Sarah has come to the counselor about her inability to show her feelings. This is the only problem she relates when she first enters the office. The counselor, who knows Sarah is coming, pulls out her medical record from the college health services. The counselor notes she has a history of headaches, which she dates from when she reached puberty at the age of 14.

Conduct a 10-minute interview during which the counselor begins the interview, starts exploring Sarah's concerns, and discovers how and under what circumstances Sarah handles social situations assertively, nonassertively, and aggressively. In the interview the counselor should integrate what the nurse and the professor say about Sarah. The counselor also shows his or her method of closing the interview.

Part 3

Listen to the tape and then for 10 minutes discuss Sarah's problem as well as the positive aspects of the counselor's approach to beginning the interview, developing the interview, using empathic understanding, and exploring social behavior in terms of assertion, nonassertion, and aggressivenes. After reviewing the positive aspects, discuss ways in which the interview may be improved.

Part 4

This is Sarah's second visit to the counselor. At this session the counselor interviews for 2 minutes each the nurse and the professor. The counselor discusses the viewpoints the nurse and professor expressed at the beginning of this exercise. Then the counselor tapes a 5-minute session with Sarah. Each subgroup listens to the tape and afterward discusses for 10 minutes the improvement and the areas for further improvement in the second counseling session.

Part 5

For 5 minutes discuss possible reasons for each individual's role selection as the professor, nurse, counselor, or Sarah.

to the classroom, she notes that she sees some dancing black spots. "Oh no," she says, "that's all I need now, a headache." A slow throbbing begins in her right eye, and Sarah knows that she is going to have a migraine. "Why didn't I say something to Ms. D.? Could have gotten some pills. Began to feel something then, that horrible gnawing feeling in my stomach."

"Nut, nut, stupid nut. Didn't say anything to him [the professor] or her [the nurse] . . . all show. Don't want anyone to know. Damn, it's getting worse. Or is it I'm making it worse? Wow! Do I feel sick, nausea, so tired, and *have* to go back into the room. Everyone is sure to look, yep, stare at me. They'll think, 'There she goes again, the snob in bo-peep clothing.' Bo-peep? What do I mean by that? Why do I always do things the wrong way? Speak up . . . say up . . . throw up. Can't give forth my feelings. No wonder Joe called me a cold fish the other day. Nut, nut—what a nut. Throbbing—oooh! The throbbing, splitting my head. 'False pride,' he said. Oooh!"

Sarah reveals a great deal in her stream of consciousness discussion. Unable to show her feelings, perhaps because she has been conditioned aversely with a rebuff such as "Don't tell me your troubles" and/or annoyance (negative reinforcement) for imperfections or any show of weakness, she has become impelled toward "doing things" and doing them "right" (negative reinforcement). Sarah seeks out situations in which she will become distraught, then she inflicts self-punishment because she is unable to assert herself with people—masochism. Her primary assertion is to be perfect. Only rarely do her feelings spill forth in aggressive attacks on people. When she does let loose, she becomes very irritable to the point of seeking to belittle and rattle the individual at whom her wrath is directed—sadism. She turns from inward punishment (intrapunitive) in the form of headaches to outward punishment (extrapunitive) in the form of anger. A review of her learning experiences confirm that she has been reinforced for both kinds of behavior—masochism and nonassertiveness and sadism and aggressiveness.

The interplay of sadism and masochism—of aggression and nonaggression against others and oneself—accentuates the fact that these behaviors often offset one another. Aggressive acts sometimes are perpetrated by the seemingly nonassertive "good and quiet" neighbor who locks himself into a room with a gun or who snipes passersby. A vicious cycle of self-satisfying consequences reinforce and sustain the repetition of these behaviors.

Before clients are ready to alter their inappropriate behavior (aggression, nonassertion), they must recognize the what, when, and how of their behavior. Then they must want to do something about it. The interviewer's work is to help clients in both of these steps toward assertion.

Assertive training procedures

Preparation of the client for change. Interpersonal living is learned. Numerous authors have discussed the many forms of behavior resulting from this learning. Adler (1964), Alberti and Emmons (1978), Horney (1954), and Wolpe (1969) make similar distinctions in explaining social behavior. Adler writes of the "ruling attitude" and the "getting type," expressed in aggressive behavior, that are similar to Wolpe's "roughshod, self-interest behavior" and Horney's description of persons "moving against others." All these labels for extreme egocentric (selfish) behavior are examples of a philosophy of "attack to conquer." In its extreme form this everything-for-self behavior becomes the sociopathic behavior of individuals who have not been reinforced to feel guilty or anxious about their behavior. They do their own thing no matter who gets hurt or how they must hurt them.

At the other extreme are nonassertive individuals whose aggression is directed inward. They feel too much guilt and too much anxiety. They are the "side-stepping" types (Adler, 1964) who avoid problems. They move toward people (Horney, 1954), often humbling themselves to attain the reinforcement of other people's approval. They may be handshakers, the backslappers, or the "yes" people who would prefer to avoid these behaviors but are keeping out of trouble in this way. In putting themselves down they avoid the challenge of proving themselves or, conversely, prove themselves by allowing others to assert themselves, thus getting the thrill of "how wonderful am I to let them fulfill themselves." They move away from people (Horney, 1954) because they are fearful of the possible rejection and/or failure of social confrontation.

Assertion requires more than being free to affirm oneself. It also requires social interest (Adler, 1964). When clients have reviewed these differences among aggression, nonassertion, and assertion, they are better prepared to assume responsibility for investigating the details of their own behavior.

One more idea may promote clients' eagerness to attempt to do something about inappropriate behavior—the concept of reciprocal inhibition. Wolpe (1969) explains that when individuals are able to assert themselves, the resulting positive feelings of accomplishment are self-reinforcing. With the gradual conditioning of new habits of assertive responses, the individuals are able to better curb their anxiety feelings. When clients do something new by word or act to move themselves forward (positive reinforcement), they inhibit former unsatisfying behavior (negative reinforcement). The new habit serves a protective function through release of feelings and, in the process, reduces anxiety. Individuals who suddenly think of something humorous while embroiled in a blazing argument find that the fire of the verbal fight begins to cool. This, too, is reciprocal inhibition.

Potential difficulties. Before the interviewer can help the client become more assertive, he or she must identify some client characteristics that result in difficulties for the client. The interviewer may encounter perplexing characteristics—generalized inappropriate behavior, fear of aggression, and the proper units for behavior change.

Generalized inappropriate behavior is a combination of behavioral characteristics that must be identified by a more complex approach than can be accomplished in the usual counseling situation. Thus a more experienced professional may be needed on a consultative basis or the client should be referred to someone else who is able to handle the more complicated problems associated with the general patterns of frustration and failure.

In contrast to the widespread theme of defeatist behavior, the more selected the conditions under which nonassertion or aggression occurs, the simpler the solution for behavioral change. The individual who is nonassertive when with individuals he or she considers more learned or who becomes extremely (and sometimes obnoxiously) forceful when debating a point with a certain person has a greater possibility for rapid success in changing to an assertive approach than the person who exhibits these inappropriate behaviors in most social situations.

Another kind of problem originates with the individual who evidences fearful responses, even to the point of being phobic (irrational, pervasive fear) about self-assertion. The anxiety-stimulating events are often extensive, and the individual may be concerned with speaking to a group of people, asking questions, or any form of social situation. Assertion either becomes the trademark for aggressive behavior that horrifies the individual or an overwhelming form of one-upmanship that the individual considers undesirable. Extreme caution must be used not to break down the barricades of coping strategies too suddenly. Whether this person should be referred to a therapist rather than a counselor must be considered before the interview process is begun.

Finally, the interviewer must plan precisely to decide on comfortable units for the assertive training process. These units of approximations toward the terminal behavior of assertion by choice should have a high probability of success. The anguish that the client has experienced from prior attempts and failures must be avoided. Sometimes failure and setback may follow when the client misinterprets a cue or is too clumsy in the newly sprouting behavior. Then the interviewer must step in to help the client understand and regain confidence.

Behavior shaping. The process of desensitization is an important element in the conditioning of assertive behavior. In desensitization a hierarchy of anxiety-producing stimuli is drafted and the client is presented with these stimuli (for example, gradual and closer exposure to feared snakes) and positively reinforced at each unit of success accomplished. This is shaping.

In the shaping process the terminal behavior is broken down into small units or single responses. These are arranged in a hierarchy of activities of increasing difficulty. Each step requires a little more of the individual. After the individual makes a successful attempt, the interviewer offers positive reinforcement either verbally or nonverbally; then the next step is assigned. Each new unit should be simple enough that the client may continue without too much stress.

The process of shaping is encouraged when the interviewer models both the inappropriate behavior the client exhibits and the appropriate behavior to be achieved. The client observes and is encouraged to assess the interviewer's modeling. Then the interviewer may once again model while the client takes the role of the other person involved in a social situation. This process may be repeated until both interviewer and client are assured that the difference between nonassertive or aggressive behavior and assertive behavior is understood (behavioral rehearsal). An additional procedure may be added during which the client role-plays himself or herself, first with the inappropriate and then with the appropriate responses. The use of videotape or an audio tape increases the feedback for the client. Practice in front of a full-length mirror helps some clients note nonverbal cues.

After the client has examined his or her own behavior as well as the interviewer's modeling behavior, the client begins the progressive steps toward the goal of assertion. During this process the interviewer is actively engaged in modeling and providing feedback to the client about the role playing by means of a discussion that is enriched with the video tape and/or audio tape.

How long the process takes depends on the client's degree of motivation, what behaviors are already possible (behavioral repertoire), the success at each step toward the goal, how carefully the interviewer has recorded the client's progress,

and the reinforcements the client receives from the interviewer and from other significant people. In addition, the decision about when to progress from practice in the security of the interviewer's office to a real social situation calls for a joint brainwork and agreement by the client and the interviewer. This may require only one visit or a series of visits to the interviewer's office.

The client who begins trying out new response patterns is more likely to succeed if the assertive responses have become automatic. The client should report to the interviewer all attempts to behave more assertively rather than with the former inappropriate nonassertion or aggressiveness, and together they should review the degree of success experienced. This may be accomplished through discussion or by means of role playing.

The final step in learning assertive responses is the acquisition of a generalized behavior pattern that permits the client to expand assertive responses to situations other than those practiced in the confines of the interviewer's office. Eventually the client realizes that the process of living entails persistent testing of one's own behavior in a multitude of situations and the ability to be self-reinforcing.

Changed self-concept. The terminal behavior to which clients are striving is assertive behavior that is satisfying. Thus clients who become sufficiently assured of their assertive ability can discriminate the situations when they will assert themselves. Since they do not have to hide or to prove themselves constantly, they can look more readily to the needs of others. They are able to wait for a favorable time for assertion when they will not be upsetting the more sensitive person or when too many "bad vibes" will make assertion fruitless.

Furthermore, they are able to admit they are wrong when they make a mistake and not compound the mistake with "assertion" colored red with the fury of aggression. Indeed, they will know when compromise is the better path to follow rather than stubborn resistance to have only their way.

To assert or not to assert depends on the insistent essential of social interest (Adler, 1964). Social interest demands that solutions be useful not only to oneself but also to others. Thus the individuals who have adopted social interest as a way of life "see with the eyes of another, hear with the ears of another, feel with the heart of another" (Ansbacher and Ansbacher, 1964), yet are aware that these are borrowed on a temporary basis. Empathy and social interest have much in common. The balancing of social and self interests that characterizes assertion is fluently expressed in the Talmudic saying, "If I am not for myself, who will be for me? But, if I am for myself alone, what am I?"

The experiential interview

The helping event of mutual support is enriched by the interviewer's empathic responses to the client's problems and concerns. Acceptance intermixed with timely and constructive confrontation encourages the client to develop greater openness and self-awareness. This fulfilling interpersonal transaction characterizes the microcosm of society that is an experiential interview.

Sometimes it is difficult to draw sharp distinctions among the information-oriented, behavior modification, and experiential interviews. The information-oriented interviews may be concerned with more than objective factual data and may seek details about attitudes, values, feelings, hopes, plans, and self-descriptions. The behavior modification interviewer also realizes that other features of the interview are significant in the changing of inappropriate behavior. Teaching a client a different set of responses to anxiety-provoking stimuli requires that the client be enlisted as an agent of the change (Nelson, 1979) and that this change be accomplished in an atmosphere of empathic understanding, nonpossessive warmth, and genuineness (Truax and Carkhuff, 1967). Otherwise, although the behavior change takes effect in a short time, it might also be of short duration (Bocknek, 1979).

Differential features. The nucleus of the experiential interview inheres in the preceding statement about the involvement of the client and the atmospheric conditions conducive to change. The

significant differentiating features are the kind of sharing and understanding that enter into the experiential interview and the aim toward some degree of personal growth for the client and for the interviewer. These features may also occur in the information interviews but are then side effects rather than primary goals.

The experiential interview stresses the human relationship between two people being together in a moment of time. The immediate situation and the sharing of thoughts in an acceptant atmosphere are essential attributes. The experiential orientation erases a hierarchy of "better than" and "worse than" and thus omits judgmental reactions. The helping-knowledgeable person and the client join in their quest for personal growth and in becoming more fulfilled individuals. How many interviews and how frequently the interviews occur are mutual decisions.

Experiential means just what the word implies, experiencing with the client. This kind of interview becomes a proving ground of life in which two people, the interviewer and the client, share feelings, understandings, and behavior—a small unit of life experience in which the individuals involved share themselves and in which the client can test his or her interpersonal relationships.

Experiential interviews and psychosocial therapy. Experiential interviewing resembles both Turner's (1978) definition of psychosocial therapy and Ivey and Simek-Downing's (1980) description of the person-environment interaction. (See Chapter 8.) Turner (1978) defines psychosocial therapy as follows:

That form of psychotherapeutic practice in which the bio-psycho-social knowledge of human and societal behavior, skills in relating to individuals, families, groups and communities, and competence in mobilizing available resources are combined in the medium of individual, group and familial relationships to help persons to alter their personality, behavior or situation, fulfilling human functioning within the framework of their own values and goals and the available resources of society.

As with the experiential interview, the conceptual basis for psychosocial therapy is interdisciplinary—a multi-faceted system that reaffirms the centrality of the client's needs, difficulties, and inclinations. Furthermore, psychosocial therapy parallels the experiential interview as well as the Ivey and Simek-Downing viewpoint in its direction toward involvement with and awareness of the impact of environmental resources such as the family, groups, and the community.

Experiential interview and person-environment approach. Ivey and Simek-Downing (1980) conceive of the person-environment interaction as follows:

□ The environment is developed by the person.
□ Persons are developed by their environment.
□ Persons and environment are constantly interacting with and changing one another.

This model proposes that the target of intervention may be the individual, a primary group (family or living companions), associational groups (clubs, classes, other activities with groups), or institutions and the community (school, church, governmental agencies). Common to all three (experiential, psychosocial, person-environment) notions is the commitment to personal and societal change with particular emphasis on individual fulfillment in societal improvement. All three approaches differ from psychodynamic counseling.

Experiential interview and psychodynamic counseling. Psychodynamic counseling—"uncovering therapy"—concentrates on disclosing the unconscious processes regulating the client's anxiety and malfunctioning. Classical psychoanalytic therapy supports the long-term goal of personality reconstruction and pays scant attention to the environmental impact of cultural and other physical, social, and interpersonal circumstances surround-

Table 5-3. *Three dissimilarities between Freud's psychoanalytic view and the experiential interview*

Freud's psychoanalytic view	Experiential interview
Deterministic: Individuals are impelled by animistic-like instincts and needs. Early childhood experiences are stressed as imprinters of life-long personality structure. Thus uncovering the past is essential for recovery. Since individuals are motivated by instincts and early childhood experiences, they are victims of these and not to be censured or held responsible for their acts.	**Existentialistic:** People are shaped by environmental events and, in turn, affect these events. Thus their motivations depend on their experiences, not their instincts. The impact of the "here and now" takes precedence over past events, and past events are significant as currently perceived. Individuals are subject to changes throughout their life, depending on their environmental interactions, and individuals learn desirable and fulfilling acts as well as undesirable and unfulfilling acts. In essence, therefore, individuals can learn responsibility for themselves, in accordance with their intellectual and other characteristics, if provided the opportunities for such learning.
Mind-body dichotomy: Individuals are composed of mind (mental functions) and body (physical functions); one influences the other, and both are dependent on cause-effect laws.	**Holistic viewpoint:** Mind and body are one, and behavior results from the interactive integration of all parts and functions of the body.
Irrationality: People lean toward irrationality rather than rationality in their responses to life events. In spite of this emphasis on the client's basic irrationality, the psychoanalytic approach depends on reasoning as part of the therapeutic process.	**Rationality:** The cognitive restructuring that is part of the problem solving of the experiential interview helps clients to identify the relationship between their self-defeating and faulty thought processes and their subsequent emotional responses and other actions. Thus people can be rational in their evaluations and responses.

ing an individual and arranging the milieu favorably or unfavorably.

Finally, the experiential interview, psychosocial therapy, and the person-environment approach differ from the psychoanalysis of Freud, in particular, in at least the three aspects listed in Table 5-3.

Psychoanalytic contributions to the experiential interview. By no means should Table 5-3 suggest that psychoanalysis has not contributed to the processes of experiential interviewing. Freud's nonmoralistic attitude and his identification of unconscious motivations clarify and support acceptance of clients' comments such as "I don't know what kept me from going to the social gathering" or "Whatever made me say that?" Individuals are often unaware of the impellents for their behavior. They may be reluctant to admit something about themselves—even to themselves. So they "forget" the thought. On the other hand, they may momentarily not recognize the origin of a particular act because of their anxiety or because so many other events have happened since that act. The experiential interview builds the client's confidence to recollect if this is essential for progress in the present interview relationship. Other contributions of Freud include his theory of personality as the first substantial theory, his accentuation of early childhood experiences, which prompted attention to child-rearing practices and instigated research, and, perhaps most consequential for the present discussion of interview techniques, his use and development of the interview as part of the helping process.

■ ■ ■

Similarities are discernible in the foregoing descriptions of information-oriented, behavior management, and experiential interviews. Besides the prerequisite basic skills of observation, recording, and reporting, the three broadly categorized interview forms also must be versatile and harmonious with the client's value system and needs. Accordingly, the helper must be sufficiently flexible to adapt interview techniques to the individuality of the client and yet be "tough" enough to aid the

client to pursue his or her objectives. The experiential interview borrows and gels methods from the information-oriented and behavior management approaches with additional characteristics such as client-centered orientation, attunement to interpersonal processes and thus to the transactions of communication, and emphasis on reciprocality in client-helper personal growth. Examples 5-4 to 5-7 present samples of information-seeking, information-sharing, behavior modification, and experiential interviews. Exercise 5-4 (p. 231) involves a a role-playing situation based on these interviews.

Example 5-4
INFORMATION-SEEKING INTERVIEW

MS. H.: *(Knocks at the door, then bends down to pick up the briefcase she has put at her feet.)*

HELEN: *(Opens the door slightly.)* Yes?

MS. H.: I am from the University of Wannuga. We are conducting a survey for the Institute for Policy Studies on current opinions toward the energy crisis. See, here are my credentials.

HELEN: *(Opens the door a little further.)* I'm really very busy today; have to finish something before I leave for an appointment.

MS. H.: Just 10 minutes. The questions won't take more than 10 minutes to answer. We have selected five houses on this block, and since yours is in this chosen sample, it would help considerably if you would give me 10 minutes of your time.

HELEN: *(Opens the door wider, and Ms. H. enters.)*

MS. H.: Thank you very much. I appreciate your assistance. You do have an attractive house. May I sit here?

Ms. H. removes the questionnaire from her briefcase and proceeds to complete the background information about the educational level, financial group, occupational level, and age group that describes Helen. Then Ms. H. asks the questions on the questionnaire, stopping to chat briefly when Helen asks for some clarification about the purpose of the study.

Example 5-5
INFORMATION-SHARING INTERVIEW

TOM: *(Enters the counselor's office at the college and sits down in the chair opposite Ms. M.)*

MS. M.: *(Looks up from her desk and smiles.)* Hello, Tom. Nice to see you again.

TOM: *(Stretching out his legs.)* I've been thinking about our conversation last week and looked into *Barron's Guide to Colleges.* Need to talk to you some more about some of my ideas.

MS. M.: *(Silent.)*

TOM: Last week I was tossing around whether I should take off 1 year after graduation, then go on to graduate school, or start grad school right away. Want to work. Just work. Doesn't matter what I do. Want to be around some people I like—people who dig me, too. Yet my parents are on my back about grad school.

MS. M.: Work or school? Difficult decision to make. So many things going for either decision.

TOM: Hmmm, that's it! When we talked about it last week, you suggested *Barron's* to see if any of the colleges turned me on. I did. Saw a few colleges—offer the program I want, in the geography I want, people I want, near enough. I could get in, but . . . (Pulls up his legs and sits forward. With his hands clasped between his knees, he looks over Ms. M.'s shoulder.)

MS. M.: (Silent.)

TOM: Gotta get away from education bullshit for a year.

MS. M.: Have you any ideas of where you would go to work for the year?

TOM: New York. Like to be around New York. Don't know where I would find work or a place. Some people said they'd come to live with me.

MS.M.: I have some information about job opportunities and apartments in New York. Would you like to look the lists over during the next week and then we can get together to talk about your decision for next year?

TOM: Thanks. Give me a start. I'll keep *Barron's*, also, and see you at 2 next week.

Example 5-6
BEHAVIOR MANAGEMENT INTERVIEW

With stooped shoulders the man and woman slowly walk into the psychologist's office. The woman holds a crumpled tissue in her right hand. The psychologist, Dr. E., rises and walks over to Mr. and Ms. R.

DR. E.: Hello, please sit down over here. (He motions to two black leather seats that face a third black leather seat.)

MR. R.: (Sliding down in the seat.) Well! This is a comfortable chair.

MS. R.: (Looking at her husband.) Oh, Tom, let's get down to it. This uncertainty is . . . Dr. E., is he . . . is Buddy really not . . . not . . .

MR. R.: Not normal—not normal. That's what we want to know. Is our child normal?

DR. E.: Dr. M. examined Buddy, and he believes Buddy has a good chance to live a satisfactory life. Buddy is a jolly 5-year-old who can do much more than he does. I administered some psychological tests and find that Buddy functions at the intellectual level of a 2-year-old, but both Dr. M. and I believe he is able to do much more.

MS. R.: But Doctor, it just can't be—can't be. What did we do to . . . Doctor, you're the fourth doctor we've seen. Just

confuses us . . . ready to give up. This doctor shopping won't do.

DR. E.: That's fine. You are ready to really help Buddy now, to help Buddy learn a great deal.

MS. R.: He looks so funny—eyes so far apart, nose so small, chin almost not there, ears so low. How can he live a happy life? He's so unmanageable, bangs his head against the wall. Have to take care of him, dress him, feed him.

MR. R.: Come now, Doris, you don't even give the kid a chance to do anything on his own.

MS. R.: What do you know? You don't have to watch the mothers of the other children look at me with pity when I have to carry Buddy up and down the steps. You don't . . .

MR. R.: Shut up, Doris. I don't want to hear you any more.

MS. R.: (Dabs at her eyes with the crumpled tissue.)

DR. E.: Buddy can do much more. It all depends on reinforcement, systematic rewards for appropriate behavior.

MR. R.: What do you mean—reinforcements? What more can Buddy do?

DR. E.: Look at it this way. Buddy learns just as anyone else would but more slowly. Behavior is caused; it can be changed by what happens after the behavior, in other words, the consequence of the behavior.

MR. R.: Yes. So, how do we do it?

DR. E.: It's much easier than you think. Both of you can help.

MS. R.: Doctor, I don't know—don't . . .

MR. R.: Doris, hear him out.

DR. E.: There are three important parts to changing behavior. First, you have to decide on the behavior you want to change. This is your target behavior, your behavioral goal. Pinpoint this behavior. What behavior bothers you most?

MS. R.: Head banging, that's it. Can't stand it; I yell at him; I hold him in my arms; I talk to him, but he does it more. When I don't let him do something, then that's the time he does it.

DR. E.: Fine. Now you have given step two, what follows the behavior, and step three, what happened before. Target behavior—head banging; reinforcement—yell, hold, talk equals attention, and you say that what happens before is stopping him from doing something. There it is, that's your formula for change.

MR. R.: Sounds easy. Is it that simple?

DR. E.: Simple, yes, but it may be made difficult because you need to be consistent, particularly at the beginning of the learning. You must decide on reinforcers to extinguish the behavior. For Buddy, ignoring the head banging would be a form of nonreinforcement. Pay attention when Buddy does not bang his head, not when he does.

The interview continues with Dr. E. practicing behavior modification with Ms. R. Whenever Ms. R. becomes upset, he ignores her. When she or Mr. R. makes a statement that demonstrates willingness to do something positive about Buddy's behavior, Dr. E. pays attention by responding.

Example 5-7
EXPERIENTIAL INTERVIEW

Dr. P. is seated at his desk when he hears a gentle knock on his office door. He rises from his chair and goes to the door, opening it slowly. Before him stands a small-framed young woman with long, blonde hair. Dr. P. notes the frown on her face and the downturned mouth.

DR. P.: Hi! I'm Dr. P., come in. *(He points to his left where there are two chairs, one straight-backed and the other upholstered in brown leather.)* Please sit down.

TERRY: *(Sits down on the straight-backed chair with her hands loosely lying in her lap and her feet pushed under the chair seat.)* I phoned yesterday. Told you about myself. A little bit. I'm Terry.

DR. P.: Yes, I remember. You said that Margie told you about me.

TERRY: *(Staring at her hands and silent.)*

DR. P.: Perhaps it would help if you would tell me a little more about how you feel.

TERRY: *(In a low voice.)* As I told you over the phone, I'm pregnant. Just found out definitely from the doctor 2 days before I phoned you. Can't tell my instant-liberal, middle-class, hung-up parents. Thought I could. Have to know what to do . . . talk to someone. I want an abortion, but don't have the money . . . don't know where to go. Haven't told Marty about it. Don't want him to know. So, I feel alone, pushed in, lousy.

DR. P.: Hmmmm. You feel confused, need someone to listen, someone to understand and help. I know that feeling.

TERRY: Yes, help. I spoke to Margie, and she said if she were pregnant, she would have the baby. She's a year older, 16, don't think that makes her readier. She belongs to the high school women's lib group. I don't. I'm too young to have a baby. Want to finish school. How would I face my parents . . . or my straight friends?

DR. P.: *(Silent.)*

TERRY: Marty is a good person, a beautiful person. He knows where he's at. Someday we may get married. Maybe not—too young to know, too much still to do. He's 18 and in his first year of college. He's the only one. We've been total for about 6 months. Don't you think an abortion is the only answer?

DR. P.: I wish I could give you a simple "yes" or "no" to your question. It might or it might not help you. But the answer is yours. I will help you try to find the answer. Some facts might help. How far along in pregnancy are you?

TERRY: Five or 6 weeks, I think. That's what the doctor thought. Wow, was that something, telling him I'm Mrs. G.

DR. P.: You do seem to have some strong feelings about being pregnant. It might help to air those feelings.

TERRY: You know, that's the odd part. Feel angry at Marty, yet like the idea. Makes me feel a little closer to him. Feel that I would like to have the baby . . . to sort of play with it. Not ready for that mother game. Feel mad at my parents because I don't trust them to let me talk about this. Feel guilty about not being careful and maybe fearful about an abortion. Feel as if I'm going back and forth. *(Sways slowly back and forth, and her hands become fists in her lap.)*

DR. P.: Yes, I see, I see.

TERRY: *(Silent.)*

DR. P.: I feel that you're saying—you seem to be telling me that you're both glad and mad at what has happened, that you wished that your parents and Marty would know about how you feel so that they might share the burden.

TERRY: *(Looks at Dr. P. and stretches her hand out toward him.)* That's it . . . mmmm . . . that's it. It seems as if I'm left alone when I need someone most. Marty should know about it without me telling him. My parents should offer their help without me asking for it. Feel good about it. Feel bad about it. If only I could wish it away, all away.

An important contribution from interviewing would be lost if all human service workers, although skillful, narrowed their professional space to a seat behind a desk and, practiced only a specific form of interviewing, fitting the client to their specialization. Some human service workers do not constrict themselves to the office-desk pattern. They expand their helping, caring, and mutuality and flexibly use a script that includes active movement to aid the person in need of help—*where the problem is*. They move into the streets to rap with the youth who hang-on in shopping centers, in the fast-food eateries, in the vacant lots. They go to clients' homes to help them plan a budget or to train them to manage their children more effectively. Human service workers strive to deal with a problem before it snowballs into a major catastrophe. Thus the office, the home, and the community can be the settings for human service workers. Bolstered by self-understanding, controlled nondirection, friendliness, and skillful interpersonal functioning, human service workers seek "wellness" (the quality of life) for themselves and their clients—not just the alleviation of illness. (See Chapter 1.) They also are alert to the configuration of influences impinging on the effectiveness of the interviewing process.

Exercise 5-4

HOW DO THE VARIETIES IN INTERVIEW GOALS DIFFER? *(should be done in a group)*

Time: APPROXIMATELY 20 MINUTES

An effective method to discover the differences in the atmosphere and the different approaches described in Examples 5-4 to 5-7 is to role-play the different situations.

Get together a group of five trainees. Three members of the group will be the observers, and two members will be the role players. The role players should continue the interviews from the point the actual conversation stopped in the examples. The three observers should take notes about different aspects of the role-playing situation. One member should note verbal cues, another member should note nonverbal cues, and a third member should observe the entire situation, noting all cues.

The two role players decide who will be the interviewer and who will be the client and then conduct an interview for 3 minutes. Stop the role playing and discuss for 5 minutes the observational cues that were recorded. Discuss the kind of interview that is developing—information getting, information sharing, behavior modification, or experiential. Suggestions should be made by all members of the group as to how the interview is effective and how it might be even more effective.

Role players resume their roles, but this time they incorporate the suggestions from the discussion. Observers once again record the verbal and nonverbal cues. After 5 minutes stop the role playing and again discuss the recorded observations.

FACTORS INFLUENCING THE EFFECTIVENESS OF INTERVIEWING

Undergirding the discussions in this book is the ecological perspective—that there is an intrinsic mutual compatibility (or incompatibility) between a person and his or her environment (Baum, Singer, and Baum, 1981; Rogers-Warren and Warren, 1977). The declaration of the fact of continuing transactions of person-environment-person and so on focuses attention on numerous attributes of the environment, including processes of communication, acquisition of knowledge, and procedures and channels for applying information. From the ecological perspective, therefore, whatever is operating in the helping situation advances or impedes the helping process. Three issues germane to this ecological orientation are explored in this section: certain personal characteristics, misdirected motivation, and interview pitfalls.

Personal characteristics

Helpers would profit from reviewing at least three characteristics that markedly modify the cli-

mate in the interview: status, roles, and interrelatedness and interrelating.

Status. Status refers to culturally and individually determined positions that stem from sex, age, ethnic origin, socioeconomic level, and education. The status of the person determines the rights and obligations of the person. How the status of the interviewer and client is handled may help or hinder the interview process.

Roles. Roles refer to culturally and individually determined patterns of expected behavior that may help or hinder an interview, depending on the meaning and worth of the roles to the individuals.

Interrelatedness and interrelating. Interrelating and interrelatedness are distinguishable. Interrelating occurs when the participants in an interview consider themselves *separated individuals* interacting with one another (an interaction interview). Interrelatedness refers to two individuals working toward a *mutual relationship*. Interrelating assumes there is respect, worth, and perhaps dignity for the client. Interrelatedness goes further by adding equality to respect, worth, and dignity.

Status, roles, and interrelatedness are all part of the social system of the transaction. In this society of the interview the interviewer and the client weave an everchanging pattern of responses.

■ ■ ■

The helper's review of his or her status, roles and interrelatedness is the first step. If the helper confirms that all these characteristics are compatible with the client's needs, the next step is somewhat more difficult because it probes into what makes the helper "tick"—the helper's motivation. It would be foolish to pretend that human service workers do not receive satisfactions from helping; there are payoffs in prestige, pride in accomplishment, increased self-confidence, and other recognition. The problem is not these kind of self-payoffs but rather misdirected motivations.

Misdirected motivation

Misdirected motivation evidences numerous subtleties among which are defensive motivation, buddy motivation, and nagging motivation.

Defensive motivation. In interviews the "knowing" person offers understanding while seeking to assist the client find satisfaction and resolutions to his or her problems. Yet one immense barrier to such transactions might arise from defensiveness. One or both participants in the interview may set up a barrier to hide an undesired revelation. If the interviewer is defensive and concerned about concealing self-centered motives (hidden agenda), trouble starts.

To appear intelligent, virtuous, capable, and correct, the interviewer may manipulate the conversation to revolve about certain safe themes. The outcome may be a sorting of messages. This selection, rejection, and evaluation results in a more stilted, less acceptant, and less honest atmosphere. The interviewer is more likely to be overrestrained in messages. The interview becomes heavily laden with distorted motivation misdirected to the interviewer rather than the client's needs.

Buddy motivation. Sometimes, to induce client motivation, the interviewer falls back on buddy motivation. The interviewer seeks responses from the client by offering friendship through an exchange of problems. At times this may amount to a barter: "Here's a problem [or confidential matter] for you. Now you tell me something."

Novice interviewers are especially prone to depend on a misconstrued conception of establishing rapport (harmonious relationship). The new interviewer frequently believes rapport is another word for friendship or for being a buddy. One jarring problem emerging from the establishment of a friendship is that such a status may encourage clients to withhold their true feelings to avoid hurting their newfound friend, the interviewer. Clients may distort their own reactions to conform more nearly to what they think will please the interviewer.

Nagging motivation. Another kind of inappropriate motivation develops when the interviewer tries too hard to establish motivation. Too many questions are asked; clients are asked over and over again what is bothering them, why they won't talk, and what is wrong with the interview. On and on the interviewer presses to get more responses and lengthier explanations from clients. When clients sense this nagging pressure, they may indicate an impatience by requesting that the interviewer stop pushing and questioning so much, being so nosey, and get on with it. Another tactic clients may use is to clam up. A stalemate may result in which whatever motivation the clients may have originally had for seeking help may be decreased. Even greater problems with motivation may appear. When clients become silent and reduce or even discontinue *working* on their problems, the interviewer had best examine whether the interview is indeed meaningful and rewarding to the clients.

■ ■ ■

Unless the client wants it to, very little will happen. The nature of the interviewer's motivation is one aspect. The encouragement and building of the client's motivation is the other aspect. Misdirected motivation in the form of defensive motivation, buddy motivation, or nagging motivation may satisfy the interviewer's needs, but rarely encourages client participation in an honest partnership of self-discovery and self-growth toward behavioral change.

The interviewer's work is to be an enabler not an enforcer of change. The helper assists in removing the blinders that keep the clients from facing their predicament honestly. Although the interviewer extends a helping hand, clients control whether they will accept the hand. Of particular importance is clients' discomfort with their present plight (degree of cognitive dissonance). The more clients are reinforced by themselves or others in their crutchlike behavior, the less they feel the need for change.

Interview pitfalls

The avoidance of interview pitfalls is the next consideration after the interviewer ascertains that his or her personal characteristics are in concert with the client's and that he or she knows how to avoid misdirected motivation.

The behaviors identified in this discussion are called pitfalls because they represent unsuspected difficulties that may snare the interviewer or the client and prevent the client from fulfilling his or her goals.

Steering. Two forms that steering may take are the Greenspoon effect and the prompting effect. Both steering devices bias the interview and disrupt the client's direction of thought.

Greenspoon effect. The Greenspoon effect is named after J. Greenspoon, who first noted the dramatic effect of certain sounds (mmm-hmmmm and huh-uh) on a client's verbal behavior (Greenspoon, 1955). Both the client and the interviewer may be unaware of the source of the bias or the extent of the influence of these sounds on the client's responses. However, unless the interviewer is aware of particular speech mannerisms, he or she may steer the client's responses away from the main issues of concern to the client.

The communication distortion that may result from the Greenspoon effect will be directly related to the suggestibility of the client. The client may

not "tell it like it is" but tell it like he or she is being reinforced to tell it.

Prompting effect. Further contamination of the interview may arise from the tendency of some interviewers to introduce their own ideas into the conversation. The interviewer may comment on a client's answers, may suggest answers, or may use nonverbal prompting. Examples 5-8 to 5-10 demonstrate some different forms that interviewer prompting may take.

Example 5-8
PROMPTING THROUGH COMMENTING

The interviewer can prompt the client by commenting on the client's answers.

MR. P.: Yes, I see how that might upset you. How did you handle it afterward?

GREG: I was on a total trip. Felt as if all stops were gone. Said things to my father that dug deep. Told him what a jerk weakling he is, screamed at him. Why doesn't he stand up to that b-b-b . . . Oh, what's the use? Done—my mother . . . *(Voice trails off.)*

MR. P.: You seem to think your mother is the cause of all your problems and your father's, too.

GREG: Mother? Hmmm, may be. Is that what you think? Maybe you're right. My mother . . . yes . . . didn't realize that. Hah! The life-giver—the living-taker. Damn her, you're right. Yes, yes, right!

Example 5-9
PROMPTING THROUGH SUGGESTING

Sometimes the interviewer prompts by suggesting answers.

LESLIE: Just have to find out. Should I go along with Ches? All my friends didn't tear their thoughts to decide on what they should do. Can't decide! What's marriage anyway? Who needs it?

DR. G.: You're really working hard at this. Do you feel as if both establishment pressures and less conventional aspirations are gnawing at your decision?

LESLIE: Yes. That's true. When Ches and I talk about us, the logic is on his side. But when I'm home with my parents . . . I wonder how they would feel. Really don't want to hurt them. Don't know what to do or say. What should I tell Ches? Should I tell my parents?

DR. G.: *(Silent.)*

LESLIE: Tell me, Dr. G., what do you think?

DR. G.: You should discuss this with your parents. Tell them that you and Ches are not ready for marriage but have a great need to be together. Tell them—ask them . . . *(Dr. G. speaks at length in answer to Leslie's question.)*

Example 5-10
PROMPTING THROUGH NONVERBAL CUES

Perhaps the most subtle form of prompting is provided by nonverbal cues.

MS. C.: Hello, Cher. *(Smiling.)* Come in, come in. Let's sit over here today. I'm sorta tired. Hard day.

CHER: All the other times . . . other times—spoke about education . . . parents—unimportant. Real issue—something else.

MS. C.: *(Sighs and moves around in her chair; puts left leg under and sits on it.)*

CHER: I . . . I . . . really don't know how to deal with it . . . can't really tell anymore . . .

MS. C.: *(Moves and puts her leg down on the floor. Raises her right eyebrow and squeezes her lips together.)* Cher, we've talked together. Let it all hang out. I'm listening. *(Ms. C. moves forward, leaning toward Cher.)*

CHER: *(Speaking rapidly.)* Men—can't stand 'em. Only another woman knows how to caress . . . how to make a woman enjoy . . . how to find those body places that stir me to excitement.

MS. C.: *(Opens her lips slightly and licks her bottom lip with short, rapid movements of her tongue. She clasps her hands tightly. Her forehead becomes creased.)*

CHER: Maybe I better come back . . . you're upset . . . you think I'm horrible; no use.

MS. C.: *(Unclasps her hands, sits back in her seat, and frowns.)* Come now, Cher, I didn't say a word. Just listening hard. How do you see me helping you . . . that's what I need to know. *(Ms. C. sneezes.)* Allergy again . . . 'xcuse me . . . and . . . tell me . . . how do you see me fitting in to helping you? *(Ms. C. straightens the collar of her jacket and taps on the desk with her left index finger.)*

CHER: I . . . well . . . class now . . . don't want to be late . . . see you.

Blatant or subtle prompts can and do steer the client into the interviewer's mold of thinking.

Allness. Some of the steering described previously may be related to the need of some interviewers to be one-up on their clients. Some interviewers revel in the client's effort to endow the interviewer with magical powers.

The interviewer's need to be all-knowing, all-powerful, and all-capable may result in a power struggle that the client often loses, leaving the client feeling more helpless and inferior. At other times the interviewer may suggest symptoms or illness to the impressionable client. In an effort to assure the client that he or she is knowledgeable the interviewer may offer more information and an untested diagnosis. Thus symptoms of a disorder are produced and sustained by the interviewer. Symptoms that originate in this fashion are called *iatrogenic.*

Insistence on the interviewer's infallibility may lead to the client's overdependence on the interviewer and the implication that no other individuals understand the client as well as the present interviewer. Furthermore, the power-driven interviewer may exaggerate findings and even argue with and badger the client.

Omnipotent (all-powerful) needs may lead the interviewer to use words and concepts over the patient's head. Then the interviewer may enjoy the client's failure when the "Great Interviewer's" words have not been followed. This sounds harsh, but there are interviewers who, because of their own unfulfilled needs for recognition, unwittingly perhaps, express themselves best in the presence of the client.

The most serious consequence may be if the interviewer enjoys or is embarrassed by the client's discomfiture even to the point of laughing. This form of cruelty to clients happens with novice interviewers who are uncertain about procedures and too eager to impress.

Mistakes in approaches to clients are bound to occur. Inconsistencies, inaccuracies, and exaggerations are not unusual. The problem goes much deeper, however. The real problem lies with the interviewer who makes no effort to correct errors. The more serious destructiveness stems from the inability of the interviewer to admit errors because of a profound need for prestige and power. The beginning interviewer is able to alter such an allness course through self-understanding before his or her reputation becomes more important than the client's welfare.

Pinch-hitting. Pinch-hitting is a trait that most humans develop to some extent. The mother who basks in the glory of "her son, the doctor," is pinch-hitting. The father who glories in the football prowess of his son is pinch-hitting. Another term for pinch-hitting is "vicarious experience." Vicarious experience refers to the satisfaction of one's own needs through substitution and imagined participation in the behavior and accomplishments of others. Vicarious living through others is not the same as being proud of another's accomplishments. Substituting someone else's experiences for one's own participation is usually accompanied by feelings of inadequacy and inferiority. Thus pinch-hitting is usually a cover-up for distress. The enveloping, yet hidden, thought of the nonproducing individual is, "If only I could do that."

Pinch-hitting by the interviewer does not promote personal growth for the client. Frequently the problems and needs of the interviewer creep into the interview. For example:

□ Because of the interviewer's dependency needs, the client's dependency may be encouraged. The interviewer may treat the client as a helpless person who needs "parenting," thus decreasing the client's possibilities for self-growth. In giving too much concern, care, and help, the interviewer may feel almost as if these behaviors were offered to him or her.

□ The sexually meek interviewer may revel in the client's sexual pursuits.

□ The interviewer who is unable to combat the infringements by parents or spouse on his or her own interests and directions may encourage the client, openly or by a nod and a smile, to talk back or to act out aggressive behavior.

Living through the client's life is most unsatisfactory for both the client and the interviewer and must be recognized as one of the barriers to facilitative helping.

Outside or inside view. Another subtle cover-up for unpleasant feelings and unmet needs may take the form of either taking only an outside view of events, making an all-out effort to be objective (overobjective), or taking only an inside view of events, becoming sentimental and overinvolved emotionally (oversubjective).

Overobjectivity and oversubjectivity are two widely divergent approaches. Overobjectivity inclines toward coldness and insensitivity. To get the facts without being aware of feelings may result in a robotlike approach to questioning and to probing. Considerable danger can spring from the interviewer's parrotlike use of bookish questions or clumsy attempts to formalize questions. Since the same word has different meanings for different people and even for the same person at different times, the approach, the word, the statement, and the question must focus on the "here-and-now" needs and expressions of the client.

Often efforts at objectivity achieve a ridigity and a one-way action-reaction that ignores signs of anxiety or other cues to the emotional distress of the interviewer or the client. Disregard for the client's feelings because the interviewer is determined to plod through a list of questions disconnects the interview situation from the client's problems. It is difficult to imagine how an interviewer intent on asking a list of predetermined questions is able to listen to, show interest in, and care for the client.

Freud was so concerned about the possibile influence of the interviewer on the client that he encouraged the client to talk about anything that came into his or her mind (free association). The client reclined on the couch, and the interviewer sat out of the client's view, behind the client. Direct questioning was sparse so as not to interfere with the client's flow of thought.

Carl Rogers also is concerned about the social situation of the counseling event. His views stress a client-centered approach in which the counselor does not respond every time the client pauses. Instead the counselor takes time to formulate a verbal response and often responds nonverbally. Rogers writes about the direct personal encounter counselors experience with clients and the necessity that counselors be themselves, aware of their feelings and the meaning of these feelings so that they do not interfere with the client's problem solving (Rogers and Truax, 1967).

In the face-to-face experiential transaction both verbal and nonverbal cues become even more important, since there is more obvious sharing and experiencing of thoughts and reasoning (cognitive aspect) and feeling (affective aspect). To note only outward behavior as expressed in words or actions or to structure interviews similarly for all clients neglects a most significant part of the process—the individuality of each client.

The effects of oversubjectivity may be just as deadening. The purpose of the interview is certainly not for both interviewer and client to share the same, or even different, crying towels. This does not infer that the interviewer must always conceal feelings but that the interviewer must not become the client.

The interviewer-turned-client may say:

☐ "I find so much pleasure in helping. I want so much to help you."

☐ "I'm lost, don't know what to do, am having such a hard time in this agency."

☐ "I have to have this interview with you or my supervisor will flunk me."

☐ "I know just how you feel. My father used to . . ."

Oversubjectivity by the interviewer may incite the client to more frequent outbursts of emotion. These outbursts may be directed at the interviewer because of the tension built up by the interviewer's emotional distress. Sometimes it may be wiser for the interviewer to discontinue an interview if the emotions are too much to handle. Awareness of feeling is sensible. Expression of feeling (by the interviewer) must be carefully apportioned. Examples 5-11 and 5-12 describe some of the problems that may occur. Which of these examples exhibits the outside or the inside difficulty?

Example 5-11
FIRST INTERVIEW

Today is the day! Carla's first interview! All the class discussion seems a mad jumble at the moment. Carla has written down some opening questions as well as other kinds of questions that may help in keeping the interview going. She even remembered to include some ending phrases.

As she waits, she looks around the small office that has been given to her for this interview. She notes the littered desk and remembers how similar it is to the desk of her instructor. This gives her some comfort. Then the door opens, and a tall black man walks in.

CARLA: Hello. Please sit down over here. I want to thank you for volunteering to speak with me. I'm new here and am studying to be a mental health technician. *(Carla wonders whether she has said too much.)*

MR. B.: Yeah, Mr. S. told me. What do you want to know?

CARLA: Just want to know about you . . . about how you came to be in this hospital. *("Why did I say that?" thinks Carla. "All the opening questions I jotted down. No use.")*

MR. B.: Came to the hospital about a week ago, I guess. Really didn't want to come. Went out to Ed's house and we put a load on. Got home stoned; the wife started at me, yelling what a bastard I am, "Drunken bastard," wouldn't stop. So I began breaking things, maybe smashed her up, too. She called the cops, here I am.

CARLA: Yes? *("What do I say or do now?" wonders Carla.)*

MR. B.: That's it. Getting dried out so I can get out of here. Need to get back to work.

CARLA: Mr. B., please tell me more. I have to have more information about you. This isn't enough to make a report. *("Wow, that is a dumb thing to say.")*

MR. B.: Ask me some questions.

CARLA: Mr. B., you are being very kind and patient with me. Hmmmm. Tell me, when did you start drinking, what age?

MR. B.: Fourteen.

CARLA: Tell me more about how you began to drink. *(Carla is frantically looking through her notes to find the question that should follow. She does not see Mr. B. clench his hand into a fist and then extend the fingers. Nor does she see the shifting of his legs from one position to another.)*

MR. B.: Drinking—everybody was drinking. At 14 ran around partying and boozing. Later drank more and more to feel the high.

CARLA: I see. Did you have a happy home life? *(Carla thinks this has to be a good question. This question should always be asked according to a book she had read.)*

MR. B.: *(Looks at Carla with raised eyebrows. He bends down from the waist and cups his chin on his hands, continuing to look at her.)*

Example 5-12
DIAGNOSTIC TURMOIL

Mrs. M. walks into the office rapidly. She goes over to one of the chairs opposite Mr. P. and sits down, also rapidly.

MRS. M.: I'm Missus M. I came to talk about my Henry. You asked me to come to discuss the tests you gave him.

MR. P.: Thank you for coming, Mrs. M. I administered several tests to Henry to help me better understand how he is functioning. His teacher is concerned that Henry might have to remain in the first grade again.

MRS. M.: *(Nods her head as Mr. P. speaks. When Mr. P. says that Henry's teacher had said Henry might remain in the first grade again, Mrs. M. suddenly straightens herself so that her back almost seems rigid.)* Oh, no! Not stay back again. Take him out of school. Henry's a bright boy.

MR. P.: I guess I jumped too fast with that explanation. You're right, Henry is a bright boy. That's one of the things I found out.

MRS. M.: *(Slumps a little bit in her chair and looks at her hands.)* What the? I . . . I . . . my husband is so angry, blames me, says I'm too easy with Henry.

MR. P.: Yes, I see how you feel. Concerned about Henry and about your husband's remarks. But what I have to say is really good news. There is a way we can help Henry.

MRS. M.: Good news? Then why does Henry need help?

MR. P.: From all the tests I gave Henry and from my conversation with him, I found out three things. Henry *is* above average in his intellectual ability. Yet he is upset because, although he is trying hard, he can't read. And Henry needs some special help because he doesn't see things in the same way other boys his age see things.

MRS. M: Are you saying Henry needs glasses?

MR. P.: Glasses? Not as far as I know. What he needs is some special training to help him read more freely and comfortably. Henry shows what is called a perceptual difficulty. Have you ever noticed that he writes his b's and his d's backward? Or, perhaps, have you seen him mirror-write? You know, it seems as if he is holding a mirror up and writing from right to left—letters backward.

MRS. M.: Maybe I did see that. I remember hearing a program on television once. They called this dys . . . dys . . . something or other.

MR. P.: Dyslexia. But labels don't tell us anything about Henry. The important thing is that we know how to help him now. And, besides, we found out about it early enough before damage is done to his education and to the way he feels about himself—and about learning.

MRS. M.: *(Begins to sob softly, and tears splatter down her face.)* Oh, what have I done? Tom was right; I was too easy on Henry.

MR. P.: Not you, Mrs. M. You did not do anything to cause this perceptual difficulty. However, you and your husband might aggravate the situation if you cannot accept Henry as he is and even help him at home with certain exercises. It's really not as horrible as you seem to think. I have dyslexia and am now studying for my doctor's degree. When I was attending school there was very little knowledge about perceptual difficulties. Today we have a good idea of how to handle it.

Missed or messed wavelength. The effort to find the client's wavelength of communication demands that interviewers first get themselves in order. Then the interviewer's tune in to the client's world.

Interviewers must realize that they are both speaker and listener at the same time. The silent speech (listening) is revealed not in the words that are being used (speaking) but rather in what is not being said. Thus the meaning of the nonverbal as well as the verbal cues to the client make the interviewing event satisfactory or unsatisfactory to the client. The wavelengths between client and interviewer get messed or missed if the speaking and listening process going on between them is not finely tuned to their understandings, their awareness, their interests, their values, their expectations, or any combination of these factors. Their translations go into tangents. Their realities are too far apart. It is up to interviewers to be able to walk in the language-shoes of the client. Interviewers must recognize the relationship between what they are saying and doing and what the client is saying and doing. Interviewers whose self-interests predominate are likely to hear only their own speaking and to avoid the meaning of the self-message as well as the client's message. Often misdirected motivations and consequent mishandling of prompting procedures emerge from interviewers' inability to commit themselves to an affiliation with the client. Because of interviewers' feelings about their uncertain identity, they avoid a partnership of intimacy with the clients, fearing ego-identity loss if they invest too much of themselves in the helping situation. Thus intimacy, a fundamental dimension of interpersonal relationships, is undermined. The interviewer expresses what Erikson (1968) labeled "distantiation"—isolation from others aggravated by self-absorption. The client, in turn, responds similarly, or may pretend intimacy in the game plan of the helping situation.

Intimacy

Intimacy is more than closeness and is integrally part of involvement. Intimacy is not merely making oneself liked and doing things for others (Cormier and Cormier; 1979). The expression of intimacy requires acceptance of the worthiness of others and commitment to a relationship with another human being. This commitment ideally becomes a two-way process—the interviewer committed to helping the client and the client committed to collaborate in the helping event (Basch, 1980). Close association, self-sharing, inclusion, and the cohesion of working and thinking together are all parts of intimacy.

In the context of the intimacy of the helping relationship, associations assume more significant and intense proportions than the comradery of the work world, the superficial amity of the passenger who "spills it all" to the stranger sitting nearby in the airplane, or even the special affinity of friendship. Intimate and nonintimate disclosures vary with social-situational determinants. In addition to these particulars, intimacy is modulated by the degree of commitment, the expected reciprocity, and the length of the continuing social relationship. Table 5-4 compares two facets of the degree of intimacy in self-disclosures: the degree of commitment to a social relationship and the expected length of time for continuing a social relationship.

Unfortunately, the word "intimacy" often is misused in the narrow meaning of contact between two people. This contact may be called "intimate" because of the secret thoughts one person reveals about himself or herself or about another. Yet these secret thoughts may be selected carefully to make points, to impress, or to conceal other contrasting or disturbing thoughts. These surface revelations are not for the sake of honesty or for enhancing understanding. Intimacy is more than knowing *about* someone conversationally or sexually. To know another person intimately there must be an exchange of thoughts and feelings, a close and confidential relationship of trust. There must be assurance that one will not be censored or rejected.

Intimacy takes many forms. The more of these forms two individuals can comfortably and forthrightly express to one another, the more complete is the intimacy of their relationship.

Cerebral intimacy. The easiest intimacy to accomplish is probably the cerebral kind. It only takes the right choice of words. Keeping oneself encased in one's skull prevents others from getting too close and in this way maintains a safe distance for the skull-hugger. The magic of words lulls many individuals into a false feeling of togetherness. "Aw, come on, you know you're rationalizing; you know you really dig this stuff" has the sound of intimacy but is actually manipulation.

Cerebral intimacy may also be deceitful. Ad-

Table 5-4. *Degrees of intimacy in self-disclosures*

Degree of commitment to relationship	Expected length of time for continuing social relationship	
	Short	Long
Low	"Stranger-on-the-train" phenomenon.* More likely for more intimate disclosures to occur more rapidly.	Disclosure of nonintimate details continues for longer time. Questionable when and whether intimate details might be revealed.
High	Social-situational factors more likely to affect degree of intimate disclosures. Disclosures in privacy more likely.	Nonintimate disclosures are likely at beginning of relationship. Disclosure of intimate topics take longer, occur about the middle of the relationship, and lessen as the relationship is terminating.

Data from Altman, 1973; Chaikin and others, 1975; Chelune and others, 1979; Derlega and Chaikin, 1975; Derlega, Chaikin, and Herndon, 1973; Jourard, 1971; Thibaut and Kelly, 1959.
*"Stranger-on-the-train" phenomenon (Thibaut and Kelley, 1959). Short-term relationships that are associated with little or no commitment tend toward more intimate disclosure that is more open and with more details. Passengers on trains, planes, and buses are likely to disclose intimacies to strangers with less concern for possible repercussions.

mitting one's deceit to others and, most important, to oneself is a difficult task. It is much easier to cover up with candy-coated lies and to create deceptions to conceal real intentions. To conceal real intentions from oneself and others may be a plan of action or manipulation.

Sincerity means one has to face oneself first. The false compliments with which one person flatters another, the mechanical words of praise, may wear the mask of intimacy but are just extravagant cerebral game playing. A dialogue can be conducted only between people of equal worth. This does not require that the individuals be equally intelligent or equally educated, nor does dialogue prevent angry expressions. As long as the cerebral battle is fair, frank, and respectful, the individuals involved are on their way to intimacy. The two counselors in Example 5-13, Mr. V. and Mr. P., are on different trips, and the client, Peter, bounds forward or springs back in accordance with their different approaches.

Example 5-13
TWO COUNSELORS—ONE CLIENT

[1]

MR. V.: Hello, Peter, nice to see you. How about the red chair? It's very comfortable. Say, aren't you the brother of. . . .

PETER: Hello, I—well, it's been a hard year for me. I guess you know my brother, Jim. We . . . he managed OK, even got a scholarship to college. Everything was OK with me until this year. Ben and I, we . . . Is this confidential?

• • •

MR. P.: *(Notices Peter's peculiar stride as he walks in on the balls of his feet with his hands jammed into his torn, black leather jacket. Hair hangs around Peter's forehead and face. Mr. P. stands and walks to Peter.)* Hi.

PETER: Huh, well—phew!! This is a real drag. My brother, Jim, told me about you. Remember him? Won a scholarship. Until this year, everything was okay. Ben and me, we . . . *(Silent.)*

[2]

MR. V.: Oh, yes, Jim—uh, mean Peter, of course, I remember your brother. Brilliant student, used to come in to chat with me, played guitar, too. Sure, remember him well. Hmmmm, so what's the problem?

PETER: *(Silent.)*

• • •

MR. P.: *(Moves his chair slightly forward and leans toward Peter. Looks at the deep lines between Peter's eyebrows and Peter's clenched hand rigidly pressing his thighs.)* Kinda hard to begin?

PETER: Mmmmm, very. So tight; how do you . . . ?

[3]

MR. V.: Come now, Pete, you can talk freely here. Trust, the very essence of interpersonal relationships, trust is an everlasting credo [belief] you must establish. The relief that comes from catharsis—you know, tell about it; get emotional release. Helpful, very helpful.

PETER: Mr. V., I dunno. Wonder if I can do it alone. Ben will get uptight if he finds out I've been talking to you.

• • •

MR. P.: Peter, seems like heavy stuff you're carting. How about starting with when you met Ben.

PETER: Ben, yes. Met him last May, no, April, at a pot party. Saw him after almost daily. Funny, never noticed him before, but suddenly he seemed to be around the same places, and then . . .

The trend of the conversation in Example 5-13 is apparent. Mr. V. is the skull-hugging individual whose pseudointimacy serves his own ends. Mr. V. delivers words but little empathic understanding. Peter finds responding to Mr. V. too difficult. Mr. P., on the other hand, indicates by means of body language (moving and leaning toward Peter) and his few well-chosen words that he is "in there" with Peter.

Words do indeed help to establish intimacy. However, overindulging in words, supercerebral intimacy, can be a front for alienation or hostility rather than honest intimacy. Social intimacy is another channel to increase or decrease closeness.

Social intimacy. Social intimacy is similar to cerebral intimacy insofar as it varies in intensity and the way it is expressed. An individual may be so eager for other people that he or she constantly seeks the company of others. Interpersonal relations become the means of survival. The question arises as to whether this is intimacy and openness or a sign of unconquerable loneliness.

On one end of the scale of social intimacy is the person who hoards privacy and keeps to himself or herself. On the other end is the individual who is almost unable to exist without the company of others. In between is the person who feels free enough to either open his or her windows to others, to be prepared to share with others, or to ask for and arrange for privacy without feeling apologetic. There is a difference between what Berne (1964) calls pastimes or games of intimacy and game-free intimacy. Pastimes are involved with a special kind of cerebral intimacy in which special words are used for certain events to achieve surface social intimacy.

DON: Hey, man, did you hear about Butch? He finally made it.

HAL: Butch? Oh, yeah, that dude; so he marked one. Whaddyaknow?

The ritualistic language and the noninvolved discussion point to intimacy that hardly scratches the surface of interpersonal transactions. One more step into social organization and games becomes the way of things—and people. Sometimes the games become grim in the attempt to be intimate. The individuals advance into a little more involvement and plan a little more carefully. However, the behavior is commanded by rituals so well regulated that spontaneity is lost. Therefore cerebral intimacy must be controlled and social intimacy carefully programed. The rigidity of contacts makes the social intimacy unreal. Friends are selected according to their ability to play along in mutual gamesmanship.

MR. C.: Yes, indeed. I enjoy these swinger groups. Jealousy? Of course not at all. My wife still is faithful to me. I've really learned a great deal about myself, even helped in my sexual relationship with my wife.

MS. L.: Know what you mean. Freedom. Manny and I, we know ourselves so well and we've gotten closer, much closer, since we joined the group. How about moving along now?

Social intimacy implies mutual availability and mutual acceptance. This does not signify that each individual is everlastingly available to the other person or even everlastingly acceptant of the other person. It does mean that privacy is expected and

practiced. It means that there is genuine cerebral intimacy. Ritual social ability and ritual avoidance do not fit into genuine social intimacy.

HELGA: Bob, it won't work; just can't get into this housewife bit. Feel guilty about your taking over.

BOB: Noticed it today, how tense you look, so uptight. I really feel where you're at. We've just got to get into this thing together.

HELGA: Well, you do . . . you are helpful, yet—wonder if my guilt is blown up because I keep sensing your annoyance. Are you really telling me like it is? Keep wondering.

BOB: Hell, Helga! You know damn well I don't like getting into the house scene any more than you do. But maybe I dislike it just a little less while you're getting into this new thing of yours. Let's not fight it; laid back as our teenager says. Let's look at it again later when there's less static for you, OK? *(Walks over to Helga and puts his hands on her shoulder and then embraces her gently.)*

The conversation between Helga and Bob brings forth some feelings of anger as well as tenderness. Yet the prevailing mood is intimacy, which is honest in Bob's cerebral, social, physical, and emotional responses. Bob's movement toward Helga went one step farther than cerebral and social intimacy to physical intimacy.

Physical intimacy. Intimacy is considered most often from the perspective of physical closeness. Perhaps it is more accurate to view the depth of intimacy on this physical level. Morris (1971) argues that physical intimate behavior is crucial to human existence. This argument is supported by others who have studied infants deprived of physical contact and found that they waste away without this kind of contact comfort. This wasting away occurred even though the infants were provided with adequate nourishment, rest, temperature, and so on. When people were assigned to rock and otherwise hold these infants, the infants began to thrive (Ribble, 1955; Spitz, 1965). Although these studies concentrated on infants in institutions, hospital personnel and pediatricians have discovered that physical contact is an important survival factor from the moment of birth. As with all forms of intimacy, physical intimacy begins with the parent being physically intimate with the infant and goes on to the child's acceptance of self-intimacy and gradually physical intimacy with others. The individual who feels comfortable with his or her own body is an "embodied self" (Laing, 1960). This person feels his or her physical self together as an organized whole. Individuals who act as if they were disconnected from their body (disembodied) reveal this feeling in the way they talk about themselves, in the way they carry their body, and in the way in which they use space. People who reject all or part of their body or fear or are ashamed of the consequences of body contact speak with displeasure of their physical dimensions, their shape, or their odor. They may tackle this distaste by calling verbal attention to their body with hostile humor or even sometimes with pretended affection.

Furthermore, individuals who feel that part or all of their body image is distasteful or even disgusting may reveal these disquieting feelings by the way in which they seem to detach themselves from their body. They may show this detachment in several ways:

□ By lack of care for their clothing or physical cleanliness
□ By a thrusting walk that gives the impression of the head, shoulders, trunk, and legs moving at different speeds as if these body parts were not joined together
□ By rigid, robotlike movements

Another response that demonstrates negative body feelings is the way an individual uses space. Hall (1959) discusses people's use of space in his book *The Silent Language*. He points out that the ranges of distance may be divided from the "very close," which is the "soft whisper" of from 3 to 6 inches, to "stretching the limits" or "hailing distance" of from 20 feet indoors to 100 feet outdoors. Interaction distances vary in different cultures and from individual to individual. Individuals who reject their own body are more than likely to reject the body of another person. They keep their distance by manipulating the physical space between themselves and another person. They place

themselves sufficiently away from the other person to require a louder voice and to discourage touching. They may pad their body with enough poundage that the body contours maintain distance from others. Limiting contact by distance hampers physical intimacy.

Physical intimacy as well as the other forms discussed transform in relation to "where," "when," and "with whom" (Archer, 1979). A carpeted room with indirect soft lighting, pictures on the walls, colorful drapes at the windows, and comfortable, cushioned couch and chairs is more conducive to intimacy than is a room with a cement or linoleum floor, bare cement-block, unpainted walls, bright lights, uncurtained windows, and straight-backed wooden chairs. The characteristics and extent of intimacy are also influenced by the location, the degree of prior contact between the persons, and the possibility for future contact (see Table 5-4). For instance:

On a long plane ride Martha sat next to a woman whom she had never met and whom she thought she was unlikely to meet again. Martha had just completed an unpleasant argument with Sam and had run off from him just in time to catch her plane. Now she was exhausted, yet the disturbing thoughts kept piling into her head. "Should she sever the 30-year marriage? At her age, what would she do? But she couldn't take it anymore. Wasn't it time she took a stand? The children were on their own—had been for awhile. Why not get into her own life." She began speaking to the woman next to her—about the weather, about where they were going, about many trivialities. The small talk became more and more personal as Martha told this stranger about her "hemmed-in feeling" because her physician-husband had a professional and social life apart from her. Gradually Martha exposed the script of the unhappy marriage and her dependent personality. The stranger seemed to be listening, but that was not important. Martha felt relieved just talking.

"Opening up" to a stranger is not unusual. Yet it is a one-time event and differs from the kind of intimacy experienced with a close friend, affectionate spouse, or counselor. Sometimes the release afforded and the opportunity of hearing oneself repeat one's concerns may lead to conclusions. This is not the same intimacy that occurs at a candlelight dinner with a desirable, empathic companion. This is different from the intimacy of the individuals working, marching, and protesting together for civil rights or at some political rally.

Fundamentally, physical intimacy varies from person to person in the situational variables of culture, the decor of the environment, the nature of the event, and the degree of familiarity and connectedness of the individuals. Sex and age are also factors. In addition, the degree of closeness an individual can comfortably handle is revealed in the space an individual arranges for conversational purposes. Withdrawn people are more likely to remain farther from other people. A rapid departure frequently results if someone invades the spatial safety limits arranged by the withdrawing individual (see Chapter 2).

Emotional intimacy. Cerebral, social, and physical intimacy are less threatening than emotional intimacy. Some people are terrified by emotional intimacy and fear that exposure of their feelings may make them so vulnerable to themselves and to others that they will be unable to deal with the results of their emotional openness.

It is not easy to establish emotional intimacy. Many individuals build up an elaborate system of game playing to avoid emotional intimacy. Aggression and even more serious consequences often result from the inability to be close and open with others. It is simpler for those who avoid closeness to sprinkle their lives with ought's and should's rather than with honest commitments to themselves and to others. Overconformity smoothly destroys individuality as well as emotional intimacy. How can one give a genuine response to another person if one becomes dependent on another person for perpetual approval? Sometimes the individual decides that the only way to break away from such dependency is through cruelty and insensitivity to the other person's feelings.

Emotional intimacy suggests two persons who are tuned in to feelings with firm roots of identity and healthy growths of togetherness. It suggests saying ''we'' or ''us'' rather than ''they,'' ''them,'' or ''that.'' It suggests pain, pleasure, and also sharing. It suggests waves of warmth that are nonpossessive of the other person. It suggests a continuous growth of these characteristics, not a level reached—striving, not finishing.

■ ■ ■

Fulfilling intimacy means all of these characteristics—cerebral, social, physical, and emotional. There is no absolute level of intimacy but rather a matter of degree. The burden of phoniness, however, is too much for intimacy to carry. Phony intimacy is paid for with lies and concealment.

Each individual asserts a personal style of emotional intimacy. This style of intimate behavior (behavioral effects) develops from an individual's background influences, psychological responses, and situational features of the immediate environment. Out of these influences, identity is shaped and intimacy comes. Commitment and engagement with others are a test of one's identity. If individuals are shaky about who they are and about their meaning for living, they are also apt to be strained and reserved in their emotional transactions with others. They cannot abandon themselves to the joys of emotional sharing if they are bewildered by their vague identity and are striving for the distinctness of their identity through extremes of independent activity, self-sufficiency, and self-containment. Benjamin Tucker aptly remarked, ''Independence is good but isolation is too high a price to pay for it'' (*Instead of a Book*, 1893).

Intimacy's opposite is separateness, remoteness, isolation, and alienation. These signs of distance encourage destruction and/or ignoring of others who may be considered dangerous to one's identity-seeking. Otherwise a desperate pseudointimacy leads this same person to try to merge his or her shaky identity with another adult, a guru, a cause, a religion or cult, or drugs. If none of these half measures works, a vicious cycle of searching and retreating, of excessive trusting or mistrusting begins.

SUMMARY

This chapter begins with the straightforward proposal that *caring* is the chief specification for effectiveness of the helping relationship. Caring is considered from the standpoint of helping other people grow and actualize themselves—a process of relating that involves development. The chapter concludes with a discussion of several forms of intimacy—cerebral, social, physical and emotional. Cerebral intimacy is presented as the easiest form of intimacy to establish, since it requires merely words that can successfully conceal the emotional coloration of one's more intense private thoughts. Both social and physical intimacy reflect only surface responses. When individuals also risk emotional intimacy, they are more prepared to face themselves; and in trusting and respecting their right to feel, they have made the first step of trusting others. Intimacy does not signify revealing only negative intimate thoughts and acts; it also indicates the declaration of the intimacy of "highs," actions by oneself or others that are exceedingly stimulating or just pleasingly comforting. The more forms of intimacy that the client feels free to express, the more satisfying and productive will be the interview sessions. It is the hope, trust, and patience of the interviewer that encourage the intimacy of the client.

The dimensions of mutuality introduce the notion of reciprocal growth, another characteristic that is associated with caring and intimacy. The extent to which reciprocal growth for the client and the helper becomes allied with increased "copeability" relates to the varieties of interview goals in information-oriented, behavior management, and experiential interviews. Information-oriented interviews include information-seeking and information-sharing interviews. Both forms of interview seek information, but in the latter type the interviewer makes a more concerted effort to share as well as to gather specific facts. The behavior management interview draws some procedures from the information-oriented interview and primarily from principles of learning. Concepts of operant conditioning, behavioral analysis, a reinforcement menu, and such procedures as thought stopping, verbal and nonverbal conditioning, and desensitization are mentioned. Assertive training procedures are added to these considerations about behavior management, and the distinctions among aggression, nonassertiveness, and assertive behavior are inspected. The experiential interview orchestrates selected procedures from information-oriented and behavior management interviews. The discussion of the experiential interview is amplified with considerations of its similarities to psychosocial therapy and the person-environment approach as well as the psychoanalytic contributions to this form of interviewing.

Discussion of these approaches to interviewing is followed by a survey of factors influencing the interviewing event: personal characteristics, misdirected motivation, and interview pitfalls. The chapter ends with an account of forms of intimacy. Each of these facets operates on the helping relationship, enriching or weakening the interviewer's effectiveness. Status, roles, and interrelatedness are the personal characteristics that can improve the helping event if the interviewer and client are harmonious. Such synchronization of characteristics would be more likely to deter the misdirected motivations (defensive motivation, buddy motivation, nagging motivation) that interfere with rapport—the empathic hand-in-hand efforts of client and interviewer to solve problems. Such accord also would be more likely to check the pitfalls of interviewing such as steering (Greenspoon effect, prompting), allness, pinch-hitting, outside or inside view, and missed or messed wavelength. Harmony, however, is not enough; it must be balanced with skills and knowledge.

From these considerations of the dimensions of the interview the next chapter moves on to an analysis of the three parts of all interviews: the opening or beginning phase, the developing or exploring phase, and the ending or terminating phase. Each phase is associated with certain specific skills and knowledge that further the effectiveness of the helping event.

Chapter 6

ALL INTERVIEWS ARE DIVIDED INTO THREE PARTS
helping the client find his or her way

The beginning phase of the interview—the greeting.

Every single interview with a client as well as each series of interviews with a client follows the same structure. This structure involves the opening or beginning phase, the developing or exploring phase, and the ending or terminating phase. These three phases overlap.

PHASE I: THE OPENING OR BEGINNING PHASE

The interview begins when the client first makes contact by telephone or in person with the interviewer or a secondary person who relays the message to the interviewer. The client's feelings about this initial contact will have much impact on what happens later in the interview process. First impressions do count, particularly with the troubled person.

The initial greeting

The where and how of greeting a client may come easily to some beginning interviewers. Others may quake at the thought of the client's first visit. The interviewer may wonder where the client should be greeted—in the reception room, as the client enters the interviewer's office, or after the client has been seated?

How should the client be greeted—with a handshake, with an introduction to the interviewer, with small talk, with ''hello'' or ''hi'' and the client's name, or with a nod and/or a smile? Should the interviewer be seated or standing when greeting the client? Should the interviewer walk toward the client? Should the interviewer greet the client by his first or last name? What name should the interviewer use—Mr., Miss, Mrs., Ms.—first and last name? Should the interviewer use his or her title?

The answers to all these questions depend on the way in which the interview is initiated, the lifestyle of both the client and the interviewer, and the age of the client.

A hearty greeting to a depressed client and a strong handclasp for a 6-year-old are obviously foolish. Such foolish greetings are possible when the interviewer is self-occupied and/or uptight. The interviewer who is immersed in his or her own problems is prevented from heeding the client's cues for a greeting.

A dominant point influencing the nature of the greeting arises from how the interview was initiated. The approach to the client-initiated interview is somewhat different from that to the other-initiated interview, particularly if the client is compelled by the courts, a school, or a parent to meet with the interviewer.

When the interview is client-initiated, the interviewer is less likely to have to deal with lack of interest, piecemeal cooperation, or outright hostility. The task of beginning is simplified if the client initiates the interview. Then, either the client begins to discuss the problem that brings him or her to the interviewer or a simple suggestion from the interviewer will spur him or her on: "Would you tell me what brings you here?"

If the interview was arranged by someone other than the client, the interviewer tries to discover who the client thinks made the request and what the client believes urged this person to refer the client. Since the interview is not client-motivated, the interviewer will have to work harder to begin the session. Some possible beginnings for this non-client-arranged interview are given in the following examples.

[1]

To the 17-year-old whose parents have asked about some educational directions for their son: "Hello, I'm Dr. Y. I have been looking at the results of your interest inventory. Let's talk about . . ." or "Have you been thinking about anything in particular after you graduate from high school?" or "There are several ways we can tackle your plans after graduation. We can . . . How would you like to begin?"

[2]

To the adult who has been asked to speak with a social worker about where she will live after she leaves the hospital: "Mr. H. was talking to me about your concerns. Let's explore the choices you have."

[3]

To the 16-year-old girl who has been arrested for shoplifting and uncontrollable behavior: "I've been asked to work with you. I know it's tough to be reporting to me regularly. Together we can work something out which will be helpful. Let's try."

[4]

To the angry client who has been brought to the interviewer against his wishes: "I can understand your anger since you did not want to come here" or "I gather you feel you were forced to come here against your wishes."

[5]

To the desperate mother of the 12-year-old severely mentally retarded boy who is a fire-setter: "The telephone call from the state institution gave me a good idea of your position about your son. Yes, I do know how frustrating it must be with no place for your son to get

the care he needs. We have to work at finding a solution until residential placement is available. Pleasant or not, this is reality."

No one can borrow another's words. The suggestions for beginning are just that—suggestions. Each person must decide on his or her own words.

Exercise 6-1 offers an opportunity for experiencing some of the methods for beginning.

Life-style. Another challenge in the early moments of the interview is the client's life-style. An individual's life-style originates from the way in which the person's parents viewed the world and develops in accordance with the individual's unique experiences. Life-style includes the values, attitudes, and behavior that an individual learns.

The conduct of a successful interview from beginning to closing must be in balance with the life-style of the client as well as the life-style of the interviewer. Some individuals are comfortable with small talk about the weather or about an item in the interviewer's office as icebreakers. Others view this small talk as disrespectful. Small talk may encourage some clients to escape their immediate problems with more small talk. As a result, the icebreaker becomes a barrier to communication.

The client's life-style also will affect his or her expectations of the interviewer's office, the interviewer's appearance, and the interviewer's approach. These expectations may be revealed by such comments as "Where's your couch?" or "You don't look like a head shrinker." The interviewer who pursues the client's line of thought may open up some fruitful channels for further communication by replying, "No couch. Don't use one. How do you feel about rapping on these comfortable chairs?" or "What do you think a head shrinker looks like?" What the client says or does not say in the first few minutes is an effective springboard for what will take place during the rest of the interview hour.

The client's life-style provides the compass to direct how and which details will be presented and how and whether the precipitating stress that stirred the client to seek help will be revealed. The inter-

Exercise 6-1
HOW DO YOU MANAGE YOUR INITIAL GREETING? *(should be done in a group)*

Time: APPROXIMATELY 25 MINUTES
Part 1

The group is divided into subgroups of four members. One member of the subgroup tapes "beginnings" to one of the following situations:

[1]   Trish walks into the counselor's office in the Sheltered Workshop. She holds a facial tissue in her hand with which she dabs at the tears falling down her cheeks. (The Sheltered Workshop is a center in which mentally retarded people are paid at a piecework rate in a more supervised and less complex training atmosphere than in competitive employment.)

[2]   Tisa, 4 years old, is pulled into the doctor's office by her mother. Tisa's face is wet with tears.

[3]   Manny slowly opens the door marked Personnel. He moves his left leg forward and then slides his right leg so that he manages to move his body round the door. His shortened right arm has a newspaper under his armpit. Manny looks around the office, and when he sees the woman seated at her desk, he says, "I have come to apply for the salesman's job."

[4]   The woman is led into the quarterway house for alcoholics. She walks slowly and clutches a hand-kerchief to her lips.

[5]   Jim is pushed into the psychologist's office by a tall man. Jim is wearing a closed safety pin stuck through his right ear. A toilet chain hung on a hoop in his left ear is attached to a link pierced through his nose. Around his neck a string of heavy dog leash is closed with a small bicycle lock. His hair, cut in geometric layers, is painted bright yellow down one side. "Punk is beautiful" is painted in purple and orange on the front of his black jacket. When Jim nears the psychologist's desk, he spits at the tall man.

The same person plays the role of both the client and the interviewer and tapes both of these roles (3 minutes). During the taping the three other subgroup members observe and record the client-interviewer role player's verbal and nonverbal behavior.

Part 2

The tape is played, and a 5-minute discussion follows the role-playing event. The discussion centers first on the positive aspects of the beginning, and the role player comments on his or her feelings during the dual roles (client and interviewer). Then all members of the subgroup make suggestions for improvement.

Part 3

The same person repeats the taping of a 2-minute role playing of client and interviewer. The three observers once again record the verbal and nonverbal cues.

Part 4

The tape is played, and the 5-minute discussion that follows focuses on:
□ What improvements did the role player make in the initial greeting?
□ How did the role player feel about the dual role?
□ How might the beginning be improved?

viewer's life-style influences the way he or she encourages the client to bring forth or hold back thoughts and words.

The interviewer who inspires the client in this beginning stage to believe "You can do it," "There are solutions," "You are capable" facilitates the client in inspecting feelings and experimenting with new approaches to solving problems.

No matter what the client's life-style may be, it is the interviewer's responsibility to offer the client instant assurance of genuineness and interest. Even the most willing, eager-to-do-something client feels some degree of fear, despair, or confusion about what might happen during the interview.

It is up to the interviewer to weigh all the cues from the client and then decide whether this particular client is ready for a handshake or would be disturbed by any form of body touching. It is up to the interviewer to treat the client with the same humanity as a guest welcomed in his or her home. Exercise 6-2 focuses on beginning interviews with people with different life-styles.

Client's age. The developmental changes in an individual as he or she ages are another cue for the initial approach to the client. The younger the client, the less the interviewer can depend on the verbal cues. The body also "speaks" to the interviewer. Body posture and movements can provide important nonverbal cues. Not only children but also adults tell a great deal by means of these nonverbal cues.

With children the initial gesture may have to be a nonverbal greeting such as offering a toy through which the child may "speak." Finger, hand, and string puppets are excellent vehicles for conversation for the interviewer as well as the child.

The younger the client, the more likely that help was sought *for* rather than *by* the client. Therefore the two questions of interest to the interviewer— "Who felt the need for help?" and "Why now?"—must be answered by someone other than the client.

Establishing rapport. Recognition and respect for the client's life-style and adaptation of one's approach to the client's age and maturity influence the initial greeting and provide clues for the establishment of rapport. Rapport is essential for a comfortable and unconditional (positive) working relationship for helper and client. It depends on mutual client-helper understanding and genuine interest and acceptance of the interviewer (Shertzer and Stone, 1974; Wright, 1980). The bond of responsiveness that originates from rapport forms a consociation. This alliance for working together with a community of thought gravitates toward the common goals for the betterment of the client's life functioning.

Rapport depends on communication skills. It means more than a smooth opening to the interview. The helper's reputation of trust and effectiveness partially influences the establishment and maintenance of rapport. Other factors include the client's reluctance to begin, friendly greetings, active listening, and the helper's reassurances.

Exercise 6-2
HOW DO YOU RESPOND TO LIFE-STYLES? *(may be done alone or in a group)*

Time: APPROXIMATELY 20 MINUTES

The group is divided into subgroups of no more than five members. Each participant writes two replies for each of the five situations presented in Fig. 4-8. In the first column the participants write replies that indicate a lack of awareness and lack of acceptance of the client's life-style on the part of the interviewer. In the second column the reply should show recognition and acceptance of the client's life-style. The replies should be discussed by the five group members; the preferred replies of the small groups can then be discussed by the class.

The client is likely to experience some reluctance to become part of the interviewing process in the beginning. Therefore the interviewer opens up the conversation with some neutral, yet relevant, topic or event—some experience, acquaintance, or activity mutually known to client and helper.

However, this is not a superficially designed social conversation. The interviewer's initial communication is brief and focuses on the purpose of the client's visit and on acclimating the client to the unfamiliar helping situation. It is not "just talk"; it is "useful talk" (Patterson, 1974). It is important for the interviewer to observe both verbal and nonverbal cues so that the interviewer's initiative in the earliest session does not restrict the client's communications to fit into the interviewer's frame of reference. This is one of the pitfalls of interviewing to be avoided (see Chapter 5). Instead the interviewer's mission is the discovery of the client's interests, directions, and needs.

The friendly greetings of the receptionist, if there is one, and of the interviewer are crucial to these beginnings. Small gestures count. Introductions, showing the client the coatrack, and offering coffee add to the hospitality that reveals the helper's solicitous and positive regard for the client. These gestures impart the atmosphere for rapport. An austere or even too lavish office can detract from these signals of friendliness. In a warm, pleasant environment the helper's emotional tone is a model for the client's responses, and the general feeling of goodwill lessens tension and hostility.

Listening—active, attentive listening to another person—triggers the mutual communication system. It permits and encourages the client to speak and act freely and goes beyond the usual manners of social conversation. Too often the "listener" does not focus attention on the speaker but only hears the speaker's sounds until it is the "listener's" turn to speak. Too often the "listener" is thinking about what he or she is going to say and blocking out what the speaker is saying.

Barbara Haimowitz

Fig. 6-1. Active, attentive listening triggers the mutual communication system. Human service workers in Somerville-Cambridge Elder Services Office, Somerville, Mass.

Without dominating the course of the initial session, the helper should take charge so that the client may be reassured that the interviewer is ready to help the client reduce anxiety and avoid undue pressures. In the process of monitoring anxiety the interviewer fosters rapport, since the client is relieved to have the interviewer as an ally in slowing down the escalation of feelings.

Of course, the establishment of rapport would be faciliated if there were a recipe or a bag of tricks that might be offered to the beginning professional. However, all that can be offered are the generalities summarized in the previous discussion and the encouragement that competence in the helping event will be boosted by experience.

In the final analysis the primary goal of the opening session is to reduce the client's defensiveness and to induce the client to sustain the striving necessary to work through his or her problems. The helper's willingness to collaborate in mutual discoveries and resolutions must have promise of usefulness so that the client will return for further sessions as needed. Rapport becomes the mainspring that sets in motion and drives on the client's tenacity to continue—rallying the client to take emotional risks and to expend time and effort because of the prospective benefits.

During these preliminary endeavors in the achievement of rapport, other interpersonal refinements are materializing. The establishment of the relationship and roles of the interviewer and of the client are among these phenomena.

Establishing the relationship and roles of interviewer and client

A client probably has preconceived ideas of what an interviewer's role should be. Some clients may think of the interviewer as a question answerer, as someone who will tell the client what to do, how to do it, and when to complete the "doing." Other clients may be searching for someone who will silently listen to their complaints and preferably agree with their solutions. It is important that the client's notions about the interviewer be part of the opening discussions.

What the interviewer does depends on the client. No roles or rules adequately specify the interviewer's behavior. The way in which the interviewer responds to the client must be in terms of what would most benefit the client. The interviewer is primarily a person committed to *help* the client— a person who is not hung-up on a particular assumed role because of his or her own unfulfilled needs.

Only one characteristic is similar for all clients. All clients *voluntarily come* or *are brought* to the interviewer for some assistance, *for help*. Only one characteristic is similar for all interviewers. All interviewers *must be functioning at a higher level than the client*. The interviewer must be the knowing person who can and will give help.

Stating the purpose of the interview

One of the first tasks in the beginning phase is to state the purpose of the interview. The similarities or differences among the expressed purposes of the client, the interviewer, and other interested parties provide the interviewer with some understanding of the degree of pressures and distortion involved in the client's problems.

From the client's viewpoint. From the client's viewpoint the purpose of the interview depends on whether the client has sought help or was sent or brought for help. The self-referred client is more likely to ease into the client role, a seeker of help. The purpose of the client's seeking help is important even if the interviewer or other sources see another picture. Establishing an *empathic* relationship requires the interviewer to see events through the client's eyes, and establishing *rapport* requires that the client view the interviewer as a trustworthy person who is collaborating in finding a way to solve the client's problems.

From the interviewer's viewpoint. From the interviewer's viewpoint the client's expressed purpose for the meeting may appear to be only a cover for a more complex bewilderment that is being concealed by surface concerns. The client may feel safe in relating only a small part of his or her concerns at this point in the interview relationship.

In the initial phase the client may be unaware of the connection of several problems.

The takeoff for the interview must be where the client states the beginning should be. The skilled and experienced interviewer will assist the client in a greater degree of self-exploration. The interviewer's job is to help the client break down the walls of the tunnel through which the client views the world. The client must be prepared to expand and delve.

From the viewpoints of other interested parties. From the viewpoints of other interested parties the client may appear to have a more or less serious problem than he or she expresses. Often the degree of seriousness is judged by others in terms of the acting-out behavior of the client. The different tolerance levels of the people around the client influence which behavior is considered a problem. A close relative may be frightened by the argumentative behavior of the client or annoyed by the unceasing complaints. Yet the withdrawn client who makes no waves in the household may be ignored.

Example 6-1 compares the purpose of an interview from the client's, the interviewer's, and client's mother's viewpoints.

Each individual in Example 6-1 has only one view of the client's problem. The purpose of the interview as the client sees it is to help him get out of a school situation that is presently overwhelming

for him. This is the *manifest* purpose for the interview—the top layer of the client's problem. The interviewer is searching for more physical and psychological information about the client. The interviewer is just scratching the surface of the client's problem. The mother describes her purpose for the interview in terms of the annoyance value of her son's behavior. Her purpose is to stop his acting-out behavior and to make him toe the line. The mother appears to have no understanding of the seriousness of the client's problem, nor is she aware of her son's drug usage. Even though the purposes of the client, the interviewer, and the mother differ, together they provide a more complete picture of what factors might be entering into the interview situation.

Understanding the expectations for the outcome of the interview

Outcome expectations are related to the expressed purposes but should extend beyond those initially stated. According to his expressed purpose, the 15-year-old boy wants out of school. Yet, as the interviewer notes, this client's problems are interwoven with maternal pressures and misunderstanding. The communication barriers between parent and son have to be removed. Therefore the initial purpose is just that, a beginning—to discover what the problem is.

Expectations for the outcome are related to one

Example 6-1
VIEWPOINTS ABOUT PURPOSE OF INTERVIEW

Client's purpose	Interviewer's purpose	Mother's purpose
FIFTEEN-YEAR-OLD BOY SPEAKING TO INTERVIEWER: "I've been smoking pot now for 2 years. Fine. Like it. Tried firing*—scared. Scared because don't feel so good. Don't want a monkey on my back. My parents and school are heavy enough. Can you get me out of school?"	INTERVIEWER THINKING TO HIMSELF: "This 15-year-old needs medical care. Looks thin and worn out. Must lead toward a medical exam soon. Wonder whether he fired only one time. Need to find out more about family relationships and school."	CLIENT'S MOTHER TELEPHONED THE INTERVIEWER: "He's a tyrant at home. Yells, uses foul language, threatens to hurt his younger brother. I don't know what's gotten into him. He either locks himself in his room, mopes around the house, or runs through the house shutting all the windows and locking all the doors. I think what he needs is discipline. Do you know of a good military school where we can send him?"

*Firing refers to injection of a drug into the vein. In this case the drug used was heroin.

other item in addition to the expressed purposes of the client, interviewer, and other interested individuals. This item is the time involved. The amount of time involved influences when the outcome can be expected and the procedure to be followed in attaining the outcome. One simple statement may be made no matter how much time is involved—the interviewer must make clear the amount of time available for the interview but should not stretch out the interview just to fill time. In addition, the interviewer must be cautious in making the available time known to the client so that the client will not feel pressured to hurry or too frustrated to continue.

The novice interviewer is more likely to find it difficult to use the allotted time for the interview. The interviewer may encourage more talk because of guilt feelings or feelings of inadequacy. The interviewer who feels that he or she has not accomplished enough pushes some more. The fee must be earned, so this interviewer continues professional services until the completion of the 45- or 50-minute "hour."

Whatever the motives of the interviewer, the client will not be helped very much after the stopping point has been reached. The interview should be stopped when both the client and the interviewer agree that all has been said. The interviewer is more effective if, when the client sends out stop signals, the interviewer comments, "Would you like to stop now? I notice you looking at your watch." The words may differ, but the sentiment should be disclosed.

Since the time factor is part of the interview process, the time framework dictates what must be accomplished. The suicidal client relating intentions and the methods to be used is in a crisis interview. The telephone becomes the vehicle to *immediately* give the client reason to live or, at any rate, a reason not to die at that moment. Thus the time involved in a crisis interview pushes together the opening, developing, and closing phases.

Short-term and long-term outcomes. In other interview situations an immediate goal may be satisfied in a single interview or the interview may become the first of a series of interviews. The client, along with the interviewer, sets the short-term outcome for each interview. The two also plan the long-term outcome for a series of interviews. The short-term and the long-term outcomes are flexible and serve as guides for the expected outcomes between the interviews. Example 6-2 relates time to outcome.

Example 6-2
TIME AND INTERVIEW OUTCOME

Enid is 10 years old. The possible diagnosis is autism (severe emotional disturbance associated with withdrawal and language disturbance; capable of object relationships but little or no interpersonal relationships).

FIRST INTERVIEW: SHORT-TERM OUTCOME
(some response to interviewer)

Enid sits in the chair near the wall. She presses her head and shoulder to the wall. Her legs are close together, her back is straight, and her arms are folded tightly on her chest. Slowly she turns her head forward with fixed eyes blankly focused straight ahead of her.

The interviewer, Ms. S., had smiled whenever she had passed Enid during the past week, since Enid arrived at Dencrest Center. Ms. S. gets up from her chair, moves closer to Enid, and stops in front of her.

Enid looks up, unfolds her arms, and places one hand on the chair next to her. Ms. S. sits down and after a few minutes places one hand on the edge of Enid's chair. Enid and Ms. S. sit silently. Enid remains sitting rigidly upright with her feet on the floor. She does not respond to Ms. S.'s hand on the edge of her chair. After about 10 minutes, Ms. S. stands before Enid, smiles, and says, "I'll see you again tomorrow, Enid. Thanks for coming."

SECOND INTERVIEW: SHORT-TERM OUTCOME
(some verbal response to interviewer)

Enid is brought to Ms. S.'s office by one of the health assistants. Ms. S. is waiting for her, seated in the same chair as on the previous day. Ms. S. places her hand on the edge of Enid's seat, and Enid rigidly walks over to the chair and sits down. Ms. S. observes that there is a difference in Enid's movements today. Enid does not push her shoulder up to the wall. Instead she places one hand on the side of her thigh. Her arm and hand near the wall are held tightly against her body. Enid's hand rests near but not on Ms. S.'s hand. Ms. S. turns slightly so that she faces Enid at an angle.

MS. S.: *(Smiles.)* I am near you, Enid.

ENID: *(Quickly looks at Ms. S.)*

MS. S.: How are you, Enid?

ENID: *(Again looks at Ms. S.)*
MS. S.: How are you, Enid?
ENID: *(Mumbles.)* Hurting.

LONG-TERM OUTCOME

☐ Establish trust in interpersonal interactions with Ms. S.
☐ Encourage conversation, first with Ms. S., then with staff, and later with peers.
☐ Begin education at center with further possibility of entering school outside of center while living at center.
☐ Further goals to be determined depending on progress.

The goals that Ms. S. proposes are based on the time factor as well as Enid's problems. Simple and concrete goals with favorable possibilities for accomplishment are planned. Since relating to people is difficult for Enid, Ms. S. includes brief exposure to the short-term outcomes of interpersonal contacts. Each new exposure is arranged to begin where the previous interview left off. Note that in the second interview Ms. S. sits in the same place with her hand held in the same way as at the end of the first interview.

Ms. S. is aware that the fuller development of trust and a relationship will take much longer to achieve than the simple responses of Enid's placing a hand on the chair next to her or mumbling something in response to Ms. S.'s question. Yet each change toward the final goal is a step forward and, for Enid, an achievement never before completed.

The time allotted to each interview is brief. The frequency of the interviews allows for small units of behavioral outcome. In another situation the arrangements would have to fit the time schedule and the client's needs.

The term "outcome" in the preceding example is only one of a number of terms with similar meanings, such as "goals," "objectives," "purpose," "target," and "endpoint." Although these terms differ somewhat in meaning, all of them signify intent, aspiration, and direction. Most of these terms are used interchangeably in the following discussion of goal setting to refer to the end result of an act or sequence of acts that a person or group intends and plans to bring about by these actions.

Selecting goals. Goal setting is best achieved by reciprocal decision making of the client and the helper (Cormier and Cormier, 1979). The process of choosing a target with the client requires an interviewer whose communication skills and knowledge of the client's needs are clear yet flexible so that the client's inclinations and priorities take precedence. The interviewer also must "read between the lines" to discern whether the risk of the particular change the client selects might have unfavorable side effects. Client and helper must weigh the advantages and disadvantages of the goals.

Advantages and disadvantages of goal setting. In general, goal construction gives direction to the helping process and provides a built-in self-correction device. For the helper, goals become the basis for using certain interviewing and counseling strategies. For the client, goals clarify the helping procedure and reduce the vagueness of the client's and counselor's roles. Goals provide a channel for continuous feedback, since progress can be monitored. Dividing the actions toward the goals into separate parts yields continuous indicators of the client's progress and of the effectiveness of the helper's interventions. These milestones of progress or lack of progress alert the interviewer to the fact that new directions and new information may be necessary.

Since goal setting is designed to be an interactive process, both client and counselor must carefully think through priorities and focus on the specific tasks of greater urgency. The client has the opportunity to share in the analysis of his or her problem, in the planning of the goals, and in the formulation of the tactics and schedule for the sequential action steps to accomplish the goal. The helper's role is that of facilitator, catalyst, supporter, and monitor. Thus the interviewer guides and protects the client and also spurs on the client when interest and incentive dwindle. In addition, the helper constantly observes and appraises the client's ongoing behavior toward the goals to make certain that progress continues.

Two significant aspects of reciprocal goal setting are (1) that the client has the prerogative to accept or reject a particular goal or action plan, and (2) that the counselor explains the goal-setting procedure to the client with explicit details about the client's responsibility to fulfill the plans. Clients who assume the obligations associated with the goal are more likely to thoroughly ponder the problem areas that need immediate attention and to seek clarification of what can be accomplished through the helping event. This definition of role, tasks, and expectations paves the way for the interviewer to cooperate with the client in realizing goals in the areas of greater concern to the client rather than aimless striving.

The advantages of goal setting as the framework for the helping event are apparent. However, certain disadvantages erect barriers to goal attainment. The client may be able to plan goals with ease but be unable or unwilling to perform the behavior leading to achievement of the goal. He or she must have the skills and want to stop smoking or nail biting, or to become more proficient in mathematics or to try out some ways to decrease marital strife. The client must demonstrate the initial push and must maintain motivation. Herein lies the crux of the dilemma—the helper cannot be sure that the selected goals and tasks are the wisest and most promising for the client to pursue, and the client may achieve the goals but fail to understand why

the changed behavior is more desirable and appropriate. Moreover, the goal-setting device is not adaptable to complex psychological problems, particularly when the client's motivations are unclear (Wright, 1980).

What matters in goal setting and attainment are the attitudes, skills, and knowledge of the helper. Success does not imply merely that goals always are arranged, that the client complies, and that the helper directs. Success means that the helper is empathic and competent and realizes when goals are to be attempted and when other forms of intervention are more appropriate.

Goal setting and problem solving. When the helper weighs all the facets of the problem presented by the client and determines with the client that goal setting is the way to go, then the helper's competence depends on knowing the procedures to be followed in selecting goals. The helper who knows and uses the problem-solving model is one step ahead. Goal analysis and establishment evolve through at least six stages: (1) specifying the goal, (2) identifying the purpose of the goal, (3) outlining the suitability and attainability of the goal, (4) exploring the possible hazards, (5) itemizing the benefits of the behavior change, and (6) determining

Table 6-1. *Models for goal setting, problem solving, and S-C-I-E-N-C-E*

Goal setting	Problem solving	S-C-I-E-N-C-E
1. Specify goals.	Develop the problem.	*S*pecify the category. *C*ollect data.
(Goals are selected to transform the behavior associated with the problem.)		
2 and 3. Identify the purpose and outline the suitability and attainability of the goal.	Analyze the problem and identify alternative solutions.	*I*dentify patterns. *E*xamine options.
4 and 5. Explore possible hazards and benefits of behavior change.	Select a solution and test its limits and potentialities for favorable outcome.	*N*arrow options. *C*ompare options.
6. Determine advantages and disadvantages of working with a particular helper.	Compare value systems with solutions and the advantages and disadvantages of the plan of action.	*E*xtend, reevaluate, and revise original plans; replace as needed.

Exercise 6-3
GOAL-SETTING MATRIX

Fig. 6-2 is a form for originating and developing relevant ideas and plan (a matrix) for goal setting. Complete this form after careful consideration of your needs for change or development. Your goal does not have to relate to altering unfavorable habits unless this is your preference; it may be the achievement of a particular skill or even of tasks that would support a trip you have always wanted to take. The important feature of this exercise is priority: choose the goal that is most important for you. Narrow your considerations to only *one* goal. If you wish, you might extend your goal-setting matrix to include a time frame for accomplishing the change in behavior.

Goal analysis	Directions: goal decisions	Your responses
Goal specified	One thing I would like to change about myself:	
Purpose of goal	Successful goal attainment would make my life circumstances different in the following ways:	
Goal suitability and attainability	I think this is a goal I can achieve because:	
Possible hazards	I think the following might be some of the drawbacks, difficulties, hazards if I make this change:	
Benefits, gains	I think the following might be the payoff for making this change:	
Goal achievement: help	If *(insert someone's name)* helped me, getting to my goal would be easier because:	
Goal achievement: barriers	If *(insert same or another name)* helped me, there would be a conflict of ideas or values because:	
	If no one helped me I would:	

Fig. 6-2. Goal-setting matrix. (Modified from Cormier, W.H., and Cormier, L.S.: Interviewing strategies for helpers: a guide to assessment, treatment, and education, Monterey, Calif., 1979; Brooks/Cole Publishing Co.)

with the client the advantages and disadvantages of working with a particular helper. These steps resemble the problem-solving approach discussed in Chapter 1 and the S-C-I-E-N-C-E paradigm for problem solving of Mahoney and Mahoney (1976). Table 6-1 compares these three approaches. Add to these comparisons the skills developed in observation, recording, and reporting, and the foundation for the professional human service worker is strengthened. Exercise 6-3 proposes a form for working through the six stages in the goal-setting model.

The work of composing suitable goals is not simple, but when germane to the needs and problems of the client, goal setting is a serviceable technique for the helper. Clearly defined goals that are noticeable and measurable serve the client and interviewer best. More structured approaches also exist, ranging from goal contracting to established scaling systems.

Structuring the goal-setting procedure. In Chapter 4 a contract is discussed from the viewpoint of the roles and responsibilities of the client and the helper. In the present context, contract refers to the formalized goals (designated through the same processes as previously presented) written in a special format and signed by the client, and helper, and all other significant persons involved with the client (Wright, 1980). This contract includes dates of beginning, of termination, and, when necessary, of renegotiation. The behavior to be changed is defined, and the amount, kind, and frequency of reinforcement are spelled out. The contract also can include rewards for steadfast, extraordinary effort and corrective effects for dilatory behavior. A pact arranged for goal achievement has the same advantages and disadvantages as mentioned for the less formalized goal-setting process plus the burden of more people to monitor. The significant persons in the client's life can prove to be a boon if reinforcements from them bolster the client and cushion the difficulties of work toward goals; however, they also can be counterproductive if they are unsuitable participants.

Contracting goals derives from behavioral counseling and favors self-regulation (Wright, 1980), as do the *Human Service Scale* (HSS) and the *Goal Attainment Scaling* (GAS) systems (see Appendix B). These scaling systems identify the client's needs and associated problems and provide measures of client change. The HSS is based on Maslow's (1970) hierarchy of needs (see Chapter 7) using a scoring system to identify the level of functioning of the client in each of seven areas. The GAS also produces an individual client plan that indicates five levels of functioning and five levels of possible outcome from goal attainment.

Setting limits

In combination with the skills and knowledge involved in the initial greeting, clarification of the relationship and roles of the participants in the helping event, statement of the purpose of the interview, and goal setting, the interviewer must set limits (time limits, behavior or acting-out limits, and process limits) with the client.

At the beginning of an interview there must be some mutually approved ideas about setting limits. The helping road is much smoother if client and interviewer agree on a cooperative pact that is satisfying and realistic for both of them.

Time limits. The security and ease of both client and interviewer are enhanced by an informational exchange about the time of appointments, what happens if appointments are to be missed, and how tardiness is to be handled. Time requirements that are too loose or too rigid disturb the effectiveness of the interview relationship. There is no fast-help, one-shot approach to finding a middle ground between too little and too much. The interviewer must adjust the time specifications in accordance with his or her own and the client's needs as well as with the client's cultural framework.

Time is judged and handled differently in various cultures. For instance, the pressure of time and getting places *on time* means more in the Western than in the Eastern cultures. Time means more to the harried businessmen who want to increase production and less to the youth of the counterculture who are turned off by the materialistic surgings of their elders.

The conditions of life make for different perspectives about time. Delaying gratifications becomes a burdensome chore for the black person, the Indian, and the Chicano who are grappling with the present satisfaction of their needs. Telling people of these cultures "You will feel better in time" often discourages their faith in the interviewer. For people from these cultures, longer periods for each interview with some apparent positive results are far more effective than interview sessions conducted over a longer period of weeks. Time has different meanings for the prisoner who is serving an indefinite sentence than for one who knows how long he or she has to serve, for the anxious person who tends to overestimate the passage of time, and for the older person who is doubtful about the future and tenaciously holds on to the present.

The interviewer who stands aloof from the world of the client loses out in setting time limits. Unfortunately, all too often interviewers have been trained to function with people similar to themselves and are not prepared "to deal with individuals who come from different racial, ethnic, and socioeconomic groups whose values, attitudes and general life styles may be at great variance" with their own (Hernandez, Haug, and Wagner, 1976). These authors also concluded:

A minority group individual may find himself in the difficult position of trying to overcome what Schofield (1964) describes as the therapist's "Yavis syndrome,"* a common tendency of the therapist to differentially select clients who are successful, young, attractive, intelligent, well educated, verbal, and introspective.

What this discussion is leading up to is the frequently repeated phrase "Time is relative." Therefore, although time limits are a necessity, considerations of age, ethnic background, and immediacy of problems as well as the impact of the client's

present situation are the foundation for arranging time provisions. Time limits exist not only to fulfill the interviewer's schedule but also for the client's advantage.

The client's attention may have to be drawn to a briefer period of time on a certain day; for instance, "Ned, we have 30 minutes today; let's see what we can accomplish." Toward the end of an interview session, the interviewer may say, "There are 15 minutes left; let's try to pull together some of the things we've talked about."

Example 6-3 suggests some responses when the client or the interviewer is late.

Example 6-3
WHEN THE CLIENT OR THE INTERVIEWER IS LATE

[1]

The first time the client is late the interviewer listens to client's explanation without comment. Approving comments such as "That's OK" may reinforce the client's behavior. In fact, the client may begin to wonder whether 45 or 50 minutes are really necessary for the interview or perhaps whether the client is really important to the interviewer.

[2]

After the client has been late once, the interviewer may say, "Sorry to hear about your clock conking out again. We will do as much as we can in the remaining 35 minutes."

[3]

When the client says, "Forgot about my appointment until it was time to leave," the interviewer's reply might be, "How did you feel when you realized you would be late?" or "I wonder, did you feel as if you really did not want to come?" If the client's answer is "yes," the interviewer helps the client explore his or her feelings. If the client's answer is "no," the interviewer holds off further discussion for another occasion. The client is probably not ready to talk about feelings at the present moment. Responsibility for the length of the appointment and for promptness must be shifted to the client.

[4]

When the interviewer is late, he or she should make adjustments so that the client will not lose interview time. It is the interviewer's responsibility to either lengthen the interview session or make up the lost time at a later session, unless the client prefers not to do this.

---

*The term "Yavis" comes from the first letters of young, attractive, verbal, introspective, and successful.

An early arrival may reveal some degree of anxiety, just as a later arrival may signify a reluctance to participate. If the early client shows by word or by gesture that he feels the interview is threatening, the interviewer reassures him by saying, "Glad to see you, Mr. A. Please wait in the reception room. I'll be with you at three. The client in my office will be finished by then." The interviewer's smile and nod also provide needed support.

Sometimes the client plays with time by making frequent requests to change the time of appointments. The interviewer's response depends on the client. For one client, changing the time occasionally may reassure the client of the interviewer's interest. For another client, providing such changes may encourage the client to attempt other manipulative devices. For still others, the interviewer would appear as disorganized as the client and thus lose face with the client.

When the client asks, "What time is it?" at frequent intervals, the interviewer should be aware of the possibility that the client may be bored, annoyed, withholding informaton until there is too little time to discuss it, comparing the present interviewer's procedure with a past one, or any number of other possibilities. Some productive interviewer comments are "You seem to be concerned about the time. Is there something you want to do?" or "Is there something you need to tell me about?"

The words must be individualized. The interviewer must look at what is happening in the client-interviewer interaction and use the preceding ideas as guidelines for responses. Time limits as well as other limits should be minimal and in accordance with the client's belief system. In addition, these limits should be applied nonpunitively.

Behavior or acting-out limits. The interviewer may be puzzled about the when and how of setting limits on the client's behavior. Reluctance to assert himself or herself or inability to establish a framework of acceptable behavior may impede the interviewer from establishing behavior limits. The important idea in setting acting-out limits is that it is acceptable for the clients to *tell about* how they

feel and what they would like to do, but there is certain behavior that *cannot be acted out.*

Some verbal comments may not fall easily on the dainty ears of some interviewers even though the spontaneous release of the feelings may help the client over a barrier. When the client shouts "Man, you're a son of a bitch! You made me remember . . .!" the explosive comment may open up a wealth of more relevant thoughts and feelings. The interviewer who becomes defensive about such tongue-lashing reveals this reaction by a comment such as "Who do you think you're talking to? Cut out the foul language." On the other hand, the interviewer may compensate for discomfort by interpreting the client's outcry in the following manner: "Aren't you feeling the same way about me as you did about your father?" Such an interpretation may shut off the client's expression of feeling because it is untimely or incorrect.

It is different, however, when the client approaches the interviewer in a menacing fashion or raises a hand as if to strike the interviewer. At such a moment the interviewer immediately must stop the client. Stopping the client from acting out hostile behavior is not only for the interviewer's protection but also to rescue the client from guilt feelings. For instance, the interviewer says, "Mrs. T., I'll listen to anything you want to say—how you feel about your brother or about me. But I won't let you hurt me," or "Bobby, it's OK to tell me you hate me, but I won't let you break that car."

The adult as well as the child client most probably is hoping to be restrained from acting out hostile impulses. Permitting the client to hurt or break something often arouses feelings of shame and increases rather than decreases anxiety feelings. The client is encouraged to express feelings verbally and restrained from expressing feelings through action.

Process limits. A third kind of setting limits is concerned in part with the client's expectations from the interviewer and in part with the degree of dependence the client desires and sometimes the interviewer encourages. Process limits refer to the degree to which the client and the interviewer are participating in the interview transaction.

The client may await the interviewer's questions or remarks and put forth little or no work effort in the interpersonal transaction. Another client may talk too much or ask continuous questions, seeking directions and answers from the interviewer. Symptom listing becomes the chief method of some other clients.

Example 6-4 provides samples of some problems and solutions for process limits.

Example 6-4
PROCESS PROBLEMS—THE CLIENT

The overdepender: "Wow, you really want me to tell you what to do. I bet together we could work out a good arrangement for your apartment searching."

"I know you want me to tell you how I would act in this same situation. But that would be *me, not you*. Do you really think that it would help you if I spelled out a step-by-step approach to the problem?"

The concealer: "Lee, I'm here to help you. Unless you come forth with your feelings, your ideas, how can I help?"

The waiter: "Cindy, tell me about the incident. Asking you questions is a drag. You're the only one who can tell it like it is to you."

The symptom recorder: The client lists symptoms, reviewing them in great detail. The interviewer guides the client into a discussion of one of his problems, "Mr. T., you have told me a great deal about your daughter's horrible behavior and your stomach pains. Let's look a little more closely at your feelings about your daughter now."

The merry- (or sad-) go-rounder: The client begins to talk as soon as he or she enters the office and rambles on about problems, all dominated by a central concern that is repeated like a broken record. The interviewer picks out the recurring theme and says, "Over and over again people seem to tell you to shut up and to mind your own affairs. How do you think you might change what's happening?"

The role reverser: The client asks personal questions about the interviewer's life. The interviewer answers if the question is pertinent to the client's problems and/or the interviewer's reply will indicate empathic understanding of the client. The client who continues these personal questions may be trying to avoid his or her own problems. In this instance the interviewer might say, "I could go on and on talking about myself. I do think we ought to get on with your distress about the people who are working with you at Xaviar Company."

The praiser: The client persists in complimenting the interviewer and repeats such statements as "I know you're the only one who can help me" and "You must know the answer, you're so capable." The interviewer answers, "Your confidence does make me feel good. I do know, however, that without your help little can be accomplished."

The self-contempter: The client asks, "How can you stand to listen to people like me all day?" or "Why do I get myself into these messes?" The interviewer responds, "I'm here to help. I believe that you have the ability to do something about the messes! Let's try to find out what can be done."

The self-pitier: The client talks freely about self but back-pedals into blaming others, martyring self for others, and excusing himself or herself for not doing things. The client seems not to be making any effort to use the interview to move toward improvement. In externalizing the causes of the problem, the client expects other people to change and removes himself or herself from the solution. The interviewer says, "I have the feeling that we are up against something that is stopping us from looking at your problems. Together, let's both search further for some solutions."

The anxiety increaser: The client bursts into tears. Talking does not seem to bring relief or reduction of feeling. Instead emotionality increases and feeds more anxiety reactions. The interviewer comments, "How do you feel now that you have cried?" "I know you feel bad. Tell me more about it so I can help," "What do you think would happen if you rode on the subway?" "How did your feelings about large crowds in department stores begin?" "What were things like before you became so upset?" "Talking seems to upset you," or "That feeling is common when a person gets upset."

The labels attached to the client's behaviors just described do not signify that there are distinctive types of clients who exhibit specific behavior. Clients are prone to behave in many different ways. Nevertheless, threads of behavior are usually detected that persist in the interview situation. It is up to the interviewer to detect these recurrent behaviors and to learn how to handle them.

In Example 6-4 the interviewer is accomplishing one or more of the following objectives in each of the sample situations:

- Guiding and involving the client in further exploration of the problem
- Pointing up the client's responsibility for participation in the interview transaction
- Encouraging the client to examine his or her feelings about his or her behavior
- Reassuring the client when necessary but urging the client to move on
- Reinforcing the client's ability to change

Sometimes it is the interviewer who needs to have process limits clarified. Example 6-5 shows behavior that restricts the interviewer's ability to function effectively.

Example 6-5
RESTRICTIONS ON INTERVIEWER'S EFFECTIVENESS

The competitor: The trainee or interviewer wants to perform better than his or her peers or teacher, or the employed interviewer wants to make point with the supervisor. This hunger to compete frequently results in a defiant approach toward peers, teachers, supervisor, and worst of all, the client.

The defender: The trainee or interviewer who fears losing approval of the teacher or supervisor covers up fears with coping strategies that temporarily conceal fears of failure. Although these patterns of behavior may reduce the anxiety feelings, these unsatisfying behaviors also dodge the interviewer's problems. As a result, the interviewer pushes energy toward self-defensive behavior and resents what he or she considers the teacher's or supervisor's infrequent or inadequate praise. Thus the self-involved interviewer diminishes sensitivity to the client's needs because of hypersensitivity to his or her own needs.

The self-blamer: The trainee feels guilty about using a client as a guinea pig, or the employed interviewer feels that someone more experienced could do a better job. Believing themselves incapable, they act incapably. Their performance is consequently lowered—just one more self-fulfilling prophecy.

The nonlistener: The interviewer is so involved in his or her own problems that he or she is unable or unwilling to listen to the client. Therefore the interviewer misses a great deal of information pertinent to the client's problem and also gives the client a feeling of nonimportance.

The speeder: The interviewer fails to give the client sufficient time and opportunity to answer a question or to complete a statement. Part of the reason for speeding up may be that the interviewer is convinced that the client's background experiences are so inadequate that the client would have little to offer to increase understanding of the problem. The interviewer diminishes the flow of the client's discussion by a bombardment of talk and explanation, or may be more direct by remarking, "That's all you have to say about it, isn't it? You're just repeating the same thing from another angle now. Let's talk about . . ."

The avoider: Fear of making mistakes stops the interviewer from speaking. Wary of saying the wrong thing, the interviewer tends to overlook situations and is quiet and passive when active intervention would be desirable. Insecure about involvement, intrusion, or a possible struggle, the interviewer proceeds overcautiously.

The outliner: The interviewer is preoccupied with the outline of required information that is part of the intake interview. Therefore the interviewer compulsively follows the formal guide. A disconnected interview of high quantity but low quality results. In addition, strict adherence to form reduces the interviewer's ability to listen to what the client is saying.

The advisor: The interviewer gives advice too readily when the client should be provided with alternatives from which to select. This does not mean that the client's request for advice should be disregarded. Some direct requests from anxious and dependent clients must be satisfied. Giving advice in this instance is proof of the interviewer's interest in the client and instills client confidence in the interviewer. Later on in the interview transaction the interviewer may offer alternatives rather than direct advice.

The interviewer's personal problems may make the interpersonal process between the client and the interviewer more complex and unsatisfactory. In the preceding discussion a number of ineffective interviewer characteristics are brought to light. The "point-maker" interviewer may become defiant in competitive efforts to get ahead and may also cover up fears of losing out by lies, by distortions of the client's problems, or by excessive self-blame. Any one of these characteristics can blunt the interviewer's ability to listen.

In addition, because of feelings of unimportance, the interviewer may seek ''points'' from the client. Such interviewers rush headlong to show the client that *they* (the interviewers) *know,* that *they are wise.* Consequently, the interviewers interrupt and speak rapidly, disregarding the client's replies. In other situations the interviewers' fear that they may mismanage the interview cuts down their comments to a minimum. Two further obstacles decrease the harmony of the interview transaction. The too-directive interviewer who oozes instructions to the client on the best course of action is similar to the interviewer who is managed by an application form. The interviewer-advisor does not permit the client the opportunity to choose from alternatives; the toe-the-form interviewer does not allow any alternative to the rigidity of the words on the intake application.

■ ■ ■

The groundwork has been laid for the opening of the interview session. Relationships and roles of interviewer and client have been clarified. The purpose and expected outcome of the interview have been established, and the interviewer has been alerted to interview pitfalls. Potential barriers have been stated that might arise from the differences between the backgrounds and experiences of the interviewer and the client. The danger of misdirected motivation as well as loss of cues has been pointed out. Communication, particularly the ''what'' and ''how'' of communication, is central to this entire discussion. The message becomes clear: the opening of the interview demands a knowledgeable and skillful helper who is prepared to help the client explore more deeply.

Fig. 6-3. Developing or exploring phase: getting into the center of the interview.

PHASE II: THE DEVELOPING OR EXPLORING PHASE

The beginning stage of the interview merges into the middle or developing phase without any obvious point of change. Certain previous concerns become even more apparent at this time, and new concerns arise.

Getting into the center of the interview

It may be assumed that the center or core of the interview has been reached when both the client and the interviewer settle into their conversational niches to begin some serious explorations.

Developing objectives. Some objectives for the developing phase are merely expansions of what has gone on in the interview up to this point. The fact-gathering process is justified only if it serves the client's needs for increased understanding. If the opening phase has been successful, the empathic interviewer has already established an acceptant atmosphere in which the client will throw more light on the current problem, be moved to discover whether other problems are involved, discuss ways in which he or she has tried to cope with his or her problems, and search for and select from alternative solutions.

Current (presenting) problem. Up to this moment in the interview the client has been generalizing about the problem. Now it is necessary to obtain more details about the client's concerns as well as to help the client recognize his or her role in the present difficulties. This closer inspection may reveal circumstances that the client has been avoiding in order not to recognize and accept involvement and responsibility for the predicament.

The competent interviewer is aware of the double bind that faces the client. The client wants help and yet is fearful that his or her self-protective behavior may be penetrated. The client therefore holds on tightly to his or her coping strategies even if they are not working.

The interviewer's skill is vital in smoothing the way for the client through what may become a rough period. It is during this search for details that the client may seek to deny his or her role in the muddled situation. The client may distort the facts to put himself or herself in a more favorable position or adopt coping devices that apparently reduce the cognitive dissonance (conflicting ideas) yet that continue tension-producing behavior. Thus the client may just move into a slightly different storm area.

Exercise 6-4 seeks different approaches to this search for details.

Other problems. The problem that the client first states, the *manifest* problem, may be the only one the client is prepared to share. This itemization of the obvious evidence of the client's distress may simply be a maneuver to allay the anxiety of what the client fears most. Fear of ridicule, of shame, and of rejection drives clients to conceal their part in the drama they enact about the relationship with their wife, child, friends, or work. The client becomes a child again, trying to buy favor from the interviewer by proving "what a good child am I." "If only someone would understand me."

Before the client will freely look at himself or herself in this elaborate system of interrelationships, a feeling of trust for the interviewer must be established. By exploring the major area of the client's functioning as child, parent, spouse, friend, student, educator, employee, or employer, the client and the interviewer arrive at disclosure of other aspects of the client's living arrangements that are influential in the initially presented problem.

When Ms. H. says that her 4-year-old son Sammy manipulates his father, fights with his sibling (the baby), and has exhibited this behavior since the age of 2 years, an alert interviewer asks, "How does your son 'twist his father' around his finger?" "What do you do when this is happening?" "Tell me about Sammy—about his fights with his baby sister." "And then what do you do?"

The blueprint for coping with the behavior that has baffled Ms. H., her husband, and her children leads into the circumstances surrounding the behavior, the antecedent events, and the consequent events reinforcing the behavior. (See the discussion of the ABC of behavior in Chapter 3.)

Exercise 6-4
HOW DO YOU MOVE INTO DETAILS? *(should be done alone and discussed in a group)*

Time: MINIMUM 60 MINUTES

Each participant completes the interviewer's and client's discussion in the following examples of behavior with three purposes in mind. First, the interviewer encourages the client to recognize himself or herself as one of the sources of the problem. Second, the interviewer reinforces the client's movement from generalities to details. Third, revised and/or new objectives are mutually planned.

After participants finish writing as much as they think is necessary for the five examples, the conclusions to the examples are discussed by the group. The group decides which interviewer responses are effective in attaining detailed client answers and examines the appropriateness of the objectives for the problem as presented by the client.

[1] Mr. D. and his wife are in th office of the marriage counselor because of what they call a "battle of ideas." Mr. D. is certain that he is right. If his wife were not a spendthrift, there would be no problem. Pointing at Mr. D., Ms. D. gnashes her teeth and says, "If only you gave me other satisfactions. The only thing I've got—the only pleasure . . . Buying things makes me feel good." The marriage counselor has heard Ms. D. say this same thing in her two previous sessions and has asked Mr. D. to join the counseling session in order to unravel some of the details.

[2] Terry is the spokesman for the group. He rapidly launches into the list of annoyances that the other students had prepared with his help. Terry says, "Here it is. They all revolve around your demands for too much meaningless work for what we want to do as human service workers. We want to find out more about ourselves. You give us mickey-mouse requirements."

[3] The situation has become worse. At least that is what the white members of the club believe. Not only are there special cliques with their own ideas, but there is also a sharp split between the white and the black members. Bob comes to the club sponsor to tell him about this split: "We sit together according to pigmentation. Blacks—whites. We—they. Just can't seem to get together."

[4] Tom enters the interviewer's office slowly. He wears jeans patched with rainbow colored cloths of different sizes and shapes. His crushed, embroidered, faded blue shirt is loosely stuck in to his jeans, which are held together with a large safety pin near the top of the fly. Strung through the loops of his jeans is a bright red macramé belt with a hand-engraved buckle. He sits down on the straight chair with one leg beneath him. On his sockless feet he wears rubbed, ripped moccasins. He says, "Wow! Weary jaunt. Promised them I would see you. No need, what for? From place to place, crash where I'm at. Hmmmm, that's it. Where I am—commune, somewhere, nowhere, anywhere. Remorse? Parents? Uptight, bourgeois mentality. I wonder sometimes if they're all wrong? Wonder?"

[5] This is Ms. H.'s second visit to the community center's social service department. She is thinking about her last visit as she walks up the steps to the interviewer's office. She mumbles, "All week— what a talk session. More like a sermon. Why am I back here? She doesn't know from a hole in her head. Need someone to tell me how to handle his temper. Blue, yes, blue he gets when he gets mad. He's 4 years old, and he twists his father around his little finger. Four! Been winding-up the family since he was 2. Has to stop. Fighting with the baby, fighting with me. It has to stop! Gotta find a way to stop it." Ms. H. enters the social worker's office.

Details are accumulated to provide the client with an enriched awareness of her role as well as her husband's role in reinforcing Sammy's behavior. Information about Ms. H.'s feeling about her husband is coupled to this awareness of the effect each member of the family has on the other. The inquiry goes on reviewing the interaction between husband and wife. Is there some other behavior of the husband or the wife that is disturbing their relationship and is being duplicated in the parental relationship with their children?

The empathic interviewer is responsive to the client's needs. Together they decide when they have reached a plateau and should stop awhile to look for other directions or have arrived at some solutions to try out. The plateau may indicate an altering of the relationships between client and interviewer, some new complications in the client's life space, or the client's desire to mull over what has occurred. Any number of possibilities may crop up.

Problem coping. Two additional facets are inspected during this developing phase: What is being done about the disturbing situation? How successful are these coping strategies in reducing the disturbance? The answers to these two questions determine alternative solutions. Sometimes the client may be reluctant to talk about how he or she tackled problems because of the unsuccessful results. In an effort to avoid criticism the client may become silent or may fabricate some success.

Some approaches promoting the client's unraveling of distressful behavior follow:

- □ "You seem to set high standards for yourself."
- □ "Seems to me you're harder on yourself than you are on anyone else."
- □ "I'm here to help you, not to criticize you."
- □ "I wonder what makes you believe you can't do well. Look at how well you handled . . ."
- □ "It isn't always possible to do things right the first time."
- □ "Come now. Here you have the *right* to be wrong. So, if it didn't turn out so well, we'll find another way."

- □ "I know you're finding it hard to talk, but I can only help when you tell me about things."
- □ "Hmmmm. Have you noticed how uptight you get when someone says something you don't like?"
- □ "What has happened between us to close you off now?"

These suggestions are meaningless unless they fit the occasion, the interviewer, and the client. The interviewer who is genuinely interested in the client's self-fulfillment knows not to use "canned" answers.

Alternative solutions. When some degree of clarity is achieved about the branching difficulties of the problem and when the existing coping strategies are apparent, then client and interviewer aks themselves, "What else might be done?" In actuality, clarity, coping, and "what else" are all being discussed to some degree at any one interview moment.

Flexibility is essential in establishing guideposts to new action. Both a reorganization of prior attacks on the problem and some innovative coping methods should be brought forward for the client's scrutiny. Underlying the framework for alternate solutions is a belief in the dignity of the client and the client's right to make decisions about change. The interviewer's role is to help the client figure out what has been going on and to seek other ways of behaving. In some instances the interviewer may make outright suggestions. However, these suggestions must be offered with clarity, simplicity, and caution.

Sometimes the interviewer must assure the client that others have experienced similar disturbances and feelings as well as the same lack of progress in finding solutions. Clients profit from reports about how others strive to face and deal with their problems. They increase their chances for coping by listening to similar but hitherto unrecognized solutions that they may try with their own difficulties. In a group the thoughtful, empathic rejoinders of other group members also can be helpful (Fig. 6-4).

In the presence of the accepting, nonpunishing

Ross Laboratories

Fig. 6-4. The middle, exploratory phase of the group interview. Sharing of problems and solutions becomes more intensive.

interviewer the client feels free to enlarge on grievances or to express hostilities. As interviewing time goes on, the client's fears or anxieties are diminished; the client becomes more secure in the interview transaction. More energy is transferred from conflicts and feelings of threat to the positive challenge associated with seeking a solution.

Thus the interviewer avoids the do-gooder attitude that regards the client as a child to be shown the right way. Since there is no one right way, emphasis is placed on the client's initiative and capacity for personal growth. This does not mean, however, that when the client needs information the interviewer refuses to give it.

Through the human relationship of the closed-off, protected social unit of the interview transaction clients are led to examine their problems, themselves, and their interactions with others. When troubled clients are assured that they are worthwhile to someone (the interviewer), they are reinforced by the social approval of the interviewer to attempt new ways of behaving.

Incubation period. Sometimes the wisest way to go forward in the interview is to stand still. The remark ''They also serve who only stand and wait'' by Milton in the poem ''On His Blindness'' appropriately fits the periods during which very little client work and progress seem to be made. Often this occurs after the client has spoken about the problem as he or she sees it. This pause permits the client to integrate the parts of the discussion. The interviewer serves the client's needs best by standing by supportively but not pushing the client into deeper exploration before the incubation period is complete.

The client may begin to say something, veer off to some other topic, and return to what he or she was saying previously. The thinking appears to be circular, but actually the client is moving to some associations with the beginning thought. These associations seem to be drawing the client somewhat astray but are meaningful to the client and in the path of his or her concerns. The client is going through the process of coordinating thoughts, seeking alternative solutions, and trying to understand what has been going on during the interview.

The incubation period is not the same as inhibiting or blocking of responses. One essential difference is observed. In the incubation period the client does not return immediately to the original statement but instead begins an entirely different, often tangential discussion. Blocking shows in behavior that is negative (the client refuses to answer), angry ("Stop getting into my head!"), coy ("Come on Doc, you don't really want to know that!"), or in some other form refuses to continue the interview.

In contrast to blocking, incubation offers the client the opportunity to shape thinking to find a more comfortable way to express a disturbing thought or to bend a little more toward solving problems. It is a process of organizing and reorganizing on a subvocal level. Incubation may be revealed nonverbally rather than verbally by the furrowed brow, the raised eyebrow, and silence. None of these signals of incubation can be interpreted out of the context of what has gone before and what continues afterward. The effective interviewer does not jump in where the client is not ready to tread.

The puzzled interviewer may wonder, "What do I do or say at a time like this?" The interviewer who is really uncertain of what makes the client slow in continuing might be honest about it and say, "Frankly, I don't understand what is making you have difficulty in continuing." In the event that the interviewer is able to note a pattern in the client's offshoots of the central concern, the interviewer may comment, "I feel it's somewhat hard for you to go on. Sit and think for awhile if it helps. I don't mind."

Shifting gears. In order to push further into the center of the interview, it is necessary to find some ways to "shift gears" from the beginning of the interview to the middle or developing phase. It may be necessary to go back to what already has been discussed or just to wait until the client gives the interviewer the "go" signal so the gears might be shifted. Four points related to shifting gears will be discussed: speed of shift, self-appraisal, client's pace, and nonverbal affirmation.

Speed of shift. Transitions from one area to another vary from rapid to slow. Sometimes the transition may be abrupt, as when the interviewer comments, "Now that you have told me your problem, tell me more about yourself—how you feel right now."

Getting clients to talk about themselves may be very difficult since they have been accustomed to looking at themselves as others see them. He is "no good" because they frown on him as a black man. She is "not wanted" because her father really wanted her to be a boy. He is an "ungrateful son" because he wants to live in a commune. These labels conceal clients' true feelings and communicate a distorted view of self. These public labels may become the private labels that clients accept.

Self-appraisal. The next step, after clients move from generalities to details, is for the clients to see themselves as they are, not solely as others see them. When the client says, "I hate being a homosexual, and I don't know what to do about it," the interviewer may reply in one of two ways. The The interviewer may respond with a statement that prompts the client to continue to look at the behavior as others perceive it, "Then why do you keep on being a homosexual? You say you hate it.

You say you can't stand what others say to you."
A contrasting comment by the interviewer is, "You
say you hate being a homosexual, but you continue.
I wonder what it really means to you?"

When the interviewer presses the client to examine what the behavior really means to him or
her; self-exploration becomes the responsibility of
the client, and the client forges ahead toward a
better understanding of self. The interviewer does
not desert the client during this self-probing but is
part of the searching team. The client provides the
lead, while the interviewer listens sensitively and
responds in the client's direction.

At times when the conversation begins to slacken
the interviewer may say, "Well, I guess that covers
the way you feel about your boss. Now let's look
some more at what you were saying about your
husband." To change the topic in this fashion, the
interviewer must not get too far ahead nor too far
behind what the client is conveying. The drift of
the interview still comes from what the client is
talking about.

Client's pace. To match the client's pace the
interviewer must avoid jumping into some point
because of his or her own craving. Helpers who
are bored, tired, or annoyed may shove the client
into a verbal situation for which the client is un-
prepared. Interviewers must observe the client's
posture, facial expressions, and gestures. On the
basis of these observations plus the client's verbal
clues, interviewers must decide when it is time to
indulge in a "pause that refreshes" or when it is
time to help the client over a hurdle with some
remark such as:

  □ "Tell me more about it."
  □ "Tell me how that fits in with what you said
    before about your . . ."
  □ "Tell me your reasons for . . ."
  □ "I'd like to hear more about your ideas
    on . . ."
  □ "How do you feel about your reationship with
    your . . . ?"
  □ "Anything else?"
  □ "What does Marcia's refusal to see you mean
    to you?"

  □ "Hmmm, tell me where that thinking leads
    you."
  □ "How did you come to that conclusion?"

Nonverbal affirmation. The interviewer may
affirm interest in the client by nonverbal cues. The
attentive interviewer sits forward looking at the
client, not above or to the side of the client's head.
A nod of the interviewer's head and a smile affirm
that the interviewer is closely following what the
client says and anticipating more discussion.

These postures are not mere gimmicks but are
means to establish trust and understanding. Shifting
gears requires a keen awareness of the meaning of
this relationship to both the client and the interviewer and also some further techniques for spurring the client on.

Techniques for spurring the client on

The interviewer brings humanness to the interview and undertakes a joint effort with the client
to accomplish the difficult, active work of mutual
understanding. In the process of spurring the client
on the interviewer is cautious not to stumble over
his or her own eagerness to make progress. Therefore the interviewer must use professional responsive skills such as minimal encouragers, eductive
techniques, and skill in coping with silence.

Minimal encouragers. Ivey and Simek-Downing (1980) write about how the interviewer can
become active and involved in the interview and
yet remain client centered so that the directional
impetus will be provided by the client's needs.
Minimal encouragers permit the client to carry
most of the conversation while the interviewer
mainly listens. By means of sparse verbal and
slightly more nonverbal reinforcements, the interviewer is able to provide feedback that sparks the
client on to deeper self-exploration. "This skill
[minimal encouragers] is concerned with helping
the client to keep talking once he has started to
talk. A minimal encourager is . . . a powerful mode
of response which represents the therapist's selective attention to key utterances of the client. . . .
[It] is by no means minimal in its effect on the
client" (Ivey and Simek-Downing, 1980). The

skills for minimal encouragement reiterate the importance of active listening and controlled nondirection (see Chapters 1 and 2).

The effective interviewer's brief verbal retorts depend on the interviewer being plugged in on the client's wavelength. Then the interviewer gives a brief response ("Hmmm," "So, " "Oh," "Then?" "And?" "Tell me more, " or "Yes, I see") or repeats a word or a few words that the client just said. Nonverbal responses may be a slow forward movement of the interviewer's shoulders, placing hand on chin, or some other characteristic motion of the interviewer.

Such brevity of interview responses tends to be less constraining on the client. The responses' impact on the client urges the client to greater self-responsibility and more self-exploration. When the interviewer who adheres to minimal encouragers considers it necessary to energize the interview with increased verbal activity, he or she is less likely to overwhelm the client with a volley of words. Exercise 6-5 offers practice in minimal encouragers.

Eductive techniques. Just as clients reinforce certain interviewer responses, interviewers encourage (positive reinforcements) or discourage (negative reinforcements) clients' responses. The interviewers train themselves, however, not to interrupt, to avoid unnecessary advice giving, and to be frugal with words and expressive with their body

---

Exercise 6-5
HOW DO YOU ACCOMPLISH THE SKILL OF MINIMAL ENCOURAGERS? *(should be done in a group)*

Time: APPROXIMATELY 40 MINUTES

Participants form subgroups consisting of four participants. Each of the four participants selects one of the following roles: client, interviewer, interpreter, or observer. The interviewer and interpreter conduct the interview. The client decides on a particular problem—real or fantasized—that he or she wishes to role-play, and a 5-minute interview is taped.

Although the interviewer may freely use nonverbal cues to convey messages of interest and caring, he or she may respond to the client with only the following words and sounds, "Yes," "So," "Fine," "And," "Oh," "Hmmmm," and "Mmmmm." Even though this may feel forced and uncomfortable at first, if the interviewer really listens to the client, he or she should become so involved in what the client is saying that the mechanical aspect of the responses becomes less noticeable. The interpreter sits beside the interviewer and puts into a longer sentence what he or she thinks the interviewer is saying. The client responds to both the interviewer and the interpreter, revealing feelings about the interviewer's words and sounds and also reactions to the interpreter's comments. The observer records the nonverbal responses of the interviewer and adds his or her own inferences about their meanings.

The tape is played back, and for 10 mintues the four participants discuss the effectiveness of both the interviewer and the interpreter in helping the client understand, feel comfortable, and move forward in the discussion. The observer of the nonverbal cues adds his or her findings to the discussion. Suggestions are made for improvement of the interview.

Another 3-minute interview is taped with this difference—the interpreter's role changes; the interpreter records the words and sounds the interviewer is making and also notes changes in volume or tone of the interviewer's responses. The client continues with the discussion, relying only on the interviewer's verbal cues. The observer continues to record nonverbal cues.

After the playback of the tape, another 10-minute discussion is held with an additional evaluation of the changes made and the degree of improvement. The subgroup considers how the interview may be further improved.

and gestures. The objective is to open the way for clients to ease into talking about themselves and whatever is troubling them. The eductive technique permits clients to speak of their concerns without feeling obligated to do so.

Talking about oneself is a hard job. It is probably the most difficult work the client has ever done. The courage to talk honestly about one's problems and the behavior associated with these problems radiates from the interviewer's empathic understanding.

As the client reports concerns, the interviewer's face-to-face presence provides a sounding board as well as a protective shield. Eductive technique refers to the process of leading forth or drawing out. Thus the interviewer's nonpossessive warmth coupled with genuineness promotes the client's feelings of self-worth and trust. Trust, in turn, assures clients that what they say during the interview will not be used as a weapon to threaten them.

In addition, clients are assured that *they* are the ones who select what they are comfortable in communicating. There is no obligation to dredge up the past for the history of present behavior. Clients invest their energy in the present, and interviewers maximize the meaning of the reality elements of the present by means of the transaction relationship established.

The success of eductive techniques depends on the shared learning experience established between interviewer and client. The process of recounting events brings the problems directly to the client's attention. The interviewer becomes the source of reinforcement and the model of learning for the client coping with problems.

Silence. Attending with words, with body, and with eyes is the foundation for feeling more comfortable with the sounds of silence. The Eastern cultures grant room for the silence of meditation. In the Western cultures, however, silence often bears the mark of incompetence. Hence in Western cultures people without a flow of words (the gift of gab) learn to be uncomfortable if they do not know what to say. They treat silence as if it has created a vacuum without meaning.

There is no question that silence should be valued more than it is. Silence should not be dressed up as a threat, a failure, or a breach of etiquette. Instead of an absence of communication, silence can be a specific form of communication that is understood in the context of the relationship between the participants.

The silence of the helping event may be noncommunicative in the sense of a social interaction, but the empathic interviewer perceives beyond the surface silence. This perception differs from the lack of reaching out of the characters, for instance, of Pinter's plays (1970) "Landscape" and "Silence." Although playwrights usually are interested primarily in the dialogue of characters, Pinter turns to a form of communication that actually is anticommunication. His plays relate tales of two kinds of silence, the silence when the flow of words are a smoke screen for noncommunication and the silence when no words are spoken. Pinter's characters are enclosed in the small space of their own egos and speak or are silent, not to be heard or noticed by anyone. These silences are not to be disregarded, nor are they to be condemned by the effective interviewer.

Interviewers need to revise their thinking if they consider the client's silence as their fault. Few beginning interviewers can accept silence as a positive form of communication. Instead they consider silence destructive, indicative that the client is holding back and therefore resistant or unmotivated. Consequently, the interviewers blame themselves for being incapable or too gruff. Clients must be assured that they will not be pressured into discussing subjects they are not ready to disclose. The compulsion to talk often stems from the fear of silence. Talking to hear oneself talk becomes the way in which the individual relates to companions and to the interviewer.

The essential fact is that the client and the interviewer should be aware of their feelings about silence during the interview; then they are able to appreciate the silence and to handle it more capably. The interviewer must hear the client's silence as well as the client's words.

The interviewer needs to make allowances for client variations in talking style. Some clients speak from the moment they enter the office. Others burst into speaking, stop, and then begin again. Still others say very little, mumble their words, or do not say anything. Whatever the style, the effective interviewer learns to listen to the language of words and of the body.

Beginning interviewers feel they must earn their bread. They think that when pauses are long, they are not doing enough for the client. This may be so. They should not be doing things *for* the client anyway. The appropriate mix of interviewer listening, pauses, and responses is one of the most difficult interviewer behaviors to learn. To evaluate the significance of a pause, the interviewer must be mindful of the timing and frequency of the silence and whether the pause was initiated by the client or by the interviewer.

There is no universal rule about how long is too long for a period of silence. Each interview and each client has to be taken on its own merit. Silence is worthwhile only as long as it is communicating something or serving some function and is not frightening the client. Recurring silence should be carefully examined by the interviewer. The interviewer should explore what he or she is doing and saying and what is happening between him or her and the client.

Silence in the early part of the interview is more apt to reflect embarrassment, resistance, or the client's fear of what the interviewer is thinking. As the interview progresses, silence gradually becomes more supportive and a medium for emotional expression and thought.

An effective rule to follow is to let the client assume responsibility for going on if the client initiated the pause. This does not mean that the interviewer sits back and awaits the client's bidding. It is important that the interviewer be alert to those situations in which the client needs support over some rough places. The interviewer's nonverbal behavior or brief comments avoid interference with the client's silence but prove the interviewer's understanding that the client is not ready to face the problems verbally. The objective is to encourage the client to take on the responsibility for both pauses and words when he or she is ready.

The client must discover that he or she can be silent and still be liked. When the interviewer accepts and respects the client's silence, the less articulate client gains a feeling of worth and acquires a feeling of acceptance for what he or she is, a quiet person.

There is value in the client spending time with someone who understands and who has faith in the client's ability to solve problems. This value is apparent even when little is said. Client self-awareness does not hinge solely on verbal exploration. What is even more important is the client's feeling that the interviewer *accepts* the client *as is* and that the interviewer does not look down on the client for what the client considers failures.

The client often uses periods of silence to delve deeply into feelings, to struggle with alternative courses of action, and to weigh a decision. Often the interviewer senses that the client is rushing too fast or pushing too hard. Then the interviewer may suggest slowing down to allow longer "think time," longer periods of silence. The interviewer says in effect, "We are not in a hurry; take it easy."

During later interviews or the latter part of a single interview the interviewer's silence tends to have a calming effect on the client. The silence technique does not signify that the interviewer is passive or uncommunicative. The interviewer must learn to talk for the right amount at the right time. The way in which the interviewer moves into the client's silence and the way in which the interviewer moves in his or her chair have bearing on how the client feels about silence. Thus silence becomes a bore, a burden, or an opportunity for getting together.

Silence is easily misunderstood. The same may be said for even the simplest verbal communication. To pause for refueling after an idea is completed is important. To pause because of negative feelings is not as productive.

Heavy silence is unproductive when it represents conformity, discomfort, confusion, or hostility.

Often the client is misguided into silence by means of unsuitable timing or reinforcement. Speaking in low, almost inaudible tones is a form of communication that resembles silence.

There are other reasons for silence, however, that make pauses valuable in the progress of the interview. "Headwork" silence is a period when the client or the interviewer quietly organizes and summarizes thoughts and creates some solutions. Finally, there is a peculiar kind of silence that shows itself by overtalkativeness. The client or the interviewer runs away from silence by chattering. The following explanations identify other bases for silence.

Toe-the-mark silence. Even though it seems unbelievable in the contemporary life scene that some parents should still insist that children should be seen and not heard, it is not as unusual as some may think. The requirements for obedience during the individual's development may have been subtle. Parents may have talked endlessly and the child was unable to pursue a thought or say a word. On the other hand, the restrictive communication style of the home may have imposed a lock on the child's mouth with no key.

The client reveals obedient wait-until-you're-addressed approach to conversation by silence, which is broken only when the interviewer asks a question or makes a comment. The client does not talk until he or she knows what the interviewer wants him or her to talk about. If the interviewer remains quiet for any length of time with this toe-the-mark client, the client feels that talking is prohibited.

How the interviewer handles it. The client must be assured of the right to be silent. With the obedient client the interviewer must take a further step. This client must be convinced not only of the right to be silent but also of the right to speak. Some appropriate interviewer comments include:

☐ "I'm interested in what you are thinking. It would help us decide on some directions for you to take."
☐ "I've told you how I feel about the complicated situation in your home. Now, how about your feelings?"

☐ "Whenever you're ready, you can tell me your ideas on the subject."
☐ "I have the feeling that a lot is going on. I wonder if you are ready to share it with me."

Awkward silence. The awkward silence is an uncomfortable pause that comes when one topic ends and the client is searching for what to discuss next. It also happens as the interviewer and client move toward the termination of the interview session and one or both of them begin to notice an empty space in their word exchange.

At other times clients may flounder because they do not know how to begin or don't want to begin talking about their problems. They have been rapping casually and then find a lull in the conversation. This turning point makes the pause awkward because the clients do not know what to say as a transition to the more serious concerns they have been avoiding.

How the interviewer handles it
☐ "I feel as if both of us have nothing more to say about this point."
☐ "Perhaps we have said all we are going to say today."
☐ "It seems to me that you are looking at me as if to say, 'Where do we go from here?'"
☐ "It's sort of hard to get down to serious business."

Hot-seat silence. The unpleasant feeling associated with the hot seat of anxiety is part of the awkward silence. The client is often fearful and feels isolated, so "clams up." Yet the client would be even more fearful if the interviewer were also silent. The interviewer's silence would make the client feel rejected. To avert the threat of the interviewer's silence, the client may become talkative or fall deeper into silence. In this way the client rejects the interviewer before the client can feel rejected.

Silence serves an important function for the client who is trying to avoid responsibility for and consequences of verbal communication. By not talking, the client avoids what he or she considers to be inevitable—unkind remarks and a feeling of being inferior.

Painful feelings may tie the client into another kind of protective shell. The desperate client may want to express feelings but may not be ready to hear the words out loud. The observant interviewer quickly picks up the muscular tension around the eyes and the mouth that signals the distressing experience.

There are other clients who are often disregarded. These are the clients who have difficulty in expressing themselves either because of language barriers, a speech difficulty, or because they have (or think they have) difficulty in putting their thoughts into words. When the interviewer assists such clients to break their barrier of silence and attempt to reveal feelings, the clients experience their first success in self-expression.

How the interviewer handles it. All clients need acceptance and support from the interviewer; the more anxious person needs it the most. The warmth communicated by the interviewer's hand on the client's shoulder or hand is a uniting of forces. The interviewer assures the client, "It is all right to be silent. I am with you and will share this quiet period with you until you think of something you want to say."

If the client feels withdrawn and isolated, the interviewer begins the conversation with some information he or she knows about the client or some item likely to ease into verbal exchange. The interviewer may say, "Up until now, we've been talking about how your father feels about you. Now, how about your feelings for your father?" Of course the interviewer is cautious about what is said and just when it is said to prevent intensified client withdrawal. Other interviewer comments include the following:

- □ "It's okay if you want to wait until the words come."
- □ "Hard to say what you want, isn't it? Give me a hint of where you're at. I'll help you find the words."
- □ "It's OK to say whatever you like. Begin wherever you want."

Jumbled silence. The client may say something that confuses the interviewer, or the interviewer may say something that confuses the client. In some instances the extended pause that follows a client-interviewer interchange signifies that both the client and the interviewer are confused.

How the interviewer handles it

- □ "I want to help you. I need to find out more about what you think and feel about this. Let's try again."
- □ "What I said just now about . . . seems to have confused you."
- □ "What I meant was . . . " Interviewer rephrases previous statement.
- □ "I really don't know where we're at. Let's try to unravel this together."

Foot-dragging silence. Clients become reluctant to speak and feel hostile for any of several reasons. They may resent the interviewer's probing and use the silent treatment as a form of defiance. On the other hand, the clients may be asserting what they consider to be their individuality and freeedom because they are opposed to the authority figure the interviewer represents. Therefore the clients reject the interviewer through silence.

On other occasions the client is not interested in the interviewer and does not think highly of the interviewer's ability. So the client clamps his or her mouth and shows annoyance by means of antagonistic silence. Passive defiance (not talking) may be the only way the client has learned to fight back when frustrated or angered.

Resistant silence frequently results when someone sends or brings the client to see the interviewer. At first the client may speak with rude words and curt phrases. Then the client envelops himself or herself in protective silence. In similar fashion the foot-dragging silence of a client may arise from reluctance to reveal what comes next in the story.

Even more serious for the angry client are fears about inability to control aggressive, destructive impulses without the cover of silence. The wordless protest and the passive defiance of silence fight back the overwhelming rage.

How the interviewer handles it. Unless the interviewer views the hostile silence as a challenge rather than as a threat, he or she will find the client's silent behavior too difficult to handle. It is important that the interviewer avoid a response that shows that the interviewer feels personally attacked. Instead the interviewer accepts the client's form of protest and says something like the following:

- □ "It seems to me that you are reluctant to talk about . . ."
- □ "I don't mind the silence. I do feel you are resenting me in some way. Wish you could tell me about it so we can find out what to do about it."
- □ "I can wait, but if there is something you're feeling, let's get it out. Let's look at it together."
- □ "I don't feel that either of us is particularly comfortable with this silence."
- □ "I don't know what to make of this silence, do you?"
- □ "You don't feel like talking just now, do you?"
- □ "Last time we got into a long silence like this you said it was something I had done. How about this time?'
- □ "Is your silence connected with anything I've said."
- □ "Who used to give you the silent treatment?"

Retreat silence. This form of silence usually happens when both the interviewer and the client speak at the same time. Then both are silent, each waiting for the other to continue what they began to say. This silence is usually much easier to remedy.

How the interviewer handles it
- □ "Sorry I got in the way. Go ahead."
- □ "What were you saying?"
- □ The interviewer smiles and nods encouragingly.

Reinforced silence. Clients are reinforced to continue or to stop their conversation or their silence by what the interviewer does in response to the client's behavior. Sometimes the client utilizes silence to reinforce the interviewer's increased conversational activity. At other times the overpowering interviewer may make a silent victim of the

client by shaping him or her to hold back. As a result, the client feels uninvolved in the interview and does not recognize his or her role in the process of personal growth. The client often becomes even more upset by his or her deficiencies and more afraid of the interviewer's prestige and power.

How the interviewer handles it. The essential issue is interviewers' awareness of their power to steer the client. If they find themselves indulging in too much or too little talking, they must pull back to examine whether they really understand the client and what is happening. Interviewers must constantly keep before them the thought that their helping (reinforcement) is for the client's personal growth, not for the interviewer's glory.

Interviewer's silence. Occasionally the interviewer is working through some thoughts and becomes silent. Fortunately, this may be just what some client needs. The interviewer's silence exerts pressure on the client to talk and thus leads the client into greater exploration of problems. However, more insecure or more hostile clients may find the interviewer's silence threatening.

How the interviewer handles it
- □ "I just have nothing to say right now. . . . I'm with you. . . . I'm here. . . . I'm listening. . . . please go on."
- □ "Truthfully, I don't know why I have so little to say today. Played out, I guess. I am with you though. Do go on."

Pseudo-silence. An interesting kind of silence develops when either the client or the interviewer speaks so quietly that the other must strain to hear. Whatever the reason may be for this whispering, it hampers communication and may give an impression of disinterest. It is often very difficult to encourage quiet-speaking individuals to increase the volume of their voice. Unless something can be done about it, the receiver of the quiet communication finds the leaning forward a back-breaking exercise in futility.

How the interviewer handles it
- □ "Sometimes I wonder. Do you really want me to hear what you are saying?"
- □ "Here goes, turning up the volume button."

☐ Interviewer says something in a very low voice. "See, it's difficult to hear me. I'm having the same difficulty with your speech."

☐ The interviewer sits back in the chair. "You see, it's something I can't do, sit forward to catch your words. You'll just have to speak louder."

Sorting-out silence. A sorting-out silence is "thinking silence," which is reflective and productive. The client or the interviewer pauses for a few seconds, during which there is a sifting through and organization of thoughts and feelings to decide what should be said next. During the client's silence the interviewer may join in meditation or may reassure, inform, or explain according to the client's request.

Sorting-out silence is both absorbing and nourishing for the interview participants. There is a cozy feeling of empathy. The client may have just finished talking about an unusual, wonderful event or a frightening, tragic experience. Mutual silence of client and interviewer follows this client disclosure, during which both people recover from the great joy or the emotional shock.

This deliberate, shared silence serves another purpose. It permits the interviewer to listen with a "third ear." Listening with a third ear is the skill of reaching usually locked-out sounds and sights. It means that an individual listens to his or her own thoughts and feelings and becomes more keenly aware of sensory impressions.

The interviewer who listens with a third ear is using thought speed to put together what the client has communicated with his or her words and motions. The interviewer is silent—not to await a turn to speak but to do some heavy listening. Listening with the third ear obliges the interviewer to keep an antenna up to catch what is happening during conversation as well as during silence. The helper hears a client's question that appears simple and direct on the surface—"Where do you live?"—and determines just what information the client is seeking. For one client it may be simply an address or a geographical location; for another it may be

an inquiry about the interviewer's philosophy of life. Thus the interviewer becomes more aware of the client's world by means of the third ear.

How the interviewer handles it. As in all periods of the client's silence, the interviewer is courteous and respects the client's inclination. The helper does not impatiently interrupt the pause and in the process shut out the client's train of thought. The interviewer responds with silence so that the client has the opportunity to pull thoughts together for the purpose of answering the interviewer's question or beginning a new topic.

Meanwhile the interviewer watches for signals that indicate that the client is reaching out for help in starting anew.

☐ "There seems to be a great deal going on. I'm ready to participate if you're ready to have me."

☐ "It must have been an experience."

☐ "I'm with you, go on. I'll wait if you're not ready to go on."

Nonverbal gestures from the interviewer affirm that the interviewer will not hurry the client into talking. Sometimes this may mean that for this particular session no words are exchanged, just companionship.

Pregnant silence. The pregnant silence frequently follows the sorting-out silence. Quiet "headwork" continues, incubating a creative idea. Interwoven in this creative silence is a feeling of fulfillment. The client discovers solutions. He or she may not want to talk about his or her brainchild immediately, but the interviewer notes the reduced tension and often the smile of understanding and satisfaction.

How the interviewer handles it

☐ "You look as if you've found something. I would be pleased if you would share it with me."

☐ "Wow! You do seem to feel better. What's it all about?"

☐ "Whenever you feel like sharing your thoughts, I'm here to share them with you."

☐ "Tell me about it."

Antisilence. Talking too much is often just as annoying as long periods of silence. Chattering clients may believe that to remain silent is impolite, unkind, or even snobbish. Interviewers also may find silence hard to bear. They may feel that they are at fault and that they immediately must remedy the silent situation. They pounce on clients and push them into talking.

Making conversation creates a wall of words to hide behind. With perpetual words, clients reveal less of their thoughts, wishes, and feelings to the interviewer and, perhaps, themselves. Overtalkativeness keeps people at a distance just as effectively as silence does.

How the interviewer handles it

☐ "Too fast, too fast. Can't follow what you are saying."

☐ "Let's stop a minute and think this through."

☐ "Whoops. Lost you there. Back up a minute. What did you just say?"

☐ "You really know how to explain about. . . . Would you retrace your steps a bit? Tell me about. . . ."

☐ "How did you feel about the . . . you just mentioned?"

■ ■ ■

Silence merits this lengthy discussion because it is so misunderstood, misused, and yet required for the effective interview.

Edward H. Richards accurately described the impact of silence in his poem, "The Wise Old Owl."

The wise old owl sat on an oak,
The more he saw the less he spoke;
The less he spoke the more he heard;
Why aren't we like that wise old bird?

This is not a plea for a silent interview but rather an appeal for a more silent interviewer. Exercises 6-6 to 6-8 should help develop an increased ability to listen to silence.

Silence clings around the fearful person and gives comfort to the composed person. Occasional periods of silence make the conversation between client and interviewer more meaningful. When words fail, silence can help settle distress. The client who is unable to put problems into words may use the sounds of silence more frequently; these sounds of silence will be detected in the client's facial expression, gestures, and body. The

---

Exercise 6-6
HOW MUCH DOES YOUR SILENT COMMUNICATION REVEAL? *(should be done in a group)*

Time: APPROXIMATELY 20 MINUTES

Person A selects a partner and sits down 5 feet away, opposite the partner. The partner, person B, selects two observers who will write down all gestures, body movements, and facial expressions that the two partners make.

For 5 minutes person A tries to tell person B how he or she feels about this partner without using any words. Person B jots down what he or she thinks person A is communicating. Then the roles are reversed, and for 5 minutes person B tries to tell person A nonverbally how he or she feels about person A. Person A notes what he or she believes person B is communicating.

After person A and person B have completed their 5-minute sessions, all four members of the group discuss their notes and verify whether the silent messages were interpreted accurately. Person A also talks about what signals encouraged the selection of person B as a partner, and person B explains what induced him or her to select the two observers. These discussions will reveal some additional nonverbal cues.

Exercise 6-7

HOW WELL DO YOU READ ANOTHER'S SILENCE? *(should be done in a group)*

Time: APPROXIMATELY 30 MINUTES

Four participants are required for this exercise. Two are the observers, who will carefully write down what they see and hear. The third member of the group is the client, and the fourth one is the interviewer.

The client carries on a 5-minute conversation, while the interviewer replies only by nonverbal messages. Then for 10 minutes group members discuss what they saw and heard and how they felt about what happened during the interview. The client and interviewer reverse roles and repeat the exercise.

Exercise 6-8

HOW DO YOU COPE WITH THE SILENT CLIENT? *(should be done in a group)*

Time: APPROXIMATELY 45 MINUTES

Four participants are required. One participant keeps detailed notes of what the client is saying and doing. Another participant notes what the interviewer says or does. The other two participants role-play the client and interviewer.

The client speaks for approximately 1 minute about any problem he or she chooses to relate; then the client becomes silent until the interviewer encourages him or her to talk. The client does not go on unless he or she wants to do so. The interviewer respects the client's right to be silent and yet proceeds to restore verbal communication when he or she deems it advisable. Then for 15 minutes the four participants discuss the following four questions:

☐ How did the client feel about the interviewer, and how did the interviewer feel about the client?

☐ What did the two observers note that the client and the interviewer were saying or doing? What messages were they sending?

☐ What successful procedures did the interviewer use to show respect for the client's silence and to help the client begin to speak?

☐ How may the interview be improved?

After the four points have been discussed, the entire exercise is repeated. The same questions are considered for 10 minutes after the second interview, with the addition of how the second interview showed improvement.

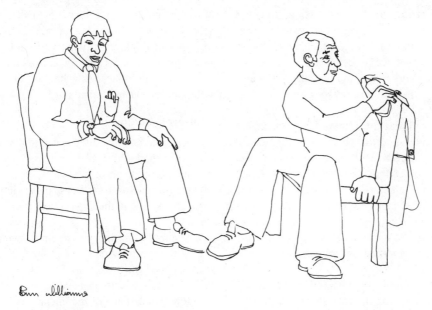

Fig. 6-5. The ending or terminating phase: concluding remarks with time boundaries.

interviewer assists (reinforces) the client in eventually ending the silence. Moving from silence to sound is not merely a matter of opening one's mouth to spill forth words. Although it may seem contradictory, words sometimes isolate people even more than silence. Words that form questions often result in barriers to communication. Questions must be few and purposefully related to the overall goal. A general rule is that the questions should be clear and short. In addition, the interviewer should anticipate the possible responses of the client as well as the further direction for the interviewer's responses.

PHASE III: THE ENDING OR TERMINATING PHASE

Often starting and ending an interview are more difficult for the beginning interviewer than is developing the interview once it is started. Time is an ally in both of these instances. The interviewer may begin with, "We have 50 minutes to rap today. Where do you want to start?" The interviewer may end with, "Ten minutes more. Hmmmmm. Let's look at what's been happening."

Time boundaries

A natural boundary line for each interview is created by the element of time. If the interviewer has initially stated that there are a certain number of minutes to the interview, this serves as the time boundary. Sometimes this time boundary may be imposed by the number of minutes allotted in a school period or by the work setting.

In spite of this time boundary, the interviewer is often concerned about how to ease the client into the home stretch. This may be of particular importance if a series of interviews has occurred and the question of closure (completing the pattern of the interview) arises.

Timing devices. The beginning interviewer may watch the clock to determine when 10 or 15 minutes remain in the interview. As the interviewer becomes more proficient, the interviewer develops a built-in timing device based on cues from the client and automatically becomes aware of when the time boundary has been reached. The client also becomes alerted to time signals. This framework of time may be a comfortable boundary for some clients; for others it may be a blunder. Cultural and other unique characteristics of the client influence the meaning of time. The empathic interviewer knows the meaning of time for the client and pursues the most effective procedures possible in the imposed framework. The time boundary may also impress the client with more responsibility to perform the interview work.

If time boundaries are imposed by outside requirements and cannot be changed in accordance with the client's needs, a 10-minute wrap-up period is a favorable procedure. No new material should be begun during this period. Instead the client should be assured that new thoughts may be discussed with the interviewer at the next interview, or the client may be referred to someone else if the material seems important and only one interview is permitted.

The introduction of new material when another client may be awaiting the interviewer's attention might result in a hasty and careless examination. Both client and interviewer are apt to become irritated. Even if the information is what the interviewer has been hoping the client would relate, rushing through the discussion of this disclosure is unfair and unsatisfying to the client.

Concluding remarks

Closing remarks may come from either the client or from the interviewer. The client indicates readiness to leave by comments that suggest he or she has shaped thoughts into some ideas for action. The client says, "That's it. I know what I want to do now. I will . . ." or "This chat has given me some things I want to think about before I decide what to do. See you next time, Mr. H."

The interviewer's comments seek to give the client the opportunity to perform the finishing touches, to plan some actions the client should accomplish in between the interview sessions, or to plan for a subsequent session. Some of the concluding remarks of the interviewer might be "We have about 12 minutes left in this interview; are there any questions you would like to ask?" "In the remainder of the time we have left today, is there anything in particular you think we have to pull together?" "In the time we have left, let's see

if we can pull together the main concerns we have talked about," "Our session is almost over; would you like to think about what you might be doing after this interview?" or "Our session is almost over; let's think ahead to what we might want to talk about at our next meeting."

Nonverbal endings

Nonverbal endings often speak louder than concluding remarks. When the client begins to shift around, look at his or her watch, or, even more obviously, reach for car keys, these signals come through clearly if the interviewer hangs in there with the client.

The interviewer may also begin the wind-up process with movement cues. He or she may straighten the papers on the desk, arise from the seat, or look at his or her watch. Depending on the age and developmental status of the client, the interviewer may hold out his or her hand to shake the client's hand or touch the client on the shoulder as a form of departure. Some form of courtesy in leave-taking is a wise interpersonal policy. Such courtesy as well as the verbal preparation for termination serves to assure the clients that they are not being pushed out and thus rejected.

The difficulty of parting may be lessened if the interviewer is not fearful of separation from the client or anxious about losing the client's confidence. The important factor is that both the interviewer and the client must be prepared for terminating the interview.

Interview series

Dealing with a series of interviews presents problems of closing each individual interview and additional problems involved with the transitions from one interview to the next and with the determination of the adequate number of interviews.

Number of interviews. In some instances an agency or individual interviewer sets forth in the beginning interview the number of interviews that will be included in the series. Thus the interviewer may latch on to the already agreed on final interview, and during the next-to-the-last interview the interviewer prepares the client for the termination.

The interviewer reminds the client of the forthcoming ending interview.

When a series of interviews is indicated, the termination of the series does not stamp the client's problems as having been completely solved. Instead the client still has to work on positive growth as well as continue to achieve appropriate coping behavior. When the client is ready for this self-sustaining growth, empathic interviewers perceive this and remove themselves before they become a heavy crutch.

"Hello-goodbye." Occasionally the client leaves too soon. Brammer and Shostrom (1977) speak of the "hello-goodbye" or "flight-into-health" phenomenon that a client may experience after only one or two interviews. The client feels relieved, relaxed, "so good." The client believes the problems have been solved because for a brief time conflicts and distress have decreased in annoyance value. However, from the client's behavior the interviewer realizes that the client is leaving by a revolving door. The client is bound to return to the same or to another interviewer.

Sometimes nothing can be done to encourage the client to remain in the interview situation for a few more sessions. When clients decide to check out, their determination has to be respected. The only further help the interviewer can offer is to assure such clients that they may return if they want to do so.

Closing devices. When clients become more certain in their discussions about themselves, they will begin to question the interviewer about ending the interviewer series. This client-determined termination is, of course, the simplest to accomplish. The interviewer need only agree: "It seems that you can operate on your own now. You've shown you can solve your problems. You're aware of when and in what way certain events trouble you. How about one or two more times together to tie things up?"

Depriving the client who is lonely or dependent of the interview relationship might be too stressful. Therefore the interviewer begins a gradual weaning process. Interviews are arranged at longer and longer intervals rather than cutting them off suddenly. If the interviews have been conducted once every week, then the spacing might be changed to every other week. Later on, depending on the anxiety level of the client, the interval between interviews may be lengthened.

Another effective device that keeps communication channels functioning even between interviews is to ask the client to write a summary letter. After a certain time the client reviews in writing what has been brought to light since the last interview and what growth the client considers still necessary. This summary letter may continue. However, the interviewer should read between the lines of the letter to make certain that the summaries do not become another crutch.

Open-door policy. The abruptness of a feeling of dismissal may be avoided also if the interviewer tells clients to "Drop in sometime when you're near the office" or "Let me know how things are going." Thus the interviewer keeps the door open so that clients know that they may contact the interviewer in times of crisis or even for a friendly chat.

Caution is necessary so that this open-door invitation for further contact does not become a pass to further dependency. The empathic interviewer understands clients and adjusts this offer accordingly.

Referral. At times referral to someone else for further interview sessions may be desirable. If only a set number of interviews are permitted with one interviewer or if the interviewer feels that because of certain problems in the interviewing relationship the client and interviewer have gone as far as they can together, then referral may be the wisest course to follow. To avoid having clients feel that failure has resulted, that they are being rejected, or that they are getting the "run-around," the interviewer must discuss the reasons for referral in such a fashion that the clients do not feel depressed or frightened. Suggesting some possible other interviewers or perhaps someone who specializes in some aspect of the clients' further developmental needs builds a bridge for clients.

Summary of Part Three

■ Part Three concentrates on an in-depth examination of the interview process. The discussion begins in Chapter 5 with statements about caring as the fountainhead of helping. Hope, trust, and patience are mentioned as the core of caring. The many meanings of helping are revealed in the assortment of settings in which assistance is offered to a customer, a foreign traveler, a client, and so on. In the interview event helping is formalized into mutuality of purpose leading to reciprocal growth.

The reciprocity of the helping relationship is explored in a variety of interviewing systems, ranging from information-oriented interviewing with less emphasis on mutual change to transactions, complementary associations, and development of the experiential interview. Furthermore, interviewing is broadly differentiated into the information-seeking, information-sharing, behavior management, and experiential interviews.

Although each variety of interview envelopes some distinguishing characteristics, there is also an inclusive wrapper extending over all forms of interview that covers the interviewer's ethical responsibility and interest in the client as well as the form of communication process.

The *information-oriented interview* is designated for obtaining and/or sharing information. This interview is usually more structured in procedure and goals than is the experiential interview. Often what is required is an answer to predetermined questions by the interviewer, client, or both.

The *behavior management interview* focuses on positive reinforcement of appropriate behavior and nonreinforcement or negative reinforcement of inappropriate behavior. Interviewers must shape their own behavior so that they will systematically reinforce the established behavioral goals. The steps in a plan for behavior modification require behavioral analysis, a reinforcement menu, and the terminal behavior that is the goal of the behavior management. Assertive training procedures are presented as one form of the behavior management interview.

The *experiential interview* incorporates information and behavior change but in an atmosphere in which human relations are the crucial elements. The interviewers themselves become important parts of the process that (1) seeks to guide and facilitate the client's exploration of behavior, concerns, and problems in the "here and now" of the interview situation, (2) strives to establish a miniature (microunit) social situation in which the client may try out interpersonal relations as well as some solutions to problems, (3) sets up an acceptant atmosphere of trust in which the client feels safe to try out some changes in behavior, and (4) provides another individual who listens, participates, and becomes an involved helper on whom the client may depend and then grow away from as the client's self-confidence increases.

Chapter 6 continues to analyze the interview process with deliberations of the three overlapping phases of the interview structure. The *opening or beginning phase* of the interview sets the stage for a productive and harmonious relationship if the helper is competent. At the onset, after the initial greeting and the establishment of rapport, both client and interviewer clarify their roles and relationships. When both client and interviewer arrive at an understanding of the "interview work" they must accomplish together and of the purposes and expectations of the interview, they commence to ease their way into exploration of what have become mutual concerns. This exploration occurs in a frame of time limits, behavior or acting-out limits, and process limits.

The discussion of the developing or exploring phase studies the techniques for getting into the center of the interview and for spurring the client on. Basic to the smooth interchange on which the effective interview is built is the attending behavior of the empathic listener. If the interviewer listens to the client's words, to the client's body language, and to the sounds of silence, he or she can respond more capably to the client. Minimal encouragers and deductive methods permit the flow of conversation in the client-interviewer dialogue to follow the client's pace and the client's lead as well as sparking new areas of exploration.

Terminating the single interview or a series of interviews requires client preparation and the avoidance of a feeling of rejection. The client and the interviewer make themselves ready for the separation. By means of mutual feedback the client and the interviewer make known new understandings and how the client has translated these notions into action. If this is the first of more than one interview, then the interviewer reinforces the client's search for some goals to work on between interview sessions.

One closing device is an ''open-door'' policy. The open-door invitation offers a helping hand that reaches beyond the ending interview. However, this invitation must be used with caution so that the client is not prodded into a dependency relationship. In addition, since the client continues to develop more self-fulfilling, appropriate behaviors, he or she should not be encouraged to use the open door as an excuse to run to the interviewer for assistance rather than working out his or her own problems.

Some considerations that might ease the closing of either a single interview or a series of interviews are time boundaries, verbal and nonverbal endings, recapping accomplishments, decreasing the frequency of visits, and referral.

The content of Part Four delves further into the skills involved in communication and in the particular form of interviewing involved in the counseling process. Chapter 7 restates the basic *a*ttitudes, *s*kills, and *k*nowledge (ASK) and the layered approach—observation, recording, reporting, and interviewing—which are the building blocks of the effective counseling relationship. Then the discussion moves into the components of the climate of trust: empathy, genuineness, nonpossessive warmth, and the expressive skills of communication—paraphrasing, summarization, reflecting, confrontation, and interpretation. Social game behavior is described as one aspect of the recognition of potential barriers to becoming oneself more fully; and stress, distress, and burnout are explained.

Chapter 8 probes beyond counseling roles for human service workers. The investigation of changing human systems begins with an analysis of the systems approach and then reports on the range and interprofessionalism of human service systems.

Part Four

FROM INTERVIEWING TO COUNSELING

the client is on the way to somewhere

**Two roads diverged in a wood, and I—
I took the one less traveled by,
and that made all the difference.**

Robert Frost (1916)
The Road Not Taken, Stanza 4

Choosing the directions for change.

Chapter 7

INGREDIENTS OF AN EFFECTIVE COUNSELING RELATIONSHIP

WE WEAR THE MASK

We wear the mask that grins and lies,
It hides our cheeks and shades our eyes,
This debt we pay to human guile;
With torn and bleeding hearts we smile,
And mouth with myriad subtleties.

Why should the world be overwise,
In counting all our tears and sighs?
Nay, let them only see us, while
We wear the mask. . . .

From Dunbar, P.L.: Complete poems of Paul
Laurance Dunbar, New York, 1965, Dodd,
Mead and Company, Inc. Reprinted by
permission of Dodd, Mead and Company, Inc.

The masks of non-genuineness.

Alice (in Wonderland) asks:

"Would you tell me, please, which way I ought to go from here?"

"That depends a good deal on where you want to get to," said the Cat.

"I don't much care—" said Alice.

"Then it doesn't matter which way you go," said the Cat.

"—so long as I get *somewhere*," Alice added as an explanation.

"Oh, you're sure to do that," said the Cat, "if you only walk long enough."

Doubts and concerns about "Which way I ought to go" are often signals of becoming and of growth. The wise Cat knows that only the individual can set the direction of where he or she wants to go or what he or she will become.

THE SIGNS TO BE FOLLOWED: BASIC INGREDIENTS

The journey toward becoming oneself more fully is a never-ending search for the client as well as for the counselor. For the client the criteria for success must be individualized in terms of the client's potential for growth. Undoubtedly, current scientific knowledge is not sufficient to assess potential accurately. The developmental approach, however, assumes that progress is possible and that each positive step the client takes advances him or her one measure forward. Robert Browning proposes this philosophy as follows:

. . . man's reach should exceed his grasp . . .
(Andrea del Sarto, 1855, 1. 97)

. . . and gain is gain, however small . . .
(Paracelsus, 1835, part IV)

Change for the counselor entails the establishment and maintenance of certain *a*ttitudes, *s*kills, and *k*nowledge (ASK) evolved through the acquisition of competencies in *o*bservation, *r*ecording, *r*eporting, *i*nterviewing, and *c*ounseling (ORRIC). These are necessary items for the journey toward the professional self.

Attitudes, skills, and knowledge (ASK)

Everyone who has any experience with other persons is in one way or another a human service worker—a helper. The concept of *professional self* featured in this book means more than one who offers sympathy, conversation, and advice. Helpers unfold this professional self through expanding their self-understanding, through values clarification, through strengthening their life-coping and problem-solving skills, and so on. Professional human service workers refine their communication style (for example, controlled nondirection) and practice behavior that expresses acceptance and friendliness. In addition, the imperative attribute of their professional self is a code of ethics that directs the helpers' behavior with their clients (Chapter 1). These "ASK" considerations are the framework for mastering proficiencies in observation, recording, reporting, and interviewing.

Observation, recording, reporting, interviewing, and counseling (ORRIC)

Just as everyone performs as an embryonic human service worker, everyone observes from birth onward and, according to some views, even in the womb. However, the accuracy of untutored observation is affected by numerous factors related to the observer, the location of the observation, and the person or group observed. Insidious myths about people can distort and prejudice the beginning as well as the long-standing human service worker. The path the helper must follow demands vigilance and a guiding ideology respecting the rights, responsibilities, and worthiness of the client as well as the helper. When the helper incorporates such an ideology and is wide awake to the intrusions of biases, then, and only then, is he or she ready to realize accurately and effectively the observational skills of active listening and looking for verbal, sound, and nonverbal cues. Subsequently the helper can move from casual observation through the stages of the observational structure—naturalistic, clinical, specific goal, standardized, and experimental (Chapter 2). The methods of recording and reporting are interwoven with these observational skills.

Recording and reporting are forms of observation feedback. Both of these feedback processes can be pushovers for stereotypical thinking. The semantic impact of the Humpty-Dumpty syndrome (Chapter 3) confuses the client, particularly if the counselor speaks in "jargonese." The counselor also is prone to confusion by this syndrome if she or he is unfamiliar with the client's utterance or enunciation. Even more serious is the plight of the client whose counselor is disrespectful, unconcerned, preoccupied with self-aggrandizement, and unable to express and control emotions appropriately. Added to these deterrents to the helping relationship is the counselor who is unable to differentiate the client's feelings. The recording and reporting of such confused, unenlightened counselors are bound to be fallible and sometimes worthless.

Recordings and reporting (Chapters 3 and 4) therefore depend on certain basic attitudes, skills, and knowledge—on accurate observations. These two procedures for data notation and transmission are refined by the ABC sequence of recording (*a*ntecedent event, *b*ehavior, and *c*onsequent event) and the use of descriptive rather than interpretive words. Another issue relates to the objective-subjective continuum. This issue questions the helper's capability to recognize and balance observations and subjective inferences. The narrative technique is more susceptible to inference than are some other recording methods such as scaling, charting, and checklists. In any case, inferences are not the center of concern, but rather, how the inferences are derived. One solution to assuring greater reliability for inferences is the multiple hunches procedure. Observational back-up supports the continuance of certain hunches and the weeding out of others. These findings form the basis for reporting.

Reporting (Chapter 4) is another aspect of communication and, as such, reflects several levels of communication from the soliloquy to the dialogue. The most meaningful reporting avoids cue distortions and relies on the transaction pattern of interpersonal relationships. Reporting and the observation and recording on which it is based are clarified and expanded with constructive questioning.

Throughout this book, the unequivocal significance of *caring* is stressed. In Chapter 5 caring is described as the fountainhead of helping, and hope, trust, and patience are described as the core of caring. The dimensions of mutuality that emerge from caring tend to lead to reciprocal growth for helper and client. This growth is the special focus of the transaction of the experiential interview and is a payoff to some extent in information-oriented and behavior management interviews. Before embarking on the interview, the caring helper examines the factors that might influence his or her effectiveness, such as certain personal characteristics, misdirected motivation, interview pitfalls, and intimacy.

All single interviews and series of interviews are

divided into three parts: the opening or beginning phase, the developing or exploring phase, and ending or terminating phase (Chapter 6). The opening phase is crucial, setting the stage for the client's favorable or unfavorable response to a return visit, if necessary. Several characteristics of this opening phase potentially benefit or hinder the helping relationship: the initial greeting, establishing the relationship and roles of the interviewer and the client, understanding the expectations for the outcome of the interview, and setting limits. The opening phase of the interview moves into the developing or exploring phase as the helping event delves into broader and deeper concerns and solutions. Certain techniques tend to spur the client on toward an examination of the dynamics of current difficulties and gravitate toward short- and long-term decision making and consequent development. These methods stress a holistic approach and self-reliance in an atmosphere of empathic support. Minimal encouragers and deductive techniques guide but do not prod or dominate the client's communications or inclinations. The competent handling of silence is another essential component of the interview process. The termination of each interview and of a series of interviews often poses problems for the novice interviewer. Preparation of the client for the eventual culmination, time boundaries, and concluding remarks are all part of the wind-up. In certain instances an open-door policy and/or referral reduces the strain of the separation.

■ ■ ■

This "backward glance o'er traveled roads"* is in preparation for an additional layer of learning—counseling. Exercise 7-1 directs attention to a creative process, serendipity, that reflects client-centered strategies unwarped by dogmatic, uncritical adherence to pedantry. Thinking rather than gathering more facts is the immediate quest.

---

*Walt Whitman, *November Boughs*. "Backward glance o'er traveled roads" is the title of the preface, 1888.

The serendipitous counselor

Chance discoveries are important for the counselor. This does not signify that "good fortune" stands alone without substantial padding from a second strongbox of facts and other competencies. Contemplations and practical application must accompany these facts. Three further attributes of effective helping belong with the fund of skills and knowledge—empathy, warmth, and genuineness (EWG). The helper who grasps the meaning and performance of EWG is less prone to precipitate misunderstanding and thwarting of the helping event. The next discussion includes the definitions of, general characteristics of, and scales for measuring empathy, warmth, and genuineness.

COMPONENTS OF A CLIMATE OF TRUST: EMPATHY, WARMTH, AND GENUINENESS (EWG)

Some research studies have indicated that empathy and warmth must go together for a successful helping transaction. Other studies support genuineness or warmth as the primary prerequisite to the interview. The order of importance of these attributes is difficult to establish, but there are indications that empathy is the outcome of the helper's skillful expression of genuineness and warmth. However, the order of the listing is unessential. It is noteworthy that the significance of these characteristics is supported by the findings from many years of research. These characteristics are referred to as the Truax triad, from Truax and Carkhuff, who first pulled together these three aspects in their book *Toward Effective Counseling and Psychotherapy* (1967).

Although other conditions are necessary to conduct an effective helping transaction, empathy, warmth, and genuiineness are the basic attributes. In effect, therefore, the preeminent fact is that either warmth or genuineness must be at a high level with empathy for an effective relationship to exist and persist.

The "halo" effect may enter into the relationship of the three attributes. This effect occurs when

Exercise 7-1

CAN YOU BE A SERENDIPITOUS COUNSELOR? *(should be done in a group)*

Time: PARTS 1 AND 2, APPROXIMATELY 25 MINUTES;
   PART 3, APPROXIMATELY 20 MINUTES

Part 1

A client is referred to you by a colleague who believes he is overidentifying with the client, whose ethnic, educational, and experiential backgrounds are similar to his own. This client, Jim, became progressively narrowed in his field of vision until there remained only a pinpoint of light. During the time of his depreciating vision, Jim earned his Ph.D. and practiced as a counselor until the age of 42, his current age. Your colleague tells you that Jim eventually will become totally blind and that he is an intelligent, creative man whose innovative research and perceptive counseling have been curtailed because of his gradual loss of vision plus associated decrease in auditory acuity. The most serious problem confronting Jim at present is his agitated depression. Jim is convinced that "he has no future . . . can't be a counselor . . . does not intend to make baskets for the rest of his life." Your colleague hopes that your "fresh outlook" can avert the difficulties of your identifying with Jim, particularly since many more dissimilarities exist between you and Jim than between your colleague and Jim. You ponder at length about this situation and recall a recent workshop at which a discussion of serendipity occurred.

You read from your notes: "*Serendipity,* the notion about making happy and unanticipated discoveries by accident, is traced to an ancient fairy tale, *The Three Princes of Serendip,* written in numerous versions. The word—'serendipity'—coined in a letter (1754) by Horace Walpole alluded to the experiences of these princes who 'were always making discoveries by accident and sagacity, of things which they were not in quest of.' This story and the word evolved from it have special meaning for the human service worker. Serendipity reflects the 'eureka,' 'aha,' 'got it,' 'at last'—the exclamations that burst forth with the elation of a chance discovery when ideas synthesize and a solution or direction is acknowledged. A serendipper is a person who in the process of acquiring knowledge and skills finds that these gel and a pattern forms with sudden insight—a new arrangement of relationships. The counselor and the client grasp the meaning of an event; the researcher, the scientist, and the counselor accidently find interesting items of information or unexpected support for a theory or directions for a procedure."

Part 2

After reading the notes about serendipity, divide into small groups of five to eight participants to consider the following questions:
   □ What do you think the foregoing notes and the word serendipity mean to you as a human service worker?
   □ Describe your most recent serendipitous experiences, particularly those which occurred in interpersonal relationships. Think hard; everyone has experienced some unsought discovery.
   □ How might you use this story in your counseling session with your newly referred client?

Part 3

Remain in your small group. Two volunteers from this group arrange their chairs so that they are visible to the remaining observers. One volunteer is the visually impaired client and the other the counselor. Before beginning the counseling session discuss how the person who role-plays the visually impaired client can actually "feel" blind. (One way is to construct a blindfold similar to that shown in Fig. 7-1.) Make the accommodations that put the client in the frame of reference of blindness. (The sex of the client can be changed as desired.) Then the counselor conducts the preliminary session (5 minutes) with the client, introducing the concept of serendipity at the propitious moment. After this session the participants of the small group assess the counseling situation by offering a positive comment, a suggestion for improvement, and then another favorable comment. The blind person describes how he or she felt, and the counselor appraises his or her procedures and reactions. Two other volunteers repeat the role performance and attempt to incorporate the suggestions for improvement. The same assessment process reoccurs.

an individual uses first or initial impressions as the standard by which to judge whatever happens afterward. For example, Melinda does it when she says, "I knew it was going to be good. He was just outta sight when I first met him." It is what the voter is doing when he says, "I don't like his looks. He can't be trusted. I'm voting for . . . whose tax policy is good." In each instance the reacting person picks out some characteristic or impression and uses it to explain all other characteristics and impressions, as if the individual were enveloped in a "halo" that describes everything.

Other items also contribute to the successful outcome of the counseling transaction. These may be the depth of knowledge of human behavior, skill in applying behavior modification techniques, and additional interpersonal skills such as an internal rather than an external frame of reference. Thus the counselor views a problem from the uniqueness of the client's position (internal) rather than from the position of an outsider (external).

Empathy

All interpersonal roads lead toward empathy. Yet the behaviors associated with empathy are complex and interrelated with all the facets of the helping process. An examination of the origin of the word "empathy" is the first step toward building an understanding. The second step requires gathering some facts about what characteristics are part of the empathic process. Finally, a procedure is presented that can lead to individual rating of the counselor's level of empathy.

The origin of the word "empathy." *Empatheia* is the Greek word that refers to affection plus passion touched by the quality of suffering. The prefix *em-* (or *en-*) signifies "in" or "into" and thus is a form of connection. The Latin word *pathos* is analogous to the Greek *-patheia* with the further refinement of "feeling perception." Still another connotation was tacked on to the term in 1897 when Theodore Lipps, a German psychologist, used the term *einfuhling* (*ein*, meaning "in"; *fuhling*, meaning "feeling")

to refer to the process of becoming totally absorbed in an external object such as work of art, vivid or powerful with meaning for the perceiver. Implied in the concept was a process of feeling-into, through the creative work of another or of an object in nature, but not specifically into the experience of another person (Barrett-Lennard, 1981).

The meaning of one person feeling himself or herself into another person's world evolved through many years' usage of the word "empathy," with

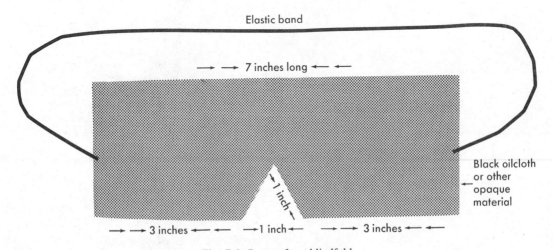

Fig. 7-1. Pattern for a blindfold.

enrichments by Edward Titchener, Gordon Allport, Alfred Adler, Carl Rogers, and others (Barrett-Lennard, 1981; Katz, 1963). Most recently, Barrett-Lennard (1981) discusses "the empathy cycle," the sequence of processes from one person's (the observer, the counselor, the friend) actively attending to another (the observed person) with an empathic set to the increased self-expression of the observed person. Fig. 7-2 diagrams the counselor-client relationship and the responsiveness and feedback processes involved.

"Feeling into" another's world is easier if one has had similar experiences. Perhaps this explains the deeper understanding of former alcoholics for other alcoholics, of former junkies for continuing drug addicts, and of people who live in the inner city for other inner-city dwellers. For example:

MARIO: How can you know what it's like to split from the scene? You're the cat who's made it.

DR. P.: Yep. You're right. I'm sitting in this foam-soft chair now, but I used to be on the street, the highly charged streets of Harlem, where verbal shootouts were just the beginning.

In essence, empathy is a special kind of observation, experiencing, and communication. Empathic helpers remain themselves yet look at the world through the client's eyes and listen with the client's ears. Thus the helpers walk in the client's shoes and try on the client's point of view so that they may experience the client's feelings. After observing *as if* they were the client and experiencing *as if* they were the client, the helper's feed back to the client what they have seen, heard, and felt. Empathy requires the helpers to personalize their communication in the client's language.

Helpers temporarily identify with the client but must constantly be aware that they are *not* the client, but rather participant-observers. It is important for helpers to have both in-sight and out-sight. In-sight helps helpers understand themselves, and out-sight helps them to understand the client intellectually. Empathy goes one step fur-

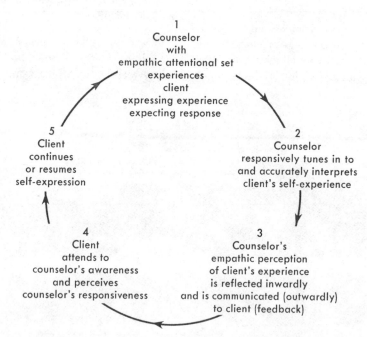

Fig. 7-2. The empathy cycle. (Data from Barrett-Lennard, G.T.: J. Counsel. Psychol. **28**(2):91-100, 1981.)

ther. Empathy starts with in-sight and adds out-sight plus a feeling for the client's meanings and emotions. Empathic helpers go beyond the client's public showing of behavior to the internal world of the client.

Empathy is not specially doled out to certain patients or clients; it is an attribute for all reasons of the helping encounter. It enhances daily relationships; it opens communications for mentally ill, mentally retarded, and physically ailing persons (Fig. 7-3). The preceding review of the etymology of "empathy" demonstrates the many characteristics that are associated with the term. Exercise 7-2 provides an opportunity to explore the application of some of these characteristics.

The empathic responses of the helper in exercise 7-2 are similar to those labeled "interchangeable" by Carkhuff (1969) and "primary" by Egan (1975). These communications demonstrate the counselor's search for the explicit meanings of the client's remarks. During this stage of empathy the counselor acts and reacts in a manner similar to the client's nonverbal and verbal level of intensity. This type of reaction probably is more productive at the beginning phases of the helping event. Later the counselor manages a more profound form of empathy, labeled "additive" by Carkhuff (1969) and "advanced" by Egan (1975) so that greater depth of exploration and the implications of the client's concerns might be explored. The exposi-

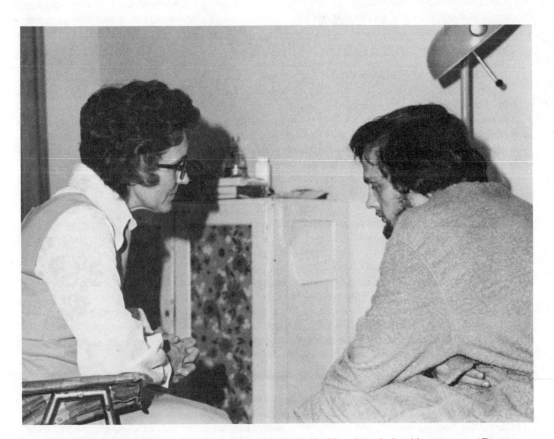

Fig. 7-3. Empathy and acceptance support the physically ill patient during his recovery. (From Mereness, D.A., and Taylor, C.M.: Essentials of psychiatric nursing, ed. 10, St. Louis, 1978, The C.V. Mosby Co.)

tion of secondary and primary process thinking by Alley and others (1979) further clarifies the significance of the helper's empathy in encouraging client's responses. Secondary process thinking focuses on practical problems and is reality oriented (for example, "How do I meet people?"). This objective, concrete problem appears to be of immediate importance to the client. However, it is the symbolic and more complicated themes of the inner life of the client—the primary process thinking—that can deter the client from making contact with others. For instance, the client may be conducting a subvocal conversation such as: "I'm just no good, no wonder no one cares to be with me," "Why is everyone against me?" or "No one is any good." Primary process thinking frequently is symbolic and associated with complicated themes regarding the client's inner life. In addition, the

---

Exercise 7-2
HOW DO YOU RATE IN EMPATHY? *(should be done in a group)*

Time: APPROXIMATELY 20 MINUTES

One way to improve the level of empathy is to role-play a variety of situations. The following procedure offers a global approach to discovering your functioning level of empathy and then assists in improving your level by means of feedback and repetition.

Part 1

Get into groups of five and select two role players and three observers. The role players select one of the three following situations and seat themselves so that the three observers will have a good view of them. One role player becomes the client, the other one the helper. The helper answers the client, and the conversation continues for 3 minutes. Then the five participants in the subgroup discuss for 5 minutes: Did the helper show awareness of the client's feelings? Did the helper answer concretely and in terms of what the client just said? Did the helper show that he or she is exploring what is happening in the interpersonal relationship between himself or herself and the client? How could the helper improve the level of empathy?

Select one of the following situations and begin your conversation.

[1]   Tess bends forward and begins to speak in a whisper that can hardly be heard: "Fed up . . . fed up. I'm fed up with lack of knowing where I am in this job. I feel as if this is a nowhere. Don't know what I'm doing or where I'm going. There's no one to speak to . . . no one pays attention."

[2]   Mrs. P. begins, "Doctor, I don't know how to say this . . . but . . . getting me down. Been married to Tom for 12 years. Last week I was putting away some shirts in his drawers and found . . . oh, my Lord! . . . found a black lace nightie, a black bra, and a sort-of leather harness. As I look back, I wonder . . . sex has been OK . . . yet, sometimes I think there has been lipstick on Tom. And . . . and . . . " Mrs. P. begins to cry.

[3]   Albert looks around the office as he walks past the doorway. He walks to a corner between two bookshelves and squeezes into the space between them. He pushes his hand through his long, blond, curly hair and rubs his index finger and thumb over his protruding upper teeth. He rapidly licks his lips with his tongue and slowly slides down to crouch between the bookcases.

Part 2

The helper and client continue their conversation for 3 minutes from the point at which they stopped in Part 1. Once again, the five participants in the subgroup discuss the questions stated in Part 1 but instead of discussing how the helper could improve they discuss how the helper has improved his or her level of empathy.

primary process issues are emotionally loaded and consequently more difficult to elicit; and as these issues emerge, they require more intricate handling. Further examination of the characteristics of empathy clarifies and fills in some gaps in procedures that free the client to penetrate the closeted sources of problems. However, this gradual shifting from more obvious to more obscure concerns requires more from the counselor than knowledge. Skill development depends on the application of this knowledge in supervised practice.

General characteristics of the empathic process. How does one go about "feeling in" with another person? Infants and young children accomplish this openly and candidly until they are trained by the do's and don'ts of social requirements. The infant cries when mom screws up her mouth and tightens her arm muscles as she holds the infant. The young child quips, "But I don't want to kiss her; she looks meanie." Very soon the infant and young child are brought into socialized, civilized controls of the culture in which they live. They learn to sense the kind of behavior expected of them, and thus become a little less genuine in their responses. Adults who seek to become helpers must undo some of the cover-ups that would stand in the way of their counseling role. They must learn to express unconditional acceptance, openness in receiving and recognizing, accurate processing of information, and concrete feedback.

Unconditional acceptance. Unconditional acceptance is discussed in Chapter 4, as is the verbal and nonverbal behavior associated with it. In this chapter there is a brief discussion of certain specific aspects such as self-acceptance, brotherly love, and altruism.

One way of looking at acceptance is to start at what must be the beginning—self-acceptance. Self-acceptance encourages genuineness and warmth, which lead to empathy. Empathy is actually acceptance of another individual. Acceptance of (and by) others increases self-acceptance. Additional increases in any of the elements of the acceptance-empathy process will have a positive effect on the interpersonal relationship.

Two additional characteristics of unconditional acceptance are important to consider—brotherly love and altruism. Brotherly love is similar to the Greek word *agape,* which refers to nonsexual, unselfish caring for another human being. Brotherly love "means the sense of responsibility, care, respect, knowledge of any other human being, the wish to further his life . . . In brotherly love there is the experience of union with all men, of human solidarity, of human at-onement" (Fromm, 1956).

Agape is intertwined with altruism. The altruistic person considers the welfare and happiness of another above his or her own welfare and happiness. Altruism encourages an individual to make possible another person's satisfactions and self-fulfillment. Unconditional acceptance is all of these aspects and more.

Unconditional acceptance is built on the groundwork of warmth and genuineness. Sincerity and openness (genuineness) as well as comforting and tender feelings (warmth) are the essential characteristics of acceptance. Empathy is both part of and the result of acceptance. One person cannot accept another without understanding the values of the other person as he or she is, not as he or she ought to be.

Openness in receiving and recognizing. Acceptance moves a person into an open relationship of receiving and recognizing. Nonacceptance of oneself and/or others tends to set up nonrelationships in which there is less self-disclosure.

Openness to sexual equality, to different value systems, and to bizarre behavior and speech is an essential characteristic of the acceptant counselor. Such openness helps the counselor develop fuller contact with the client. The counselor then encourages and receives information more freely and recognizes the gaps in the information presented.

Openness helps counselors listen more attentively, sensitively, and calmly. It keeps counselors in touch with the ways in which clients are like them and the ways in which they differ. Finally, openness tells the client, "I am here with you." All these aspects are part of acceptance and empathy.

Accurate processing of information. The sorting or processing of information is one of the counselor's goals. The counselor sets in order his or her experiences of the client and systematically and constantly sifts through, groups together, and screens the feelings, moods, and inclinations of the client. Out of the assorted jumble the counselor files some ideas about the client (see discussion of multiple hypotheses in Chapter 3) and some approaches for alternative solutions to the client's problems. At the appropriate moment the counselor shares these findings with the client so that he or she also may sift, screen, and group. Then the client shapes his or her own words and images. Part of the client's work is to use this new awareness to discover what his or her purposes are, how he or she is fulfilling these purposes, and how he or she may better fulfill these purposes.

Concrete feedback. Concrete, moment-to-moment, appropriate counselor feedback is basic for the client to go forward in searching and becoming. This feedback is directly related to the counselor's degree of accuracy in processing the interpersonal relations between the client and himself or herself. The counselor "cools it" in the return message (feedback) to the client. Although sensitive to the client's feelings and experiencing, the helper does not lose the balance between being inside the client's world (empathic) and yet sufficiently outside (objective) to be able to be exact, immediate, and compact in reporting to the client.

Another requirement for concrete feedback is the counselor's moment-to-moment tryout of impressions to make certain that he or she thoroughly grasps the client's meaning. For example:

MS. R.: You seem to feel that it's the scar on your face that keeps people away from you. Is that what you're saying?

HENRIETTA: That's it, almost, but . . . well. Oh, hell, if only people were color-blind. White on the outside, black on the inside—that's me.

MS. R.: I'm hearing something else now. Is it that . . . are you really more upset because of your parents? You said earlier you wished you had "come out black"—would have been easier.

Ms. R. has caught the inadequacy of her interpretation of Henrietta's problem. Henrietta is using her facial scar to conceal her real distress, which appears to be her discomfort with looking and passing as a white woman when her mother is black. Henrietta seems to be telling the counselor that her life would be simpler and less frustrating if both her parents were black.

Moment-to-moment tryouts check the counselor's errors before they get too far off the beam. This immediacy of experiencing, reporting, and correcting allows for a more direct, complete, and positive relationship. Immediacy also firms up the client-counselor partnership and exploration of the transactions that come about from their relationship. The more empathic counselor responses are the following:

☐ Those which fall into place with what's happening in the client-counselor relationship.

☐ Those which are responsive to the "good," "bad," and/or mixed-up feelings implied by the client's discussion of an event

☐ Those which are more likely to concentrate on deeper exploration of fewer topics

In essence, the counselor unconditionally accepts the client, is open to clearly receive and recognize the client's feelings, and puts together all that he or she understands about the client. The counselor who is functioning at a higher level also continuously checks the accuracy of findings by concretely and specifically reporting them to the client. In this way the counselor prepares and encourages the client to explore and disclose deeper feelings and experiences.

Empathy scale (Table 7-1). The empathy scale serves as a means to rate the counselor's functioning level of empathy. This scale is adapted from several sources (Barrett-Lennard, 1962; Carkhuff, 1969; Truax and Carkhuff, 1967). The characteristics (dimensions) contained in the empathy scale include the degree of the counselor's awareness of feelings expressed, the concreteness of the counselor's responses, the immediacy of the counselor's relationship, and the depth of self-exploration. The five levels of the Truax-Carkhuff scale are retained

Table 7-1. *Scale for rating functioning level of empathy**

Awareness of feeling	Concreteness	Immediacy	Self-exploration
Level 1			
C. responds in a distant and unrelated manner. C. shows little awareness of even Cl.'s obvious feelings. C. may try to understand but from own viewpoint.	C. leads discussion or responds to Cl. in an unclear, nonspecific, over-intellectualized manner, avoiding personally significant situations or feelings.	C. deals with many items but does not attend to or speak of them in relation to the words and feelings of the client-counselor relationship even though Cl. refers to C. in his or her remarks.	Cl. mechanically talks about self and his or her problems or feelings. C. fails to encourage Cl. to produce personal and/or emotional material. Cl., in effect, does not reveal self, either because of lack of encouragement from C. or because Cl. actively avoids discussing more personal concerns.
Level 2			
C. shows poor understanding of the meaning of Cl.'s expressions. C. often responds accurately to Cl.'s obvious (surface) feelings but overlooks the depth of Cl.'s feelings. Sometimes C. jumps to the conclusion that Cl. feels more strongly or is more concerned than he or she actually is.	C. may talk about Cl.'s feelings and experiences, but the discussion is unclear, intellectualized, and not sufficiently specific.	C. seems to disregard most of Cl.'s verbal and nonverbal expressions that may refer to C.	Cl. often responds mechanically without exploring the meaning of experiences and does not attempt to unveil or understand feelings. When C. tries to encourage Cl. to discuss personally relevant materials, Cl. may agree or disagree, change the subject, or refuse to respond. Cl. does not produce new information related to problems.
Level 3 (minimal facilitative level)			
C. accurately responds with understanding of Cl.'s obvious feelings but does not realize how intensely Cl. feels about some of the material discussed. C. may misinterpret deeper feelings.	At times C. enables Cl. to directly discuss more personally significant material clearly and concisely. In some areas of discussion C. does not assist Cl. to be sufficiently specific.	C.'s verbal and nonverbal behavior is appropriate for Cl.'s comments about others and to some extent about C. in the counselor-client relationship but is not sufficiently clear in relation to the client-counselor relationship.	Some personally relevant and new material is willingly produced but discussed as if it has been rehearsed by Cl. Cl. shows some degree of either feeling or spontaneity but often not both responses.

*C., counselor; Cl., client.

Continued.

Table 7-1. *Scale for rating functioning level of empathy—cont'd*

Awareness of feeling	Concreteness	Immediacy	Self-exploration
Level 4			
C. is sensitive to Cl.'s obvious and deeper feelings and accurately communicates understanding to Cl., thus enabling Cl. to express feelings he or she was unable to talk about previously. C. tries to see things through Cl.'s eyes.	C. often helps Cl. discuss personally significant feelings and experiences in specific and concise terms.	C. openly, yet in some ways cautiously, pulls in Cl.'s comments to refer to the client-counselor relationship.	Some personally relevant and new material is willingly introduced and openly discussed with emotional expressiveness. Cl.'s verbal and nonverbal behavior fits the feelings and the information discussed. C. begins to help Cl. get deeper into relationships with others (interpersonal), yet Cl. is not fully enabled to discuss these relationships.
Level 5			
C. accurately responds to Cl.'s obvious and even most painful feelings. C. is tuned in to Cl.'s deeper feelings but is not burdened or distressed by them. Together C. and Cl. explore feelings deeper than what Cl. was able to express previously. C. appreciates the meaning and importance of Cl.'s experiences.	C. enables Cl. to freely and fully discuss personally significant feelings and experiences in specific and concise terms regardless of the emotions expressed.	C. openly responds and directly pulls in and interprets Cl.'s comments to refer to the client-counselor relationship.	Cl. is able to be himself or herself as well as to explore himself or herself. Cl. actively and willingly engages in careful inward searching (intrapersonal) and discovers new views about self and his or her feelings and experiences. Cl. arrives at some choice for a new view of others as well as of self.

as is the idea that level 3 is the minimal facilitative level for effective counseling. A score sheet (Fig. 7-4) provides a method for determining the counselor's functioning level.

In the following exercises two different approaches to raising the level of empathy are described. In Exercise 7-3 the trainee discovers his or her general approach to understanding the meaning of the client's experiences and to recognizing the client's feelings. Exercises 7-4 to 7-6 focus on more specific aspects of empathic ability.

The words fuse into each other when feelings, concreteness, immediacy, and self-exploration are considered. These have been divided into separate categories for discussion purposes, yet these words are inseparable and interdependent. Empathy is the catchall word for all the characteristics of accurate understanding. The expression of warmth enriches

Place check under *one* of the levels for *each* characteristic. The empathy level equals the total number of checks under each category divided by 4, the total number of categories. This is the average level of all the characteristics.

EXAMPLE:	Feeling	Level 2	
	Concreteness	Level 3	
	Immediacy	Level 2	
	Self-exploration	Level 1	
		Total = 8	
		Divided by 4 = 2 (level 2)	

Characteristics	Levels				
	1	2	3*	4	5
Awareness of feeling					
Concreteness					
Immediacy					
Self-exploration					
Total No. of checks under each category					

*Minimum facilitative level

Fig. 7-4. Score sheet for empathy scale.

the communication of an empathic relationship. Although obsolete, two words euphoniously synchronize the notions of empathy and warmth—"fellowfeel" and "boonfellow." Fellowfeel signifies to share another's feelings, and boonfellow refers to a warm companion (Sperling, 1977). Skills in applying the characteristics of warm companionship are the focus of the following discussion.

Warmth

Warmth is readily expressed by gestures, touch, and facial expression. Tone of voice and to some extent the words used are other ways of expressing warmth. Warmth is similar to genuineness, since it is related to trust. However, warmth is not enough. Too much warmth loses its effectiveness and, in fact, can be overwhelming. Nonpossessive warmth permits the weaning of the client because it does not encourage dependency. Instead nonpossessive warmth cultivates the resources of an-

other person by offering support in an acceptant atmosphere of goodwill peppered with alternative choices and nurtured by self-exploration of both client and counselor.

Nonpossessive warmth. The term "nonpossessive" may be more easily defined if the "non" part of the word is temporarily removed and "possessive" is examined first. "Possessive" brings to attention both ownership and the occult or mystic meaning of possession, that is, control by an invading being or thing. These two ideas together give a more complete meaning. Both the materialistic notion of using an individual for one's own gain or profit (ownership) and the manipulative notion of control by someone other than oneself are combined. Nonpossessive is obviously the opposite of these notions.

Nonpossessiveness is unconditional, that is, with no strings attached. Nonpossessiveness refers to self-direction, self-control, and consequently self-choice in decision making. Nonpossessiveness re-

Exercise 7-3
DO YOU GET THE MESSAGE? *(may be done alone and discussed in a group)*

Time: APPROXIMATELY 35 MINUTES

Messages are conveyed through speech, art, poetry, and the like. Sometimes the message is clear and concrete. At other times the message is wrapped in a camouflage of sights and sounds. The empathic counselor accepts the straight message, "I'm bored, don't want to discuss this any more." The empathic counselor also penetrates the disguise of the same message delivered by a client who often conceals from self as well as from the counselor the actual intent of the message. In Fig. 7-5 are examples of three different forms of communication. In the spaces next to the message group members write the "meaning" as they perceive it and also the reply they would give to the client. No more than 5 minutes should be spent on each message. After completing the first part of the exercise, the group members form subgroups of four members and for 15 minutes compare their comments about meanings and replies to clients. Table 7-1 may be used to scale each participant's replies, and these replies may be rated in accordance with the categories in Fig. 7-4.

Exercise 7-4
ARE YOU SPEAKING TO THE POINT? *(may be done alone and discussed in a group)*

Time: APPROXIMATELY 25 MINUTES

Rate the following counselor responses according to the degree of concreteness on a scale from 1 to 5. Refer to the second column (concreteness) in Table 7-1 for characteristics at each level. After completing your ratings, compare your scoring with others in your group.

MAC: I find your explanation of my father's insistence on my going to medical school unacceptable. How can it be either/or?

Possible replies by Mr. J., the counselor:

- ☐ "I see. So you don't believe it can be either/or?"
- ☐ "You know you don't have to agree with me."
- ☐ "I see what you mean. Maybe you can tell me more about how you see it so I might better understand how you feel."
- ☐ "Well, perhaps it's because you really don't want to understand."
- ☐ "You mean that you can't see your father's viewpoint?"
- ☐ "Hmmmmm. Lots of sons find it difficult to understand how their fathers feel."
- ☐ "You know, you've got something there. Let's look at this some more."
- ☐ "Yes, I did make a broad statement. Just because three generations have been doctors doesn't mean that either you have to be one or leave home. Hmmm, let's see."
- ☐ "I understand your feeling. Feel hemmed in—is that it? Maybe we can look at other possibilities."
- ☐ "I guess in some ways I understand you. We need to talk some more about specifics."
- ☐ "Sometimes you feel like I don't really understand what you are saying. Is that it?"
- ☐ (Insert your own response if none of the above satisfies your concept of concreteness.)

Client's message	Meaning	Empathic answer
Speech "I don't know whether I should tell you this, Dr. P., but one of your former patients told me you hold on to your patients—you know, money—more money. I don't really believe him."		
Art The client brought this drawing to the counselor and said, "Here, here's what I think about my mother."		
Poetry earth could not answer me sky could not comfort me you could not be with me so death was my destiny		

Fig. 7-5. Message, meaning, and answer.

Exercise 7-5
HOW DO YOU PULL IN THE CLIENT-COUNSELOR RELATIONSHIP? *(should be done in a group)*

Time: APPROXIMATELY 30 MINUTES

Three participants are needed for this exercise—a client, a counselor, and a doubling counselor. The client presents a problem, either one of his or her own or one of the situations given here.

The client is free to discuss the problem in any way he or she wishes. The counselor, however, may answer in only one sentence. The doubling counselor listens to both the client and the counselor. If the doubling counselor does not think that the counselor has accurately dealt with the client's statement, he or she may add to what the counselor has said, but with only one sentence. Anyone in the rest of the group who is still unsatisfied with the responses to the client may tap the doubling counselor on the shoulder after which the doubling counselor leaves. Then the new doubling counselor adds what he or she considers appropriate. This counseling session should take no more than 10 minutes. Then the third column (immediacy) of Table 7-1 is used to determine the functioning level of the counselor and the doubling counselor. After the discussion a second counseling session of no more than 10 minutes is conducted and the evaluation procedure is repeated.

[1]   Two weeks ago Helen gave birth to a boy. She is disturbed by her ambivalent feelings of love and hate for the infant. When she sees him, she wants to touch him and hold him, but then she thinks of how annoying his crying is and she ''can't stand him.'' She is afraid she might hurt the baby if she touches him because her ''hatred is so bad.'' She phones a counselor to talk to him about what she should do.

[2]   Jan is a weekend social drinker. Although he spends most of his time drinking over the weekend, he doesn't consider himself to be an alcoholic, but ''just one of the boys.'' ''After all,'' he comments to his wife, ''I do have a responsible position and only drink a little with my business associates.'' He refuses to see anyone about his drinking. ''Don't need to,'' he says. His wife, Martha, is upset and is seeking help from Dr. M.

Exercise 7-6
HOW DO YOU ACHIEVE DEEPER SELF-EXPLORATION? *(should be done in a group)*

Time: APPROXIMATELY 30 MINUTES

The group divides into pairs. Each pair role-plays one of the following situations. Afterward, the fourth column (self-exploration) in Table 7-1 is used to determine the functioning level of the counseling situation.

[1]   Two people talk to each other with nonsense syllables (mft, hpt, and so on), not words. Each person tries to convey feelings as well as ideas with nonwords for 5 minutes. Afterwards the two participants discuss for 5 minutes whether the nonword messages were understood accurately.

[2]   Person A is from Earth, and person B is from Mars. Person A must interview person B for 5 minutes for an article to appear in a newspaper. He or she must find out how person B feels about meeting A, an earthling. Afterward persons A and B discuss for 5 minutes how effectively person A conducted the interview and whether he or she got information from person B about person B's feelings.

[3]   The client tries to conceal some thought and/or feelings from the counselor. For 10 minutes the counselor encourages the client to open up and explore this feeling or idea.

quires that the helper be open to the client's point of view and avoid imposing on or taking over with his or her own viewpoint.

Nonpossessiveness puts limitations on warmth only insofar as the feeling of warmth must be expressed for the client's welfare, not for the glory of the helper. Warmth goes beyond involvement; it takes in the tender feeling of caring and the comfortable freedom of expressing feelings with no limits. The helper who expresses warmth is accepting. This helper accepts the client "where he or she's at" at the moment of the helping session.

Nonpossessive warmth, accordingly, may be defined as the expression of commitment, concern, and respect for another human being *as he or she is, not as he or she ought to be.* Nonpossessive warmth is a positive feeling of closeness that overlaps and intertwines with accurate empathy and genuineness.

Exercise 7-7 examines the verbal expression of nonpossessive warmth.

The manifestation of warmth solely with words is not as reassuring or satisfying as other modes of expression. Warmth, often, is more readily demonstrated and realized by gestures, touch, and facial expression (Fig. 7-6).

General characteristics of nonpossessive warmth. Nonpossessive warmth is more difficult to explain than empathy and genuineness, since it is so dependent on the expression of feelings. Transactional analysis explains warmth as positive stroking, which is preferably unconditional. Learning theorists stress warmth as reinforcement of appropriate behavior by means of some form of approval. Several characteristics are included in the concept of warmth—equal worth, absence of blame, nondefensiveness, and closeness. The list may be extended even further, but these seem to

Fig. 7-6. The warmth of tenderness and care. (From Poland, R.G.: Human experience: a psychology of growth, St. Louis, 1974, The C.V. Mosby Co.)

Exercise 7-7
HOW DO YOU RATE WARMTH? *(should be done in a group)*

Time: APPROXIMATELY 15 MINUTES
Part 1

Select a partner and answer at least two of the following questions by using what may be called a reverse-mirror approach. One person replies to the situations and questions presented in this exercise by comments that show that he or she does *not* care, does *not* like, does *not* feel warmth or feels *possessive* warmth toward the person in the situation described. In other words, one person's (person A's) answer will demonstrate all of the negative, incorrect approaches to nonpossessive warmth. The other person (person B) mirrors the first person's reply with a reverse image of the first person's answer. Person B's answer shows nonpossessive warmth. Read Part 2 before you begin Part 1.

Example: "How would you deal with Josh? He says that he is being given all of the unimportant work to do since Bill has become his supervisor."

Person A answers with the negative, incorrect approach: "I would tell Josh that he has to do what he is asked to do. If he doesn't like it, he could always find another job."

Person B mirrors what person A said but changes the words so that caring, liking, respect, and consequently nonpossessive warmth are demonstrated: "I would tell Josh that what he is doing is important to the whole project we are conducting. If he doesn't like it, we should sit down together and discuss his role in the project further so he gets a better understanding."

[1]   Sam is an 18-year-old student in one of your college classes. He comes to you, his psychology professor, and says, "I need to talk to someone, someone who can straighten my thoughts out. I love ballet . . . love to study ballet. I have been taking lessons for 4 years. When I told Hal about this, he said, 'Isn't that faggy?'" What would you say to Sam?

[2]   S.G. is sitting at the table in a sheltered workshop for mentally retarded adults. Parts to a bicycle horn have been arranged in boxes placed in front of him. S.G. picks up one piece and tries to push it down on the large screw he holds in his left hand. He is unable to do anything with the piece. He sits at the table, looks around, bites his lip, and whispers, "Can't, can't." What would you do and say to S.G.?

[3]   Sue is a new member of the group. She sits just outside the circle and has not entered into the conversation during the three sessions since she joined the group. Laurie turns toward Sue and says, "Come on in. Get with it." Sue looks around the group and then turns to you, the group leader, "Must I?" As group leader, what would you say?

[4]   Carrie's mother has just come into the room. Carrie is stretched out on her bed, and Glen is sprawled on the bed next to her. What does Carrie's mother say?

Part 2

After person A and person B reply to a situation, they use Table 7-2 to explore the level of nonpossessive warmth demonstrated. Circle the number that best describes your estimation of the degree of the characteristic your partner showed.

NOTE: The replies of person A to the example about Josh would be represented by circling the 5's, since person A's answer did not show any of the characteristics. Person B's answer would be represented by 3's, 2's, and 1's. Before you begin your replies to the question, you and your partner rate person B's answer.

Table 7-2. *Ratings for nonpossessive warmth*

Characteristic	Yes		To some extent		No
Shows caring	1	2	3	4	5
Shows liking	1	2	3	4	5
Shows friendliness	1	2	3	4	5
Shows respect	1	2	3	4	5
Shows kindness	1	2	3	4	5
Shows interest	1	2	3	4	5
Shows acceptance	1	2	3	4	5
Shows closeness	1	2	3	4	5
Shows appreciation	1	2	3	4	5
Shows nonpossessive warmth	1	2	3	4	5

be the characteristics mentioned most often in the literature. Other characteristics are further extensions of those just mentioned. In fact, the listed items overlap and are divided primarily for discussion purposes.

Equal worth. Equal worth is basic to the quality of warmth, and acceptance is the related factor. Acceptance embraces human equality as one of its elements. If one individual considers another individual equally worthy, it follows that he or she will uphold the other person's right to be different. This acceptance of difference is not attached to approval or agreement with the individual's difference. Nevertheless, no weight of lesser or greater worthiness is given to the other individual's self-experiences. For the counselor, viewing the client as having equal worth promotes a positive regard for the client, and this regard does not fluctuate with the counselor's measurement of the value of the client's life-style.

Nonblame. Equal worth demands a nonjudgmental attitude, and this nonjudgmental attitude results in absence of blame. Nonblame, however, does not suggest the clients' lack of responsibility for their acts. Instead, nonblame suggests that if the counselor were in the client's circumstances he or she would be likely to act in a similar fashion. Nonblame may also imply that clients are accepted even though they feel unacceptable. Underlying this concept of nonblame is the idea that the counselor accepts the client because he or she *is.*

Therefore clients feel safe enough to freely express themselves in the nonthreatening counseling situation. In an atmosphere of safety from blame clients learn to trust the counselor and also themselves. They move toward greater assurance in their ability to handle their own destiny.

Nondefensiveness. Through self-understanding the counselor becomes more open to the client. Counselors who attain sufficient insight about their own needs and how they may fulfill these needs are less likely to expect the client to satisfy their needs. Counselors are also more likely to be open to the client's background, goals, and value system if they do not feel defensive about their own background and beliefs.

Another outcome of the counselor's self-understanding and self-acceptance is increased ability to honestly reveal feelings to the client. The counselor is able to air feelings of pleasure as well as those of anger. Properly balanced doses of warmth and anger may actually induce greater cooperation from the client (Johnson, 1971a), particularly if the counselor's angry response is immediately followed by assurance of warmth.

Revealing anger clears the air and admits the counselor's humanness. However, the expression of anger must be accomplished with caution. The empathic counselor is sensitive to the impact on the client of the counselor's disclosure of feelings. Anger or any other emotional expression may alienate the client (turn the client away from the counselor) unless this expression is handled sensitively.

Closeness. Anger and/or anxiety may have another effect that detracts from warmth. These negative emotions tend to make the psychological distance greater between counselor and client. A more distant (standoffish) relationship between counselor and client turns into coldness and less give-and-take between counselor and client.

Closeness has two possible explanations, depending on the direction the closeness takes. When individuals are close to themselves, they lean toward a tight-lipped secretiveness and keep to themselves and away from others. Such people are apt to maintain an area of psychological and probably also physical space around them. In other words, they are "cold" and keep their distance from others.

The opposite meaning for closeness shrinks the person-to-person distance. Closeness implies coming in contact either psychologically, through understanding and acceptance, or physically, through touch. Often both physical and psychological contacts coexist. This meaning of closeness suggests a fellowship of warmth. When one person says of another, "He is someone with whom I dare to be me" or "She knows my faults and yet she likes me," then closeness exists. It is this sense of the word "closeness" that is essential to the teammate companionship of the effective client-counselor relationship. Furthermore, it is easier to connect, to rap, with someone who considers one worthy of respect, who does not blame, who really tries to understand, who is not defensive about what he or she says, and who does not become closeted into self thinking.

There is one note of caution about warmth. Counselors who feel and exhibit warmth increase their personal attraction to clients and consequently elicit greater cooperation from their clients. However, an overabundance of warmth associated with excessive liking may lead to overdependent clients. If this should occur, counselors should examine their motives—are they actually striving for dependent clients?

Clothing. Empathy, warmth, and genuineness are essential considerations in helper-client and leader-group relationships. In either situation the connectedness of warmth or the distancing properties of coldness can be loudly proclaimed by the clothes the counselor or leader wears. Clothes reflect certain feelings about others as well as about oneself. This can be envisioned in the dissimilar images of a woman dressed in an Yves St. Laurent couturier silk dress and high-heeled suede boots with "well-manicured" hair and carefully applied makeup and another woman in jeans and sweatshirt, with her jeans tucked into her high, laced Frye boots and her hair hanging in long strands of tight, uncombed ringlets around her cosmetic-free face. How differently would these second skins—the clothes and general appearance of these women—convey warmth to the client living in a large expensive modern private home in an exclusive neighborhood compared with another client struggling with insufficient funds in a government-subsidized apartment? It is possible that the garb and style of both women would be unappealing. Men, too, convey messages with their clothes, depending on whether the degree of casualness or conventionality in dress fits the clients and the neighborhood. The counselor's or leader's interpersonal impression begins at this first "look." There is no magic formula for identifying the best clothes for a certain client or for a group of people. The helper's alertness to the effect of clothes and the expectations of the clients is the only guideline. Clothes can initiate the atmosphere of warmth, and warmth contributes to the client's conviction that the helper respects and acts with positive regard.

Warmth scale (Table 7-3). Two factors are included in this scale—positive regard and respect. The items for the scale for degree of warmth are based on those of Truax and Carkhuff (1967) and Carkhuff (1969).

Each person shows regard for things and people,

Table 7-3. *Scale for rating functional level of warmth**

Positive regard	Respect
Level 1	
C. actively offers Cl. advice and is indifferent to and uninterested in Cl. C. is heedless of Cl. as a person. C. feels responsible for Cl. and often indicates that he or she knows what would be best for Cl. C. is actively critical of Cl., approving or disapproving of Cl.'s behavior. C. may in fact dislike Cl. and reveal impatience with Cl. C's overconcern for Cl. interferes with C.'s open and clear discussion and with Cl.'s free responses.	C.'s verbal and nonverbal expressions communicate a clear lack of appreciation and esteem for Cl. C. conveys to Cl. that Cl.'s feelings and experiences are not worthy of consideration and that Cl. is incapable of acting constructively. C. is more concerned with self and shows contempt of Cl. In fact, C. may focus on self to such an extent that C. tells Cl. more about his or her own opinions and feelings than Cl. wants to know. C. is actually concentrating on "blowing his or her own horn," on increasing his or her own self-respect.
Level 2	
C. ignores Cl., showing little interest or genuine kindness. C. responds mechanically and is often passive, as if not attending to Cl. Sometimes C. is cold and disapproving, but C.'s feelings toward Cl. vary considerably and are dependent on Cl.'s response to C.	C.'s verbal and nonverbal expressions indicate lack of appreciation and esteem for Cl. However, C.'s interest in and response to Cl. depend partly on what Cl. is talking about and how Cl. is feeling about himself or herself; at times C. may respond with some recognition and appreciation of Cl.'s worth, and at other times C. may be unresponsive to Cl.'s worth as a person.
Level 3 (minimal facilitative level)	
C. shows positive caring in that he or she communicates to Cl. that Cl.'s feelings and behavior matter to him or her (C.). C. sees self as responsible for Cl. and is thus semipossessive, telling Cl., "I want you to . . ." and "It's important to me that you . . ."	C.'s verbal and nonverbal expressions indicate some degree of appreciation and esteem for Cl.'s feelings, experiences, and potentials. C. shows that he or she values most, if not all, of Cl.'s opinions and expressions about self.
Level 4	
C. shows deep commitment, interest, and concern for Cl.'s welfare and accepts Cl. as a person free to be himself or herself with little evaluation or criticism of Cl.'s beliefs or feelings. However, C. conveys to Cl. expectation that Cl. be mature (adult) and not regress (retreat into earlier forms of behavior).	C.'s verbal and nonverbal expressions indicate appreciation and esteem for Cl.'s feelings, experiences, and potentials. C.'s responses enable Cl. to feel worthwhile and that Cl.'s expressions about self are important. C. serves as a model for Cl. rather than as a manipulator of Cl.'s behavior.
Level 5	
C. shows unrestricted thoughtfulness, kindness, and consideration for Cl.'s worth as a person, no matter what Cl.'s beliefs and feelings may be. Thus Cl. feels free to be himself or herself, even if this means regression, defensiveness, or disliking and rejecting C. C. attends to and shares Cl.'s happiness, hopes, and successes as well as depressions, despair, and failures. C. makes one requirement of Cl.—work; that is, Cl. is expected to communicate personally relevant material.	C.'s verbal and nonverbal expressions indicate appreciation, genuine pleasure, and deep esteem for Cl.'s feelings and experiences. C.'s recognition of Cl.'s potential to handle his or her own concerns encourages Cl.'s problem solving and decision making as a free agent of his or her own affairs. C. recognizes Cl. as *somebody* of importance to self, to C., and to others.

*C., counselor; Cl., client.

Exercise 7-8
HOW DOES YOUR WARMTH COMPARE WITH THE "GRATE" WARMTH?
(should be done in a group)

Time: APPROXIMATELY 50 MINUTES

A phenomenon has been disturbing the persons who walk by several streets in Troglodyte City. Men and women are sleeping on the grates trying to warm themselves in the recent frigid weather. Temporary shelters were offered to these "grate people," but many of them refused to accept this "handout" because they said that they did not want to be shepherded by "do-gooders" and were "damn better off" in their freedom. Some of them eagerly preserved their anonymity and indignantly spurned the meals, bed, and warm shelters because they insisted on remaining nameless and addressless—unburdened by material things and avoiding the glare of publicity. This publicity exploded onto the front pages of several newspapers when two men and one woman froze while lying on the grates. No one could explain what made these three people remain on the grates in the snowstorm while others sought and found makeshift shelters.

The mayor has called upon the expertise of a well-known human service worker to arrange a group meeting with as many of these people who will attend. This worker is asked to use his or her problem-solving skills and leadership skills to reassure these people that they are respected, considered with positive regard, and neither condemned nor commended for their "grate" behavior.

The group members form a circle. One person volunteers to be the human service worker, and the remaining participants become the "grate people," who respond as they wish to the leader while empathizing with the plight and their interpretation of the philosophy of the "grate people." After 5 or 10 minutes the leader stops the group process, and the participants rate (Table 7-3) and score (Fig. 7-7) the warmth skill of the leader. These findings are discussed in the group for 10 minutes. This same procedure may be repeated as often as time permits, with a new leader continuing with the group discussion wherever the previous leader stopped. Sufficient time should be planned for a wrap-up session with the group discussing the following questions:

☐ What have you learned from this exercise?

☐ Are there any changes you will try to make in your behavior as a result of this exercise? If you do plan to change, present your planned changes. If you have no inclinations toward change, explain how you consider your current functioning satisfactory so that changes are unnecessary.

☐ How would you change this exercise to make it more meaningful for you?

Place check under *one* of the levels for *each* characteristic. The warmth level equals the total number of checks under each category divided by 2, the total number of categories. This is the average level of all the characteristics.

EXAMPLE: Positive regard   Level 3
                        Respect   Level 2
                                         Total = 5
                    Divided by 2 = 2.5 (level 2+)

Characteristics	Levels				
	1	2	3*	4	5
Positive regard					
Respect					
Total No. of checks under each category					

*Minimum facilitative level

Fig. 7-7. Score sheet for warmth scale.

evaluating them favorably or unfavorably. The more positive or favorable regard one person feels for another, the more likely this person would be to consider the other person's needs and attend to the satisfaction of these needs. However, heeding the call for help is not quite the same as respect. Respect goes one step beyond regard and adds another dimension that distinguishes each individual as unique and recognizes each individual for particular potentials.

There is a fine line between regard and respect, since their characteristics do overlap. Another distinction accentuates the dissimilarity. Since regard may be either positive or negative, one person may consider another (regard) in an unkindly, unconcerned, uninterested manner (negative regard) or in a kindly, concerned, interested manner (positive regard). Respect, on the other hand, can only be positive and varies only in degree and not in direction of negative or positive. Therefore both regard and respect are included in the characteristics of warmth to provide a fuller picture. Exercise 7-8 provides an opportunity to explore how positive regard and respect are shown.

■ ■ ■

A provocative question intrudes the preceding considerations of empathy and warmth—how does the human service worker, in fact anyone, separate plain-spoken and dependable communications from those which are chiefly based on social facade? The question is made more complex in a technological society in which depersonalization and dehumanization permeate many interpersonal dealings and reinforce stylization of responses. It is *genuineness*, the third attribute of the Truax triad, that embellishes the trust that is fundamental to the helping event.

Genuineness

This above all—to thine own self be true;
And it must follow, as the night the day,
Thou canst not then be false to any man.

(William Shakespeare, *Hamlet*, act 1, scene 3)

Shakespeare caught the essence of genuineness in the preceding comment by Polonius, who realizes that genuineness begins with oneself.

Genuineness is the process of self-disclosure in which individuals are sufficiently aware of and accept their own feelings and experiences so that they are able to freely and appropriately communicate their feelings and experiences to someone else; they are also open to the communication of feelings and experiences from other persons. In addition to openness to oneself and to others, genuine persons develop the ability to honestly tell the difference between their own feelings about the experiences of other persons and other persons' experiences of their own feelings. Thus when genuine persons get caught up in thinking, "What a jerk she is. She thinks she's superior to me," they know they are surrounded by their own prejudices. They must sift through their feelings and see the other person's point of view: "She does put on a superior air. Something about the way she looks at me makes me wonder if she feels comfortable with me."

Two words are closely related in explaining the meaning of genuineness—congruence (when one's words and actions correspond) and authenticity (when one is himself or herself, not a phony). Basic to all three of these words is the idea of being real. The most *real* individual is the infant who has not as yet learned the mask of politeness or the unreliability of distrust. The infant is born *genuine* (to be natural) and is conditioned to adopt a front that diminishes self-disclosure.

Exercise 7-9 explores the various meanings of certain events. After completing this exercise, the members of the group might discuss what genuineness in response means to them.

Genuineness and trust. Genuineness eventuates from being "true" to oneself, and from this trust is derived. In other words, to trust others, one must trust oneself—to be both trustful and trustworthy. The helper avoids the put-on of "airs" and of phoniness. Basically, counselors remember their own humanness and respect the humanness of clients. Relating to people, being oneself, and

---

Exercise 7-9
WHAT DO YOU REALLY MEAN? *(may be done alone or in a group)*

In the situations listed in Fig. 7-8 several meanings can be interpreted. Read the statements in the first column, and in the second column briefly write two different explanations for the possible intent of the persons and the situations. If you are completing this exercise with a group, discuss your explanations with other group members after you have written them.

Situation	Explanations
Mary ran over to Obie, threw her arms around him, held him closely, and said, "Where the hell have you been?"	
Lester took the gun out of the cowboy holster and slid across the floor toward his mother. "Bang, bang," he said, "You're deader than dead." Lester ran away laughing.	
Chris spoke in a quiet voice. Her eyebrows were drawn together and her forehead was wrinkled. She held her hands tightly clasped as she spoke and cleared her throat several times. "Hmm. Guess I can go along with the idea. Sounds as if it will work."	

Fig. 7-8. The genuine meaning.

interdependence (harmonious balance between dependence and independence) are the traits to be desired and acquired. The counselor seeks self-fulfillment through commitment to helping rather than solely through self-satisfaction.

Stages of growth toward self-fulfillment. An examination of the stages in growth toward self-fulfillment assists in understanding some of the needs to be satisfied in order for a comfortable self-competency to develop.

In Fig. 7-9 Maslow's (1970) and Erikson's (1963a,b) concepts of the stages of growth toward self-fulfillment are diagrammed. Both Maslow and Erikson stress that an individual must turn on to self before he or she can turn outward toward others. As the steps of the pyramid in Fig. 7-9 show,

there is a gradual development of the child from self-interest to interest in others. This *natural* characteristic at birth is distorted if the following needs are not satisfied:

- The need for air, food, water, physical comfort, rest, and activity
- The need for freedom from fear, insecurity, and danger and threat
- The need to be *somebody,* first in the family group and later on in other groups
- The need to be loved (cared for and comforted) and to love
- The need to feel worthwhile and competent

Out of the gradual satisfaction of these needs emerges a feeling of fulfillment, an outward seeking to know—to understand oneself and later to

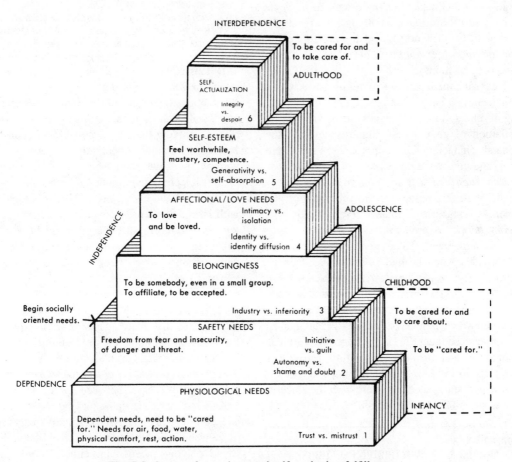

Fig. 7-9. Stages of growth toward self- and other-fulfillment.

understand the world and other people. All the needs are present at each stage of personal growth. However, certain needs are more important at certain ages. The redevelopment of genuineness therefore requires that the individual learn to trust, to feel autonomous (self-directed), to be comfortable in trying out new experiences (initiative), to work at learning and achieving (industry), to be developing who "I am" and becoming "who and what I want to be" (identity), and to care for oneself and for others (generativity). In essence, to be genuine is to be more oneself.

General characteristics of genuineness. Out of genuineness arise self-understanding, understanding of others, and a willingness to be known. The definition of genuineness suggests several other general characteristics: congruence, self-disclosure, and confrontation.

Congruence. The term "congruence" is the one single word that represents the substance of genuineness. This term originates from the Latin word *"congruere,"* a verb signifying "meeting together" or "agreement." Shakespeare selected the gist of this idea when he had Hamlet say, "suit the action to the word, the word to the action" (act III, scene 2). The harmonious results that occur when words and actions correspond are not easily achieved when defensive feelings or antagonism lead to concealment. These feelings often are barriers to free and open communication. Example 7-1 depicts an instance in which hidden agendas of unrevealed annoyances interfere with the sincerity that is essential to genuineness.

Example 7-1
ANN AND HANK—A CONSTRICTED RELATIONSHIP

[1]

Ann fears rejection from Hank.

HER FEELINGS: I love him, really love him. But, does he love me?
HER STATEMENTS: Come on now, let's not get too close into things. Won't work.
HER ACTIONS: She bites her lower lip, tightens her jaw, and sits back in her chair with her legs loosely placed on the floor, one ankle bent, the other leg stretched out.

[2]

Hank doesn't want to get too involved with anyone right now, but he would like a casual sexual arrangement with Ann.

HIS FEELINGS: Better watch out for this chick. She's scrounging for ties.
HIS STATEMENTS: Why not? Getting close is what it's all about, pleasant being, got a lot to share.
HIS ACTIONS: He pulls his lip up to one side in a half smile, raises one eyebrow slightly, squints his eyes, and leans forward with his hands tightly clasped between his knees.

Defensive maneuvers are evident in both Ann's and Hank's statements. The words spoken evaluate the relationship instead of describing how Ann and Hank feel. Ann says that getting close won't work. She is implying that she fears taking a chance on Hank's uncertainty. Apparently Ann would like to control the interrelationship to defend herself against rejection and emotional hurts. She reveals by her facial and body cues that she is not leveling with Hank. She tenses her face, stretches out one leg, and partially pulls the other leg back at the ankle. Instead of speaking her feeling, she says with certainty what she is afraid might happen ("won't work").

Hank is also defensive and not leveling with Ann. He tries to cover up his own concerns with some tactics that guard against revealing his flight from real intimacy and self-disclosure. He pretends he wants closeness, yet he is pulling himself both toward (leans forward in chair) and away from Ann (hands tightly clasped between his legs).

Ann and Hank are game-playing. Gameplaying is the artificial social device that individuals use to relate to one another in order to avoid being hurt. Game playing means you either "don't make waves" or when you do, you arrange the waves carefully. Game playing for counselors may mean that they do not let their humanness show; they play the counseling role with only their techniques showing. Under these conditions counselors cannot say what they mean nor can they mean what they say. The counselors, in other words, are not genuine. Exercise 7-10 directs attention to the need for correspondence between verbal and nonverbal behavior.

Words, thoughts, and actions—sometimes these fit, and on other occasions discrepancies disturb and distort the message. Exercise 7-10 arranges situations to explore these incongruities. The clues for identifying these behaviors depend on keen observation of whether *what* the person says and *how* the person says it agree. In other words, does the smiling person say, "I hate you"? Does the man say, "Doesn't hurt a bit," while his eyebrows move closer and closer into a frown and his jaw and fists become tighter and tighter? Congruence, or the harmony and correspondence of verbal and nonverbal cues, is an essential point. Correspondence between verbal and nonverbal behavior is essential to genuineness, and self-disclosure is a natural outcome of this correspondence.

Self-disclosure. Self-disclosure signifies the willingness to be known. This term may be simply defined as the offer of personal information. In the counseling situation this offer must be according to the client's desire to know about the counselor as well as the counselor's understanding of which of his or her experiences would best fit the client's needs. The counselor's willingness to share with the client encourages similar self-disclosure by the client. Mutual exchange of information is encouraged.

In general, people need to feel free to reveal information as well as to conceal; this applies to the counselor as well as to the client. The main difference between the degree of concealment is that the counselor, as compared with the client, has more open space (see discussion of Johari's window in Chapter 1) that he or she can comfortably share with the client *for the client's benefit*. This last phrase is very important, for the purpose of the counselor's disclosure is to prompt similar disclosure by the client. The goal is not a confession to absolve the sins of either the counselor or the client. The goal is mutual sharing for the client's benefit.

Confrontation. From the counselor's standpoint self-disclosure serves as a form of self-confrontation. Not only does the counselor reveal to the client his or her experiences but also, in this process of revealing, the counselor must consider and weigh the meaning of these experiences. Facilitative (effective and reinforcing) counselors are more alert to and inclined to tell about differences in their emotional experiences. More contented and more satisfied counselors, in fact, are more able to identify, accept, and respond nondefensively to their own reflections and disclosures.

Confrontation has at least two purposes. It provides informational feedback for both the client and the counselor. At first feedback (confrontation) arises from the counselor's efforts to discover self; then it comes from the counselor to the client. Later the client begins to give feedback to the counselor, and finally both the counselor and the client give feedback on the feedback.

■ ■ ■

The assessment of genuineness encompasses the three aforementioned characteristics: congruence, self-disclosure, and confrontation. Although separated for discussion purposes these three aspects are interdependent. The phony person covers up by word or act and in this concealment camouflages the obscured message.

Genuineness scale (Table 7-4). The scale for measuring the functioning level of genuineness incorporates the five progressive levels of congruence, self-disclosure, and confrontation (Truax and Carkhuff, 1967). The interrelationship among these three characteristics is evident when one looks at one of the levels described. At level 1, if the counselor is clearly defensive and contradictory in responses to the client (low level of congruence), he or she is more likely to be close-mouthed in voicing feelings and beliefs (low level of self-disclosure) and also less likely to be aware, or at any rate less likely to reveal, awareness of the client's inconsistencies in behavior. On the other hand, the counselor may point out the inconsistencies in a manner destructive to the client's self-esteem. The

Exercise 7-10
HOW DO YOU MAKE VERBAL AND NONVERBAL BEHAVIOR GO TOGETHER?
(should be done in a group)

Time: APPROXIMATELY 35 MINUTES

This exercise starts from what should not be and then goes into what should be genuineness. In this way, by going from "wrong" to "right," an individual becomes more aware of how phony behavior interferes with the counseling transaction.

Arrange a group of five participants. Two of the participants are to be a client and a counselor. The three other participants are observers. Figs. 7-10 and 7-11 are the score sheet forms for rating the level of congruence during the first and second role performances.

The counselor selects one of the situations below, and the client role-plays the problem. The counselor exaggerates his or her behavior to show self-interested purpose—to do his or her *worst* in order to get a rating at the lower end of the interpersonal scale. The counselor tries to conceal the fact that he or she hates this role-playing requirement, is really not interested in the client, and thinks the person role-playing the client is a jerk. The counselor must be as phony as possible.

After the role playing the group discusses for 10 minutes the ratings of the counselor's congruence and points out the verbal and nonverbal behaviors that reveal the counselor's lack of interest in and respect for the client. Examples of the lack of congruence between verbal and nonverbal behavior also are discussed. Group members make suggestions for the counselor's improvement. Then the same incident is role-played for 5 more minutes. This time the counselor respects the client, is interested, and thus is genuine and trustworthy. The three other participants shift their observations so that they are observing different behavior than during the last counseling episode—for example, a participant might observe verbal behavior this time if he or she observed nonverbal behavior last time. The observers rate the counselor on this second role playing; a second general discussion follows for 10 minutes in which the observers include examples of the counselor's improvement in genuineness (congruence between verbal and nonverbal cues).

[1] Mr. P. is counseling a 30-year-old Mexican-American man who has been having difficulty in getting a job. Mr. P. does not believe that those foreigners should remain in the United States using up welfare and taking jobs from solid Americans. Mr. P. thinks as he looks at the brown skin and blue shirt and jeans of the client, "Mess, what a mess. That's the trouble with these Chicano guys. Talk about machismo, macho [manliness], and are really just weak sisters. If a man wants to work and better himself, he can get a job, an education. This union stuff is un-American. Gotta be nice to the guy; damn supervisor is all for this minority stuff."

[2] Ms. I. believes she is a liberated woman who is "unshockable." However, she really does get disgusted with these drug freaks who try everything. "These young long-hairs who make the drug rounds like this 15-year-old, flipped-out kid, Marcia, seeing me, can't take the world. Got to make her see I really understand and accept her." Marcia is telling Ms. I. that she has been smoking angel dust* and feels "far away, moving back and forth from my arms and legs; can't find my legs. Mmmmm, feel, mmmmmmm, so empty—shrinking, shrinking. Oh my God, I won't beeeeeeee . . . ! Got to find my shoes, my feet." Ms. I. is displeased and thinks, "Don't want to handle another one of those. But who else can do it?" She says, "I'm here with you, Marcia."

---

*Angel dust is the name sometimes given to phencyclidine (PCP), a psychoactive or consciousness-expanding drug that depresses the central nervous system and results in a state resembling alcohol intoxication, with muscular incoordination, generalized numbness of the extremities, sensory disturbance, muscular rigidity, and probable loss of contact with one's environment. Large doses may produce convulsions. Sometimes other side effects such as vomiting, nausea, drowsiness, confusion, and other nonpleasant effects result. PCP is also referred to as "PeaCe Pill" and Hog (STASH notes, 1973).

	Always (consis-tent)	Usually	No real incon-sistency (cues not observable)	Usually	Always (incon-sistent)	
Posture						Posture
Movement						Movement
Position						Position
Distance maintained						Distance maintained
Gestures						Gestures
Facial expression						Facial expression
Breathing						Breathing
Eye contact						Eye contact

Nonverbal cues *fit* spoken words (left)   Nonverbal cues do *not* fit spoken words (right)

Fig. 7-10. Score sheet for congruence: first role performance.

	Always (consist-ent)	Usually	No real incon-sistency (cues not observable)	Usually	Always (incon-sistent)	
Posture						Posture
Movement						Movement
Position						Position
Distance maintained						Distance maintained
Gestures						Gestures
Facial expression						Facial expression
Breathing						Breathing
Eye contact						Eye contact

Nonverbal cues *fit* spoken words (left)   Nonverbal cues do *not* fit spoken words (right)

Fig. 7-11. Score sheet for congruence: second role performance.

Table 7-4. *Scale for rating functioning level of genuineness**

Congruence (correspondence)	Self-disclosure	Confrontation
Level 1		
C.'s verbal responses are clearly defensive and unrelated to what he or she is feeling at the moment, as shown in what he or she is saying and in the sound of his or her voice. Contradictions appear in what he or she says. C.'s only genuine responses are negative (unfavorable) remarks to the Cl.	C. remains removed from Cl. and is close-mouthed about his or her own feelings or personal beliefs. If C. does disclose self, he or she does so in a way that is not tuned in to Cl.'s needs, and C. may make disclosures about self that may disturb Cl. C. tries to turn off Cl. from asking personal questions.	C.'s verbal and nonverbal behavior disregards or passively accepts inconsistencies in Cl.'s behavior.
Level 2		
C.'s verbal responses are slightly unrelated to what he or she is feeling at the moment. When C. does respond appropriately with the right words, his or her voice and general manner have a "canned quality," as if C. were reading from a book or imitating a "professional air." Thus C. responds carefully and correctly but without the expression of real, felt emotions. C. may respond genuinely but with negative remarks concerning Cl. C. does not seem to know how to use negative reactions to Cl. as a basis for exploring the relationship between C. and Cl.	Although C. does not always appear to be actively avoiding self-disclosure, he or she never offers any personal information about self. C. may respond briefly to direct questions from Cl. but does so unwillingly and answers only what Cl. specifically requests.	C. shows by verbal and nonverbal behavior disregard of Cl.'s inconsistencies in behavior. C. remains silent about Cl.'s inconsistencies yet shows by some behavioral expressions that he or she is aware of and not accepting the inconsistencies. However, C. does no more than hint at this awareness.
Level 3 (minimal facilitative level)		
Although C. does not show any real inconsistency between what he or she says, how he or she says it, and what he or she does while saying it, C. still does not give any definite cues that response is genuine. C.'s behavior hints at possible underlying defensiveness or professionalitis (Chapter 1).	C. offers personal information about self, which may be tuned in to Cl.'s needs. However, this information is often indistinct and too general to really describe C. C. does give impression of willingness to disclose more about self but is less free in dealing with feelings about Cl. and about the transactions going on between them.	C.'s verbal and nonverbal behavior reveals awareness of the inconsistencies in Cl.'s behavior, but C. does not relate directly and specifically to these inconsistencies. C. may ask questions about inconsistencies without pointing out the disagreements and/or inconsistencies in Cl.'s answer.

*C., counselor; Cl., client.

Table 7-4. *Scale for rating functioning level of genuineness—cont'd*

Congruence (correspondence)	Self-disclosure	Confrontation
Level 4		
C. responds with many of his or her own feelings and is positively genuine and nondestructive in responses to Cl. What C. says corresponds with what he or she is feeling, but C. is somewhat hesitant to express feelings fully. C. is able to handle favorable as well as unfavorable feelings toward Cl. as a basis for further exploration of the interpersonal relationship. There is no evidence of false front, of defensiveness, or of professionalitis by C.	C. freely offers personal information about ideas, attitudes, feelings, and experiences that fit into Cl.'s interests and concerns. In fact, C. may discuss intimate ideas in both depth and detail, and his or her expressions clearly reveal him or her as a distinct individual.	C.'s verbal and nonverbal behavior attends directly and specifically to inconsistencies in Cl.'s behavior. When C. confronts Cl., he or she does so honestly and sensitively.
Level 5		
C. is freely and deeply himself or herself in an unselfish, caring relationship with Cl. C. is nondefensively open to experiences of all types, both pleasant and hurtful, and is able to use these experiences comfortably and constructively for deeper exploration for self and for Cl. Verbal and nonverbal expressions match.	C. offers even intimate and detailed information about self in tune with Cl.'s needs. C. gives impression that he or she is holding nothing back and freely presents both ideas and feelings to Cl.	C.'s verbal and nonverbal behavior is sharply tuned in to the inconsistencies in Cl.'s behavior. C. confronts Cl. in an honest, sensitive, understanding manner when inconsistencies in Cl.'s behavior appear.

counselor's own inconsistencies are covered up and the client's inconsistencies are ignored or harmfully reported.

Two serious obstacles deter the transformation to a more genuine approach: (1) the nongenuine person sincerely believes that honesty is *not* the best policy, and (2) some individuals have kept a lid on their feelings for so long that their forthrightness is tucked away under layers of socialized other-directed responses. They have learned the behavior of dissembling, and its works. Example 7-2 describes the behavior of one such person, an alcoholic whose fabrications are supported by the bluffs of alcoholic reasoning ("alcologia"). Exercise 7-11 is based on this example.

Example 7-2
CONFRONTING "ALCOLOGIA"

Mr. R. is certain that his wife is wrong. He is not an alcoholic. He thinks to himself, "Why, just the other day, last Friday, it was, when I realized that all that beer drinking was just making me gain too much weight, when I was getting so fuzzy. Couldn't work. So what did I do? I cut down on liquids; 'No more beer,' I said, 'Take too much.' So decided to drink bourbon and soda. Don't drink as much now. My wife, she just doesn't understand the willpower I have."

For a few months he drinks bourbon and soda only as a pick-me-up when he gets up in the morning and a few to be social with the fellows at lunchtime, and, of course, just a couple before dinner. When his wife "nags him" because he "doesn't look well," he has to "drink away" his "uncomfortable feeling." He decides to switch to bourbon and water. "After all, it must be the carbonation in the soda. That fizz makes me have indigestion."

His wife tells him she can't take his behavior any more and that she has gone to some meetings of Al-Anon. Maybe he ought to go to that doctor who treats alcoholics. That will shut her up, at least. After all, all he needs to do is stop drinking the bourbon with the water. It is the water that is giving him the gas, his embarrassing hiccups, and resounding burps. "So, I'll drink bourbon on the rocks. Who says you have to drink bourbon with soda or water?" considers Mr. R.

At first Ms. R. pours all the bourbon down the sink so that Mr. R. will not find any to drink. She soon discovers that this is foolish because Mr. R. either manages to have a bottle hidden in the oddest places, such as the baby's diaper pail or behind the toilet bowl, or he travels miles, if necessary, to get some. She also is comforted by the Al-Anon meetings, which assure her that she is not at fault. It is Mr. R.'s responsibility. All she can do is to be there when he needs her and show that she cares for his welfare. "The situation might go on forever," Ms. R. sadly supposes, "or at least until his liver deteriorates completely." However, Mr. R. begins drinking more to "feel comfortable" or to "tide himself over the ugly feeling between drinks" and goes home later. One evening he remains at the bar a little longer than usual, drinking even more than usual. In fact, he is now drinking bourbon straight, since when the "rocks" melt he is still getting too much liquid.

Mr. R. lives in the suburbs, and in the 10 years that he has been working and drinking he has managed to escape having any serious accidents. Tonight he wobbles from the bar to his car in the garage near his office. "Sure, I'm fuzzy, must be tired," he slurs. He pulls out of the garage and slams into an oncoming car.

In the hospital Mr. R. awakens to see his wife and some bearded guy. Despite the pain in his bandaged head, Mr. P. manages a question, "Who're you?" The bearded man answers, "I'm Dr. McNeil; your wife has asked me to see you. Just saying hello today. I'll be back tomorrow when you are feeling a little better."

The key to the effectiveness of the helping relationship continues to be communication—what, how, and when the client and the counselor communicate. Words labeling the aspects include the acronyms ASK and ORRIC and other classifications: empathy, warmth, and genuineness. Yet, the nuts and bolts issue remains the message sent and

---

Exercise 7-11
HOW DO YOU CONFRONT "ALCOLOGIA"? *(should be done in a group)*

Time: APPROXIMATELY 60 MINUTES

"Alcologia" is the term used "to describe the combination of denial and rationalization typical of alcohol reasoning" (Twerski, 1973). The importance of confronting Mr. R. with his inconsistencies is crucial. It may be difficult to make a wedge in the distorted thinking that is part of alcologia, yet it is essential to do so in order for the alcoholic to learn to face his responsibility for the act of drinking.

Two group members role-play this exercise. One role-plays Mr. R., and the other role-plays Dr. McNeil. The rest of the group should each have a copy of the scale for rating functioning level of genuineness (Table 7-4) and of the score sheet for genuineness (Fig. 7-12). The observers take notes on the counselor's confrontation incidents and note how the client accepts or rejects the counselor's confrontations. The counseling session may take up to 30 minutes. After the group rates and scores Dr. McNeil, a general discussion follows of Dr. McNeil's confrontation procedures and level of genuineness. Suggestions are made for improvement.

The entire procedure is then repeated for 15 minutes. The discussion after rating of Dr. McNeil should include examples of how confrontation procedures and level of genuineness have or have not improved.

the message perceived. The meticulous counselor in quest of more polished communication skills augments his or her competencies in the expressive skills of paraphrasing and summarization, reflection, confrontation, and interpretation.

EXPRESSIVE SKILLS OF COMMUNICATION

The educational status of the helping person is not as important as the helper's belief that people have the capacity to grow. Therefore the interviewer, the counselor, and the psychotherapist may differ in characteristics such as their level of training and extensiveness of experience, in the functions they perform, and in the settings in which they work, but they all must develop the same basic skills of observation, listening, and responding. In addition to these basic skills are the more specific communication skills that the counselor uses to clarify ideas, to convey the meaning or feeling, and to indicate that the client's message has been received accurately.

Paraphrasing and summarizing

The interviewer has to learn what the client is conveying. This does not imply that the client's word meanings are the same as the counselor's but that the counselor is able to listen so well as to understand the client's frame of reference. In other words, the helper is on the client's wavelength. The alert counselor makes every effort to understand and to share understanding with the client.

Paraphrasing and clarification. Paraphrasing is a form of translation. The message receiver (the listener) rewords what he or she has just heard to pull together the chief points. The primary purpose of paraphrasing is to make clear what has been said by restating what the message sender (the speaker) has said. Repeating, highlighting, and coordinating are interrelated characteristics of paraphrasing.

Repeating. In some instances, paraphrasing merely repeats.

MANNY: I have a galloping case of depression. Emptiness just grows. The hollow yearning for something runs through me more and more frequently. There are no

---

Place check under one of the levels for *each* characteristic. The genuineness level equals the total number of checks under each category divided by 3, the total number of categories. This is the average level of all the characteristics.

	EXAMPLE:	Congruence	Level 1
		Self-disclosure	Level 2
		Confrontation	Level 2
			Total = 5
			Divided by 3 = 1.7 (level 1+)

Characteristics	Levels				
	1	2	3*	4	5
Congruence (correspondence)					
Self-disclosure					
Confrontation					
Total No. of checks under each category					

*Minimum facilitative level

Fig. 7-12. Score sheet for genuineness scale.

more daily dividends of joy, not even my quiet feeling. I feel remote, even here with you. Confused, just confused. A prisoner of my depression. *(Stops talking suddenly and leans forward to look at the counselor, Ms. R.)*

MS. R.: Depression? (Or "Prisoner of depression?")

Paraphrasing by repeating is the least complicated method used to focus the client's attention on certain aspects of the communication. By repeating one or several words the counselor shows that he or she is listening. The counselor also steers the client to continue a particular direction of discussion.

A flow of repetition, however, results in a dull and probably less effective session. Clients who are exposed to too frequent repetition sometimes ask, "Don't you hear me?" or "Something wrong with the words I use?" A greater variety of responses requires deliberate listening and keener "headwork" on the part of the counselor in order to catch the feeling and meaning of the client's remarks.

Highlighting. Another form of paraphrasing requires that the counselor concentrate on the client's train of thought. In highlighting, the counselor emphasizes the main points in several of the client's last remarks. These counselor comments may not be in the sequence in which the client has just expressed them but in accordance with a theme the counselor has begun to notice. Ms. R. might respond to Manny by saying:

MS. R.: Hmmmmm. A galloping case of depression, confined by depression. No more joy, just isolation and emptiness.

By means of highlighting the counselor pulls together and repeats several of the client's words or phrases. The difference between shallow repeating and purposeful highlighting lies in detecting the recurrent theme of the ideas in the client's last statements. Highlighting serves to assure Manny that Ms. R. is trying to see events through his eyes. It also draws Manny's attention to the central concerns in his statements.

Coordinating. Contrary to repeating one or more words or to highlighting the main points of the client's statements, coordinating is the process of organizing and rewording the client's message. The counselor tackles the coordinating procedure cautiously so that the meaning of the client's statements is kept intact. Ms. R. would coordinate Manny's outlook as follows:

MS. R.: Sounds like you're telling me that your depression is increasing rapidly and is becoming more annoying . . . and you are seeking something—something that will break up the emptiness with a comforting feeling.

Changing some of the words may have altered the poetic sound of Manny's statement, but the counselor's message still carries the meaning of his comments. Ms. R. emphasizes Manny's increasingly annoying depression and his hope for a change in his feelings. Although she may not comment on the way in which Manny presents his thoughts, that is, his particular choice of words, she remembers and records these words. These words may have some bearing on Manny's distress and on the quality of his contact with social realities, even though at this counseling moment she is unable to determine the significance of his words.

Exercise 7-12 provides an opportunity to practice the three types of paraphrasing just discussed.

Summarization. Summarization overlaps with paraphrasing. Clarification is sought by feeding back to the client the substance of what he or she has been talking about. The primary difference between paraphrasing and summarizing is the amount of material covered. Paraphrasing concentrates on the client's immediate comment; summarization restates what the client has been saying during an entire counseling session or a series of counseling sessions. Another difference is that paraphrasing concentrates on the idea content rather than the feelings expressed, whereas summarization may pull together ideas, feelings, or both.

Summarization of content. The counselor may summarize the themes and thus the meaning of the client's discussion. This summarization may occur at the beginning, at the end, or sometimes during the counseling session.

At the beginning of the session the counselor starts the conversation by recalling the main ideas of the previous interview or series of interviews. The client is urged to continue where the prior session stopped. Summarization at the beginning of a session is of particular value if the client is having some difficulty in starting the conversation. This review also aids the client in noting what has been expressed so far on a particular topic.

Either the client or the counselor may summarize. The counselor may seek to encourage the client to summarize by saying "Do you recall what we talked about the last time we met? Try to recap it. It will help us go ahead from our ending point."

When the counselor decides it would be best for him or her to summarize, the counselor might initiate the summary with "If I recall correctly, you were saying at our last session . . . " The counselor prefaces the remarks with "If I recall correctly . . . " or "If I understood what you said . . . " to leave the way open for the client to correct any errors in the counselor's understanding.

Summarization of feeling. Accuracy in condensing the feelings the client expresses during one or more sessions depends on whether the counselor has been intensively and sensitively tuned into the client's feeling "vibes." One difference between summarization and reflection of feelings is the time span and the range of feelings covered. Both reflection and summarization of feelings pursue clarification for the client and the counselor. In sum-

Exercise 7-12
HOW DO YOU PARAPHRASE? *(may be done alone and discussed in a group)*

Time: APPROXIMATELY 20 MINUTES

For 10 minutes write your paraphrases of Ms. H.'s following statements in the form of repeating, highlighting, and coordinating. Discuss your responses with others in your group for 10 minutes.

MS. H.: Ms. M., I've heard about you from my friend, Zita Camshum. She says she belongs to the same women's liberation group as you do. Been reading books about women's liberation movement and am more and more angered by the marketing outlook of many, no, I mean most, men. "What's a woman got to give?" "Why should a woman take away a man's job?" That's what I hear them saying. So my consciousness is raised. Now I see how I have been exploited by the masculinist. Hell, I've got ideas. I've got skills. Not feminine ideas, not feminine skills—just ideas, just skills . . . no sexism with them. So where am I at? Beginning to be torn between husband, home, children, and me. Does it have to be this way?

Exercise 7-13
HOW DO YOU SUMMARIZE CONTENT AND FEELINGS? *(may be done alone and discussed in a group)*

Time: APPROXIMATELY 20 MINUTES

Read the comments of Ms. H. described in Exercise 7-12. Then write summarization of content and of the feelings expressed in Ms. H.'s remarks. Discuss your responses with others in your group.

marization, however, the feelings discussed involve an entire session or series of sessions and also include a wider variety of feelings.

Empathic understanding is necessary for this review of feelings. The counselor who is attending to the client notices the consistent patterns of positive, negative, and/or ambivalent emotions (Chapter 3). When summarizing, the counselor must be wide awake and sharp-witted to correctly echo the client's feelings.

Since errors in summarizing feelings are possible, the wise counselor adds to the summarizing remarks: "I think you have been telling me you feel . . . Does it seem this way to you?" or "The feeling you expressed in the last few sessions made me think you . . ."

Exercise 7-13 uses Ms. H.'s comments in Exercise 7-12 to practice summarizing content and feelings.

Reflection

Recognition and reflection of feelings may help the client become aware of the degree to which behavior is molded by his or her feelings. Reflection is a very difficult expressive response to accomplish and should not be attempted by the untrained individual. Accurate reflection depends on skills of attentive listening and empathic understanding.

Explanation of reflection. Reflection is often referred to as the Rogerian mirror. The technique of reflecting feelings was first clarified in Carl Rogers' book *Counseling and Psychotherapy* (1942).

Definition. Reflection is more than echoing the feelings that the client has put into words. It is the act of uncovering and making known in fresh words the feelings that lie within the client's comments. Thus the counselor brings the client's feelings to the client's attention without adding or subtracting from what the client is saying.

TOM: All I keep thinking is "Man, you blew it. You got the dream but not the drive." I'll end up hangin' 'round the shopping center with all the other freaks.
MR. A.: I hear you saying that you're feeling pretty hopeless at this point.

Reflection and other expressive skills. Reflection borders on summarization of feelings and confrontation. Reflection of feelings is a step beyond summarization. In reflection the counselor feeds back those feelings the client has just labeled and also labels the intent of the feelings the client has described in ideas. Summarization of feeling merely pulls together the feelings that the client has labeled during one or more sessions. The following is an example of reflection of feeling:

STAN (a Vietnam veteran): So many years ago and still need to erase their faces as we shot them down. Want to forget their twisting and turning, their death dance . . . to forget the shot of pleasure when I killed my first 15-year-old for democracy.
DR. R.: Yes, I know what you mean. I was there. The guilt gnaws at you.

If Dr. R. were summarizing Stan's feelings, he would have waited until Stan stated his theme of guilt over a longer period of conversation. If Stan has been speaking of feelings similar to those in his preceding statement, Dr. R. might summarize the feelings as follows:

DR. R.: I hear you saying that you want to *forget*, to forget the look on their faces as they died, the pleasure you felt when you killed your first 15-year-old—forget the memories.

A form of reflection that goes beyond reflection of feeling and approximates confrontation is reflection of experience. The reflection of the client's experience focuses on contradictions between what the client says and what the client shows by nonverbal cues. The client is faced with the discrepancy between his or her words and feelings. Confrontation delves further into the similarities, differences, and confusions that the client is and has been expressing in ideas and feelings over one or more sessions.

Types of reflection. Reflection "puts feelings on the line" so that the client may become more aware of them as well as realize that it is OK to feel. The counselor works at sending the client the message, "I am here to share the burden of your feelings with you until you are prepared to shoulder them alone. I am with you, trying very hard to understand how you feel.'' In this way reflection increases the client-counselor involvement.

Reflection of feelings. Recognition and reflection of feelings help the client to inspect feelings and to note how they relate to behavior. The counselor's empathic understanding and skillful approach in reflecting these feelings are of paramount importance. Not only may possible distortion irritate the client, but even suitable and accurate verbal reflection may result in an increase in the client's unpleasant feelings. When the counselor's reflection is acceptable to the client, it supports the client's further exploration of feelings.

The client hears his or her feelings discussed twice. First the client remarks directly and/or indirectly about these feelings. Then the counselor, who accepts and respects the client, describes the client's feelings. This double exposure helps clear up any undercurrents of sadness, anger, frustration, and dejection suggested in the client's word content. Reflection of feeling provides opportunity for the client's self-understanding but is not the primary goal of counseling. The client must learn both to trust the expression of feeling and to control emotional behavior.

When reflecting the client's feelings, the counselor usually precedes the remark with ''You feel,'' ''You think,'' ''You seem to feel,'' ''You sound as if,'' or ''I hear you say.'' The counselor, Mr. A., illustrates reflection of feeling in his comments to Bonnie:

BONNIE: How do you tell a big-shit, white, businessman churning it up in a motel that you're not for hire . . . working as a maid, a black maid, cleaning up his damned mess. Then he offers me . . . *(Begins to sob.)*

MR. A.: Angry, I hear your anger, and I hear frustration. I do understand. Are you also asking how to handle a white man's prejudice?

From the moment that the counselor begins to reflect the client's feelings, he assures the client that he is not just a spectator in this interpersonal transaction. Often the counselor goes a step beyond the role of spectator, to that of participant and sharer of experiences.

Reflection of experience. In reflecting experience the counselor advances to more complex helping. The counselor tells the client, ''I am listening to you very carefully. I am looking at you intently. I not only sense your feelings, but I hear and see that what you say and what your eyes, hands, body do just don't fit together.'' By means of this thought process the counselor becomes more than an echo or a mirror; the counselor now shares his or her own experiences *of* the client *with* the client.

Other terms that may be used for reflection of experience are ''congruence'' and ''genuineness.'' All three refer to the consistency between what the client says and what is implied by the client's facial expression, gestures, and tone of voice. Inconsistency between the client's or the counselor's verbal behavior and nonverbal signals often indicates that the individual is not prepared to be open about some aspects of experience.

Such absence of consistency on the part of counselors sets limits to their empathic understanding, since they are unable to be honest and direct in what they convey. Lack of honesty and directness is also suggested for inconsistent clients who, like the counselors, feel threatened by the counseling situation and consequently wrap themselves up in a tightly protective, uncommunicative package.

To determine the client's level of consistency or congruence, the counselor listens to the client's words and observes his or her posture, gestures, eyes, and tone of voice. Then the counselor brings to the client's attention the contradictions in what the client says he or she feels and what the counselor notes the client's nonverbal language is ''saying'' (see Example 7-3).

Example 7-3
THE WORDS AND ACTS DON'T MATCH

[1]

MS. B.: You say that you are happy about your new job, but you clench your fists and your eyes seem to tell me you're hurting.

[2]

DR. T.: I wonder whether you know that whenever you talk about how wonderful your mother is, your lips begin to quiver and your brow wrinkles.

On some occasions counselors may go even further and express their own feelings about the client's behavior. They may say, "I know you just said you want to 'let yourself go' to enjoy life . . . but then you lean back in your chair and hold onto the arms. I wonder? I feel uncomfortable because you are so sad. Yet, I get the feeling that you won't let yourself *feel* any other feelings."

When counselors are forthright in their own feelings about the client's responses, they risk more than when they merely reflect the incongruence in what the client says and does. They not only risk being incorrect in the reflection but also risk exposure of their personal feelings. In other words, the counselors make themselves vulnerable to an attack on their feelings. Only experienced counselors, well grounded in theory and nourished by supervised practice, who are congruent themselves can successfully share experiences with the client.

Since reflection calls for highly developed skills, the beginning counselor is more apt to commit errors in reflecting. These errors relate to the more mechanical problem associated with timing as well as to the more complicated results of misunderstanding the client's meaning.

Errors in reflecting. Four forms of errors of reflecting are considered: timing, worn-thin phrases, too deep or too shallow responses, and adding or subtracting. Since these are interrelated, the beginning counselor frequently exhibits more than one.

Timing. The error of timing, which on the surface appears simple to avoid, is a constant difficulty. The greatest barrier to learning the "when" of reflecting stems from the lack of development of other skills such as attending to and understanding what the client says in addition to identifying feelings.

The essential generality about timing is that the

counselor should not wait too long to reflect the client's feelings or the client may become confused by too many diverse feelings. At times, therefore, the counselor may need to interrupt the client's flow of words to focus on some important feelings.

Aside from this basic generality, the timing of reflection also depends on the counselor's empathic understanding of the client's life-style, of the meaning of the client's words, of the significance of the client's actions, and of the underlying feelings. The alert counselor makes certain that the client is ready for a comment. Readiness is not solely determined by when the client stops talking but also by when the client has conveyed a feeling that seems to need clarification.

Suitable and unsuitable timing are contrasted in Example 7-4.

Example 7-4
MAKING THE TIMING FIT THE HELPING NEEDS

[1]

ROGER: Wow, you're a great counselor! Man, no one has been able to get to me as well as you do. Really want to stop speeding up [use of methedrine, a form of amphetamine]. I feel great! Used to get all uptight and . . .

MR. J.: Hold it, man, you're laying it on thick. Let's put it on the table. Feel good, want to stop. Swell, man, swell. Hearing something else though, coming from your drawn eyes, your pull-in body, your tightly clenched arms. Level with me.

[2]

SEPH: You don't understand, how could you? Pig-lover, in with the cops, whaddya know about the street? That's where it's at—slaughter jungle. Nowhere, man, nowhere. No bread [money]—pieces of living. Gotta fox [woman]. Coke [cocaine] . . . sick with no dope. Whaddya know?

DR. K.: It seems to me that you are jumping to conclusions. I *do* understand. You believe all people are the same. You're angry, very angry. Isn't it time you looked at all this another way?

It should be noted that Dr. K. is missing the intense feeling of frustration and depression Seph is expressing. Seph's comments result in a standoff that permits him to avoid full responsibility for his actions. Since there are elements of truth in what Seph is saying, Dr. K. misses the meaning by calling attention only to the anger expressed. It would have been more productive timing if Dr. K. had stopped Seph's rambling at an earlier point, when he was revealing the hopelessness of his relationship with Dr. K. An honest admission by Dr. K. of his feeling of discomfort and his lack of knowledge of the street would have placed both Seph and Dr. K. on a more even relationship. Another essential feeling that Dr. K. missed was Seph's remark that he is a street addict. This is a crucial factor, since the street addict often relates more readily to his peers than to authority figures, as represented by Dr. K.

Worn-thin phrases. The frequency of timing errors is surpassed only by the rut some counselors dig themselves by means of monotonously using the same canned phrase to begin their remarks. "You feel" is the worst offender in this respect. The beginning of the counselor's remarks is worn thin by overuse. When the counselor regularly initiates comments reflecting feelings with any one phrase, the result is either a client's deaf ear or an annoyed comment. These routine starters are used automatically. The very fact that they are automatic detracts from their impact and suggests that the counselor is doing too little "headwork."

Many other introductory phrases are available to provide some variation. Some of these are "You sure are," "It seems that you feel," "You believe," "Do I hear you say you feel," "As I get it, you feel that," "It sounds like," "In other words, you feel . . . , is that it?" and "Mmmhmmmm, I see; you're saying."

In addition to these openers, the counselor may come directly to the point of the feeling expressed by labeling the emotion as in Example 7-5.

Example 7-5
IDENTIFYING EMOTIONAL BEHAVIOR

DELORES: If I have to clean up after these kids one more time, I think I'll kill myself. Need some time alone. Someone older than 5 to talk to. Blood pressure is soaring . . . tired of it all.
MS. F.: Uptight, frustrated, depressed . . . that's what I hear you saying. Let's get into this. Tell me more about what you would rather be doing.

Another possible counselor response to Delores might have been, "I gather that you've had it. You sound frustrated, depressed, and lonely."

Too deep or too shallow responses. Improper timing and worn-thin phrases may occur more frequently but are less difficult errors to overcome than the counselor's lack of sensitivity to the depth of the client's feelings. When counselors load their response to the client's remarks too heavily (too deep) or tend not to go far enough in their response (too shallow), they reveal lack of understanding and/or inadequate expressive skills. One factor that may result in an inappropriate counselor response might be the counselor's level of regard for the client. The level of regard refers to the degree of respect and positive feelings (affective responses) that one individual has for another.

The counselor's reflection would most likely be inaccurate if his or her feelings toward the client were negative, too positive, or even neutral. Negative feelings arise when the counselor finds the client unappealing, distasteful, or objectionable. Neutral responses occur when the client just leaves the counselor cold and uninvolved. Too positive responses are just as serious, since the counselor is apt to become too involved and overidentify with the client. Either extreme, negative or positive regard, or neutral regard contributes to too deep or too shallow a reflection of feeling and/or experiences. Furthermore, the counselor whose regard varies with the client's moods is likely to communicate these changing feelings through too deep or too shallow reflections.

A consistent level of regard that leans toward positive feelings for the client encourages more accurate reflections. Adequate regard, empathic understanding, and satisfactory expressive skills turn out reflections that neither go beyond what the client intends (too deep) nor are less than the client implies (too shallow). Example 7-6 shows the contrast between too deep and too shallow reflection.

Example 7-6
REFLECTION: SHALLOW, DEEP, MORE SUITABLE

CHUCK: Where do I go from here? Wish I were different. Want to get into law yet don't feel in the bookgrind mood.

[1]

MS. O.: I hear you say you're feeling that you want to be a lawyer but you would rather not study. *(Too shallow)*

[2]

MS. O.: Chuck, I hear you say you're distressed because you are different, confused by your conflict. You want to study law but feel antagonistic toward the rigor of books. *(Too deep)*

[3]

MS. O.: Chuck, I hear you say you feel uncertain about whether you really want to get into the book scene . . . yet you are interested in law. *(Preferable response)*

Adding or subtracting. The counselor who tacks a thought or feeling onto the client's comments may be evidencing lack of skill, an attempt to exhibit counseling power, or several other failings. This error in reflection is similar to the too deep reflective remark. Subtracting from the client's meaning or feelings is similar to the too shallow reflective expression. The counselor does not understand or does not listen carefully and so misses something important in what the client is saying.

The dissimilarity between adding and subtracting and too deep and too shallow remarks comes from the fact that in adding and subtracting the actual meaning of the client's statement is distorted. In too deep and too shallow remarks the meaning is not lost but the feelings are not responded to appropriately. (See Example 7-7.)

Exercise 7-14 deals with the avoidance of errors in reflecting.

Example 7-7
ADDING AND SUBTRACTING COMMUNICATIONS

DONNA: I just can't see myself as a librarian all my life. It makes me feel hemmed in. I need a job where I move around and see people.

[1]

MR. I.: You don't think you could be tied down to the clerical work, the routines, the mechanical aspect of library work. What you need is a fast-moving job so you won't feel so restricted. Satisfaction of your need for people is vital to you. *(Adding)*

[2]

MR. I.: You just don't like being a librarian. *(Subtracting)*

[3]

MR. I.: I hear you saying you're feeling so uptight you don't know whether you can stand it much longer. You seem to want to break loose so you may meet more people. *(Too deep)*

Exercise 7-14
HOW DO YOU AVOID ERRORS IN REFLECTING? *(may be done alone and discussed in a group)*

Time: APPROXIMATELY 35 MINUTES

Write counselor responses for the following client remarks. For client remark No. 1 show subtracting and too shallow responses; for client remark No. 2 show worn-thin phrases, adding, and too deep responses; and for client remark No. 3 show inappropriate timing and too deep responses. Also write a suitable response to each client. After you have completed writing your responses, discuss them in your larger group for 15 minutes.

[1] "I cannot help but pity my child. Twelve years old and he can hardly make himself understood; he has cerebral palsy [motor disturbance due to nonprogressive damage to the brain]. I'm sad about him, yet so ashamed—want to hide him."

[2] "The nighttime is when it's worse. I have the same recurring nightmare—being choked. Wake up suddenly in a sweat, frightened, panic."

[3] "Something I can't seem to help. Walk along the street and eye every man. Sex is my joy, the only act that turns me on. Think about it all of the time."

[4]

MR. I.: You feel you want a new job so you will be around people. *(Too shallow)*

[5]

MR. I.: Want to stop feeling hemmed in. You really are ready to start thinking about a new job, one that will have more to do with people. *(More suitable response)*

Confrontation

The term "confrontation" has the tint of antagonism. Yet to confront suggests a much broader range of feelings. When the word "confront" is traced to its Latin roots, *con* is found to come from *com,* meaning "together" and *front* from *frons,* meaning "forehead" or "front." The original meaning of the word is to face, stand, or meet face to face. There are also three other meanings: to face or oppose boldly, defiantly, or antagonistically; to bring face to face; and to set side by side to compare. From these various definitions the concept of confrontation acquires negative hints of antagonism, positive glimmers of honest communication, and suggestions of objective gathering of facts for comparisons.

All these definitions are used when one considers confrontation as an expressive skill. As an expressive skill confrontation implies one additional thought; that is, the counselor confronts the client to close a gap that the counselor feels is separating the client from deeper self-exploration or from the counselor as a participant in the counseling session.

As an expressive skill confrontation is a form of communication that may be defined as a process

Fig. 7-13. Confrontation. (From Hernandez, C.A., Haug, M.J., and Wagner, N.N., editors: Chicanos: social and psychological perspectives, ed. 2, St. Louis, 1976, The C.V. Mosby Co.)

of calling attention to and/or challenging another person. This act brings the client face to face with the following:

- ☐ Discrepancies between the counselor's observations of the client's behavior and the client's statements about experiences and feelings
- ☐ Some facts about self the client does not know or experiences only vaguely
- ☐ Something the client knows but thinks others don't know

These differences between the open and closed areas of the person's self-concept are described more fully in Chapter 1 (see discussion of Johari's window).

The counselor who functions at higher levels often confines comments (confrontations) to the client's adequacies and resources rather than to the client's shortcomings. Furthermore, confrontation is a reciprocal process insofar as the counselor becomes vulnerable to the client's counterconfrontation. Thus both the client and the counselor may become unmasked by means of the tactic of "undenial"—confrontation that "tells it like it is."

No matter how constructive the confrontation, it still has a tendency to cause distress; the counselor must have well-developed empathic understanding to assess what should be uncovered, when this recognition should be revealed, and how the screen of denial, aversion, and deception should be removed. Surprise, humor, and sometimes a forceful manner become channels by which the client's awareness is sharpened. Confrontation may be approached in a light vein with a simple question, "I wonder?" or may tend toward a direct frontal attack such as "Cut the bull!"

Forms of confrontation. Confrontation pulls up short the confronted person. Some act of the confronter, of which he or she may or may not be aware, is a stimulus for the other person. This act of confrontation has many forms, which may either promote growth or be destructive.

Confrontation may vary from a light challenge to the client to examine and mobilize resources for deeper self-recognition or constructive action in his or her own behalf to a thrust that may temporarily disturb the client's personal and social equilibrium. Daytop, Synanon, and some of the marathon groups are more likely to replace tact with brutal frankness. Although the "hot seat" is not comfortable, punishment is not the primary intention of the attack. Instead, in this electric group no holds are barred, and everyone undergoes the same penetrating and attacking scrutiny. Each individual is brought face to face with what others think and feel about him or her.

Communication may become more or less confronting, depending on the people involved; the words, gestures, and tone of voice used; and the time when the particular remarks are made. In addition, confrontation may be favorable and pleasant (positive) or unfavorable and repugnant (negative); it may respect individuals for their humanness (unconditional) or for what they do (conditional). Confrontation also can be a symbol of one human touching another verbally or by means of nonverbal language (stroking).

General purposes of confrontation. Long ago in Plato's "Apology" Socrates was quoted as follows: "I say again that daily to discourse about virtue and of those other things about which you hear me examining myself and others, is the greatest good of man and that the unexamined life is not worth living." Synanon adds another thought to the purpose of confrontation. When what a person claims to be doing does not show in the person's behavior, Synanon challenges this person with the criticism that he or she is "talking the talk but not walking the walk." Embedded in the two preceding quotes, which are centuries apart, are the purposes of confrontation.

Self-exploration. The essential purpose of confrontation is to produce suitable circumstances that encourage an individual to look at and hopefully to find ways to change his or her behavior. Confrontation is an invitation to examine oneself and to reflect on one's behavior. The primary objective of confrontation is to free the confronted individual rather than to restrict, punish, or destroy this person.

In order to avert increased self-depreciation,

comments about weaknesses or limitations should be accompanied by comments about strengths or resources. Telling a person "You talk too much" can be devastating if the statement is not combined with "You have important ideas to contribute to the discussion. I wonder, are you aware that you talk so much that others don't have a chance for their contributions?"

Self-exploration may arise from some feelings of discomfort by the individual or from the remarks of others. In either situation the value of confrontation comes from its immediacy and pertinence to the person's problems.

When someone else originates the confrontation he may say, "It seems to me that . . . I wonder how it seems to you?" Whenever counselors confront a client, they control the event by means of their selection of what they say or do (verbal and nonverbal cues). Because of their empathic understanding of the client, they are alert to what the client is ready to hear and what would be better omitted. Counselors confront clients to focus their attention on a situation, not to mold them into a preconceived notion of what is right for them.

When clients attempt self-exploration, they turn to the counselor, with whom they feel they may safely explore themselves and their difficulties. The clients may need a relationship of trust and honesty that they feel they do not experience in daily activities. In such an atmosphere clients discharge accumulated frustrations and begin to confront their role and responsibility in these frustrations. Whether these revelations become an active surge toward discovery of routes for behavior change or result in inhibiting the clients depends on the counselor's skill in the give and take of confrontation.

Confrontation that leads to self-exploration is, in essence, a process of reality-testing, with the ultimate goals of more effective intrapersonal (self-satisfying) and interpersonal (socially satisfying) living. In order to move toward these goals it is necessary to help clients remove the screen through which they see themselves and their experiences. Freud considered this as forcing the unconscious into consciousness.

In some instances this self-exploration may require the realization that the supposed freedom of choice an individual believes he or she has is actually compulsive behavior. Mary, for example, who says that she will date whomever she pleases, no matter what race or religion or "whatever my mother doesn't like," may be just as tied down by trying to do the opposite of what her mother demands as if she were adhering closely to her mother's requests. The question for Mary to examine would be "How do you want to restrict your freedom, by self-imposed compulsions or mother-imposed demands? What other solutions are available for you?" Mary is not told what to do; she is just confronted with the reality of her choice.

Another example of confrontation is of particular importance for individuals who are physically disabled or even temporarily ill. In either event the individuals must be confronted with their existing limitations. Then the individuals explore for themselves the ways in which they must learn to live in the limits of their disability or illness as well as the possibilities for them *in spite of* their limitations. At an even higher level of confrontation disabled individuals may be helped to realize that they are able to express themselves even better *because of* the disability, for they have gained a broader and deeper understanding of living. Then the clients can focus on abilities rather than on disabilities.

Behavioral change. Self-exploration initiated by confrontation is the foundation for behavioral change. For behavioral change to occur, the individual must go beyond self-examination to self-challenge and/or challenge by others. Before behavioral change may come about, the individual must develop an awareness of the behavior that should be changed (self-exploration) and also the alternatives for change from which he or she may select. Confrontation provides the necessary challenge to the client. The counselor underlines how his or her experiencing of the client and the client's expression of his or her own experience are dissimilar. The counselor says to the client, "You say you're perfectly satisfied with your sexual relationships with your present husband. How, then, do you explain what you said after your recent 'fling' with your former husband?''

Self-exploration and behavioral change are forerunners to becoming oneself more fully. The counselor confronts the client with ideas or feelings of which the client is oblivious or is avoiding. By awakening the client to these hidden areas the counselor strives to initiate or to improve the client-counselor relationship or to open pathways toward solutions of the client's problems. This encouragement to action plus the challenge to the client to integrate, to become one with his or her experiences, offers the client the opportunity to become more fully sincere and in contact with self, strengths, and resources as well as self-destructive behavior.

Becoming oneself more fully. A continuous theme throughout this discussion of confrontation differentiates confrontation from other skills of communication. This difference stems from the fact that confrontation acts more as an initiator of new directions for the client (an act) than as a response to the client (a reaction). Confrontation does more leading than following; it steers the client away from the self-fulfilling prophecy behavior that makes him or her become a loser, a helpless and pathetic failure. The counselor charges the client to consider, ''How much failing would you avoid if you honestly told your boss he gives you too much work? Look at what you do. You take on more work to outdo the others because you think you have to prove that you are not a loser. Then you find you can't finish. So you feel that you are a failure, and you do fail to finish. So you've proved to yourself and to others—you are a loser. You're throwing your own boomerang. Do you see that?''

The counselor confronts clients to spur them on to remove their ''front.'' The counselor helps clients either accept themselves as they are or find a new self-image, a new way of behaving, that would be more satisfying. In this way the counselor seeks the clients' increased awareness and acceptance of their identity as an outcome of confrontation.

Stopping game behavior. The falsity that *game behavior* produces in interpersonal transactions is another target for confrontation. Alcoholics Anonymous speaks of the ''stinkin' thinkin' '' of those members who play the rationalizing game. Berne (1964) writes of the numerous social games in which individuals indulge. Although certain games are expected because of the conventions of social living, blind adherence to these rituals or game behavior that becomes a way of life interferes with fulfilling living.

''Calling the other's behavior'' to stop game playing can be a troublesome confrontation. If the effort to stop game interaction is not handled competently, calling attention to it may reinforce it and result in branching out into further games.

Forms of games. The games people play are endless, and the ways to cope with these games vary.

The sick game. Clients may use ''symptoms'' to cover up their real intentions. The client may be so tired, nervous, upset, and misunderstood that he or she is unable to work. The client actually wishes to stop working and to live a slow, leisurely pace but is unable to do so because of certain obligations or certain feelings about the work ethic.

The sick game has many variations. A young child may say that his throat feels ''sore'' and so he can't attend school that day and at frequent intervals thereafter. A wife who has nightly ''headaches'' may be unable to understand why her husband is annoyed with her lack of sexual response. The man who ''just can't find the woman who could take care of him'' may actually find most women annoying. Each of these individuals hides a game under certain conventions; the counselor must listen carefully to pick up the subtle messages that conceal the problems. Individuals play games to manipulate the people around them so that they may accomplish their goals.

The helpless game. Many individuals indulge in the pastime of helplessness for their own amusement or to score points with someone. Students ask questions for which they know the answers. They question because they have ''psyched'' the professor who enjoys the superior status of answerer. This kind of game is not serious unless it becomes the primary way in which an individual relates to other people. At times the helpless game becomes involved in such serious phobic behavior (excessive and unreasonably overwhelming fears) that the victim becomes unable to remain alone in a room or to walk out of doors alone. Clients do indeed become prisoners of their own symptoms.

The insight game. This game is much more subtle and possibly more manipulative than the sick or the helpless game. On the surface it appears that the individuals are seeking better understanding of their problems. They keep searching for greater insight. However, the search is endless, for the individuals are actually defending their present behavior by means of their quest. They appear to be making progress as they grasp each new insight, yet this is just an illusion to keep them safe from change. The insight game is similar to intellectualization and often is associated with emotional insulation.

■ ■ ■

There are many more games, some of them everyday social events and others barriers to effective living. Some games should not be changed, for individuals have such a strong inclination for their game behavior that without their games they would function at a lower level. On the other hand, the three games just mentioned are often stumbling blocks in the counseling situation that detract from the client's ability to move toward self-fulfillment. Skillful, empathic confrontation at a suitable time may draw the game player toward more constructive behavior.

Game coping. There is a risk in confrontation, but without it there may be no further growth for the client. The risk is increased even more if an untrained, inexperienced, and therefore unskilled individual attempts confrontation.

Knowing the game one is playing does not in itself make it possible to change. After the counselor confronts the client with the game behavior, alternative behaviors must be offered for change.

Withdrawal of reinforcement, calling the game, and the asocial response (Beier, 1966) are three interrelated methods of coping with game behavior.

The client whose behavior becomes bizarre may be playing a particular type of the sick game. Ignoring this client when he or she puts slacks on inside out, is unwashed, or has uncombed hair is a form of withdrawal of reinforcement. The client is also ignored when he or she jumbles words at high speed so that the speech cannot be understood. By ignoring the client's inappropriate behavior (nonreinforcement) and attending to the client's appropriate behavior (positive reinforcement) the counselor attempts to weaken and eventually to extinguish the socially destructive behavior.

The counselor calls the client's game when, instead of ignoring, he or she brings certain inconsistencies to the client's attention, as described in Example 7-8.

Example 7-8
PROJECTING THE GAME

[1]

The client implies that someone else must change before the problem can be solved.

TOM: If only my wife wouldn't make so many demands on me, I wouldn't drink.
MR. O.: Ten years you've been drinking, Tom. You've been married for 5. How come you drank before you were married?

[2]

The client suggests that past events force him or her to act as he or she does.

WILMA: My mother was just like that. I know I'm like her. She and my father would argue about such petty things as how high or how low the window shade should be. Then she would get more and more upset . . . throw up . . . my father would shut up. I'm just like her.
DR. N.: Are you saying that you can't be different just because of your mother?

In both instances in Example 7-8 the counselor strives to confront the client by interrupting the associations the client brings forth in support of the game behavior. This is not done to condemn the client but rather to confront the client with new ways of looking at the behavior.

Beier writes of the "beneficial uncertainty" he establishes when he removes himself from the client's game with an asocial statement. This asocial statement is a shocker that brings the client up short. The client is uncertain about what the counselor is trying to accomplish. However, in the beneficial atmosphere of the acceptant, nonthreatening counseling session, the client is more likely to attain greater freedom of response. The asocial response (Example 7-9) does not fit into the usual rituals required by conventional conversation, and the client must do a fast turnabout to a new trend of discussion.

Example 7-9
THE ASOCIAL RESPONSE

[1]

TED: You're a jerk. You don't understand anything.
MR. R.: Aren't you foolish talking to a jerk who doesn't understand?

[2]

MARTHA: Hey! Wait a minute. I think you're manipulating me.
MR. T.: So?

Underlying the counselor's remarks is a challenge to encourage the client to spread the nature of interactions. In the supportive counselor-client relationship the counselor confronts the client with the offbeat remark so that the client must rise to new ways of relating. This asocial response also has the effect of inducing cognitive dissonance.

Reducing cognitive dissonance. The word "cognitive" comes from the Latin *cog-nascere,* meaning "to get to know"; " dissonance" stems from the Latin *dissonant,* meaning "disagrees in sound" and therefore out of harmony. Hence cognitive dissonance refers to the process of receiving information (getting to know) that is not harmonious (dissonant) with one's already existing beliefs and/or knowledge. Confrontation induces this state of conflict when beliefs or assumptions are challenged by the contradictory information the counselor presents to the client.

When this dissonance occurs, clients feel uncomfortable and seek to correct the difference between what they believe and the new information by convincing themselves that the differences do not exist (denial or intellectualization), by adopting some other kind of defensive coping strategies (rationalizing), or by controlling the flow of information (withdrawal or fantasizing). It is the counselor's responsibility to help clients over this distress of cognitive dissonance so that the experience is helpful rather than destructive. One way to do this is to suggest new actions that contradict the negative attitudes.

The assumption underlying the promotion of new actions is that changing behavior induces a change in attitudes. The individual who complains of inability to speak on the telephone because of stuttering is urged to make phone calls. Although the act of phoning does not cure the stuttering, the successful act, if repeated, gradually decreases the withdrawal attitude.

It is up to the counselor to confront clients with the facts that they distort or screen out so that they cannot continue to maintain and protect their misbeliefs. After this awareness the clients are assisted in engaging in the behavior they have avoided because it has created negative attitudes. When individuals commit themselves to certain behavior, they also make an effort to reduce the dissonance. Gradually the negative attitudes change, and the individuals decide that the behavior is not so bad after all.

Example 7-10 describes Bill, who committed himself to a change of behavior and in turn changed his attitudes toward himself.

Example 7-10
BILL MAKES THE CHANGE

A brief examination of Bill exemplifies how commitment altered both attitudes and certain self-destructive behavior.

Bill grew up in an affluent middle-class suburb.

Through high school he remained a conformist to the customs of the establishment. He wore his hair clipped short and dressed in the prescribed slacks with a belt, shoes below the ankle bone, and socks to match. He was, as he later stated, "a real square." He graduated from high school in 1966, wearing the traditional gown with the mortar board correctly placed on his still closely cut hair. He also bit his nails.

He went off to the conservative college he had selected. During his first year at college, away from the close scrutiny of his liberal, yet "square," parents, he encountered some new ideas. He discovered that smoking pot was not so bad. He found that the dudes with long hair whom he had avoided during high school were interesting and pleasant friends. By the end of his first year at college his hair was longer and he wore faded jeans and a tie-dyed tee shirt. Gradually his nonpolitical approach to life was disturbed by some of the injustices he heard about. The Vietnam War rattled his calm, yet his negative attitude toward participating in mass sitdowns continued. He also continued to bite his nails.

During his second year at college he joined a sensitivity group and met Raina. In the sensitivity group he voiced his anxieties and was confronted with disagreements, with a radical political philosophy, and with an acceptant, supportive atmosphere for change. He became aware of different viewpoints and very much aware of Raina. Raina's life-style was a free one. She reveled in experiences. She liked to travel. She enjoyed and was comfortable with people. She was distrustful of the way in which the government functioned. Bill and Raina had spritely conversations about their differing viewpoints. Bill began to wonder and still bit his nails.

The third year of college was a year of decision. Bill went on a trip and left his razor at college. After the itchy period of the newly sprouting face hair, a shaggy beard and moustache began to grow. The hair spread, and by the time he went home his parents were confronted by a shaggy-haired, bearded, tall young man whose ideas were more radical than theirs. He spoke of the blacks and the rip-off they experienced. He condemned the administration for the war. He joined demonstrations against the war. Bill had advanced from cognitive dissonance to a commitment, to behavior change. He was trying to let his nails grow.

College graduation was a hassle. Bill was pleased that he was graduating but resented the requirement that he wear a cap and gown. He decided to join several others who were protesting by sitting in the audience rather than participating in the ceremonies. He asked his parents to join him in the audience, and they complied with his wishes. He had stopped biting his nails for a few months but recently had begun to bite them again.

After graduation, Bill drove to the West Coast with some of his friends. They stopped at the homes of various friends, crash-padding along the way. He enjoyed the freedom of the trip and the company of his friends as they camped under the vast expanses of the open spaces. The stares of people at the shops where they bought their supplies did not disturb him as much as the reaction of the cousin of one of his friends at whose home they were supposed to stay overnight. The cousin asked them to leave because her husband hated long-haired hippie types. However, the support of his friends and their mutual annoyance made the twinges of distress less painful. He knew he would be likely to bite his nails.

Bill decided to move to the "haven of culture" and to his "kind of people" in Boston. He wanted a year of work before he decided what he would do next. Raina was still in his thoughts, but by this time they both had found other friends. Bill felt so different about everything. He moved into an apartment with some friends. Together they collected furnishings from Goodwill, The Salvation Army, parents, and other friends. He decided that he liked where he was at—that he liked what he was doing. He thought he would like to become a poverty lawyer. He decided to stop biting his nails and did just that.

Interpretation

Interpretation is another form of an expressive skill. The skill involved is more difficult to attain, since interpretation requires counselors to color their remarks with their own way of thinking. Thus counselors introduce their own frame of reference into the counseling session.

The challenge to counselors is immense. The counselors must state their view of the client's beliefs in language that the client can understand and, hopefully, accept. Therefore counselors must talk the client's talk even though they add a thought or view an idea somewhat differently.

Some counselors and psychotherapists cloak their interpretations in complex explanations about how the past explains the present. This grows out of the notion that the client's history accounts for the present story. These interpretations require extensive knowledge of symbolic formulas that link the past with the present.

Other counselors and psychotherapists seek interpretations based on the client's present behavior and the way in which the client sees the past in the here and now. The characteristics that tie all interpretations together are empathy, creativity, and well-developed listening skills.

Explanation of interpretation. Interpretation brings new facts or rearranges existing facts so that clients may see their behavior in a different light.

Definition. Interpretation is a suggestion that goes a little farther than the client's suggestions about his or her ideas and feelings. Interpretation is a contrast in which the counselor mixes together two or more of the client's dissimilar ideas.

A broad, general definition of interpretation is the slanting of the client's comments from another standpoint. This slant provides the basis for the client to view concerns with a fresh start. The counselor binds together the client's words and feelings with the counselor's altered choice of words, uniting these words with additional relevant information. Thus interpretation differs from:

- Paraphrasing, which focuses on repeating, highlighting, or coordinating of the content of the client's immediate conversation
- Summarization, which repeats, highlights, and coordinates the content and feelings of the client's conversation over an entire session or a series of sessions
- Reflection, which is the act of sharpening the client's attention to the feelings and experiences he or she is expressing
- Confrontation, which brings the client face to face with some gaps in what he or she is saying and/or some facts that may be vague or unknown to the client

Interpretation contains all the characteristics of the previously described expressive skills as well as something else. This something else is the particular meaning or significance added to the client's

discussions. Example 7-11 compares these expressive skills.

Example 7-11
THE VARIATION IN EXPRESSIVE SKILLS

STUDENT: I feel terrible, really worried, about being absent from class so much.

[1]

INSTRUCTOR: Worried because you've missed several classes. *(Paraphrase)*

[2]

INSTRUCTOR: You sound upset and worried. *(Reflection of feeling)*

[3]

INSTRUCTOR: Yes. You have had so many absences that your grade is very likely to be affected. What do you plan to do about it? *(Confrontation)*

[4]

INSTRUCTOR: You've missed so many classes . . . now you're worried about your grades. Have you thought about the possibility that you may actually be setting yourself to fail? *(Interpretation)*

In each response in Example 7-11 there are elements of observation, description of behavior, and explanation. In general, the primary purpose of interpretation is to provide clients with a new look at themselves and their problems.

Primary goals of interpretation. The working hypotheses present some guesses about the significance of the client's behavior so that the client may coordinate thoughts and feelings. In the process of coordinating thoughts and feelings the client attains a new outlook (reconstruction) of the meaning of his or her behavior. Finally, out of the original hypothesis, the coordination, and the reconstruction comes about an expansion of awareness and self-realization.

Hypothesis. The counselor explains his or her guesswork, or hypothesis, about the client's problems according to the counselor's orientation. If insight is the counselor's eventual goal for the client, then the counselor seeks to make conscious the hidden meanings of the client's behavior patterns. The counselor guesses about (hypothesizes) the underlying conflicts and needs driving the client toward certain forms of behavior.

If reduction of symptoms and changed behavior are the primary goals, then the counselor sets forth a hypothesis about the inappropriateness or appropriateness of the client's behavior. The client follows through by testing the counselor's hypothesis by trying out new ways of behaving both in and out of the counseling session.

The counselor in either an insight-oriented or behavior-oriented approach states the hypothesis in words familiar to the client. Thereafter the hypothesis becomes the signal that prods the client to work through problems. Putting together the hypothesis and the changes in behavior is, of course, dependent on the client accepting the counselor's guesswork. The accepted hypothesis, in this way, becomes the building block for coordination.

Coordination. The counselor assembles observations of the client, the client's comments about his or her feelings and about other people, and the counselor's frame of reference. This coordination of observation, feelings, and frame of reference is submitted to the client to decide whether it *fits*.

By means of this coordination the counselor accomplishes at least two purposes. First, the counselor emphasizes the similarities and differences of the client's and the counselor's views of the client's behavior. Second, the counselor compares the client's past and present behavior. Coordination of these various aspects clarifies the client's thoughts and feelings and helps focus attention on some important issues.

In one sense the counselor's coordination interferes with the client's ongoing behavior and leads the client into constructing new or reconstructing old ways of behavior. In the fourth response in Example 7-11, when the instructor coordinated the student's absences and worry with the interpretation of the student setting himself to fail, the instructor was stating a hypothesis and was coordinating the behavior and the feelings into meaning. The student might respond in many ways; he might resist the interpretation (deny it) or begin to wonder about himself (reconstruction).

Reconstruction. As clients become able to talk more freely about the present as well as earlier conditions of anxiety arousal, they also begin to display new responses to the present situation. Apparently the clients are now able to handle daily affairs with a lower anxiety level. Their reconstructed behavior (new responses) begins to appear outside the counseling office. As this occurs, clients move toward termination of the counseling sessions.

Sometimes the client switches to resistance rather than to reconstruction. Sufficient self-reinforcement or reinforcement by others may act as a counterforce to the reconstructed behavior. For this reason the drug addict continues shooting up even though it is becoming more difficult to steal enough money to buy the increasing number of bags of dope. The sudden, pleasant flush from the injection or the avoidance of the pain and discomfort of a drugless existence is far more impressive and thus maintains the habit in spite of the counselor's hypothesis: "Has it ever occurred to you that this self-destruction has something to do with your guilt feelings?"

The resistant client finds it extremely difficult to give up behavior even though it is inadequate and not completely satisfying. The client is reluctant to reconstruct behavior because the promise of other reinforcement is insufficient to take the risk. The counselor's hypothesis and subsequent coordination do not fit the client. Example 7-12 describes the difficulties an individual has in restructuring behavior even though he accepts the interviewer's interpretation.

Example 7-12
INTERPRETATION: BERNIE ACCEPTS, MARTHA REJECTS

Bernie returns to his home after a session with Dr. L. and says to his wife:

BERNIE: Martha, this is it. I *am* going to stop drinking. Doc has been saying it, now I know it. Alcoholic, I'm an alcoholic.

MARTHA: Yes, so what's new?

BERNIE: Martha, I'm trying to tell you something. Something it's taken almost 20 years to accept. I'm a souse, a lush.

MARTHA: OK. So you drink too much. I've known that. What is that guy, Dr. L., trying to get you to do? Pulling you down this way. You oughtta stop seeing him. He's a quack!

BERNIE: But, Martha, that's not it—not it at all. In the group, and alone with Doc, I've been putting things together. How I've done things, not able to work, a weekend drunk. Many Mondays, no go, and you . . .

MARTHA: Yeah, now you're going to blame me. I make you drink, don't I?

BERNIE: No, wasn't going to say that. But, Martha, Martha, listen. Remember when I stopped for a month? No piling it on, on weekends, for 1 month. Remember how mad you were when I wanted you to just sit and talk to me? To go out into the woods? Let loose? Once you even said I should get something to wet me down. You wanted to be left alone.

MARTHA: See. I thought so. It's that Dr. L.; he's trying to get you to hate me, to blame me, for your drinking.

BERNIE: No, Martha, that's not it. Oh, what the hell! *(Walks to the door swiftly, swings it open, slams it behind him, and leaves the house.)*

One might question whether Dr. L. has sufficiently helped Bernie to prepare for this attempted reconstruction of his behavior. It seems that Bernie accepts the hypothesis that he is an alcoholic. There are numerous facts to support this notion. Also, he is ready to coordinate his feelings about himself, about his wife, and about his relationship with his wife. He is even ready to do something about changing his behavior. Every item fits except for the way he must learn to deal with his wife. The interpretation was inadequate, since it did not help Bernie determine how he might handle himself outside of the counseling situation.

Martha interpreted also. She interpreted Dr. L.'s speculations as a threat to her. She may also have been reluctant to release Bernie from his dependent role. She preferred reinforcing the dependence that alcohol encouraged in Bernie. This newfound strength of Bernie's to change was not to her liking. Bernie needs to know more about her interpretation.

Bernie is ready to change. He is prepared to become more self-sufficient and less dependent. The counselor has brought Bernie to this stage by means of the hypotheses, which pointed out the reinforcements for Bernie's continuing alcoholism. However, Martha places hurdles before Bernie. If Bernie is sober, he wants Martha's companionship. If Bernie doesn't drink, he is more capable of handling his own affairs. Martha interprets this as a form of rejection. She is reinforced by Bernie's weakness.

Insofar as Bernie is concerned, the goal of independence looks farther away. An additional negative outcome might be Martha's rejection of him if he stops drinking. Martha reinforces the goal of "sickness," rather than "wellness."

Clients may have to be exposed to numerous interpretations of their behavior and the behavior of those around them. They must be prepared for the outcomes of behavior change (reconstruction) on the relationships involved as well as for the expanding realization of their personal growth.

Expanding boundaries. Broadening self-knowledge makes it easier to deal with the shoulds and the should nots that are often hurdles in the way to fulfillment. People who do mostly what they should do when they should do it are not free enough and usually not aware enough to change their behavior. Interpretation may open new doors to experience and change for these clients.

Clients who can look at themselves through the eyes of the counselor and then become their own observer are on the way to experimenting with new behaviors. At first the clients must be amply reinforced, with sufficient time to try out alternative roles. Gradually they find their own more effective role, their own pattern of behavior, their reconstructed life-style.

This broadened base of functioning may be compared with the completion of a puzzle in which one of the pieces is turned the wrong way or is missing. Someone, in this instance the counselor, turns the piece around or provides the missing piece. After this assistance, this interpretation, the client is able to put the puzzle together. The next time, or it may take one or more similar "pieces" of interpretation, the client expands awareness of the possible difficulties with the situational puzzle and takes over.

Another way of looking at this expanding awareness is to think of the client as someone who has developed an unsuitable, undesirable script for behavior. This script contains conversations and hypotheses that the client has acquired from early infancy. The counselor points out the hypotheses of the client's script; shows the way to compare, coordinate, and change; and reinforces reconstruction of behavior. The client becomes more informed about how to solve problems and tries to get along on his or her own.

Interpretation may also be considered as a form of learning to discriminate. Clients build up freer, more effective functioning because they learn the difference between their own view of their behavior and the counselor's hypothesis about their behavior. As a result of these interpretations and differentiating reinforcements, the clients break up their rigidity and establish more positively active and flexible behavior.

SUMMARY

Chapter 7 is mainly about communication—of empathy, warmth, and genuineness and of the expressive interactions of paraphrasing, summarizing, reflecting, and confronting. The chapter ties together the ideas presented earlier in the book, beginning with an overview of the basic ingredients of the helping process: *a*ttitudes, *s*kills, and *k*nowledge (ASK) and *o*bservation, *r*ecording, *re*porting, *i*nterviewing and *c*ounseling (ORRIC). Three recurring and interlocking words are mentioned throughout this book—*understanding, acceptance,* and *caring.*

These are hook-ups to humanness. From self-understanding (insight) emerges the openness, the self-disclosure, and the self-evaluation that are the foundation for empathy, warmth, and genuineness (EWG). These three interpersonal skills are the central ingredients for change. Empathic counselors exhibit both in-sight and out-sight, since they work at understanding themselves as well as others. They look at the world through the client's eyes and listen with the client's ears *as if* they were the client. They must experience closeness (warmth) with the client as well as remain alert to the messages the client sends. Observation and recording of verbal and nonverbal behavior are the keys to the counselor's understanding. The client "talks"

with words, with sounds, and with his or her body. The counselor uses similar language to convey messages, which are enveloped in empathy, enriched with warmth, and trustworthy because of their genuineness.

Genuineness involves the counselor's willingness to be known. This ability to reveal himself or herself to the client aids the client to untangle some of his or her feelings. The counselor tunes in to the client's needs to know how and what ideas and feelings to share with the client. This sharing becomes a form of self-confrontation for both client and counselor. They both feed information about themselves to each other and also hear what they are saying. Thus there is not only mutual feedback but also self-feedback.

EWG may be measured by scales that describe the different levels of verbal expressions. It may also be measured by observation of the kinds of words and nonwords (sounds and nonsense syllables) used. In addition, the language of the body, its movement forward or backward, gestures, physical distance, and eye contact are cues for determining the level of EWG.

The counselor's expression of warmth increases his or her personal attraction for the client. This personal attraction is advantageous, since it encourages greater cooperation from the client. However, too much warmth, too much liking, too much attraction, and too much cooperation are apt to result in an overdependent client. If this should occur, the counselor must examine motives—is the counselor striving to satisfy his or her own needs by creating an overdependent client?

Out of warmth emerges intimacy. This freedom to feel and be close to someone hinges on the development of identity. An individual establishes a sense of selfness, of continuity, and of wholeness. Establishment of these physical and psychological boundaries of self is the springboard from which an individual can relate to others.

Identity develops from attachment (dependent) to detachment (independent) to involvement (interdependent). The troubled individual who comes or is brought to the counselor and the beginning counselor go through stages similar to the growing infant and child. They move from one stage to the next, gradually defining or redefining their identity.

Involvement takes at least two different directions. An individual becomes involved with others, interdependent, and intimate. Another individual becomes self-involved and either dependent on someone and overintimate or independent and aloof from people. The individual involved with others is comfortable in approval-giving; the individual who is self-involved is often approval-seeking.

Involvement and intimacy are locked together. They both share the same body of characteristics that include acceptance, sharing, and inclusion. Intimacy includes involvement but delves deeper into feelings. There are several forms of intimacy; each of them alone leaves something wanting in the human transaction. These forms are cerebral, social, physical, and emotional intimacy. All these forms put together make for a more complete human transaction.

Counselors whose identity is assured, who feel comfortable with themselves most of the time, do not consider their planning, changing, and learning as a finished product. They tackle not only clients' problems but also the societal problems that make it difficult for clients to express themselves freely. They keep watch over stereotypes and other prejudices and handle labeling with caution.

Woven into the tapestry of these foregoing ideas are the skills and knowledge that are the backbone of effective interviewing—accurate *o*bservation, *r*ecording, and *r*eporting (ORR). Interviewing, an organized form of feedforward and feedback, depends on ORR during the three parts of the interview process. All interviews are divided into the opening or beginning phase, the developing or exploring phase, and the ending or terminating phase. There are no sharply defined boundaries between these phases. Suitable skills and knowledge can motivate the client to return for help after the first session, can spur the client to explore problems more extensively and intensively during the de-

veloping phase, and can ease the separation of client and counselor during the terminating phase. The serendipitous counselor sometimes can "do it better." Happy and unanticipated discoveries about the client and/or the counselor spark the findings and directions for the helping event. If applied prudently, this "aha" or unexpected insight can be a crucial factor in the client's development.

Helping skills revolve around getting in touch with people through verbal and nonverbal communication. The expressive skills of communication discussed in Chapter 7 propose procedures that transfer information joining the interviewer and the client in the interpersonal relationships of message sender and message receiver. Five forms of expressive skills are described in this chapter: paraphrasing, summarization, reflection, confrontation, and interpretation. Paraphrasing depends on rewording in the form of repeating, highlighting, or coordinating. Summarization of content or of feeling is similar to paraphrasing except that summarization covers interview material for an entire counseling session or a series of such sessions. Reflection echoes and labels the intent of the feeling and experiences of the client and at times of the interviewer. Since reflection depends on a more complex level of skills, the novice interviewer is more likely to commit errors such as timing, worn-thin phrases, too deep or too shallow responses, and adding or subtracting. Confrontation goes beyond paraphrasing, summarization, and reflection, since this form of communication calls attention to and/or challenges a person to fill a gap in self-exploration and to stop destructive social game playing. Thus confrontation seeks to assist clients in becoming themselves more fully by establishing a state of cognitive dissonance. Interpretation includes pieces of all expressive skills plus the coloring of the counselor's remarks with his or her own frame of reference. The counselor brings new facts or rearranges existing facts. The end result of expressive skills points to one important goal— to expand the boundaries of the client's and counselor's self-knowledge so that they can be more positively active and flexible in their problem solving.

Chapter 8 explores ideas for innovative intervention procedures.

■ ■ ■

And all of this leads to each individual's somewhere. The somewhere of dignity and hope, but . . .

Before people can concern themselves with fulfillment of their own potential, they need to be assured of satisfaction of basic wants (Abraham Maslow).

Chapter 8

BEYOND COUNSELING ROLES FOR HUMAN SERVICE WORKERS

The Grandparents Program, a Janus-type human service program that serves two age cohorts. It fosters the esteem and helping role of the older person and provides a nurturant relationship for the younger person.

Title II of the Domestic Volunteer Service Act, PL 91-113

The Queen in Lewis Carroll's *Through the Looking Glass* says:

It takes all the running you can do, to keep up in the same place. If you want to get somewhere else, you must run at least twice as fast as that.

NEW OCCASIONS AND NEW DUTIES

Through the Queen in *Through the Looking Glass* Lewis Carroll expressed the rapidity of political changes during the nineteenth century. Today Alice would have to run even faster to "get somewhere," and a view of the future portends more rapid transformations. Some forecasters proclaim that the future is now: "Never before have human lives changed faster or in so many fascinating ways."* The present is so close to the twenty-first century that the challenge of that century looms as a significant factor for human systems. In 1967, almost four decades before the twenty-first century, the Commission on the Year 2000 adopted the following premise:

The future is not an overarching leap into the distance; it begins in the present. It is mandatory to indicate now the future consequences of present public policy decisions, to anticipate future problems, and to begin the design of alternative solutions so that our society has more options and can make a moral choice, rather than

*From Cornish, E., editor: 1999 The world of tomorrow: selections from the Futurist, 1978, p. 5. The FUTURIST, published by the World Future Society, 4916 St. Elmo Avenue, Washington, DC 20014.

be constrained, as is often the case when problems descend upon us unnoticed and demand an immediate response (Bell, 1967).

These alterations affect and will continue to modify every phase of life—living arrangements, family life, life-styles, interpersonal relationships, and social, economic, and political activities. Adaptations in political philosophy, education, services, and roles are imperative to meet the gargantuan tasks of a pluralistic society with changing human systems. James Russell Lowell in *The Present Crisis,* stanza 18 (1844) appropriately remarked:

New occasions teach new duties; time makes ancient good uncouth;
They must upward still, and onward, who would keep abreast of truth.

However, it is not the changes of the present nor of the future that can foreshadow the global cataclysm or the Golden Age, but the people in the system who invent these changes and what people do to cope with these changes.

In this framework of innovation this chapter examines some current and future trends and the human service networks and roles that exist, those which will be honed and polished and then prevail with certain refinements, and those which will metamorphose into novel patterns and methods. Both synergism and serendipity (Bell, 1967) are part of this evolving structure of human services.

Instead of being "divided from ourselves," a total effect that is greater (and different) from the sum of the individual effects (synergism) can be triggered by cooperative action at various levels of human systems. Marcus (1978) cautions as follows:

All interventions have consequences, and one of these things we should learn to keep in the forefront of our consciousness is that the most important consequences of any intervention almost always turns out to be the consequences that were not intended.

Therefore the synergistic effect can be favorable or unfavorable for the helper and the client. A happy circumstance from cooperation can emerge; and unsought, valuable, agreeable consequences can eventuate if the basic ideologies of the persons involved in decision making are developmentally oriented—facilitating individuations rather than computerizing people.*

The revolutions in human services

In essence, change is not only imminent, it is current. However, it is incorrect to presume that the twenty-first century will promote the first revolution in human services. In 1964 Hobbs cited three mental health revolutions.

The first and second mental health revolutions. The first mental health revolution may be identified with the names of Phillipe Pinel in France, William Tuke in England, and Benjamin Rush and Dorothea Lynde Dix in America. It was based on the heretical notion that the "insane" are people and should be treated with kindness and dignity.

This revolution, more than 180 years ago, did not have sufficient clout to influence services and "snake pits" for the mentally ill. Misconceptions about the mentally retarded continued even after

---

*Individuation stresses the concept of becoming a single, homogeneous being—one's own self. Computerizing people suggests that individuals may be treated as parts of a complex "factory" of productivity with little or no respect for t he dignity and individuality of each person.

the second revolution, which originated with the charismatic leadership of Sigmund Freud in the latter part of the nineteenth century. Freud shaped "our culture, our beliefs about man . . . bringing passionate attention to the intrapsychic life of man" (Hobbs, 1964).

The third mental health revolution. Hobbs continues, describing the third revolution as follows:

The third mental health revolution, the one we are now challenged to further, is not readily identified with the name of a person but is evident in the common theme that runs through many seemingly disparate innovations of the last 15 years. The therapeutic community, the open hospital, the increased interest in children, the growth of social psychiatry, the broadened base of professional responsibility for mental health programs, the search for new sources of manpower, the quickened concern for the mentally retarded, the proposed comprehensive mental health centers, these developments are evidences of a deep-running change, [indicating that] . . . *the concepts of public health have finally penetrated the field of mental health.*

The disease model of mental illness is being replaced by the dis-ease model (unsuitable coping skills and discomfort). The concept of *well-being,* not just health as the opposite of disease, has been reloading the stockpile of services with revised and innovative intervention strategies and roles for human service workers. The paraprofessionals (beginning professionals), a new breed of worker, have arrived in this third revolution.

The fourth human services revolution. There is still another revolution to come, the fourth one. Its advance notices are infiltrating contemporary procedures and staff usage. Its advent is trumpeted by the statistics about the "baby boom" with the subsequent exacerbation of the aging population in the twenty-first century. Women in the work world plug in their needs for child care. The direction toward "communiticizing" human services has implications for education, inservice training, staffing, and the interdisciplinary approach. Cohen (1973) labels this interdisciplinary form of intervention as "collaborative co-professionals." She writes as follows:

> The mental health professional in the community must readjust his traditional skills so that he can move more effectively with teams made up of new kinds of professionals and paraprofessionals and with lay groups.

The list is much longer. The message is clear. What is happening today has implications for "better or worse" for tomorrow—in the medical as well as the nonmedical human services.

The altering views of medical human service workers

Leininger (1976) considers the altering viewpoints among medical human service workers in a creative article about the gnisrun and enicidem with an anthropological perspective. With tongue in cheek she presents a transcultural study of these two tribes of health services and proposes an enlightening description of the restructuring of the subcultural norms of the professions of nursing (gnisrun) and medicine (enicidem).

Nursing. Leininger (1976) mentions changes such as the following:

☐ More nurses are achieving graduate degrees (master's and doctorates).

☐ Nurses have been asserting their competence to make independent decisions rather than to depend on the doctor's constant directions or to function solely as assistants to physicians.

☐ Nurses have been functioning as psychotherapeutic agents who are expected to be skillful interviewers and interactors with individuals and groups of patients concerning their health problems.

This last item is pertinent for all human service workers, since it emphasizes that clinical nurses are prepared for interventions that incorporate skills and knowledge dependent not only on empathy, warmth, and genuineness but also on the ORRIC skills.

Medicine. Physicians (the enicidem) have been divided in their acceptance of the changing role of nurses while undergoing a metamorphosis of their own culture. Some physicians are refocusing their direction and are moving out of their office enclosures to interact and collaborate with nonmedical human service workers. For example, certain psychiatrists have recognized the merit of furthering their knowledge about normal persons of various ages. They visit the elderly peoples' housing projects to help them with their coping strategies; implement public education programs in community mental health and comprehensive health centers; and in schools and classrooms they consult, teach, and counsel young students, their teachers, and the administrators of educational programs. Brody and Schneider (1973) describe their experiences as consultant-teachers in an eighth grade class about personal and family life. Teaching adolescents had a two-way effect. Brody and Schneider gained a more extensive view of the community; a better grasp of the teacher's problems, thus improving their consultant functions; new information and understanding of the educational process; and an opportunity to observe a broad spectrum of normal adolescent behavior. The adolescents profited from exposure to psychiatrists in the less threatening atmosphere of their own turf—their classroom. Both teachers and students benefited from the psychiatric expertise in dealing with "resistance and transference; promoting catharsis, ego-strengthening and insight; and encouraging reality-testing and verbal expression" (Brody and Schneider, 1973). In addition, the consultant-teachers readily became aware of students' psychological problems and handled these problems themselves or through suitable school personnel without referral to a mental health center. Crucial to this approach were the empathic relationships the consultant-teachers developed with school administrators, counselors, psychologists, teachers, and students. They all shared common experiences and attained mutual understandings. The psychiatrists shed the mystic cape of jargonese that might have interfered with relevant dialogue. They realized that they were unable to function without the educational competencies of the teachers and relied heavily on team efforts that provided a platform for a new psychoeducational approach in the classroom.

Dentistry. Dentists also warrant mention in this survey of changing roles and practices of medical human services. Over the years dentists have been moving away from mores that emphasized teeth as their sole concern. They have expanded their focus from the removal of decaying or malformed teeth to a wide variety of efforts to induce people to use their services less grudgingly and more regularly to preserve their teeth and consequently further their "wellness." For more than 50 years the contributions of the social and behavioral sciences have been important in dental procedures (Phipps, 1972; Public Health Service, 1980). Some dentists have used unusual methods to attract patients. A few have set up offices in department stores, and others have donned costumes representing animals or characters in literature to dispel the threat of the dentist's chair.

Still other dentists have devised methods for informing the public about some of the dangerous practices that contribute to decaying teeth in the young child. Shulman (1980) produced an educational technique to inform parents about nursing bottle caries. He wrote and recorded a videotape and slide cassette show about the suspected causes and results of "nursing bottle syndrome." This presentation warned mothers in simple and informative language of the effects of putting a bottle into children's mouths when they are placed in their beds.

In many ways psychology and dentistry have become allies in reducing people's anxiety, fears, and phobias about a visit to the dentist.* The rumblings of change become stronger. Medical and nonmedical human service workers are beginning to establish teamwork alliances leading toward a comprehensive continuum of human services—a holistic effect.

---

*For further discussions of psychology and dentistry see Ayer and Hirschman, 1972; Corah, 1972; Corah and Pantera, 1972; Evans and others, 1972; Gale and Ayer, 1972; and Phipps and Marcuse, 1972.

Now: halfway down or up

The challenge now remains—halfway up or halfway down? Milne (1924) cleverly describes this dilemma in his poem "Halfway Down."

Halfway down the stairs
Is a stair
Where I sit.
There isn't any
Other stair
Quite like
It.
I'm not at the bottom,
I'm not at the top;
So this is the stair
Where
I always
Stop.

Halfway up and becoming. Halfway up focuses on the present and the future; halfway down focuses on the past. "Up" or "down" is more than gameplaying; it presents two different viewpoints. People who are halfway down are looking at what they have learned and what is happening around them, and they are satisfied with or at any rate slow to do anything about themselves or the world around them. People who are halfway up are aware of what they have learned but continue to search for more knowledge and increased competence. The first think they *have* become; the latter *continue* becoming. The first sit tight on their status quo; and the latter acknowledge and are involved in the changing role and prospects for human service workers. Anti-shrinkthink and progressive counseling present some of these innovations in human systems.

Anti-shrinkthink. The simplest method of dealing with the protests of minority groups, women's lib groups, and radical revolutionary or disenchanted people is to deny they exist. If one of these dissenting noisemakers happens to push his or her way into one's consciousness, all one has to do is to find that halfway-down stair, stop, and sit. Then it is easy to shut one's ears to unpleasant remarks about the needs of people or the impact of an unsatisfying and/or hostile society. Conversely, the person who finds stopping on the stair uncomfortable and feels compelled to move up and out must then search for the sources of discontent and do something about them.

"Anti-shrinkthink" (Dilley, 1972) is one of the ideas proposed to make the helping profession more answerable to people and to their problems. It is a plea:

☐ For recognition of the need to support beginning professionals in their roles as helpers
☐ For a shake-up of the stereotypes about women's roles
☐ For a recognition of the prejudices against and pressures on minority group members and the poor
☐ For opposition to the label "mental illness" and to the indiscriminate use of any labeling
☐ For the right of all individuals to find their own way toward satisfaction and self-fulfillment

Progressive counseling. How about counseling? Would the anti-shrinkthinkers find that most counselors are restricting conformists who repress their clients? Several critics of the counseling profession have presented it as reactionary (Banks and Martens, 1973) in spite of the fact that the counseling movement has typically supported change in the schools as well as in society (Adams, 1973).

The *Personnel and Guidance Journal* devoted its entire March 1980 issue to the theme "Revolution in Counseling—A Second Look." The articles of this issue contribute examples of novel ideas and procedures in counseling, such as:

☐ The widespread acceptance of the behavioral counseling movement. (However, controversy continues about the "directive" quality of shaping and modifying behavior as well as the apparent omission by behavioral counselors of philosophical topics related to values [Barclay, 1980; Hosford, 1980; Krumboltz, 1980; Stulak and Stanwyck, 1980]).
☐ The problem-solving model for consultation (McBeath, 1980).

☐ The innovative counseling procedures that are sensitive to the needs of women (Worell, 1980).
☐ The challenge to the counselor to move out of the office and get involved with the "whole person" (Sprinthall, 1980).

Is the counseling profession experiencing an identity crisis that is not easy to resolve? Are the proponents of behavioral counseling "intolerant zealots"? Are those who espouse the client-centered approach closer to the "right" approach (Rogers, 1951, 1961; Rogers-Warren and Warren, 1977)? Are the behavioral counselors and the client-centered supporters coordinating their views with the recognition that behavior and perception play a reciprocal role in the process of change (Barclay, 1980) and that the efforts of behavioral counselors must be directed to help clients change their own behavior (Hosford, 1980)?

A human services system manifesto for change. On the one hand, counselors support clients in their right to select alternative life-styles and yet do not recognize or are uncomfortable with the need for significant changes in educational, social, and economic institutions to support these varieties of individual life-styles. Counselors are more prone to emphasize the need for change in their clients so that the clients may live more satisfactorily in society. The "Catch 22" in this effort is that if the clients do learn to live in society, they lose some of their uniqueness. Yet, if these clients do not learn to live in society, they are likely to become outcasts, living on the fringes or gathering in isolated places to live differently.

The basic assumption that the problem is rooted in the client's inability to adjust upholds the notion that one cannot change society, one can only change the person. This opinion ignores "one-half of the relationship of the individual and the society. Working only to implement the individual has the effect of giving implicit approval to the society" (Adams, 1973). A proposal for a person-environment position statement for the human service worker integrates individual and societal responsibilities of the helping relationship as follows:

Human service workers should be prepared to explain their changing roles to both administrators and to others. They also should be knowledgeable about the following issues and should have developed an effective level of skills to deal with the populations with whom they are involved in a helping relationship. Human service workers should be ready to do the following:

☐ To provide counseling and other assistance to special groups such as abortion counseling groups, drug crash pads, women's liberation chapters, and minority groups

☐ To interact with youth in the neighborhood settings

☐ To establish rap groups in shopping centers and other places that are accessible to people of various ages

☐ To become involved in outreach activities such as organizing community groups according to community interests

☐ To practice the precepts related to the holistic model of human needs and behavior

☐ To recognize that *loss* touches all people throughout their lives, not only in extreme cases of change such as death, war, or natural disasters, but also, possibly, in getting promoted, graduating, moving to a new community, or having a baby (Frears and Schneider, 1981) (Helpers should become able to cope with their own losses and grief and help their clients develop coping skills with their own losses.)

☐ To develop and support introductory and continuing education programs for themselves and for other human service workers

☐ To realize that social problems are not neatly stable with "once-for-all solutions," and not to expect that their solutions to social problems, once stated, be universally accepted and terminated (McGrath, 1980)

The foregoing "manifesto" recalls what Carkhuff (1972) tagged as the outlook for the "militant humanist," an agent for self-change as well as for social change. Not all human service workers are expected to accrue the same level of knowledge and skills, and not all wokers would function in similar roles. However, a new constellation of factors—both domestic and international—does not permit the luxury of recommending more of the same in a variety of areas (President's Commission for a National Agenda of the Eighties, 1980). When all these thoughts are tied together, they evoke an all-inclusive question: Does the helping profession dare to design a new approach to helping that is identified with human fulfillment rather than the patching of psychological wounds? (Does it dare not do so?)

■ ■ ■

The comments about changes in both nonmedical and medical human services and the proposals offered for counseling and other practices establish the groundwork for the innovative approaches to be described in this chapter. One point is certain—a Neanderthal view of human services has no place in the contemporary concepts of human systems.

The human systems approach will be introduced with an exploration of the concept of levels of human systems and the role of the human systems consultant as an intermediary and catalyst in the process of change. Some degree of stress is associated with change. This stress can produce growth, or life's challenges can become a threat even to the person's existence during stress overload. Physical ailments and behavioral dysfunction derive from this excessive burden of stress. Stress management, burnout, relaxation techniques, and the role of the human service worker are discussed as integral components of the system of human services.

Psychoeducation, psychosocial rehabilitation, and the present and projected roles of paraprofessionals (beginning professionals) are further subjects of inquiry in the remainder of this chapter. These concepts have been given increased emphasis in recent years. The chapter ends with a brief examination of trends for human service systems.

CHANGING HUMAN SYSTEMS AND THE HUMAN SYSTEMS CONSULTANT

Each person lives within a system of human and other environmental interactions and interdependence. Discussions of systems may begin with the smallest unit of the system, the human cell (microsystem), or the more refined stage of the atom. It may begin with the human being and the inner and outer environmental factors affecting the human condition, with the universe (cosmos), or with the individual, one small speck within this complex system (the macrosystem) (E.D. Schulman, 1980).

The behavior of the whole system cannot be predicted from the behavior of its parts, since a synergistic effect results from the interactions of the parts. Thus an individual adds to or subtracts from the unity of the system when he or she becomes part of a group of individuals. The group becomes organized into a pattern that is different than the mere sum of its parts—of the individuals that make up the group.

The organization of the system

The organization of the system is affected by the number of parts or elements involved and the relationship between. and properties of these parts. The larger the number of parts, the more complex the system; the effect of each part depends on the proximity and emotional or other responses of the individuals and events forming the components of these parts (E.D. Schulman, 1980).

Changes in the system

Any change in a unit (element, component, or part) of the system changes the relationships of the entire system. The change may be favorable, leading to greater strength and development of the system, toward synergy—harmony and order—or may lean toward entropy —discontinuity and disorganization (E.D. Schulman, 1980).

The system is influenced by:

1. The number of components

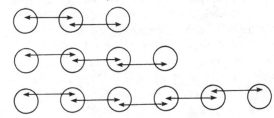

2. The arrangements and relationships among the components

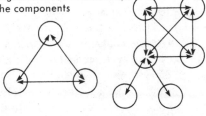

Peripheral relationships

3. The distance between the components

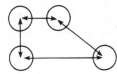

4. The size or significance of the components

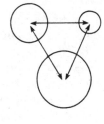

Fig. 8-1. Number, relationship, and properties of parts of a system. (From Schulman, E.D.: Focus on the retarded adult, St. Louis, 1980, The C.V. Mosby Co.)

These changes are dependent on the properties that are diagramed in Fig. 8-1: the number of components, the arrangements and relationships among the components, the distance between the components, and the size or significance of the components.

To understand a person, one must know about the person, other persons impinging on his or her life space (number, arrangements, and relations of components), the community, the government, and so on (distance between components and size or significance of components). Furthermore, these data are clarified by an exploration of the levels of the human systems in which the person participates.

Levels and characteristics of human systems
(Capelle, 1979; Kuhn, 1976; McPheeters, 1979; Von Bertalanffy, 1968)

Input, throughput, and output are characteristic aspects of each level of human systems from the microsystem of the atom to the macrosystem of the universe. Each system receives input from some source, whether this input is food, sounds, bright lights, materials, service in a clinic, or other resources. These stimuli or inputs are digested, registered, and associated in the brain. They are experienced as nourishment, counseling, consultation, or other transactions and undergo changes in the process of throughput. The output occurs in the form of excretions, verbal or nonverbal communication, higher functioning clients and communities, or some other form of productivity or lack of productivity.

For each system there also are interdependent boundaries and environments. The boundary is limited by the specific system level under consideration, ranging from one-to-one events at the interpersonal level to worldwide episodes at the level of the universe. Environments therefore are narrowed or spread in accordance with the dimensions of boundaries. The life-space in which an individual moves and encounters people, things, and other sensory stimulations can be narrowed by incarceration, sensory impairment, or disabling conditions

or can be widened by innovative procedures that provide horse's legs for the person previously confined to a wheelchair and open new vistas for the mentally retarded person and the autistic individual.

Fig. 8-2 and the diagram of problem solving in Fig. 1-12 depict the classifications that illustrate the functional relationships among the levels of systems; analyze developmental stages and other general factors; and link these into the five steps of the problem-solving procedure. The systems approach in Fig. 8-2 integrates the person into the constellation of influences in the extending network.

From intrapersonal to universal human systems levels. The expression of uniqueness enriches human systems from the intrapersonal through the universal levels (Snyder and Fromkin, 1980). The attributes of uniqueness are symbolized in names, for instance, the person's name such as Kathy or Fred, the name of states or a group of states such as the United States, and the name of a continent such as Europe. Differences are signified further in attitudes, beliefs, and behavior. When the environment, during turbulent and/or repressive events, forces deindividuation (loss of uniqueness), then the pursuit of individuality (individuation) is thwarted. When barriers to individuation are imposed, the system—the person, the community, the state—tends to falter in progress toward human fulfillment and is inclined to "satisfice" (Capelle, 1979) rather than maximize decisions regarding individual needs. Rationalizations for economy and for individual restraint abound, and dissatisfactions erupt. This is a time ripe for systems analysis.

Systems analysis. The human systems consultant begins with an analysis of the various facets of the problem to determine (1) the appropriate systems level for intervention, (2) developmental and other factors, and (3) change potential. After this basic information has been gathered, the human services consultant and the human system that is the client (4) set criteria for the preferred outcome, (5) generate alternative solutions, (6) make decisions and develop action steps to fulfill the

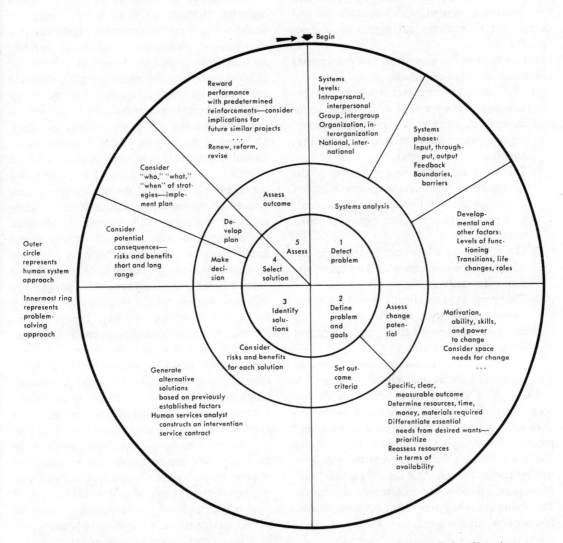

Begin

Reward performance with predetermined reinforcements—consider implications for future similar projects
...
Renew, reform, revise

Systems levels:
Intrapersonal, interpersonal
Group, intergroup
Organization, interorganization
National, international

Consider "who," "what," "when" of strategies—implement plan

Systems phases:
Input, throughput, output
Feedback
Boundaries, barriers

Consider potential consequences—risks and benefits short and long range

Developmental and other factors:
Levels of functioning
Transitions, life changes, roles

Outer circle represents human system approach

Innermost ring represents problem-solving approach

Assess outcome

Systems analysis

Develop plan

5 Assess

1 Detect problem

Make decision

4 Select solution

3 Identify solutions

2 Define problem and goals

Assess change potential

Motivation, ability, skills, and power to change
Consider space needs for change
...

Consider risks and benefits for each solution

Generate alternative solutions based on previously established factors
Human services analyst constructs an intervention service contract

Set outcome criteria

Specific, clear, measurable outcome
Determine resources, time, money, materials required
Differentiate essential needs from desired wants—prioritize
Reassess resources in terms of availability

Fig. 8-2. Human systems analysis and problem solving. (Data from Capelle, R.G.: Changing human systems, Toronto, 1979, International Human Services Institute.)

outcome criteria, (7) determine the implications of the consequences (outcome) for the present and for future similar projects, (8) reinforce the appropriate performance with predetermined rewards, and then (9) continue, as needed, with preestablished procedures for maintaining and improving changes (see Fig. 8-2).

On the basis of this analysis, the human systems consultant identifies certain issues:

□ The human systems level at which intervention procedures are needed, for instance, intrapersonal, interpersonal, group, intergroup, organization, interorganization, community, national, or international

□ The factor or combination of factors of the human system that requires specific attention in relation to input, throughput, output, feedback, boundaries, or other aspects of environment

□ The efficiency, effectiveness, and appropriateness of the functioning of the human system under study

□ The human systems client's objectives, roles, communication style, and reward system, and the client's power and allotments of time and space for improvement

□ The client's motivation to change as well as the client's ability and skills for change

These issues plus the costs and materials (resources) required and the potential benefits and risks of change are considerations in constructing programs for rectifying the problem. It is apparent that the consultant functions from the problem-solving perspective and that decision making and consequent solutions can take several directions. The following discussion describes consultants' functions as change agents in a variety of directions.

Human service: the helping change agents

The human systems consultant is one of the more contemporary roles in the human services network (Ivey and Simek-Downing, 1980; Kurpius, 1978; Shertzer and Stone, 1974). This helper is asked to assist the client, for instance to improve produc-

tivity in mental health agencies, provide consultation and education, and establish and enrich an employee assistance program.

To improve productivity in mental health agencies. McPheeters (1979), in a working paper he submitted to the Department of Health and Human Services, proposes a method of accountability for community mental health centers. This method includes procedures for assessing input (resources) and output (products or successfully functioning people) to increase the productivity index (obtaining more mileage out of the cost of services). McPheeters, the director of the Commission on Mental Health and Human Services of the Southern Regional Education Board, acted in the role of a consultant who analyzed the human system services of the community mental health centers, gathered data, and organized these findings into areas that are the prime aspects of a community mental health agency's operations. This thorough study differentiates input and output criteria, emphasizing that these are integrally related in a productivity ratio and pointing out that output assumes several forms such as income, services, hours of client services, and number of clients served successfully. What happens to the recommendations proposed in this working paper depends on the responses from the federally funded community health centers and the implications for the federal government at the national level. From the human systems viewpoint, several systems levels are involved—from the intrapersonal (how the people in the community mental health system assess and respond to the system) to the national (the prevailing ideology concerning federal funding of local services). From the viewpoint of roles for human service workers preparing, evaluating, organizing, communicating, and implicating consultant functions, McPheeter's proposal requires administrative functions of a program director, communication skills, group process skills, research functions, and so on.

To provide consultation and education. The Cutler Counseling Center cosponsored by the Norfolk Mental Health Association and the Massachusetts Department of Mental Health with a 12-town area offers consultation and education (C and E) services to a number of community agencies such as schools, courts, police, clergy, the Visiting Nurse Association, daycare centers, and other human service agencies. Cutler also participates in the delivery of mental health educational programs to the community in the form of lectures, seminars, and group discussions (K. Schulman, 1980). Community education and information also are furthered by means of a quarterly newsletter, "The Reporter," which contains information about the activities of the center and other articles.

Consultation is arranged through each school system's Special Services Administrator or Pupil Personnel Director by means of the direct assistance of the C and E school consultant or by referral of the pupil to a psychiatrist, psychologist, social worker or other staff member at the Cutler Center. School counselors, psychologists, teachers, and administrators profit from unraveling problems concerning pupils; interpersonal, group, or intergroup communication difficulties; and so on. C and E extends its services to the enrichment of present professional skills and to the establishment of new skills. Referrals also are provided to supplementary community resources such as other counseling centers, funding sources, and training seminars.

Consultation to the schools is augmented by K. Schulman (1981) who is involved in the planning and in certain instances the actual training of special personnel such as nutrition site managers, friendly visitors, and senior aides. The identification of mental health and social service needs in the communities sparks these efforts and proposes others such as a holistic health workshop, a program for women returning to work or to school, and single parenting.

These C and E programs and other services of this organization are of particular interest to human service workers because of the diversification of roles and functions assumed by staff members as well as the broadened services offered to a number of community residents and agency professionals. Several levels of human systems are represented in the services offered—from individual client services to interagency collaborative efforts extending to the national level through federal grants.

To provide consultation as researchers for an employee assistance program. Another area of expertise is tapped in the consultation researcher who uses problem-solving skills to seek solutions in a business or industrial setting. For example, human systems consultants were requested to identify intervention strategies for handling problem drinkers and to increase employee utilization of the employee assistance programs. These major issues were addressed by the Project Railroad Employee Assistance Programs (REAP) and consultants from other organizations. These consultants conducted a 2-year study and concluded that it cost railroad companies more to dismiss a drinking-rule violator than to rehabilitate him or her. The consultant researchers recommended educative and restorative discipline rather than punitive practices, increased availability of REAP services to handle a larger caseload, increased focus on primary prevention, and increased Federal Railroad Administration support of railroad companies in researching efforts to control on-the-job drinking (NIAAA Information and Feature Service, 1981b).

■ ■ ■

Improved productivity, consultation and education, and research for needs assessment and proposed services are only three examples of the kind of consultation that human service workers can contribute. Consultation unravels some of the problems at various human systems levels and also launches innovative functions for human service workers.

The consultant's role as part of the helping process

The consultant's role is one of the strategies involved in the helping process. Helping is the general framework, the fundamental ideology fostering assistance to an individual or to a more complex pattern of interrelationships at some level of human systems. In this helping framework are intervention

Table 8-1. *The helping matrix of human systems intervention strategies*

Strategies	Intervention level	Primary focus	Degree of intensity and time span	Interrelationship with other intervention strategies
Helping	General framework for human systems intervention	Assistance and training for individuals and groups in problem solving and decision making	Depends on particular intervention strategy and human systems level	Basic to all strategies
Interviewing	Intrapersonal or interpersonal; group or intergroup	Information gathering and sharing; typically concerned with employment, placement, careers	Usually short-term but may lead to counseling or psychotherapy	Differentiation between interviewing and other intervention strategies often blurred
Counseling	Intrapersonal or interpersonal; group or intergroup	"Normal" persons aided in goal achievement and more effective functioning	More intense process of seeking solutions	Interviewing as part of counseling process; sometimes psychotherapeutic procedures are used
Psychotherapy	Intrapersonal or interpersonal; group or intergroup	More disturbed individuals; personality reconstruction	Longer process and more intensive helping relationship to effect personality changes	Interviewing and counseling as part of psychotherapeutic process
Consulting	Usually occurs at interpersonal and more complex levels of human systems	Helping the consultee directly and the client and the problem indirectly	More extensive relationships affecting more people; intensive study and analysis required to provide data for consultation and human systems level for intervention	Interviewing, counseling, research, group process, and other strategies involved in the change process

strategies such as interviewing, counseling, psychotherapy, and consulting. The helping matrix in Table 8-1 indicates the relationship and some general differentiating characteristics of these procedures.

The boundaries between strategies. There are no stringent boundaries between strategies. The distinctions depend on the characteristics and severity of the presenting problem, the length of time the problem has existed, the estimated length of time for problem resolution and the establishment of coping skills, and the degree of personality reconstruction considered desirable. The orientation and the particular training of the helping person are additional determining factors in the strategies preferred and used.

Appropriately trained and effective helpers are essential, particularly in this twentieth century that has been labeled "the century of fear" by Alexander Camus and the "age of anxiety" by W.H. Auden (Kutash and others, 1980). The President's Commission for a National Agenda for the Eighties (1980) adds another tag—a "decade for choices." There are many warning signs of the effect of these stress-producing pressures. The role of human service workers in dealing with burnout and stress management is crucial.

It can be argued that increased awareness has itself ballooned stress and bloated its effects. Whether this is an accurate concern is not as central as the issue of the efforts to diminish the negative effects of distress. The damaging effects of distress are apparent in every phase of human existence.

STRESS, BURNOUT, AND STRESS MANAGEMENT HELPERS

At first glance the support of stress as a constructive experience appears to be strange. Yet Shakespeare recognized mortals' stress-seeking behavior when he had Hecate in Macbeth speak as follows (act III, scene 5):

And you all know, security
Is mortal's chiefest enemy.

Selye, the originator of many of the concepts about stress, is even more resolute in his statement: "Complete freedom from stress is death" (Selye, 1980). Selye describes four basic variations of stress as diagramed in Fig. 8-3. He distinguishes good stress (eustress) from bad stress (distress) and overstress (hyperstress) from understress (hypostress). These differentiations clarify the significance of stress as motivation, a constructive experience, and stress as an inhibitor of capable accomplishments—distress. Sensory and cognitive stimulations also are gauged in the understimulation of hypostress (sensory deprivation) and the overstimulation of hyperstress (sensory overload). An analysis of these facets of experiencing aids the helper in assessing the client's problems at various human systems levels.

Stress and dis-stress

Shakespeare had Hecate speak lines that described a human being's rejection of a shield of safety from any degree of tension and a preference for the prick of stimulation. In essence, stress can be sought as a positive and constructive experience—when it is "eustress" (Bernard, 1968; Selye, 1975, 1976, 1980). Bernard (1968) uses Max Weber's term "eudaemonism"* to describe the human being's "lust for life" and the "unending struggle" of stress-seeking behavior.

Stress as a constructive experience

The truck swerved to the side to avoid the small boy pulling his fire engine into the street, and crashed into the light pole that fell across the child's legs. The mother rushed to her son, and summoning unbelievable strength, she lifted the heavy pole a few inches and pushed it away from his bleeding legs (Oken, 1974).

Stress equipped this mother with adrenaline triggered by messages to her brain activating the hypothalamus to stimulate the sympathetic nerves and the pituitary to step up the adrenaline supply from

---

*Max Weber: The protestant ethic and the spirit of capitalism, New York, 1948, Charles Scribner's Sons.

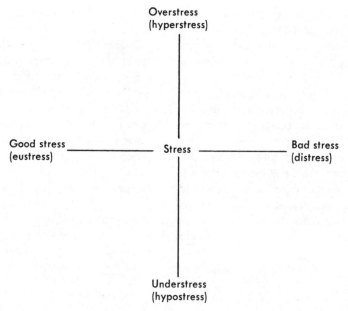

Fig. 8-3. Four basic variations of stress. (From Selye, H.: The stress concept. In Kutash, I.L., and others: Handbook on stress and anxiety, San Francisco, 1980, Jossey-Bass, Inc., Publishers.)

the adrenal gland, which stimulated the cardiovascular system (heart and blood pressure) with upsurging muscle strength, lung capacity and blood flow, prodded the functioning of the liver, spleen and other vital organs, and decreased the activity of the digestive system and other organs not essential for the effort she must expend (Oken, 1974).

General adaptation syndrome (GAS). Selye (1975, 1976, 1980) labeled the stress mechanism described by Oken (1974) the general adaptation syndrome. The GAS has three stages; arbitrary divisions of a continuous process.

Stage one: alarm reaction. At first the individual reacts with body responses indicative of *shock;* the body processes slow down. Almost immediately, unless the shock has been too injurious to the body, a countershock reaction triggers increased defensive stress mechanisms as related in the previous example by Oken. From the flight of the body into decreased adaptability, the body gets

prepared to "fight." The next stage continues the adaptive processes.

Stage two: stage of resistance. The individual develops almost *tunneled responsiveness* to the stressful event and rallies energy to the task at hand. Meanwhile other functions such as digestion are decreased. Trite, but accurate, is the admonition "Don't eat when you're upset." The energy needed for continuing reponses to stressful events varies, and each individual has a different "breaking point." Therefore the stage of exhaustion deters continuation of adaptations if the stressful event is of too long duration or too severe for the particular person's coping skills.

Stage three: stage of exhaustion. Various symptoms appear or reappear, usually with increasing harmfulness. These take many forms, from behavioral disorders to psychotic dysfunction; from headaches and indigestion to even death during extremely stressful events. Example 8-1 cites illustrations of extreme effects.

Example 8-1
EXTREME STRESS AND EXTREME EFFECTS

[1]

It is estimated that a third of the population died of 'The Black Death' between 1347 and 1350 and shortly after 1350 large numbers of survivors were observed to be expressing sadistic behaviors such as: ritual whippings, mass persecution of the Jewish people, bizarre outbreaks of prolonged dancing, child wanderings, and persons running and howling through fields and graveyards fantasizing that they were wolves (lycanthropy) (Rahe, 1979).

[2]

During the first two months of 1940 during the bombing of London, sixteen hospitals in London reported a highly significant increase in stomach and duodenal perforations secondary to ulcers. The high incidence of these ailments continued until the end of the bombing raids in 1951 (Rahe, 1979).

[3]

Two elderly ladies lived alone within a half mile of each other. They had been much alike in circumstances and general outlook before going blind. They were members of the same church and had similar interests. Their reactions to blindness, however, contrasted sharply. The one revolted against fate: "Why me? What have I done to deserve it?" Her friends and neighbors were kind and attentive, but she was so engrossed in her own misery that she never seemed to appreciate their thoughtfulness; and as the years passed she became hard, bitter, complaining. She resisted, but never succeeded in overcoming her disability; rather, she seemed to be increasingly at variance with herself and her lot.

The other woman was altogether different. When it first seemed evident that she would go blind, she made a conscious resolution to accept the fact and triumph over it. She learned Braille, began to take an interest in work done for the blind, and accepted blindness as a new experience. She seldom mentioned her blindness, and never referred to it as an affliction. On one rare occasion she told a friend, "Since I have been like this I have learned so much. The world is a different place. Sounds mean more to me now than they did before; I appreciate music more than I did; people's voices mean more to me; and I recognize people by the sound of their walk." (Brandon, 1979).

Local adaptation syndrome (LAS). The three preceding examples are just a few illustrations of the suffering and pain of an overload of stress or distress. The general impact is demonstrated in physical ailments, behavioral oddities, and maladaptive actions. Sometimes the effects of "bad stress" are milder, of brief duration, and localized rather than generalized as in the general adaptation syndrome in the form of the local adaptation syndrome (LAS). "Tired eyes," "sore muscles," and "inflamed tissues" may be signals of distress, announcing that these organs have been overused, or may be harbingers of emotional stress, giving notice of more widespread consequences in GAS. LAS is the protective mechanism proclaiming the need for rest, a change of activity, or some assistance in coping with a difficult situation.

None of these comments suggests that individuals should avoid stress. In fact, deprivation of stimulation—of stress—is the most significant factor in the lack of development of the mentally retarded person and impels the socially isolated older person to deteriorate. People constantly expose themselves to risks, often without even realizing they are doing so. Most people recognize that risk is involved in certain physical activities such as mountain climbing and sky diving. They also would admit that gambling is a risky business. Horse-racing, poker games, and the stock market are "chancy events" (Bem, 1971). Other people reluctantly admit that they are taking risks by smoking cigarettes or drinking alcohol. How many would accept that driving a car and some of life's supposedly pleasant happenings—marriage, pregnancy, birth, changing one's job to a better position, retiring—are also examples of risk taking? It is apparent that individuals venture on some risk in nearly every action of their daily lives. The consequence of this stress-seeking behavior depends on chance factors and the person's experiences, coping skills, age, state of health, and the like. Any of these factors can influence probability of successful or unsuccessful outcomes.

Even more interesting is the dual position of stress as a motivator of behavior and an outcome of behavior.

A young woman, Chessie, finds that she needs that extra push of finishing her paper at the last moment. Somehow the tension of brevity and the concern about a failing grade push her on to meet the final deadline. She is very tired; her eyes are red and beginning to tear.

What keeps her going is the fact that she will take a rest . . . big rest . . . after this is finished. Right now she gets up and walks around. Sometimes gets a coke . . . then back to the "grind." Of course, Chessie knows that if she had started sooner she would not be under this pressure. Yet she knows her "ways." Last minutes always make her work harder.

Chessie is one of many—students, professional people, authors—who seek the tension of stress as a spur to completing a task. The lure of competition, the challenge of attempting something new, and the avoidance of the "easy way out" are all part of some individual's behavior. Stress seeking and responses to stress are individualized, as are all other characteristics of the individual.

Myths about stress

Greenberg and Valletutti (1980) list a number of myths about stress and comment on their accuracy. Two of these myths have just been discussed and rebutted: that all stress is bad or negative and therefore should be avoided at all cost. Life without stress would be dull and uninteresting, and the zest for living would be absent. To avoid stress is to avoid living. Therefore the tranquilized, drug-dependent or addicted person is actually using temporary stopgaps. It is a myth that drugs can eliminate stress. Drugs may mask stress and may also incapacitate the individual with serious ailments.

Stress in the work place. Another group of myths concerns the work place, the types of work, and all forms of regulated activity. The occupation itself is not the cause of stress. Environmental as well as personal factors produce stress. In addition, increased responsibility for certain professionals or executives does not precipitate distress; the individual's perception of the events and his or her coping skills also are part of the picture. Individuals who are part of the problem-solving and decision-making process and who perceive the results of their productivity are less likely to experience the boredom, frustration, and loss of self-esteem that arouse distress. Human service workers confront a special kind of situation, particularly if they become involved or seriously identify with their clients. For some human service workers such as the police and nurses the boredom of routine tasks becomes overwhelming, particularly on the midnight-to-morning shift (Greenberg and Valletutti, 1980).

Executives do not contend with more distress than employees in midmanagement or first-level positions. In fact, according to a 1979 Cornell University Medical College study mentioned by Greenberg and Valletutti, "executives experienced only 60% of the expected incidence of heart disease." These findings reaffirm the notion that it is not the event itself—work, leisure, and so on—but the meaning of the event to the individual that makes it eustress or distress. However, the human service worker is bound to be exposed to stressors more frequently as well as to more extreme stressors than individuals in other work places.

There are several demonstrable facts about stress and its effects:

- □ All human beings experience stress, children as well as adults.
- □ The person's perception of the event as well as the person's age and health condition, the locus of the stressful event, and the other people around at the stressful moment influence responses.
- □ Environmental factors such as weather, geography, time, and space also affect the possible responses.
- □ The kind of stress—the stressor—only partially explains the person's possible behavior.

Stressors

Stressors are significant variables that provoke stress. These potential disturbances should be exposed and examined carefully so that their prospective impact can be alleviated or in certain instances eliminated. Two antecedents are associated in the chain of events determining the effect of stressors—the psychological vulnerability of the individual and, more important, the roots of the psychological vulnerability, that is, cognitive processes (Minter and Kimball, 1980; Selye, 1980). In other words, what people think about certain stressors and their affective processes (emotional reactions) join with specific stressors and add clout to the annoyances. In addition, certain biological stress factors predispose the individual to a greater or lesser reaction to stress. These factors may be genetic or congenital or due to prior illness or the aging process; they can be noted in a biochemical imbalance. Thus these two aspects—psychological vulnerability and the cognitive-affective roots—foreshadow the possible consequences of the stressor. Schafer (1978) comments further as follows:

Stressors vary in many ways or along many dimensions. They may originate inside or outside the person. They may be pleasant or unpleasant. They may be few in number or many. They may be mild or intense; chronic or acute, new or familiar. And they may be easily changed or difficult or impossible to change.*

Five kinds of stressors will be discussed: physical settings and environmental influences, psychosocial stressors, stimulus overload, stimulus underload, and life events. These cannot be sharply compartmentalized, since there is an interweaving of effect among them. However, for discussion purposes these stressors are separated.

Physical settings and environmental influences. It is no surprise to the environmental psychologist, the human systems consultant, and the office space manager that offices can be designed for efficiency as well as for workers' productivity (Baum, Singer, and Baum, 1981). The arrangement of desks, office machinery, and even the parts of machinery can be "stressful, harmful, or otherwise unpleasant [and] lead to such costly management problems as excessive sick leave, high absentee rate or frequent employee turnover" (Yenckel, 1981a).

Organizations such as the Facility Management Institute in Michigan are training individuals to plan worker-oriented office arrangements. The Buffalo Organization for Social and Technological Innovation (BOSTI), funded by the U.S. General

*From Schafer, W.: Stress, distress, and growth, Davis, Calif., 1978, International Dialogue Press, p. 27.

Services Agency and several large U.S. corporations, has been conducting a 2-year study of 10,000 workers in 100 offices to identify the characteristics of the work place that contribute to worker satisfaction (Yenckel, 1981a). The current findings of this study indicate that productivity and morale are higher in the *systems office design,* which groups workers together according to tasks with flexible partitions to provide a sense of privacy. The work space is shaped to harmonize with the requirements of the tasks to be performed. These studies and the ecological orientation confirming the importance of physical environment on workers' proficiency offer novel roles for human service workers as industrial designers, person environmental planners, and the like (Zimring, 1981).

Crowding. Consideration of the use of space has been afforded a great deal of attention in recent years (Epstein, 1981). Crowding in general and the effects of space usage and changes on the elderly are two areas of concern. The definition of crowding has been refined to distinguish between density, the number of people per spatial unit (the physical aspect), and a psychological concept describing the individual's striving to increase spatial dimensions (Keating, 1979). Research findings have supported the notions that a variety of aspects of crowding can become stressors, such as too many or too few people making up population density and the interactive qualities of interferences and stimulus overload. "Temporal, social, personal, as well as spatial factors contribute to the experience of feeling crowded; and *feeling* crowded has been found to be associated with social pathology and physical symptoms" (Keating, 1979). The key word is "feeling." Spatial considerations considered in isolation do not explain the differential reactions of individuals. The human service worker finds an important niche in the counseling/consultant role to be assumed in the prevention, intervention, and postvention phases of person-environmental changes and effects. Rowles (1980) studied in great detail the person-environment relationships of five people from 68 to 83 years of age living in a working class urban neighborhood for a long period of time.

The objective is to identify the principal dimensions of the participants' total involvement with the spaces and places of their lives, and to integrate these dimensions within a holistic conceptual framework which can serve as a model for interpreting the changing relationship between the older person and an environmental context.

Thus Rowles explored the geographical experience of these individuals from a multilayered framework that integrated social, psychological, and physical dimensions of the spatial transactions. Symbolic and emotional meanings prominently appeared in his deliberations. Several findings emerged from Rowles's study. Considerations of the design of the surroundings is particularly pertinent to the present discussion of environmental influences as potential stressors. This design is decisive:

. . . in the location [and] site planning . . . of both community housing facilities and institutional living spaces [as well as] consideration of more subtle components of the older person's orientation within, and feelings for space. Designers are already beginning to acknowledge the significance of the surveillance zone (a realm within the general schema) in recognizing older residents' preference for designs which offer potential for monitoring scenes of bustling activity instead of the dull tranquility of bucolic vistas. We might enrich the lives of even the most physically restricted, by creating surveillance zones through the judicious design of "lowered" window sills to provide a view of the world outside from a sitting position, by placing beds by windows, or by facilitating visual access to the bustle of corridor activity.

The environmental significance of physical settings, space, density, and crowding is interlaced with the personal experience of these aspects. This personalization of space enriched by suitable physical settings can provide appropriate doses of stimulation and socialization. Human service workers prepared as systems consultants can join forces with architects and other environmental analysts and designers to humanize blueprints for residential, work, educational, and other environmental arrangements.

Coping with rural to suburban changes. The interrelation between physical settings and psychosocial stressors is apparent in the concept of the person-environment relationships. Sager (1981) describes an instance of coping with a changing environment from rural to suburban characteristics in a once staunchly rural, plank-fenced farm county in Virginia with "the proud rural heritage of thoroughbred horses. . . . New residents . . . escaping more crowded cities . . . brought with them their urban problems: unemployment, inflation, the stress of making ends meet . . . [and] the funding for the services . . . is not there." Former residents as well as the new residents are exhibiting behavioral disorders and psychotic episodes that have exacerbated the need for mental health services. An emergency services program has been organized that "seems to be a model of old-time cooperation among the local hospital, mental health workers, law enforcement officers and the Department of Social Services." The crowding—increased density of population— that has occurred because of the six percent annual population growth for the past ten years, plus the changing psychosocial stressors, has been handled in the creative interdisciplinary Emergency Service Program.

Psychosocial stressors. The person-environment relationship with stressors and their effects has emphasized the physical environment in the preceding discussion. Another aspect of environmental clues regarding the strength and effect of stressors recognizes the impact of the social environment. Psychosocial stressors can substantially alter the best environment to become unfavorable.

One of the responses to psychosocial stressors is an increase in tonic (ventricular contractions) heart rate, which can be triggered by social pressures rather than deficiencies in the heart itself. Cox, Evans, and Jamieson (1979) conducted a study to investigate whether aerobic power is related to how people respond to psychosocial stressors. The psychosocial stressor sought to evoke an aggressive (angry) response to the experimenter by means of remarks disparaging the participant's ability to perform a task. Heart rate increased in the experimental subjects, but those exhibiting high aerobic power displayed stress responses for shorter time periods. The ramification of this study goes beyond the evidence that high aerobic power is a determining variable in the speed of recovery from stress. The more important implication is that to experience a situation as a psychosocial stressor, the reacting person must perceive that the incident is intended to "make me angry." The meaning of the event assumes negative qualities. In essence, therefore, this study supports notions similar to those introduced in the previous discussion of physical settings. Stressors are interpreted as favorable or unfavorable according to the unique perceptions of the individual; the meaning of the event depends on these perceptual markings, not solely on the physical or the social environments.

Pleasant events as psychosocial stressors. The provocative aspect of the study of psychosocial stressors is that both pleasant and unpleasant events can be stressors. The person who experiences a severe migraine headache after successfully completing a difficult task for which he or she is complimented is just as uncomfortable as the individual whose spouse is dying of cancer. Cory (1980) labels this unfavorable response to what might be considered favorable events the "sore-winner response." Oscar Wilde recognized this response in his comment:

> In this world, there are only two tragedies.
> One is not getting what one wants; and the other is getting it.
>
> (*Lady Windermere's Fan*, III, 1892)

Studies of negative, unpleasant situations have predominated in the research literature, but more recently research has begun to spread into the larger perspectives of the social disruption accompanying supposedly favorable psychosocial stressors. Cory (1980) reports on a study by Abramson at the University of Connecticut. Abramson reviewed the reactions of 164 men and women who "won be-

tween $100 and $100,000 in the 1977 and 1978 Connecticut lotteries" and found that the responses were highly individualized depending on the lottery winners' attitudes to their "right" to their winnings and their general attitudes toward people and how they thought others would view their winning.

Societal views of impairments as psychosocial stressors. Societal attitudes degrade individuals with impairments and evoke psychosocial stressors for these individuals. Physical settings that establish barriers to accessibility as well as employers who demean the competencies of the physically disabled, the mentally disabled, the mentally retarded, the blind, the deaf, and so on erect psychosocial obstacles to acceptance of these individuals. The narrowing of life's opportunities and of life-space is a consequence of these infringements of rights. Often these hurdles are fortified with the stigma of adverse labels, including the implications of the term "handicap." The psychosocial stressors are not as apparent with the use of words such as "impairment" and "disablement" that specifically refer to the limitation of certain abilities but do not efface the other strengths. However, "handicap" is a pejorative term imposed by society; its only value emerges from its political significance for funding. Recently there have been several dramatic efforts to portray the difficulties of individuals with a disability or disfigurement. Example 8-2 describes the problems of the "elephant man."

Example 8-2
THE ELEPHANT MAN

Pomerance's (1979) interesting play *The Elephant Man* points out some of the psychosocial stressors that are associated with the disfigurement that occurs with neurofibromatosis (NF). This usually non-life-threatening ailment is hereditary or sometimes due to spontaneous mutations. The psychosocial stressors develop as the individual's coffee-colored spots on the skin, multiple benign tumors, and often appearing spinal curvatures make his appearance more and more disfigured. The play is based on the experiences of Joseph Merrick, the original "elephant man." Merrick was accidentally discovered by an English surgeon, Frederick Treves, who cared for him, photographed him, and described his enormous, misshapen head, his other malformations, his brownish skin, and his growths with sickening stenches (Lattin, 1980). The play "dramatically presents the emotions that Merrick dealt with as he tried to separate intended compassion from resultant cruelty"(Lattin, 1980). From sideshow to hospital, people responded to Merrick as a freak until Merrick in his efforts to become a more identifiable part of his benefactors may have precipitated his own death in his attempt to sleep in the "normal" way of others.

NF sufferers are pleased, for the most part, that *The Elephant Man* has brought their plight to the attention of the public. There is no cure for NF, and the progress of the disease multiplies the number of tumors that frequently require surgical removal. Some persons with NF are able to accept their plight most of the time but find that the psychosocial stressors involved in presenting themselves to others is sometimes extremely traumatic. Others isolate themselves to avoid the stares of astonished viewers. Still others eventually become debilitated and some die because the tumors form in the brain and spinal cord. Others have impaired vision or hearing because the tumors spread to the optic or auditory nerves. Both biological stressors (Selye, 1980) and psychosocial stressors are illustrated in NF, as is the interactive quality of these stressors.

What is particularly interesting about NF as well as other stressors is the paradoxical associations of stimulus overload and stimulus underload as additional related events. Biological stressors tend to overload the individual with sensory stimulations such as pain and thus may discourage an individual from participating in interpersonal or other events, resulting in stimulus underload. Other facets of stimulus "load" also have potential as stressors.

Stimulus overload. The earlier discussion of stress-seeking behavior promoted the notion that stress is an impellent to action and in fact is a necessity for development and even for living. High levels of stimulation—overloads—occur when social and nonsocial inputs are too frequent, too dense, too loud, and the like. Crowding is one example of social overstimulation. However, crowding must be accompanied by certain cogni-

tive mediators (the meaning of crowding) that allot crowding a high dose of negative connotations for the individual. Stimulus overload also may derive from interpersonal distance (physical or psychological), the size of an area enclosing individuals, seating arrangements, the shape of the room, turf possessiveness, and the like (Suedfeld, 1979). Proximity to others may prove to be more intimacy, physical or psychological, than an individual is prepared to accept. "Don't invade my space!" means more than keep out of my physical setting.

Stimulus overload eventuates from other sources such as information and noise overstimulation. Students as well as workers are aware of the difficulty in remembering facts that seem to be excessive. Whatever the problem may be, deficient listening skills, auditory or visual impairments, psychosocial or physical stressors, and the amount of information that overburdens depends on the individual and on principles of learning that suggest procedures for information delivery. Noise presents another idiosyncratic aspect that can be related to information presentation and processing. Some people prefer to listen to music or other programs on the radio while studying, working, painting, and so on. Some like it loud, some like it soft, and still others like it quiet. Noise overload need not be loud to be disturbing. Its effect depends on the individual's need for sounds. The dripping faucet can "drive a person batty," whereas Dolby sound in the movie theater and rock and roll at high decibels can be satisfying, even soothing. The stressor effect of noise as well as information overload must consider the person to detect the presence of overload. The important idea is that the aversive consequence of excessive stimulus overload is avoidable.

Stimulus underload. The desire for privacy (Journal of Social Issues, 1977) is not the same as stimulus underload that is evoked by low social stimulation. Aloneness usually is a voluntary act; loneliness is an imposed condition. Enforced isolation of children in time-out areas as part of behavior management, the seclusion of the psychotic patient during the acute, agitated phase of mental illness, the placement of the seriously ill person in a quiet, darkened room have led to conjectures about the effectiveness of these procedures as well as support for the restorative function of confinement. Suedfeld (1979) proposes that "isolation and stimulus restriction in natural settings are frequently accompanied by other circumstances that are anxiety arousing and debilitating. Some of the symptomatology that results may erroneously be attributed to the social-reduction aspect of the environment. . . . Prisoners in solitary confinement may be harrassed or even tortured by their captors; be deprived of adequate clothing, food and medical care; suffer from feelings of hopelessness and helplessness; and worry about their own fate and about the fates of the people with whom they are associated."

Individuals in concentration camps and hostages separated from their families and from other hostages vary in their responses to the stimulus underload that results. In fact, for some it may not be stimulus underload. One person in the concentration camp may write an autobiography on a stolen role of toilet tissue; others may conjure up scenes of their future or concoct mental or physical games, thus providing self-stimulation.

In the constriction and restriction of the prisoner or hostage, self-stimulation may preserve contact with self and reality. However, for the autistic or the mentally retarded person self-stimulation may be a signal of stimulus underload that deters progress in development. The autistic child twirling around in robotlike movements might profit from another person moving into his or her stimulus-world by imitating the child's actions so that the stimulating environment is spread with the participatory presence of another individual. The mentally retarded person sitting in a chair moaning low grunting sounds needs an interested and capable person to introduce eye contact and the sounds of speech and to initiate interpersonal stimulation.

Isolation can be deadly—both figuratively and literally. Sylvia Plath (1966) felt so "out of life's

stream" that she eventually committed suicide, leaving in her poetry such disquieting thoughts as*:

A vulturous boredom pinned me in this tree.

(The Hanging Man, Ariel)

I smile, a buddha, all
Wants, desire
Falling from me like rings
Hugging their lights.

(Paralytic)

The stress of living led to her withdrawal from a world she considered overwhelmingly bombarded by distressful signals and undernourishment of her urgent plea for pleasant psychosocial experiences. She was unable to cope with her grievously disturbing self-imposed isolation.

Isolation is being used in many ways, including as a method of self-exploration and for therapeutic purposes. The film *Altered States* (1980) relates the story of an experiment revealing the combined effects of hallucinogenic drugs with immersion in a water tank. This tale evokes imaginative scenes of the beginning of consciousness, primitive behavior and even physical changes. Immersion (isolation) tanks are being used for chic self-seeking experiences by private individuals as well as for psychotherapeutic purposes. Restricted Environmental Stimulation Therapy (REST) is a stimulus underload technique used with hospitalized psychiatric patients, alcoholics, persons seeking weight reduction, and persons striving to cease smoking (Suedfeld, 1979; Suedfeld and Ikard, 1974).

■　■　■

It is apparent from the preceding discussions that stimulus overload or underload is only part of the antecedent events that determine behavioral reactions. Other components dependent on the individual's interpretation of and prior experiences with

*From Plath, S.: Ariel, New York, 1966, Harper & Row, Publishers, Inc., pp. 69 and 78. Copyright © 1965 by Ted Hughes. Reprinted by permission of Harper & Row, Publishers, Inc., and Faber & Faber.

the event also are implicated. This constellation of influences is applicable in relation to physical settings, environmental influences, psychosocial stressors, stimulus overload or underload, and to the life events at any human systems level.

Life events. Birth, infancy, childhood, adolescence, adulthood, middlescence (middle age), senescence—at each of these broadly divided stages life changes occur and are associated with physical, psychological, and cultural stressors. These stressors evolve from the developmental tasks associated with the physical, intellectual, emotional, and psychosocial expectations imposed by a particular culture. The accomplishment of tasks depends on physical maturation and opportunities for training and expression as well as practice in the requisite competencies.

Sarason, Johnson, and Siegel (1979) constructed a self-report *Life Experience Survey* (LES) to measure the stress of life events frequently experienced by people. The LES (see Appendix B) provides a tool for self-assessment of the favorable (positive) and unfavorable aspects of life-change events. Coddington (1981) also has produced a 50-item adolescent life-event scale containing "good and bad" life events. Coddington's scale is currently being tested to determine its predictive value regarding the risk of illness of adolescents under frequent and severe stress.

Change does cause stress, which becomes a serious matter if the individual's hormonal balance and immune system are unable to combat the destructive effects. Although most individuals would agree with Jonathan Swift that "there is nothing in this world constant, but inconstancy," ("A critical essay upon the faculties of the mind," 1707) there are life events that reach a peak at certain times because of the person's perception and/or the impositions from physical or social pressures. Some of these life events will be discussed: changing women's roles, marriage, parenthood, and age points. These life-events are viewed as potential stimulators for innovative roles for human service workers.

Women's roles. Probably the more drastic changes in women's roles began with the onset of industrialization, when a wife joined her husband in the factory and worked alongside him, thus augmenting the family income. This life change lessened the authority of the father when the mother realized that she had become a contributing member of the household upkeep from another standpoint than homemaking. A new kind of stressor emerged for both men and women. Their changed status led to power plays that became amplified with advancing women's assertiveness. Other sociocultural events can be traced through the nineteenth and twentieth centuries with the recognition of women's voting rights (nineteenth amendment) in 1920 and the initiation of efforts to obtain an Equal Rights Amendment (ERA) in 1923. This amendment was approved by Congress in 1972 but still has not received ratification by the 38 states required for adoption.

For some women the changing roles induced a sharp turn toward what is described as "the natural order of a matriarchal society" patterned after the Amazon women of Greek mythology. These women espouse the superiority of women and are members of the Society for the Promulgation and Encouragement of Amazon Conduct and Attitudes (SPEACA) (Yates, 1980). The views and behavior of this group have been questioned as an extreme measure of dealing with the stressors associated with changing roles. For many men and women the stress of the growing shift in interpersonal relations has posed problems (Behavior Today, 1981e; Voydanoff, 1980).

In spite of increased freedom for women, socioeconomic stressors have aggravated their difficulties. The woman's salary is usually lower for performing the same job functions as men, and her advancement in the corporate structure often is undermined. (Krucoff, 1981a; Riger and Galligan, 1980). "Genuine career equality will require a profound change in social, economic, and educational spheres . . . [with] non-discriminatory hiring practices" (ILO, 1980). Thus the need for human service workers specializing in women's problems becomes a serious target for training. Vocational guidance, career assistance for the displaced homemaker (EDC, 1980; Zawada, 1980), personnel techniques that can elicit the skills derived from homemaking and volunteer experiences, and a gamut of other competencies are needed at present and in the years ahead (Worell, 1980). Additionally, since changes in roles of women affect men also, a fresh examination of man-woman relationships, for example in marriage, would suggest innovative functions for the human service worker.

Marriage. The advent of marriage sometimes triggers maladaptive reactions. For instance, a young woman who had recovered from claustrophobia reverted to her phobia about enclosed places when her boyfriend pressured her to marry him (Moulton, 1980). Of course, there were numerous other background stressors issuing from conflicts with her parents that had incited prior depression and self-effacement, but the threat of being hemmed in by a "static marital trap" sparked the renewed claustrophobic behavior; and sociocultural events such as the "new feminism" posed the dilemma of autonomy evoked by what she considered a restrictive state of affairs.

The "new feminism" of the 1960s and 1970s has wielded a dual-edged sword. It has cut through some of the restraints on women's achievements, but it also has cut away some of the comfort and satisfactions. Twenty-five years of exceedingly rapid and crucial changes have honed the stressors to sharp effects. Sexual attitudes and behavior as well as marriage and divorce have altered. Female submission has shifted to equal participation in man-woman encounters as well as in sexual satisfactions. For some marital partners the stress of dual careers, children, and equal participation in marital affairs has led to "role sharing" in which husbands and wives "share traditionally male and female family duties" (Haas, 1980). These include the breadwinner role, the domestic role, the handyman role, the kinship role, the childcare role, and the major and minor decision-maker roles. "Specialization within any of these roles would be compatible with role-sharing, as long as the specific tasks are not assigned to a spouse on the basis of sex . . . and as long as the overall responsibility for the duties of each role is evenly shared" (Haas, 1980). These role-sharing items were the ideal, Haas reports from her 1976 study of 31 role-sharing couples, who revealed self-fulfillment benefits in the egalitarian arrangement. The marital relationship was happier with less one-sided burdens from homemaking functions or child care. Parent-child relationships were improved, and the mothers preferred their expanded world, since it was not peopled primarily by children. Children received dual parent care, and the strengthened role of the father in the home proved advantageous.

Role sharing did create some problems. The egalitarian division of domestic chores evoked the most difficulty; next in importance was the handyman role for women. Previous training and experience had not prepared these marital partners for these roles. There also were conflicts in other spheres—in jobs, the location of new job opportunities, increased responsibilities, and interference of job or study responsibilities with homemaking necessities. The benefits as well as the stressors suggest the desirability of a full-sized commitment of both partners in the marital role-sharing arrangement and preparation for these altering family relations.

The changing life-styles of marital relationships and the subsequent stressors do not always have simple solutions. Sometimes the stressor is so intense that there are serious and even brutal consequences such as wife abuse (Yenckel, 1981b). The precipitating aspects of wife abuse are numerous, but the results are similar: there are quarrels that are frequent and continue for hours, sometimes ending with a slap and often with other injuries to the face or body. The need for assistance to these women has created a new role for the human service worker—a domestic violence specialist.

The Arlington County Domestic Violence Program got started in Arlington, Va., about a year ago when county officials decided to do something about the alarming incidence of a problem that is plaguing communities all across America. Statistics show that one in twenty women nationally suffer chronic abuse at the hands of their spouses. And a survey done in Arlington County last year (1979) showed the county has a problem of its own. . . . On the recommendation of the Task Force on Violence of the County Commission on the Status of Women [the board of supervisors] authorized the creation of a position for a domestic violence specialist within the county Department of Human Resources. . . . [This specialist] oversees a staff of 24 part-time volunteers . . . [who staff] a 24-hour telephone crisis line in eight-hour shifts over the course of a week (Steele, 1980).

Parenthood. When a child enters the marital scene, still another life change occurs that potentially can originate severe stressors. "Children are no longer an economic necessity for helping to provide the family, but instead additional consuming units that have to be fed, clothed, and socialized" (Nickols and Nickols, 1980). Child abuse became distinctly noticeable in the United States when the baby boom came to parenthood.

The homicide rate for children aged 1-4 tripled between 1950 and 1975 and is now a greater cause of childhood mortality than any disease. In the late 1970's, the age group that felt the largest percent increase in homicide was, sadly, 1-4. An estimated two million children are abused physically each year. Granted that some of the increase is a reporting phenomenon—doctors, for example, are better able to identify child abuse cases now—the incidence of child abuse is still high enough that experts deliberately use the word "epidemic" (Jones, 1980).

The inability to cope exemplified in child abuse is particularly evident in parents under thirty and teen-age mothers, especially those who are unmarried. A different kind of abuse occurs with black children in the United States who have a greater chance (one in two) of being born into poverty and are twice as likely to die during the first year of life (Denton, 1981). Physical illness, mental retardation labels, lowered scholastic expectation, less schooling, more probability of delinquency, and greater probability of becoming homicide victims are some of the additional difficulties and abuses that are more frequent for black as compared with white children (U.S. Department of Commerce, 1979, 1980; U.S. Department of Health, Education, and Welfare, 1979; U.S. Department of Labor, 1979). Discouragement, anger, and continuance of socioeconomic problems, and lack of self-confidence are the outcomes of these oppressive deprivations. Child abuse of all forms—obvious and subtle—demands innovative human service approaches as well as social, political, and economic changes.

Age points. The American society thinks in numbers. Elementary school begins at 6; beer and other alcoholic beverages are permitted at certain ages; registration for the military draft is imposed at a specific age; voting is set at 18; marriage without parental approval occurs at certain ages (usually younger ages for women than for men); social security allotments can be initiated at 62. Many other age points are designated during the individual's life. There also are other points that are socioculturally rather than legally earmarked. The expectations, new roles, and responsibilities can ripen into stressors when conflicting demands, undeveloped coping skills, and inadequate opportunities interfere with achievements. For instance, there are transition ages that seem to presage malcontent.

If suicide, homicide, and perhaps accidents, cancer, and major cardiovascular diseases can be attributed, to some extent, to stressors, then the Metropolitan Life Insurance Company's 1979 statistics presented in Fig. 8-4 represent singular age points linked with stressors. For men suicide and accidents peak at about the age of 15 and then decrease gradually, whereas homicides continue to rise to age 20, then decrease until after the age of 30, when a slow rise reappears. A rise in cancer and major cardiovascular diseases also occurs. The high point for accidents first appears at about the age of 10 for females but never equals the frequency of accidents for males. Female suicides and

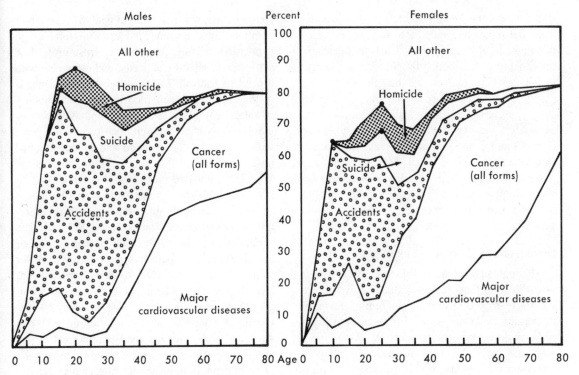

Fig. 8-4. Percent of deaths from selected causes, 1979. Standard ordinary policyholders—Metropolitan Life Insurance Company. (From Metropolitan Life Insurance Statistical Bulletin **61**(4), 1980.)

homicides both peak at about 20, then decrease until after 30, when once again they evidence a gradual rise similar to that for males. According to these statistics, the crucial stressor age points for women generally occur later than for men, and women do not reach the statistical frequencies of men for suicides, homicides, and accidents. The conjectures that explain these differentiations include socioeconomic and other pressures that are more severely imposed on young boys and the biological explanations regarding hormonal differences emerging from the biochemical reactions of women's XX chromosomes as compared with the XY chromosomes of men. Whatever the explanation may be, the fact remains that women do live longer than men—4 to 5 years longer.

Human service workers must be prepared to deal with crises of life. Levinson and others (1978) call

attention to the "severe and stressful period for men of the 'Age Thirty Transition.' The provisional, exploratory quality of the twenties is ending and a man has a sense of greater urgency. . . . Life is becoming more restrictive, more . . . real."

This urgency is translated into the imperatives to plunge in and "do it now" or it will never be accomplished. For many women, aging primarily signals the wrinkles that must be treated with special creams and lotions and covered with other cosmetics.

Reaching adolescence propels the individual through several age points that become especially burdensome for some because of the physiological changes of puberty and culturally imposed demands. Reaching 30 almost heralds another type of adolescence—the coming of middlescence. Another age point is reached, but this time it presents a spectacle of the past and the future. As the person ages, the future becomes narrower. Yet the stress of aging can be diminished. "Chronic illness may presumably be postponed by changes in life style and it has been shown that the physiologic and psychologic markers of aging may be modified. . . . The older person requires opportunity for expression and experience and autonomy and accomplishment, not support and care and feeding and sympathy" (Fries, 1980). Thus the formula for preventing and dealing with dis-stress depends on human interaction and helpers prepared to analyze human systems and intervene as needed. Copeability can be developed.

Dis-stress as a destructive experience

Although stress is inevitable and, in fact, desirable, dis-stress tends to be a destructive experience. Dis-stress is excessive stress emerging from harmful, disagreeable stressors. This reaction to stressors may originate and demonstrate symptoms in numerous ways. Physical distress evoked by the discomfort of sunburn, by the congested nostril of a cold or sinus condition, by the chest pains (angina) of cardiac dysfunction, or by the ravages of cancer can be associated with both the result of dis-stress and the cause of the dis-stress.

Dis-stress and food compulsions. Emotional dis-stress concomitant with physical symptoms is frequent. The origin of the emotional distress often is complex, and the symptoms may be represented in high blood pressure, arthritis, insomnia, backaches, or anorexia nervosa. Anorexia nervosa is a nervous disease exhibited by lack of appetite. Obesity, anorexia nervosa (eat a bare minimum of foot) and bulimarexia (binge and purge) are contemporary problems that usually plague women more than men (Madway, 1980; Rovner, 1980a, 1980b; Schafer, 1979). The effects of the three food compulsions are different, but the crucial fact is that the intake, refusal, or regurgitation of a single stimulus—food—is associated with the stressors that precipitated the eating or not eating constellation of events. These individuals are re-sponding to emotional and physical distress. Their emotions have become tied up with food as an expression of their resentment, frustration, low self-esteem, affectional needs, and often also with a need to control. They control others by means of the amount of their food intake. Their history of antecedent events is complex, and the maladaptation has evolved through a series of life events with which they have coped and failed, avoided unsuccessfully, and, in general, found disturbing. What constitutes too much food or too much weight is not the question. The problem is that the obese person is unhappy with a self-imposed or other-imposed label of the "fat person." Yet he or she continues to build a wall of fat around himself or herself. The obese person is more likely to suffer from diabetes, gallbladder disease, hypertension, and heart disease, which can lead to serious complications, including death. The person who is a victim of anorexia nervosa or bulimorexia can starve to death. There is another important difference in the effects of these compulsive acts—the obese person is more readily detectable and has access to a multitude of intervention strategies. Individuals whose actions decrease food consumption are not easily identified until their condition becomes obviously severe because of their emaciated appearance and inability to function (Rahe, 1979; Wolf, 1979). There is a serious need for more study of this area of food compulsions, and there are creative functions for the human service workers in the alleviation of the distress that may lead to such compulsions. These compulsions occur as individual responses to stressors. However, community disasters have a far-reaching impact on larger numbers of people.

Disasters and dis-stress. Conflict, crisis, and loss of status are themes that recurrently appear in the literature describing the origin of distress. The effects of this distress are manifested in the association of physical and other components with social and psychological factors, which is vividly demonstrated in community disasters (Haas and Drabek, 1970).

Extreme crises are prompted by catastrophic events such as:

☐ The volcanic eruption of Mt. St. Helen's in 1980

☐ The past 50 years of annual (on the average) earthquakes in California

☐ The floods of Johnstown in 1889 and 1936

☐ Hurricane Agnes and its destruction along the Eastern Coast of the United States in 1972

☐ The nuclear blast in Hiroshima in 1945

☐ The nuclear mishap in Three Mile Island in 1979

☐ The instigating factors and the subsequent mass suicides of the Jim Jones religious cult in Jonestown, Guiana in November 1978

☐ The riots in the Los Angeles neighborhood of Watts that began after a 21-year-old black man was arrested for reckless driving

☐ The prison riots in the New York Attica Correctional Facility in 1971

☐ The riot in Oklahoma State Penitentiary in 1973

The foregoing are a few examples of community disasters resulting in costly material damage and even more cataclysmic instabilities of social relationships. Sudden and violent changes become unsurmountable when individuals are unable to rally restorative procedures because prior experiences and modes of behavior do not prepare them for coping with the unusual and often unpredictable events. Sometimes, as with the Californians, the ardent residents seemingly become inured to the apparent regularity of the earthquakes; yet their anxiety is exhibited after a quake by frantic telephone calls, rushing to their children's school or to the work place of a spouse, relative, or friend, and hastening to find safety. The shock of the calamity is distressing and disruptive.

The kinds of problems that people experience following a disaster and consequently the kinds of services required relate not to classic mental health problems; but to grief around the death of loved ones, loss of home and/or possessions and general problems of living and coping with a major life disruption. While the physical impact of a disaster may be over in a few minutes, other consequences extend for weeks, months and even years. What is important after the anguish of the first days is the disruption of family and community life, the marked alterations in routine patterns, social and occupational expectations, and day-to-day personal habits that follow in the disaster's wake (Richmond, 1979).

The gap in services and trained personnel to perform services during a disaster originated the enactment of Public Law 93-288 (The Disaster Relief Act of 1974). This law provides funding for certain projects through the National Institute of Mental Health. An innovative program has been established in Belmont, California, by Caminar, a voluntary, nonprofit corporation (see Appendix E). This program provides "specialized training for mental health and other human service professionals and paraprofessionals in the unique field of disaster crisis intervention; and for the provision of direct disaster volunteers in times of community catastrophe" (Richmond, 1979).

A course is offered through the California Department of Mental Health, Manpower Management and Development Branch in collaboration with Caminar, entitled, "How to Train Professionals for Psychosocial Intervention in a Community Disaster." This course intends to train the participants in disaster preparation techniques, symptoms of distress, and approaches to dealing with victims of disaster; and to train trainers who can spread their accrued skills and knowledge to others. An interesting sidelight is that these innovatively prepared helpers are trained to facilitate the coping of "normal" people under pronounced duress. Instead of severe pathology, these distressed individuals are more likely to exhibit signs of dis-stress that are amenable to alteration if suitable procedures are instituted promptly.

■ ■ ■

Innovative programs and innovative helpers emerge from this type of relief. Thus far the discussion of stress and dis-stress has focused on stress as a constructive and dis-stress as a destructive experience, on dispelling the myths about stress, on the variety of stressors, and on the catastrophic effects of community disasters. Two further areas of information are of singular importance: burnout and stress management.

Burnout

The electric bulb that no longer lights up, the fire that is just glimmering, and the energy that is diminishing metaphorically chronicle a cursory description of burnout. The term "burnout" describes a group of attitudes and feelings about work (or any project), such as boredom, apathy, exhaustion, and low motivation. The behavioral patterns associated with burnout include absenteeism, lowered responsiveness to and decreased concern for clients or to other workers, social withdrawal, alcoholism or other drug abuse, and job changes.

Cherniss (1980) writes as follows:

Before 1974, the term burnout had not appeared in print . . . [but] few topics during the last five years have generated so much animated discussion among practitioners. . . . Speeches, symposia, workshops, and published papers on the topic . . . as well as the few available research studies, suggest that staff burnout is indeed a major problem and concern in the human services.

The costs of involvement with other human beings—the human cost of acting human—often leads to disillusionment. What makes this happen? What are the sources for excessive stress?

Sources of burnout. The antecedent of burnout may be external, internal, or a combination of these two (E.D. Schulman, 1980).

External antecedents include the following:

☐ *Institutional factors* such as policies, procedures, administrative practices, and repressive working conditions that are excessively demanding, ambiguous, or constantly changing. These factors are especially noticeable in some organizational designs in which tasks and duties are allocated (the role structure) unevenly so that some individuals are more stimulated and involved, thus experiencing role-satisfaction, while others perceive just

the opposite: role conflict, role overload, or role underload (Cherniss, 1980).

☐ *Client factors* such as client's low level of responsiveness to being helped, difficult behavior pattern and differing value systems.

☐ *Personal factors* (often unrelated to the work place) such as marital and family concerns, social relationships, and daily events.

Internal antecedents include the following:

☐ *Expectations* from other people and oneself that require predetermined levels of performance for which one does not have the resources.

☐ *Responses* to stressful situations that *fail to reduce stress* to a manageable level.

☐ *Interpersonal relationships* that usurp the person's dignity and sense of responsibility for himself or herself.

In general, burnout can be designated as a transactional process (Cherniss, 1980). The antecedents of burnout—external or internal—initiate the stressful situation. When the demands of these stressful stimuli cannot be suitably satisfied with the available resources, tension and dis-stress ensue. These amplify and generate other symptoms that burgeon into irritability, emotional detachment, cynicism, rigidity, derogation of other workers or clients, and so on. Even more insidious is the consequent disillusionment and its contagion in the work place.

Disillusionment and contagion in the helping profession. Frustration is another feeling in the cycle of distress experienced during burnout. Often the person senses that he or she is unable to scrounge for any more time to spend on a particular task, or the task appears unachievable because of lack of other resources. Frustration and disillusionment become associated with helplessness and hopelessness; these not only are self-perpetuating but also are conveyed to other personnel.

Prevention of burnout is difficult because it is so gradual. The warning signals appear, but the worker does not recognize them. For instance, "a primary warning signal is that the worker expends increasing effort, but accomplishes less" (Daley,

1979b). Increased awareness and alertness are the safeguards to avert continuing discomfort and the spreading of disappointments. When Ben constantly complains about how much work he has and how much energy he expends in trying to keep up, other workers tend to speak of and even embellish tales of similar conditions. Ben's feelings are reinforced, and the cycle of contagion, distress, and dissension continues as other workers agree or disagree with Ben's evaluation of work demands. To help Ben or any other worker distressed by burnout—stress management—a problem-solving approach is essential.

Stress management

The human systems analysis and problem-solving model diagramed in Fig. 8-2 are useful in designing a paradigm for stress management. Thus, before any specific strategies are planned and implemented, the particular problem must be analyzed and identified and the level of intervention and methodology for resolution determined. MacNeill (1980) states that the extensive research in occupational stress can be related to the study of the burned out human service worker. He urges that the beginning for burnout theory should be the person-environment fit.

Analyzing the stress variables. An analysis of the variables involved in burnout must account for the stressors that are part of the person's behavioral repertoire, those that are external to the person, and the relationships between these two—the person-environment fit. The factors that make the person or the environment not fit must be discovered to move on to the steps of generating alternative solutions to ameliorate the psychosocial strain. Example 8-3 describes Sandie's burnout problems and their possible origins.

Example 8-3
BURNOUT AND THE PERSON-ENVIRONMENT FIT

Sandie's first day at work is uneventful. She shares an office with Paul, a social worker, and he is helpful in "showing her the ropes" and introducing her to other people in the partitioned office cubicles. The cubicles

bother her. Voices drift over the tops of the offices, and the person in the cubicle next to her plays popular music all day. She hates popular music . . . but does not know just how to deal with this annoyance tactfully. She quickly gets involved in planning inservice training as dictated by her supervisor's identification of staff needs. She realizes later that this was her first mistake. She had responded to the supervisor's suggestions but had neglected to include the view of the people for whom the inservice is planned. After the first plan for orientation of new employees and the inservice for those in the job for longer time periods, the negative feedback from a majority of the staff "exasperates" her.

The supervisor is satisfied with her attempts until he too, receives adverse criticism. Sandie asks Paul, "What's up Paul? Why the verbal pile?" Paul tries to be tactful but truthful: "Sandie, the people around here think you're high-handed and are getting special privileges from old 'Scrooge.' Surely you know how they feel about him. He treats each hour as an accordion, stretching it with his expectations from us and constricting it so that his business is negligble. He needs inservice more than the staff."

Several priority duties by her supervisor interfere with the time Sandie can allot to planning inservice, and her supervisor makes a complete turnabout, commenting to Sandie, "They [the staff] don't have any idea what's good for them. Forget their displeasure. You continue with the same discussions and same subjects that you had previously."

These requests do not suit Sandie, but she is reluctant to relate her concerns to her supervisor. "More aggravation," thinks Sandie. "Why does Paul get a salary raise and my salary gets zilch?" Strike two for the job! The work piles up, and Sandie works incessantly, becoming "tired all the time." She wishes her kids would not be so demanding when she gets home. She wishes she wouldn't fly off the handle so easily at home. She is beginning to feel a little confused and desperate. She decides to gather staff suggestions without consulting her supervisor and is determined to make changes in accordance with the staff's ideas.

One obvious direction is to adjust the inservice topics and procedures to the number of years the staff member has been with the agency. This means that staff members would attend different inservice meetings depending on their gaps in skills and knowledge and their previous experiences in the organization. It sounds so logical; most of the staff members like it. But there are some who resent the fact that because they are more recent employees they might have to attend more frequently than others. Some of them complain, not to Sandie, but to Paul and to the supervisor. Even though more individuals praise than denounce the training, the supervisor speaks to Sandie about the failures rather than the successes. In fact, Sandie recalls that he once mentioned that, "If I don't say anything, you don't need to worry about anything. I'll tell you if you're wrong." Sandie gritted her teeth . . . even in her sleep, her husband told her. "It was too much."

She feels the growing annoyance and knows she is more tired—exhausted, indeed! She wonders, "What am I doing in an agency that does not claim that its primary purpose is to help the clients?" She cannot figure out why she remains in a job where she is not appreciated. So many things bother her—red tape for the clients, no recognition for her, her family life is more intolerable, Paul is obviously a chauvinist, the supervisor is impossible. She quits!

Several points spring forth from Sandie's problems. The person-environment lack of fit is aggravated by her lack of resources in energy, time, and skills to deal with the demands of her job. The policies and demands of her supervisor create a role structure for her that conflicts with the furtherance of the objectives for inservice training. Psychosocial strain grows for her in the work place, in her home life, and in her feelings about herself. Her resignation from her job may be considered a failure, since she did not develop coping strategies in that particular work place. However, for Sandie, under the controlling circumstances, was not quitting the wisest solution?

Managing interpersonal stress. How can stress be managed? How can an individual develop a self-satisfying, flexible, and empathic approach to human service working relationships? Is the answer to reduce stress in interpersonal situations by agreeing with the opinions of other people? Would it be wiser to reject the other person as incompetent or not understandable? Or, perhaps the better way is to devaluate the importance of disagreements, in fact of any event, discounting the frequency or the extent of annoyance? (Steiner, 1970). These may

work some of the time for some of the people. However, stress management is far more complex, and the coping strategies discussed in this chapter represent only a few of the possible directions that can be useful. Stress filter, neutralizing the stressors, relaxation procedures, and biofeedback are just the beginning.*

The stress filter and neutralizing the stressors. To establish a stress filter, the person must become aware of the stressors that "gets his or her goat" the most and must identify how he or she is dealing with these stressors. Then attempts to neutralize the stressor begin. Each person must consider questions such as, "Can certain demands of the job or the family be reduced or eliminated? Can personal goals, preferences, and expectations be altered in some way to make them less stressful? Are there skills or knowledge that might further competency and attainment of goals? Is there any other method that would be useful to bolster one's esteem, one's energy level, one's level of tension?" Some individuals who can answer the foregoing questions honestly and satisfactorily can subsequently experiment with the changes until they find their effective stress filter(s). In neutralizing the stressors they discover valuable procedures in stress management.

Relaxation procedures. Some people gain even more satisfaction from relaxation procedures. Research supports the contention that the strain of excessive stress increases muscle tension (Cautela and Groden, 1978). A pain in the neck has many subtle meanings about stress and strain. It follows therefore that tension reduction tends to reduce strain, and, in turn, the individual finds tackling dis-stress more possible. The individual who can identify the muscles that he or she tends to tighten during stress has moved forward toward relaxation. Individuals who are aware of their primary tensed

---

*For further information on stress see Blake and Mouton, 1980; Carney, 1971; Cherniss, 1980; Edelwich and Brodsky, 1980; Greenberg and Valletutti, 1980; Klausner, 1968; Kutash and others, 1980; McGrath, 1970; Pines and Aronson, 1981; Sarason and Spielberger, 1979; Schafer, 1978; and Selye, 1975, 1976, 1980.

muscles and have learned relaxation procedures relax before undertaking a possible stressor and thus neutralize the effect of possible strain. Before or after a stressful situation relaxation relieves tension. It takes practice, however. Individuals who have high blood pressure must be cautious, since the exercises that teach relaxation initially tense the body, thus increasing blood pressure. However, when a person with high blood pressure develops the ability to relax, blood pressure can be lowered significantly.

A person learns to relax by sitting in a comfortable chair and proceeding to tighten and relax muscle groups beginning with the forehead or the toes and proceeding downward or upward as appropriate. Each muscle group is tensed: the forehead, the eyes, the nose, the mouth and lips, the tongue, the jaw, the neck, and so on (see Exercise 2-8). Cautela and Groden (1978) present a carefully designed program for relaxation in their manual.

Relaxation also can be accomplished by means of leisure activities. Leisure serves many purposes, but it frequently is relegated to the third "box of life" (Bolles, 1981). Leisure activities have been considered primarily the province of the later retirement years and have been given connotations of worthlessness. Bolles decries the designation of education for the first part (box) of the life cycle, work for the second part (box), and leisure as the box that is left for old age. Others such as Neulinger (1974) have espoused the importance of leisure as bracing relief, actually a stimulant, that sustains a more positive outlook toward work. Garte and Rosenblum (1978) describe their leisure consciousness workshops for "lighting fires in burned-out counselors." They define "leisure therapy as the process of utilizing leisure activities for the purpose of increasing personal and professional effectiveness," and write that at the "conclusion of the workshop, participants develop personal prescriptions for an individually oriented treatment program for the use of their leisure time." Small group processes and workshop exercises encourage participants to examine their attitudes and values with regard to work and leisure. Exercise 8-1 presents two examples of activities related to work and leisure.

Biofeedback and other stress management measures. Yoga breathing, meditation, and anxiety-decreasing drugs are additional approaches available for controlling responses to stressors. Biofeedback uses an electronic technique that "can enhance discrimination of subtle physiological functioning . . . [by producing] and external 'effect' whereas previously the effect was below awareness" (Budzynski and Peffer, 1980). Biofeedback of sympathetic nervous system activity is being used increasingly to manage stress-related symptoms. Instruments for measuring signs of stress are used in clinical settings, and smaller, less costly units are being produced with which an individual can be trained to self-monitor temperature and skin resistance changes (Thought Technology, 1981). Voluntary control of psychophysiological* processes is the primary objective of biofeedback relaxation systems.

The pivotal component in stress management is the person in distress. No one technique is the supreme answer for every person. Kutash (1980) expressed the notion as follows:

If stress can be experienced in the interpersonal environment, the physical environment, the mental environment, and the physiological environment, prevention is certainly a multi-faceted enterprise and needs to involve multidisciplinary input to be effective. Psychological, sociological, ecological, biological, and medical factors all figure in the equation. Ultimately, however, each person must become involved in his own individual program, as both client and practitioner on the individual level and as agitator and effector on the global level.

These conclusions support the urgency for psychoeducators, psychosocial developers and other creative expansions of human services.

---

*Interrelationships among and interactive responses of emotional (affective), sociocultural, mental (cognitive) and other psychological characteristics of an individual and somatic (physiological) factors.

Exercise 8-1
HOW DO YOU FEEL ABOUT YOUR WORK AND LEISURE ACTIVITIES?
(may be done individually and discussed in the group)

Time: APPROXIMATELY 30 MINUTES

For this exercise think of work as those activities you are required to perform, whether these are education or employment. Leisure includes those "play" activities you choose to do. Each participant follows the directions in Parts 1 and 2. If small groups are formed, the individual responses are discussed in the group.

Part 1

If you had sufficient funds and might be supported in whatever you needed to do for the remainder of your lifetime, what would you do? List the activities in Fig. 8-5 and then rank them in terms of priority from "most wanted" to "least wanted." Use the number "1" for most wanted and continue from that number. In the column marked "W" check the items you consider to be *work;* in the column marked "L" check those you consider *leisure*. Which of the items predominate—work or leisure? Which are the priority items? What does your list tell you about your attitudes and values regarding work and leisure?

Part 2

What activities have you found most enjoyable during the past 6 months? List these activities in a copy of Fig. 8-5 and follow a similar procedure as in the first part of this exercise, rating your activities from most enjoyable (number "1") to least enjoyable. Also approximate the frequency with which you performed these activities during the past 6 months. What do the results of this list reveal to you about your more satisfying activities?

Modified from Garte, S.H., and Rosenblum, M.L.: Lighting fires in burned-out counselors, Personn. Guid. J. **57:**158-160, 1978.

List of activities	Rank from most wanted (1) to least wanted	Work activities (W)	Leisure activities (L)
	Total number		

Fig. 8-5. Free-to-be-me list of work and leisure.

PSYCHOEDUCATORS

Psychoeducation focuses on skill training and regards the person seeking problem solution as a learner—a student. The underlying assumption is that it is commonplace for people to have problems and to experience frustrations and that three questions must be considered to optimize the learner's need satisfaction: (1) Would redesigning the person's social system further his or her self-determination and self-esteem? (2) Would the development or refinement of specified personal limitations lead to improved health and more appropriate and satisfying interpersonal relationships? (3) Would specific training advance the person's educational, employment, and leisure goals? (Guerney, 1978; Ivey and Authier, 1978; Ivey and Simek-Downing, 1980). As "learners" psychoeducators become competent in life-sustaining and socialization skills and in turn help the clients—their students—to learn these skills (Ivey and Authier, 1978). Psychoeducation has wide applicability in many problem-solving areas. Six of these are briefly mentioned in this discussion: parent-child relationships, rural helping systems, corrections personnel, management attitudes, mental illness, and public education.

Parent-child relationships

Parents, are the first significant nurturing forces in the child's life, must take an active role in family management. Yet, in spite of the crucial impact of these originators, many parents flounder. The following paragraphs mention several procedures that train parents in the skills of parenting: behavior management system, helping parents to help themselves, parenting skills, systematic parent training, systematic training for effective parenting, and tough love. Finally, some brief comments are included about organizations that aid parents of mentally ill offspring.

Behavior management system. Normile (1971) proposes a behavior management system (BMS) that directs parents in the observation of their child's behavior so that more successful parent roles and children's development results. BMS depends on the establishment and preservation of the child's self-esteem, a frequently forgotten need for children. The psychoeducator's role is to help the parent deal with children's desired behavior with positive reinforcement and to become skillful in denying reinforcement for undesirable behavior. Parental skills are trained and strengthened through practice and discussions with the psychoeducator, who frequently models the skills for parents to observe, practice with their children (under supervision), and later continue on their own with consultations with the psychoeducator as needed.

Helping parents to help themselves. A unique behavioral approach to training of the mentally retarded was instituted by Elliott and others (1978) in Florida. The goal was to teach parents from a wide range of socioeconomic and educational backgrounds the skills to train their children. Parents were provided with observational, reinforcement, and activities skills in the class sessions that were reaffirmed in home visits. Project staff noted the easing of family tensions and positive changes in children's behavior.

Parenting skills. A trainer's manual and a workbook are the tools for developing a greater sense of competence and comfort for parents about their role and practices. Group sessions and home practice assignments enrich and reinforce the skills developed. Two major keys are emphasized: "I am worthwhile" and "Competence and responsibility." After the parent-child relationship has been evaluated, the following major areas are considered: building a relationship with the child, discipline and managing children's behavior, parents' management of their feelings, and principles of behavior management, including techniques for recording and reinforcing behavior (Abidon, 1976a,b).

Systematic parent training (SPT). SPT includes a training text for clinicians and a wide variety of community agents in the field of child mental health. This social learning approach to helping children with disturbing behavior requires a minimum of professional time and effort with more intensive involvement of parents. Five major interventions are used in SPT: (1) social learning concepts, (2) basic discriminational training, (3) home contingency programs, (4) punishment procedures, and (5) parent counseling (Miller, 1975).

Systematic training for effective parenting (STEP). STEP is a nine-session 6- to twelve-member parent-study group program developing parenting skills that foster mutual respect, cooperation, responsibility, and self-reliance. A kit contains a parent's handbook, five cassette recordings, charts, discussion guide charts, posters, and a leader's manual. The nine steps answer questions about such concerns as children's behavior and misbehavior, children's manipulation of parents with emotional behavior, the difference between a "good" parent and a "responsible" parent, differentiating between praise and encouragement, listening and "closed" and "open" responses, the exploration of alternatives contrasted with advice giving, development of responsibility through logical rather than natural consequences, decision making, family meetings, and development of parental confidence and potential (Dinkemeyer and McKay, 1979).

Tough love. In Pennsylvania a program called "tough love" (Krucoff, 1981d) seeks to teach parents to establish a "bottom line" for their children's behavior. Parents are trained to assert themselves as family managers, responsive to their children's acceptable behavior and "tough" in their responses to unacceptable behavior. The Yorks, originators of the method, help parents whose children have similar drug problems to band together and collaborate in setting comparable limits and standards of behavior. Offspring are expected to "toe the line," and no infringement of established rules is allowed. Parents emphasize their tough love by predictable reactions if rules are disregarded and by making certain that their offspring have an alternative place to stay if they are not permitted into their home. Frequently parents need ego-bolstering from one another or from the psychoeducator to maintain their tough love stance. The procedure is not applicable for all parents be-

cause of the stringency of its methods, but others support its value in behavioral change. Tough love offers fertile research possibilities to identify the variables involved in its procedures as well as its level of effectiveness.

Families of the mentally ill. Families of the mentally ill also profit from psychoeducation. There are formal programs conducted by professionals and support groups for families organized as self-help discussion groups. In Silver Spring, Md., Threshold Alliance for the Mentally Ill conducts monthly meetings at which speakers present information about housing for the deinstitutionalized mentally ill person, wills to provide for chronically mentally ill relatives, and other pertinent facts. Threshold maintains a group with an empathic atmosphere to which, as one mother stated, "I can turn to someone who knows how I feel—who is standing in my feet." Support, advocacy, and information are some of the objectives of Threshold, which recently affiliated with the nationwide coalition of state and local advocacy groups (National Alliance for Mentally Ill) dedicated to better care and treatment for the chronically mentally ill (see Appendix D).

Rural helping systems

The problems of families and of disabilities exist in all communities. Rural areas, particularly those which are isolated, depend on helping systems that are unique to the rural environment. Three categories of helping systems are noted by Hanton (1980): (1) *the primary helping system* (natural helpers)—a voluntary effort in which neighbor helps neighbor with direct help and also acts as a gatekeeper, selecting individuals who may become part of the primary group, thus minimizing change; (2) *the informal helping system*—churches, schools, institutions, agencies, and programs indirectly involved with providing services for people; and (3) *the formal helping system*—institutions, agencies, and programs directly responsible for the provision of helping services.

The human service worker in rural areas discovers that the formal helping system often is sought last, usually in crisis situations after all resources of the primary and informal helping systems have been exhausted. Distance plus hours of availability may be at the root of this infrequent utilization. Therefore skillful helpers coordinate their efforts with primary and/or informal systems. Through training of these two fundamental systems, these groups become a source for client identification. For example, teachers and administrators, properly trained, identify and report suspected instances of child abuse and neglect and also act as a referral service in the absence of the social worker (Hanton, 1980).

Training natural helpers focuses on the primary helping system and prepares these individuals to be psychoeducators. Kelley and Kelley (1980) describe a training program in Iowa that originated after studies indicated an extreme shortage of mental health services in rural areas. These trainers recognized that specialized clinical techniques appropriate in urban areas were not as effective with rural clients. In fact, the small primary community in rural areas tended to blunt the benefit of help for those persons soliciting services from "outsiders." The training program included consultation from staff members of the local mental health center and a competency-based model of education, including Carkhuff's (1969) characteristics of "good helpers"—communication of empathy and respect, concreteness, genuineness, self-disclosure, confrontation, and immediacy of relationship as well as interviewing skills, family dynamics, recognition and management of depression, when and how to make referrals, and when to seek professional consultation. Through this process of psychoeducation the natural helpers were offered professional services, and because of their increased competencies, their skills and knowledge had a ripple effect, aiding others in their community. Community control and self-reliance were bolstered, and the existing folk system is now supported through this program with professional assistance available as needed (Kelley and Kelley, 1980).

Corrections personnel

The Stay'n Out Program established by the New York Regional Chapter of Therapeutic Communities of America identifies and rehabilitates substance abusers and sensitizes corrections personnel to appropriately confront drug offenders with the chronicity of their problems. Treatment and education rather than containment are the primary objectives of the program. At Bayview Correctional Facility for Women the vigorous program requires the incarcerated women to abide by two sets of rules: the institution's and those of Stay'n Out. After the orientation to the program the women receive group and individual counseling; family and significant others also are involved, if possible. The women can enroll in high school or college courses, classes in English as a second language, or homemaking skills training. All the women are expected to attend seminars on subjects such as employment, education, finding housing, and familiarization with contemporary society. During the final phase of the program the women may be parolled into therapeutic communities (NIAAA Information and Feature Service, 1981a).

In spite of the exacting requirements of Stay'n Out, the focus on rehabilitation encourages the offender to examine her maladaptive behavior, to learn new skills or refine former skills, and to begin to assume responsibility for her actions. "This program has been effective in its goals of reducing recidivism—more than 80 women have graduated from the Bayview program since it began in 1978, and only 8 have returned to prison" (NIAAA Information and Feature Service, 1981a).

Management attitudes

Psychoeducation may be accomplished by human systems instructors or trainers from several disciplines. It can take place in a classroom, club house, home, mental health center, or other setting. It teaches the troubled person, the family, the psychologist, the educator, the employee, and the manager of a corporation the skills needed for improved interpersonal relationships, a higher functioning level, and more satisfactory productivity. An innovative example of a form of psychoeducation with management personnel is demonstrated by the International Center for the Disabled (ICD) of New York City. ICD has initiated a corporate management training program—"The Awareness Factor: A Management Skills Seminar"—which is described as

an innovative approach to helping corporations meet the requirements of Equal Employment Opportunity (EEO) and affirmative action programs for disabled persons. The program is designed to explore and clarify negative attitudes that affect the decision-making process, to improve problem-solving skills, and to provide information critical to effective implementation of affirmative action compliance. . . . "The Awareness Factor" signals the increased responsiveness of the rehabilitation profession to the needs of the business community, and seeks to build a more effective working partnership among disabled job seekers, rehabilitation specialists and employers (Schweitzer and Deely, 1980).

The *awareness factor* to which the seminar directs attention concerns attitude clarification. In-

formation about disabilities or about affirmative action is insufficient to alter negative attitudes. Unless an individual has direct or indirect experiences with disabilities, facts alone are insufficient to prompt attitudinal change. The seminar encompasses modules that include the *affective* component—attitude exploration and clarification; the *behavioral* component—problem solving and decision making; and the *cognitive* component—information and resource materials.

Exercise 8-2 exemplifies some of the components just described. The purpose is similar—consciousness raising, an increased awareness to "feel" the experiences of a blind person.

Mental illness

Psychotherapy and psychosocial rehabilitation overlap with psychoeducation. The objectives—the client's self-fulfillment with higher functioning levels—are similar, but the labels, training, competencies, and staff titles differ. Since psychoeducation is geared to skill development and involves a student-trainer relationship, it emphasizes

---

Exercise 8-2
HOW WOULD YOU DEAL WITH BLINDNESS? *(should be done individually and discussed in the group)*

Time: VARIES DEPENDING ON ACTIVITIES PURSUED

Individuals who depend on their lenses for distance vision can readily experience the increased visual impairment—the fuzziness—that ensues when their lenses are removed. These people can observe their own behavior as well as the reactions of others to their lowered degree of visual acuity. An even more cogent experience occurs if you cover your eyes with a mask such as the one drawn in Fig. 7-1. Use a cane (white, if available) if you wish. The simulated blindness should be tried out at home for about an hour and then attempted, if feasible, in different physical settings such as a shopping mall, a store, the street, and in someone's home. For safety you should have the assistance of a friend or relative when not in the familiar surroundings of your home.

Other experiences with impairments may be added to your experiential repertoire, such as auditory impairment with the use of ear plugs, cotton, or ear muffs—use a pad to communicate; lameness with the use of a cane, crutches, or a loosely bandaged (elastic bandage) leg or part of the leg or arm.

A follow-up of these experiments in physical challenges might be accomplished in group discussion of your feelings and the reactions of others. Note your coping style, and compare it with that of others. Think about what you have learned from these experiences, what else you would like to know, and how these simulated disabilities could assist you if you are a psychoeducator.

a different scope of expertise that encompasses several levels and fields of education. The previous discussions cited the application of psychoeducation with parent-child relationships, rural human services, corrections personnel and offenders, and management attitudes. Psychoeducation also is used with autistic and psychiatric patients.

Autistic adults. At Napa State Hospital in California the behavioral approach used with autistic adults is based on task analysis to fill in the gaps in the individual's development. A film, *Teaching Makes the Difference,* describes the sequential conditioning program and the reinforcement employed to increase eye contact, communication, conceptualization, money management, and other skills for moving into the "real world" (Walsh, 1980). This film, a teaching device for staff members, portrays the student-patients in the process of skill development.

Psychiatric patients. Psychoeducation was also used to create a pool of former psychiatric patients in a New York State institution who could provide sophisticated "self-help" for people still undergoing treatment. A local community college serves as the source for the educative effort.

La Guardia Community College and Transitional Services for New York, Inc., recently concluded the first semester of a unique joint project to provide college level training for mentally handicapped persons who wish to become mental health workers. . . . Former psychiatric patients have not been universally acceptable or accepted in the professional helping role. Despite the normal anxiety aroused by the stresses and mini-crisis of being a student, those involved appear to have gained a heightened awareness of their human potential. . . . They unabashedly verbalize their renewed hopes and goals, their energy levels have risen, along with an evident capacity for new experiences and self-direction. . . . The intrinsic value of this experience in the overall program of Transitional Services has yet to be evaluated. . . . Staffs believe it to be an outstanding and productive educational model that is succeeding (Williams, 1980).

The variables involved in this program are numerous and have not been identified as yet. However, the important point is that these trained helpers gain momentum toward "wellness" and become role models for other patients who are still hospitalized.

Public education

The most effective psychoeducation is ineffective if the rehabilitated individual is not accepted in the community. David Gilmour Blythe voiced this disillusionment blatantly in a letter he sent to Hugh Gorley in 1857:

. . . I have grown
Almost gray and half-demented
In trying to find some place where I could
        Get acquainted.
Some place where man and man might "dwell
Together in unity," and not tell
Lies on one another . . .
I've never found
Such place. And though I've hunted 'round
Perhaps with goggles on, I'll just
Bet my life it don't exist
        On top of ground.

Perhaps, above all other goals, the singular role of psychoeducation is to sensitize the public to "What if I couldn't?" Yet attitudinal change is a complex matter. The following two attempts to educate the public employ diverse approaches—one aims at providing actual experiences, and the other provides information.

Experiencing disabilities. To dispel some of the fallacies and myths surrounding physical and mental handicaps, Boston's Children's Museum assembled a participatory exhibition for the 1981 International Year of Disabled Persons. This display traveled throughout the United States, encouraging the public to explore feelings about various disabling conditions and possible solutions. The exhibit included Braille clocks and typewriter, wheelchairs, crutches, and devices to help mentally retarded and hearing impaired individuals. Individuals' remarks as they were leaving emphasized their astonishment at "how much these people could do" and "how tough to cope with these difficulties but these people really weren't helpless or hopeless.'' The Boston exhibit also contained information about the various disabilities that was enriched by the reality of temporary ''tryouts.''

Telephone counseling. Another form of public education concentrates on fact-giving by means of a telephone counseling service. This program, Counseline, is provided as a public service of the Psychiatric Institute of Montgomery County, Md. and the Mental Health Association of the District of Columbia. The library contains 50 tapes on subjects such as assertiveness, self-confidence, emotional problems, sexuality, marriage, divorce and separation, interpersonal relationships, family relationships, suicide, and alcohol and drugs. This free, confidential service is obtained by a telephone call to request from the operator the program number selected from the distributed brochure. The service provides information and suggestions for resources for assistance when needed.

■ ■ ■

The examples of psychoeducation programs just described present only a cursory glance at an immense and varied source. This model of service delivery is summarized by Guerney (1978) as follows:

[It] calls for teaching basic psychosocial skills to every adult (and child) who wants to learn them as soon as possible, dropping stigmatizing labels such as ''neurotic'' or ''maladjusted'' and making no greater distinctions among clients than would be made between those in a class for the mathematically inclined versus those who don't like math. In place of a one-to-one system of treatment, curricula with appropriate texts, films, behavioral homework, etc., would be designed to be used on a massive scale. Each program would be so designed as to encompass a broad range of individual differences in capacity for learning those particular behaviors. Eventually, individual tutoring would be reserved for those who already had failed to benefit from the programmatic group instruction, or for those who desire and could afford the luxury of private tutoring.

Challenge to psychoeducation

Arbuckle (1977) challenges the ''skills approach to counseling'' proposed by psychoeducation as a packaged means of instant mental health that omits certain human values. These values are essential for coping as well as for individual expansion toward changing unsuitable environments. Since psychoeducation is comparatively new in the history of human service systems, evaluation is not extensive. Perhaps the safeguard remains in the fact that there can not be one answer; many procedures are necessary for the diversified views and needs of both helpers and clients. Psychoeducation, for example, provides training in psychosocial skills. Psychosocial rehabilitation adds other dimensions.

PSYCHOSOCIAL REHABILITATION

Psychosocial rehabilitation is not so much a process as a model for preparing an individual to function more satisfactorily and satisfyingly in a community with other people. Psychoeducation is part of the process of rehabilitation. Thus psychosocial development is important for the person with mental illness, the mentally retarded person, the physically disabled, and so on. Psychoeducation would be the channel for the skills training that would prepare the individual to increase his or her level of functioning. The differentiations between psychosocial rehabilitation and psychoeducation are not clearcut, except that the rehabilitator is usually referred to as a counselor and the psychoeducator is called a teacher. Client and student also have different connotations.

Psychoeducation and psychosocial rehabilitation

Psychoeducation and psychosocial rehabilitation are similar; both ''labels'' legitimatize skills training for persons with disabilities.

Historically, the psychiatric treatment of those with mental illness has paid more attention to discovering the ''causes and cures'' of mental illness than to the rehabilitation of persons with psychiatric disabilities. . . .

Treatment approaches focused rather exclusively on changing the client's psychodynamic functioning. Rehabilitation intervention was thought to be unnecessary if the client's symptoms could be either eliminated or reduced, or if the client could acquire insight into personal behavior. However, these approaches did not produce sustained improvements and many previously treated psychiatrically disabled persons had to be rehospitalized. A need was recognized for a rehabilitation program that prevented further deterioration or reoccurrence of psychiatric disability and that consequently would lead to a more lasting rehabilitation (Rehab Brief, 1980).

Interpersonal skill development. Rehabilitation builds on the person's strengths and resources, establishes a systematic program to teach (or reteach) new (or former) skills, and assists the individual in coping with deficits that cannot be altered. Interpersonal skill development is a crucial aspect of this training, since relationships with others often are the determining factors in career choices and successes as well as in a variety of daily encounters (Gerrard, Boniface, and Love, 1980; Guerney, 1977). Exercise 8-3 offers one way to examine interpersonal skills.

Exercise 8-3
INTERPERSONAL SKILLS SCALE *(should be done individually)*

Time: APPROXIMATELY 45 MINUTES

This rating scale is to help you think about your ability to initiate, develop, and maintain effective and fulfilling relationships with other people. After each item circle the number in the rating scale that you think best describes your own behavior. Your responses will reflect your opinions more accurately if you *do not read the note at the end of the questions until you have responded to the 24 questions.*

	Not at all				All the time
A. When I talk with another person, I usually:
1. Appear comfortable and relaxed	1	2	3	4	5
2. Appear disinterested and bored	1	2	3	4	5
3. Look the person in the eye	1	2	3	4	5
4. Interrupt the other's talking	1	2	3	4	5
5. Compete for "talking time"	1	2	3	4	5
6. Follow the other's comments	1	2	3	4	5
B. When I talk with another person, I usually:
7. Sense the feelings of that person	1	2	3	4	5
8. Am able to notice if the person is tense	1	2	3	4	5
9. Am unable to identify hidden meaning in what is said	1	2	3	4	5
10. Find that I misunderstand what the person is saying	1	2	3	4	5
11. Find that it is necessary to let the other person know I understand what is being said	1	2	3	4	5
12. Do not note reactions to my comments	1	2	3	4	5
C. When I talk with another person, I usually:
13. Tell others only part of what I think and feel	1	2	3	4	5
14. Am able to express anger toward the person	1	2	3	4	5
15. Hide my emotions	1	2	3	4	5
16. Am able to disagree openly when I want	1	2	3	4	5
17. Am able to express warm feelings	1	2	3	4	5
18. Have difficulty expressing gratitude	1	2	3	4	5

Continued.

Exercise 8-3—cont'd
INTERPERSONAL SKILLS SCALE *(should be done individually)*

	Not at all				All the time
D. When I tell another person something about himself or herself, I usually:					
19. Try not to judge the person	1	2	3	4	5
20. Make vague, general comments	1	2	3	4	5
21. Try to make constructive comments	1	2	3	4	5
22. Do not consider the other's needs	1	2	3	4	5
23. Find my communication clear	1	2	3	4	5
24. Impose my values on the other	1	2	3	4	5

NOTE: The *Interpersonal Skills Scale* consists of four skill factors:

A. *Attending behavior:* the interpersonal skill that allows the listener to appear comfortable and relaxed, to maintain comfortable eye contact, and to follow the verbal comments of the other person. Items 1, 3, and 6 indicate positive attending behavior (see Chapter 2).

B. *Sensitivity and listening:* the interpersonal skills that allow the listener to hear, to accurately understand, and to communicate to the other his or her understanding of both the feelings and content expressed. Items 7, 8, and 11 indicate favorable sensitivity and listening skills (see Chapter 3).

C. *Expression of feelings:* the interpersonal skill that allows one to express emotions clearly and to share them easily with others. Items 14, 16, and 17 indicate skill in openness, sharing and expression of feelings (see discussion of Johari's window in Chapter 1 and Chapters 3 and 5).

D. *Feedback:* the interpersonal skill that allows one to give helpful, descriptive, nonjudgmental, specific, and immediate observations and reactions to others. Items 19, 21, and 23 indicate positive feedback skills (see Chapter 4).

Modified from *Interpersonal Skills Scale*, Student Counseling Center, Normal, Ill., Illinois State University.

Components of psychosocial rehabilitation. Interpersonal skill development is only one aspect of the six related dimensions of psychosocial rehabilitation (E.D. Schulman, 1981) (Fig. 8-6):

□ *Psychiatric and psychological services*—crisis stabilization, symptom amelioration, medication management

□ *Family services and other social services*—back-up support (financial, counseling, respite care), income maintenance, finances management, counseling for the client

□ *Community services*—training for community living, community involvement and development activity, community education

□ *Educational services*—enriching educational resources, filling in educational gaps, furthering educational opportunities as needed

□ *Vocational services*—identifying work interests and work-skill resources, work training (work habits, job opportunities, placement assistance)

□ *Sociorecreational services*—social and leisure skills developed, opportunities for day, evening and weekend activities

Each of the six components of the psychosocial rehabilitation spectrum contributes to the quality of life, but each component varies in significance for an individual. Often, psychosocial rehabilitation fails in part or completely because the human services do not heed cultural differences. This occurs on an international scale when people from one culture immigrate and settle in another. It occurs from the national perspective when the approaches used with the urban population are trans-

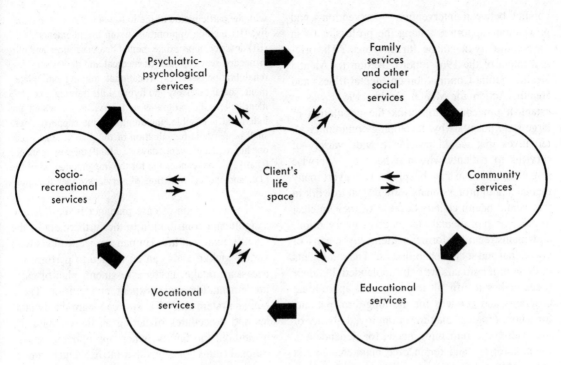

Fig. 8-6. Six components of the psychosocial rehabilitation spectrum. (Data from Schulman, E.D.: Rehabilitation of the mentally ill: an international perspective, Washington, D.C., 1981, President's Committee on Employment of the Handicapped.)

ferred to the rural setting or when minority viewpoints are disregarded.

Deinstitutionalization

Deinstitutionalization is based on an ideology closely allied with psychosocial rehabilitation. Two unrelated phenomena sparked the concept of deinstitutionalization. In the 1950s the tranquilizer chlorpromazine (Thorazine) was discovered. It is a calming agent that controls certain symptoms of mental disorders so that patients could be released from institutions sooner. In the 1960s the Kennedys supported efforts to noninstitutionalize and deinstitutionalize the mentally retarded. "Training" became a key word, with increased expertise in furthering mentally retarded persons' abilities. There was an increasing realization, however, that drugs and/or therapy alone did not prepare these formerly institutionalized persons for comfortable community living. Other services were required to establish and maintain suitable behavior. Gradually, innovative programs arose, partially because of grass-roots movements and partially in response to civil rights initiatives.

The case manager. Legislation and the United States Constitution have mandated effective community alternatives through affirmative action, but neither of these guarantees can follow mentally retarded and the mentally ill persons into the community to secure their welfare. Sometimes concerted efforts do attain the letter but not the spirit of the law because the philosophy of the institution finds its way into the planning and development of community services (Gostin, 1980). Many perplexing questions provoke consternation among human service workers: Have the expectations for deinstitutionalization been too unrealistic? too simplistic? too extensive? too rapid? Is there a basic conflict between intervention—postvention—and prevention supporters among the professionals in the community mental health movement? The original intent of the 1961 report "Action for Mental Health" (Joint Commission on Mental Illness and Health, Action for Mental Health, 1961) was to establish procedures to shrink the population of large state hospitals by developing community alternatives that would provide a wide variety of services to patients who had been or otherwise might have been in state hospitals. However, many mental health professionals were drawn to work in the mental health centers because of their interest in prevention of mental illness, crisis intervention, and mainstreaming former patients by means of vocational and social rehabilitation. The sentiments of these professionals are to be applauded, but their focus makes it difficult to implement appropriate programs and services for the long-term patients for whom progress may mean improved quality of life with some remaining needs for dependency, for monitoring, and for income maintenance and other public support (Lamb, 1981). Are there channels for altering the lack of suitable programs so that clients avoid falling between the cracks?

The Mental Health Systems Act. No one answer will satisfy every community for the same reason that no one innovative program can be transferred unaltered from one community to another. Cultural, geographic, and human differences make fixed transplantations unsuccessful. In spite of this cultural diversity, there is value in the cross-fertilization of ideas added to the core of fundamental skills and knowledge of the human service worker. The case manager plan is one of these ideas incorporated into the 1980 Mental Health Systems Act (P.L. 93-398). The functions of the case manager are described in this act as follows:

Each inpatient mental health facility shall develop a written treatment and services plan for each chronically mentally ill individual to be discharged or diverted from the facility . . . in consultation with a case manager in the community mental health center or other appropriate entity in the mental health service area. . . . Such plan shall (I) to the maximum extent feasible, be developed with the participation of the individual . . . and the family; (II) include appropriate living arrangements . . . ; (III) describe appropriate mental health services and other needed services such as medical and dental services, rehabilitation services, vocational training and placement, social services, and living skills training; and (IV) identify specific programs and services for which the individual is eligible, including income support. There shall be periodic reevaluation of the plan at least every one hundred and twenty days . . . [and] the case manager [shall] . . . be responsible for the implementation of the plan and the coordination of services under the plan.

The conception of case manager is feasible and a significant contribution to the furtherment of the client's quality of life. Human service workers with varied backgrounds can be trained to perform the necessary intake, needs assessment, plan of care, implementation, reassessment, and revision. These human system change agents can learn the dynamics and procedures of acting as liaison with the institution; the family, when appropriate; the vocational counselors and other medical and nonmedical human service workers; the prospective employers; the community human systems; and, most important, the clients. Several states and the District of Columbia believe this plan is practicable and "do-able." Mental health personnel are being retrained, and new recruits are becoming part of the human service network. A proposed plan for Montgomery County, Md., is cited in the following description.

Montgomery County Mental Health Association. The Montogomery County Mental Health Association (1980) recently proposed a case management program for deinstitutionalized mental patients with the following objective: "to provide chronically mentally ill individuals who have been hospitalized for more than one year a coordinated mental health, and related social support service as they return to the community."

The case manager would become knowledgeable about the whole spectrum of community resources and act as a link between the institution and the community, expediting and advocating on the client's behalf when indicated and developing a supportive relationship to fulfill the person's needs and to facilitate his or her assimilation into the community. The program proposes the use of work-study students from a local 2-year community college. These students would be trained at the college and at the Mental Health Association during their 20-hour-a-week paid employment. Thus the students enrich their skills and are offered a practical opportunity to determine whether the case management role is harmonious with their interests and goals. To round out the services, other programs of the association, such as the Volunteer Corps and the Hotline, would collaborate in the arrangement and implementation of transitional planning and aftercare for deinstitutionalized persons. The concept of case management is not new, but the expansion of functions and networks to bridge the transitions and settlement of the deinstitutionalized person moving into the community adds a new dimension and specific training for human service workers.

Developmental programing. The case manager is a promising role for the training and employment of human service workers. Other innovations in community programs introduce programing directed to the development of the potentials and self-awareness of physically, emotionally, mentally, and socially impaired individuals. Gloria Blum of Feeling Good Associates in Mill Valley, Calif., is the originator of Feeling Good, Yes, No, and Project MENCH. By means of a file (or videotape), a book, a deck of cards, and workshops therapists, counselors, teachers, parents, and clients are trained in self-awareness, acceptance of feelings and sexuality, and assertiveness. The central aim of the program is the cultivation of self-esteem.

Project MENCH (Meaningful Education Now for Citizens with Handicaps) is planned for mentally retarded adolescents. This project's objectives add a new purpose to self-enrichment skill training; the newly trained personnel from this program are expected to serve other clients labeled retarded by assisting them in developing self-esteem, social skills, sexual information, and sexually appropriate

behavior. Eventually, the more competent of the trained group also are expected to become the leaders of new groups of mentally retarded adolescents. Each group becomes the model of success for the next group (Blum and Goldenberg, 1979). In essence, this is psychoeducational methodology for psychosocial development that seeks to promote the socialization of the mentally retarded adolescent as a part of the human service network and to modify the concept of normality to include the variation in competencies of these individuals.

Community alternatives

The case manager described in the previous discussion provides the bridge between the institution and the community, and developmental programing exemplifies the fundamental skills for self-actualization especially important for individuals often considered failures by themselves and others. Additional human service roles and unique functions in augmented community alternatives are essential to further the community acceptance of persons with disabilities. A brief sampling of a few of the innovative programs and of creative staffing is presented in the following paragraphs.

Rehabilitation Mental Health Services, Inc., San Jose, Calif. Degrees are not the primary criterion for employment at RMHS. Previous experience, an ideology supporting respect for clients, a positive outlook, and team compatibility are foremost considerations. The functions and titles vary, but all personnel are expected to work together as a staff team and with the residents and other program participants as a total team. The services include psychiatric evaluation, counseling, recreation, and vocational rehabilitation. A number of residential support services similar to RMHS exist elsewhere in California and throughout the United States. However, the uniqueness of RMHS programs emerges from the precedents it has originated, such as the following:

☐ A residential program with primary focus on providing vocational and job placement services

☐ A residential program that demonstrates that clients viewed in need of state hospitalization could be more effectively served in a community residential program

☐ An alternative to institutionalization for acute patients who formerly might have been placed in a locked hospital setting

☐ The use of paraprofessionals in the provision of health and human services

The last item is of particular significance for human service workers whose credentials include the appropriate attitude, skills, and knowledge but who lack advanced degrees. (See Appendix D for additional details.)

Caminar, Belmont and Redwood City, Calif. Caminar is another organization that provides diversified residential arrangements and services for clients as well as programs for staff development. There are five community living arrangements with varying levels of supervision, a disaster crisis intervention program (described earlier in this chapter), and a consultation, education, and training program. Transitional living is the keynote that is similar to the orientation of the RMHS objectives. Psychosocial rehabilitation is the focus of the services offered. The degree of staff monitoring of client activity is coordinated with peer prompting. Thus residents are encouraged to control themselves and to superintend each other. (See Appendix D.)

Our Plac (Outpatient Unit Rehabilitation Program for Living with Accomplishment in the Community), Los Angeles, Calif. Our Plac is a psychiatric satellite clinic for outpatient veterans. This clinic occupies four stories of a spacious old building and is staffed with personnel from Brentwood Hospital. The staff includes psychiatrists, nurses, social workers, mental health associates,* program evaluators, student nurses, and student and community volunteers. The program and services incorporate educational, social, and vocational experiences; training in physical grooming; and opportunities for arts and crafts, recreation, and physical fitness. Relaxation techniques and the development of communication and assertive skills are integrated in the program to enrich the veteran's ability to cope with problems of daily living. Individual, conjoint, and family therapies are provided in accordance with the veteran's needs.

An interesting device is utilized at Our Plac to present a graphic display of the specific services assigned for the program participants. The Dix* Total Program Display Board is a magnetic board with color coding and rearrangeable accessories. This board visually displays data about the client's living arrangements, needs, programs, progress, program and service changes, and staff members responsible for the client. According to Dix, this board has "helped improve staff communication and encouraged both staff and client interaction." It also serves as a graphic basis for describing the procedures of Our Plac to professionals interested in constructing similar devices.

PACT (Patient's Advisory Consultation Team), Los Angeles, Calif. PACT began in 1973 as an organization of former and continuing patients of the Veteran's Administration Brentwood Hospital. Members (about 20 at present) meet every 2 weeks in a cottage made available to them on the grounds of the hospital. They act as consultants about patients' needs to the administrator and the hospital staff, are role models and advocates for inpatients, contribute to the identification and securance of hospital and community resources, and facilitate communication with ward staff and patients. PACT states its mission as follows:

PACT is not a therapy group. Its work is not directed toward the rehabilitation of individual group members but rather toward . . . providing patient in-put which will benefit the total hospital operation (PACT, Patient's understand).

---

*Mental health associates are 2- or 4-year college graduates, usually with HSW (human service workers) titles.

*Originated by J.M. Dix, a human service worker employed at Our Plac.

Educational offerings, with outside speakers as well as hospital personnel, are included occasionally, but the primary emphases are on resources development and social interaction with self-help orientation.

The peer support system exemplified by PACT extends the social bonds so that individuals with similar problems afford one another mutual assistance (Innovations, 1980a,b). The Senate Committee report (S. 1177) accompanying the Mental Health Systems Act mentions self-help groups among supportable activities. Professionals and professional care-giving institutions are becoming more involved in initiating, sponsoring, and in other ways furthering the self-help mutual aid systems so that consumers may assume more control of their own destinies. Collaboration with these self-help groups is sought so that effective integration of goals and services can result. Many reasons have been offered for the trend toward this coordination of efforts; chief among them is the recognition that consumers do have an impact on planning and implementation of services and that there can be negative aftermaths from overselling dependency on professional helpers. PACT is an example of mutual aid of human service workers and consumers; four other examples are reported in the following paragraphs.

The Center for Independent Living (CIL), Berkeley, Calif. CIL illustrates several aspects of interest to human services. This organization primarily serves physically impaired individuals and has been expanding its services to other groups such as the elderly and the mentally retarded. Paid and volunteer "natural" helpers* perform the functions that emphasize independent living as the dominant goal. Any newcomer wandering through the streets of Berkeley is impressed by the scurrying wheelchairs manipulated by intent and often conversing young and older men and women. Berke-

ley's traffic is aware of these rapid vehicles, and their "drivers" are so secure that occasionally they risk speed and caution in their movements through the crowded streets. There is always a happy note in the socialization on the streets, in the walkways of the nearby campus of the University of California, and in the center. CIL is located in a large store front structure flanked by two mobile units that contain additional offices; other offices—the Law Resource Center—are across the street.

The entrance to the large store front is filled with people in earnest conversation, individuals clatter through the hallways in their motorized or hand-driven wheelchairs or with their crutches. Many forms of communication are noted. Oral speech, sign language, and communication by quadraplegics with their unicorn (a long, pointed stick) pointing to the words and letters on a board. The excitement and upbeat atmosphere are obvious, and the mutuality of concerns and assistance also is apparent.

Fountain House, New York City. A comparable atmosphere of activity and friendliness is exhibited in Fountain House. This facility has been the prototype for many similar houses in the United States and in some foreign cities such as Lahore, Pakistan. Each facility adapts its organization and functions to blend with the local culture, geographic guidelines, and other educational and occupational requirements and opportunities. The chief purpose of all these houses is to facilitate community adjustment of individuals with a history of mental illness. Often there is a proviso added to the qualification for membership—that persons whose primary diagnosis is substance abuse (alcohol or other drugs) and those who have a background of criminal or antisocial behavior are excluded from the house's program. Fountain House emphasizes that the participants of the facility are members, not patients, and this fact of belonging and openness can be observed by the numerous visitors to the house who are guided through the units of activities by trained members. Although there are degreed social workers as director and associate director,

---

*Natural helpers are individuals who do not necessarily have educational backgrounds or degrees in the human service fields but are or have been participants, in some way, in problems similar to those of their clients.

as well as other credentialed staff, it is obvious that the members are an integral part of the administration and of the rehabilitative milieu (Beard, 1976; Dietz, 1980; Glasscote and others, 1969; Robinault and Wiesinger, 1979).

Center Club, Boston, Mass. Center Club and Montgomery House are psychosocial centers patterned after Fountain House. Center Club is one of the three major subdivisions of Center House, Inc., a private organization providing housing and social and vocational rehabilitation facilities for emotionally disabled and mentally handicapped adults. The club is located on the third floor of the YMC Union building in the middle of downtown Boston near public transportation. The club's inclusion in this multipurpose building is its unique feature; the members are not segregated from the nondisabled population. The facility is open 7 days a week, offering social and prevocational opportunities as well as luncheons planned, prepared, and served by the members with staff guidance. Some paid employment in office work, maintenance, and kitchen programs is available at the club for members who are ready and suitable for the work. Prior experience and comprehension of rehabilitation principles rather than degrees are the criteria for the selection of staff members. These resemble the qualifications for the staff at Fountain House, where members have become paid staff after they have developed sufficient stability and competency. Degrees held by staff members range from 2- and 4-year college degrees to master's degrees in social work (Center Club).

Montgomery House, Gaithersburg, Md. Montgomery House is a recently established program that is the first psychosocial rehabilitation center in Montgomery County. The program is geared to the needs of adults at least 18 years old who have experienced disabling psychiatric problems, excluding those with substance abuse complications. The house is staffed with social workers, rehabilitation counselors, practicum students, and volunteers. The long-term goal of this facility is to assist its members to gain self-confidence, to become motivated, and to develop the skills neces-

sary to be reintegrated into community living. The allocation of funding is unique, since there is interagency collaboration of federal, state, and local agencies. The Family Service Agency of the county acts as the conduit for federal Department of Education funds, and other funds are provided by the Maryland State Department of Health and Mental Hygiene, Threshhold (a local private organization of parents and other relatives of the mentally ill), and the Upper Montgomery County Mental Health Center (Montgomery House, brochure, The transitional employment program).

■ ■ ■

The rehabilitation goals of Postgraduate Center West, Altro Health and Rehabilitation Services, and ICD correspond with those of the programs described in the previous paragraphs. However, the program structure and in some instances the participating population differ.

The Postgraduate Center West (PCW), New York City. PCW is located between eighth and ninth avenues on West 36th Street in a much trafficked and crowded business district of New York City. Thus members are in the midst of the rapidly paced culture of a busy urban crowded environment. PCW includes the Social Rehabilitation Clinic, a Vocational Workshop, and the General Psychiatry Program; it is a service of the Postgraduate Center for Mental Health. The center offers multidisciplinary postgraduate training, therapeutic services, research and community consultation, and comprehensive mental health services. Innovative programs are provided for a variety of clients' interests and levels of functioning. These programs seek to develop self-care and social, vocational, community-living, and consumer skills. Intake, progress notes, and aftercare records are carefully and thoughtfully organized and maintained in a confidential, securely clasped folder. New clients are welcomed with a letter that includes a list of names of staff with whom they may be in contact. A New Member Group assists clients to unravel the stroboscopic puzzle of their self-feelings and their concerns about the unfamiliar environment. Clients are given a weekly schedule with daily designations of group meetings from which they select their activities. (See Appendix D for additional details.)

Altro Health and Rehabilitation Services, Bronx, New York. Altro resembles PCW in that it serves the rehabilitation needs of severely psychiatric patients. However, its program differs in scope. This multifaceted model is associated with a wide spectrum of workshops that offer specific training to educationally disadvantaged and mildly retarded as well as psychologically handicapped and emotionally disturbed persons. The workshops have expanded from the range of services offered since Altro's inception in 1915. Currently they include training in work settings simulating the atmosphere of actual factories and/or business establishments with specially trained business or industrial supervisors. Useful and saleable products are the outcome of the workers' efforts in the garment shop, mechanical and hand assembly program, machine shop, commercial and office services division (including microfilming), data processing unit, and print shop. Highly sophisticated contemporary equipment and training procedures prepare Altro's clients to transfer to positions in the business and industrial setting. (See Appendix D for additional details.)

International Center for the Disabled (ICD), New York City. ICD includes rehabilitation, research, professional education, and comprehensive outpatient services, including a placement preparation program for all disabled persons, including the psychiatrically disabled. It has pioneered numerous approaches to rehabilitation plus unique testing procedures such as Micro-TOWER (Backman) and TOWER (Rosenberg, 1977). ICD publishes informational pamphlets as well as the *Program Evaluation Newsletter*. Recently its research division published the third edition of its handbook "Mobilization of Community Resources" by Robinault and Weisinger, 1979 (E.D. Schulman, 1981).

ICD also conducts several training programs. Some are associated with New York University,

and others are integrated in ICD's paraprofessional programs. One example of the latter program is the Human Service Assistant (HSA) project that was initiated in 1971 as the Rehabilitation Aide Program. This 24-week training incorporates selected clients (for instance, those with a history of as well as those with hospitalization for mental illness or alcoholism) and prepares these "paraprofessionals" as follows:

Graduates of the program will have the basic skills and techniques to function effectively as paraprofessionals; aides; assistants; subprofessionals in rehabilitation, education, health, criminal justice, recreational and social service settings. In addition to practical work under supervision in ICD service areas, the trainees will receive specialized talks on medical, social, psychiatric and vocational topics. . . . The clients will have an opportunity to apply their skills . . . by participating in work-study programs in community facilities at private institutions under ICD's staff supervision.* (See Appendix D.)

ICD's client-trainee project expands vocational opportunities for both established and beginning human service workers. The established workers undertake roles as part of a process of psychoeducation merged with psychosocial rehabilitation. The beginning workers gain an essential element in rehabilitation—involvement in the helping process—as learners and later transfer their competencies to the job market.

CORPORATE SUPPORT FOR RECREATION

For those who have been isolated form the mainstream of community living, being productive members of the community is a paramount goal. However, *wellness* requires a unity—a balanced view of work tempered by recreation for the disabled as well as the nondisabled. Bolles (1981) graphically underscores the difficulties encountered by "boxed-in" workers, a vast amount of literature discussing the burnout consequences of

---

*Personal communication from Jean Goldklank, Administrative Assistant, Social Adjustment Services, ICD, 1981.

occupational stress has been published. Physical fitness as a pathway to wellness is recognized by human service workers, and corporations concurring in this view sponsor recreational activities as "good business."

The number of corporations encouraging and to some extent financing recreational outlets has multiplied in the past 20 years (Peters, 1981). Companies have confirmed the desirability of their support of physical fitness, since it has demonstrated increased productivity and decreased absenteeism. Statistics support these contentions (Zink, 1981):

Researchers estimate that in 1977, heart attacks alone cost industry a whopping 132 million workdays, $3 billion in illness and $25 billion in premature deaths of employees. . . .

After a two-year study, the National Industrial Health Board of Great Britain concluded that insufficient recreation was the cause of approximately 20 percent of employee absenteeism.

A six-month study of top business executives by NASA determined that people who exercise regularly are able to maintain a higher level of productivity throughout the day.

Corporations in many states "are getting their employees involved in athletics. A few have even built fitness centers for their workers, complete with swimming pools, running tracks and trails, weight equipment, and more" (Peters, 1981). In some companies more than half the personnel participate in some recreational activity. For example, over 60% of the staff of a division of the Gillette Company, the Gillette Research Institute in Rockville, Md., engage in recreational programs that the Institute supports in some manner, such as by providing uniforms, league or court-use fees, or instructional videotapes.*

Physical fitness and mental health

The effect of physical fitness on mental health is a comparatively new field of study that is the concern of researchers from diverse professional

---

*Personal communication (April, 1981) with James Solan, a Gillette employee who participates in the recreational program.

orientations as well as corporations. Folkins and Sime (1981) recently reviewed a variety of studies related to this subject and concluded that "only about 15% of the studies reviewed . . . qualified as true experiments, and most of these studies were on clinical populations." These reviewers highlight the following implications regarding theory and research of physical fitness:

The research suggests that physical fitness training leads to improved mood, self-concept, and work-behavior; the evidence is less clear on cognitive functioning, although it does appear to bolster cognitive performance during and after physical stress. Mentally retarded children demonstrate psychological improvement following physical fitness training, but no conclusions can be reached regarding the effects of physical fitness with other clinical syndromes.

Physical fitness and human service workers

Even though the research does not as yet assuredly affirm the impact of physical exercise on a person's physical, psychological, cognitive, interpersonal, affective, and environmental processes, the holistic system approach that emphasizes the *whole* person-environment complex proposes such interactive effects. Human service workers who accept the holistic model also must acknowledge the fundamental principle that a change in one element of a system affects other elements of the system. Carlson and Ardell (1981) consider this intermeshing of the benefits of physical fitness and wellness and suggest strategies for counselors with an annotated bibliography. These authors' comments encompass a broad perspective that expands considerations of physical fitness outlets to concepts such as psychocalisthenics, jogotherapy, stretching, aerobic sports and dancing, the martial arts, the Alexander technique, Rolfing, the Feldenkraus method, and biofeedback. Furthermore, Carlson and Ardell urge counselors

to break away from their limiting therapeutic rituals, habits, and routines and learn to encompass a spectrum of multimodal intervention strategies. . . . Physical exercise seems to be a highly appropriate helping strategy. The physical dimension, because it is the most concrete, serves as a good starting point for change. The suggested changes are simple to follow and easy to measure. . . . Counselors and others in the helping professions should dwell less on client problems and more on the positive life enhancing things the individual can do for himself or herself. . . . Counseling programs, mental health centers, and certain other treatment facilities should be reorganized to promote positive health and to minimize the attention devoted to symptoms and negative life situations.

Physical fitness as one of the dimensions of an integrated life-style, good business for corporations, and a human service strategy for enhancing total well-being are the salient points of the preceding paragraph. These points suggest a breadth of human services that reiterates the broader scope of human service roles and functions.

THE SCOPE OF HUMAN SERVICES

The scope of human services includes many fields of human relationships as indicated by the new occasions and new duties described in this chapter—from the fourth mental health revolution to physical fitness as part of the human system network. Uhlmann's (1981) definition aptly proposes the far-reaching dimensions of human service systems:

Human services include all services provided within a community that are designed to meet the personal and social needs of its residents. In addition to mental health services, this broad definition encompasses areas such as social services, health care, recreation, law enforcement, employment services, seniors' services, youth services, and vocational rehabilitation.

There are even more services that can be specified in these categorizations. A few of these are discussed in the following paragraphs, including: the psychiatric autopsy, the control of speeding, and creative outlets. These diverse areas are similar in at least one respect—these provide innovative roles for many levels of human service workers.

The psychiatric autopsy

The psychiatric autopsy is based on what amounts to a psychological postmortem examination. This technique dates to the 1950s, when "Edwin Schneidman, a professor of thanatology

[the study of death and dying], and some associates in Los Angeles pioneered its use to help coroners determine whether a death was a homicide, a suicide, or just an accident. Schneidman labeled the method 'the psychological autopsy', but the Phoenix [Arizona] psychiatrists prefer 'psychiatric autopsy' to encompass medical as well as behavioral factors" (Alsop, 1980).

The methods of the psychiatric autopsy depend on a review of a person's entire life, not just an examination of the happenings on the day when the death occurred. Data are gathered from relatives, co-workers, clergy, club members, and other channels for general information and details about previous aggressive acts against self or others. These facts form the particulars for decisions such as the appropriate heirs in inheritance disputes, the competence of the deceased person, insurance conflicts, and the guilt or innocence of a homicide suspect. A variation of the psychiatric autopsy, labeled psychohistory or psycho-profiling, has appeared in some books and magazines. These accounts compose a psychological portrait of a living politician or celebrity or a historical figure. However, distortion, omissions, or additions result if the author of the profile fails to gather sufficient data or prepares a biased, unsubstantiated profile.

The "autopsy," scientifically implemented and analyzed, can provide the essential links to clarify a person's life-style that can be useful for the family, for certain forms of conflict resolution, and for matters of litigation.

Psychology and the control of speeding

Human services are closely involved with legal matters in many aspects besides the lawsuits often associated with the requests for psychiatric autopsies. One novel example is described in the following paragraphs about control of speeding.

A new technique has been devised to control speeding on urban highways. Several methods have been used, such as posting speed limits, increasing police patrolling, enforcing speed limits, and imposing stiffer penalties. However, only the posting of speed limits has had any significant impact. The other methods have proved to be ineffective or too costly (Van Houten, Nau, and Smith, 1980). An ingenious approach was devised by psychologists at Mount St. Vincent University with the Chief of Dartmouth City Police Department in Nova Scotia. A large feedback sign was installed at the first posting of the maximum speed limit:

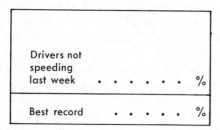

The feedback provided by the weekly insertion of the percentage of drivers not speeding was at least "ten times more cost effective in reducing speeding than was high visibility police patrolling and ticketing. . . . It produces large effects with a minimum of time and effort [and] . . . works selectively reducing the speed of the faster drivers while not causing drivers already traveling at the speed limit to slow down further. . . . [In addition, the] technique has a positive influence on police community relations. Rather than relying on ticketing and coercion, our procedure relies on voluntary compliance and the community spirit of our citizens" (Van Houten, Nau, and Smith, 1980).

These researchers caution that their findings cannot be generalized beyond the situation of a speed limit on an urban highway at the beginning of a residential zone, but they speculate that "the public posting of feedback about drivers' speeds should prove to be an extremely valuable technique for use by urban and small town police departments."

An interesting note that emerges from the speeding study is the notion of self-control rather than policing methods. This idea concurs with the procedures recommended by self-help groups and also is in harmony with a source not often realized—creative outlets.

Creative outlets

Originative human service workers utilize creative expression for more than its aesthetic poten-

tials, for instance, to communicate ideas, to provide a channel for conflict resolution, to offer a safety valve for stress and aggressive feelings, and coincidentally to serve as skill development. In addition, creative outlets make possible the betterment of self-control. Creative outlets have become part of psychosocial rehabilitation as art therapy, music therapy, drama therapy, and the like. Numerous approaches exist.

The intriguing aspect about creative outlets is the revelation that individuals who have been considered incapable of certain motions with their arms or legs manage actions on a canvas or a stage with visible pleasure and also with more obvious control that would have been deemed possible. The young man with cerebral palsy who is confined to a wheelchair and whose arms and legs seem to escape from his body in wild untamed motions, slowly and painstakingly places his large-handled paintbrush in a jar of paint, wipes it on the edge of the jar, and applies the still dripping brush to the large paper, arranging the drippings in an interesting pattern. This happens in Creative Growth.

Creative Growth. Creative Growth is a community-based program in Oakland, Calif., described by Ludins-Katz and Katz (1978) as follows:

[It is] dedicated to the idea that all people—including those with physical, mental, and emotional handicaps—have the capacity to grow and develop as happier, more productive human beings through creative art experiences. . . . The instructors act as stimulators. When needed, they give help with artistic problems but they do not take the lead. Students interact with them and with the other students, but they come to their own artistic decisions. This is a new and valuable autonomy for some. . . . The people in Creative Growth have grown and developed—at their own pace and their own direction. They are respected as contributing members of society—some for being artists in their own rights, some in being able to take care of themselves, some by being ready to enter the vocational world.

Creative Growth is more than an experience with water colors, oil painting, or sculpturing with clay. It provides counseling with staff members who exchange views with art instructors about their observations and methods for utilization of creative channels for expanded expressiveness or greater control. Participants with a wide range of abilities, disabilities, and ages work together. The effectiveness of the method of Creative Growth has been recognized with its designation as "a national model site" by the National Committee—Arts for the Handicapped, an affiliate of the Kennedy Center for the Performing Arts in Washington, D.C.

Theater Unlimited. The enthusiasm of visitors to Creative Growth's large, busy art center is repeated in the reactions to Theater Unlimited, a dramatic ensemble committed to expanding the aesthetics of the theater with an integrated group of disabled, mentally retarded, and nondisabled individuals. This program is one of many sponsored by the San Francisco Recreation Center for the Handicapped funded by local, state, and federal grants. The individual labeled "disabled" perform as enthusiastically, spontaneously, and capably as the so-called nondisabled. Self-discoveries, concentration, relaxation, and controlled interactions are only some of the attributes of the togetherness of this ensemble, and their "work is built on discipline and imagination" (Theater Unlimited, 1981).

The group experience incorporates what traditionally might be termed dance therapy, drama therapy, and music therapy but actually integrates all these into training that contributes to specific skills. Task analysis and physical sensitivity training underlie the individual movements and initiative. The developmental approach to performance is conducted in group and individual performances that provide a dynamic flow of actions of able-bodied and disabled persons, of instructors and students, and of individuals and the group. With the guidance of human service workers, task-oriented creative outlets are offered for both disabled and nondisabled participants (Heus and McCommons, 1980).

∎ ∎ ∎

The foregoing comments about innovative roles beyond counseling have omitted many functions. However, the primary purpose is not to be all-inclusive, but to demonstrate that the human service system embraces a wide circle of activities. The compass directing the remainder of the twentieth century is pointed toward a different world —a different social and physical environment. Goethe must have been considering similar stirrings when he commented, "I find the great thing in this world is, not so much where we stand, as in what direction we are moving." These directions are the focus of the next discussion.

THE FUTURE FOR HUMAN SERVICES

Human services have been and continue to be shaped by a number of societal and environmental features such as population shifts, societal changes, energy transitions, and cultural diversity. Each of these facets of change signal certain trends for human services and demand accountability and continuing education.

Population shifts

The remainder of the twentieth century entails crucial decisions, particularly for two groups in the United States—the "baby boom" population, which has grown into adulthood and young adults of high school age; and the aging population (65 years of age and older) emerging from this mid-twentieth century peak of births (Jarvik, 1978; Woodruff and Birren, 1975). The unemployment rate of this age cohort (from the years 1950 through 1965) reached a high point in 1980 that is predicted to diminish slowly in the next decade (Havighurst, 1980). Human service workers have pivotal roles in assisting people in these groups with educational goals, career developments, job-seeking skills, and mid-life crises (Cytrynbaum and others, 1980).

Projected statistics indicate that significant increases in the aging population will continue until about the year 2025, when they will begin to taper off. The following human service areas must be initiated, revised, or expanded:

☐ Preretirement counseling (Jones), retirement preparations, and coping with changed living arrangements are essentials (Sherman, 1979; Sinick, 1977; Leung and Eargle, 1980).

☐ Group work with the elderly must go beyond the traditional busywork to satisfy the needs of a larger, more knowledgeable, even more heterogeneous "young-old" and "old-old" group of people (Capuzzi and Gross, 1980; Neugarten, 1968, 1974, 1980).

☐ Bereavement counseling bolstered by preventive measures supplied by education about losses, in general, and about death and dying is necessary. Specially trained helpers should be on the staff of hospices that serve patients with terminal illnesses and their families (Cheiken, 1979; Hartley, 1980).

☐ Continuing education, leisure counseling, and recreational opportunities must be expanded or initiated (Goodman, 1981; Neulinger, 1974; Poon, 1980; Remer and O'Neill, 1980).

☐ Women must be offered specific community supports and protective services as displaced homemakers, widows, and so on. Their needs may be greater, since their life-span is longer than men (Bell, 1980; Lopata, 1980).

☐ Stress management and careful consideration of the discovery of measures that prolong men's lives are important in this pressurized society (Kutash and others, 1980; McGrath, 1970; Sparks and Ingram, 1979; Van Auken, 1979).

☐ The origination and strengthening of life-span developmental opportunities and counseling are focal roles for human service systems (Baltes and Brim, 1979; Drum and Knott, 1977; Riedesel, 1979).

These are just a smattering of human service needs predicated on population shifts; societal changes also are affected and affect other alterations.

Societal changes

At the beginning of the twentieth century people age 65 and over were only a small percentage of the total population; while the percentage of the population under 15 was three times as great. During the beginning 1900s there were still some traces of an agricultural economy, which was being altered to industrialization. The industrial economy changed working relationships and family struc-

ture. By the 1970s economists and other social scientists stated that the socioeconomic milieu deemphasized the production of goods and accented the provision of services, highlighting a postindustrial society (Bell, 1973). Havighurst (1980) describes this shift as follows:

The occupational areas claiming a growing proportion of the labor force today are professional, technical, managerial, clerical and sales. Factory workers, transport workers, and skilled craftsmen are barely holding their own; and farming now claims only 5% of the labor force. These developments point clearly to the increasing centrality of education in the white-collar middle-class society . . . [and for all races and ethnic groups].

Education rather than property inheritance may become the ingress to status and income. The training of educators, counselors, and other human service workers will most likely have to be revised. In fact, the educational system warrants an overhaul to realize the lifelong needs for learning, work, and recreation. The educational system eventually may have to assume definitive counseling activities with minority and other students as well as juvenile probationers and other young people with problems (Lee and Olejnik, 1981; McBeath, 1980; Schauble and others, 1979).

Broad societal changes also are noticeable in the insistence of individuals that they assume improved control of their existence and their futures. Self-help groups have burgeoned (Gartner and Riessman, 1977; Lieberman and others, 1979; Remer and O'Neill, 1980). The use of group processes has expanded to a variety of populations, particularly since it is cost-effective and serves as a laboratory for interpersonal relationships and social skills. Group leadership is being viewed critically and has been modified so that it is more receptive to the participants, more eclectic in its methods, and ever mindful of the salience of confidentiality (Chadbourne, 1980; Davis, 1980; Golembiewski and Blumberg, 1977; Landreth and Berg, 1979; Masson and Jacobs, 1980; Van Dyck, 1980).

More human service workers accept the fact that individuals must be viewed as active change agents in their own behalf and as potential helpers in the enlarging scope of tasks assumed by paraprofessionals (Alley, Blanton, and Feldman, 1979; Alley and others, 1979; Nash, Lifton, and Smith, 1978; Social Action Research Center, 1978). Trained human service workers are beginning to learn to accept their clients as allies in community change and to train them in problem-solving and decision-making skills (Fessler, 1980; Remer and O'Neill, 1980).

Concepts related to social impact are becoming more essential elements of the aggregrate of resources of human service systems. Population growth and the enlarging interdependence of people magnify the significance of knowledge and application of social outcome, since "it is becoming more and more important to understand both the positive and negative ways in which people have impact on each other and to design our physical and social environments so as to manage the quality of life for all" (Latane, 1981).

A narrow interpretation of human services is too restrictive for the broad societal changes emerging. In addition to the aforementioned functions, some human service workers must learn skills that prepare them to be brokers, mediators, and consultants with individuals, with groups, and in business and industry (Cristiani and Cristiani, 1979; Hersey and Blanchard, 1972; Kessler, 1979; Splete and Bernstein, 1981). They must be able to perform in decentralized community center efforts "as group process consultants . . . [to help] organizations like cooperative or neighborhood associations [which after an initial spurt of enthusiasm] . . . often encounter severe difficulties because of inadequate planning, organization or leadership" (Kasman, 1981). "Professionals are already providing such support as leadership, training, education, skill sharing to a wide range of volunteer and self-help groups" (Rossman, 1976).

Since coordination of the service system is critical especially for deinstitutionalized individuals, case managers provide a decisive service without which community supports would be less successful (Lamb, 1980).

Energy transitions

Population shifts, societal changes, and energy transitions have been disturbing issues of the twentieth century. There has been a compelling push to weather the multitude of challenging events and to umpire the problems and conflicts ensuing from the altering social and physical environment. The specter of an exhausted supply of petroleum and natural gas by the year 2000 has led to an exacerbated energy crisis. "Economists and technologists talk of a transition of modern society away from an energy-intensive technology to a more labor-intensive technology: in other words, using more worker hours with less mechanical energy to do the work" (Havighurst, 1980).

Many persons do not recall previous great energy transitions that also produced social changes. "For example, the substitution of coal for wood and wind in Europe accelerated and refashioned the industrial revolution. Later, the shift to petroleum altered the nature of travel, shrinking the planet and completely restructuring its cities."* Solutions have taken and will take several forms—technical, social, educational, and occupational. Shifts in the work world induce new perspectives for the content and goals of vocational counseling and the training of these human service workers. Clients' skill development as well as career choices and conversions must become part of the educational and skill background of counselors.

Energy transitions do have pervasive consequences. Technological conversions are only one aspect of these transformations. The depletion of petroleum and other raw materials also affects the means for heating and cooling homes, the weight of and material for clothing, and the provisions for transportation. Many who "escaped" to the large open areas of suburbia have returned to the inner city to avoid the cost and difficulties of purchasing gas. Urban builders are concentrating on middle-

*From Hayes, D.: The coming energy transition. In Cornish, E., editor: 1999 The world of tomorrow: selections from the Futurist, 1978, p.86. THE FUTURIST, published by the World Future Society, 4916 St. Elmo Avenue, Washington, DC 20014.

class housing units, especially town houses and apartment condominiums. Families are smaller; single parent households are frequent. Housing needs change. Beautification of cities has become a central concern of business and urban governments. The energy crisis has vitalized reforms in a wide variety of human systems.

Cultural diversity

The population increases and the other metamorphoses discussed have been interwoven with cultural diversities. A surging infiltration of Hispanics, Asians, and persons of other ethnic and racial groups has led to cities and some suburbs bulging with confused people who require special bilingual and other services. Culture shock has been a two-edged sword, impacting on established residents as well as the newcomers. This migration of minorities calls for culturally aware mental health services and culture-specific educational programs for counselors and teachers as well as for minority groups (Barnes, 1980; Rogers, 1979; E.D. Schulman, 1981; Wilson, Reis, and Bokan, 1980).

Other future progress notes

The telephone is bound to be a key tool in the future. Travel has been curtailed with the use of the telephone for national and even international conferences. By the year 2000 telecommunication and computers most likely will be used in the office as well as for medical and other human services.

The telephone is speeding the development of the electronic office. Computer terminals may be arranged in homes and offices will become obsolete. Consultants may have portable computers and/or telephones to confer with their clients. Copying machines, facsimile transmission devices, television, tape recorders will be added to the electronic office. Human service workers will have to learn to communicate and listen to this new electronic client.*

By [the year] 2150 there could be more people living in space than on earth. . . . Earth might serve mainly as a tourist attraction—a carefully preserved monument to man's origin. . . . The establishment of an ecologically independent colony would require a global perspective as well as psychological considerations explored by spaceship efforts.*

Prevention may be the emphasis of the future in all forms of human services and people will probably become increasingly group-oriented and more highly organized. These changes will affect the origin of psychosocial stresses. Computers will be used widely for: hospital record storage, data retrieval, medical history taking, to prescribe medicine, to conduct psychotherapy and counseling, and to "learn" from experience so that transformations would be possible. Conference videophones will be used for group therapy and counseling; and interactive TV will monitor the older population in their homes (Lesse, 1978; Maxmen, 1976).

An outcome of these changes, some gradual and others more rapid, is an increase in social inventions that alter the way in which people relate to one another. Laws, organizations, and procedures are even now in the process of reforming (Conger, 1978). Human service systems should be readied to create new ways. Accountability and continuing education are necessary to undertake the challenge of change.

Accountability and continuing education

The trends outlined in the previous paragraphs oblige human system services to establish procedures for accountability and continuing education. Accountability should be viewed as a fundamental component of the learning and improving process rather than as a punitive measure. The evaluation of human service workers' effectiveness thus would serve to re-*form* and re-*new* rather than depreciate and emphasize failures (Riggs, 1979). Continuing education would not be tacked on as required for credentials or when occasionally de-

---

*Modified from Vail, H.: The automated office. In Cornish, E., editor: 1999 The world of tomorrow: selections from the Futurist, 1978, p.74. THE FUTURIST, published by the World Future Society, 4916 St. Elmo Avenue, Washington, D.C. 20014.

*Modified from O'Neill, G.: Space colonies. In Cornish, E., editor: 1999 The world of tomorrow: selections from the Futurist, 1978, p. 74. THE FUTURIST, published by the World Future Society, 4916 St. Elmo Avenue, Washington, D.C. 20014.

sired, but would be an ongoing life-long process. Productivity in human services can assume the same positive hue of accomplishment in the framework of quality of services (McPheeters, 1979). The gist of these suggestions is that the preparation of human service workers, both nondegreed and degreed, cannot be considered a completed process. With these caveats as part of the human service systems credo, it would follow that educational, societal, and environmental changes could spark revolutionary improvement in the structure, goals, and methods of human services (Day and Sparacio, 1980; Frey and Raming, 1979; Haber, 1979; Krumboltz, 1980; Stulac and Stanwick, 1980). Education, work, and leisure would be recycled with flexible life-scheduling and alternative plans to suit individual needs and the transformation in a fast-changing world.

Summary of Part Four

■ Part Four presents the layer of the ORRIC approach that integrates the processes of observation, recording, reporting, and interviewing with counseling. Chapter 7 initiates the discussion with the concept of the serendipitous counselor whose openness to ideas, for the client's benefit, permits creative thinking. This counselor develops the attitudes, skills, and knowledge (ASK) that integrate empathy, warmth, and genuineness as well as the expressive skills of communication. These skills include paraphrasing and summarizing, reflection, confrontation, and interpretation. The astute counselor applies these skills appropriately and becomes adept at recognizing and stopping the client's game behavior such as the sick game, the helpless game, and the insight game.

Chapter 8 explores new territory—beyond counseling. Innovations in the human service system can be traced to at least four revolutions. The first revolution occurred more than 180 years ago, when professionals from several countries made definitive commitments to improve services for "the insane." The second revolution in the nineteenth century was instituted by Freud's personality theory, which emphasized the importance of the intrapsychic life. The recognition of the significance of public health in mental health is part of the third revolution. The fourth revolution is contemporary, giving rise to a new breed of professional, the paraprofessional, and a new kind of cooperative effort, the interdisciplinary form of intervention—collaborative co-professionals.

These revolutions indicate that human services are at several crossroads. Many decisions must be made, and innovations considered and implemented. Traditional roles need regeneration in the emerging framework of population shifts, societal changes, energy transitions, cultural diversity, and other aspects of future progress. New occasions indicate new duties such as consultants, stress management helpers, psychoeducators, psychosocial rehabilitators, and human service workers prepared for services in a new work world with electronic tools. Deinstitutionalization and decentralization to community-centered services has led to a variety of novel and expanded service necessities. Accountability, continuing education, and flexible life-scheduling of education, work, and leisure have become crucial components of the structure, goals, and methods of the human service worker's professional preparation. There are projections for the future and also many unknowns, but Antoine de Saint-Exupery's comment (*The Wisdom of Sands,* 1948) can be reassuring:

As for the future, your task is not to foresee, but to enable it.

APPENDICES

Appendix A

GLOSSARY

abnormality Term used with several meanings: (1) maladaptive behavior that is not in accordance with cultural requirements or environmental demands expected for age level, sex, or social role and (2) behavior away from or deviating from the norms (standards) of a particular society.

action-reaction interview Refers to a form of specialized conversation in which a one-directional, more or less impersonal form of communication between client and interviewer occurs.

actual self Includes all the behavioral and physical characteristics of an individual at any one moment, whether or not the individual or other people are aware of these characteristics.

adult ego state Term used in transactional analysis that refers to an individual's behavioral style (ego state), which is primarily logical, positive, and factual.

affective level Refers to the level or frequency of change of an individual's feelings or emotions.

ahistorical Approach to the study of people that concentrates on the here-and-now, present events.

alcologia Combination of the denial and rationalization typical of the alcoholic's reasoning.

alienation Process by which individuals detach themselves from others and hide within themselves in a form of self-attachment.

ambivalent feelings Refers to simultaneous sensations of positive and negative emotions, for example, loving and hating the same person.

antecedent event (A) Refers to the stimulating or beginning events that happen before behavior (B).

anxiety hierarchy Refers to a reconditioning process in which a series of steps are planned in order to reduce the degree of anxiety associated with an object, person, or event.

appropriate behavior May be explained as the terminal behavior established by the behavior-changer (interviewer) and the client as the behavior to be strengthened or the coping mechanisms (learned behavior) that are tension-reducing for an individual and that result in a harmonious relationship with environmental events and with people around the individual.

assertive training Conditioning process during which an individual becomes better prepared to express self in relationships with people.

attending Refers to the process by means of which individuals selectively concentrate (focus) their eyes, ears, body position, etc. toward a particular person, event, thought, and so on to achieve sensory clearness, vividness of experience, and accurateness of information.

authenticity A characteristic of genuineness that refers to being oneself or being ''real'' and not a phony.

automated interviewing Form of behaviorally oriented interview in which the computer is programed to ask the client questions on printouts.

autonomy Self-direction and independence in decision making.

baseline data Refers to the frequency (number of times) of certain behavior in specified time periods.

behavior (B) May be explained as acts and feelings of an individual that may be seen and/or heard or concealed; what an individual says or does after the antecedent event (A).

behavior modification Process of changing behavior by means of reinforcement principles based on experimentally discovered laws of learning.

behavioral analysis Process of defining the target behavior to be eliminated and the terminal behavior to be strengthened.

belongingness Feeling of being part of, accepted by, and secure in relationships with one or more individuals.

blind-alley career Job that keeps worker locked into one kind of job and usually at one salary level.

body language Refers to the physical distance between people, the orientation or direction of the body (proxemics), and the motion of the body (kinesics).

boonfellow A warm companion.

brotherly love Nonsexual, unselfish caring for another human being.

burnout The term burnout assembles a group of attitudes and feelings about work, such as boredom, apathy, exhaustion, and low motivation. The behavioral patterns associated with burnout are exhibited in one or more of the following: absenteeism, lowered responsiveness to clients and/or to other workers, social withdrawal, alcoholism and other drug abuse, job changes.

caring An interpersonal skill demonstrated by helping another person to grow, change, actualize as a separate person in accordance with his or her needs and potentials.

case history Scientific biography of an individual, an institution, or group of people.

casual observation Nonscientific, unplanned "looking and listening" that is often biased and incomplete.

chaining Refers to a sequence of behaviors or a habit in which one conditioned behavioral response is the cue for the next response, for example, moving one foot after the other in order to walk.

child ego state Term in transactional analysis referring to an individual's behavioral style (ego state) that is likely to be impulsive, dependent, and open to parentlike demands of authority as well as carefree and joyful.

client-centered counseling Emphasizes the leading role of the client in decision making during the interaction between the client and the counselor.

clinical observation Organized form of naturalistic observation, for example, a case history.

closed-ended questioning Form of questioning that contains possible answers in the question, for example, multiple-choice questions.

code Set (pattern) of signals or symbols used to convey a message, for example, letters or numerals.

code of ethics, professional Refers to the rights of the client and the responsibilities of the helping person in maintaining the client's rights.

cognitive dissonance Process of receiving information that conflicts with an individual's beliefs and/or knowledge.

cognitive factors Include those thought processes involved in acquiring comprehension, judgment, memories, and reasoning for problem solving and the further application of these competencies in directing one's own conduct effectively. Cognitive development is dependent on opportunities for learning (stimulating environment) and the capacity to learn and to use appropriately (intelligence) what one has learned.

cognitive process Act or processes involved in thinking.

compensation Attempt to overcome feelings of inferiority or dissatisfaction with real or supposed weakness by developing strength in some other area.

conditioning Process of learning in which a new stimulus becomes associated with a former response (classical conditioning) or a new response is acquired when this response satisfies a need (operant conditioning).

confrontation Form of communication that calls attention to a person's behavior and challenges him or her to examine the effect of this behavior on self and other people.

congruence A characteristic of genuineness that refers to behavior in which an individual's words and actions fit together.

connotation The idea or notion culturally or individually associated with a word or phrase.

consequent event (c) Event that follows behavior; the reinforcement that either strengthens or weakens the continuation of behavior.

consociation Complementary communion of give-and-take.

consultant, human-systems Any individual who assists a person or group of persons (human systems) to develop toward increased effectiveness, in terms of both the internal functioning of the system and its relationship to the environment. Human systems consultants include psychiatrists, psychologists, social workers, marriage counselors, family therapists, clergy, management consultants, and staff-training and development specialists. Other members of the society may perform this role, including parents, teachers, managers, and supervisors in organizations.

contingencies Refer to behavior plus its consequences.

contingency management Conditioning process by means of which a relationship is established between behavior and the consequences or reinforcements of this behavior.

continuum Series of things, people, or events that have some relation to one another and differ in either degree or some quantity or quality.

controlled nondirection Form of interviewing in which the interviewer offers alternatives for problem solving and reinforces the client's self-selection.

coordinating/paraphrasing An expressive skill in which the listener organizes and rewords the speaker's message but maintains the speaker's sentiments.

coping The individual's behavioral responses to environmental demands and self-needs.

coping mechanisms Learned ways of behaving in the process of satisfying needs; acquired in order to curb the distress and/or tension resulting from environmental demands antagonistic to the satisfaction of needs. Coping mechanisms are similar to coping strategies and defense mechanisms.

counseling Form of interviewing that is concerned with self-exploration and/or behavioral examination.

covert behavior Refers to behavior (actions) that cannot be directly seen or heard by an observer but can be inferred from measurement of certain bodily responses, from the observation of subsequent behavior of the client, or from the client's verbal report.

cue Refers to the stimulus, the excitant, or the signal that elicits certain behavior.

daydreaming Process of thinking (imagining) while awake, which often serves to satisfy unfulfilled needs (wishes).

decode Translate a coded message into understandable language for a selected person or persons.

demographic factors Statistical information about such items as the distribution of people in neighborhoods and their age, race, sex, birthplace, socioeconomic status, and education.

denial Form of behavior in which an individual avoids painful events or thoughts by pretending that they do not exist.

denotation The actual, direct, explicit meaning of a word or term uncontaminated by cultural or individual significance.

dependent variable Behavior that follows the antecedent event.

depth interview Stresses and carefully explores the impact of underlying attitudes, feelings, and self-understanding on the client's behavior and problems.

descriptive words Words that explain what is seen or heard in behavioral terms, for example, "walks" or "hits."

desensitization Conditioning process by means of which the level of anxiety associated with certain events (stimuli) is gradually reduced.

developmental approach Method of determining manpower needs that begins with exploration of needs and problems of the clients, their families, and their communities and then determines the tasks and activities that will satisfy these needs.

developmental tasks The physical, intellectual, emotional, and psychosocial expectations imposed by a particular culture. The accomplishment of these tasks is dependent on biological maturation and opportunities for training and expression.

dialogue Form of communication in which both the message sender and the message receiver are listening and responding to one another.

didactic Refers to teaching that concentrates on theory, facts, and sometimes moral instruction.

direct questioning Information-seeking question that asks for a specific answer, for example, "What is your address?"

displacement Response to a situation considered threatening by an aggressive act against an object or a person other than the threatening source.

dis-stress Disturbances and annoyances (stress) perceived by an individual as excessive, too frequent, and unpleasant.

duelogue Communication in which two individuals arm themselves with word weapons and carry on a verbal duel.

duologue Similar to two monologues in which two individuals speak and try to control the conversation at the same or at separate times.

dyslexia Lowered ability to read and/or to understand what is read; thought to be caused by minimal brain dysfunction.

ecology Refers to the study of natural systems emphasizing the interdependence of each element of a system with all other elements. Human ecology features a holistic framework, and ecologists contend that data about surroundings are essential to understand any one element of the system.

eductive technique Approach to an interview that encourages clients to talk about their concerns yet assures them that they are not obligated to do so.

ego state Organized system of feelings and actions that is expressed as a parent, adult, or child behavioral style.

ego-alien Rejection of a problem or characteristic that individuals feel does not fit the way they think of themselves.

ego-syntonic Acceptance of a problem or characteristic that individuals feel fits into the way they think of themselves.

emotional insulation Behavior that is indifferent, detached, and unemotional to protect the individual from emotional distress.

empathy Active, persistent, and respectful tuning in of one person to another's point of view to receive and share the other person's meaning and feelings about his or her experiences.

encode Refers to the act of arranging a message into forms or symbols (a code of figures or words) that is understandable to a particular person or persons.

ethnic Refers to groups of people thought to be biologically and/or culturally related.

experiential interview Stresses the human relationship involved with two people "being" together, sharing and changing thoughts and feelings in an acceptant atmosphere.

expressive feelings Free discussion of feelings (ventilating) that helps to relieve tension and usually gives the individual additional energy to achieve new understanding of problem.

expressive skills Communications that attempt to accurately feed back the meaning and/or feeling of a message in order to bring new understanding.

external frame of reference Stresses viewpoints and/or observations that focus on behavior that can be seen or heard and objective observations made from the viewpoint of an outsider looking at the behavior of another person.

extrapunitive Refers to the act of directing anger, blame, and guilt outward toward and against other persons, events, or ideas. Extrapunitive behavior may be expressed by means of sarcastic remarks, hostile acts, or destructive humor.

facial language Includes any movement or change in the face, for example, the wrinkled brow, the smile, or eye contact.

fantasizing Imaginative attempts that may result in a plan and action or a substitute for action.

fatalism syndrome Refers to a pattern of behavioral actions and reactions that emphasize a negative outcome for habilitation or rehabilitation intervention strategies with certain, or sometimes all, forms of disability.

feedback Refers to the return message from the message receiver to the message sender.

fellowfeel Refers to the act of empathically sharing another's feelings and experiences.

field observation Form of naturalistic observation that explores the behavior of animals and humans in their natural settings.

filial therapy Process of training parents with specific guidelines in the treatment of their disturbed children in a play group that includes other disturbed children.

fugue Individual's physical escape from usual surroundings by more or less forgetting past identity and events.

functional professionals Individuals selected on the basis of their existing abilites in a given area who are trained to a high level of expertise in that area.

funnel questioning Forms of questions that begin with generalities and proceed to more specific questions.

generalist Refers to concern for the whole individual and his or her needs and also to training in a job that is related to working with people.

generalized behavior pattern Gradual expansion of certain newly learned ways of behaving to other similar situations.

generativity Interest in the production of offspring and/or in a parent role; also a creative process that includes caring for oneself and others with the goal of guiding the fulfillment of potentials.

generic Term referring to a whole class or group of activities or professions that have similar general goals. Human service is categorized as a generic term, since the general goal of all specialties included is the helping of individuals or groups.

genuineness Awareness and acceptance of one's own feelings and experiences and ability to freely and honestly communicate these feelings and experiences to someone else.

gestalt observation Process of picking up cues about the observed person through all channels of communication and putting these all together for the pattern of behavior that emerges.

gestural language Movements of the body or parts of the body that substitute for or emphasize words.

goal End result (outcome) of an act or sequence of acts that a person or group intends and plans to bring about.

Greenspoon effect Refers to the reinforcing impact of sounds such as "mm-hmmm," "huh-uh," or other speech mannerisms as well as visual cues that tend to sustain (or sometimes diminish) the client's responses in a certain direction.

"halo" effect Influence of the first impression of a person, event, or object that colors all later impressions either favorably or unfavorably.

"hello-goodbye" phenomenon Describes the behavior of the client who feels so much better after one or two interviews that he or she stops interview visits, falsely believing the problems have been solved.

highlighting-paraphrasing An expressive skill in which the listener repeats several of the speaker's remarks that seem to be similar in meaning.

historical question Question that asks about past events.

human services, professional Generic term for all acts performed by individuals who have acquired the appropriate attitudes, skills, and knowledge essential for an effective helping relationship with people and with organizations. Human services include mental health associates and technicians, counselors, psychologists, social workers, court officers, ministers, physicians, nurses, educators, and developmental assistants.

human system Refers to any system involving people. These systems may be intrapersonal, interpersonal, group, intergroup, organization, interorganization, community, national, or international.

hypotheses "Educated guesses," interpretations, inferences, and hunches to explain the relationship between various factors and human behavior or other events.

iatrogenic Refers to ailments or behavioral disorders produced and sustained by a physician's or counselor's words or actions.

identification Behaving like one's interpretation of the characteristics of significant people or objects; defining one's identity.

identity The unique ideas an individual has about his or her role and status in society that provides a sense of wholeness and of self-continuity over a period to time.

identity diffusion Inability to establish a feeling of wholeness and uniqueness of one's ideas, values, and feelings.

impunitive Refers to behavior in which individuals do not blame themselves or others but direct efforts to correcting mistakes and changing toward more appropriate and self-satisfying behavior. Impunitive persons may display embarrassment and shame but not anger or feelings of inability to do something about altering the situations.

inappropriate behavior Coping mechanisms that result in behavior that is bothersome or destructive to the individual; the target behavior that has been established by the behavior changer (interviewer) and the client as the behavior to be eliminated.

incidence Occurence of new cases of the subject of inquiry during some specified time period.

inclusion Feeling of being important, worthy, and part of a group; similar to belongingness.

incorporation Early form of recognizing external reality and of identification in which the infant and the young child take into themselves the behavioral qualities of another individual.

incubation period Time of silence during an interview when the client or the interviewer is putting together the pieces of the problem and/or his or her thoughts.

independent variable Antecedent event; the factor that is changed in an experiment to determine its effects on some form of behavior (dependent variable).

indigenous human service worker An individual usually living in the same geographic area, belonging to the same income or ethnic group, and/or having experienced similar problems as the client.

indirect questions Questions that explore for further communication and understanding by asking for information with broad, general statements; for example, "Tell me more about that situation."

individuation Becoming a single, homogeneous being—one's own self. This does not imply selfishness; instead it signifies fulfillment as an individual and as a member of a collectivity and the wholeness achieved in contact with one's surroundings.

inference Refers to a conclusion or implication arrived at through a process of reasoning. When this conclusion is validly based on existing data, new scientific knowledge or understanding is achieved, but when influenced by biases and unscientific guesswork, distorted assumptions and negative labeling can result.

information-seeking interview Directed to gathering data about people, places, or products.

information-sharing interview Goes one step beyond information seeking, since the data collected are not solely for the interviewer's purposes but are also to be shared with the client.

insight game Persistent pursuit of understanding by means of questioning and discussion that is a cover-up for defending and continuing existing behavior, similar to intellectualization.

insight interview Focuses on the discovery of relationships among events, often of past experiences with present behavior; uses interpretation of the client's unconscious conflicts and behavioral responses as the basis for establishing the relationships, and concentrates on the client's unconscious processes as the originators of the client's symptoms.

intellectualization Defensive maneuver (coping strategy) that uses lengthy explanations and small details to conceal turbulent emotions and/or undesired thoughts.

intelligence May be defined according to the device that measures this ability—intelligence is what the intelligence test measures; qualitatively—intelligence is the increasing competence of an individual that develops in four main stages toward logical thinking (Piaget, 1952); and as a tool—a personality characteristic that serves in the process of adapting and/or problem solving.

interaction interview Specialized form of two-directional communication in which the interviewer listens to and responds to the client to assist the client in problem solving and decision making.

interdependence Feelings and behavior demonstrated in a cooperative and sharing approach in one's dealings with other people; making one's own decisions (independence), yet caring enough to help and be helped by others (dependence).

intermittent reinforcements Rewards and/or punishments given at preplanned intervals of time for the purpose of strengthening or weakening a particular behavior.

internal frame of reference A viewpoint that seeks understanding about another individual "from the inside looking out"; understanding gained through the examination of events from the viewpoint of the behaving person rather than from the viewpoint of the observer.

internalization Process of making certain ideas, standards, and behavior part of an individual's behavior pattern.

interpretation An expressive skill by which the counselor introduces his or her viewpoint in remarks about what the client is saying.

interpretive words Words that evaluate, pass judgment, and label behavior as "crazy," "dumb," "good," and so on.

intervention May be defined in at least two ways. (1) As direct confrontation that is appropriately used in crisis situations when life and death issues are at stake. This form of intervention sometimes raises ethical and legal issues regarding the person's well-being and civil rights. (2) More effective intervention involves caring and empathic help when requested by the client or in certain situations at the request of a relative. Such intervention seeks to preserve order, to protect the client from threats or negative emotional outbursts, and to ensure that an atmosphere of objective fairness is maintained.

interviewing Specialized pattern of communication with defined goals and with emphasis on some degree of interpersonal relationship.

intimacy Refers to closeness plus acceptance of the worthiness of another person and also some degree of responsibility for the other person's welfare.

intrapunitive Refers to the directing of anger, blame, and guilt inward against oneself. Intrapunitive behavior is often expressed by self-criticism, depression, self-belittling remarks, and negative comments about one's accomplishments and about one's potential for accomplishment.

introjection Process of adopting other people's values, attitudes, and behavior as one's own for the purpose of avoiding conflicts and in order to feel accepted by others.

inverted funnel questioning Form of questioning that begins with requests for specific information and proceeds to more general areas.

job-factoring approach Focuses on an analysis of the specific tasks and related activities that various levels of workers perform.

Johari's window Diagram of the interpersonal behavior of individuals that reveals the degree of openness with which they meet other people and their level of awareness of themselves.

journalistic interview Information-seeking interview conducted by a reporter to gather answers to the five W's: *Who? What? When? Where? Why?* and sometimes *How?*

kinesics Study of communication meanings of movements of the body and of the face.

leading questions Similar to closed questions that restrict answers to certain choices by including the expected answer within the question, for example, "You don't really want to go, do you?"

learning style Individual's preferred method of achieving understanding that is conditioned in early childhood by the important people around the child, for example, through hearing, viewing, or touching.

life space The "world" of an individual that includes home, the people and the geographical area in which he or she moves, and the interaction of his or her needs and goals with these external factors.

life-style Behavior pattern of the individuals that includes appearance, values, attitudes, goals, and the procedures they use to achieve goals.

manipulative feelings Refer to emotional behavior used to urge or embarrass another individual to perform acts desired by the controlling individual.

matrix A form (diagram) for originating and developing relevant ideas and plans.

mechanism General term for habits or behavioral acts by means of which individuals meet environmental demands while satisfying and protecting their needs.

mental retardation Impairment in adapting to natural and social demands of one's environment that may be shown in lower level of maturation of skills such as sitting, crawling, walking, talking, self-help, and social interactions; the inability to learn—to acquire knowledge from one's experiences; and lowered ability to maintain oneself independently and responsibly in the community and in gainful employment.

mental status examination Part of a psychiatric interview that takes into account emotional and intellectual functioning and primarily serves a diagnostic purpose.

microcounseling Brief and carefully planned series of steps with immediate feedback in which an individual is training in specific interviewing and counseling behaviors.

milieu therapy Refers to the creation of a treatment or rehabilitation environment conducive to improve a person's role performance. This strategy emphasizes the improvement of psychosocial functioning.

minimal encouragers Procedure that encourages the client by means of respectful listening and well-timed remarks to carry on most of the conversation.

modeling In behavior change refers to the training procedure in which the human service worker performs certain behavior that is imitated by the client.

monologue Communication process in which an individual takes over the conversation and expresses thoughts out loud, disregarding the interests or responses of others.

motivation Refers to the external or internal stimulations for behavior.

multiple questions Contain two or more ideas, for example, "Would you like to stop here or go on?"

naturalistic observations On-the-spot running records of observations that begin and end at any point with no planned attempt to change the environment or the observed person.

need Refers to (1) a lack or deficiency of whatever is required for the health or well-being of an individual, or (2) a state of tension or dissatisfaction felt by a person, between persons, within a group, or within any human systems level. Needs may lead to goals for living satisfaction or goals such as sacrificing one's life for a cause.

negative reinforcements Unpleasant consequences of behavior whose avoidance or removal increases the recurrence of the desired terminal (appropriate) behavior.

neurofibromatosis Hereditary disease characterized by presence of neurofibromas (tumors) in the skin or along the course of peripheral nerves.

nonjudgmental attitude Refers to behavior that does not place one's own values, estimates of worth, or criticisms on the opinions and/or behavior of the other person.

nonpantomimic gestures Actions that accompany words and modify or regulate the meaning of the words.

nonpossessive warmth Expression of commitment, concern, and respect for other human beings as they are, not as they ought to be, and "with no strings attached."

nonprofessional Usually refers to nontraditionally trained workers without educational degrees who do not meet qualifications set by professional groups.

nonverbal cues Visual messages without sound that include body language, facial language, and gestures.

normality Refers to the usual, the average, or accepted behavior within a certain culture.

norms Values or criteria of behavior established for certain characteristics and/or for certain groups that become the standards by which normality is judged.

objective process The process of eliminating biases and distortions in perception and description and centering one's attention on what actually can be seen, heard, touched and the like—an overt observation. When a number of individuals agree and report about their subjective experiences, subjective responses become culturally objective reality that can be shared. The term "objectivity" is based on these characteristics referring to the capacity of the observer to perceive the world as it "actually" is.

observation, scientific Cautiously planned, orderly process of fact gathering through one's senses.

obsessive Refers to idea or impulse that persists even though the person may prefer to be rid of it.

open-ended questioning Broad general request that invites the answerer to express views and feelings, for example, "How do you feel about this glossary?"

operant conditioning Process of strengthening or weakening certain voluntary and unprompted behavior by means of consequences (reinforcements).

overt Refers to behavior (action) that is observable (can be seen or heard).

pantomimic gestures Actions that substitute gestures for words.

paraphrasing Form of translation in which the listener expresses the sense of what he or she has just heard so that the chief points are pulled together.

paraprofessional Individual functioning in a similar but secondary role that resembles the activities of the professionals with whom they work.

parent ego state Organized system of feelings and behavior that arises from experiences with parental figures and in which the behavioral style is judgmental, moralistic, and caring for the other person.

participant observation Careful "looking at and listening to" the observed person while becoming involved in the activities of the observed person.

perception Sensory impressions (seeing, hearing, smelling, feeling, and touching) modified and given meaning by life experiences.

person-environment fit The degree of congruence between an individual's needs, capacities, and aspirations and the environment's resources, demands, and opportunities.

personnel interview Information-seeking, sometimes information-sharing, interview conducted for the purpose of job placement and resolution of job or personal problems.

phobia (phobic) Intense, unreasonable fear that goes beyond the seriousness and/or danger of the object or situation.

positive reinforcements Pleasant consequences of behavior with the goal of strengthening appropriate behavior.

prevalence Refers to the total number of active cases of a particular subject of inquiry during some specified time period.

privileged communication Stresses that conversation between client and interviewer must be considered private and confidential.

process limits The degree and manner in which the client and the interviewer are expected to participate in an interview situation.

professional Describes an individual who is knowledgeable about a particular area, skilled in procedures to be used in this area, functioning at a level that uses these skills for the client's benefit, and maintaining a code of ethics.

professional self Behavior resulting from training in knowledge and skills in order to satisfy established qualifications for certain levels of responsibility, competence, and also a code of ethics.

professionalitis Describes the interviewer who may feel uncomfortable in the interviewer role and hides behind complicated explanations and high-sounding words to hide uncertainty and discomfort.

projection Refers to the shifting of one's unacceptable thoughts, feelings, and other undesired qualities onto someone else so that the blame for those thoughts or feelings is apparently transferred to the other person.

prompting Interviewer's verbal or nonverbal behavior that encourages the client to continue a certain behavior (discussion or action).

proxemics Study of body orientation and direction.

psychoanalysis Viewpoint about behavior of individuals that focuses on unconscious processes and the inner conflicts that initiate and maintain the client's symptoms.

psychodynamic The systemized study, theory, and information of the cognitive and affective processes underlying (motivating) human behavior. Psychodynamic data are based on the assumption that at any one time a person's responses (both internal and external) are the consequence of past and present interactions of genetic endowment and environmental influences.

psychoecology Focuses on the interdependent influence of people, animals, things, and physical surroundings on an individual's behavior.

psychoeducation Refers to an intervention strategy in which the human service worker assumes a teacher or training role and the client becomes the student actively involved in the change process. The techniques of this strategy emphasize the development of higher functioning levels of coping skills.

psychological tests Standardized (experimentally constructed and scaled) measures of characteristics such as interests, attitudes, achievements, and intelligence.

psychophysiological Refers to the interrelationships and interactions of emotional (affective), sociocultural, mental (cognitive), and other psychological responses with somatic (physiological) factors.

psychosocial Refers to the interpersonal behavior of the individual involving social interactions and sequential sociocultural tasks.

psychotherapy Specialized pattern of verbal and nonverbal interaction with specific purposes that goes deeper into self-exploration and self-disclosure than counseling and in which basic personality reorganization is usually one of the goals.

public opinion interview Information-seeking interview that surveys the opinions and/or attitudes of people toward some event or person.

Pygmalion effect Refers to the effects of training and labeling on the achievement level of individuals and attributes the extent of progress or nonprogress to the increased interest and attention associated with positive or negative expectations from one's surroundings.

rapport Refers to the harmonious relationship established in an interpersonal transaction.

rational Process of reasoning and logical problem solving.

rational-emotive therapy Concentrates on the origin and development of emotional disturbance from irrational and illogical thoughts and philosophies.

rationalizing The effort to appear reasonable in order to cover up feelings, thoughts, or acts.

reaction formation Shifting of unacceptable thoughts, feelings, and behavior into their more socially acceptable opposites, for example, masking a feeling of hostility with behavior expressing love and/or sympathy.

reciprocal affect Process by means of which one individual expresses a certain emotion (affect) that calls forth similar emotional behavior in the other person.

reciprocal effect The process by means of which one person's response elicits (brings about, results in, effects) a similar response in another individual.

reciprocal growth The process by means of which one person's constructive gain in knowledge, satisfactions, or positive change in behavior influences the other person to similar constructive changes (mutual growth).

reciprocal inhibition Gradual reduction of anxiety feelings about a person, idea, or event by means of the introduction of behavior antagonistic to the anxiety-provoking stimuli that suppresses and eventually weakens the anxiety reaction, for example, relaxation when presented with the feared object.

reflection Act of uncovering and making known in fresh words the feelings that lie in the client's comments.

rehabilitation The selection, blending, and use in appropriate sequence and relationships—for the individual's needs—of medical, psychiatric, educational, mechanical, social, emotional, and auxiliary therapeutic services.

reinforcement Concerned with the positive and negative consequences and punishments that either strengthen and continue or weaken and discontinue certain behaviors.

reinforcement menu Refers to the list of negative consequences to be used in eliminating one kind of behavior (target behavior) and the positive consequences (rewards) for strengthening the appropriate behavior (terminal behavior).

repeating/paraphrasing Feedback of one or more words in order to direct the speaker into further discussion of a certain topic and to assure the speaker he or she is being understood and attended to carefully.

regression Return to less mature behavior that is representative of an earlier developmental level.

repression Unaware (unconscious) holding back or covering up of ideas, feelings, or acts that an individual considers too painful to self or to others or that he or she feels would be socially unacceptable.

response repertoire Refers to a collection of skills and knowledge that an individual learns and performs comfortably and effectively.

right to treatment Client's right to demand help and to receive adequate treatment, to refuse a particular kind of treatment, and to seek another kind of help elsewhere.

role reversal Occurs when one individual changes behavior and acts as if he or she were another person.

role-playing Training method in which individuals test and receive immediate feedback about approaches to a situation by acting out the handling of a situation and/or by trying out new skills.

roles Individually interpreted patterns of culturally expected behavior.

script analysis Term used in transactional analysis referring to the exploration and careful examination of the individual's life plan that serves as the basis (motivation) for the individual's behavior.

secondary source observation Information about the observed person obtained from files, reports, or other people.

self-actualization Process of recognizing and accepting oneself, developing abilities and satisfying interests, and establishing a harmonious relationship between individual expression and social interest.

self-assertion Act of responding rather than holding back in social situations that may be expressed either with respect for the goals of others (assertion) or disregarding the goals of others (aggression).

self-concept An individual's values, attitudes, abilities, and behavior that he or she recognizes as his or her own and evaluates favorably or unfavorably.

self-fulfilling prophecy Refers to an individual's expectations regarding a situation; because the individual believes certain results inevitable, he or she acts in such a way as to influence the expectations to actually happen, thus strengthening the belief in the self-fulfilling prophecy, for example, acting aggressively because he or she expects the other person to be aggressive.

self-fulfillment Similar to self-actualization with the possible difference that self-fulfillment focuses on satisfying an individual's needs, whereas self-actualization is also concerned with the needs of others.

self-help organizations Mutual help networks that are formalized in a systematic organization and program. The helping interactions depend on the participants sharing a common problem with which one of them previously has successfully coped and thus has developed an expertise based on experience and ability to solve a particular problem. These persons are "natural helpers" as distinguished from "professional helpers." Alcoholics Anonymous is one of the best known self-help groups.

semantic differential The rating of an object, idea, or concept on a series of scales that reflect the rater's attitude toward the item noted—the meaning (semantics) or significance of the item to the rater.

semantics The study of symbols that is concerned with the current and changing means of these symbols. It also includes the feelings (positive versus negative) associated with these symbols.

serendipity Refers to the accidental or chance discovery of a valuable, agreeable, or creative finding in endeavors such as research, human services, and interpersonal relationships.

shaping Procedure in which terminal behavior is broken into small units or single responses that are conditioned and each small unit of behavior builds on (chaining) behavior already learned (conditioned).

site permeability An ecological variable referring to the self-imposed boundaries an individual erects that have both physical and behavioral components.

social system Refers to the effect on behavior of variations in the interaction of two or more persons as well as the environmental factors around these individuals.

soliloquy Act of speaking to oneself out loud.

spectator observation Careful "looking and listening" through a one-way mirror or within the same room but not near the observed person.

standardized observation Carefully planned and controlled "looking and listening."

standards Expected levels of performance that are determined by the individual, by other people, or by institutions.

status Refers to culturally and individually determined positions stemming from sex, age, race, and education that determine the rights and obligations of a person.

stimulus situation Refers to a pattern of antecedent events.

stressor Refers to potential disturbances (stimuli) that provoke stress. These may vary in many ways or along many dimensions, and may originate "inside" or "outside" of the person.

structural analysis Term used in transactional analysis that refers to the progressive analysis of the organization and interaction of ego states.

subjective process Refers to the action or the form of observation that reflects the individual's private and unique experience of an object, person, or event. Subjectivity tends to be biased and unscientific. Inferences derived solely from these subjective observations are likely to be distorted.

subprofessional Describes an individual whose responsibilities are less complicated than the professional and whose functioning is usually expected to be subordinate to that of the professional.

summarization An expressive skill in which there is a restatement of what the speaker has been saying or feeling during an entire counseling session or a series of counseling sessions.

suppression Form of voluntary forgetting that is usually temporary.

survey interview Information-seeking interview that seeks data about attitudes, for example, preferences for certain boxes for a new food product.

sympathism Sympathy-seeking behavior that asks for emotional support by dwelling on misfortunes and/or physical complaints; openness to the influence of someone's suggestions.

sympathy Many forms of expression that range from pity to compassion; differs from empathy, since it signifies that the sympathetic individual shares the same feelings as the other individual and it sometimes implies a value judgment that the sympathetic person is more capable or ''better off'' than the individual who is pitied.

syndrome A pattern of characteristic acts occurring together identifying a specific type of behavior or sequence of behavioral acts.

synergy Working together cooperatively so that the total effect of the combined efforts is greater than the individual actions.

thought-stopping Program of conditioning in which annoying thoughts are gradually weakened and finally eliminated by means of reinforcement such as saying ''Stop'' whenever the disturbing thoughts arise.

time interval or time-sampling Requires observations at predetermined times of the day or night and usually for a set length of time.

transaction contract Mutually designed written or oral listing of the client's and the interviewer's objectives and procedures.

transaction interview Social system of shared responsibilities in which client and interviewer establish rules for self-discovery and personal growth and in which the relationships that result influence both client and interviewer to change.

transactional analysis Focuses on the discovery and script analysis of the predominant ego state of parent, adult, or child and the influence of the behavioral style of this ego state in helping or hindering the individual in encounters with people and other events.

triangulation Refers to the pulling in of the interviewer or some other person as an ally against someone whom the client finds disturbing.

Truax triad Refers to the three characteristics—empathy, genuineness, and nonpossessive warmth—that are considered essential to the effective counseling situation.

undoing Way of escaping painful events or thoughts by constantly atoning for real or imaginary sins.

ventriloquizing Refers to an individual who speaks as if he were commenting for someone else, for example, ''Lots of people are asking about how you feel about this book.''

want The personal or socioculturally determined craving or desire for goods, services, and other items that satisfy—and also stimulate—these wants. Food is a goal to satisfy a hunger need; ice cream is a goal to satisfy a hunger want.

withdrawal Pattern of behavior in which an individual removes himself or herself physically or psychologically from disturbing circumstances.

Appendix B

SELECTED PSYCHOLOGICAL TESTS FOR HUMAN SERVICE WORKERS

The Adjective Check List, H.G. Gough and A.B. Heilbrun, Consulting Psychologists Press, 577 College Avenue, Palo Alto, Calif. 94304.
Gives 300 adjectives commonly used to describe attributes of a person; may be used for self-evaluation or be rated by someone other than subject.

The Adolescent Value of Orientations, R. Ulin, School of Education; University of Massachusetts, Amherst, Mass.
Focuses on choices. Contains 42 either/or situations with two of following values in conflict: peer group, family, athletics, sex, financial security, upward mobility, academic achievement.

Assessment of conceptual level: paragraph completion method (PCM), revised 1976, D.C. Hunt, L.F. Butler, J.E. Noy, and M.E. Rosser.
Mimeographed manual for PCM, obtained from D.C. Hunt, Ontario Institute in Education, Toronto, Canada.

Caring Relationship Inventory, E.L. Shostrom, Educational and Industrial Testing Service, San Diego, Calif. 92107.
Measures the essential elements of caring or love.

Conceptual Systems Test (CST), O.J. Harvey: Teacher beliefs, classroom atmosphere and student behavior, Education Research Journal **5**:151-165, 1968.
Objective instrument designed to assess values and beliefs called conceptual systems, content of respondent's belief system, and degree to which these beliefs are cognitively complex, consistent, abstract and open to new information.

Consumer's Measurement Scale (CMS), W.G. Hills: Evaluating vocational rehabilitation programs, Norman, 1973, University of Oklahoma, Regional Rehabilitation Research Institute.
Provides information about client's view of impact of rehabilitation services and a follow-up to determine employment experiences and satisfaction.

Defining Issues Test (DIT), J.R. Rest and others: Judging the important issues in moral dilemmas—an objective test of development, Developmental Psychology **10**(4):491-501, 1974. See also J.R. Rost: Manual for the defining issues test, Minneapolis, 1974, University of Minnesota.

The Differential Value Profile (DVP), 1963, W.L. Thomas, W. & J. Stone Foundation, Chicago, Ill.
For college students. Takes 30 to 45 minutes. Measures personal thoughts and feelings about six factors: aesthetic, humanitarian, intellectual, material, power, and religious.

Fowler's Faith Interview, J. Fowler, Caudler School of Theology, Emory University, Atlanta, Ga. 30322.
Structural developmental approach to study of character and how individuals give meaning to and orient their lives.

Goal Attainment Scaling (GAS), T. Kiresuk and others, 1972, The program evaluation project: overview, Program Evaluation Project, Minneapolis, Minn.
Developed for use in mental health center settings to provide an individualized client evaluation. Major client problems specified with numerical values assigned to each problem area, ranking its importance to client's rehabilitation. Behavioral description developed for each of five outcome levels with rehabilitation expectation levels associated with numerical values. After assessment of basic level of functioning with five-point scale, services are identified. At closure of services same scale is used to determine goal-attainment progress.

Group Environment Survey (GES), 1974, R.H. Moos, D.M. Insell, and B. Humphrey; Consulting Psychologists Press, Family Work and Group Environment Scales, Palo Alto, Calif.
Standardized objective instrument originally designed to assess the social environment or climate of therapeutic, task-oriented, and social groups. Contains 80 statements, each with 9 subscales.

405

Gruen-Korte-Stephens Internal-External Scale, G.B. Gruen, Department of Psychological Services, Purdue University, West Lafayette, Ind.

Concentrates on extent to which individuals perceive their degree of control of their lives.

The Human Service Scale (HSS), S.P. Kravetz: Rehabilitation need and status: substance, structure, and process, unpublished doctoral dissertation, 1973, University of Wisconsin—Madison.

Takes about 35 minutes. Measures degree of client change insofar as unmet needs are reduced during rehabilitative processes. Based on Maslow's need hierarchy. Has 80 items, 7 areas of needs. Can be administered at intake and again at any time after closure of services.

IPAT Anxiety Scale Questionnaire, R.B. Cattell, Institute for Personality and Ability Testing, Champaign, Ill. 61820.

Arrives at six scores: self-sentiment development, ego strength, protension of paranoid trend, guilt proneness, ergic tension, and total anxiety.

Jastak Wide Range Test Series, Guidance Associates of Delaware, Inc., 1526 Gilpin Avenue, Wilmington, Del.

Four instruments for the assessment of various aspects of human behavior, such as integration factors, interest and opinion, employment sample, and achievement.

The Jones-Mohr Listening Test, J.E. Jones and L. Mohr, University Associates, Inc., La Jolla, Calif.

Test developed for use in education and training designs and as an evaluative tool. The parallel forms of the test, forms A and B, can be used independently or together in numerous ways. Album contains cassette and test forms.

Kuder Occupational Interest Survey, Science Research Associates, Inc., 155 North Wacker Drive, Chicago, Ill.

For grade 11 to adult. Contains 10 scales, report form, and manual. Reports 124 occupational scores and 48 college major scores.

The Learning Style Inventory (LSI), D.A. Kolb, Tests and Scoring Division, McBer & Co., 137 Newbury Street, Boston, Mass.

Self-scoring test that provides a profile of individual's preferred learning style. LSI test, profile sheet, self-scoring booklet, and/or technical manual.

Life Experience Survey (LES), I.G. Sarason and others: Assessing the impact of life changes: development of the life experience survey. In I.G. Sarason, 1979 (see reference list).

A 57-item self-report measure. Respondents indicate events they experienced in past year and rate the desirability or undesirability as they perceive the event.

Loevinger's Sentence Completion Test, J. Loevinger, and others: Measuring ego development, vols. 1 and 2, 1970, Jossey-Bass, Inc., Publishers, San Francisco, Calif.

Contains 36 sentence stems. Scoring manual provides characteristics to be expected at each scoring level and examples of responses grouped into categories. Rating by matching the content of responses to the content of examples.

The MEPS (Menas-Ends Problem-Solving) Procedure, 1975, J.J. Platt and G. Spivak, Hahnemann Medical College and Hospital, Philadelphia, Penn.

Set of 10 stories depicting real life situations testing person's capacity to create and choose means of meeting aroused needs. Person is asked to provide middle of story to ending in which problem has been resolved.

Multiple-Input Measurement of Social and Affective Needs, Educational Skills Development, Inc., Department PG, 179 East Maxwell Street, Lexington, Ky.

Contains assessment measures for early childhood, classroom climate, and learning needs inventory for students in junior high school through junior college.

Personal Orientation Inventory for the Measurement of Self-Actualization, E.L. Shostrom, Educational and Industrial Testing Service, San Deigo, Calif. 92107.

Emphasizes mentally healthy and actualizing qualities rather than pathological characteristics. Growth toward self-actualization may be assessed by administering this to trainees at the beginning and toward the end of training. May be used for similar purpose with clients.

The Projective Assessment Aging Method (PAAM), 1979, B.D. Starr, M.B. Weiner, and M. Rabetz, Springer Publishing Co., New York, N.Y.

Consists of a series of pictures of various scenes related to the aging process and themes of aging. In making up stories about the pictures, the respondent reveals feelings, attitudes, and perceptions. Should be part of a battery of techniques for assessment purposes or may be used to spark discussions in intake or other interviewing procedures.

The Relationship Inventory, G.T. Barrett-Leonard: Dimensions of a therapist response as causal factors in therapeutic change, Psychol. Monogr. **76:**(whole no. 562)43, 1962.

Paper-and-pencil test for client and/or counsel to assess level of certain characteristics of client-counselor relationship, such as empathy, level of regard, and congruence. Adapted by B. Mann and K.C. Murphy: Timing of self-disclosure and reactions to an initial interview, J. Counsel. Psychol. **22:**304-308, 1975.

Rokeach Value Survey, Halgren Tests, Sunnyvale, Calif.
Takes about 15 to 20 minutes. Provides two sets of alphabetically arranged values with brief phrases defining them. One set (18 values) refers to end states (terminal values); the other set refers to modes of behavior (instrumental values).

Rotter's Internal-External Locus of Control Scale, J.B. Rotter: General expectancies for internal vs. external control of reinforcement, Psychol. Monogr. **80:**(whole no. 609)1, 1966.
Assesses individuals' perception of degree of control of their lives.

Rotter's Interpersonal Trust Scale, J.B. Rotter: A new scale for the measurement of interpersonal trust, J. Personality **35:**661-665, 1967; J.B. Rotter: Interpersonal trust, trustworthiness, and gullibility, Am. Psychol. **35:**1-7, 1980.

Schedule of Recent Experiences (SRE), T.H. Homes and R.H. Rahe: The social readjustment rating scale, J. Psychosomatic Research, **11:**213-218, 1967.
Self-administered questionnaire with list of 43 events. Respondents check the events they have experienced in the past year (or past 6 months). Significance of these events in terms of stress impact is assessed by established scores regarding degree of social readjustment required.

Sixteen Personality Factor Questionnaire (16 PF Test), R.R. Cattell, Institute for Personality and Ability Testing, Champaign, Ill. 61820.
Measures 16 main dimensions of personality. Has two forms each with 187 items (forms A and B) and one shorter form (C) with 105 items.

Social Adjustment Scale (SAS), M. Williams and others: An evaluation of an intensive group living program with schizophrenic patients, Psychol. Monogr. **14:**(whole no. 543), 24, 1962.
Contains subscales for self-responsibility index, daily living skills, living setting, and social participation.

Strong-Campbell Interest Inventory, 1974, D.P. Campbell, Stanford University Press, Stanford, Calif.
Presents statements on occupations, school subjects, amusements, characteristics of people, and activities found to be associated with the interest patterns of persons in various occupations. Respondent indicates preferences with "like, indifferent, or dislike" scoring. Interest inclinations indicated by degree of similarity of respondent's replies with patterns of established and "successful" representatives in various occupations.

Study of Values (SV), G.W. Allport, P.E. Vernon, and G. Lindzey: Study of values, ed. 3, 1960, Houghton Mifflin Co., Boston, Mass.
For high school students and adults. No time limit. Usually takes about 20 minutes. Focuses on relative importance of six basic interests; theoretical, aesthetic, social, religious, political, social.

Survey of Interpersonal Values (SIV), V.V. Gordon: The survey of personal values: manual for the survey, 1960, Science Research Associates, Inc., Chicago, Ill.
For grades 9 through 16 and adults. Takes about 15 minutes. Contains social and interpersonal perspectives: support, conformity, recognition, independence, and leadership.

Survey of Personal Values (SPV), V.V. Gordon: The science of personal values, 1960, Science Research Associates, Inc., Chicago, Ill.
For grades 11 through 16 and adults. Takes 15 minutes. Focuses on determining relative importance an individual ascribes to practical-mindedness, achievement, variety, decisiveness, orderliness, and goal orientation.

Tennessee Self-Concept Scale, 1964, W.H. Fitts, Counselor Recordings and Tests, Nashville, Tenn.
Distinguishes between psychiatric and nonpsychiatric populations. Contains 100 self-descriptive items to which the respondent replies on a five-point scale ranging from completely true to completely false.

Thorndike Dimensions of Temperament (TDOT), R.L. Thorndike, The Psychological Corp., 757 Third Avenue, New York, N.Y. 10017.
A forced-choice inventory through which the individual describes self with respect to 10 dimensions of temperament: sociable—solitary, ascendant—withdrawing, cheerful—gloomy, placid—irritable, accepting—critical, tough-minded—tender-minded, reflective—practical, impulsive—planful, active—lethargic, responsible—casual. The inventory presents 20 sets of 10 statements; in each set the alternatives are matched for social desirability.

Vocational Decision Scale; Adult Decision Scale, 1977, L. Jones, North Carolina State University, Raleigh, N.C.
Adult Decision Scale is adaptation of Vocational Decision Scale. Measures improvements in decision-making skills, plans for realism, logic, and completeness.

Watson-Glaser Critical Thinking Appraisal, G. Watson and E.M. Glaser, The Psychological Corp., 757 Third Avenue, New York, N.Y. 10017.
Measures five aspects of the ability to reason critically: drawing inferences, recognizing assumptions, reasoning by deduction, drawing conclusions, and evaluating arguments.

Ways to Live, C.W. Morris: Varieties of human values, 1956, University of Chicago Press, Chicago, Ill.

Values questionnaire. Takes about 20 to 30 minutes. For college or general adult population. Contains 13 different "ways to live." Useful as a projective device for client's reactions.

Work Environment Preference Schedule, L.V. Gordon, The Psychological Corp., 757 Third Avenue, New York, N.Y. 10017.

Measure of individual's commitment to kinds of attitudes, values, and behaviors that tend to be rewarded by bureaucratic organizations. High scores are earned by persons who accept authority, prefer specific rules to follow and imper-sonalized relationships, and seek the security of organizational identification. Useful to counselors and employers in identifying similarities and differences between the orientation of an individual and that of an organization to which he or she belongs or may be applying.

INFORMATION ABOUT TESTING PROCEDURES AND LEVELS OF COMPETENCY FOR ADMINISTRATION OF TESTS

Standards for Educational and Psychological Tests and Manuals, 1966, 1974, American Psychological Association, 1200 Seventeenth Street, N.W., Washington, D.C. 20036.

Appendix C

SOURCES FOR AUDIOVISUAL AND OTHER AIDS FOR HUMAN SERVICE CURRICULA AND HUMAN SERVICE WORKERS

CASSETTES, TAPES, RECORDS

Assertiveness: Self-Directed Assertiveness Training, BMA Audio Cassette Publications, New York, N.Y.

Four audio cassettes plus instruction manuals for teaching and reinforcing assertiveness in clients. Audio guide features interaction with real-life situations; listeners try out various responses through role rehearsal and other cognitive and behavioral exercises.

Communicating Empathy, J. Milnes and H. Bertcher, University Associates, La Jolla, Calif.

Designed to teach participants how to make appropriate verbal empathic responses and to assess the effectiveness of empathic reactions in self and others.

Helping Skills, D.C. Kinlaw, University Associates, La Jolla, Calif.

A facilitator's package consisting of a guide and a 30-minute cassette, instructions for skills practice and feedback, and descriptions of various skills and relationships to each other and to the helping professions.

Initiating Marital Therapy, BMA Audio Cassette Publications, New York, N.Y.

Clinical demonstration of a first interview.

Progressive Relaxation Training, D.T. Shanon, Research Press Co., Champaign, Ill.

Biofeedback Tapes, G.D. Fuller, Thought Technology, Ltd., Montreal, Canada 44A 2N5.

Color videotapes consisting of sampler, introduction, instrumentation, procedures, case studies, and troubleshooting problems.

Suicide Prevention and Crisis Intervention, A.J. Enelow, The Charles Press Publishers, Inc., Bowie, Md.

Six cassettes detailing problems of persons in crises situations. At various choice points the listener is asked to choose the preferred response to the troubled person. Response sheets for choice points are provided, and preferred choices are presented afterwards.

An Anthology of Human Communication, revised 1974, P. Watzlawick, Science and Behavior Books, Inc., New York.

Text and 2-hour reel tape. Provides introduction to some basic concepts of communication as related specifically to patterns of interaction between human beings. Focuses on speech and its analysis, the statistical theory of communication problems of redundancy, semantics, syntactics, etc.

Environmental Records, J. Cook, Ft. Lauderdale, Fla.

Recordings on separate records of sounds: nature sounds, water sounds, rain sounds, thermopsych sounds. For relaxing and other psychological effects.

DRAMA

Plays for Living, Family Service Association of America, 44 East 23rd Street, New York, N.Y. 10010.

One-act, half-hour plays about specific problems or issues written by professional playwrights, for example, "Who says I can't drink?" about adolescent alcohol abuse. Deal with such subjects as aging, parent-child relations, race relations, and venereal disease. Purposefully leave an unresolved end to stimulate audience discussion.

FILMS
BEHAVIORAL TREATMENT

Harry: Behavioral treatment of self-abuse, Hospital and Community Psychiatry Service, American Psychiatric Association, Washington, D.C.,

38 minutes, 16mm. Documentary presenting the successful behavioral treatment for a mildly retarded young man.

INSTITUTIONALIZATION

Any Place but Here, Hospital and Community Psychiatry Service, Washington, D.C.,

50 minutes, color, 16mm. Originally made as a TV documentary, focuses on what happens to former state hospital patients after their release to the community.

How to Create a Non-person, Hospital and Community Psychiatry Service, Washington, D.C..

18 minutes, black and white, ¾ inch videotape. Series of brief, humourously presented vignettes illustrating how thoughtless and inconsiderate behavior on the part of staff can cause unnecessary frustration and humiliation for hospitalized patients.

INTERPERSONAL SKILLS

Carl Rogers counsels an individual on hurt and anger, American Personnel and Guidance Association, Order Services Department, Two Skyline Place, Suite 400, 5203 Leesburg Pike, Falls Church, Va. 22041.

60 minutes, 16mm, color and sound.

Carl Rogers: The Right to be Desperate, American Personnel and Guidance Association, Order Services Department, Two Skyline Place, Suite 400, 5203 Leesburg Pike, Falls Church, Va. 22041.

52 minutes, 2 reels, 16mm color and sound.

Centron Films, 1621 West 9th, Box 68, Lawrence, Kan. 66044.

Films about handling information at the personal level and about contemporary problems of society.

Discussion: An interpersonal theory of everyday communication, American Personnel and Guidance Association, Order Services Department, Two Skyline Place, Suite 400, 5203 Leesburg Pike, Falls Church, Va. 22041.

14 minutes.

Inquirer role and function, American Personnel and Guidance Association, Order Services Department, Two Skyline Place, Suite 400, 5203 Leesburg Pike, Falls Church, Va. 22041.

50 minutes, 2 reels.

Interpersonal skills and roadblocks, American Personnel and Guidance Association, Order Services Department, Two Skyline Place, Suite 400, 5203 Leesburg Pike, Falls Church, Va. 22041.

52 minutes, 2 reels.

RECALL

Client recall, *3 films;* **Interviewer recall,** *4 films;* **Mutual recall,** *7 films;* American Personnel and Guidance Association, Order Services Department, Two Skyline Place, Suite 400, 5203 Leesburg Pike, Falls Church, Va. 22041.

RELATIONSHIPS IN FAMILY

Just like a family, American Personnel and Guidance Association, Order Services Department, Two Skyline Place, Suite 400, 5203 Leesburg Pike, Falls Church, Va. 22041.

Part I—33 minutes; Part II—35 minutes; each is 16 mm, color and sound. Present life crisis situations such as divorce, single parenthood, and lack of roots due to geographic mobility.

Step-parenting, American Personnel and Guidance Association, Order Services Department, Two Skyline Place, Suite 400, 5203 Leesburg Pike, Falls Church, Va. 22041.

20 minutes, 16mm color and sound. Defines problems that occur in remarriage when children are involved.

STRESS

Facing interpersonal stress, American Personnel and Guidance Association, Order Services Department, Two Skyline Place, Suite 400, 5203 Leesburg Pike, Falls Church, Va. 22041.

4 films.

TRAINING MATERIALS—CASSETTES, TAPES, FILMS, PAMPHLETS

Resource List on Dentistry for the Handicapped, Bureau of Health Education and Audiovisual Services, American Dental Association, 211 East Chicago Avenue, Chicago, Ill.

Try another way, Marc Gold and Associates, Inc., 708 West Oregon, Urbana, Ill. 61801.

Catalogue of materials.

WOMEN AND PROBLEMS

Francesca, Baby, Walt Disney Educational Media Co., Burbank, Calif.

A 17-year old trying to cope with her mother's alcoholism.

The maturing woman, American Personnel and Guidance Association, Order Services Department, Two Skyline Place, Suite 400, 5203 Leesburg Pike, Falls Church, Va. 22041.

30 minutes, 16mm color and sound, with leader's guide. Stimulus film to help the viewer to identify attitudes and beliefs about aging.

The Woman's Resource and Research Center, University of California at Davis, Davis, Calif. 95616.

Catalogue of films on women and/or sex roles.

HANDBOOKS AND MANUALS

Choices and decisions: A guidebook for constructing values, M. Bargo, University Associates, La Jolla, Calif.

Guidebook and manual for facilitators. Guidebook contains activities, worksheets, and exercises.

Consultation as a counselor intervention, R.D. Myrick, American School Counselor Association, Washington, D.C.

Differentiates between counseling and consultation. Provides counselors with theoretical considerations as well as adaptable techniques and procedures for the consultation process.

Job Club Counselor's Manual, 1981, N.H. Azrin, and V.A. Besalel, University Park Press, Baltimore, Md.
A behavioral approach to vocational counseling.

Leisure counseling materials, Constructive Leisure, Los Angeles, Calif.
Contains manual, interview sheets, survey interpretations, activity surveys, interview interpretations, time study, and questionnaire, plus 45-minute cassette tapes.

The Nature and Treatment of the Stress Response, G.S. Everly and R. Rosenfeld, Plenum Publishing Corp. New York, N.Y.
Manual on the nature of psychophysiological stress and its treatment. Designed as a "how to" handbook for practicing clinicians and clinical students.

Needs Assessment, D.G. Hays and J.K. Linn, American School Counselor Association, Washington, D.C.
Step-by-step procedures for accomplishing needs assessment from initial step of obtaining commitment to outcome of improved program planning and development.

The Relaxation and Stress Reduction Workbook, M. Davis and others, New Harbinger Publications, Richmond, Calif.
Compilation of effective treatment strategies for stress with step-by-step directions.

Role Playing, M.E. Shaw and others, University Associates, La Jolla, Calif.
A manual for group facilitators. Describes the role play method and its use and application to resolve a variety of problems.

Transactional Analysis: Guide for Use of Life-Script Questionnaire, P. McComick, Transactional Publishers, Berkeley, Calif.
Specific questions to ask, ways to interpret responses, life-script interviews, and examples for arranging treatment contracts.

Understanding and Managing Stress, J.D. Adams, University Associates, La Jolla, Calif.
Facilitator's guide for the leader of a stress management workshop; workbook with informative material and instruments to gain understanding of the concept of stress, and book of readings with 14 articles about stress and stress management.

Workshop Evaluation System Manual, E. McCallon, Learning Concepts, Austin, Tex.
Provides procedure for participant evaluation of workshop in seven dimensions: organization, objectives, presenter (consultant), ideas and activities, scope (coverage), beneficiality, and overall effectiveness.

REFERENCE BOOKS

Developing a Community Human Service Directory, H.L. Nix, University of Georgia, Institute of Community and Area Development, Athens, Ga.
Aims to assist organizations and citizens to inventory or survey available and needed human services and to develop a community human service directory.

Diagnostic and Statistical Manual of Mental Disorders, DSM III, ed. 3, 1980, American Psychiatric Association, Washington, D.C.

Handbook of Psychiatric Rating Scales, 1978, S.B. Lyerly, National Institute of Mental Health, Rockville, Md.

The Mental Health Almanac, R.D. Allen and M.K. Cartier, Garland STPM Press, New York, N.Y.
Contains statistics, legal concerns, existing mental health organizations, available treatment programs, sources, and references in the field of mental health, including vocational questions.

National Directory of Mental Health, Edited and prepared by Neal-Schuman Publishers, Inc., and John Wiley & Sons, Inc., Somerset, N.J.
Contains data about staff, types of treatment, and fees for 3,600 mental health outpatient centers servicing adults.

Psychiatric Dictionary, ed. 5, 1981, R.J. Campbell, Oxford University Press, New York, N.Y.

The Selective Guide to Publications for Mental Health and Family Life Education, Marquis Academic Media, Chicago, Ill.
Listing of books, pamphlets, plays, and other publications.

Training and Resource Directory for Teachers Serving Handicapped Students K-12, 1977, P.M. Kapisovsky and others, Technical Education Research Centers, Cambridge, Mass.
Compiled under the auspices of the Office of Civil Rights to alert elementary and secondary level teachers about resources that assist teachers in accomodating to students with physical and mental handicaps. Lists inservice opportunities, agencies, and organizations as sources for materials, services, and technical assistance, plus literature and media on educational services and technical assistance.

RADIO READING SERVICE FOR THE DISABLED

Closed channel radio reading of newspapers, magazines, and best-selling books for visually impaired and other disabled persons. Special equipment is designed to receive these programs, and eligible persons are provided a Subsidiary Communications Authorization receiver. Stations exist in certain locations of 36 states (including the District of Columbia area). Further information from Association of Radio Reading Services, 176 Brehl Avenue, Columbus, Ohio 43223.

STRUCTURED EXPERIENCES
GAMES AND EXERCISES

Fantasy Encounter Games, H.A. Otto, Harper & Row Publishers, Inc., New York, N.Y.

Interpersonal gaming to encourage imaginative approaches, enrich self-awareness, and expand communication.

Feeling Good, Feeling Good Associates, Mill Valley, Calif.

Deck of 80 playing cards. Each card asks a question with no "right" answers expected, only individual responses. A sheet of rules describes the game procedures. To encourage self-expression and communication, creative thinking, values clarification, and decision making.

50 Strategies for Experiential Learning, book 2, L.B. Thayer, University Associates, La Jolla, Calif.

Strategies presented in order of complexity and in four major categories: the get-acquainted process, self-development, interpersonal relationships, and sharing and group dynamics.

A Fuzzy Tale, C.M. Steiner, 135 Westminister, Kensington, Calif. 94708.

A fantasy that leads to a discussion of empathy.

Growth Games, H.R. Lewis and H.S. Streitfeld, Bantam Books, New York, N.Y.

Non-verbal Group Exercises, K.T. Morris and K.M. Cinnamon, Applied Skills Press, Kansas City, Mo.

Contains 160 nonverbal group exercises and 85 exercise variations with specifically stated goals related to human relations training.

Problem Solving, Education Research, P.O. Box 4205, Warren, N.J.

Business game to guide the systematic analysis of problems. Employs the technique of programmed simulation to involve participants in a hypothetical yet realistic situation. Individual assumes role of consultant to solve operating problems of an organization.

Stress Survival, Education Research, Warren, N.J.

Business game to help identify stressors and to control stress build-up. Employs programmed simulation technique in which participant assumes role of a manager supervising a staff of people and is operating under stressful conditions.

Verbal Group Exercises, K.T. Morris, and K.M. Cinnamon, Applied Skills Press, Kansas City, Mo.

Structured exercises to assist in getting acquainted, developing empathy, gaining skill in listening, and others.

Winning with People, D. Jongeward and M. James, Addison-Wesley Publishing Co., Reading, Mass.

Group exercises in transactional analysis. A training tool for learning the principles involved.

SIMULATION EXPERIENCES

Simulation Exercises for Policy Makers, Southern California Association of Governments, Los Angeles, Calif.

Simulations regarding roles, decision-points, and issues (mental retardation, drug abuse, and others).

Simulation/Games and Training for Education, R.E. Horn and A. Cleaves, ed. 4, Sage Publications, Beverly Hills, Calif.

Listing of available low-to-moderate price range materials suitable for ages junior high through adult.

Turn-on, A. Lauffer and others, Gamed Simulations, Inc., New York, N.Y.

Designed to be played with 42 participants, but roles may be added or deleted depending on size of group. Primary function is to develop or coordinate programs responsive to the needs of older people.

TRAINING ACTIVITIES

Activities for Trainers, C.R. Mill, University Associates, La Jolla, Calif.

Collection of resource materials to meet a variety of training and consulting needs. Contains activities, structured experiences, exercises, questionnaires, instruments, guides, and checklists.

A Skills/contract Approach to Human-Relations Training in Groups, G. Evans, Brooks/Cole Publishing Co., Monterey, Calif.

Deals with interpersonal living.

Personal Effectiveness, R.P. Liberman, and others, Research Press, Champaign, Ill.

Package of training materials, including a programs guide, client's introduction, film, and manual to guide participants to assert themselves and improve their social skills.

Perfecting Social Skills: A Guide to Interpersonal Behavior Development, R.M. Eisler, and L.W. Frederiksen, Plenum Publishing Corp., New York, N.Y.

Provides background, knowledge, and skills for conducting social skills training with case examples, sample forms, and other illustrations.

Straight Talk, S. Miller and others, 1981, Rawson, Wade Publishers, Inc., New York, N.Y.

Based on Couple Communication Program with techniques, dialogues, and exercises related to listening, recognizing, and facing issues, and method to avoid misinterpretation with goal of more precise and intimate communication.

JOURNALS AND NEWSLETTERS

Administration in Mental Health, Rockville, Md.

Subjects covered: community psychology, mental health administration, and administration.

American Journal of Nursing, New York, N.Y.
Articles on nursing and health care.

American Journal of Orthopsychiatry, American Orthopsychiatric Association, New York, N.Y.
Multidisciplinary approaches to mental health and prevention and treatment of mental illness.

American Psychologist. Official journal of American Psychological Association. nonmember cost for calendar year (January through December) 1981: $50.00 domestic.
Discussion of current issues in psychology.

American Rehabilitation. Official bimonthly publication for the Rehabilitation Services Administration. Subscription: Superintendent of Documents, Washington, D.C. 20402. Annual cost: $11.75.
Articles about current status of rehabilitation procedures and services, administrative strategies, governmental funding, and new publications.

Amicus. Published by the National Center for Law and the Handicapped, Inc., P.O. Box 477, University of Notre Dame, Notre Dame, Ind. Annual cost: individual, $10.00. Published six times a year.
Articles about recent occurrences related to physically and mentally disabled regarding legislative and court matters as well as advocacy, rights, and other national concerns.

Assert: The Newsletter of Assertiveness Behavior, Impact Publishers, Inc., Department A., P.O. Box 1094, San Luis Obispo, Calif. 93406. Six issues yearly.
Presents advances in techniques of assertiveness training and current events related to assertiveness training.

Behavioral Counseling Quarterly. Journal for counseling and community interventions. Published quarterly by Human Sciences Press. Annual cost: individual, $20.00; Institution, $40.00.
Interdisciplinary articles with social learning orientation espousing the scientific method, empirical testing, and explicitly stated concepts and strategies.

Behavior Today, ATCOM Publishers, New York, N.Y. Annual cost: individual, $47.00; institution, $63.00. Newsletter published weekly.
Articles related to human services, representing several disciplines: psychiatry, psychology, social work, sociology, anthropology, and the like.

Community Mental Health Journal, Human Sciences Press, New York, N.Y. Published quarterly.
Coordinates emergent approaches to mental health and social well-being. Subjects covered: crisis intervention, planned change, suicide prevention, social system analysis, early care finding, family therapy, milieu therapy, human ecology, high-risk groups, and antipoverty programs.

Contemporary Psychology, American Psychological Association, Washington, D.C. Subscription cost for calendar year (January through December): nonmembers of American Psychological Association, $30.00 domestic.
Journal with critical reviews of new and significant books, films, and tapes in psychology.

Counseling and Human Development, Love Publishing Co., Denver, Colo. Annual cost: $15.00. Newsletter, published monthly except July and August as a service to school counselors and those engaged in human services.
Focuses on children and youth.

Directions, National Institute on Drug Abuse, Rockville, Md. Experimental bulletin about substance use and abuse. Published quarterly. Sent on request to individuals and agencies involved in human services.

Environment and Behavior. Journal published bi-monthly by Sage Publications, Inc., in cooperation with the Environmental Design Research Association (EDRA). Annual cost: Individual, $24.00; Institution, $48.00.
Reports experimental and theoretical work on the study, design, and control of the physical environment and its interactions with human behavioral systems.

Evaluation and the Health Professions. Journal published quarterly. Sage Publications, Inc. Annual cost: individual, $18.00; institution, $36.00.
Articles related to development, implementation, or evaluation of health programs stressing the philosophical, technical and political aspects of evaluation unique to the health professions.

Family and Child Mental Health Journal, Human Sciences Press, New York, N.Y. Bi-annual. Annual cost: individual, $30.00; institution, $14.00.
Interdisciplinary approach to family and child therapy. Articles relating to theoretical and therapeutic advances.

The Gerontologist. Publication of the Gerontological Society of America, Washington, D.C. Bi-monthly journal. Cost per fiscal year: $25.00. Developments in aging field.

Gerontopics, Human Sciences Press, New York, N.Y. Bi-monthly. Annual cost: individual, $14.00; institution, $30.00.

Handicapped Rights and Regulations. Newsletter published bi-weekly by Business Publishers, Inc., Silver Spring, Md. Annual cost: $97.00
Significant developments and effects from federal, state, and local laws and regulations requiring equal opportunities for handicapped citizens in phases of living such as education, employment, transportation, and accessibility.

Holistic Health Review, Human Sciences Press, New York, N.Y. Published quarterly. Annual cost: individual, $16.00; institution, $39.00.

Blend of scholarly articles, news, and consumer service related to holistic health, including political and social ramifications of the holistic health movement.

Hospital and Community Psychiatry. Published monthly by American Psychiatric Association. Annual cost: $21.00.
Articles relating to mentally ill, mental health services, crisis intervention, psychopharmacology, hospitalization, deinstitutionalization, and the like.

Human Services Monograph Series, Project Share, Department of Health and Human Services, Washington, D.C. Distributed on request to human service workers.
Monograph series survey the state of the knowledge and of literature in selected subject areas of importance to the human service community.

Innovations, American Institutes for Research in collaboration with the National Institute of Mental Health, Palo Alto, Calif. Distributed on request to human service workers.
Experimental magazine to communicate information to mental health service personnel about innovative programs and techniques and procedures to implement.

International Journal of Health Services, Baywood Publishing Co., Farmingdale, N.Y. Annual cost: individual, $25.00; institution, $55.00.
Worldwide developments in health care sector.

International Journal of Therapeutic Communities. Published quarterly by Human Sciences Press. Annual cost: individual, $23.00; institution, $48.00.
Interdisciplinary journal related to field of therapeutic communities, therapy, and the psychodynamics of large groups, natural groups, and both small- and large-scale therapeutic institutions.

Journal of Counseling Psychology. Published bi-monthly by the American Psychological Association. Annual cost for 1981: nonmember of APA, $30.00; APA member, $14.00.
Articles about counseling of interest to psychologists and counselors in schools, colleges, universities, private and public counseling agencies, and business, religious, and military settings. Subjects related to counseling processes and interventions; theoretical articles about counseling and studies dealing with evaluation of applications of counseling and counseling programs.

Journal of Environmental Systems, Baywood Publishing Co., Farmingdale, N.Y. Annual cost: individual, $27.00; institution, $51.00.
Focuses on articles about analysis, design, and management of environment as related to system-complexes making up total societal environment.

Journal of Gerontological Nursing, Charles B. Slack, Inc., Thorofare, N.J. Annual cost: $18.00.
Articles related to nursing profession's role with the aging population.

Journal of Holistic Medicine, Human Sciences Press, New York, N.Y. Annual cost: individual, $14.00; institution, $28.00.
Examines philosophy and practical applications of diagnosis and treatment from the point of view of the whole person's physical, nutritional, environmental, emotional, spiritual, and life-style needs and values.

Journal of Human Service Abstracts, Project Share, Rockville, Md. Sent on request to agencies related to human services.
Articles abstracted related to planning, management and delivery of human services.

Journal of Prison Health. Published bi-annually by Human Sciences Press. Annual cost: individuals, $14.00; institutions, $26.00.
Interdisciplinary journal with articles related to medicine, law, corrections, and ethics directed to physicians, prison health professionals, lawyers, inmate advocates, and correctional managers.

The Journal of Psychohistory. Published quarterly by the Association of Psychohistory, Inc. Annual cost: individual, $18.00; institution, $28.00.
Articles on childhood and the family, past and present psychohistory in its broadest terms, individual or group, applied psychoanalysis except for purely literary studies, political psychology, and the psychology of historical movements.

The Journal of Social Issues. Published quarterly by the Society of the Psychological Study of Social Issues. Annual cost: individual, $18.00; institution, $32.00.
Articles related to scientific findings and interpretations about human problems of the group, the community, and the nation as well as those which have no national boundaries.

Journal of Social Service Research. Published quarterly by Haworth Press, New York, N.Y. Annual cost: individual, $24.00; institution, $42.00; and library, $48.00.
Articles related to empirical policy studies of social and behavioral scientists internationally.

Occupational Therapy in Mental Health. Published quarterly. Haworth Press, New York, N.Y. Annual cost: individual, $24.00; institution, $40.00; library, $48.00.
Articles related to psychosocial occupational therapy focusing on the complex, interactive, dynamic interactions of environmental events, persons, and the therapeutic interventions of occupational therapy.

Pathfinder. Printed six times a year by the National Rehabilitation Information Center (NARIC). Annual cost: individual, $10.00; braille edition, $12.00.
Information on the rehabilitation of physically and mentally impaired individuals.

Personality and Social Psychology Bulletin. Published quarterly, Sage Publications, Inc. Annual cost for nonmembers of the Society for Personality and Social Psychology, Inc.: individual, $20.00; institution, $40.00.

Theoretical and empirical articles related to interpersonal and group memberships.

The Personnel and Guidance Journal. Official journal of American Personnel and Guidance Association. Published 10 times a year, monthly, Sept. through June. Annual cost to nonmembers of APGA: $25.00.

Articles related to counseling research, findings, strategies with individuals and groups.

Programs for the Handicapped. Bi-monthly publication, subscription from Office for Handicapped Individuals.

Contains current governmental and some private sector information about programs and services for a variety of disabilities; and listings of resources for additional information.

Psyc Scan (3 publications) Applied Psychology, Clinical Psychology, Developmental Psychology. Four quarterly issues. American Psychological Association. Washington, D.C. Annual cost for each publication: nonmember, $10.00; members, $8.00.

Abstracts from journals in fields related to subject-areas of specific Psych Scan.

The Psychology of Women Quarterly. Published quarterly by Human Sciences Press. Cost per academic year: $40.00.

Contains empirical studies, critical reviews, theoretical articles, and invited book reviews related to psychobiological factors, behavioral studies, role development and change, career choice and training management variables, education, discrimination, therapeutic processes, and sexuality.

Rehab Brief. Prepared by Rehabilitation Research Institute (RRI). Copies available from University of Florida, RRI.

Current research and information about rehabilitation.

Rehabilitation Counseling Bulletin. Published September, November, January, March, and May by the American Rehabilitation Counseling Association. Division of American Personnel and Counseling Association. Annual cost: individual, $12.50; agency, $11.25.

Articles related to theory and practice as well as innovations in the field of rehabilitation counseling.

Self-Help Reporter. Published bi-monthly by National Self-Help Clearinghouse.

Articles about the activities of new and existent self-help groups for a variety of problems about the impact of federal legislation on various human problem areas, and about resources for information in specific areas.

Social Action and the Law, Center for Responsive Psychology. Bi-monthly. Annual cost: individual, $6.00; institution and library, $10.00.

Magazine designed to bring relevant social science information to the attention of the practitioner and the legal, judicial, and correctional fields in nontechnical language.

Special Report of the President's Committee on Employment of the Handicapped, Washington, D.C. 20210. Sent to individuals and agencies in field of rehabilitation on request.

Contains brief descriptions of programs for employment and care of the disabled.

This Month in Mental Health. Published monthly by the Office of Mental Health, State of New York, for people working, involved, or interested in the mental health programs of New York State and concerned with the prevention of mental illness and promotion of mental well-being. Subscription fee not stated.

Up Front, UPF, Inc., Johnstown, Pa. Published 11 times a year. Annual cost: $12.00.

Newspaper for and about physically and mentally disabled people.

ADDRESSES FOR PUBLICATIONS—JOURNALS AND NEWSLETTERS

American Institutes for Research
P.O. Box 1113
Palo Alto, Calif. 94302

American Personnel and Guidance Association
Two Skyline Place, Suite 400
5203 Leesburg Pike
Falls Church, Va. 22041

American Psychiatric Association
1700 18th Street, N.W.
Washington, D.C. 20009

American Psychological Association
Subscription Section
1400 North Uhle Street
Arlington, Va. 22201

The Association of Psychohistory, Inc.
2315 Broadway
New York, N.Y. 10024

Baywood Publishing Co., Inc.
120 Marine Street
Post Office D
Farmingdale, N.Y. 11735

Behavior Today, ATCOM Publisher
2315 Broadway
New York, N.Y. 10024

Business Publishers, Inc.
P.O. Box 1067
Silver Spring, Md. 20910

Center for Responsive Psychology
Brooklyn College
Brooklyn, N.Y. 11210

Gerontological Society
1835 K Street, N.W.
Washington, D.C. 20006

The Haworth Press
149 Fifth Avenue
New York, N.Y. 10010

Human Sciences Press
72 Fifth Avenue
New York, N.Y. 10011

Love Publishing Company
Executive and Editorial Offices
1777 South Bellaire Street
Denver, Colo. 80222

National Institute on Drug Abuse
5600 Fishers Lane, Room 102-56
Rockville, Md. 20857

National Rehabilitation Information Center (NARIC)
The Catholic University of America
4407 Eighth Street, N.E.
Washington, D.C. 20017

National Self-Help Clearinghouse
Graduate School and University Center/CUNY
33 West 42nd Street, Room 1227
New York, N.Y. 10036

Office for Handicapped Individuals
Office of Special Education and Rehabilitative Services
Department of Education
Room 3631 Switzer Building
Washington, D.C. 20202

Office of Mental Health, State of New York
44 Holland Avenue
Albany, N.Y. 12229

Project Share
P.O. Box 2309
Rockville, Md. 20852

Rehabilitation Research Institute (RRI) (UF-RRI)
College of Health Related Professions
University of Florida (UF)
Gainesville, Fla. 32610

Sage Publications, Inc.
275 South Beverly Drive
Beverly Hills, Calif. 90212

The Society for the Psychological Study of Social Issues
Caroline Weichlein, Executive Secretary
P.O. Box 1248
Ann Arbor, Mich. 48106

Superintendent of Documents
U.S. Government Printing Office
Washington, D.C. 20402

Up Front, Inc.
90 Cherry Street, Box 519
Johnstown, Pa. 15907

RESOURCES FOR INFORMATION

Academy of Dentistry for the Handicapped and **National Foundation of Dentistry for the Handicapped,** 1726 Champa, Suite 422, Denver, Colo. 80202.
ADH Membership Roster of dental professionals involved in oral health of special care patients.

Accent on Information, P.O. Box 700, Bloomington, Ill.
Computerized retrieval system, operated by Accent on Living, Inc., provides disabled persons and professionals with information for specific problems concerning everyday living.

Bureau of Census, Foreign Demographic Analysis Division, Room 705, 711 14th Street, N.W., Washington, D.C. 20230.

Center for Health Statistics, Health Resources Administration, 5600 Fishers Lane, Rockville, Md. 20852.

Clearinghouse on the Handicapped, Room 3631, Switzer Building, 330 C Street, S.W., Washington, D.C. 20202.
Agency collects and categorizes descriptions and addresses of national, state, and local organizations supporting information on disabilities, and refers individuals to relevant information providers in the public and private sector.

Expand Associates NIA Epid, 8630 Fenton Street, Suite 508, Silver Spring, Md. 20910.
Single publications from National Institute on Aging (free).

General Accounting Office Reports, U.S. General Accounting Office, Document Handling and Information Services Facility, P.O. Box 6015, Gaithersburg, Md. 20760.
On request name can be inserted on monthly distribution list of GAO Reports—available to human service workers.

Materials Development Center (MDC), Stout Vocational Rehabilitation Institute, University of Wisconsin—Stout, Menomiee, Wis. 47551.
National central source collecting, developing, and disseminating information and materials in the areas of vocational evaluation and work adjustment.

Mental Health Materials Center. The selective guide to publications for mental health and family life, ed. 4, 1981, Chicago, Ill., Marguis Academic Media.
Contains listing of 469 books, plays, and pamphlets recommended in area of mental health.

National Center for Paraprofessionals in Mental Health, National Education Center, 18 Professional Center Parkway, San Rafael, Calif. 94903.

National Clearinghouse for Mental Health Information, National Institute fo Mental Health, 5600 Fishers Lane, Rockville, Md. 20857.

Provides access to scientific information on all areas of mental health and provides custom searches, computer searches, and computer printouts of citations and abstracts.

National Clearinghouse of Rehabilitation Training Materials (NCHRTM), 115 Old USDA Building, Oklahoma State University, Stillwater, Okla. 74074.

Maintains a large collection of materials relevant to rehabilitation education and staff development. Bibliography can be produced of materials in a specific area from their collection, consisting primarily of documents emerging from Rehabilitation Services Administration (RSA) and NIHR. Sponsors training or research efforts. NCHRTM also provides a quarterly newsletter, Memo (free subscription), which includes information on recent acquisitions as well as news of general interest in the field.

National Council on the Aging, (NCOA) Inc., 600 Maryland Avenue, S.W., West Wing 100, Washington, D.C. 20024.

National Institute on Drug Abuse (NIDA) Clearinghouse, 5600 Fishers Lane, Rockville, Md. 20857.

Catalog of services, research, and newsletter.

National Institute of Mental Health. Directory of Halfway Houses and Community Residences for the Mentally Ill, 1977, U.S. Department of Health, Education, and Welfare, Washington, D.C.

National Referral Center for Science and Technology, Science and Technology Division, Library of Congress, Washington, D.C. 20540.

Provides names, addresses, telephone numbers, and brief descriptions of significant organizations, institutions, and individuals who are able to provide desired information. A subject-index computer file and print-outs are available for individual requests at no charge.

The National Rehabilitation Information Center (NARIC), The Catholic University of America, Eighth and Varnum Streets, N.E., Washington, D.C. 20017.

Provides information (including bibliographic searches) on many topics in rehabilitation and helps locate answers to specific reference questions. Nominal charges for photocopying, duplicating of audiovisual materials, and searching computerized data bases other than NARIC's for rehabilitation-related information.

National Technical Information Services (NTIS), 5285 Port Royal Road, Springfield, Va. 22161.

Office for Handicapped Individuals, Human Development Services, Directory of National Information Sources on Handicapping Conditions and Related Services, DHEW Pub. No. (OHDS) 80-22007-1980, U.S. Government Printing Office, Washington, D.C.

The Paraprofessional Manpower Branch, National Institute of Mental Health, Parklawn Building, Room 8C02, 5600 Fishers Lane, Rockville, Md. 20852.

Information about service programs, making effective use of paraprofessionals, and special training programs oriented toward paraprofessionals.

People to People Committee for the Handicapped, Suite 1130, 152 K Street, N.W., Washington, D.C. 20005.

The Directory of Organizations Interested in the Handicapped, an extensive listing of organizations that give information about techniques, training, treatment, devices and procedures used for helping the disabled person.

Regional Rehabilitation Research Institute on Attitudinal, Legal and Leisure Barriers, 1828 L Street, N.W., Suite 704, Washington, D.C. 20036.

Research and Program Development Institute National Center on Employment of the Handicapped at Human Resources Center, Albertson, N.Y. 11507.

Attitudes Toward Persons with Disabilities, a compendium of related literature by J.G. Schroedel, 1979. Other literature and information about innovative training programs available.

The Social Action Research Center, 2728 Durant Avenue, Berkeley, Calif. 94704.

Has annotated bibliography (1977) related to the use of paraprofessionals in community mental health. Can provide information about service programs about the use and training of paraprofessionals.

Survey and Reports Section, Biometry Branch, NIMH, (NIH), Rockville, Md. 20852.

United States Department of Justice, Law Enforcement Assistance Administration, National Criminal Justice Reference Service, Washington, D.C. 20530.

University Center for International Rehabilitation (UCIR), D-201 West Fee Hall, Michigan State University, East Lansing, Mich. 48824.

Provides information on research practices, technological devices, and policies developed and implemented by other countries. Produces a newsletter, Inter-Connector, selected bibliographies, a TV series, "International Perspectives in Rehabilitation," workshops, seminars, consultation, and an inquiry-response program.

Yale University, The Center for Paraprofessional Evaluation and Continuing Education, Department of Psychiatry, 1221 Chapel Street, New Haven, Conn. 06511.

Appendix D

ADDED DETAILS ABOUT SELECTED INNOVATIVE PROGRAMS

Altro Workshops
3600 Jerome Avenue, Bronx, N.Y. 10467

Altro began as the Committee for the Care of the Jewish Tuberculosis victims to aid them through comprehensive services. Three basic tenets that originated with this Committee are still sustained by Altro:

☐ Whether a person's illness is physical or emotional, he or she must be restored at least to a level of health that allows community living.

☐ Every individual's potential to contribute to society regardless of manner or degree should be realized.

☐ The individual's family and inherent capabilities form an important influence on client's personal problems.

Since Altro recognizes that depreciated self-worth is often the basis for the client's inadequate motivation, the client's self-evaluation is added to by the Robert J. Levy Evaluation and Day Treatment Services team (a subdivision of Altro). This team carefully analyzes the client's aptitude and mental and physical condition to determine each person's unique needs and the most effective procedures for increasing the client's existing proficiency or for establishing new achievements. Clients are offered the opportunity to explore every type of vocational training available at Altro, and there is a coordination of the various services leading to personal-social-occupational adaptations. Thus the client's individualized plan is collaboratively developed by the Altro psychiatrist with other members of the professional staff and the referring institution. All these efforts are integrated with the vocational services of the Altro Workshops, since this source of industrial therapy is considered a significant aspect of rehabilitation. The ideology undergirding Altro's services is expressed in the following brief excerpt (Altro):

> "Success" is a relative word. Altro's philosophy is based on the principles that each patient be viewed as an individual; allowed to proceed at his or her own pace and be guided to their own level of productivity.

Caminar
720 El Camino, Belmont, Calif. 94002

Caminar is a voluntary, nonprofit corporation that has, since 1967, specialized in the planning, development, and direct operation of social rehabilitation programs and related training components. The agency provides a continuum of services to both acutely and chronically emotionally disabled individuals through graduated levels of treatment and care. Four of the living arrangements are located in California (Belmont, Redwood City, and Vallejo); one is in Las Vegas. The following details derived from a Caminar brochure describe Redwood House, Satellite Housing, and El Camino House.

Redwood House. Living arrangements are provided as a crisis-oriented alternative to hospitalization for adults experiencing acute psychiatric distress, ranging from temporary inability to cope with life stress to exacerbation of long-term mental disability. Residents are accommodated for periods from 24 hours to 3 weeks. At the daily meeting of the "community group" residents discuss their feelings, develop communication skills, and establish a supportive and interactive network with other residents. The counselor acts as role model for relating to people. On certain evenings members of the nearby community are invited to join the residents in the group discussions. No television sets are permitted at Redwood House so that residents concentrate on self-exploration and interpersonal skill development. The counselors and their assistants are available to assist in sudden crises situations. The living arrangement is an open house, but because of the severity of the crises and reactions of the residents, residents are expected to sign out when leaving Redwood and to sign in on their return. A prescribed daily routine and a curfew are additional aspects of the structure.

Satellite Housing Project. Another living arrangement is provided for individuals requiring less structure with continuing support to live in the community and cope with life events. Apartments, duplexes, and other types of homes comprise the housing units for the Housing Project. These units offer the

418

residents affordable housing, furniture, appliances and rental subsidies. Weekly small group meetings of staff and residents provide interpersonal and other support plus problem resolution and training in daily living skills. Recreational and social activities, including a therapeutic social club co-sponsored by Caminar and the San Mateo Mental Health Services, also are available.

El Camino House. A third kind of arrangement, sometimes referred to as a "halfway house," maintains a homelike atmosphere that affords residents opportunities to participate in homemaking activities, caring for pets, decision making about new residents as well as their own activities, and a special type of friendship role to orient new residents—a "buddy." Residents are required to be involved in therapy and some structured activity during the day. Group meetings serve a multitude of purposes:

□ The new residents are expected to attend weekly meetings at which they are encouraged to discuss their feelings and pose questions and problems related to their move to an unfamiliar environment. After 6 weeks their attendance is voluntary.

□ Residents contemplating major life changes (changing jobs or personal relationships or moving to another residence) attend a planning group for 6 weeks to air their concerns and intentions.

□ All residents are required to attend house meetings to resolve issues concerning group actions and for the assignment of homemaking responsibilities.

Most residents remain at El Camino from 6 to 12 months. In addition to problem resolution by means of group processes, special programs are available, such as art and dance therapy, yoga, sexual understandings, family therapy, and housing assistance.

Center for Independent Living
2539 Telegraph Avenue, Berkeley, Calif. 94704

CIL is not a residential club, although lists of accessible housing possibilities are made available to prospective residents who are physically impaired. CIL offers job-training programs, wheelchair repairs, a low-cost transportation service, an automotive shop where vans and cars are specially fitted for the disabled, and advice on public funds. Services are available to the blind, the deaf, the elderly, and the physically disabled. Eventually they also will be extended to the mentally disabled. CIL participants become involved in diversified activities, helping one another through their social interactions or as peer counselors. Counselors with life experiences in physical disability and substance abuse or other difficulties work with individuals, families, couples, and groups who have problems similar to their own. Peer counselors are selected on the basis of their attitudes and experiences. Training is not formally structured but rather flows with the hands-on experiences and in-

formation derived from contact with troubled persons. Staff members meet regularly and discuss their clients; suggestions are offered, and observation and supervision by the more established counselors serve as the training format.

The Community Care Homes of the Veteran's Administration
Seattle, Wash.

The Community Care Homes Project of the Veteran's Administration Hospital* in Seattle, Wash., represents another category of living arrangement—foster homes. The Veterans Administration project director selects, screens, and trains the sponsors of these homes. A variety of settings are established, in which veterans who are former patients are matched with suitable care-givers. A representative from the project regularly conducts home visits and monitors the veteran's progress and the appropriateness of the care provided. Needed resources are made available for sponsor and veteran, as are crisis services for significant relatives and guardians.

Fountain House
425 West 47th Street, New York, N.Y. 10036

Fountain House was founded in 1948 as the WANA (*We Are Not Alone*) Society by a small group of psychiatric patients from Rockland State Hospital with two volunteers from the community. Later, as the membership increased, they moved into a brownstone house with a fountain and thus the title "Fountain House." Currently this house is a five-story brownstone located in an area often referred to as "Hell's Kitchen." Members must be actively involved in some form of therapy to participate in the activities. Socialization is an essential part of the clubhouse atmosphere; it is accomplished by formal and informal member and staff contacts during the extensive daily, evening, and weekend social and recreational activities as well as the prevocational and vocational training opportunities. The program includes training units for homemaking, clerical, and other vocational and daily living skills. The Transitional Employment Program (TEP) provides half-time job placement for members in entry level jobs in business firms in New York City. These jobs offer experience in competitive employment settings under the supervision of a responsible and responsive staff member from Fountain House. This person learned the tasks of the job and trained the first worker; after a prescribed number of weeks or months, this worker trained the succeeding worker; and so on. This employment is important for the training opportunity it affords in a "normal" work setting and because it supplies the member with a current employment record and references

---

*Based on personal communication from Alan F. Castle, Veteran's Administration Hospital, Seattle, Wash.

that fill in the gaps of no work because of hospitalization or other reasons.

In 1957 an apartment program was initiated. Fountain House seeks apartments, signs leases, furnishes the apartments, and makes them available at a moderate rental fee to two to four Fountain House members. These residents may assume the lease when they are sufficiently self-assured and economically secure.

International Center for the Disabled (ICD)
340 East 24th Street, New York, N.Y. 10010

The ICD Human Service Assistant (HSA) Training Program is structured in 8-week periods, with the first 8 weeks' assignment to one of ICD's work areas in which trainees learn about the work skills and interact with the working clients. During the second 8 weeks the client-trainees transfer to another work unit. The final 8 weeks consist of introductory visits to three or four organizations so that the trainees can explore their preferences for subsequent work experience outside of ICD. The content of the training begins with the principles and practice of behavioral observation skills applied to the client-trainees by the staff and later by the trainees to their own "clients." Other subjects included are ethics in rehabilitation, skills in organizing, program planning and technical writing, the role of the paraprofessional, interpersonal relationships, and other specific topics related to medical aspects and rehabilitation techniques.

Initially, prospective HSAs complete a questionnaire regarding their reasons for wanting to be a paraprofessional, a self-evaluation of their strong points and weak points, and their concepts of the attributes of an aide. Applicants also are presented with samples of situations and asked to respond to the inquiry "What would you say and/or do?" Several other questionnaires and checklists are used in the HSA training program. For example, bi-monthly progress reports are maintained on a checklist with behavioral items related to work habits. Other forms focus on the identification of unsuitable behavior such as irritating habits and odd or inappropriate behavior that might interfere with job performance and interpersonal relationships.

About 75% of the HSA graduates obtain jobs in the human service systems. The remainder shift to other fields or find alternative activities. Those who become employed obtain positions in a wide variety of work settings with miscellaneous job titles and functions, such as family or child care workers, evaluators, counselors for residential care (halfway) houses or for substance abusers, aides for social casework or for occupational or physical therapy, outreach or recreational workers and administrators of programs. The category of paraprofessional trained by ICD has been recognized by a New York State job classification designated as "Mental Health Aide."

Rehabilitation Mental Health Services (RMHS), Inc.
86 South 14th Street, San Jose, Calif. 95112

RMHS* began in 1953 as a committee of volunteers. Currently it is a private, nonprofit, tax-exempt corporation providing residential treatment and rehabilitation services for Santa Clara and Santa Cruz county residents with psychiatric problems. RMHS has been an innovator and assumed a leadership role in the provision of services that are alternatives to institutional placement.

The philosophy underlying RMHS's services is expressed in the social rehabilitation model and focuses on the whole person. Clients are viewed as people with strengths and weaknesses, yet worthy of respect, dignity, and rights. A positive view accepts the assumption of the client's competency for improvement; clients are encouraged to build on their strengths and to learn to solve their problems.

The concept of the therapeutic community milieu stresses the importance of the physical environment with an open, unlocked, residential, noninstitutional atmosphere. A normal schedule is maintained, with structured program activities required and arranged during the day time hours of weekdays. Evenings and weekends are unstructured and more or less supervised (depending on clients' needs). Client self-sufficiency and community government by the clients are emphasized, as is encouragement of the use of appropriate community resources.

The importance of the influence of every staff member is realized. The cook and maintenance personnel are recognized as part of the rehabilitative process as they relate to and are sought out by the clients. Residents engage in activity programs in the residences and share in housekeeping and maintenance tasks planned and assigned at the weekly meetings of the community government of each residential center.

RMHS currently administers seven residential programs for adults (approximately 18 to 65 years of age) and two programs for adolescents (13 to 19 years of age). The residential arrangements emphasize a transitional goal with movement toward less restrictive living arrangements in accordance with the mentally ill person's developmental progress. The length of expected residence ranges from approximately 3 weeks to 5 months, depending on the focus of the living arrangement and the needs of the residents. The residential centers offer a nonmedical approach with goals such as the following:

☐ Provision of a residential treatment and rehabilitation center as an alternative to hospitalization or institutional placement

---

*The information about RMHS is based on observations during personal visits to the various locales, actual participation with the clients in their activities, and discussions with administrators, staff members, and clients.

□ Adjustment to community living with the aim of decreasing the possibility of rehospitalization

□ Social rehabilitation services with psychiatric consultation support as needed for both the acute and chronically mentally ill

□ Training in life management skills

□ Preparation for meaningful, productive vocational activity

Back-up services provided for the residents include the following:

□ A work-activity center for men clients whose long-term psychiatric problems and level of functioning makes them ineligible for rehabilitation services in the community

□ A day-time activity center that provides occupational therapy and prevocational and vocational skills development

□ A school operated by the Santa Clara Office of Education for adolescents living in the Adolescent Residential Centers who are considered able to realize greater benefit from a specialized school program

RMHS has historically pioneered the use of a multidisciplinary team staff. Except when degrees are required by law (for example, psychiatrist), RMHS will employ individuals who demonstrate the ability to effectively provide quality mental health services to clients regardless of degrees and credentials. RMHS is committed to staffing programs with individuals who reflect the cultural, ethnic, and linguistic characteristics of the client population.

REFERENCES

Abidon, R.A.: Parenting skills: trainers manual, New York, 1976a, Human Sciences Press, Inc.

Abidon, R.A.: Parenting skills workbook, New York, 1976b, Human Sciences Press, Inc.

Ackerman, N.W., editor: Family process, New York, 1970, Basic Books, Inc., Publishers.

Adams, H.J.: The progressive heritage of guidance: a view from the left, Personn. Guid. J. **51**:531-537, 1973.

Ad hoc Committee on Ethical Standards in Psychological Research: Ethical principles in the conduct of research with human participants, Washington, D.C., 1973, American Psychological Association, Inc.

Adler, A.: Social interest: a challenge to mankind, New York, 1964, G.P. Putnam's Sons. (Translated by J. Linton and R. Vaughan.) (Paperback edition by Capricorn Books.)

Adler, G., and Myerson, P.G.: Confrontation in psychotherapy, New York, 1973, Science House, Inc.

Agranoff, R., Pattakos, A., and Tomczak, J.: Inventory of mental health, developmental disability and substance abuse services, Executive Summary, SHR-0003196, Rockville, Md., 1978, Project Share.

Agranoff, R., and others: Planning for mental health, developmental disability and substance services, Executive Summary, SHR-0003195, Rockville, Md., 1979, Project Share.

Aguilera, D.C., and Messick, J.M.: Crisis intervention: theory and methodology, ed. 4, St. Louis, 1981, The C.V. Mosby Co.

Ahmed, P.I., and Coelho, G.V., editors: Toward a new definition of health: psychosocial dimensions, New York, 1979, Plenum Publishing Corp.

Albee, G.W.: Mental health manpower trends, New York, 1959, Basic Books, Inc., Publishers.

Alberti, R.E., and Emmons, M.L.: Your perfect right, San Luis Obispo, Calif., 1978, Impact Publishers, Inc.

Allen, G.: How your daughter grows up to be a man, Humanist **40**(2): 34-38, 1980.

Alley, S., Blanton, J., and Feldman, R., editors: Paraprofessionals in mental health: theory and practice, New York, 1979, Human Sciences Press, Inc.

Alley, S., and others, editors: Case studies of mental health paraprofessionals: twelve effective programs, New York, 1979, Human Sciences Press, Inc.

Alley, S.R., and Blanton, J.: Report to NIMH contract #NEC 1 T31, Mental Health 15414-01, Sept., 1978.

Allport, G.W.: Becoming: basic considerations for a psychology of personality, New Haven, Conn., 1955, Yale University Press.

Allport, G.W.: Pattern and growth in personality, New York, 1961, Holt, Rinehart & Winston.

Allport, G.W.: ABC's of scapegoating, New York, 1979, Anti-Defamation League of B'nai B'rith.

Allport, G.W., Vernon, P.E., and Lindzey, G.: Study of values, ed. 3, Boston, Houghton Mifflin Co.

Alsop, R.: Psychiatric autopsy, Social action and the law **6**(4):57-58, 1980.

Altman, I.: Reciprocity of interpersonal exchange, J. Theory Social Behavior **3**:249-261, 1973.

Altman, I., and Lett, E.E.: The ecology of interpersonal relationships: a classification system and conceptual model. In McGrath, L.C., editor: Social and psychological factors in stress, New York, 1970, Holt, Rinehart & Winston.

Altman, S., and Taylor, D.A.: Social penetration theory: the development of interpersonal relationships, New York, 1973, Holt, Rinehart & Winston.

Altro Health and Rehabilitation Services, Inc.: Brochure, New York, Altro Health and Rehabilitation Services, Inc.

Altro Workshops: Brochure, Bronx, New York, Altro Workshops.

American Personnel and Guidance Association: Support personnel for the counselor: their technical and nontechnical roles and preparation, Personn. Guid. J. **45**:857-861, 1967.

American Personnel and Guidance Association: Code of ethics, Washington, D.C., 1974, APGA.

American Personnel and Guidance Association: Labels seen as harmful to young, Guidepost **23**(9):1, 7, 1980.

Amerikaner, M., Schauble, P., and Ziller, R.: Images: the use of photographs in personal counseling, Personn. Guid. J. **59**:68-73, 1980.

Anderson, D.: Culturally relevant intermediacy: the role of mental health specialists in the community. In Nash, K.B., and others: The paraprofessional, New Haven, Conn., 1978, Advocate Press, Inc.

Ansbacher, N.L., and Ansbacher, R.R.: Alfred Adler, superiority and social interest, Evanston, Ill., 1964, Northwestern University Press.

Anthony, W.A.: The principles of psychiatric rehabilitation, Baltimore, 1980, University Park Press.

Arbuckle, D.S.: The counselor: who? what? Personn. Guid. J. **50**:785-790, 1972.

Arbuckle, D.S.: Where have I heard that song before? Canadian Counselor, **12**:76-79, 1977.

Archer, R.L.L.: Role of personality and the social situation. In Chelune, G.J., and others, editors: Self disclosure, San Francisco, 1979, Jossey-Bass, Inc., Publishers.

Ard, B.N., Jr., editor: Counseling and psychotherapy, Palo Alto, Calif., 1966, Science & Behavior Books, Inc.

Argelander, H.: The initial interview in psychotherapy, New York, 1976, Human Sciences Press, Inc. (Translated by H.F. Bernays.)

Argyris, C.: Integrating the individual and the organization, New York, 1964, John Wiley & Sons, Inc.

Arnhoff, F.N., Rubenstein, E.A., and Speisman, J.C., editors: Manpower for mental health, Chicago, 1969, Aldine Publishing Co.

Aspy, D.N.: Empathy—congruence—caring are not singular, Personn. Guid. J. **40**:637-640, 1970.

Association for Counselor Education and Supervision: Standards for the preparation of counselors and other personnel services specialists, Washington, D.C., 1973, American Personnel and Guidance Association.

Austin, J.: Professionals and paraprofessionals, New York, 1977, Human Sciences Press, Inc.

Austin, M.F., and Grant, T.M.: Interview training for college students disadvantaged in the labor market: comparison of five institutional techniques, J. Counsel. Psychol. **28**(1):72-75, 1981.

Austin, M.J., Skelding, A.H., and Smith, P.L.: Delivering human services: an introductory programmed text, New York, 1977, Harper & Row, Publishers, Inc.

Authier, J.: The psychoeducational model: definition, contemporary roots and content, Canadian Counselor **12**:15-22, 1977.

Avila, D.L., Combs, A.W., and Purkey, W.W.: The helping relationship sourcebook, Boston, 1971, Allyn & Bacon, Inc.

Ayer, W.A., and Hirschman, R.D., editors: Psychology and dentistry: selected readings, Springfield, Ill., 1972, Charles C Thomas, Publisher.

Backman, M.E.: The development of Micro-TOWER: a battery of standardized work samples for assessing vocational aptitudes, New York, ICD Rehabilitation and Research Center.

Bahm, A.J.: Ethics as a behavioral science, Springfield, Ill., 1974, Charles C Thomas Publisher.

Baker, E.J.: The mental health associate: a new approach in mental health, Community Mental Health J. **8**:281-291, 1972.

Baker, E.J., and McPheeters, H.L.: Middle-level workers: characteristics, training and utilization of mental health associates. In Nash, K.B., and others: The paraprofessional, New Haven, Conn., 1978, Advocate Press, Inc.

Baltes, P.B., and Brim, O.G., Jr.: Life-span development and behavior, vol. 2., New York, 1979, Academic Press, Inc.

Banks, G.: Black confronts white: the issue of support in the interview situation. In Carkhuff, R.R.: The development of human resources, New York, 1971, Holt, Rinehart & Winston, Inc.

Banks, W., and Martens, K.: Counseling: the reactionary profession, Personn. Guid. J. **51**:457-462, 1973.

Banville, T.G.: How to listen—how to be heard, Chicago, 1978, Nelson-Hall Publishers.

Baratz, S.S.: Effect of race of experimenter, instructions, and comparison population upon level of reported anxiety in Negro subjects, J. Pers. Soc. Psychol. **7**:194-196, 1967.

Barclay, J.R.: The revolution in counseling: some editorial comments, Personn. Guid. J. **58**:457, 1980.

Barnes, F.F.: A psychiatric unit serving an international community, Hospital Community Psychiatry, **31**(11): 756-758, 1980.

Barnett, M.A., and others: Antecedents of empathy: retrospective accounts of early socialization, Personality Social Psychology Bull. **6**(3):361-365, 1980.

Baron, R.: Contrasting approaches to social knowing: an ecological perspective, Personality Social Psychology Bulletin. **6**(4):591-600, 1980.

Barrett-Lennard, G.T.: Dimensions of therapists as causal factors in therapeutic change, Psychol. Monogr. **43**:76, 1962.

Barrett-Lennard, G.T.: The relationship inventory, Armindale, Australia, 1964, University of New England.

Barrett-Lennard, G.T.: Empathy in human relationships: significance, nature and measurement, Australian Psychologist **11**:173-184, 1976.

Barrett-Lennard, G.T.: The relationship inventory: later development and adaptations, JSAS Catalog of Selected Documents in Psychology, **8**:68, 1978 (MS No. 1732).

Barrett-Lennard, G.T.: The empathy cycle: refinement of a nuclear concept, J. Counseling Psychology **28**(2):91-100, 1981.

Barrow, J., and Hayashi, J.: Shyness clinic: a social development program for adolescents and growing adults, Personn. Guid. J. **59**:58-61, 1980.

Basch, M.F.: Doing psychotherapy, New York, 1980, Basic Books, Inc., Publishers.

Baum, A., Singer, J.E., and Baum, C.S.: Stress and the environment, J. Social Issues, **37**(1), 1981, 4-35.

Bayes, M., and Neill, T.K.: New roles for paraprofessionals in human services. In Nash, K.B., and others, editors: The paraprofessional, New Haven, Conn., 1978, Advocate Press, Inc.

Beard, J.H.: Psychiatric rehabilitation at Fountain House. In Meislin, J.: Rehabilitation medicine and psychiatry, Springfield, Ill., 1976, Charles C. Thomas, Publisher.

Beauregard, R.A.: From isolation to organization: structural barriers to client-induced accountability in the human services, J. Sociology Social Welfare **4**:1109-1121, 1977.

Beck, K., and others: Manual on state mental health planning, Washington, D.C., 1977, A.D. Little, Inc.

Behavior Today: Arguments for daycare, Behavior Today **8**(12):1, 1977a.

Behavior Today: Working parents choose home-based child care arrangements, Behavior Today, **8**(12):1, 1977b.

Behavior Today: Court treats girls more harshly than boys, Behavior Today **11**(49):4-5, 1980a.

Behavior Today: Ex-hostages and POW's: serious emotional problems develop—later, Behavior Today **11**(43):1-2, 1980b.

Behavior Today: Special report: comparative study: Iranian and American self-images, Behavior Today **11**(44):3-4, 1980c.

Behavior Today: Give ex-hostages and families some space, advises psychological group, Behavior Today **12**(6):6, 1981a.

Behavior Today: More mental health funding cuts equal more Atlanta syndromes? Behavior Today **12**(10):1-2, 4, 1981b.

Behavior Today: Parents of murdered children say they have "unique" grief problems, Behavior Today **12**(10):4-5, 1981c.

Behavior Today: Special report: Colorado state hospitals' Hispanic Treatment Program, Behavior Today, Part III, **12**(3):5-6; Part IV, **12**(4):5, 1981d.

Behavior Today: Therapist helps companies deal with male/female employee stress, Behavior Today **12**(12):7-8, 1981e.

Beier, E.G.: The silent language of psychotherapy, Chicago, 1966, Aldine Publishing Co.

Beik, L.L.: Organization for the Integration of Human Services, J. Hum. Serv. **5**(3):210, 1980.

Bell, D.: The coming of post-industrial society, New York, 1973, Basic Books, Inc., Publishers.

Bell, D.: The year 2000—the trajectory of an idea, Daedalus, J. American Academy of Arts and Sciences **96**(3):639-651, 1967.

Bell, I.P.: The double standard. In Hess, B.B., editor: Growing old in America, ed. 2, New Brunswick, N.J., 1980, Transaction Books.

Bem, D.J.: The concept of risk in the study of human behavior. In Carney, R.E., editor: Risk-taking behavior, Springfield, Ill., 1971, Charles C Thomas, Publisher.

Bennis, W.G.: Toward a "truly" scientific management: the concept of organizational health, General Systems Yearbook **7**:271-296, 1962.

Benton and Bowles, Inc.: Men's changing role in the family of the '80's: an American consensus report, New York, 1980, Benton & Bowles, Inc.

Beppler, M.C., Bortz, F.E., and Milligan, M.A.: 4-H leader's guide: let's look at 4-H and handicapped youth, University Park, Pa., The Pennsylvania State University Cooperative Extension Service.

Berger, M.M., editor: Videotape techniques in psychiatric training and treatment, rev. ed.: New York, 1978, Brunner/Mazel, Inc.

Berman, J.S.: What makes psychotherapy work? Discovery **5**(1):24-27, 1980.

Bernard, J.: The eudaemonists. In Klausner, S.Z., editor: Why man takes chances: studies in stress-seeking, Garden City, N.Y., 1968, Anchor Books, Doubleday & Co., Inc.

Bernard, J.: The good-provider role: its rise and fall, American Psychologist **36**(1):1-2, 1981.

Berne, E.: Transactional analysis in psychotherapy, New York, 1961, Grove Press, Inc.

Berne, E.: Games people play, New York, 1964, Grove Press, Inc.

Bernier, J.E.: Training and supervising counselors: lessons learned from deliberate psychological education, Personn. Guid. J. **59**:15-20, 1980.

Berry, J.B.: Counseling older women: a perspective, Personn. Guid. J. **55**:130-131, 1976.

Berry, J.W.: Human ecology and cognitive style: comparative studies in cultural and psychological adaptation, New York, 1976, Sage Publications, Inc.

Bertcher, H., and others: Role modeling, role playing: a manual for vocational development and employment agencies, Washington, D.C., Manpower Sciences Service.

Bertinetti, J.: Prejudice in the world of work. In Mortenson, R.A.: Prejudice project, New York, 1980, Antidefamation League of B'nai B'rith and the University of Nebraska at Omaha College of Education.

Beschner, G., and Thompson, P.: Women and drug abuse treatment: needs and services, No. (ADM) 81-1057, Washington, D.C., 1981, National Institute on Drug Abuse, U.S. Department of Health and Human Services.

Best, F.: Recycling people. In Cornish, E., editor: The world of tomorrow, Washington, D.C., 1978, World Future Society.

Bialer, I., and Sternlicht, M.: The psychology of mental retardation: issues and approaches, New York, 1977, Psychological Dimensions, Inc.

Bird, B.: Handicapism, sexism, and racism: implication for rehabilitation, unpublished article, 1980, Washington, D.C., National Public Radio.

Birdwhistell, R.L.: Kinesics and context, Philadelphia, 1970, University of Pennsylvania Press.

Bitter, J.A.: Introduction to rehabilitation, St. Louis, 1979, The C.V. Mosby Co.

Black, B.J.: Transitional and sheltered workshops for the mentally ill. In Meislin, J.: Rehabilitation medicine and psychiatry, Springfield, Ill., 1976, Charles C Thomas, Publisher.

Blake, R.R., and Mouton, J.S.: The managerial grid, Houston, 1964, Gulf Publishing Co., Book Division.

Blake, R.R., and Mouton, J.S.: Grid approaches to managing stress, Springfield, Ill., 1980, Charles C Thomas, Publisher.

Blake, R.R., and others: The social worker grid, Springfield, Ill., 1979, Charles C Thomas, Publisher.

Blanton, J., and Alley, S.: Models of program success in New Careers Programs, J. Community Psychology, **5:**359-371, 1977.

Blocher, D.H.: Developmental counseling, ed. 2, New York, 1974, Ronald Press.

Blocher, D.H.: Developmental counseling revisited, Counseling and Human Development **13**(4):1-7, 1980.

Bloom, M.: The paradox of helping: introduction to the philosophy of scientific practice, New York, 1975, John Wiley & Sons, Inc.

Blum, G.: Feeling good; Yes, No; and Project MENCH, brochure, 1980.

Blum, G., and Goldenberg, G.: A wholistic educational program, San Francisco, 1979, MENCH Project.

Blum, R.H., and Ezekiel, J.: Clinical records for mental health services, Springfield, Ill., 1962, Charles C Thomas, Publisher.

Bocknek, G.: Understanding and managing anxiety. In Eisenberg, S., and Patterson, L.E.: Helping clients with special concerns, Chicago, 1979, Rand McNally College Publishing Co.

Bolander, D.O., and others: Instant quotations dictionary, Mundelein, Ill., 1968, Career Institute.

Bolles, R.N.: The three boxes of life: and how to get one of them, rev. ed., 1981, Berkeley, Calif., Ten Speed Press.

Bolton, R.: People skills: how to assert yourself, listen to others, and resolve conflicts, Englewood Cliffs, N.J., 1979, Prentice-Hall, Inc.

Bosk, C.L.: Occupational rituals in patient management, N. Engl. J. Med. **303:**71-76, 1980.

Boy, A.V., and Pine, G.J.: Avoiding counselor burnout through role reversal, Personn. Guid. J. **59:**161-163, 1980.

Bradburn, N.M., and others: Improving interview method and questionnaire design: response effects to threatening questions in survey research, San Francisco, 1979, Jossey-Bass, Inc., Publishers.

Bradley, V.J.: Deinstitutionalization: social justice or political expedient, Amicus, **5**(2):82-87, 1980.

Bradshaw, B., and Straker, M.: A special unit to encourage giving up patienthood, Hospital Community Psychiatry **25:**164-165, 1975.

Brager, G., and Holloway, S.: Changing human service organizations: politics and practice, New York, 1978, The Free Press.

Brammer, L.M.: Who can be a helper, Personn. Guid. J. **45:**303-308, 1977.

Brammer, L.M., and Shostrom, E.L.: Therapeutic psychology: fundamentals of counseling and psychotherapy, ed. 3, Englewood Cliffs, N.J., 1977, Prentice-Hall, Inc.

Brandon, O.: Approaching the tragic triad. In Fabry, J.B., Bulka, R.P., and Sahakian, W.S., editors: Logotherapy in action, New York, 1979, Jason Aronson, Inc.

Brasch, P.: A helping hand from the boss, Parade, pp. 6, 8, 17, June 8, 1980.

Brody, E.M.: A million procrustean beds. In Hess, B.B., editor: Growing old in America, ed. 2, New Brunswick, N.J., 1980, Transaction Books.

Brody, M., and Schneider, O.B.: The psychiatrist as classroom teacher: school consultation in the inner city, Hospital Community Psychiatry **24**(4):248-251, 1973.

Brofenbrenner, M.: Poverty, exploitation, alienation, American Behavioral Scientist **23**(3):382-392, 1980.

Brown, R.: The autobiography of my mother, New York, 1976, Doubleday & Co., Inc.

Brown, W.F.: Effectiveness of paraprofessionals: the evidence. In Nash, K.B., Lifton, N., and Smith, S.E., editors: The paraprofessional: selected readings, New Haven, Conn., 1978, Advocate Press, Inc.

Brownlee, A.T.: Community, culture, and care: a cross-cultural guide for health workers, St. Louis, 1978, The C.V. Mosby Co.

Bruch, H.: The golden cage: the enigma of anorexia nervosa, Cambridge, Mass., 1978, Harvard University Press.

Buber, M.: I and Thou, ed. 2, New York, 1958, Charles Scribner's Sons. (Translated by R.G. Smith.)

Budzynski, T.H., and Peffer, K.E.: Biofeedback training. In Kutash, I.L., and others: Handbook on stress and anxiety, San Francisco, 1980, Jossey-Bass Publishers, Inc.

Bureau of Census, U.S. Department of Commerce: Statistical abstract of the United States, DHEW Pub. No. (OHDS) 79-2006-1978, Washington, D.C., 1979, U.S. Government Printing Office.

Bureau of Health Manpower, Division of Nursing: Nurse practitioners and the expanded role of the nurse, J. Hum. Serv. **5**(3):224-225, 1980.

Burke, W.W., and Goodstein, L.D., editors: The role of OD in systemic change, organization development interventions, training and OD and professional and personal issues confronting OD consultants, La Jolla, Calif., 1981, University Associates, Inc.

Butler, R.N.: Overview on aging. In Bisdin, G., and Hofling, C.: Aging, New York, 1978, Brunner/Mazel, Inc.

Butler, R.N., and Lewis, M.I.: Aging and mental health: positive psychosocial and biomedical approaches, ed. 3, St. Louis, 1981, The C.V. Mosby Co.

Butts, H.F.: Psychoanalysis and unconscious racism, Fort Lee, N.J., 1972, Behavioral Sciences Tape Library. (Cassette.)

California Department of Mental Health: Patent rights handbook, Sacramento, Calif.

Caminar: Brochure, Belmont and Redwood City, Calif., Caminar.

Capelle, R.G.: Changing human systems, Toronto, 1979, International Human Systems Institute.

Capuzzi, D., and Gross, D.: Group work with the elderly: an overview for counselors, Personn. Guid. J. **59**:206-211, 1980.

Carey, R.G.: Counseling the terminally ill, Personn. Guid. J. **53**:124-126, 1976.

Carkhuff, R.R.: Helping and human relations: a primer for lay and professional helpers, vols. I and II, New York, 1969, Holt, Rinehart & Winston, Inc.

Carkhuff, R.R.: Development of human resources, New York, 1971, Holt, Rinehart & Winston, Inc.

Carkhuff, R.R.: Credo of a militant humanist, Personn. Guid. J. **51**:237-242, 1972.

Carkhuff, R.R.: The art of problem-solving: a guide for developing problem-solving skills for parents, teachers, counselors and administrators, Amherst, Mass., 1973, Human Resource Development Press.

Carkhuff, R.R., and Berenson, B.G.: Beyond counseling and therapy, New York, 1967, Holt, Rinehart & Winston, Inc.

Carkhuff, R.R., and Pierce, R.M., Trainer's guide: the art of helping, Amherst, Mass., 1975, Human Resource Development Press.

Carkhuff, R.R., Pierce, R.M., and Cannon, J.R.: The art of helping, III, Amherst, Mass., 1977, Human Resource Development Press.

Carlson, J., and Ardell, D.B.: Physical fitness as a pathway to wellness and effective counseling, Counseling Human Development **13**(7):1-12, 1981.

Carlson, K.: Self-help handbook: a step by step guide to neighborhood improvement projects, New York, 1978, Citizens Committee for New York City, Inc.

Carney, R.E.: Attitudes toward risk. In Carney, R.E., editor: Risk-taking behavior, Springfield, Ill., Charles C Thomas, Publisher.

Carney, R.E., and Carney, J.R.: Motivational factors in risk-taking. In Carney, R.E., editor: Risk-taking behavior, Springfield, Ill., 1971, Charles C Thomas, Publisher.

Cautela, J.R., and Groden, J.: Relaxation: a comprehensive manual for adults, children, and children with special needs, Champaign, Ill., 1978, Research Press.

Center Club: what is it? Boston, The Center House,, Inc.

Chadbourne, J.: Training groups: a basic life-cycle model, Personn. Guid. J. **59**:55-58, 1980.

Chaikin, A.L., and others: Neuroticism and disclosure reciprocity, J. Consulting Clinical Psychology **43**(1):13-19, 1975.

Chayefsky, P.: Altered states, New York, 1976, Harper & Row, Publishers, Inc.

Cheiken, M.: The counselor in the hospice: a new role, Personn. Guid. J. **58**:186-189, 1979.

Chelune, G.J., and others: Self-disclosure: origins, patterns and implications of openness in interpersonal relationships, San Francisco: 1979, Jossey-Bass, Inc., Publishers.

Cherniss, C.: Staff burnout: job stress in the human services, Beverly Hills, Calif., 1980, Sage Publications, Inc.

Christmas, J.J., Wallace, H., and Edwards, J.: New careers and new mental health services: fantasy or future. In Nash, K.B., Lifton, N., and Smith, S.E.: The paraprofessional: selected readings, New Haven, Conn., 1978, Advocate Press, Inc.

Claiborn, C.D., Ward, S.R., and Strong, S.R.: Effects of congruence between counselor interpretations and client beliefs, J. Counsel. Psychol. **28**(2):101-109, 1981.

Clearinghouse for Sexuality and Population Education Program Materials: Empahsis **1**(2):5, 1981.

Coddington, R.D.: Adolescent life-event scale, New Orleans, 1981, Department of Pediatric Psychiatry, Louisiana State University Medical Center.

Cohen, N.A.: The non-MSW: overlooked conflicts in under-valued personnel, J. Social Service Research **3**(4):411-427, 1980.

Cohen, R.E.: The collaborative coprofessional: developing a new mental health role, Hosp. Community Psychiatry, **24**(4):242-245, 1973.

Cohen, R.E., and Ahern, F., Jr.: Handbook for mental health care of disaster victims, Baltimore, 1980, The Johns Hopkins University Press.

Cohler, B.J., and Grunebaum, H.V.: Mothers, daughters and grandmothers, New York, 1980, John Wiley & Sons, Inc.

Cole, H.P., and Sarnoff, D.: Creativity and counseling, Personn. Guid. J. **59**:140-146, 1980.

Collins, R.T.: Managing stress on the job, Stress, **25**(1):48-54, 1974, Blue Cross Association.

Conger, D.J.: Social inventions. In Cornish, E., editor: The world of tomorrow, Washington, D.C., 1978, The World Future Society.

Connolly, S.G.: Changing expectancies: a counseling method based on locus of control, Personn. Guid. J. **59**:176-180, 1980.

Cooper, C.L., and Marshall, J., editors: White collar and professional stress, New York, 1980, John Wiley & Sons, Inc.

Cooper, C.L., and Payne, R., editors: Current concerns in occupational stress, New York, 1980a, John Wiley & Sons, Inc.

Cooper, C.L., and Payne, R., editors: Stress at work, New York, 1980b, John Wiley & Sons, Inc.

Corah, N.L.: Development of a dental anxiety scale. In Ayer, W.A., and Hirschman, R.D., editors: Psychology and dentistry, Springfield, Ill., 1972, Charles C Thomas, Publisher.

Corah, N.L., and Pantera, R.E.: Controlled study of psychologic stress in a dental procedure. In Ayer, W.A., and Hirschman, R.D., editors: Psychology and dentistry: selected readings, Springfield, Ill., 1972, Charles C Thomas, Publisher.

Corbitt, P.M.: Basic video equipment. In Berger, M.M., editor: Videotape techniques in psychiatric training and treatment, rev. ed., New York, 1978, Brunner/Mazel, Inc.

Cormier, W.H., and Cormier, L.S.: Interviewing strategies for helpers: a guide to assessment, treatment, and education, Monterey, Calif., 1979, Brooks/Cole Publishing Co.

Cornish, E.: Introduction: welcome to the future. In Cornish, E., editor: 1999 the world of tomorrow: selections from the future: a journal of forecasts, trends, ideas about the future, Washington, D.C., 1978, World Future Society.

Cory, C.T., editor: The sore winner response, Psychology Today **14**(5):18, 1980.

Coulton, C.J.: Developing an instrument to measure person-environment fit, J. Social Science Research **3**(2):159-174, 1979.

Cox, J.P., Evans, J.F., and Jamieson, J.L.: Aerobic power and tonic heart rate responses to psychosocial stressors, Personality Social Psychology Bull. **5**(2):160-163, 1979.

Cristiani, T.S., and Cristiani, M.F.: The application of counseling skills in the business and industrial setting, Personn. Counseling J. **58**(3):166-169, 1979.

Currents: The Philadelphia Hispanic Project, Currents **3**(2):13, 1979.

Cytrynbaum, S., and others: Midlife development: a personality and social systems perspective. In Poon, L.W., editor: Aging in the 1980's: psychological issues, Washington, D.C., 1980, American Psychological Association.

Dahms, A.M.: Emotional intimacy, Boulder, Colo., 1972, Pruett Publishing Co.

Daley, M.R.: 'Burnout': smoldering problem in protective services, Social Work **24**(5):375-379, 1979a.

Daley, M.R.: Preventing worker burnout in child welfare, **58**(7):443-450, 1979b.

Danish, S.J., and Smyer, M.A.: Unintended consequences of requiring a license to help, Am. Psychol. **36**(1):13-21, 1981.

Darley, J.M., and Fazio, R.H.: Expectancy confirmation processes arising in the social interaction sequence, Am. Psychol. **35**(10):867-881, 1980.

D'Augelli, A.R., and others: Helping skills: a basic training program-leader's manual, New York, 1980, Human Sciences Press, Inc.

Davenport, D.S.: A closer look at the "healthy" grieving process, Personn. Guid. J. **59**:332-334, 1981.

Davenport, J.A., and Davenport, J.: Boom towns and human services: a model for multidisciplinary learn approaches in impacted communities, Laramie, Wyo., 1979, Wyoming University Department of Social Work.

Davis, K.L.: Is confidentiality in group counseling realistic? Personn. Guid. J. **59**:197-201, 1980.

Day, R.W., and Sparacio, R.T.: Structuring the counseling process, Personn. Guid. **59**:246-249, 1980.

Demone, H.W.: Stimulating human service reform, New Brunswick, N.J., 1978, Rutgers State University Graduate School of Social Work.

Denmark, F.L.: Psyche: from rocking the cradle to rocking the boat, Am. Psychol. **35**(12):1057-1065, 1980.

Denton, H.H.: Black children's future still seen bleak, Washington, Post, pp. A1 and A10, Jan. 7, 1981.

Depue, R.A., editor: The psychobiology of depressive orders: implications for effects of stress, New York, 1979, Academic Press, Inc.

Derlega, V.J., Chaikin, A.L., and Herndon, J.: Are demand characteristics responsible for disclosure reciprocity? Norfolk, Va., 1973, Department of Psychology, Old Dominion University.

Derlega, V.J., and Chaikin, A.L.: Sharing intimacy: what we reveal to others and why, Englewood Cliffs, N.J., 1975, Prentice-Hall, Inc.

Deutsch, M.: The disadvantaged child and the learning process. In Reissman, F., Cohen, J., and Pearl, A., editors: Mental health of the poor: new treatment approaches for low income people, New York, 1964, The Free Press.

Diasio, K.: Occupational therapy in mental health: a time of challenge, Occupational Therapy in Mental Health **1**(1):1-10, 1980.

Dietz, J.: Place where mental patients can thrive, Boston Globe, pp. 53-57, Nov. 30, 1980.

Dilley, J.S.: Anti-shrinkthink, Personn. Guid. J. **50**:567-572, 1972.

Dinkmeyer, D., and McKay, G.D.: Systematic training for effective parenting (STEP), Circle Pines, Minn., 1979, American Guidance Service.

Dodenhoff, J.T.: Interpersonal attraction and direct-indirect supervisor influence as predictors of counselor trainee effectiveness, J. Counsel. Psychol. **28**(1):42-52, 1981.

Donahue, D.L.: Frustration: a feedback activity. In Thayer, L., editor: 50 strategies for experiential learning-book one, San Diego, Calif., 1976, University Associates, Inc.

Doyle Dane Bernbach, Inc.: Husbands say, "Don't rock my boat": they recognize the changing role of women, but are somewhat dubious about its desirability: Soundings from DDB, No. 6, Sept. 1980.

Drum, D., and Figler, H.: Outreach in counseling: applying the growth and prevention model in schools and colleges, New York, 1973, Intext.

Drum, D.J., and Knott, J.E.: Structured groups for facilitating development: acquiring life skills, resolving life themes, and making life transitions, New York, 1977, Human Sciences Press, Inc.

Dunham, C.S.: Social-sexual relationships. In Goldenson, R.M., editor: Disability and rehabilitation handbook, New York, 1978, McGraw-Hill, Inc.

Dunham, J.R., and Dunham, C.S.: Psychosocial aspects of disability. In Goldenson, R.M., editor: Disability and rehabilitation handbook, New York, 1978, McGraw-Hill, Inc.

Durand, H.F., and others: A developmental approach to outreach services for counseling centers, Personn. Guid. J. **59**:38-42, 1980.

D'Zurilla, T.J., and Goldfried, M.R.: Problem solving and behavior modification, J. Abnorm. Psychol. **78**:107-126, 1971.

EDC: Vocational counseling for displaced homemakers: a manual, Newton, Mass., 1980, Education Development Center.

Edelwich, J., and Brodsky, A.: Burn-out: stages of disillusionment in the helping professions, New York, 1980, Human Sciences Press, Inc.

Edwards, P.B.: Leisure counseling techniques: individual and group counseling step-by-step, rev. ed., Los Angeles, 1977, University Publishers.

Edwards, P.B., and Bloland, P.A.: Leisure counseling and consultation, Personn. Guid. J. **58**:435-440, 1980.

Egan, G.: The skilled helper: a model for systematic helping and interpersonal relating, Monterey, Calif., 1975, Brooks/Cole Publishing Co.

Eggert, G.M., and others: Community-based maintenance care for the long-term patient, Waltham, Mass., 1976, Brandeis University, Florence Keller School for Advanced Studies in Social Welfare.

Elliott, C.B., and others: Happiness is helping parents to help themselves: a guide for training parents to teach, Tallahassee, 1978, Florida Department of Health and Rehabilitative Services.

Ellis, A.: Rational-emotive psychotherapy, New York, 1966, Jeffrey Norton Publishers, Inc.

Ende, A.: Battering and neglect: children in Germany, 1860-1978, J. Psychohistory **7**(3):249-279, 1979/1980.

Ennis, B., and Siegel, L.: The rights of mental patients, New York, 1973, Avon Books.

Ennis, K.: Elephant man's gift: hope for NF sufferers, Washington Post, pp. 1, 5, Jan. 29, 1981.

Enting, A.D.: Mid-life counseling: prognosis and potential, Personn. Guid. J. **55**:112-114, 1976.

Epstein, R.E.: Maryland Department of State Planning, Baltimore Human Resources Planning: a guidebook, Baltimore, 1978, Maryland Department of Social Planning.

Epstein, Y.M.: Crowding stress and human behavior, J. Social Issues **37**(1):126-144, 1981.

Erikson, E.H.: Childhood and society, ed. 2, New York, 1963a, W.W. Norton & Co., Inc.

Erikson, E.H., editor: Youth: change and challenge, New York, 1963b, Basic Books, Inc., Publishers.

Erikson, E.H.: Identity: youth and crisis, New York, 1968, W.W. Norton & Co., Inc.

Ethical practice: preserving human dignity, Personn. Guid. J. **50**:special issue, 1971.

Evans, R.I., and others: Fear arousal, persuasion and actual versus implied behavior change. In Ayer, W.A., and Hirschman, R.D., editors: Psychology and dentistry: selected readings, Springfield, Ill., 1972, Charles C Thomas, Publisher.

Falck, H.S.: Consultant as insider and change agent: the problem of boundaries in social systems 1976, Administration in Mental Health **5**(1):55-67, 1977.

Fast, J., and Fast, B.: Talking between the lines: how we mean more than we say, New York, 1980, Pocket Books.

Feinstein, B., and Cavanaugh, C.: New volunteerism: a community connection, Cambridge, Mass., 1978, Schenkman Publishing Co., Inc.

Fessler, D.R.: Facilitating community change, La Jolla, Calif., 1980, University Associates, Inc.

Festinger, L.: A theory of cognitive dissonance, Stanford, Calif., 1957, Stanford University Press.

Fetsch, R.J., and Surdam, J.: New beginnings: group techniques for coping with losses due to divorce, Personn. Guid. J. **59**:395-397, 1981.

Fichte, J.G.: The vocation of man, New York, 1956, The Bobbs-Merrill Co., Inc. (Edited with an introduction by R. Chisholm; originally published in 1800.)

Figley, C.: The Iranian crisis: caring for families of catastrophe, American Association for Marriage and Family Therapy Newsletter **11**(5):3, 7, 10, 1980.

Finch, W.A.: Manpower utilization in human science settings, J. Social Science Research **2**(3):311-321, 1979.

Fine, R.: Interpretation: the patient's response. In Hammer, E.F., editor: Use of interpretation in treatment, New York, 1968, Grune & Stratton, Inc.

Finley, M.H., and Krey, R.D.: A model for implementing career education within the existing curriculum, paper presented at the American Personnel and Guidance Association Convention, New York, March 1975.

Finley, M.H., and Lee, T.A.: The terminated executive: it's like dying, Personn. Guid. J. **59**:382-383, 1981.

Fishman, S.H.: Losing a loved one to incarceration: the effect of imprisonment on family members, Personn. Guid. J. **59**:372-375, 1981.

Foersterling, F.: Sex differences in risk taking: effects of subjective and objective probability of success, Personality Social Psychology Bull. **8**(1):149-152, 1980.

Folkins, C.H., and Sime, W.E.: Physical fitness training and mental health, Am. Psychol. **36**(4):373-389, 1981.

Forman, K., and Schafer, W.: Stress, distress and growth: a student manual, Davis, Calif., 1978, International Dialogue Press.

Fountain House: Brochure, New York, Fountain House.

Frankl, V.F.: Man's search for meaning. Boston, 1963, Beacon Press.

Frears, L.H., and Schneider, J.M.: Exploring loss and grief within a holistic framework, Personn. Guid. J. **59**:341-346, 1981.

Fretz, B.: Postural movements in a counseling dyad, J. Counsel. Psychol. **13:**335-343, 1966.

Fretz, B.: Evaluating the effectiveness of career interventions, J. Counsel. Psychol. **28:**71-90, 1981.

Freud, S.A.: General introduction to psychoanalysis, New York, 1938, Garden City Publishing Co. (Translated by J. Riviere.)

Frey, D.H., and Raming, H.E.: A taxonomy of counseling goals and methods, Personn. Guid. J. **58:**26-33, 1979.

Friedman, H.S., DiMatteo, M.R., and Mertz, T.I.: Nonverbal communication on television news: the facial expressions of broadcasters during coverage of a presidential election campaign, Personality Social Psychology Bull. **6:**426-435, 1980.

Fries, J.F.: Aging, natural death, and the compression of morbidity, N. Engl. J. Med. **303:**130-135, 1980.

Fritz, D.: Advocacy agency and citizen participation: the case of the administration on aging and the elderly 1978, J. Health and Human Resources Administration **1**(1):79-108, 1978.

Fromm, E.: The art of loving, New York, 1956, Harper & Row, Publishers.

Fuller, R.L.: The satellite housing program, Belmont, Calif., 1977, Caminar, Inc.

Gale, E.N., and Ayer, W.A.: Treatment of dental phobias. In Ayer, W.A., and Hirschman, R.D., editors: Psychology and dentistry: selected readings, Springfield, Ill., 1972, Charles C Thomas, Publisher.

Galvin, M., and Ivey, A.E.: Researching one's own interviewing style: does your theory of choice match your actual practice? Personn. Guid. J. **59:**536-541, 1981.

Ganikos, M.L., editor: Counseling the aged: a training syllabus for educators, Washington, D.C., 1979, American Personnel and Guidance Association.

GAO, Report to Congress: Returning the mentally disabled to the community: government needs to do more, Washington, D.C., January 7, 1977, General Accounting Office.

GAO, Report to Congress: Jailed inmates' mental health care neglected: state and federal attention needed, GGD-81-5, November 17, 1980, Washington, D.C., General Accounting Office.

Gardner, J.: Sexist counseling must go, Personn. Guid. J. **49:**705-714, 1971.

Gardner, R.: Dorothy and the lizard of Oz, Cresskill, N.J., 1980, Creative Therapeutics.

Garrison, J., and Werfel, S.: Greater Lyon Community Mental Health Program: network approach to clinical social work, Clinical Work J. **15**(2):108-117, 1977.

Garte, S.H., and Rosenblum, M.L.: Lighting fires in burned-out counselors, Personn. Guid. J. **57:**158-160, 1978.

Gartner, A.: The preparation of human service professionals, New York, 1976, Human Sciences Press, Inc.

Gartner, A., and Riessman, F.: Self-help in the human services, San Francisco, 1977, Jossey-Bass, Inc., Publishers.

Garwick, G.B., and Brintnall, J.E.: Introduction to goal attainment scaling, Minneapolis, 1977, Technical Assistance for Program Evaluation.

Garwick, G.B., and Brintnall, J.E.: Catalogue-assisted and the idea book: 550 indicators for use in setting goals, Minneapolis, 1978, Technical Assistance for Program Evaluation.

Gaw, A.C.: An integrated approach in the delivery of health care to a Chinese community in America: the Boston experience. In Kleinman, A., and others, editors: Medicine in Chinese cultures, DHEW Pub. No. (NIH) 75-653, Washington, D.C., 1975, U.S. Government Printing Office.

Gaylin, W.: Caring, New York, 1976, Avon Books.

Gazda, G.M.: Group counseling: a developmental approach, ed. 2, Boston, 1978, Allyn & Bacon, Inc.

Gazda, G.M., and Brooks, D.K., Jr.: A comprehensive approach to developmental interventions, J. Specialists in Group Work **5**(3):120-126, 1980.

Gerontological Society: Working with older people: a guide to practice, Washington, D.C., 1978, The Gerontological Society.

Gerrard, B.A., Boniface, W.J., and Love, B.H.: Interpersonal skills for health professionals, Reston, Va., 1980, Reston Publishing Co., Inc.

Gillespie, D.F., and Marten, S.E.: Assessing service accessibility, Administration in Social Work **2**(2):183-197, 1978.

Glaser, B., and Kirschenbaum, H.: Using values clarification counseling settings, Personn. Guid. J. **58:**569-574, 1980.

Glasscote, R., and others: Fountain House. Reprint from Partial hospitalization for the mentally ill, Washington, D.C., 1969, The Joint Information Service of the American Psychiatric Association and the National Association for Mental Health.

Glasscote, R., and others: Rehabilitating the mentally ill in the community, Washington, D.C., 1971, American Psychiatric Association.

Glock, C.Y., and others: Adolescent prejudice, New York, 1975, Harper & Row, Publishers, Inc.

Goldband, S., Katkin, E.S., and Morell, M.A.: Personality and cardiovascular disorder: steps toward demystification. In Sarason, I.G., and Spielberger, C.D.: Stress and anxiety, vol. 6, Washington, D.C., 1979, Hemisphere Publishing Corp.

Goldfried, M.R., and Goldfried, A.P.: Cognitive change methods. In Kanfer, F.H., and Goldstein, A.P., editors: Helping people change: a textbook of methods, ed. 2, New York, 1975, Pergamon Press, Inc.

Goldschmitt, M., Tipton, R.M., and Wiggins, R.D.: Professional identity of counseling psychologists, J. Counsel. Psychol. **28**(2):158-171, 1981.

Goldstein, A.P., and Simonson, N.R.: Social psychological approaches to psychotherapy research. In Bergin, A., and Garfield, S., editors: Handbook of psychotherapy and behavior change, New York, 1971, John Wiley & Sons, Inc.

Golembiewski, R., and Blumberg, A., editors: Sensitivity training and the laboratory approach, ed. 3, Itasca, Ill., 1977, F.E. Peacock Publishers, Inc.

Goodman, H.H.: Adult education and counseling: an emerging synthesis, Personn. Guid. J. **59**:465-469, 1981.

Goodyear, R.K.: Counselors as community psychologists, Personn. Guid. J. **54**:513-516, 1976.

Goodyear, R.K.: Termination as a loss experience for the counselor, Personn. Guid. J. **59**:347-349, 1981.

Gostin, L.: The institution in England and Wales: its advent and its demise, Amicus **5**(1):24-33, 1980.

Greenberg, S.F., and Valletutti, P.J.: Stress and the helping professions, Baltimore, 1980, Paul H. Brookes Publishers.

Greenspoon, J.: The reinforcing effects of two spoken sounds on the frequency of two responses, Am. J. Psychol. **68**:409-416, 1955.

Gross, S.J.: The holistic health movement, Personn. Guid. J. **59**:96-100, 1980.

Grosser, C., Henry, W.E., and Kelley, J.G., editors: Nonprofessionals in the human services, San Francisco, 1969, Jossey-Bass, Inc., Publishers.

Gubrium, J.F., editor: Time: roles and self in old age, New York, 1976, Human Sciences Press.

Guerney, B.G., Jr.: Psychotherapeutic agents: new roles for nonprofessionals, parents and teachers, New York, 1969, Holt, Rinehart & Winston, Inc.

Guerney, B.G., Jr.: Relationship enhancement, San Francisco, 1977, Jossey-Bass, Inc., Publishers.

Guerney, B.G., Jr.: Foreward. In Ivey, A.E., and Authier, J.: Microcounseling: innovations in interviewing, counseling, psychotherapy and psychoeducation, ed. 2, Springfield, Ill., 1978, Charles C Thomas, Publisher.

Guerney, B.G., Jr., and Flumen, A.: Teachers as psychotherapeutic agents for withdrawn children, J. School Psychol. **8**:107-113, 1970.

Guerney, B.G., Jr., Guerney, L., and Stollak, G.: The practicing psychologist as an educator: an alternative to the medical practitioner model, Professional Psychology **2**:276-282, 1971.

Guerney, B.G., Jr., and Stover, L.: The efficacy of training procedures for mothers in filial therapy, Psychotherapy: Theory Research and Practice **4**:110-115, 1967.

Guest, J.: Ordinary people, New York, 1976, The Viking Press.

Haas, J.E., and Drabek, T.E.: Community disaster and system stress: a sociological perspective. In McGrath, J.G., editor: Social and psychological factors in stress, New York, 1970, Holt, Rinehart & Winston.

Haas, L.: Role-sharing couples: a study of egalitarian marriages, Family Relations **29**(3):289-296, 1980.

Haase, R.F., and DiMattia, D.J.: Proxemic behavior: counselor, administrator and client preference for seating arrangement in dyadic interaction, J. Counsel. Psychol. **17**:319-325, 1970.

Haase, R.F., and Tepper, D.T., Jr.: Nonverbal components of empathic communication, J. Counsel. Psychol. **19**:417-424, 1972.

Haber, R.A.: What they didn't tell me about counseling in graduate school, Personn. Guid. J. **58**:204-205, 1979.

Hackney, H., and Cormier, L.S.: Counseling strategies and objectives, ed. 2, Englewood Cliffs, N.J., 1979, Prentice-Hall, Inc.

Hahn, N.F.: Too dumb to know better: cacogenic family studies and the criminology of women, Criminology **18**(1):3-25, 1980.

Haley, A.: Roots, New York, 1976, Doubleday & Co., Inc.

Hall, E.T.: The silent language, Garden City, N.Y., 1959, Doubleday & Co., Inc. (Paperback edition by Fawcett.)

Hall, E.T.: The hidden dimension, Garden City, N.Y., 1966, Doubleday & Co., Inc. (Paperback edition by Anchor Press.)

Halpern, S., Hicks, D., and Crenshaw, T.: Rape: helping the victim, Oradell, N.J., 1978, Medical Economics Co., Book Division.

Hamilton, V., and Warburton, D.M.: Human stress and cognition, New York, 1979, John Wiley & Sons, Inc.

Hanton, S.: Rural helping systems and family typology, Child Welfare **59**(7):419-426, 1980.

Harper, R.G., Wiens, A.N., and Matarazzo, J.D.: Nonverbal communication: the state of the art, New york, 1978, John Wiley & Sons, Inc.

Harris, G.G., editor: The group treatment of human problems: a social learning approach, New York, 1977, Grune & Stratton, Inc.

Harris, T.: I'm OK—you're OK, New York, 1970, Harper & Row, Publishers, Inc.

Hartley, M.P.: Coping with life after death: the counselor's response ability, Personn. Guid. J. **59**:251-252, 1980.

Havens, L.: Participant observation, New York, 1976, Jason Aronson, Inc.

Havens, L.: Explorations in the uses of language in psychotherapy complex empathetic statements, Psychiatry **42**(1):40-48, 1979.

Havighurst, R.J.: Developmental tasks and education, ed. 3, New York, 1972, David McKay Co., Inc.

Havighurst, R.J.: Social and developmental psychology: trends influencing the future of counseling, Personn. Guid. J. **58**:328-333, 1980.

Hayes, D.: The coming energy transition. In Cornish, E., editor: The world of tomorrow, Washington, D.C., 1978, World Future Society.

Hayes, R.L.: High school graduation: the case for identity loss, Personn. Guid. J. **59**:369-371, 1981.

Hearn, M.P.: The annotated Wizard of Oz (from Baum, L.F., The wonderful wizard of Oz, 1900), New York, 1973, Clarkson N. Potter, Inc., Publishers.

Heath, D.H.: Maturity and competence: a transcultural view, New York, 1977, Gardner Press, Inc.

Heath, D.R.: Wanted: a comprehensive model of healthy development, Personn. Guid. J. **58**:391-399, 1980.

Heine, R.W.: The Negro patient in psychotherapy, J. Clin. Psychol. **6**:373-376, 1950.

Hendricks, S.S.: Spinal cord injury: a special kind of loss, Personn. Guid. J. **59:**355-358, 1981.

Heppner, P.P., and Dixon, D.D.: A review of the interpersonal influence process in counseling, Personn. Guid. J. **54:**542-550, 1981.

Hernandez, C.A., Haug, M.J., and Wagner, N.W.: Chicanos: social and psychological perspectives, ed. 2, St. Louis, 1976, The C.V. Mosby Co.

Herr, J.J., and Weakland, J.H.: Counseling elders and their families, New York, 1979, Springer Publishing Co., Inc.

Hersey, P., and Blanchard, K.: Management of organizational behavior: utilizing human resources, ed. 2, Englewood Cliffs, N.J., 1972, Prentice-Hall, Inc.

Hess, B.B.: America's aged revisited: who, what and when and where? In Hess, B.B., editor: Growing old in America, ed. 2, New Brunswick, N.J., 1980, Transaction Books.

Hesse, K.A.F.: The paraprofessional as a referral link in the mental health delivery system. In Nash, K.B., Lifton, N., and Smith, S.E., editors: The paraprofessional: selected readings, New Haven, Conn., 1978, Advocate Press, Inc.

Heus, R., and McCommons, W.R.: The theatre unlimited, Disabled USA **3**(3):7-10, 1980.

Hicks, R., Okonek, A., and Davis, J.M.: The psychopharmacological approach. In Kutash, I.L., and others: Handbook on stress and anxiety, San Francisco, 1980, Jossey-Bass, Inc., Publishers.

Hilts, P.J.: Mental care revolution: clearing 'warehouses,' Washington Post, pp. A1-A3, October 27, 1980.

Hobbs, N.: Mental health's third revolution, Am. J. Orthopsychiatry **34:**822-833, 1964.

Hodges, E.J.: The three princes of serendip, New York, 1964, Atheneum Publishers.

Hoffman, A.M.: Paraprofessional effectiveness, Personn. Guid. J. **54:**494-497, 1976.

Hoffman, M.L.: Empathy, role taking, guilt and development of altruistic motives. In Lickona, T., editor: Moral development and behavior, New York, 1976, Holt, Rinehart & Winston.

Hogan, R., and Dickstein, G.: A measure of moral values, J. Counsel. Clin. Psychol. **39:**210-214, 1972.

Holmes, M.B., and Holmes, D.: Handbook of human services for older persons, New York, 1979, Human Sciences Press, Inc.

Holmes, T.H., and Holmes, T.S.: How change can make us ill. In Miller, E., editor: Stress, Chicago, 1974, Blue Cross Association.

Holmquist, D.: Opinionnaire regarding the handicapped. In Mortenson, R.A., editor: Prejudice toward hiring the handicapped, New York, 1980, Anti-Defamation League of B'nai B'rith.

Holmquist, D.: Prejudice toward hiring the handicapped. In Mortenson, R.A.: Prejudice Project, New York, 1980, Anti-Defamation League of B'Nai B'rith.

Honzik, M.P., and MacFarlane, J.W.: Personality development and intellectual functioning from 21 months to 40 years. In Jarvik, L.F., Eisdorfer, C., and Blum, J.E.: Intellectual functioning in adults, New York, 1973, Springer Publishing Co., Inc.

Hopkins, J., and Sugarman, D.: No one here gets out alive, New York, 1980, Warner Books, Inc.

Horney, K.: Neurosis and human growth, New York, 1954, W.W. Norton & Co., Inc.

Horowitz, M.J.: Psychoanalytic therapy. In Kutash, I.L., and others: Handbook on stress and anxiety, San Francisco, 1980, Jossey-Bass, Inc., Publishers.

Hosford, R.E.: The Cubberley Conference and the evolution of observational learning, Personn. Guid. J. **58:**467-472, 1980.

Howard, J.A.: Person-situation interaction models, Personality Social Psychology Bull. **5**(2):191-195, 1979.

Howell, L.: Epilepsy. In Goldenson, R.M., editor: Disability and rehabilitation handbook, New York, 1978, McGraw-Hill, Inc.

ICD Rehabilitation and Research Center: Human Service Assistant Project, New York, ICD Rehabilitation and Research.

ILO: Women bosses: Why so few? ILO Information **8**(5):1-2, 1980.

Innovations: Enhancing supports: family, friends and facts, Innovations **7**(2):18-19, 1980a.

Innovations: Extending social bonds: friends in need and deed, Innovations **7**(2):22-24, 1980b.

Innovations: Rural roundup: special problems, Innovations **7**(3):20-23, 1980c.

Insel, S.A.: On counseling the bereaved, Personn. Guid. J. **55:**127-129, 1976.

Ivey, A.E., and Authier, J.: Microcounseling: innovations in interviewing, counseling, psychotherapy and psychoeducation, ed. 2, Springfield, Ill., 1978, Charles C Thomas, Publisher.

Ivey, A.E., and Simek-Downing, L.: Counseling and psychotherapy: skills, theories and practice, Englewood Cliffs, N.J., 1980, Prentice-Hall, Inc.

Jackson, K.W.: Community needs and resources assessment guidebook, In J. Hum. Serv. **5**(1):66, 1980. (Abstract.)

Jaeger, M.E., Anthony, S., and Roskow, R.L.: Who hears what from whom and with what effect: a study of rumor, Personality Social Psychology Bull., **6**(3):473-478, 1980.

Jahoda, M.: Current concepts of positive mental health, New York, 1958, Basic Books, Inc., Publishers.

Jarvik, L.F.: Discussion: patterns of intellectual functioning in later years. In Jarvik, L.F., and others: Intellectual functioning in 65-67 year old adults, New York, 1973, Springer Publishing Co., Inc.

Jarvik, L.F., editor: Aging into the 21st century: middle-agers today, New York, 1978, Gardner Press, Inc.

Johnson, B.: Hello Carol, Washington Post, October 7, 1980, p. B13.

Johnson, C., and Kravitz, M.: Halfway houses, Rockville, Md., 1978, National Criminal Justice Reference Service.

Johnson, D.W.: Effects of the order of expressing warmth and anger on the actor and the listener, J. Counsel. Psychol. **18**:571-578, 1971a.

Johnson, D.W.: The effects of warmth of interaction, accuracy of understanding, and the proposal of compromises on the listener's behavior, J. Counsel. Psychol. **18**:207-216, 1971b.

Johnson, D.W.: Reaching out: interpersonal effectiveness and self-actualization, ed. 2, Englewood Cliffs, N.J., 1981, Prentice-Hall, Inc.

Johnson, D.W., and Noonan, P.M.: Effects of acceptance and reciprocation of self-disclosures on the development of trust, J. Counsel. Psychol. **19**:411-416, 1972.

Johnson, H.W., editor: Rural human services: a book of readings, Itasca, Ill., 1980, F.E. Peacock Publishers, Inc.

Johnson, J.H., and Sarason, I.G.: Moderator variables in life stress research. In Sarason, I.G., and Spielberger, C.D., Stress and anxiety, vol. 6, Washington, D.C., 1979, Hemisphere Publishing Corp.

Johnson, J.M., editor: Instructional strategies for curriculum units for secondary behavioral sciences, Plattsburg, N.Y., State University of New York, College of Arts and Sciences, 1973.

Johnson, R.P., and Riker, H.C.: Retirement maturity: a valuable concept for preretirement counselors, Personn. Guid. J. **59**:291-295, 1981.

Johnson, T.H., editor: The complete poems of Emily Dickinson, Boston, Little, Brown & Co.

Johnson, W.: People in quandaries: the semantics of personal adjustment, New York, 1946, Harper & Row, Publishers.

Joint Commission on Mental Health: Challenge for the 1970's, New York, 1970, Harper & Row, Publishers, Inc.

Joint Commission on Mental Illness and Health, Action for Mental Health: Final report of the Commission, New York, 1961, Basic Books, Inc., Publishers.

Jones, G.B., Dayton, C., and Gelatt, H.B.: New methods for delivering human services, New York, 1977, Human Sciences Press, Inc.

Jones, J.E., and Mohr, L.: The Jones-Mohr listening test: a tape-assisted learning program, San Diego, 1976, University Associates, Inc.

Jones, L.Y.: Great expectations: America and the baby boom generation, New York, 1980, Coward, McCann & Geoghegan, Inc.

Jones, M.K.: Pre-retirement counseling program, unpublished manuscript.

Jones, W.H.: Loss in a hospital setting: implications for counseling, Personn. Guid. J. **59**:359-362, 1981.

Jordan, R.: Thanksgiving, New York, 1971, E.P. Dutton & Co.

Joseph, S.M.: The me nobody knows, New York, 1969, Avon Books.

Jourard, S.M.: The transparent self, ed. 2, New York, 1971, D. Van Nostrand Co.

Jourard, S.M., and Jaffe, P.E.: Influence of an interviewer's disclosure on the self-disclosing behavior of interviewees, J. Counsel. Psychol. **17**:252-259, 1970.

Journal of Social Issues: Privacy as a behavioral phenomenon, J. Social Issues **33**(3), 1977.

Kadushin, A.: The social work interview, New York, 1972, Columbia University Press.

Kahle, L.R.: Methods for studying person-situation interaction, San Francisco, 1979, Jossey-Bass, Inc., Publishers.

Kahn, A.J., and Kamerman, S.B.: Course of personal social service, Public Welfare **36**(3):29-32, 1978.

Kahn, R.L., and Cannell, C.F.: The dynamics of interviewing, New York, 1957, John Wiley & Sons, Inc.

Kahn, R.L., and French, J.R.P.: Status and conflict: two themes in the study of stress. In McGrath, J.E., editor: Social and psychological factors in stress, New York, 1970, Holt, Rinehart & Winston.

Kanfer, F.H., and Goldstein, A.P., editors: Helping people change: a textbook of methods, ed. 2, New York, 1980, Pergamon Press, Inc.

Kaplan, H.B.: Sociological theories. In Kutash, I.L., and others: Handbook on stress and anxiety, San Francisco, 1980, Jossey-Bass, Inc., Publishers.

Kasman, J.: Manifest and latent functions of psychological services, Am. Psychol. **37**(1):290-299, 1981.

Katz, R.L.: Empathy: its nature and uses, New York, 1963, The Free Press.

Kaufman, R.: Identifying and solving problems: a system approach, La Jolla, Calif., 1976, University Associates, Inc.

Kaul, T.J., and Schmidt, L.D.: Dimensions of interviewer trustworthiness, J. Counsel. Psychol. **18**:542-548, 1971.

Kavanaugh, R.E.: Facing death, Baltimore, 1974, Penguin Books.

Keating, J.P.: Environmental stressors: misplaced emphasis. In Sarason, I.G., and Spielberger, C.D., editors: Stress and anxiety, vol. 6, Washington, D.C., 1979, Hemisphere Publishing Corp.

Kegan, R.: Making meaning: the constructive developmental approach to persons and practice, Personn. Guid. J. **58**:373-380, 1980.

Kelley, A.E., and Claude, J.P.: Group therapy for abusive parents and their children, J. Specialists in Group Work **6**(1):8-12, 1981.

Kelley, E.W., Franklin, V.S., and Jackson, G.C.: Counseling in public housing, Personn. Guid. J. **54**:520-522, 1976.

Kelley, P., and Kelly, V.: Training natural helpers in rural communities. In Johnson, H.W.: Rural human services: a book of readings, Itasca, Ill., 1980, F.E. Peacock Publishers, Inc.

Kelly, G.F.: Loss of loving: a cognitive therapy approach, Personn. Guid. J. **59**:401-404, 1981.

Kessler, S.: Counselors as mediators, Personn. Guid. J. **58**:194-196, 1979.

Kiesler, C.A.: Mental health policy as a field of inquiry for psychology, Am. Psychol. **35**(12):1066-1080, 1980.

Kimmel, D.G.: Adult development: Challenges for counseling, Personn. Guid. J. **55**:103-105, 1976.

Kiresuk, T., Salasin, S., and Garwick, G.: The program evaluation project: overview, Minneapolis, 1972, Program Evaluation Project.

Klausner, S.Z., editor: Why man takes chances: studies in stress-seeking, Garden City, N.Y., 1968, Anchor Books.

Kleinman, A., and others, editors: Medicine in Chinese culture, DHEW Pub. (NIH) No. 75-653, Washington, D.C., 1975, U.S. Government Printing Office.

Kluchohn, F.R., and Strodtbeck, F.L., Variations in value orientations, Evanston, Ill., 1961, Row, Peterson & Co.

Knapp, M.L.: Nonverbal communication in human interaction, New York, 1972, Holt, Rinehart & Winston.

Knight, P.H., and Bair, C.K.: Degree of client comfort as a function of dyadic interaction distance, J. Couns. Psychol. **23**:13-16, 1976.

Koile, E.A.: Listening as a way of becoming, Waco, Tex., 1977, World Books.

Kolb, D.A.: Learning style inventory (technical manual), Boston, 1976, McBer Co.

Krasner, L., and Uhlmann, L.P., editors: Research in behavior modification, New York, 1973, Holt, Rinehart & Winston.

Kravas, C.F., and Kravas, K.J.: Negative feedback: a training experience. In Thayer, L., editor: 50 strategies for experiential learning-book one, San Diego, Calif., 1976, University Associates, Inc.

Kravetz, S.P.: Rehabilitation need and status, structure and process, unpublished doctoral dissertation, Madison, Wisc., 1973, University of Wisconsin—Madison.

Kremer, E.B., Zimpeer, D.G., and Wiggers, T.T.: Homosexuality, counseling and the adolescent male, Personn. Guid. J. **54**:94-99, 1975.

Krucoff, C.: Fitness: obsessed, Washington Post, C-5, Oct. 17, 1980.

Krucoff, C.: Careers: women at work, Washington Post, Jan. 22, 1981a, p. D-5.

Krucoff, C.: Coping: lowdown on energy, Washington Post, Jan. 6, 1981b, p. B-5.

Krucoff, C.: Private lives: super language, Washington Post, p. B-5, Jan. 5, 1981c.

Krucoff, C.: 'Tough love': the bottom line, Washington Post, p. D-5, Feb. 24, 1981d.

Krumboltz, J.D.: A second look at the revolution in counseling, Personn. Guid. J. **58**:463-466, 1980.

Krumboltz, J.D., and Thoresen, C.E.: Behavioral counseling, New York, 1969, Holt, Rinehart & Winston.

Kubler-Ross, E.: Death: the final stage of growth, Englewood Cliffs, N.J., 1975, Prentice-Hall, Inc.

Kuhn, A.: The logic of social systems, San Francisco, 1976, Jossey-Bass, Inc., Publishers.

Kuriloff, P.J.: The counselor as psychoecologist, Personn. Guid. J. **51**:321-327, 1973.

Kurpius, D.: Consultation theory and process: an integrated model, Personn. Guid. J. **56**:335-338, 1978.

Kutash, I.L.: Prevention and equilibrium: disequilibrium theory. In Kutash, I.L., and others: Handbook on stress and anxiety, San Francisco, 1980, Jossey-Bass, Inc., Publishers.

Kutash, I.L., and others: Handbook on stress and anxiety, San Francisco, 1980, Jossey-Bass, Inc., Publishers.

L'Abate, L.: Toward a systematic classification of counseling and therapy theorists, Personn. Guid. J. **59**:263-265, 1981.

Lacroursiere, R.B.: The life cycle of groups: group development stage theory, New York, 1980, Human Sciences Press, Inc.

Laing, R.D.: The divided self, London, 1960, Tavistock Publications, Ltd.

Laing, R.D.: The politics of experience, New York, 1967, Pantheon Books, Inc.

Lamb, H.R.: Therapist-case managers: more than brokers of services, Hospital Community Psychiatry, **31**(11):762-764, 1980.

Lamb, H.R.: What do we really expect from deinstitutionalization, Hosp. Community Psychiatry **32**(2):105-109, 1981.

Lamb, H.R., and others: Rehabilitation in community mental health, San Francisco, 1971, Jossey-Bass, Inc., Publishers.

Landreth, G.L., and Berg, R.C.: Overcoming initial group-leader anxiety: skills plus experience, Personn. Guid. J. **58**:65-67, 1979.

Latane, B.: The psychology of social impact, Am. Psychol. **36**(4):343-356, 1981.

Lattanzi, M.E.: Coping with work-related losses, Personn. Guid. J. **59**:351-354, 1981.

Lattin, D.: The elephant man, Disabled USA **3**(3):2-5, 1980.

Lawton, M.P., and Nahemow, L.: Ecology and the aging process. In Eisdorfer, C., and Lawton, M.P., editors: The psychology of adult development and aging, Washington, D.C., 1973, American Psychological Association.

Lax, E.: Techniques in job development and placement for ex-addicts: a success story, DHHS Pub. No. (ADM) 81-1041, Washington, D.C., 1981, National Institute on Drug Abuse, U.S. Department of Health and Human Services.

Lazarus, A.A.: Behavior therapy and beyond, New York, 1971, McGraw-Hill, Inc.

Lee, R., and Olejnik, S.: Professional outreach counseling can help the juvenile probationer: a two-year follow-up study, Personn. Guid. J. **59**:4-15, 1981.

Leininger, M.: Two strange health tribes, the gnisrun and enicidem in the United States, Human Organization **35**:253-261, 1976.

Lesnoff, C.G., editor: Health care of the elderly: strategies for prevention and intervention, New York, 1980, Human Sciences Press, Inc.

Lesse, S.: The preventive psychiatry of the future. In Cornish, E., editor: 1999 The World of Tomorrow, Washington, D.C., 1978, World Future Society.

Lesser, W.M.: The relationship between counseling progress and empathic understanding, J. Counsel. Psychol. **8**:330-336, 1961.

Leung, P.: Clinical counselors, Personn. Guid. J. **54**:113-114, 1975.

Leung, P., and Eargle, D.: Counseling with the elderly living in public housing, Personn. Guid. J. **58**:442-445, 1980.

Levenson, R.M.: Physical activity and heart disease. In Proceedings of the Conference on Stress, Strain, Heart Disease and the Law, Washington, D.C., 1979, U.S. Government Printing Office.

Levine, S., and Ursin, H., editors: Coping and health, New York, 1980, Plenum Publishing Corp.

Levinson, D.J., and others: Seasons of a man's life, New York, 1978, Alfred A. Knopf, Inc.

Levinson, H., and others: Men, management and mental health, Cambridge, Mass., 1962, Harvard University Press.

Lewis, M.: Developmental theories. In Kutash, I.L., and others: Handbook on stress and anxiety, San Francisco, 1980, Jossey-Bass, Inc., Publishers.

Lewis, R.A., and Gilhousen, M.R.: Myths of career development: a cognitive approach to vocational counseling, Personn. Guid. J. **59**:296-299, 1981.

Liberthson, R.R.: Physical activity and sudden death. In Proceedings of the Conference on Stress, Strain, Heart Disease and the Law, Washington, D.C., 1979, U.S. Government Printing Office.

Lieberman, M.A., and others: Self-help groups for coping with crisis: origins, members, processes, impact, San Francisco, 1979, Jossey-Bass, Inc., Publishers.

Lifton, R.J.: The broken connection: on death and the continuity of life, New York, 1979, Simon and Schuster, Inc.

Lippman, L.: Attitudes toward the handicapped: a comparison between Europe and the United States, Springfield, Ill., 1972, Charles C Thomas, Publisher.

Lombana, J.H.: Counseling the elderly: remediation plus prevention, Personn. Guid. J. **55**:143-144, 1976.

London, M., and Brag, D.W.: Ethical issues in testing and evaluation for personnel decisions, Am. Psychol. **35**(10):890-901, 1980.

Long, A.: Implementation of a personalized clothing policy for long-stay psychiatric patients: a study of communication, J. Adv. Nurs. **4**(4):415-427, 1979.

Lopata, H.Z.: Excerpts from widowhood in an American city. In Hess, B.B., editor: Growing old in America, ed. 2, New Brunswick, N.J., 1980, Transaction Books.

Love, K.D., and Aiello, J.R.: Using projective techniques to measure interaction distances: a methodological note, Personality Social Psychology Bull. **6**(1):102-103, 1980.

Lowry, R.P.: Toward a sociology of secrecy and security systems. In Tefft, S.K.: Secrecy, New York, 1980, Human Sciences Press, Inc.

Luce, G.G., and Peper, E.: Learning how to relax. In Miller, E., editor: Stress, Chicago, 1974, Blue Cross Association.

Ludins-Katz, F., and Katz, E.: The creative growth experience, Disabled U.S.A. **1**(7):6-8, 1978.

Luft, J.: Of human interaction, Palo Alto, Calif., 1969, National Press Books.

MacKinnon, R.A., and Michels, R.: The psychiatric interview in clinical practice, Philadelphia, 1971, W.B. Saunders Co.

MacNeill, D.H.: The relationship of occupational stress to burn-out, paper presented at the eighty-eighth annual convention of the American Psychological Association, September, 1980, Montreal.

Madway, M.: Anorexia nervosa, Montgomery County, Md., Sentinel, pp. 1, 5, October 23, 1980.

Mahoney, M.J., and Mahoney, K.: Permanent weight control: a total solution to the dieter's dilemma, New York, 1976, W.W. Norton, Inc.

Manion, V.Y.: Preretirement counseling: the need for a new approach, Personn. Guid. J. **55**:119-121, 1976.

Mann, J.: Society catches up with the Tillyers, Washington Post, pp. B1, B3, Dec. 24, 1980.

Mann, J.: Women's health care needs a closer look, Washington Post, pp. B1, B6, Jan. 9, 1981.

Maple, F.F.: Shared decision-making, Beverly Hills, Calif., 1980, Sage Publications, Inc.

Marcus, S.: Their brother's keepers: an episode from English history. In Gaylin, W., and others, editors: Doing good: the limits of benevolence, New York, 1978, Pantheon Books, Inc.

Mark, E.W., and Alpen, T.G.: Sex role differences in intimacy motivation, Psychol. Woman **5**(2):164-169, 1980.

Markeny, K.: Counselors as environmental engineers, Personn. Guid. J. **49**:439-444, 1971.

Marlatt, G.A., and Perry, M.A.: Modeling methods. In Kanfer, F.H., and Goldstein, A.P., editors: Helping people change: a textbook of methods, New York, 1975, Pergamon Press, Inc.

Martin, G.L., and Osborne, J.G., editors: Helping in the community: behavioral applications, New York, 1980, Plenum Publishing Corp.

Martin, T.L., Jr.: Malice in blunderland, New York, 1980, McGraw-Hill Book Co.

Maryland Institute for Emergency Medical Service Systems, Second National Symposium: Psychosocial factors in emergency medicine, Baltimore, May, 1981, Maryland Institute for Emergency Medical Services Systems.

Maslach, C.: Helping the troubled: the costs of involvement, Washington Post, pp. C-1, C-5, Sept. 19, 1976.

Maslow, A.H.: Toward a psychology of being, ed. 2, Princeton, N.J., 1968, Van Nostrand Reinhold Co.

Maslow, A.H.: Motivation and personality, ed. 2, New York, 1970, Harper & Row, Publishers.

Maslow, A.H.: The farther reaches of human nature, New York, 1971, The Viking Press, Inc.

Masson, R.L., and Jacobs, E.: Group leadership: practical points for beginners, Personn. Guid. J. **59**(1):52-58, 1980.

Matarazzo, J.D.: Changing concepts: care and caregivers, three points of view, Ment. Hyg. **52**:163-164, 1968.

Matarazzo, J.D., Saslow, G., and Matarazzo, R.: The interaction chronograph as an instrument for objective measurement of interaction patterns during interviews, J. Psychol. **41**:347-367, 1965.

Mathias, B.: Children: patients without fear, Washington Post, p. B5, April 14, 1981.

Maxmen, J.: The post-physician era: medicine in the 21st century, New York, 1976, Wiley-Interscience.

Mayeroff, M.: On caring, New York, 1971, Harper & Row, Publishers, Inc.

McBeath, M.: Consulting with teachers in two areas: grief and mourning: relaxation techniques, Personn. Guid. J. **58**:473-476, 1980.

McDaniel, R.R., and Morris, S. A.: Effective use of personnel in human service systems, Austin, Tex., 1978, Texas University.

McDonald, P.J.: Reactions to objective self-awareness, J. Research Personality, **14**:250-260, 1980.

McDonald, P.J., and Eilenfield, V.C.: Physical attractiveness and the approach/avoidance of self-awareness, Personality Social Psychology Bull. **6**(3):391-395, 1980.

McFarland, D.D.: The aged in the 21st century: a demographer's view. In Jarvik, L.F., editor: Aging into the 21st century: middle-agers today, New York, 1978, Gardner Press, Inc.

McGrath, J.E., editor: Social and psychological factors in stress, New York, 1970, Holt, Rinehart & Winston.

McGrath, J.E.: Social science, social action and the Journal of Social Issues, J. Social Issues **36**(4):109-124, 1980.

McKeachie, W.J.: Psychology in America's bicentennial year, Am. Psychol. **31**:819-833, 1976.

McKeachie, W.J.: National symposium on the applications of psychology to the teaching and learning of music, Am. Psychol. **36**(4):408-410, 1981.

McLuhan, M., and Fiore, Q.: The medium is the message, New York, 1967, Bantam Books, Inc.

McNett, I.: Privacy bill dies, but issues still alive, APA Monitor, **12**(1):1, 12, 14, 1981.

McPheeters, H.L.: Improving productivity in mental health agencies, Atlanta, 1979, Southern Regional Education Board.

McPheeters, H.L., and Baker, E.J.: Community college programs in mental health technology, Atlanta, 1969, Southern Regional Education Board.

McPheeters, H.L., and King, J.B.: Plans for teaching mental health workers, Atlanta, 1971, Southern Regional Education Board.

Mehrabian, A.: Communication without words, Psychol. Today **2**(4):53-55, 1968.

Mehrabian, A.: Significance of posture and position in the communication of attitude and status relationships, Psychol. Bull. **71**:359-372, 1969.

Mehrabian, A.: Silent messages, Belmont, Calif., 1971, Wadsworth Publishing Corp.

Mehrabian, A., and Epstein, N.: A measure of emotional empathy, J. Personality **40**:525-543, 1972.

Meichenbaum, D.: Cognitive behavior modification, Morristown, N.J., 1974, General Learning Press.

Meichenbaum, D., and Turk, D.: The cognitive-behavioral management of anxiety, anger and pain. In Davidson, P., editor: Behavioral management of anxiety, depression and pain, New York, 1976, Brunner/Mazel, Inc.

Melnick, J., and Stocker, R.: An experimental analysis of the behavioral rehearsal with feedback techniques in assertiveness training, Behav. Ther. **8**:222-228, 1977.

Mermelstein, J., and Sundet, P.: Women acceptance and credibility in the rural environment. In Johnson, H.W., editor: Rural human services: a book of readings, Itasco, Ill., 1980, F.E. Peacock Publishers, Inc.

Merton, R.K.: The self-fulfilling prophecy, Antioch Review **8**:193-210, 1948.

Merton, R.K.: Social theory and social structure, New York, 1957, Free Press of Glencoe.

Mickelson, D.J., and Stevic, R.R.: Differential effects of facilitative and nonfacilitative behavioral counselors, J. Counsel. Psychol. **18**:314-319, 1971.

Middleman, R.R.: The non-verbal method in working with groups, New York, 1968, Association Press.

Miller, E., editor: Stress, Chicago, 1974, Blue Cross Association.

Miller, G.A., editor: Communication, language and meaning, New York, 1973, Basic Books, Inc., Publishers.

Miller, R.I.: Helping the volunteer get started: the role of the volunteer center, Washington, D.C., 1972, National Center for Voluntary Action.

Miller, S.M., and Mishler, E.G.: Social class, mental illness, and American psychiatry: an expository review. In Reissman, F., Cohen, J., and Pearl, A., editors: Mental health of the poor: new treatment approaches for low income people, New York, 1964, The Free Press.

Miller, W.H.: Systematic parent training, Champaign, Ill., 1975, Research Press.

Milne, A.A.: When we were very young, New York, 1924, E.P. Dutton & Co., Inc.

Minter, R.E., and Kimball, C.P.: Life events, personality traits, and illness. In Kutash, I.L., and others: Handbook on stress and anxiety, San Francisco, 1980, Jossey-Bass, Inc., Publishers.

Minuchin, S., and others: Psychosomatic families: anorexia nervosa in context, Cambridge Mass., 1978, Harvard University Press.

Mitchell, K.M., Bozarth, J.D., and Krant, C.C.: A reappraisal of the therapeutic effectiveness of accurate empathy, non-possessive warmth, and genuineness. In Gurman, A.S., and Razin, A.M., editors: Effective psychotherapy: a handbook of research, Oxford, England, 1977, Pergamon Press.

Montgomery County Mental Health Association: Case manager program, Montgomery County, Md., 1980, Montgomery County Mental Health Association.

Montgomery House: Brochure, Gaithersburg, Md., Montgomery house.

Montgomery House: The transitional employment program, Gaithersburg, Md., Montgomery House.

Moore, H., and Strickler, C.: The counseling professions response to sex-biased counselling, Personn. Guid. J. **59:**84-87, 1980.

Moreno, J.L.: Psychodrama, New York, 1946, Beacon House.

Morgan, C.H.: Special national agency working on mental health services in jails, Washington, D.C., 1979, National Institute of Law Enforcement and Criminal Justice.

Morgan, D., Felsenfeld, H., and Heus, R.: Theatre unlimited, San Francisco, 1981, Theatre Unlimited.

Morgan, L.B.: The counselor's in suicide prevention, Personn. Guid. J. **59:**284-286, 1981.

Morris, D.: Intimate behavior, New York, 1971, Random House, Inc.

Mortenson, R.A.: Prejudice project, New York, 1980, Anti-Defamation League of B'nai B'rith.

Morton, T.L.: Intimacy and reciprocity exchange: a comparison of spouses and strangers, J. Pers. Soc. Psychol. **36:**72-81, 1978.

Moses, S.: Employment services for the elderly: program development handbook for state and area agencies, Washington, D.C., 1977, Administration on Aging.

Moulton, R.: Anxiety and the new feminism. In Kutash, I.L., and others: Handbook on stress and anxiety, San Francisco, 1980, Jossey-Bass, Inc., Publishers.

Muro, J.J., and Engels, D.W.: Life coping skills through developmental group counseling, J. Specialists in Group Work **5**(3):127-130, 1980.

Mussen, P., and Eisenberg-Berg, N.: Roots of caring, sharing and helping, San Francisco, 1977, W.W. Freeman & Co., Publishers.

Myers, N.: Surviving the loss of self-identity, Personn. Guid. J. **59:**405-406, 1981.

Nadler, A.: Good looks do not help: effects of helper's physical attractiveness and expectations for future interaction of help-seeking behavior, Personality Social Psychology Bull., **6**(3):378-383, 1980.

Naperstek, A.J.: Community mental health empowerment model: assumptions underlying the model: review of the literature, Washington, D.C., 1978, University of Southern California, Washington Public Affairs Center.

Nash, K.B., Lifton, N., and Smith, S.E., editors: The para-professional: selected readings, New Haven, Conn., 1978, Advocate Press, Inc.

The National Association of Private Psychiatric Hospitals Mental Illness: its myths and truths, Washington, D.C., 1969, National Association of Private Psychiatric Hospitals.

National Institute on Aging: acccidental hypothermia, NIH Pub. No. 81-1464, Washington, D.C., 1980, U.S. Department of Health and Human Services.

Nelson, R.C.: Effective helping with young children. In Eisenberg, S., and Patterson, L.E.: Helping clients with special concerns, Chicago, 1979, Rand McNally College Publishing Co.

Neugarten, B.L., editor: Middle age and aging: a reader in social psychology, Chicago, 1968, University of Chicago Press.

Neugarten, B.L.: Age groups in American society and the rise of the young-old, Annals of the American Academy of Social and Political Science **415:**187-198, 1974.

Neugarten, B.L.: Middle age and aging. In Hess, B.B., editor: Growing old in America, ed. 2, New Brunswick, N.J., 1980, Transaction Books.

Neulinger, J.: The psychology of leisure, Springfield, Ill., 1974, Charles C Thomas, Publisher.

NIAAA Information and Feature Service: NCAE develops minority course, The National Clearinghouse for Alcohol Information, IFS No. 78, p. 5, Dec. 1, 1980.

NIAAA Information and Feature Service: Alcoholism treatment services provided to female offenders, The National Clearinghouse for Alcohol Information, IFS No. 80, p. 10, Jan. 30, 1981.

NIAA Information and Feature Service: Study examines EAPs at major railroad companies, The National Clearinghouse for Alcohol Information, IFS No. 80, p. 9, Jan. 30, 1981.

Nickols, S.Y., and Nickols, S.A.: Ethical issues in changing life-styles, J. Home Economics **72**(2):24-27, 1980.

Nisenholz, B., and McCarty, F.H.: Teaching concerns focus game: exploring solutions. In Thayer, L., editor: Affective education, La Jolla, Calif., 1976, University Associates, Inc.

NMHA: The case-aide programs at Medfield State, Norwood, Mass., Norfolk Mental Health Association, Inc.

NMHA: Volunteer case-aide program, Norwood, Mass., Norfolk Mental Health Association, Inc.

Normile, R.H.: The behavior management system, Binghamton, N.Y., 1971, R.H. Normile and K.L. Normile.(Reprint.)

Nussbaum, M.A., and Piasecni, J.R.: Attitudes toward the mentally disabled: research perspectives and priorities, Philadelphia, Horizon House Institute.

O'Connell, A.N.: Karen Horney: theorist in psychoanalysis and feminine psychology, Psychol. Woman Quarterly, **5**(1):81-93, 1980.

O'Connor, W.A., Klassen, D.S., and O'Connor, K.S.: Evaluating human service programs: psychosocial methods. In Ahmed, P.I., and Coelho, G.V., editors: Toward a new definition of health: psychosocial dimensions, New York, 1979, Plenum Publishing Corp.

Odell, C.E.: Counseling for a third of a lifetime, Personn. Guid. J. **55**(3):145-147, 1976.

Office for Human Development Services, Administration on Aging: Facts about older Americans, DHEW Pub. No. (OHDS) 79-2006-1978, Washington, D.C., 1978, U.S. Department of Health, Education, and Welfare.

Ohlsen, M.M.: Group counseling, ed. 2, New York, 1977, Holt, Rinehart & Winston.

Oken, D.: Stress: our friend, our foe. In Miller, E., editor: Stress, Chicago, 1974, Blue Cross Association.

Okun, B.F.: Effective helping: interviewing and counseling techniques, North Scituate, Mass., 1976, Duxbury Press.

O'Neill, G.: Space colonies. In Cornish, E., editor: 1999, the world of tomorrow, Washington, D.C., 1978, World Future Society.

Osborn, A.F.: Applied imagination: principles and procedures of creative problem-solving, ed. 3, New York, 1963, The Scribner Book Companies, Inc.

Osgood, C.E.: The nature and measurement of measuring, Psychol. Bull. **49**:197-237, 1952.

Osgood, C.E., Suci, G.J., and Tannenbaum, P.H.: The measurement of meaning, Urbana, Ill., 1957, University of Illinois Press.

Osgood, M.H.: Rural and urban attitudes toward welfare. In Johnson, H.W., editor: Rural human services: a book of readings, Itasca, Ill., 1980, F.E. Peacock Publishers, Inc.

Our PLAC: brochure, Los Angeles, Veterans Administration Brentwood Hospital, Satellite Clinic.

Our PLAC: Outpatient Unit Rehabilitation Program for Living with Accomplishment in the Community, Los Angeles.

PACT: Patients understand patients' problems, Los Angeles, Brentwood Veterans Administration Hospital.

Paraprofessional Manpower Development Branch of National Institute of Mental Health: Rockville, Md., 1979, NIMH.

Parnes, S.J.: Creative behavior guidebook, New York, 1967, The Scribner Book Companies, Inc.

Passons, W.R.: Gestalt approaches in counseling, New York, 1975, Holt, Rinehart & Winston.

Patterson, C.H.: Relationship counseling and psychotherapy, New York, 1974, Harper & Row, Publishers, Inc.

Pattison, E.M., and others: A code of ethics for a community mental health program. In Nash, K.B., Lifton, N., and Smith, S.E., editors: The paraprofessional: selected readings, New Haven, Conn., 1978, Advocate Press, Inc.

Payne, P.A., Weiss, S.D., and Kapp, R.A.: Didactic, experiential, and modeling factors in the learning of empathy, J. Counsel. Psychol. **19**:425-429, 1972.

PCEH: newsletter: deinstitutionalization, Washington, D.C., 1981, The President's Committee on Employment of the Handicapped.

Pederson, P.B., and others: Counseling across cultures, rev. ed., 1981, Honolulu, The University Press of Hawaii.

Perlman, H.H.: Relationship: the heart of helping people, Chicago, 1979, University of Chicago Press.

Perloff, E., editor: Values, ethics, and standards in evaluation, San Francisco, 1980, Jossey-Bass, Inc., Publishers.

Personnel and Guidance Journal: Revolution in counseling—a second look, Personn. Guid. J. **58**(7):entire issue, 1980.

Peters, K.: In America, corporate fitness is an idea whose time is now, Runner's World **16**(4):55-57, 1981.

Peterson, J., and Park, D.: Values in career education: some pitfalls, Phi Delta CaMay 1975.

Phipps, G.T.: Foreword. In Ayer, W.A., and Hirschman, R.D., editors: Psychology and dentistry: selected readings, Springfield, Ill., 1972, Charles C Thomas, Publisher.

Phipps, G.T., and Marcuse, F.L.: Anxiety and dental caries. In Ayer, W.A., and Hirschman, R.D., editors: Psychology and dentistry: selected readings, Springfield, Ill., 1972, Charles C Thomas, Publisher.

Piaget, J.: The origins of intelligence in children, ed. 2, New York, 1952, International Universities Press. (Translated by M. Cook.)

Piasecki, J.R.: Community response to residential services for the psychosocially disabled: preliminary results of a national survey, Philadelphia, 1975, Horizon House Institute for Research and Development.

Pines, A.M., and Aronson, E.: Burnout: from tedium to personal growth, New York, 1981, The Free Press.

Pinter, H.: Landscape, silence and night, New York, 1970, Grove Press, Inc.

Plath, S.: Ariel, New York, 1966, Harper & Row, Publishers, Inc.

Polski, M.E.: Let's improvise: becoming creative, expressive and spontaneous through drama, New York, 1980, Prentice-Hall, Inc.

Pomerance, B.: The elephant man, New York, 1979, Grove Press, Inc.

Ponzo, Z.: Integrating techniques from five counseling theories, Personn. Guid. J. **54**:414-419, 1976.

Poon, L.W., editor: Aging in the 1980's psychological issues, Washington, D.C., 1980, American Psychological Association.

Pope, B.: The mental health interview/research and application, New York, 1979, Pergamon Press, Inc.

Portner, D.L.: Hospitalization of the family in the treatment of mental patients, Health Soc. Work **2**(3):111-122, 1977.

Postgraduate Center West (PGC): Brochure, New York, Postgraduate Center for Mental Health.

Prescott, D.: The child in the educative process, New York, 1957, McGraw-Hill Book Co.

President's Commission for a National Agenda of the Eighties: A national agenda for the eighties, Washington, D.C., 1980, U.S. Government Printing Office.

Previn, D.: On my way to where, New York, 1971, Bantam Books, Inc.

Proctor, E.K., and Rosen, A.: Expectations and preference for counselor race and their relation to intermediate treatment outcomes, J. Couns. Psychol. **28**(1):40-46, 1981.

Programs for the Handicapped: Martin faces new challenge and opportunity in the new Department of Education, Programs for the Handicapped, Washington, D.C., Office for Handicapped Indiviuals, July/August 1980a, No. 4, pp. 1-2.

Programs for the Handicapped: New Department of Health and Human Services, Washington, D.C., Office for Handicapped Individuals, 4, July/August 1980b, pp. 3-4.

Proshansky, H.M., and others: The role of physical settings in life-crisis experiences. In Sarason, I.G., and Spielberger, C.D., editors: Stress and anxiety: vol. 6, Washington, D.C., New York, 1979, Hemisphere Publishing Corp.

Public Health Service: Indian Health Service Dental Newsletter, **18**(3): April 15, 1980.

Puryear, D.A.: Helping people in crisis, San Francisco, 1979, Jossey-Bass, Inc., Publishers.

Rahe, R.H.: Relationship between life change and illness onset: life changes and illness studies: a selected review and synthesis. In Proceedings of the Conference on Stress, Strain, Heart disease and the Law, Washington, D.C., 1979, U.S. Government Printing Office.

Rapp, H.M., Arnheim, D.L., and Lavine, B.J.: The roles of a parent discussion group leader, Personn. Guid. J. **54**:110-112, 1975.

Rappaport, V., and Cleary, C.P.: Labeling theory and the social psychology of experts and helpers. In Gibbs, M.S., Lachenmeyer, J.R., and Sigal, J.: Community psychology, New York, 1980, Gardner Press, Inc.

Raths, I.E., Harmin, M., and Simon, S.: Values and teaching, Columbus, Ohio, 1966, Charles E. Merrill Publishing Co.

Rehab Brief: A skills training approach in psychiatric rehabilitation, Rehab Brief **IV**(1):1-4, 1980.

Rehabilitation Mental Health Services (RMHS): Brochure, San Jose, Calif., Rehabilitation Mental Health Services, Inc.

Reissman, F., Cohen, J., and Pearl, A., editors: Mental health of the poor: new treatment approaches for low income people, New York, 1964, The Free Press.

Rejeski, W.J., and Lowe, C.A.: Nonverbal expression of effort as causally relevant information, Personality Social Psychology Bull. **6**(3):436-440, 1980.

Remer, P., and O'Neill, C.: Clients as change agents: what color could my parachute be? Personn. Guid. J. **58**:425-429, 1980.

Ribble, M.: The personality of the young child: an introduction for puzzled parents, New York, 1955, Columbia University Press.

Rice, N., Satterwhite, B., and Pless, I.B.: Family counselors in a pediatric speciality clinic setting. In Nash, K.B., Lifton, N., and Smith, S.E., editors: The paraprofessional, New Haven, Conn., 1978, Advocate Press, Inc.

Richmond, C.: A proposal for a disaster crisis intervention

training and direct service program for human services professionals and paraprofessional, 1979.

Riedesel, B.C.: Toward full development of the person, Personn. Guid. **57**:332-337, 1979.

Riger, S., and Galligan, P.: Women in management: an exploration of completing paradigms, Am. Psychol. **35**(10):902-910, 1980.

Riggs, R.C.: Evaluation of counselor effectiveness, Personn. Guid. J. **58**(1):54-59, 1979.

Rimm, D.C., and Masters, J.C.: Behavior therapy: techniques and empirical findings, New York, 1974, Academic Press, Inc.

Robinault, I.P., and Weisinger, M.: Mobilization of community resources: a multifacet model for rehabilitation of post-hospitalized mentally ill, ed. 3, New York, 1979, ICD Rehabilitation and Research Center.

Robinson, E.H.: Introduction: life coping skills through group medium, J. Specialists Group Work **5**(3):117-119, 1980.

Rogawski, A.S., editor: Mental health consultations in community settings, San Francisco, 1979, Jossey-Bass, Inc., Publishers.

Rogers, C.R.: Counseling and psychotherapy, Boston, 1942, Houghton Mifflin Co.

Rogers, C.R.: Client-centered therapy, Boston, 1951, Houghton Mifflin Co.

Rogers, C.R.: The characteristics of a helping relationship, Personn. Guid. J. **37**:6-16, 1958.

Rogers, C.R.: On becoming a person: a therapist's view of psychotherapy, Boston, 1961, Houghton Mifflin Co.

Rogers, C.R.: Encounter groups, New York, 1970, Harper & Row, Publishers, Inc.

Rogers, C.R.: Groups in two cultures, Personn. Guid. J. **58**:11-15, 1979.

Rogers, C.R., and Truax, C.B.: The therapeutic conditions antecedent to change: a theoretical view. In Rogers, C.R., editor: The therapeutic relationship and its impact, Madison, 1967, The University of Wisconsin Press.

Rogers-Warren, A., and Warren S.F., editors: Ecological perspectives in behavior analysis, Baltimore, 1977, University Park Press.

Rokeach, M., Rokeach Values Survey, Sunnyvale, Calif., 1973, Halgren Tests.

Rokeach, M., and Regan, J.F.: The role of values in the counseling situation, Personn. Guid. J. **58**:576-582, 1980.

Roles and functions for different levels of mental health workers, Atlanta, 1969, Southern Regional Education Board.

Rose, S.D.: A casebook in group therapy: a behavioral-cognitive approach, Englewood Cliffs, N.J., 1980, Prentice-Hall, Inc.

Rosenberg, B.: The development of TOWER: a world standard for vocational evaluation of the handicapped, New York, 1977, ICD Rehabilitation and Research Center.

Rosenthal, R., and Jacobson, L.: Pygmalion in the classroom:

teacher expectations and pupils' intellectual development, New York, 1968, Holt, Rinehart & Winston.

Rosow, I.: And then we were old. In Hess, B.B., editor: Growing old in America, ed. 2, New Brunswick, N.J., 1980, Transaction Books.

Rossman, M.: Self-help marketplace, Social Policy **7:**86-91, 1976.

Roth, P.: The ghost writer, New York, 1979, Farrar, Straus & Giroux, Inc.

Rovner, S.: Health talk: dieting to death, Washington Post, p. C-5, Aug. 1, 1980a.

Rovner, S.: Healthtalk: facts on fat, Washington Post, p. E-5, Oct. 10, 1980b.

Rowles, G.D.: Prisoners of space? Exploring the geographical experiences of older people, Boulder, Col., 1980, Westview Press, Inc.

Rowse, A.L., editor: The annotated Shakespeare, vol. III, The tragedies and romances, New York, 1978, Clarkson N. Potter, Inc.

Rudnick, D.T., and Wallach, E.J.: Women in technology: a program to increase career awareness, Personn. Guid. J. **58:**445-448, 1980.

Rusk, H.A.: Rehabilitation medicine, ed. 4, St. Louis, 1977, The C.V. Mosby Co.

Russell, M.L., and Thoresen, C.E.: Teaching decision-making skills to children. In Krumboltz, J.D., and Thoresen, C.E., editors: Counseling methods, New York, 1976, Holt, Rinehart & Winston.

Rutman, I.D., and Baron, R.C.: Community careers: an assessment of the life adjustment of former mental hospital patients, Philadelphia, 1975, Horizon House Institute for Research Development.

Ryback, R.S., Fowler, D.R., and Longabaugh, R.: The problem oriented record in psychiatry and mental health care, rev. ed., New York, 1981, Grune & Stratton, Inc.

Sabatelli, R.M., Buck, R., and Dreyer, A.: Communication via facial cues in intimate dyads, Personality Social Psychology Bull. **6**(2):242-247, 1980.

Sager, M.: Coping with stress in Loudoun, Washington Post, pp. B-1, B-4, Feb. 15, 1981.

Salter, A.: Conditioned reflex therapy: the direct approach to the reconstruction of personality, New York, 1949, Capricorn Books.

Saperstein, A.: Mom kills kids and self, New York, 1979, Ballantine Books, Inc.

Sarason, I.G., Johnson, J.H., and Siegel, J.M.: Assessing the impact of life changes: development of the Life Experiences Survey (LES). In Sarason, I.G., and Spielberger, C.D., editors: Stress and anxiety, vol. 6, Washington, D.C., 1979, Hemisphere Publishing Corp.

Sarason, I.B., and Spielberger, C.D., editors: Stress and anxiety, vol. 6, Washington, D.C., 1979, Hemisphere Publishing Corp.

Satir, V.: Cojoint family therapy: a guide to theory and technique, Palo Alto, Calif., 1964, Science & Behavior Books, Inc.

Satir, V.: Peoplemaking, Palo Alto, Calif., 1972, Science & Behavior Books, Inc.

Savary, L.M., and Ehlen-Miller, M.: Mindways: a guide for exploring your mind, San Francisco, 1979, Harper & Row, Publishers, Inc.

Schafer, R.B.: The self-concept as a factor in diet selection and quality, J. Nutrition Education **11:**37-39, 1979.

Schafer, W.: Stress, distress and growth, Davis, Calif., 1978, International Dialogue Press.

Schauble, P.G., and others: Taking counseling to minority students, Personn. Guid. **58:**176-180, 1979.

Scheflen, A., and Aschcraft, N.: Human territories: how we behave in space-time, Englewood Cliffs, N.J., 1976, Prentice-Hall, Inc.

Schmidt, J.: Cognitive restructuring techniques, Personn. Guid. J. **55:**71-74, 1976.

Schneider, D.J., Hastorf, A.H., and Ellsworth, P.C.: Person perception, Reading, Mass, 1979, Addison-Wesley Publishing Co., Inc.

Schneider, J.: Growth from bereavement. In Proceedings of the 1980 International Congress on Death and Dying, London, 1980, Pittman Medical Publishers.

Schneider, M., and Robin, A.L.: The turtle technique: a method for the self-control of impulsive behavior, unpublished manuscript, State University of New York at Stony Brook, 1975.

Schnike, S.P.: Teenage pregnancy: the need for multiple casework services, Social Casework **59:**406-410, 1978.

Schofield, W.: Psychotherapy: the purchase of friendship, Englewood Cliffs, N.J., 1964, Prentice-Hall, Inc.

Schuerger, J.M.: Understanding and controlling anger. In Einenberg, S., and Patterson, L.E.: Helping clients with special concerns, Chicago, 1979, Rand McNally College Publishing Co.

Schulman, E.D.: Baltimore's social interaction program, Jr. College J. **37:**34-36, 1966.

Schulman, E.D.: Mental health technician: the new professional, paper presented at the Maryland Psychological Association meeting, 1967.

Schulman, E.D.: From a social interaction focus to a mental health technician worker, paper presented at the American Psychological Association meeting, Sept. 3, 1968.

Schulman, E.D.: The four ''W's'' of the mental health technologist's field work placement, paper presented at the Eastern Psychological Association meeting, April 14, 1970.

Schulman, E.D.: Focus on the retarded adult: programs and services, St. Louis, The C.V. Mosby Co. 1980.

Schulman, E.D.: Rehabilitation of the mentally ill: an international perspective, Washington, D.C.: 1981, President's Committee on Employment of the Handicapped.

Schulman, K.: Cutler in the seventies: a special issue of the annual report—1979 of the Cutler Counseling Center, Norwood, Mass., 1980, Cutler Counseling Center.

Schulman, K.: News from Cutler, The Report (Norfolk Mental Health Association, Inc.) January, 1981.

Schumacher, E.F.: Small is beautiful: economics as if people mattered, New York, 1975, Harper & Row, Publishers, Inc. (Paperback by Perennial Library.)

Schumacher, R.: Parenting group: a process for change, J. Specialists in Group Work 5(3):135-139, 1980.

Schweitzer, N.J., and Deely, J.: The awareness factor: a management skills seminar, unpublished paper, 1980, New York, ICD Rehabilitation and Research Center.

Scott, R.B., and Maxwell, L.: Contractual counseling sets goals and duties, Research Review 2(3):4-5, 1975.

Selee, J.: Prejudice: a universal problem. In Mortenson, R.A.: Prejudice project, New York, 1980, Anti-Defamation League of B'nai B'rith.

Sells, S.B.: On the nature of stress. In McGrath, J.E., editor: Social and psychological factors in stress, New York, 1970, Holt, Rinehart & Winston.

Selye, H.: Stress without distress, New York, 1975, New American Library, Inc.

Selye, H.: The stress of life, rev. ed., New York, 1976, McGraw-Hill Book Co., Inc.

Selye, H.: The stress concept. In Kutash, I.L., and others: Handbook on stress and anxiety, San Francisco, 1980, Jossey-Bass, Inc., Publishers.

Shaffer, D.R., and Graziano, W.F.: Effects of victims, race and organizational affiliation on receiving help from blacks and whites, Personality Social Psychology Bull. 6(3):366-372, 1980.

Shapiro, D.H., Jr.: Meditation, Hawthorne, N.Y., 1980, Aldine Publishing Co.

Sherman, S.R.: The retirement housing setting: site permeability, service availability, and perceived community support in crises, J. Social Science Research 3(2):139-157, 1979.

Shertzer, B., and Stone, S.C.: Fundamentals of counseling, ed. 2, Boston, 1974, Houghton Mifflin Co.

Shrene, S.R.: Children of power, New York, 1979, Macmillan, Inc.

Shulman, S.: A nursing bottle caries prevention program: an educational media program for high incidence areas in the Indian health service, Indian Health Service Dental Newsletter, U.S. Dept. of Health, Education and Welfare (Public Health Service), April 15, 1980.

Sielski, L.M.: Understanding body language, Personn. Guid. J. 57:238-242, 1979.

Silverman, P.R.: Mutual help groups: a guide for mental health workers, U.S. Dept. of Health, Education and Welfare DHEW Pub. No. (ADM) 78-646, Rockville, Md., 1978, National Institute of Mental Health.

Simon, S.B.: Values clarification in family groups, J. Specialists in Group Work 5(3):140-147, 1980.

Simon, S.B., Howe, L., and Kirschenbaum, H.: Values clarification, New York, 1972, Holt, Rinehart & Winston.

Simonson, N.R.: The impact of therapist disclosure on patient disclosure, J. Couns. Psychol. 23(1):3-6, 1976.

Simonson, N.R.: Self-disclosure and psychotherapy, Amherst, Mass., 1973, Department of Psychology, University of Massachusetts.

Simos, B.G.: A time to grieve, New York, 1979, Family Service Association of America.

Simpson, M.E.: Societal support and education. In Kutash, I.L., and others: Handbook on stress and anxiety, San Francisco, 1980, Jossey-Bass, Inc., Publishers.

Sinick, D.: Counseling the dying and their survivors, Personn. Guid. J. 55:122-123, 1976.

Sinick, D.: Counseling older persons: careers, retirement, and dying, New York, 1977, Human Sciences Press, Inc.

Skotko, V.P., and Langmeyer, D.: The effects of interaction distance and gender on self-disclosure in dyads, Sociometry 40(2):178-182, 1977.

Slater, A., Gordon, K., and Gordon, R.: Role differences of mental health workers: observations of four sites. In Nash, K.B., Lifton, N. and Smith, S.E., editors: The paraprofessional: selected readings, New Haven, Conn., 1978, Advocate Press, Inc.

Smith, E.J.: Counseling black individuals: some stereotypes, Personn. Guid. J. 55:390-396, 1977.

Smith, W.D., and Martinson, W.D.: Counselors' and counselees' learning style on interview behavior, J. Couns. Psychol. 18:138-141, 1971.

Snyder, C.R., and Fromkin, H.L.: Uniqueness: the human pursuit of difference, New York, 1980, Plenum Publishing Corp.

Sobey, F.: The nonprofessional revolution in mental health, New York, 1970, Columbia University Press.

Social Action Research Center: Paraprofessionals in mental health: an annotated bibliography from 1966 to 1977, Berkeley, Calif., 1978, Social Action Research Center.

Sommer, R.: Personal space: the behavioral basis of design, Englewood Cliffs, N.J., 1969, Prentice-Hall, Inc.

Sommer, R.: Small group ecology. In Weitz, S., editor: Nonverbal communication, New York, 1974, Oxford University Press.

Sparks, D., and Ingram, M.J.: Stress prevention and management: a workshop approach, Personn. Guid. J. 58:197-200, 1979.

Sperling, S.K.: Poplollies and bellibones: a celebration of lost words, New York, 1977, Clarkson N. Potter, Inc.

Sperry, L.: Counselors and learning styles, Personn. Guid. J. 51:478-483, 1973.

Spiro, M.E.: Supernaturally caused illness in traditional Burmese medicine. In Kleinman, A., and others, editors: Medicine in Chinese culture, Pub. No. (NIH) 75-653, Washington, D.C., 1975, U.S. Government Printing Office.

Spitz, R.A.: The first year of life, New York, 1965, International Universities Press.

Splete, H., and Bernstein, B.: A survey of consultation training as a part of counselor education programs, Personn. Guid. J. **59:**470-472, 1981.

Sprinthall, N.A.: Guidance and new education for schools, Personn. Guid. J. **58:**485-487, 1980.

STASH notes: Phencyclidine (PCP), STASH Capsules **5**(2):1-2, 1973.

Staub, G.E., and Kent, L.M.: The paraprofessional in the treatment of alcoholism: a new profession, Springfield, Ill., 1979, Charles C Thomas, Publisher.

Steele, L.: Virginia program tries to help abused wives, Guidepost, **23**(9):1, 6, 8, 10, 1980.

Steenberger, B.N., and Adernab, D.: Objective self-awareness as a nonaversive state, J. Personality **47:**330-339, 1979.

Stein, L.I., editor: Community support systems for the long-term patient, San Francisco, 1979, Jossey-Bass, Inc., Publishers.

Steiner, I.D.: Strategies for controlling stress in interpersonal situations. In McGrath, J.E., editor: Social and psychological factors in stress, New York, 1970, Holt, Rinehart & Winston.

Steinhuasen, G.W.: Sex-role, sexism and stereotyping: curriculum module. In Mortenson, R.A., editor: Prejudice Project, New York, 1980, Anti-Defamation League of B'nai B'rith.

Stelovich, S.: From the hospital to the prison: a step forward in deinstitutionalization? Hospital Community Psychiatry **30**(9):818-820, 1979.

Stillman, S., and Resnick, H.: Does counselor attire matter? J. Couns. Psychol. **19:**347-348, 1972.

Stoltenberg, C.: Approaching supervision from developmental perspective: the counselor complexity model, J. Couns. Psychol. **28**(1):59-65, 1981.

Stone, G.L., and Morden, C.I.: Effect of distance on verbal productivity, J. Couns. Psychol. **23:**486-488, 1976.

Storr, A.: The art of psychotherapy, New York, 1980, Methuen, Inc.

Stotland, E.: The psychology of hope, San Francisco, 1969, Jossey-Bass, Inc., Publishers.

Stover, L., and Guerney, B.G., Jr.: The efficacy of training procedures for mothers in filial therapy, Psychotherapy: Theory, Research and Practice **4**(3):110-115, 1967.

Straus, M.A., Gelles, R.J., and Steinmetz, S.K.: Theories, methods, and controversies in the study of violence between family members, Arlington, Va., 1973, ERIC Document Reproduction Service.

Strupp, H.H., Wallach, M.S., and Wogan, M.: Psychotherapy experience in retrospect: questionnaire survey for former patients and their therapists, Psychol. Monogr. **78**(11):whole No. 588, 1964.

Student Counseling Center: Interpersonal skills scale, Normal, Ill., Illinois State University.

Stulac, J.T., and Stanwick, D.J.: The revolution in counseling: a sociological perspective, Personn. Guid. J. **58:**491-495, 1980.

Sudnow, D.: Dead on arrival, Transaction/Society **9**(1/2):36-43, 1971.

Sue, D.W.: Counseling the culturally different, New York, 1981, John Wiley & Sons, Inc.

Suedfeld, P.: Stressful levels of environmental stimulations. In Sarason, I.G., and Spielberger, C.D., editors: Stress and anxiety, vol. 6, Washington, D.C., 1979, Hemisphere Publishing Corp.

Suedfeld, P., and Ikard, F.F.: The use of sensory deprivation in facilitating the reduction of cigarette smoking, J. Consulting Clinical Psychol. **2:**888-895, 1974.

Suinn, R.M., and Deffenbacher, J.L.: Behavior therapy. In Kutash, I.L., and others: Handbook on stress and anxiety, San Francisco, 1980, Jossey-Bass, Inc., Publishers.

Swensen, C.H.: Ego development and a federal model for counseling and psychotherapy, Personn. Guid. J. **58:**382-387, 1980.

Teune, H., and Mlinar, Z.: Developmental logic of social systems, Beverly Hills, Calif., 1978, Sage Publications, Inc.

Thayer, L.: 50 strategies for experiential learning: book one, San Diego, 1976, University Associates, Inc.

Theatre Unlimited: Playbill, San Francisco, Theater Unlimited, 1981.

Thibaut, J.W., and Kelley, H.H.: The social psychology of groups, New York, 1959, John Wiley & Sons, Inc.

This Month: Living arrangements for chronic patients, This Month **3**(10):2, 1981.

Thought Technology: GSR 1, GSR 2, GSR/Temp 2 Biofeedback relaxation systems, Montreal, 1981, Thought Technology, Ltd.

Timmer, I.: Human services: a guide to county planning and decision making, St. Paul, Minn., 1979, Minnesota State Planning Agency, Human Resources Planning Unit.

Trexler, L.D., and Karst, T.O.: Rational-emotive therapy, placebo, and no-treatment effects on public speaking anxiety, J. Abnormal Psychol. **79:**60-67, 1972.

Trop, J.L., and Gold, C.: Patient-to-patient contact: the outpatient as a therapeutic agent, Hosp. Community Psychiatry **28:**249, 1977.

Truax, C.B., and Carkhuff, R.R.: An introduction to counseling and psychotherapy: training and practice, Chicago, 1966, Aldine Publishing Co.

Traux, C.B., and Carkhuff, R.R.: Toward effective counseling and psychotherapy, Chicago, 1967, Aldine Publishing Co.

Tucker, G.J., Turner, J., and Chapman, R.: Problems in attracting and retaining psychiatrists in rural areas, Hosp. Community Psychiatry **32**(2):118-120, 1981.

Tucker, R.C., and Tucker, L.M.: The role of paraprofessionals: an administrative dilemma. In Nash, K.B., Lifton, N., and Smith, S.E.: The paraprofessional: selected readings, New Haven, Conn., 1978, Advocate Press, Inc.

Turner, F.J.: Psychosocial therapy, New York, 1978, The Free Press.

Turner, J.C., and Ten Hoor, W.: The NIMH community support program: pilot approach to a needed social reform, Schizophrenia Bulletin **4**(3):319-348, 1978.

Turock, A.: Effective challenging through additive empathy, Personn. Guid. J. **57**:144-149, 1978.

Turock, A.: Immediacy in counseling: recognizing client's unspoken messages, Personn. Guid. J. **59**:168-172, 1980.

Twerski, A.: Alcologia, Behavior Today **4**(19):2, 1973.

Uhlmann, J.M.: Boom towns: implications for human services. In Wagenfeld, M.O., editor: New directions for mental health services: perspectives on rural mental health, San Francisco, 1981, Jossey-Bass, Inc., Publishers.

Up Front: Independence in clothing, Up Front **1**(1):3, 1980.

U.S. Department of Commerce, Bureau of the Census: Characteristics of the population below the poverty level, 1979, Series P-60, No. 119, Washington, D.C., U.S. Government Printing Office.

U.S. Department of Commerce, Bureau of the Census: Marital status and living arrangements, March 1979, Current Population Reports, Series P-20, No. 319, Washington, D.C., 1980, U.S. Government Printing Office.

U.S. Department of Health, Education, and Welfare: Annual summary for the United States, 1978: births, deaths, marriages, and divorces, Monthly Vital Statistics Report 27 (13), Hyattsville, Md., Aug. 13, 1979, National Center for Health Statistics.

U.S. Department of Labor, Bureau of Labor Statistics: Employment and earnings, July 1979, 26 (8), Washington, D.C., Aug. 1979, The Department.

Usdin, G., and Hofling, C.K.: Aging: the process and the people, New York, 1978, Brunner/Mazel, Inc.

Vail, H.: The automated office. In Cornish, E., editor: 1999 the world of tomorrow, Washington, D.C., 1978, World Future Society.

Van Auken, S.: Youth counselor burnout, Personn. Guid. J. **58**:143-144, 1979.

Vandergoot, D., and Engelkes, J.: The relationship of selected rehabilitation counseling variables with job seeking behaviors, Rehabilitation Counseling Bulletin **24**(2):173-177, 1980.

Van Dyck, B.J.: An analysis of selection criteria for short-term group counseling clients, Personn. Guid. J. **59**:226-230, 1980.

Van Hoose, W.H., and Kottler, J.A.: Ethical and legal issues in counseling and psychotherapy, San Francisco, 1977, Jossey-Bass Inc., Publishers.

Van Houten, R., Nau, P., and Smith, R.C.: Psychology and the control of speeding, Social action and the law, Canadian Police Chief **69**(3):6-18, 1980.

van Rooijen, L.: Widow's bereavement: stress and depression after 1½ years. In Sarason, I.G., and Spielberger, C.D., editors: Stress and anxiety, vol. 6, Washington, D.C., 1979, Hemisphere Publishing Corp.

Velasquez, J.S., and McCubbin, H.I.: Towards establishing the effectiveness of community-based residential treatment: program evaluation by experimental research, J. Social Service Review **3**(4):337-359, 1980.

Victor, J.S.: Privacy, intimacy and shame in a French community. In Tefft, S.R., editor: Secrecy: a cross-cultural perspective, New York, 1980, Human Services Press.

Volkan, V.D.: Narcissistic personality organization and "reparative" leadership, International J. Group Psychotherapy **XXX**(2):131-152, 1980.

Von Bertalanffy, L.: General system theory, New York, 1968, George Braziller, Inc.

Vontress, C.E.: Counseling middle-aged and aging cultural minorities, Personn. Guid. J. **55**:132-135, 1976.

Vontress, C.E.: Cross-cultural counseling: an existential approach, Personn. Guid. J. **58**:117-122, 1979.

Voorde, C.: Major legislation of interest to psychology, APA Monitor **21**(1):13, 1981.

Voydanoff, P.: Perceived job characteristics and job satisfaction among men and women, Psychol. Women **5**(2):177-185, 1980.

Vriend, T.: High performing inner city adolescents assist low performing peers in counseling groups, Personn. Guid. J. **47**:897-904, 1969.

Wagenfeld, M.O., editor: New directions for mental health services: perspectives on rural mental health, San Francisco, 1981, Jossey-Bass, Inc., Publishers.

Walsh, G.: Teaching makes the difference, Los Angeles, 1980, The Association for the Severely Handicapped. (Film and presentation.)

Warren C., and Laslett, B.: Privacy and secrecy: a conceptual comparison. In Tefft, S.K., editor: Secrecy, New York, 1980, Human Sciences Press.

Watson, D.L., and Tharp, R.G.: Self-directed behavior: self-modification for personal adjustment, Monterey, Calif., 1972, Brooks/Cole Publishing Co.

Webster, S.D.: Humanness: the one essential, Personn. Guid. J. **51**:378-379, 1973.

Weick, K.E.: The "ess" in stress: some conceptual and methodological problems. In McGrath, J.E., editor: Social and psychological factors in stress, New York, 1970, Holt, Rinehart & Winston.

Whiston, S.K.: Counseling sexual assault victims: a loss model, Personn. Guid. J. **59**:363-366, 1981.

Wicklund, R.A.: The influence of self-awareness on human behavior, Am. Scientist **67**:187-193, 1979.

Wicks, R.J.: Helping others: ways of listening, sharing and counseling, Radnor, A., 1979, Chilton Book Co.

Widgery, R., and Stackpole, C.: Desk positions, interviewee anxiety and interviewer credibility: an example of cognitive balance in a dyad, J. Counsel. Psychol. **19**:173-177, 1972.

Wiener, M., and others: Nonverbal behavior and nonverbal communication, Psychol. Rev. **79**:185-214, 1972.

Williams, C.: Former patients take college training, This month, **3**(4):6, 1980.

Wilmer, H.A.: Defining and understanding the therapeutic community, Hosp. Community Psychiatry **32**(2):95-98, 1981.

Wilson, L.G., Reis, R., and Bokan, J.: Transcultural psychiatry on an American psychiatric ward, Hosp. Community Psychiatry **31**(11):759-762, 1980.

Wilson, S.J.: Recording: guidelines for social workers, New York, 1980, Free Press.

Winnicott, D.W.: The maturational process and the facilitating environment, New York, 1965, International Universities Press, Inc.

Witkin, H.A., and others: Psychological differentation, New York, 1962, John Wiley & Sons, Inc.

Wolf, S.: Counseling for better or worse, Alcohol Health and Research World, Winter: 27-29, 1974/75.

Wolf, S.: Relationship between emotional stress and illness onset. In Proceedings of the Conference on Stress, Strain, Heart Disease and the Law, Washington, D.C., 1979, U.S. Government Printing Office.

Wolpe, J.: The practice of behavior therapy, New York, 1969, Pergamon Press, Inc.

Wolpe, J., and Lazurus, A.A.: Behavior therapy techniques, New York, 1966, Pergamon Press, Inc.

Woodruff, D.S., and Birren, J.E.: Aging: scientific perspectives and social issues, New York, 1975, D. Van Nostrand Co.

Woody, R.H.: Psychobehavioral counseling and therapy: integrating behavioral and insight therapy, New York, 1971, Appleton-Century-Crofts.

Woody, R.H., editor: Encyclopedia of clinical assessment, vols. 1 and 2, San Francisco, 1980, Jossey-Bass, Inc., Publishers.

Worell, J.: New directions in counseling women, Personn. Guid. J. **58**:477-484, 1980.

World Health Organization: Modern management methods and the organization of health services, Public Health Papers No. 55, Albany, N.Y., 1974, World Health Organization Publications (Q Corporation).

World Health Organization: Organization of mental health services in developing countries, Geneva, 1975, World Health Organization.

Worthington, E.L., Jr., and Shumate, M.: Imagery and verbal methods in stress innoculation: training for pain control, J. Counsel. Psychol. **28**(1):1-6, 1981.

Wright, G.N.: Total rehabilitation, Boston, 1980, Little, Brown & Co.

Wright, L.B., and LaMar, V.A., editors: Hamlet, New York, 1961, Washington Square Press, Inc.

Yamamoto, J., and others: Racial factors in patient selection, Am. J. Psychiatry **124**:630-636, 1967.

Yankelovich, D.: New rules, New York, 1981, Random House, Inc.

Yates, R.: Look out, men—it's Velvet Rhodes, The Washington Post, October 22, 1980, D-11.

Yenckel, J.T., Offices: designs for efficiency, Washington Post, p. D-5, Feb. 26, 1981a.

Yenckel, J.T.: Private lives: curbing the cycle of violence, Washington Post, p. E-5, Feb. 10, 1981b.

Yonce, L.J.: Availability of human services in urban and rural areas, Ann Arbor, Mich., 1977, Michigan, University.

Young, D.M., Beier, E.G., and Beier, S.: Beyond words: influence of nonverbal behavior of female job applicants in the employment interview, Personn. Guid. J. **57**:346-350, 1979.

Zawada, M.A.: Displaced homemakers: unresolved issues, Personn. Guid. J. **59**:110-113, 1980.

Zimmer, J., and Anderson, S.: Dimensions of positive regard and empathy, J. Counsel. Psychol. **15**:417-426, 1968.

Zimring, C.M.: Stress and the designed environment, J. Social Issues, **37**(1):145-171, 1981.

Zink, V.: At Texas Instruments, fitness is good business, Runner's World **16**(4):58-59, 1981.

Zirkie, K.E., and Hudson, G.: The effects of residence hall staff members on maturity development for male students, J. College Student Personnel **15**:30-33, 1975.

Zung, W.W.K., and Cavenar, J.O., Jr.: Assessment scales and techniques. In Kutash, I.L., and others: Handbook on stress and anxiety, San Francisco, 1980, Jossey-Bass, Inc., Publishers. 348-363.

Zunker, V.G.: Students as paraprofessionals in four-year colleges and universities, J. College Student Personnel **16**:282-286, 1975.

INDEX

444